The Fine Art Index

ISSN 1057-8269

ISBN 0-9629816-5-6

ISSN 1057-8269

The Fine Art Index

INTERNATIONAL EDITION

Volume I

INTERNATIONAL ART REFERENCE • CHICAGO

C R E D I T S

Publisher:
N. David Shiba

Director of Finance and Administration:
Matthew J. Chan

Director of Marketing:
Daniel S. Chan

Director of Production and Design:
Peter B. Chu

Production Assistants:
Patrick Andresen
Allen Chan
Brian Chan

Business Advisor:
Casey Cowell

Editorial Staff:
Sue Lechner
Michelle Natividad

National Account Representatives:
Hubert H. Moy
Shan Shan Sheng

Circulation and Fulfillment:
Jonathan Chan
Aquan Ecford

Design:
International Art Reference, Inc.

Cover Art:
David Salle
Courtesy of The Gagosian Gallery, New York

Typography:
Sung-In Printing America, Inc.

Color Separations:
Sung-In Printing America, Inc.

Printing / Manufacturing:
Sung-In Printing America, Inc., Korea

Editorial, Advertising and Book Sale Offices:
International Art Reference, Inc.
938 North Honore
Chicago, Illinois 60622
312.384.1113
312.384.1199 FAX

PRINTED IN KOREA

C O N T E N T S

I N T R O D U C T I O N

Welcome to the third edition of *The Fine Art Index*.

We at International Art Reference appreciate the opportunity to present some of the finest contemporary art from around the world to you.

As I am sure you have noticed, the format of the Index has been changed. Based on your suggestions, we have divided the book into two volumes. *Volume I*, which you are holding in your hands, contains the provocative survey of art for which *The Fine Art Index* has become well known. *Volume II*, available separately and as part of a two volume set, contains the gallery, museum and corporate collection listings; artist indexes; and business services listings used primarily by fine art professionals.

Another change has been the expansion of editorial coverage to include artists and galleries from around the world. For the first time, you will see artwork from London, Madrid and Shanghai, as well as New York, Chicago and Los Angeles.

We have also added a 24 page summary of a dozen important museum shows that have, or will be appearing in major cities around the world. The Museum Year-In-Review section will give you a taste of some very exciting exhibitions being presented outside of your location.

As always, I hope that you find *The Fine Art Index* both engaging and attractive. Enjoy!

Sincerely,

N. David Shiba
Publisher

MUSEUM EXHIBITIONS

TERRA MUSEUM
OF AMERICAN ART

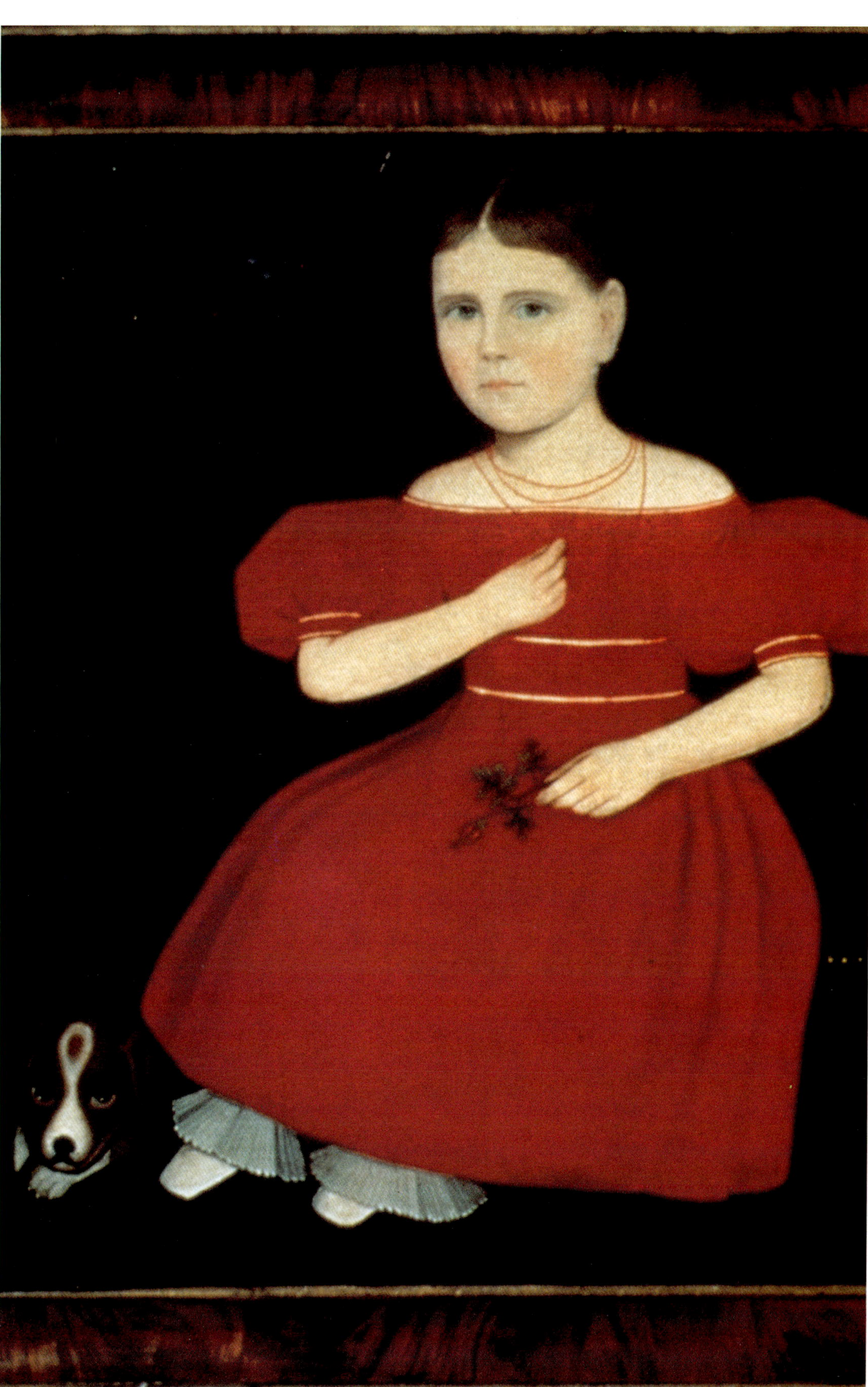

Ammi Phillips
Girl in a Red Dress
1830-1835,
Oil on canvas,

Exhibition:
Revisiting Ammi Phillips:
Fifty year of American
portraiture
Oct. 8–Dec. 31, 1994

THE MUSEUM OF
MODERN ART
NEW YORK

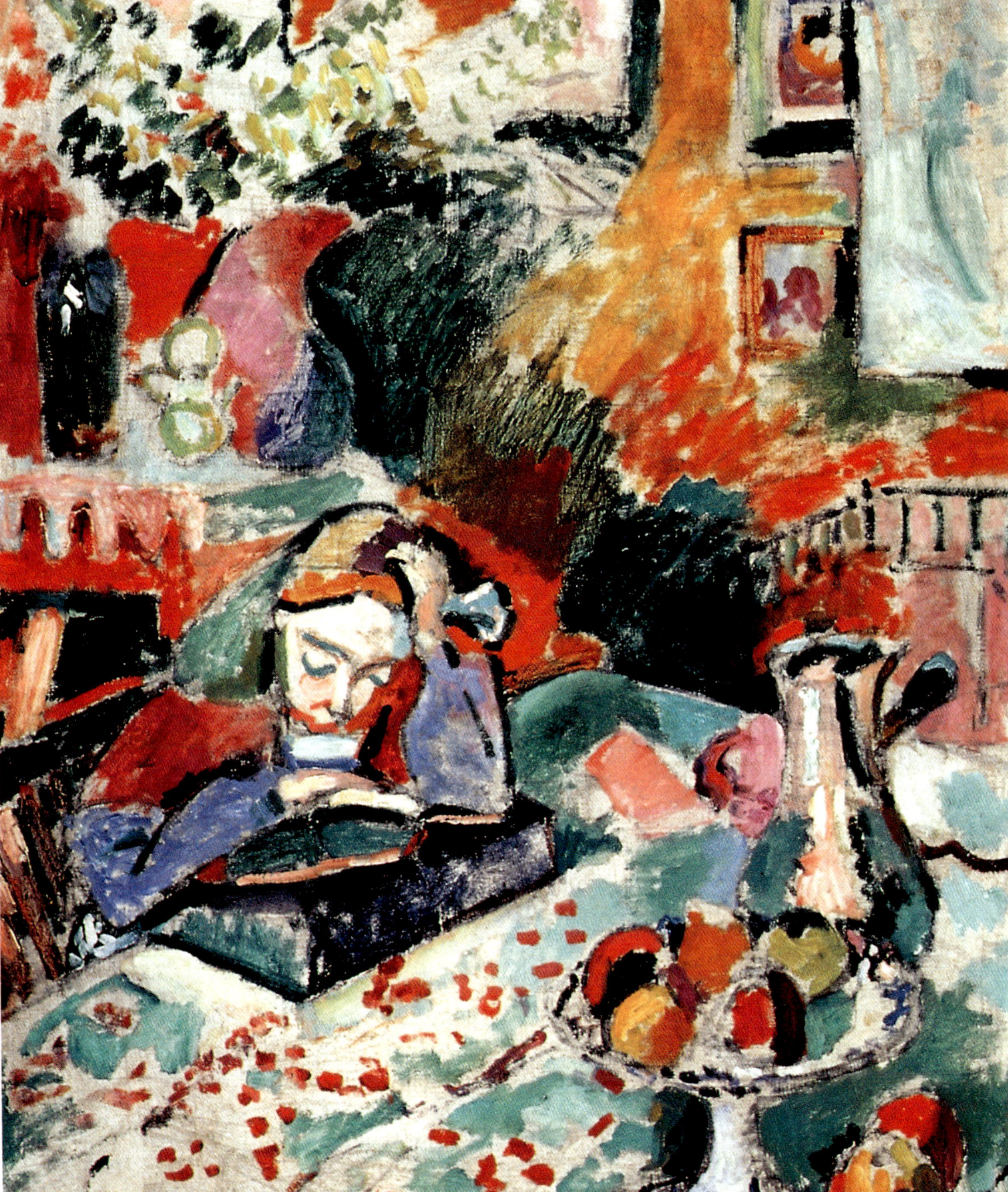

Henri Matisse
Interior with Young Girl
Girl Reading
1905-1906,
Oil on canvas,
28⅝" x 23½"

Exhibition:
Masterpieces from the
David and Peggy
Rockefeller Collection:
Manet to Picasso
June 9 – September 6, 1994

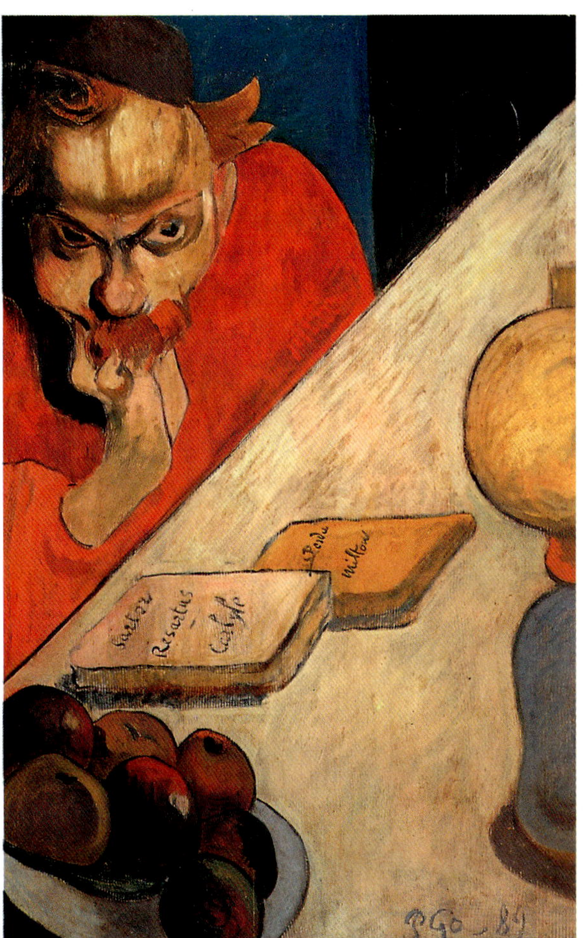

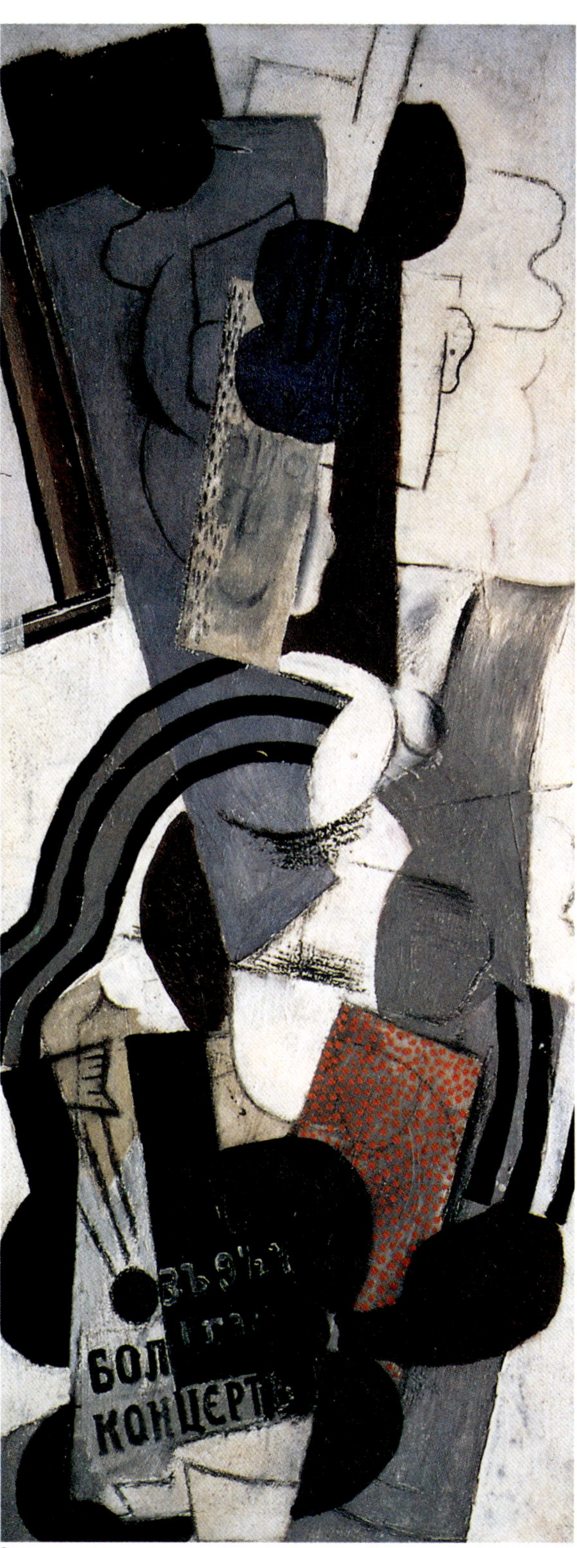

THE MUSEUM OF
MODERN ART
NEW YORK

1. **Paul Gauguin**
   Portrait of Jacob Meyer de Haan
   1889, Oil on wood,
   31³⁄₈ " × 20³⁄₈"

2. **Pablo Picasso**
   Woman with a Guita
   1914, Oil, sand and charcoal on canvas
   45½" × 18⅝"

Exhibition:
Masterpieces from the
David and Peggy
Rockefeller Collection:
Manet to Picasso
June 9–Sept. 6, 1994

NATIONAL
MUSEUM OF
AMERICAN ART

Thomas Cole
The Falls of Kaaterskill
1826, Oil on canvas,
43" × 36"

Exhibition:
Thomas Cole:
Landscape Into History
March 18 – August 7, 1994

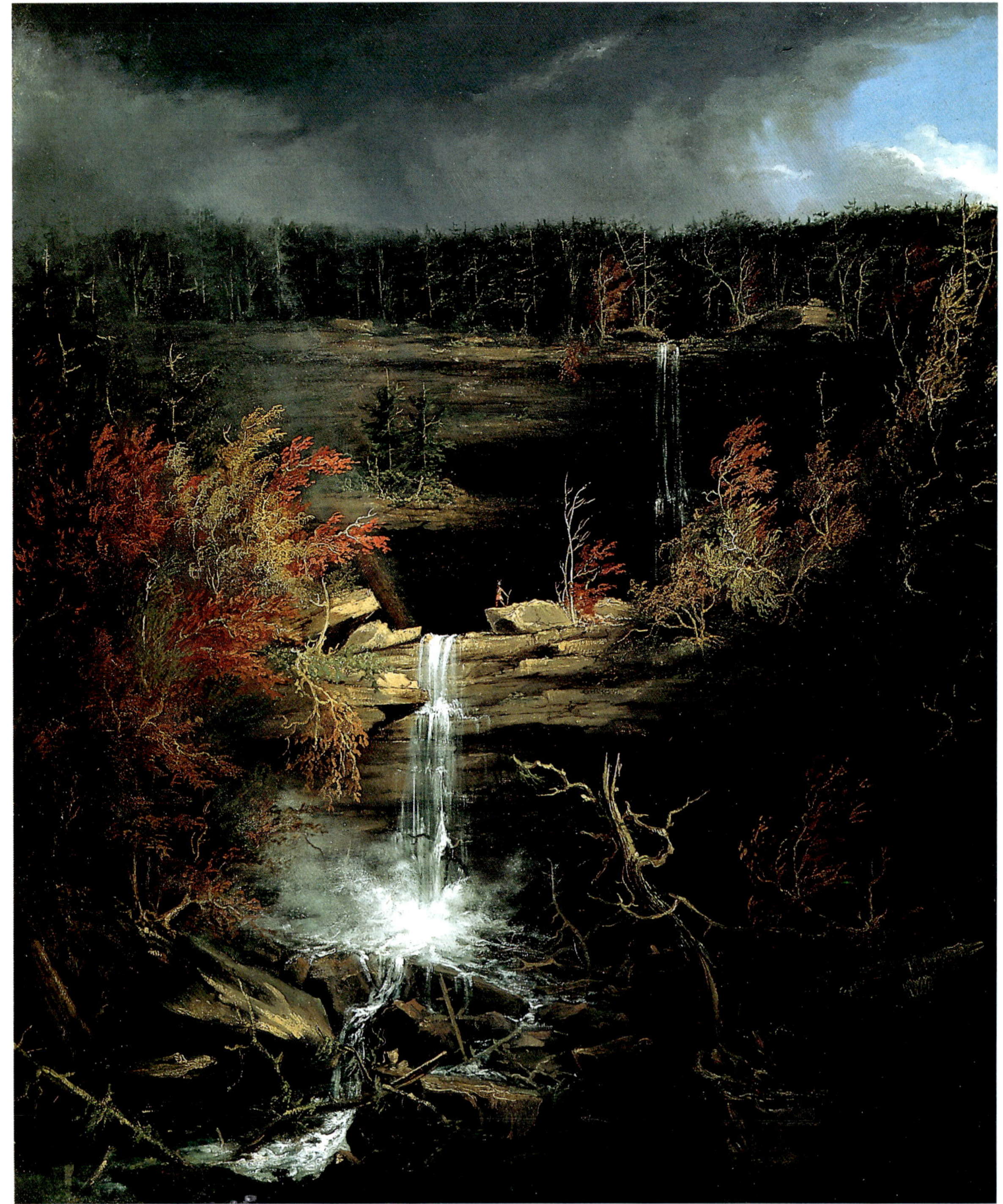

NATIONAL
MUSEUM OF
AMERICAN ART

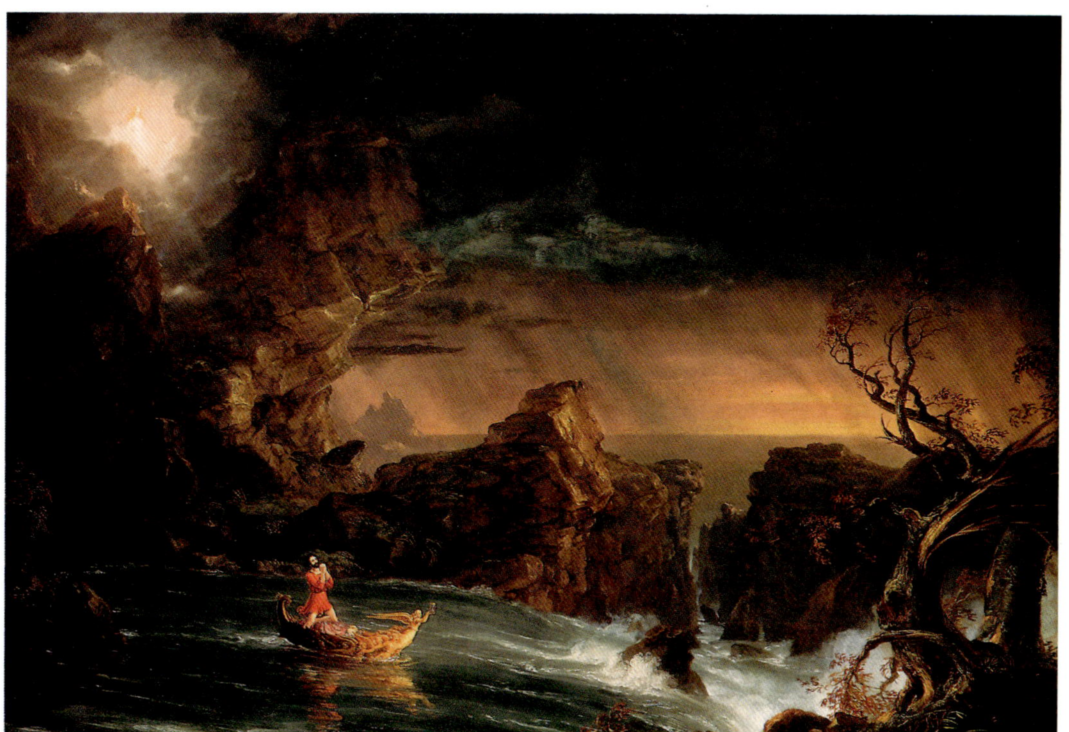

1. **Thomas Cole**
*The Voyage of Life:
Manhood*
1842, Oil on canvas,
52⁷/₈" × 79³/₄"

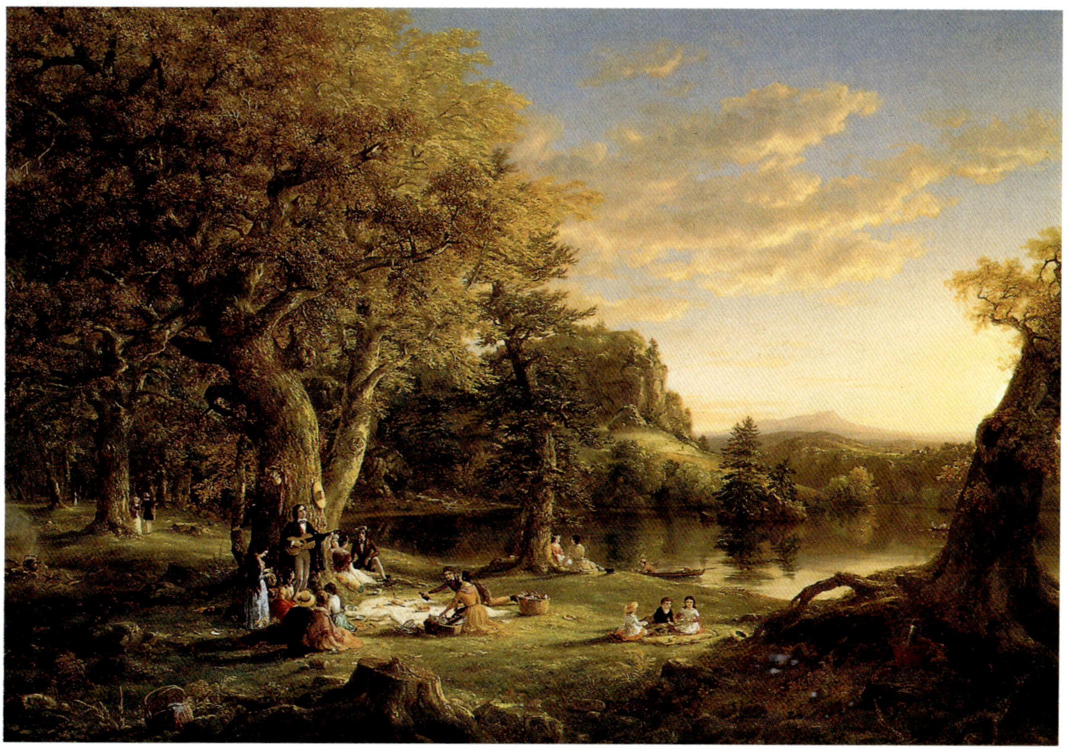

2. **Thomas Cole**
The Pic-nic
1846, Oil on canvas,
44⁷/₈" × 71¹/₈"

Exhibition:
Thomas Cole:
Landscape Into History
March 18 – August 7, 1994

THE J. PAUL GETTY
MUSEUM

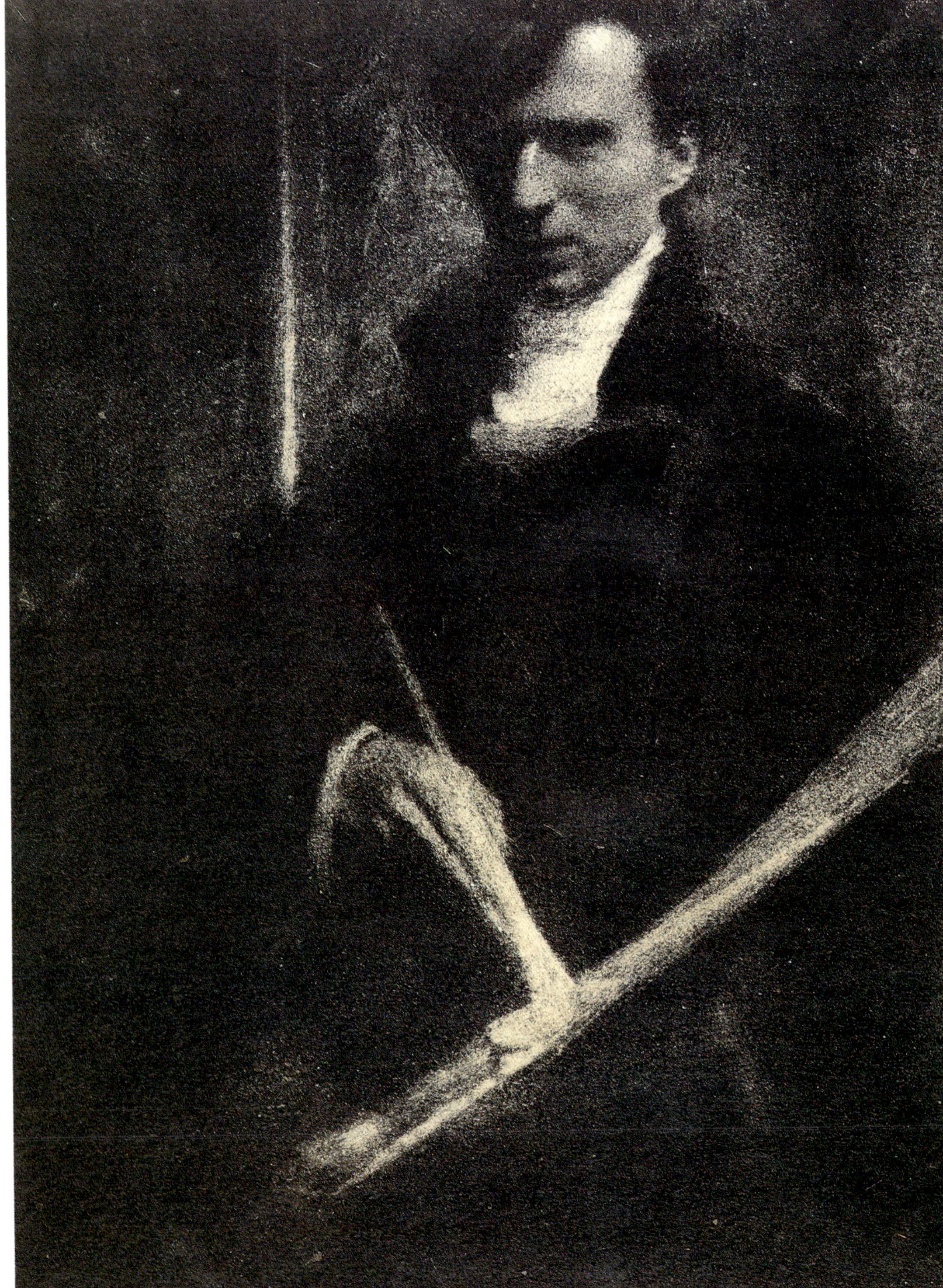

Edward Steichen
Self-Portrait
1901, Pigment,
8¼" x 9¼"

Exhibition:
Photography as a Fine Art:
Handcrafted Prints,
1898-1914
March 15 – June 19, 1994

THE J. PAUL GETTY
MUSEUM

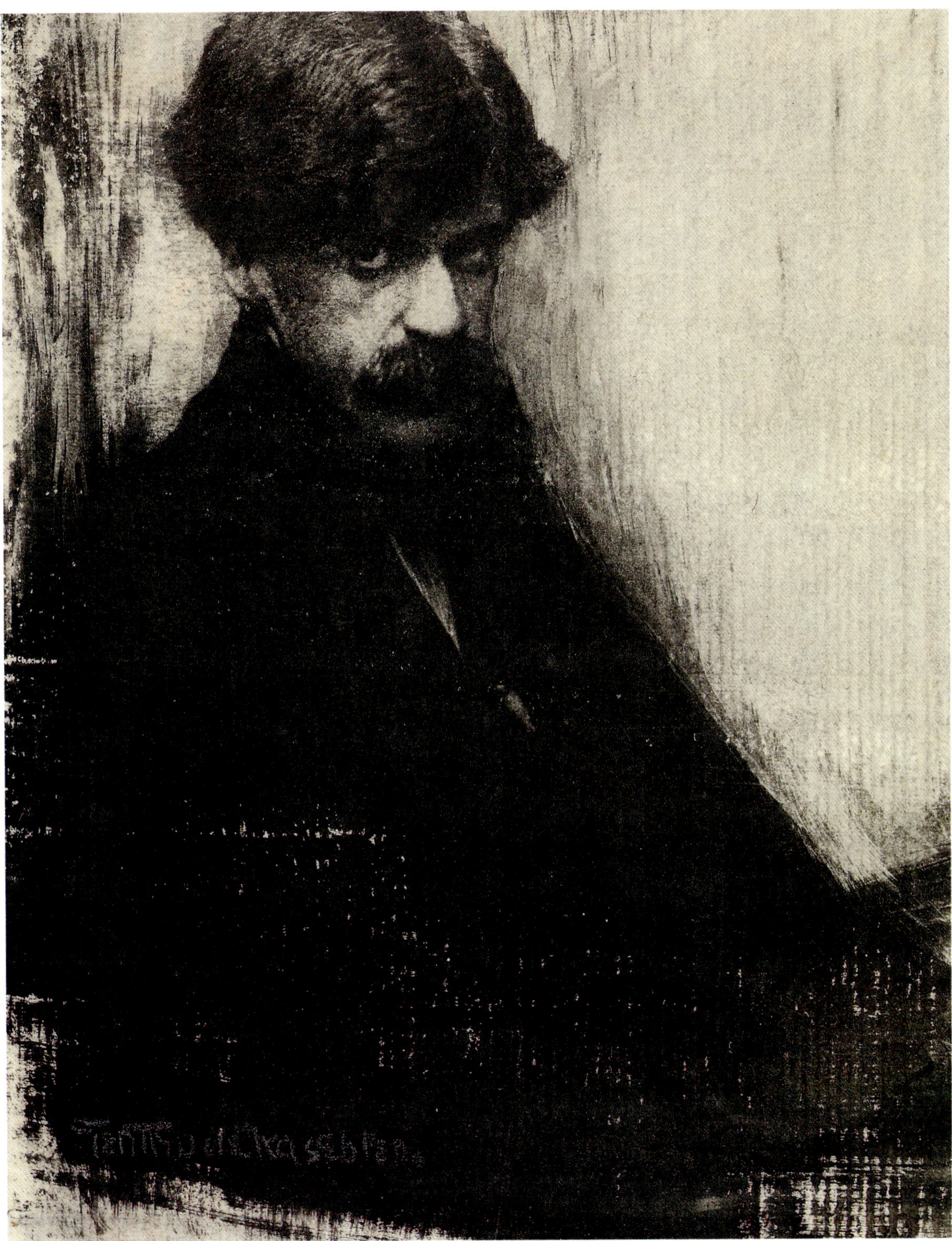

Gertrude Kasebier
Alfred Stieglitz
1968, Gum bichromate,
11³⁄₈" x 9¼"

Exhibition:
Photography as a Fine Art:
Handcrafted Prints,
1898-1914
March 15 – June 19, 1994

THE NATIONAL
MUSEUM OF
WOMEN
IN THE ARTS

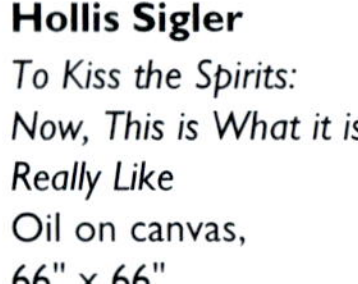

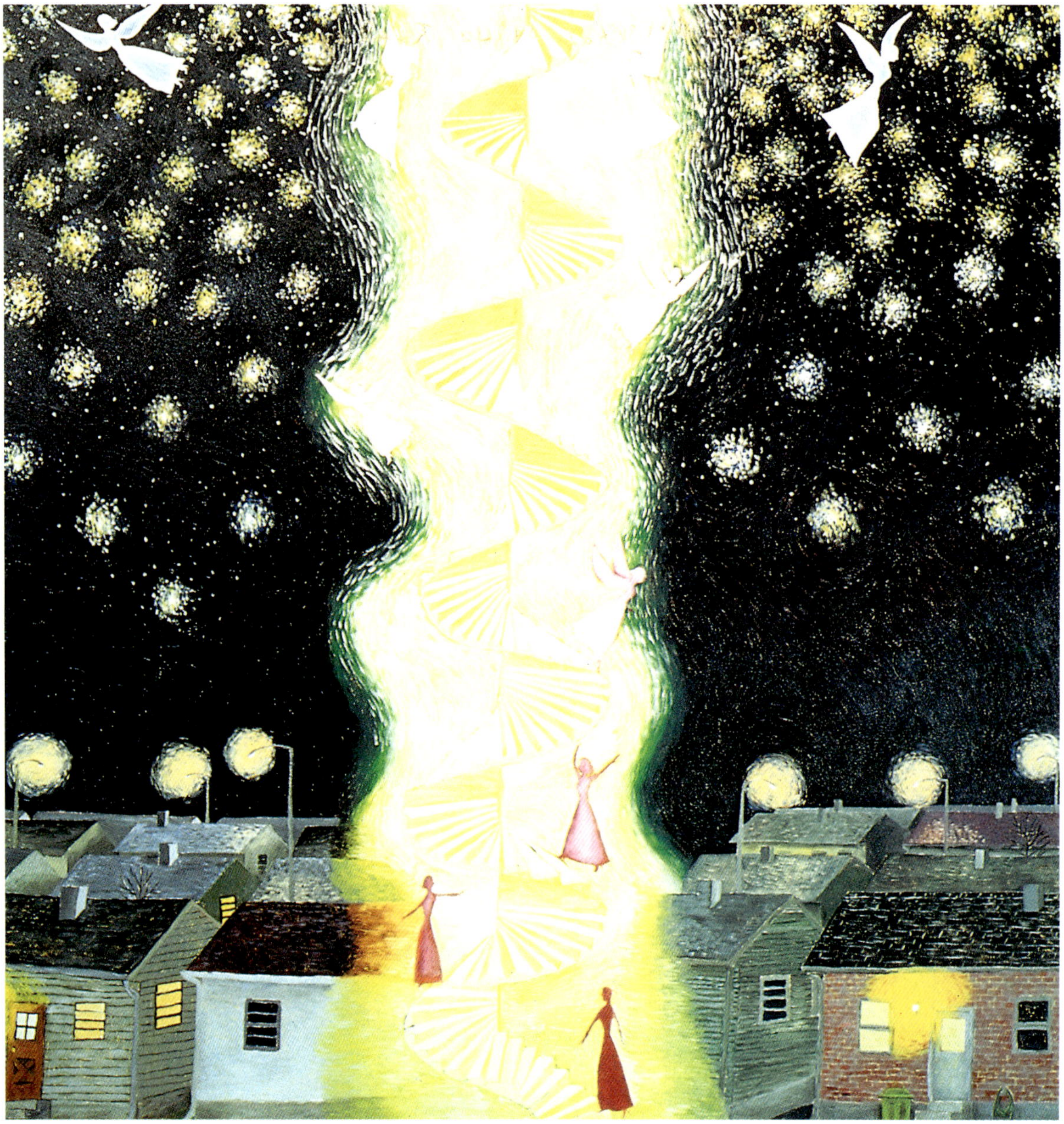

Hollis Sigler
To Kiss the Spirits:
Now, This is What it is
Really Like
Oil on canvas,
66" x 66"

Exhibition:
Breast Cancer Journal:
Walking with the Ghosts
of My Grandmothers
Sept. 2 – Nov. 14, 1993

MODERN ART
MUSEUM OF
FORT WORTH

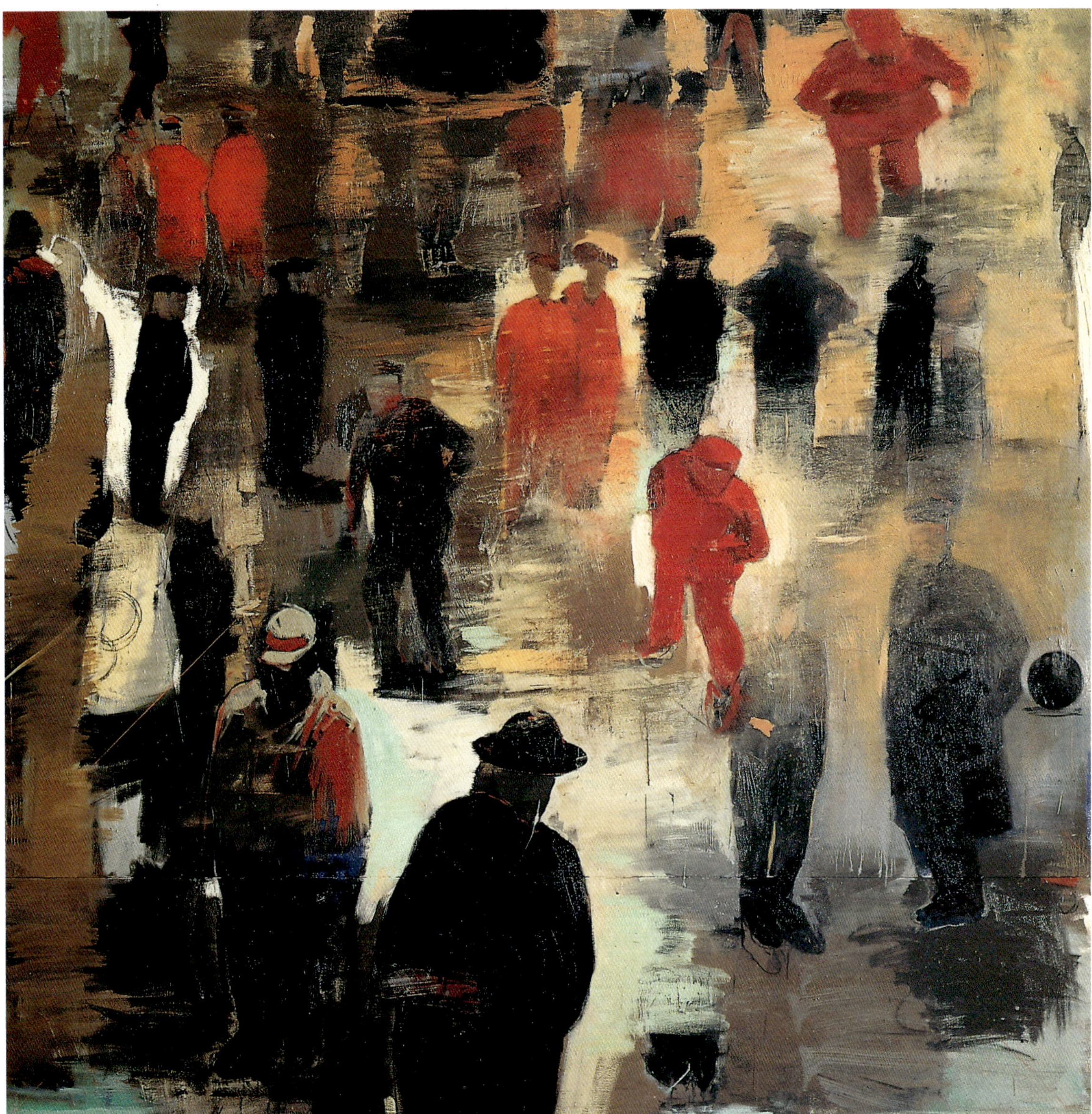

Christopher Brown
November 19, 1863
1989, Oil on canvas,
104" × 104"

Exhibition:
Christopher Brown:
Collection of the Modern
Art Museum of Fort Worth,
Museum Purchase,
the Ann Burnett and
Charles Tandy Foundation
Endowment Fund
January 15 – March 5, 1995

WHITNEY MUSEUM
OF AMERICAN ART

Joseph Stella
Neapolitan Song
1927-28, Oil on canvas,
66¼" x 28¼"

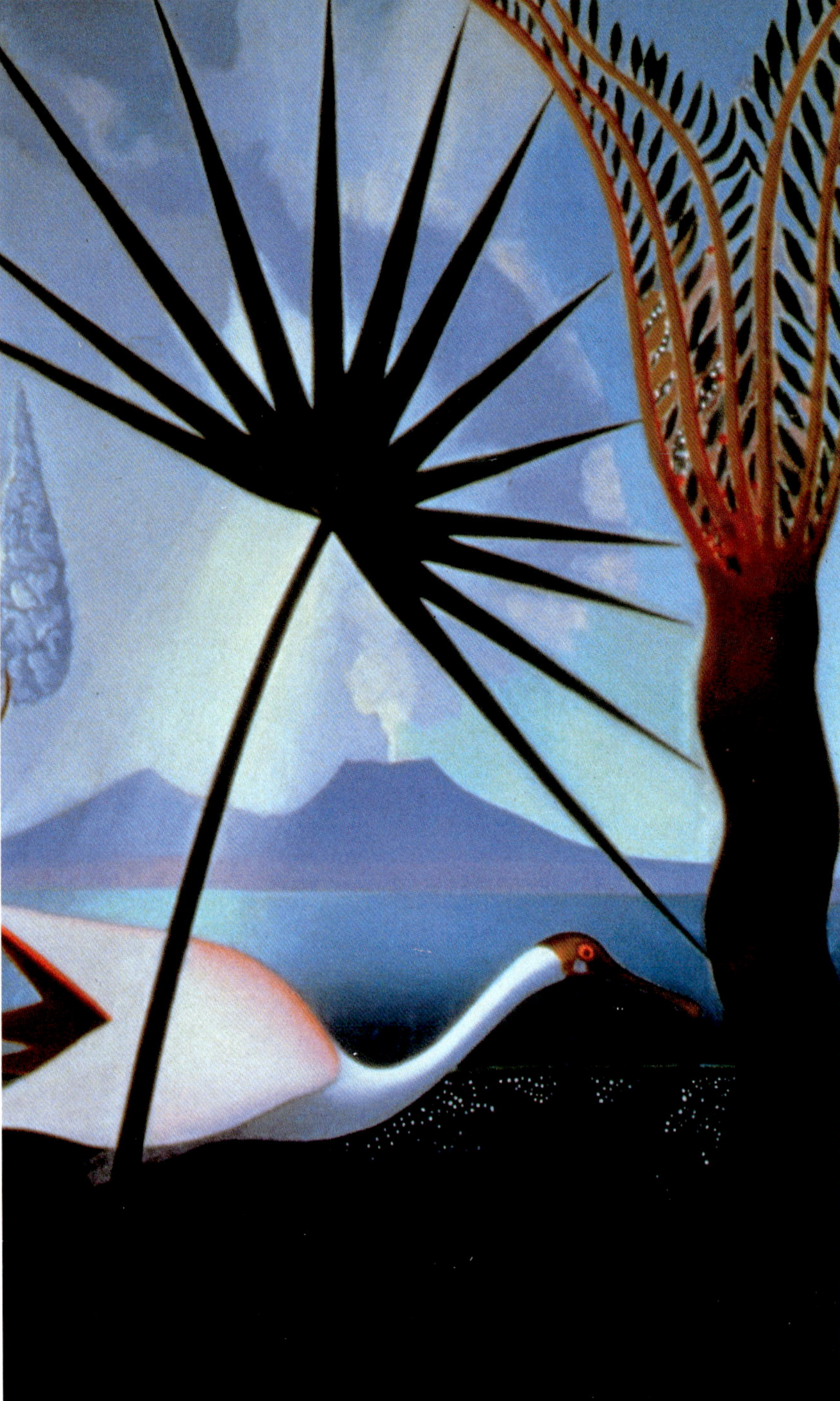

Exhibition:
Joseph Stella: The first
museum retrospective in
over thirty years
April 22 – October 9, 1994

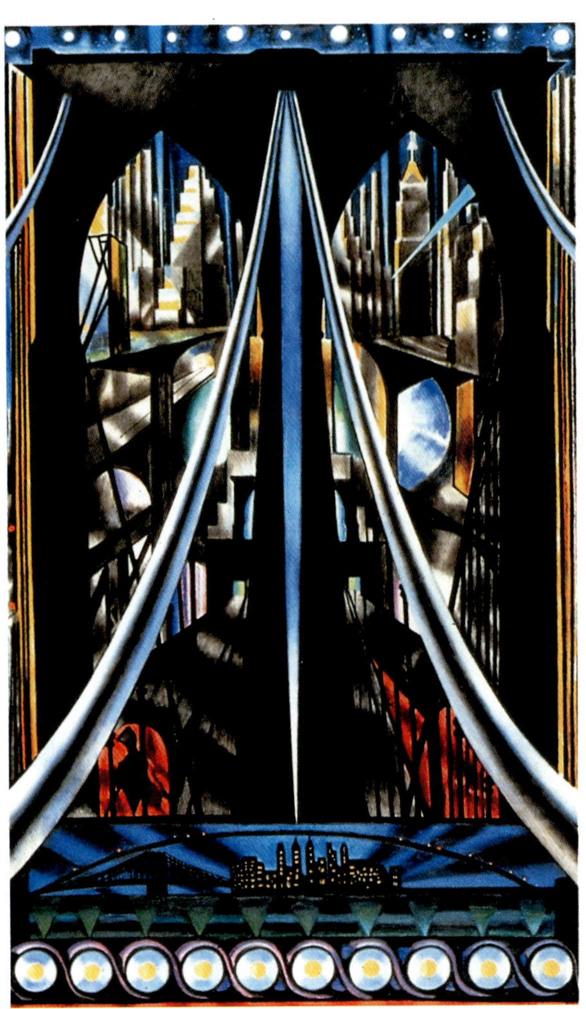

1

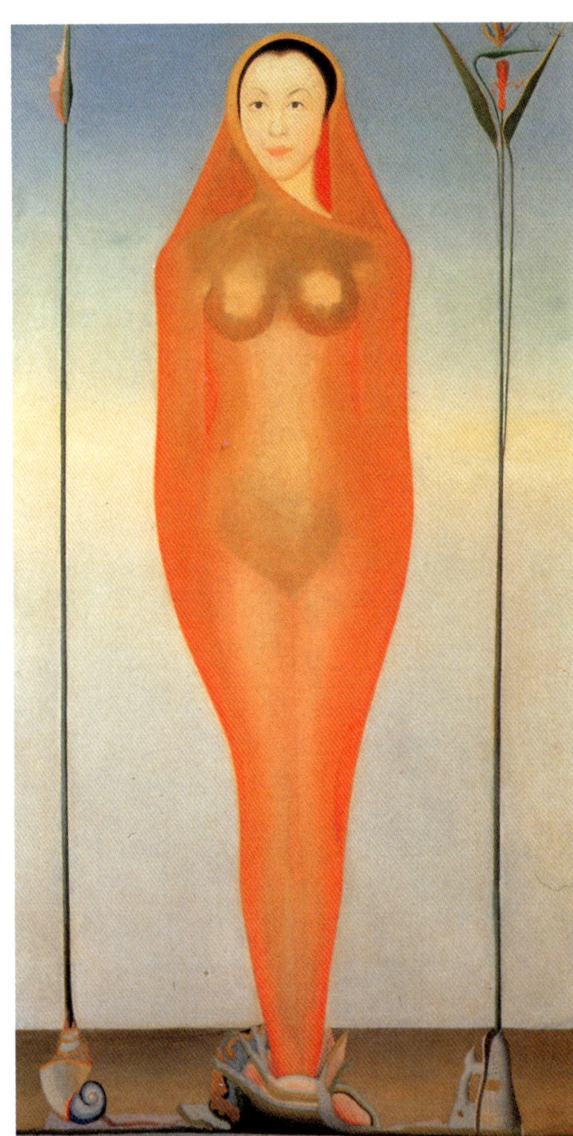

2

1. **Joseph Stella**
   The Brooklyn Bridge:
   Variation on an Old Theme
   1939, Oil on canvas,
   70" x 42"

2. **Joseph Stella**
   A Vision
   1925-26, Oil on canvas,
   80" x 40"

Exhibition:
Joseph Stella: The first
museum retrospective in
over thirty years
April 22 – October 9, 1994

SAN FRANCISCO
MUSEUM OF
MODERN ART

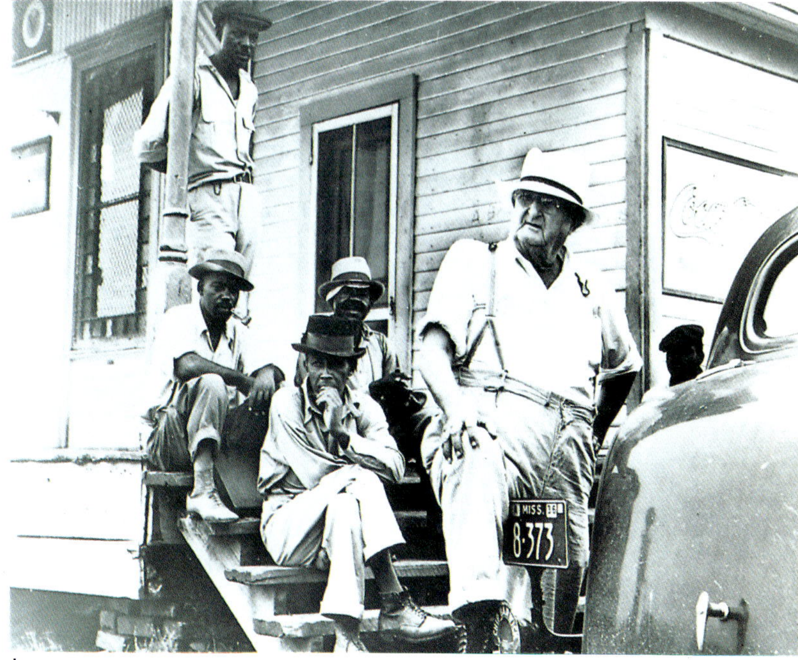

1

1. **Dorothea Lange**
   *Plantation Overseer and
   His Field Hands,
   Mississippi*
   1936, Photography,
   19.7" x 24.3"

2. **Dorothea Lange**
   *Migratory Cotton Picker,
   Eloy, Arizona*
   1940, Photography,
   19¼" x 12⅞"

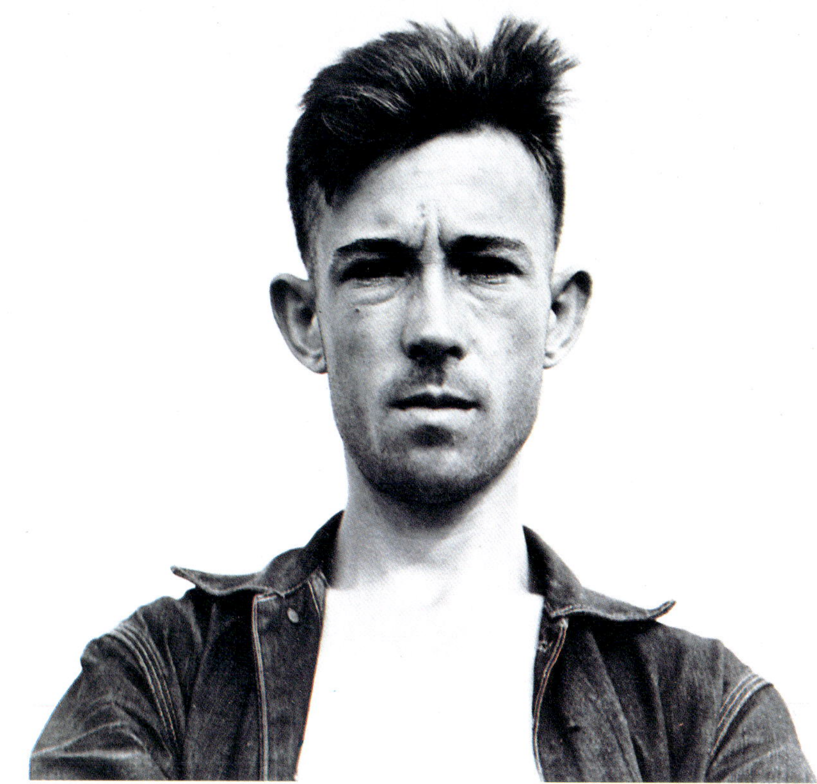

2

Exhibition:
Dorothea Lange:
American Photographs
May 19 – September 4, 1994
Lange in Context
May 19 – September 4, 1994

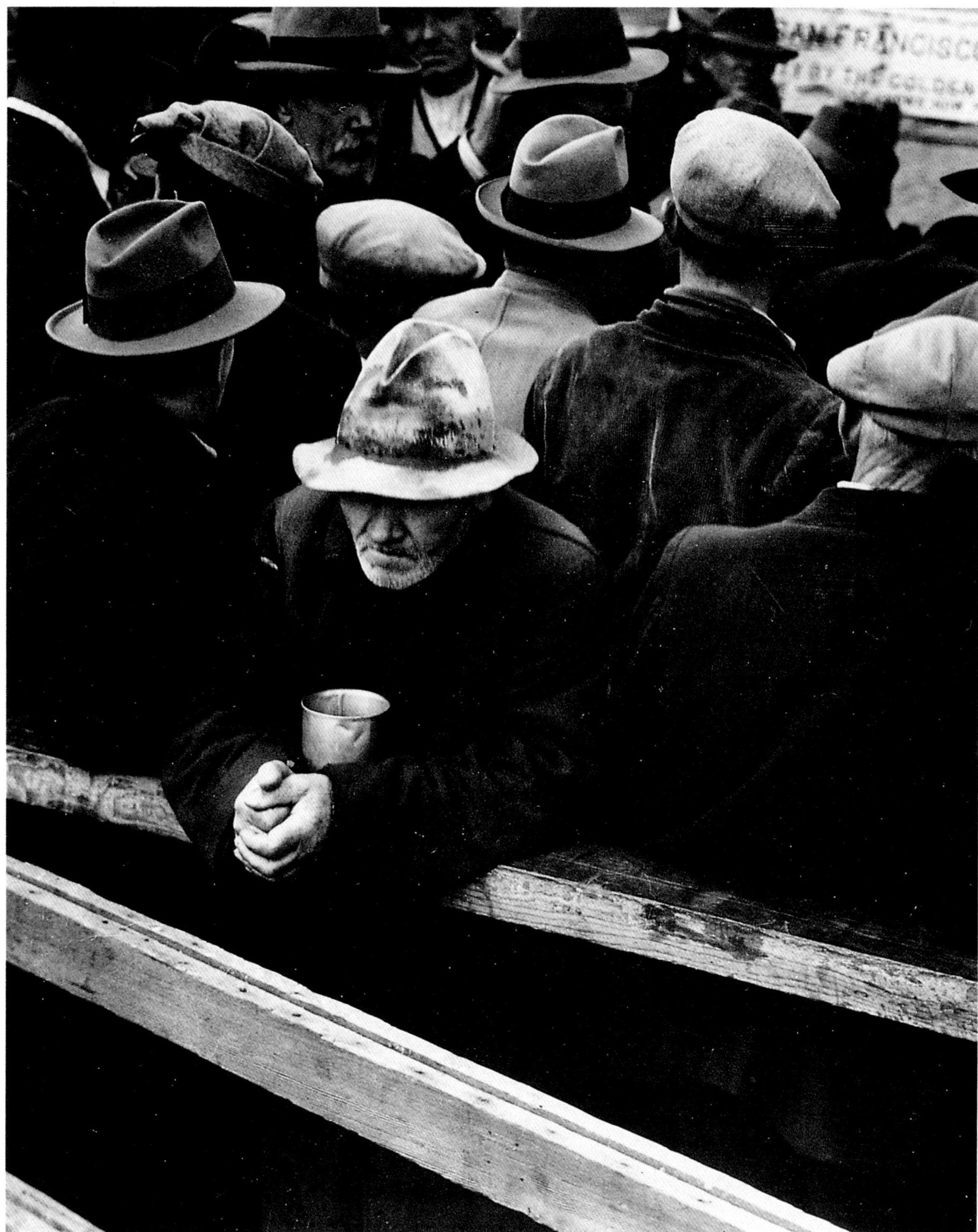

SAN FRANCISCO
MUSEUM OF
MODERN ART

Dorothea Lange
*White Angel Breadline,
San Francisco*
1933, Photography,
12¼" x 10¼"

Exhibition:
Dorothea Lange:
American Photographs
May 19 – September 4, 1994
Lange in Context
May 19 – September 4, 1994

SOLOMON R.
GUGGENHEIM
MUSEUM

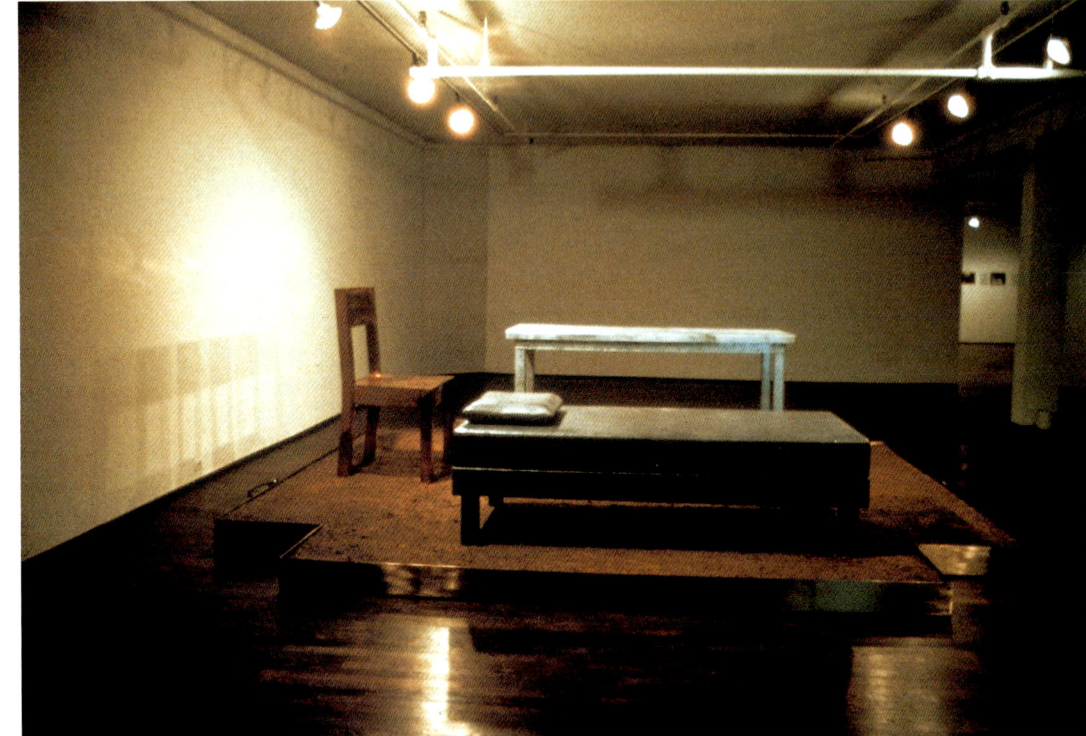

1. Robert Morris
   Hearing
   1972, Installation
   William College Museum of Art,
   Williamstown, Mass
   Photo Courtesy Leo Castelli
   Galler, New York

1

2. **Robert Morris**
   House of the Vetti
   1983, Felt, steel bracket,
   and metal grommets
   94$\frac{1}{2}$" x 96" x 36" overall
   Private Collection, Madrid

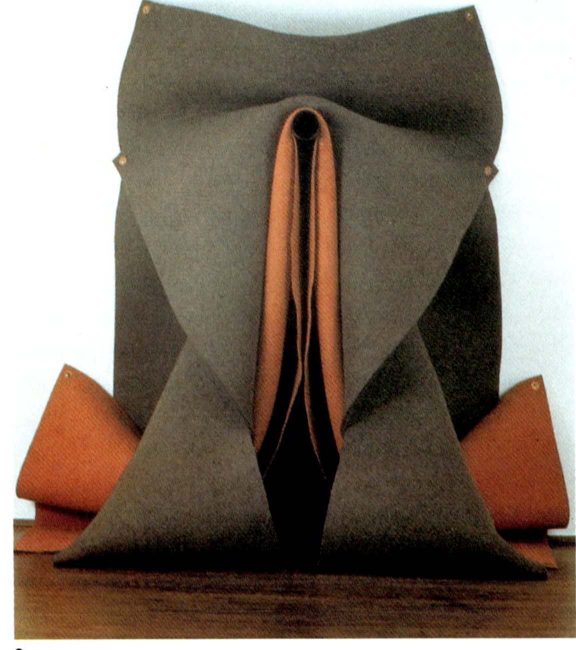

Exhibition:
Robert Morris:
The Mind/Body Problem
February 4 – April 17,1994

2

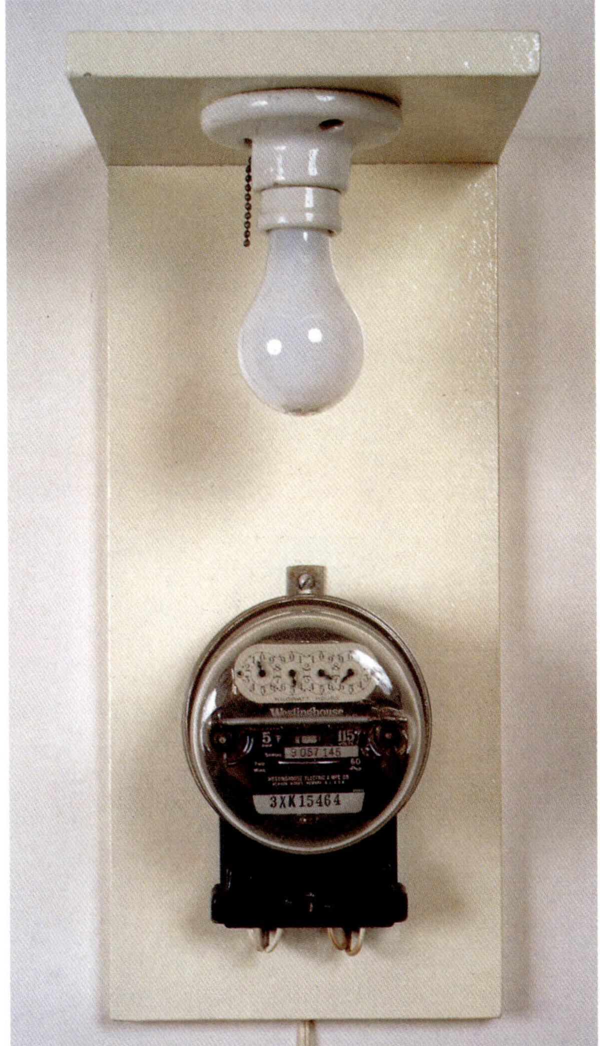

GUGGENHEIM
MUSEUM, SOHO

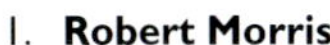
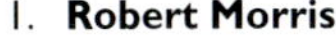

2

1. **Robert Morris**
   I-Box
   1962, Painted plywood
   cabinet covered with
   Sculptmetal containing
   photograph
   19" x 12³/₄" x 1³/₈"
   Collection Leo Castelli, Photo
   Dorothy Zeidman

2. **Robert Morris**
   Metered Bulb
   1963, Light bulb,
   ceramic socket with
   pull chain, and electricity
   meter, mounted on
   painted wood
   94³/₄" x 8" x 8¹/₄"
   Collection Jasper Johns,
   Photo Dorothy Zeidman

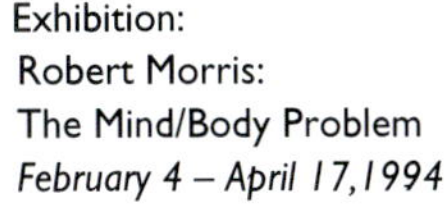

Exhibition:
Robert Morris:
The Mind/Body Problem
February 4 – April 17, 1994

1

MUSEUM OF CONTEMPORARY ART SAN DIEGO

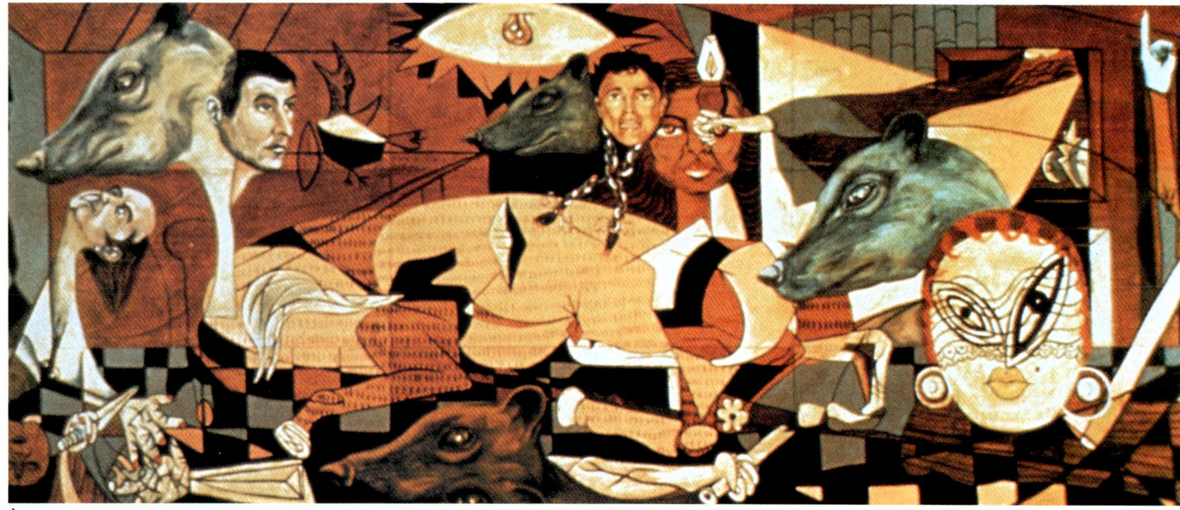

1

1. **Ray Smith**
   Guernimex
   1989, Oil and wax on wood,
   108" x 242"

2. **Anne Wallace**
   Ma Sa Sa 'Lack' Ol? from Amando en Tiempo de Guerra Suite
   1989-91, Eucalyptus
   15" x 20" x 33"

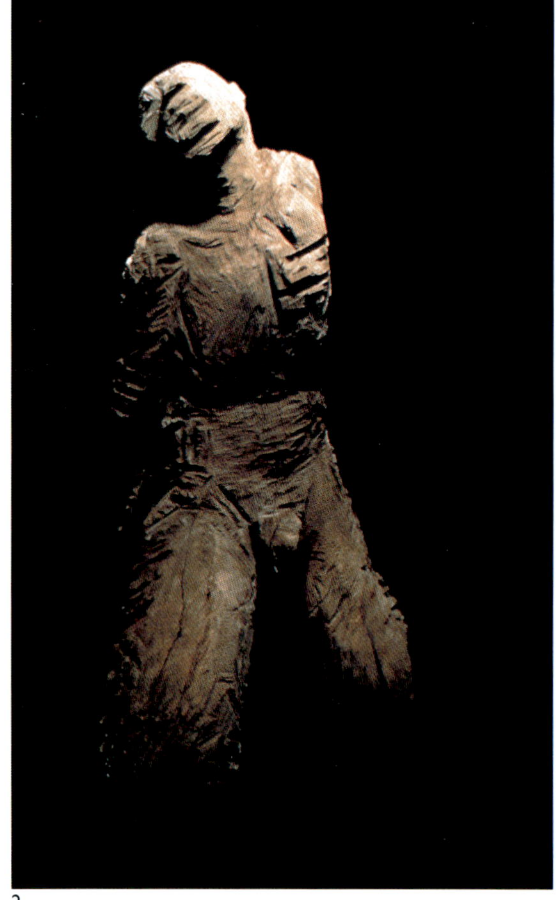

2

Exhibition:
La Frontera/The Border
Art about the
Mexico/United States
Border Experience
March 6 – May 22, 1993

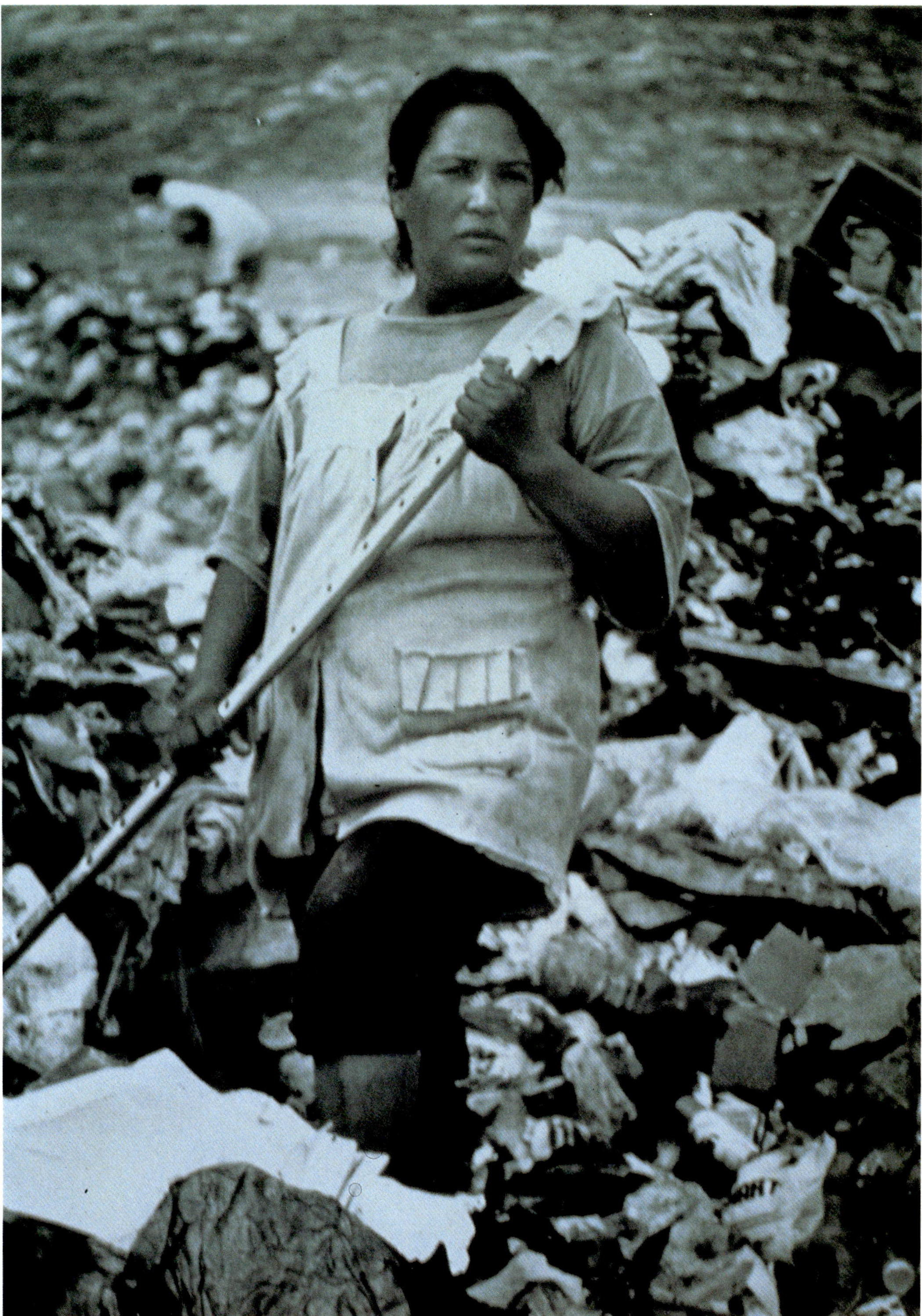

MUSEUM OF
CONTEMPORARY
ART SAN DIEGO

Carmen Amato
*Mujer Selecciondora
de Basura (Female
Sanitary Worker)*
1991, Black-and-White
Photograph
16" x 20"

Exhibition:
La Frontera/The Border
Art about the
Mexico/United States
Border Experience
March 6 – May 22, 1993

PHILADELPHIA
MUSEUM OF ART

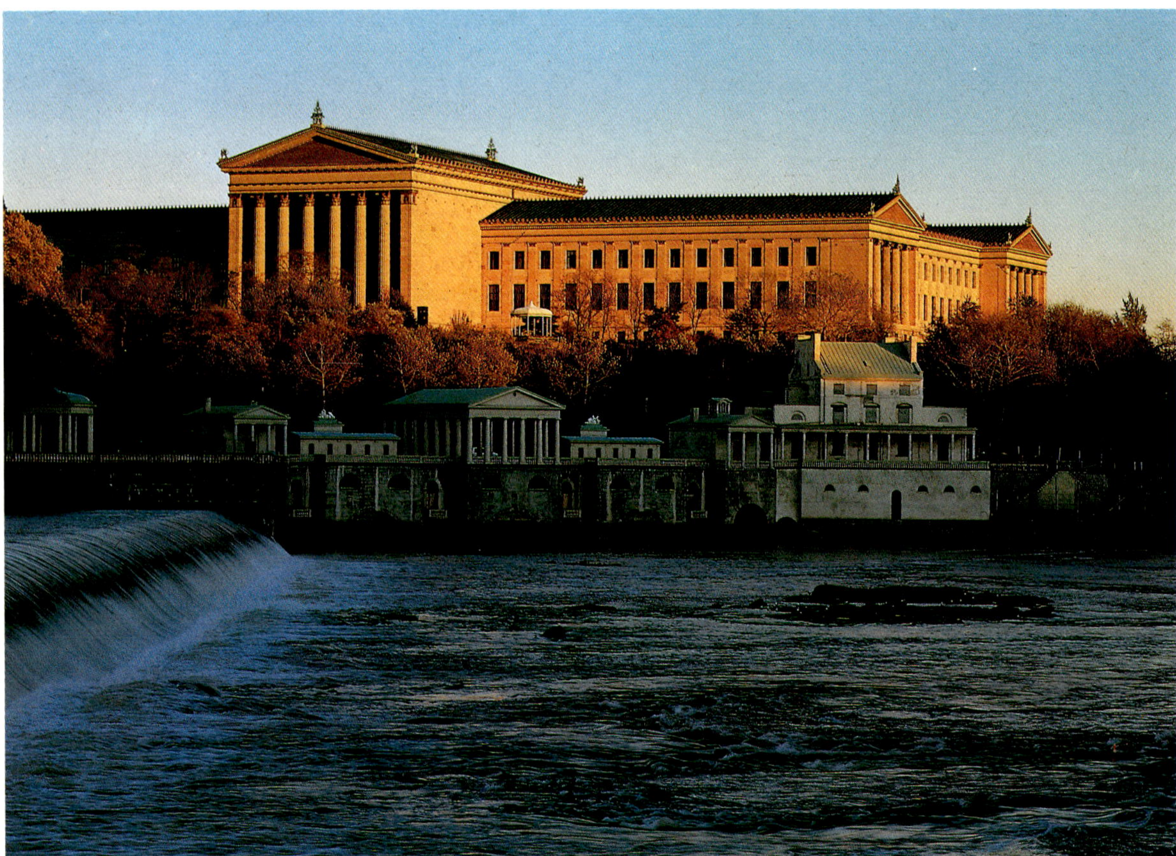

*Philadelphia Museum of
Art West View*

Exhibition:
Philadelphia Museum of Art
Collection

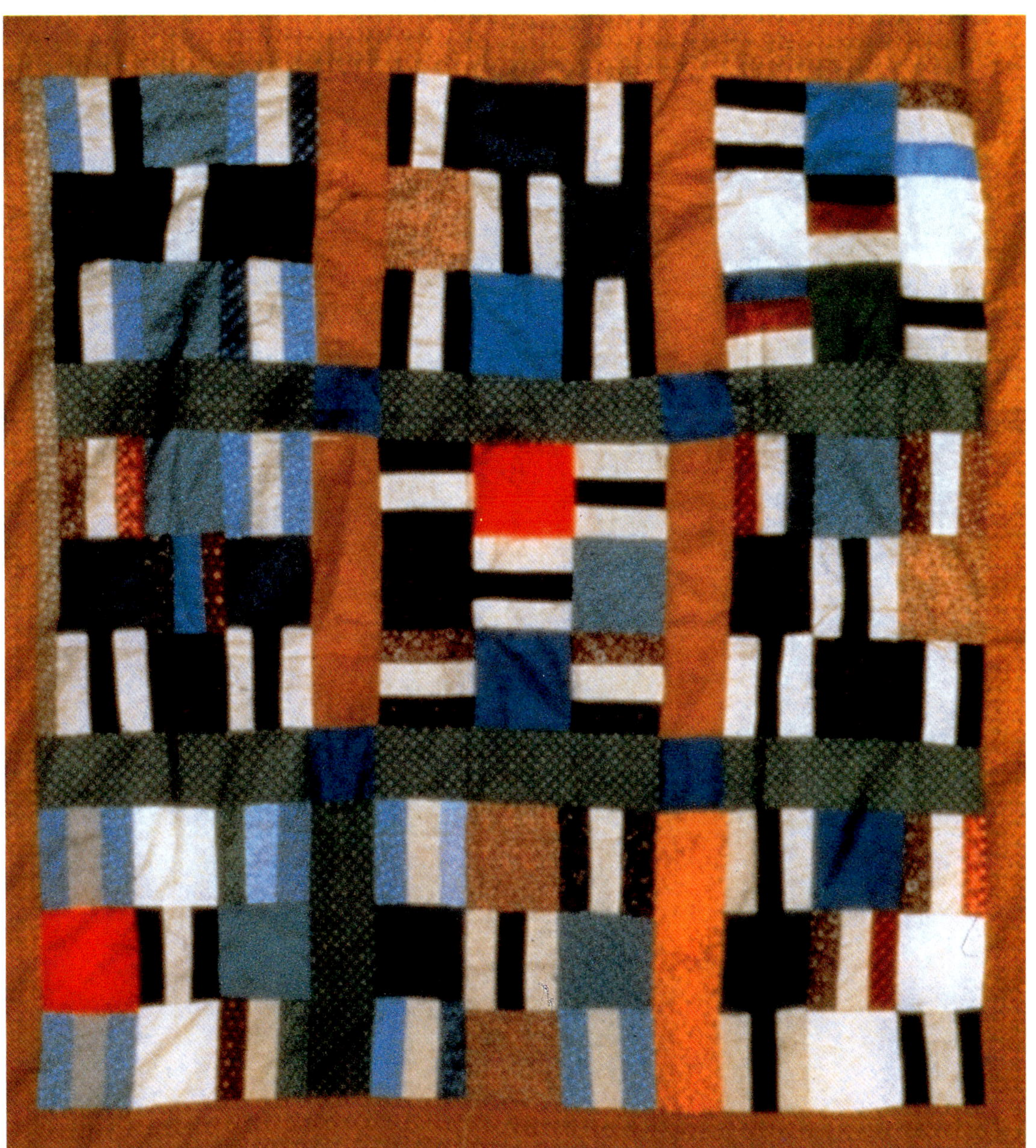

PHILADELPHIA
MUSEUM OF ART

Plummert Pettway
Nine-Patch Quilt
193 x 190 cm

Exhibition:
Community Fabric:
African American Quilts
and Folk Art
February 13 – April 10, 1994

MUSÉE D' ART
CONTEMPORAIN DE
MONTRÉAL

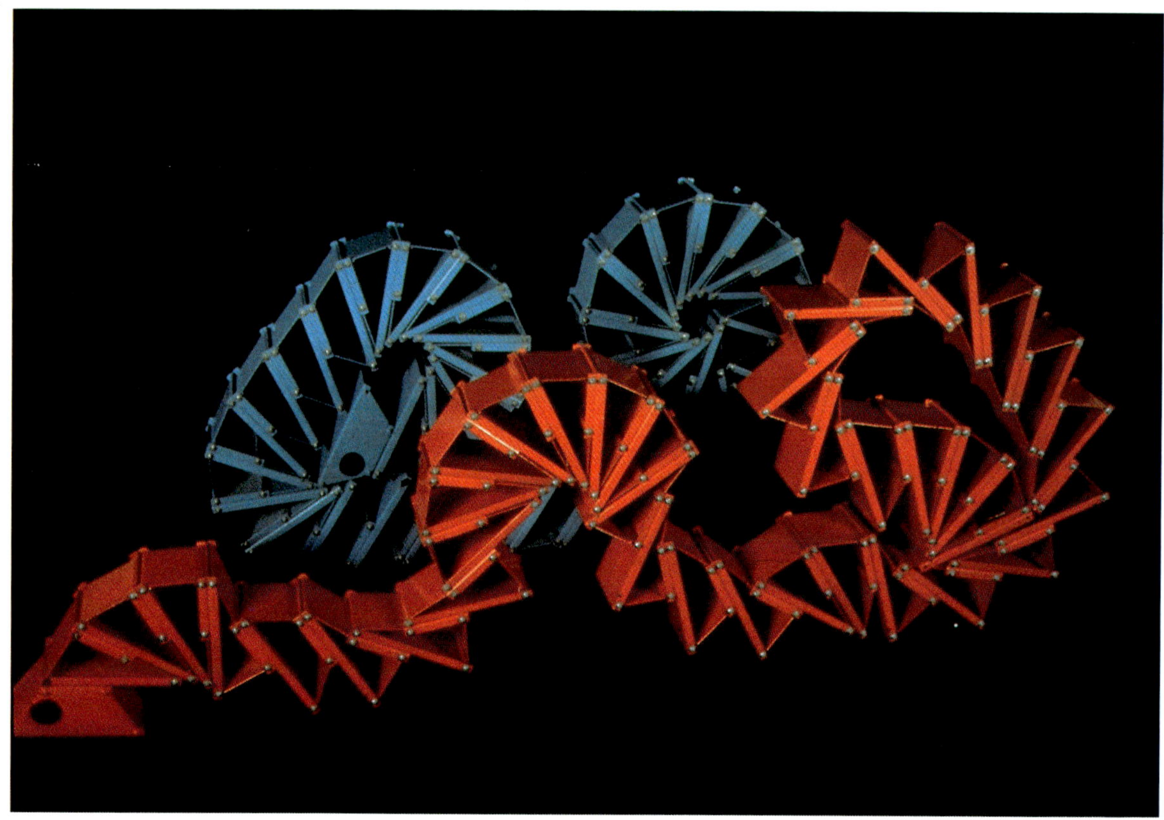

Gertrude Kasebier
Alfred Stieglitz
1968, Gum bichromate,
11⅜" x 9¼"

Exhibition:

Henry Saxe:
The first retrospective
dedicated to Henry Sax,
One of Canada's most
important sculptors
May 20 – Sept. 25, 1994

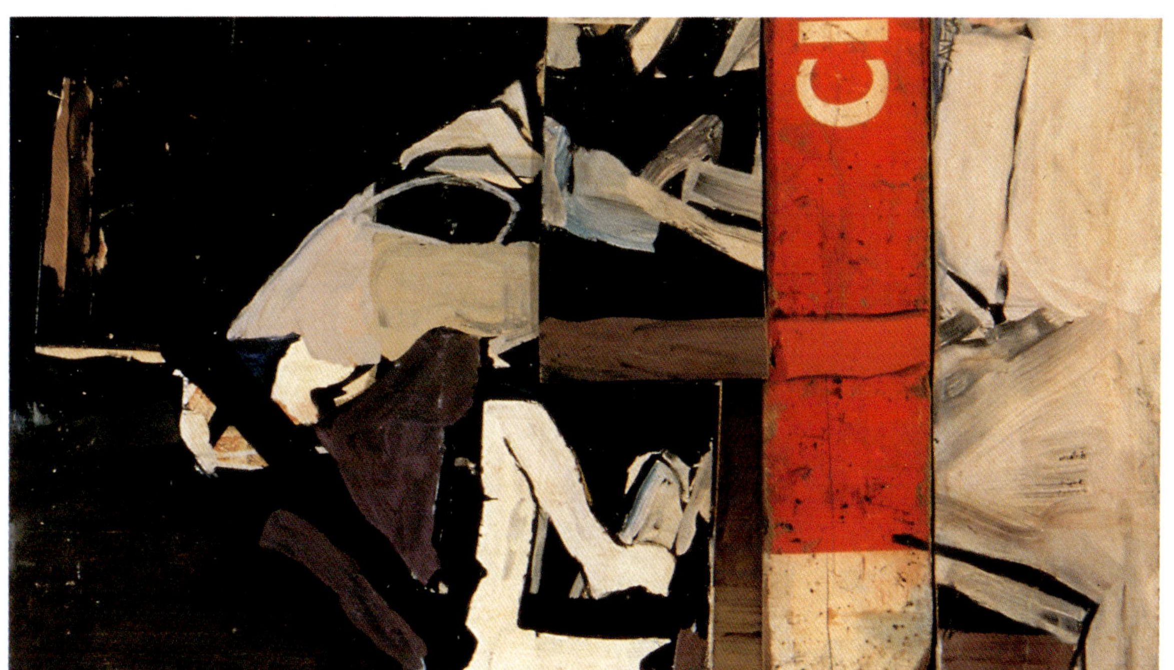

MUSÉE D' ART
CONTEMPORAIN DE
MONTRÉAL

Gertrude Kasebier
Alfred Stieglitz
1968, Gum bichromate,
11 ⅜" x 9¼"

Exhibition:
Henry Saxe:
The first retrospective
dedicated to Henry Sax,
One of Canada's most
important sculptors
May 20 – Sept. 25, 1994

THE MUSEUM OF CONTEMPORARY ART, LOS ANGELES

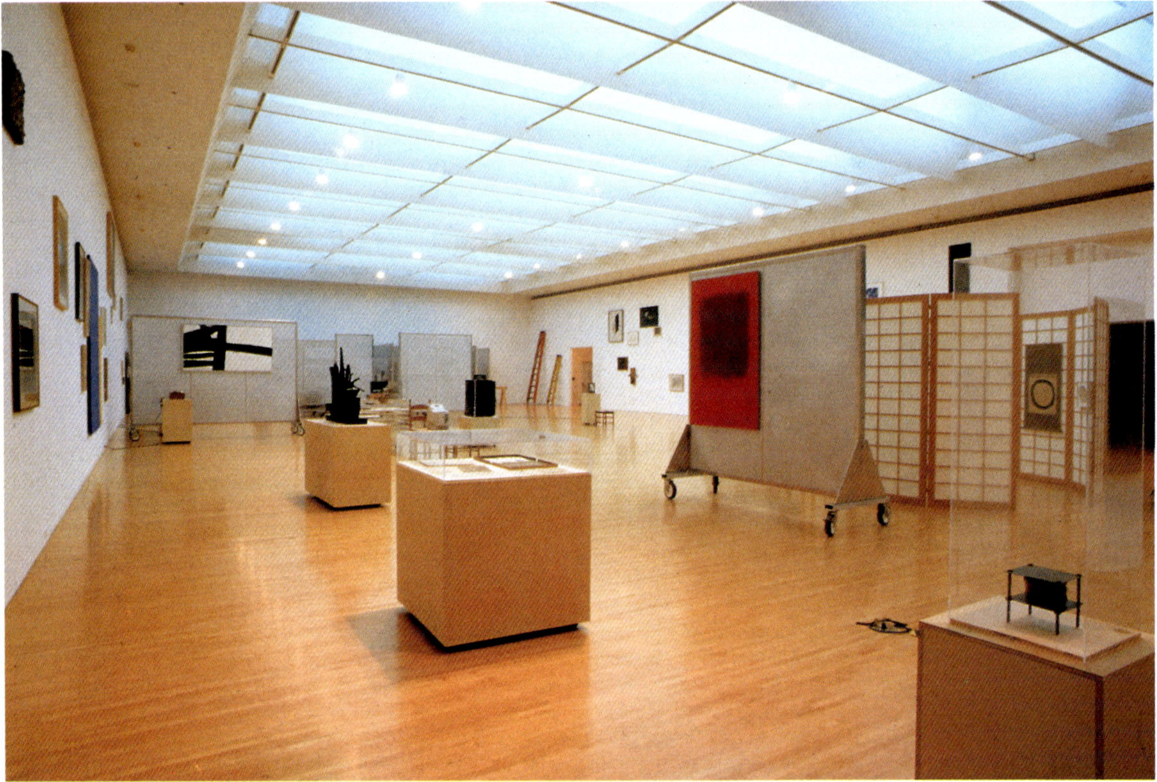

Rolywholyover A Circus
Installation view,
South Gallery,
Gallery in which
artworks are moved
according to a "chance-
generated score"

Exhibition:

"Rolywholyover A Circus,"
for museum by John Cage,
Organized by the Museum
of Contemporary Art, Los
Angeles, the exhibition
will be on display at the
Guggenheim Museum SoHo
through July 31. Its International tour than continues
to Art Tower Mito
Contemporary Art Center,

Continued on next page

THE MUSEUM OF
CONTEMPORARY
ART, LOS ANGELES

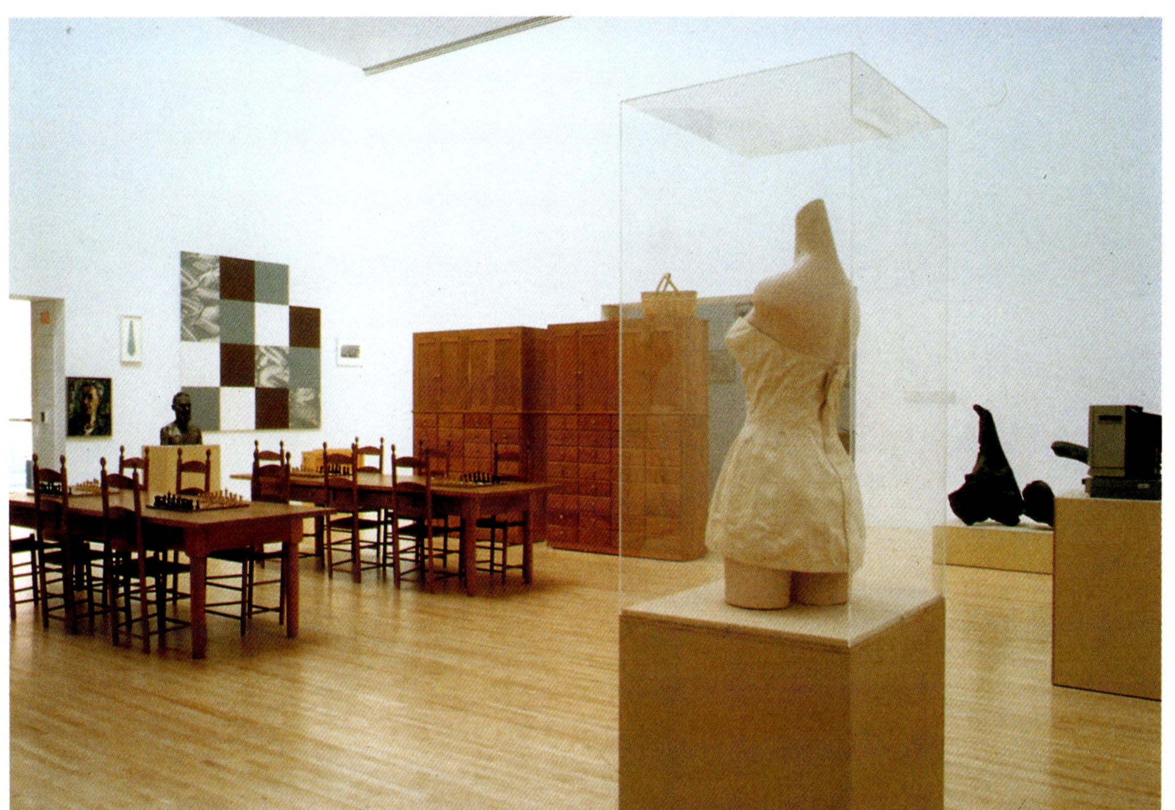

Rolywholyover A Circus
Installation view,
South Gallery
Gallery Housing
"Museumcircle" project

Continued from page 32
Japan (*Nov. 3, 94 – Feb. 26, 1995*); and Philadelphia
Museum of Art
(*May 21 – July 30, 1995*).
The exhibition premiered
at MOCA from
Sept. 12 – Nov. 28, 93

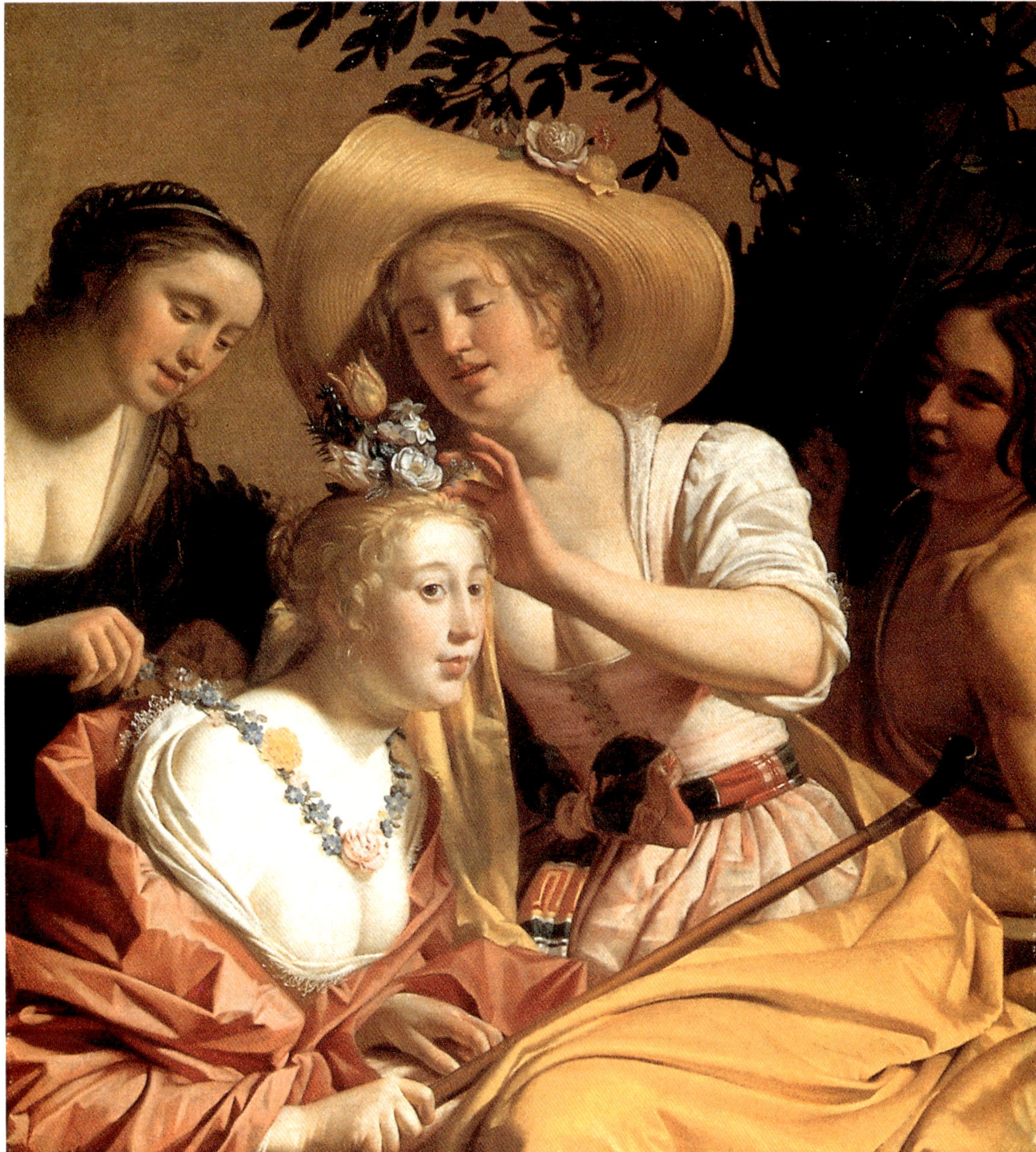

Gerrit Van Honthorst
Pastoralle
Oil on canvas

Exhibition:
A Gift to America:
Masterpieces of European
Painting from the Samuel H.
Kress Collection
Sept. 15 – Nov. 2, 1994

PAINTINGS

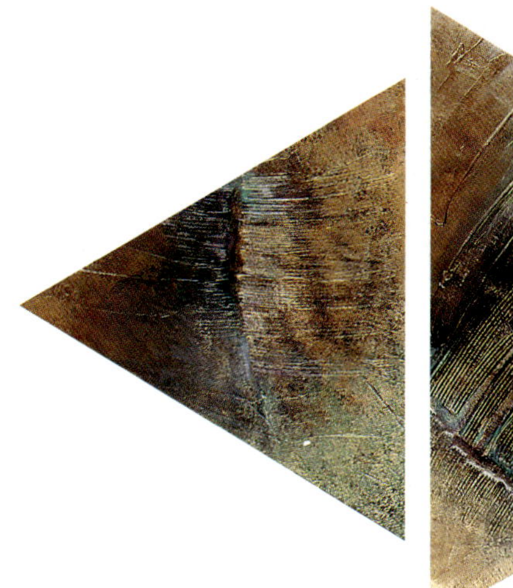

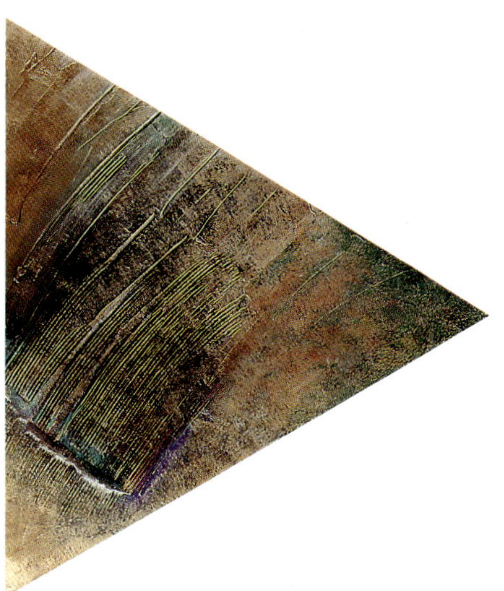

1

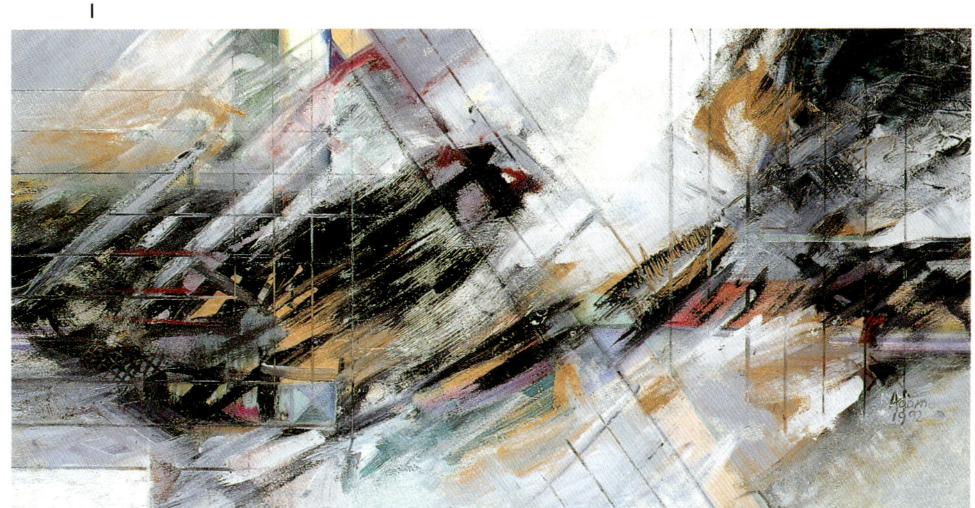

2

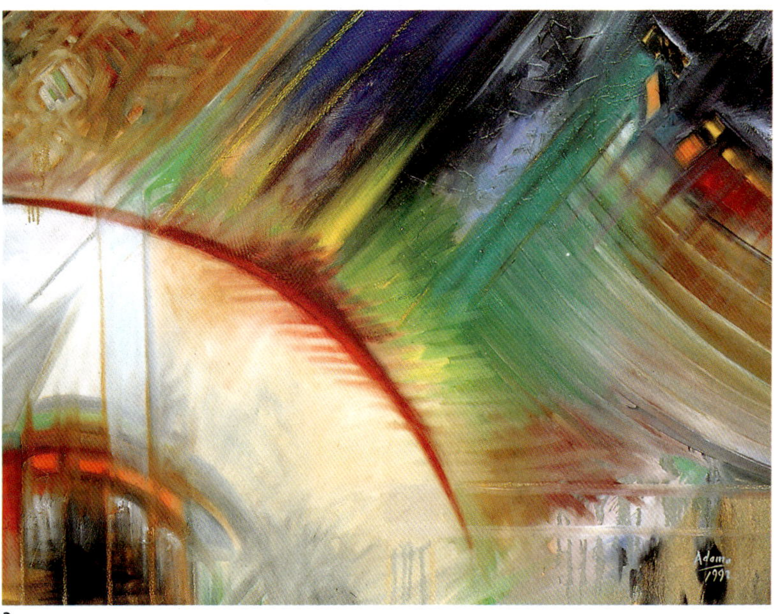

3

ROCFERN
INTERNATIONAL
GALLERIES, INC.

80 Carlauren Road Unit17
Woodbridge (Toronto),
Ontario L4L 7Z5 Canada
905.850.7647
905.850.8062 FAX

Contact:
Rocco Pannese
Fernando Rocco

Pietro Adamo

1. *Tanker Barbados*
   1992,
   Mixed media on canvas,
   30" x 30" x 30"
   40" x 40" x 40"

2. *Pythagoras*
   1992, Mixed media on
   canvas, 36" x 72"

3. *Plume*
   1992, Oil on canvas,
   40" x 54"

Selected Biography:

1994 Rocfern International
      Galleries, Woodbridge,
      Ontario, Canada

      Lerner Gallery
      Beverly Hills, CA

1993 Art Frankfurt
      Frankfurt, Germany

1992 Free & Free Gallery
      Boca Raton, FL

      Art Gallery of Hamilton
      Hamilton, Ontario

      Arte
      New York, NY

GALLERY
ART AND PEACE

1545 Palmer Avenue
Winter Park, FL 32789
407.629.6308
407.629.9206 FAX

Contact:
Susan League, Director

Exhibiting:
Contemporary painting
and sculpture

Jim Allen

Woman of Peace
1992, Fresco tempera,
84" x 60"

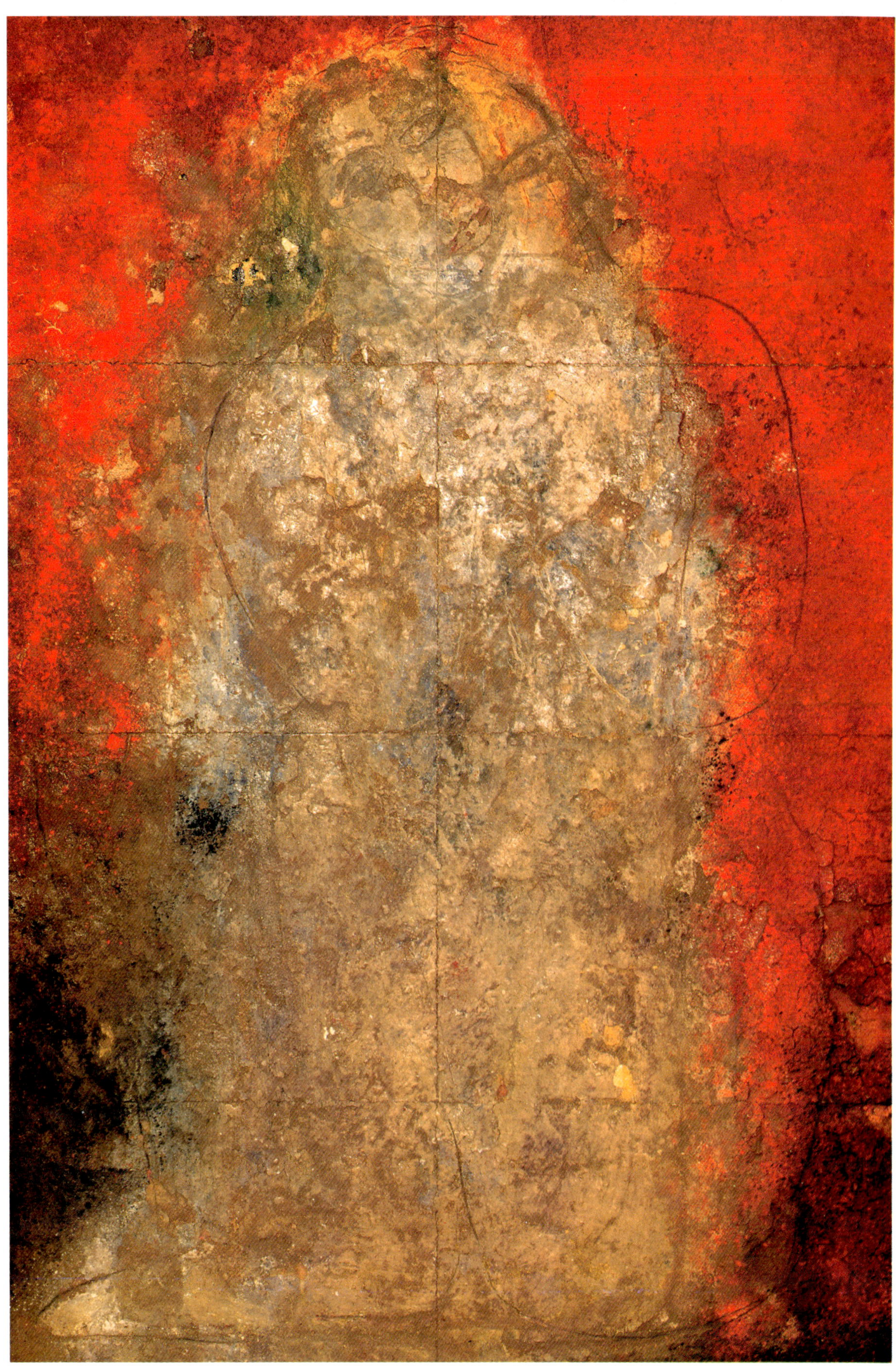

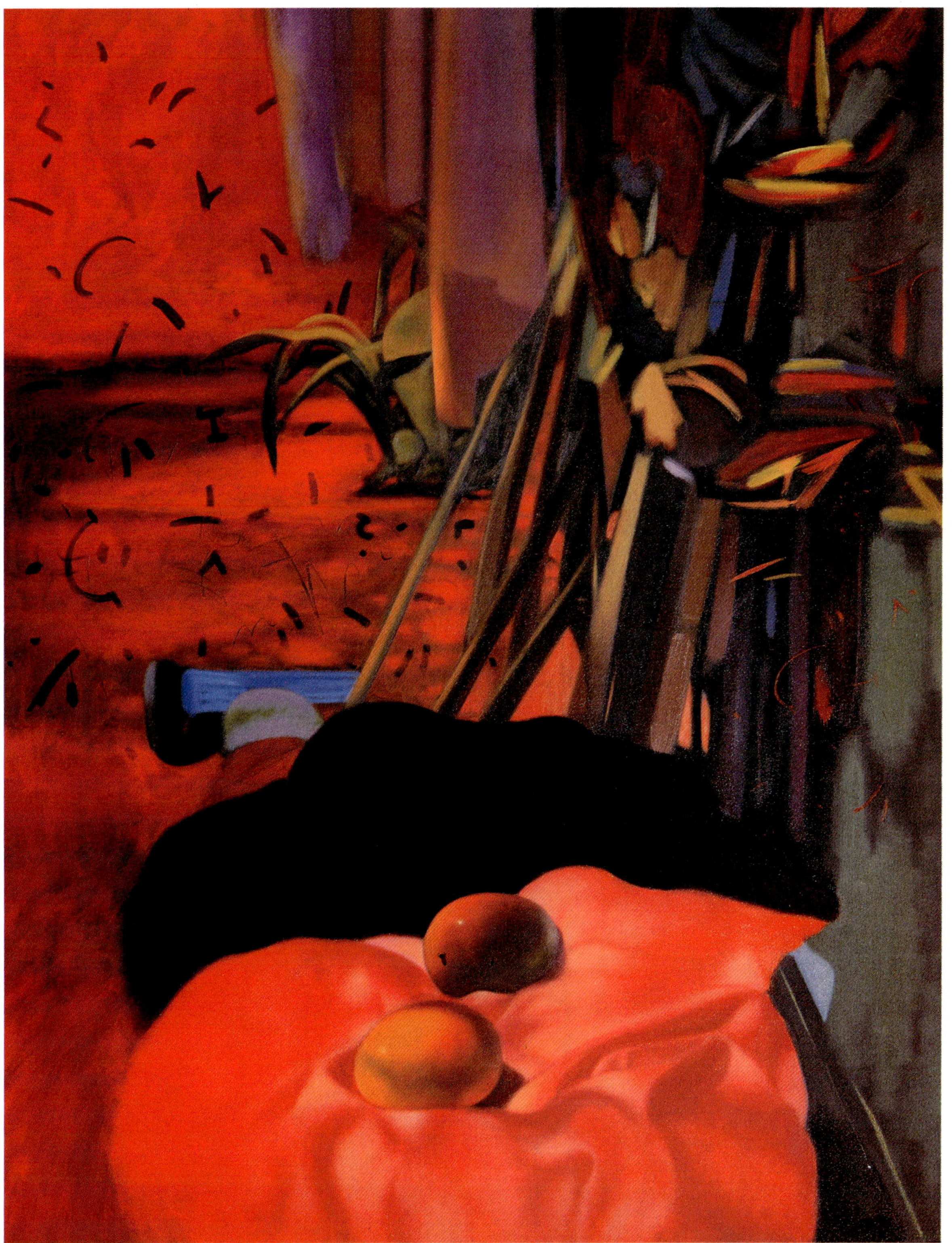

NADER ART GALLERY
Atarazana No. 9
Santo Domingo,
Dominican Republic
809.544.0878
809.565.6204 FAX

George Nader
Francisco Nader

NICOLAS ART GALLERY
2722 Ponce De Leon Blvd.
Coral Gables, FL 33134
305.446.5404
305.448.5993 FAX

George Nader
Patricia Nicolas

Exhibiting:
Latin American Art

Enriquillo Rodriguez Amiama

America, Land of Passions
1993, Oil on Canvas,
70" x 56"

Selected Biography:

1994 Art Miami 94, Miami, FL

1993 Chicago International
Art Exposition, FIA,
Chicago, IL

1992 Solo Exhibition:
Bastidas's house, a
modern art museum of
the Dominican Republic,
Traveling group show in
museums of Israel

1987 Group show at the
History and Art Museum
of San Juan, Puerto Rico

1986 "Signs and Symbols of
the Dominican Republic",
OAS Museum of
Washington

ANDREAS GALLERIES, INC.

8545 Leesburg Pike
Vienna, VA 22182
703.448.2222
703.356.3328 FAX

Contact:
Ursula Andreas, Director
Ruth Hughes

Exhibiting:
Contemporary European and
American art

George Andreas

1. *Oedipal Stage*
   1986, Oil on canvas,
   55" x 70"

2. *Repressive Action*
   1993, Ink, gouache
   and commercial labels
   on paper,
   40" x 30"

3. *Untitled*
   1992, Ink, gouache and
   photographs on paper,
   24" x 18"

Selected Biography:

1993 Galerie Vigny,
Munich, Germany

ART MIAMI '93
Miami Beach, FL

1992 SADI International
Art Festival,
Washington DC

1990 School of Visual Arts,
Urbino, Italy

1988 Rochester Institute of
Technology, Bevier
Gallery, Rochester, NY

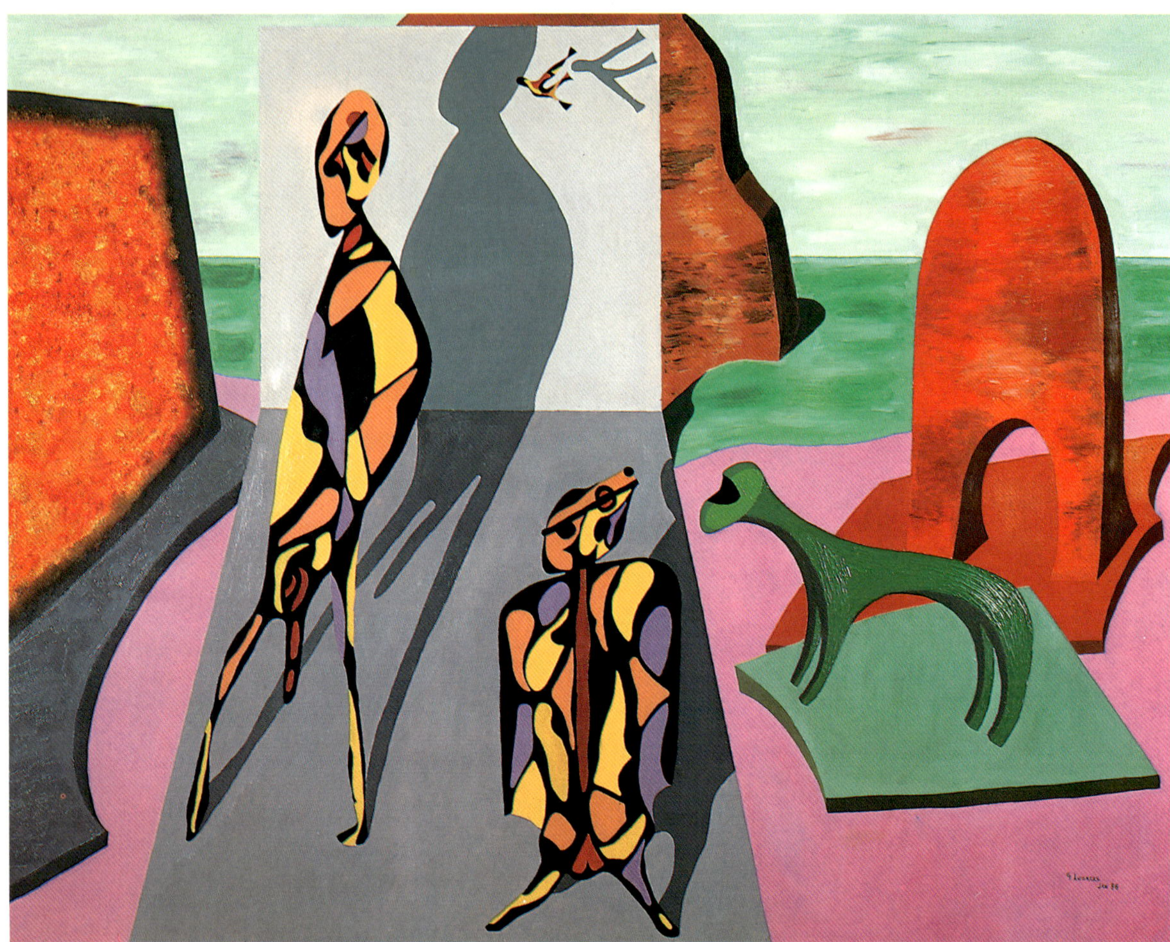

1

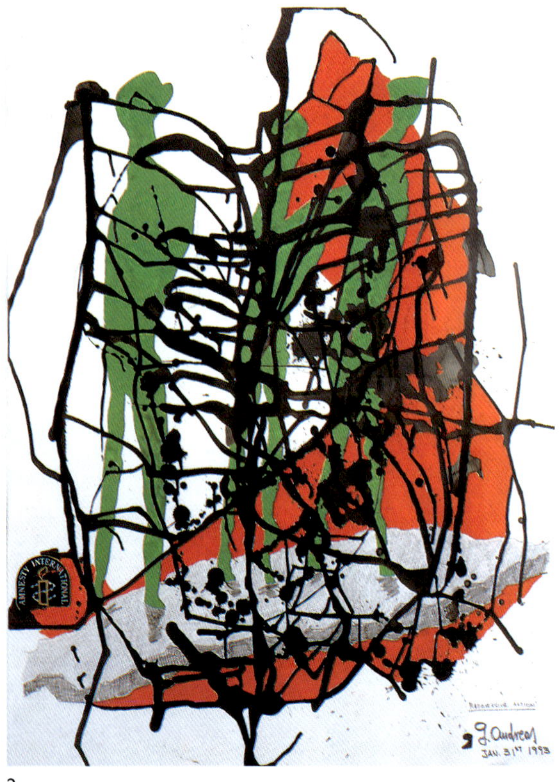

2

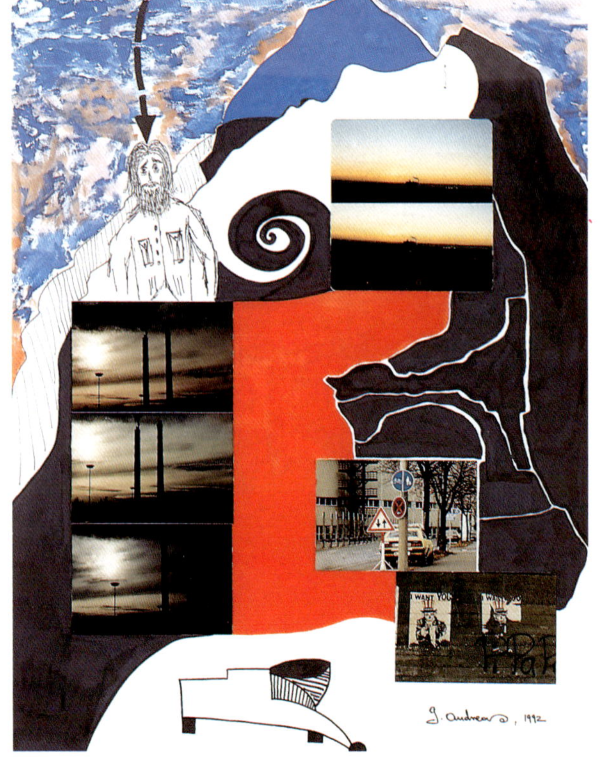

3

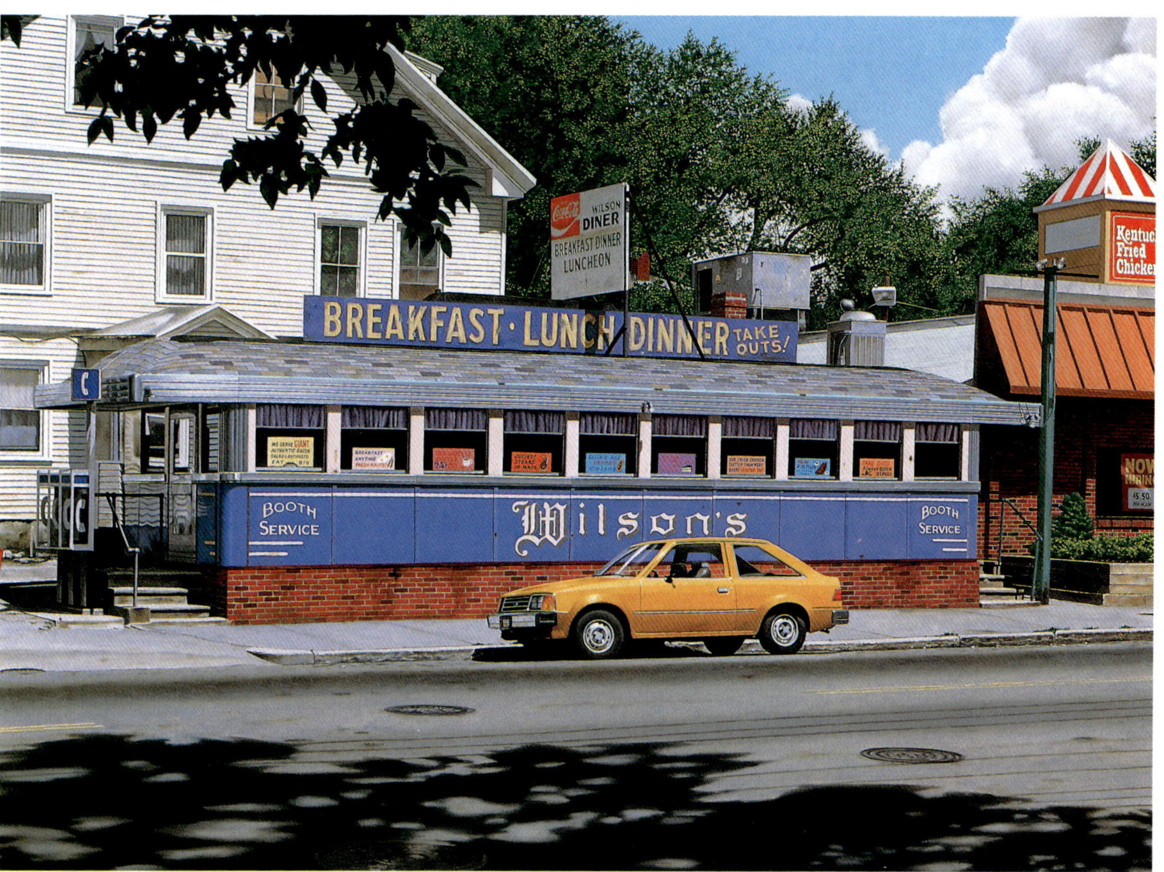

O. K. HARRIS
WORKS OF ART

383 West Broadway
New York, NY 10012
212.431.3600

Contact:
Ivan C. Karp

Exhibiting:
Contemporary American
And European painting,
sculpture, photography,
collectables and memorabilia

John Baeder

*Wilson's Diner
(Waltham, MA)*
1989, Oil on canvas,
46" x 66"

Selected Biography:

1994 "American Realism:
-93 The Urban Scene,
Selections from the
Glenn C. Janss
Collection," Boise Art
Museum, Boise, ID

1993 O. K. Harris Works Of
Art, New York, NY;
In/Sight: Late 20th
Century Art at the
Virginia Museum
of Fine Arts,
Richmond, VA

1992 "Photorealism from
Nashville Collections",
Cheekwood Fine Art
Center, Nashville, TN

EUGENIA CUCALON GALLERY

145 East 72nd Street
New York, NY 10021
212.472.8741
212.472.8741 FAX

Contact:
Eugenia Cucalon
Marta Newman

Exhibiting:
Contemporary Art by
North and South American
and European Artists

Waldo Balart

4 Modules 5x4,
2.3.4.5.7., 55 degrees
1993,
Acrylic paint on linen,
118" x 29$\frac{1}{2}$"

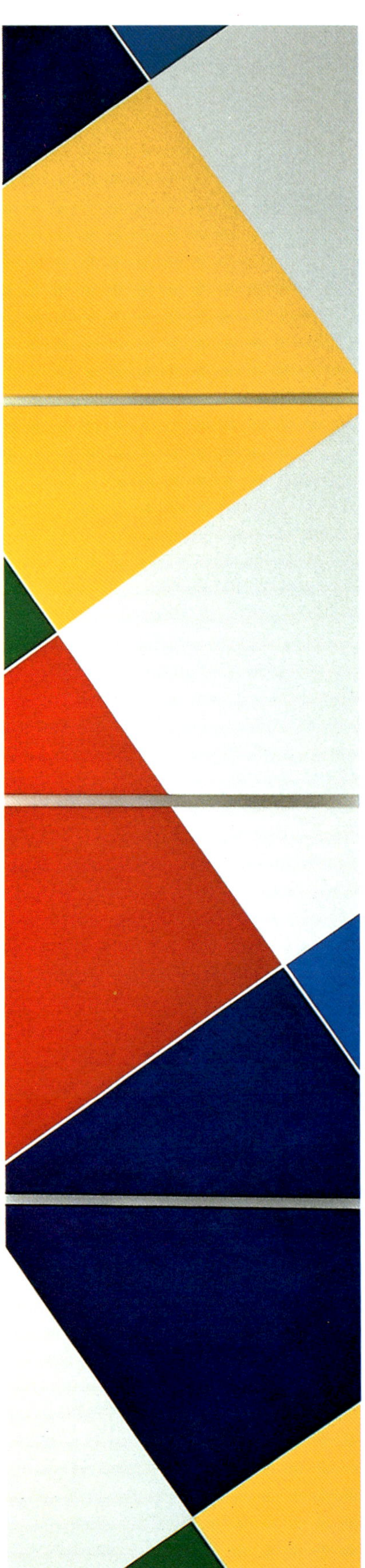

Selected Biography:

1994 Eugenia Cucalon
Gallery, Miami Art Fair

1993 One man show,
Eugenia Cucalon
Gallery, New York

Eugenia Cucalon
Gallery, Iberoamerican
Art Fair, Caracas,
Venezuela

1992 One man show,
Cyan Gallery,
Liege, Belgium

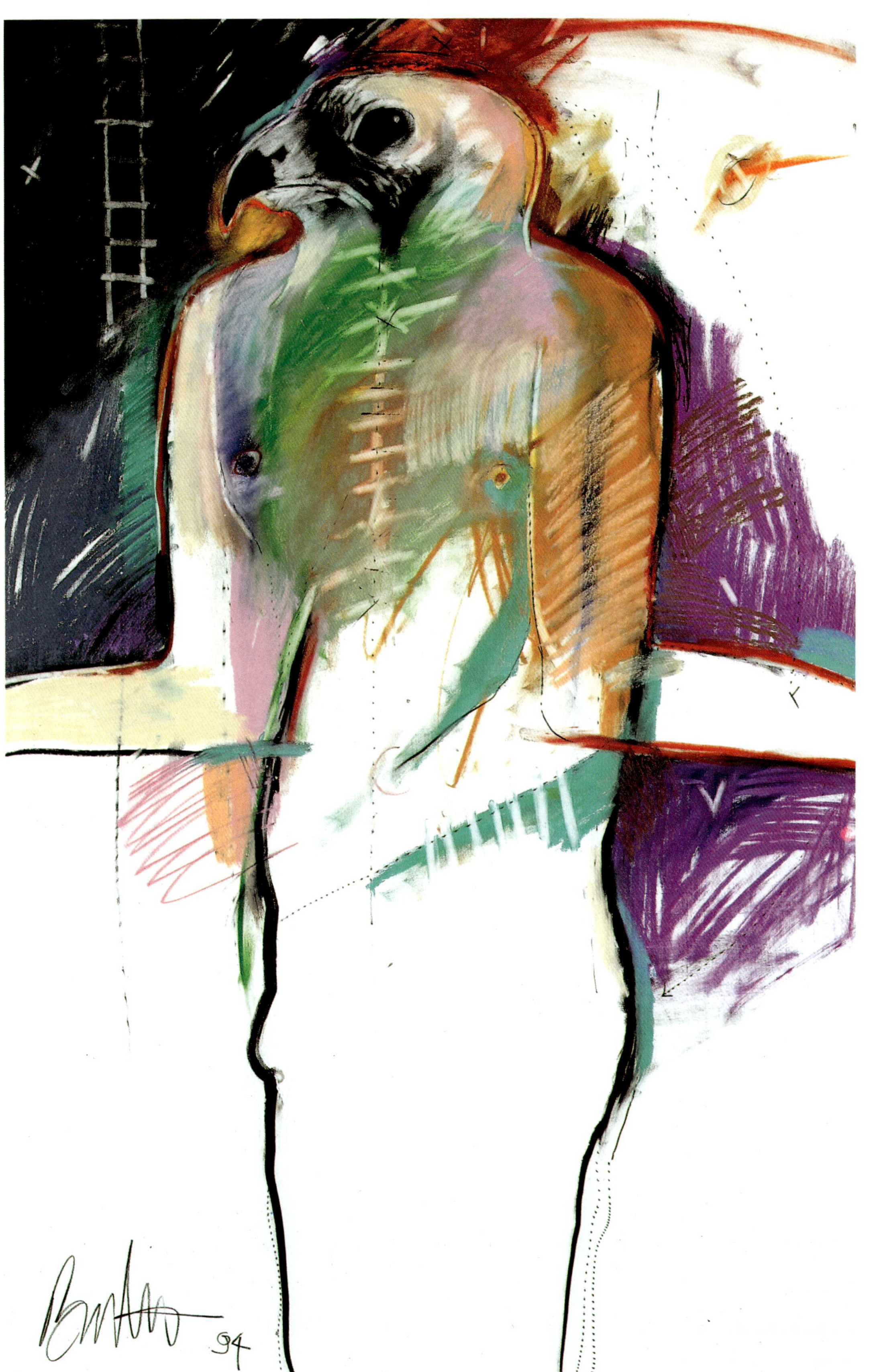

JAMISON THOMAS GALLERY

1313 NW Glisan
Portland, OR 97209
503.222.0063
503.222.1167 FAX

Contact:
William Jamison
Charles Froelick

Exhibiting:
Contemporary and
Self-Taught; painting,
sculpture, drawings, prints
and photography

Rick Bartow

Hawk and Ladder
1994,
Graphite and pastel on
paper, 40" x 26"
Photo Credit: Bill Bachhuber

Selected Biography:

1994   "My Eye Your Eye,"
-85   JamisonThomas
        Gallery, Portland, OR

1994   "Questions of Belief,"
        Yanagisawa Gallery,
        Tokyo, Japan

        Peiper- Riegraf Gallery,
        Frankfurt, Germany

        "Artists Who are
        Indian," Denver Art
        Museum, Denver, CO

1993   "Truth Abandoned,"
        Gallery of Tribal Art,
        Vancouver, BC

FORUM GALLERY

745 Fifth Avenue 5th Floor
New York, NY 10151
212.355.4545
212.355.4547 FAX

Contact:
Robert Fishko, Director

William Beckman

My Father
1988-1993,
Oil on panel,
73" x 57¼"

Selected Biography:
Solo exhibitions:
Forum Gallery, NY;
Hudson River Museum,
NY; Allan Stone, NY;
Allan Frumkin, NY;
Stiebel Modern, NY;
Indiana University
Art Museum,
Bloomington, IN
Group exhibitions:
Richard Feigen,
Chicago; Art Institute
of Chicago; The
Cleveland Museum of
Art; Wildenstein & Co.,
NY; National Portrait
Gallery; Hirshhorn
Museum; Whitney
Museum

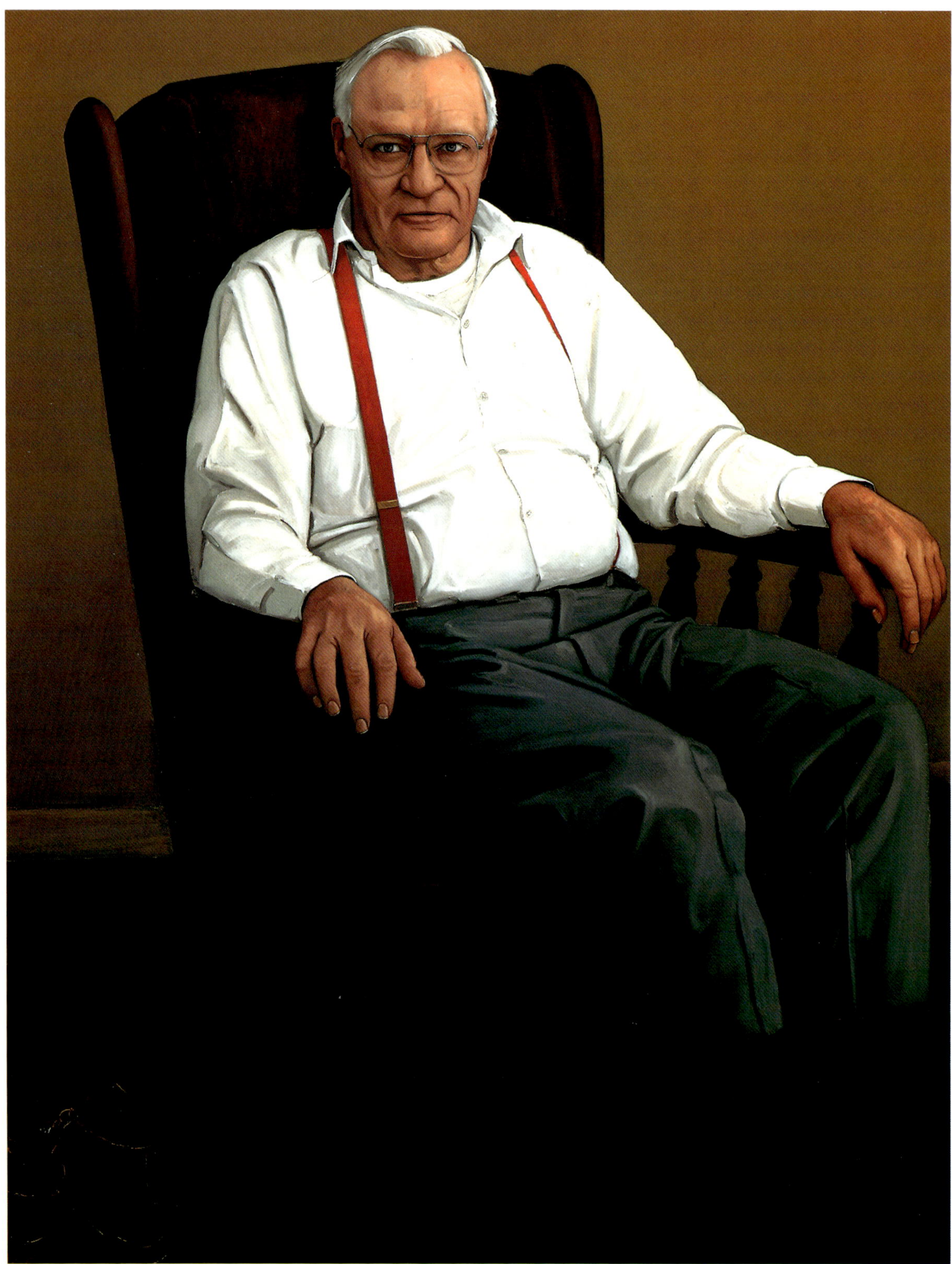

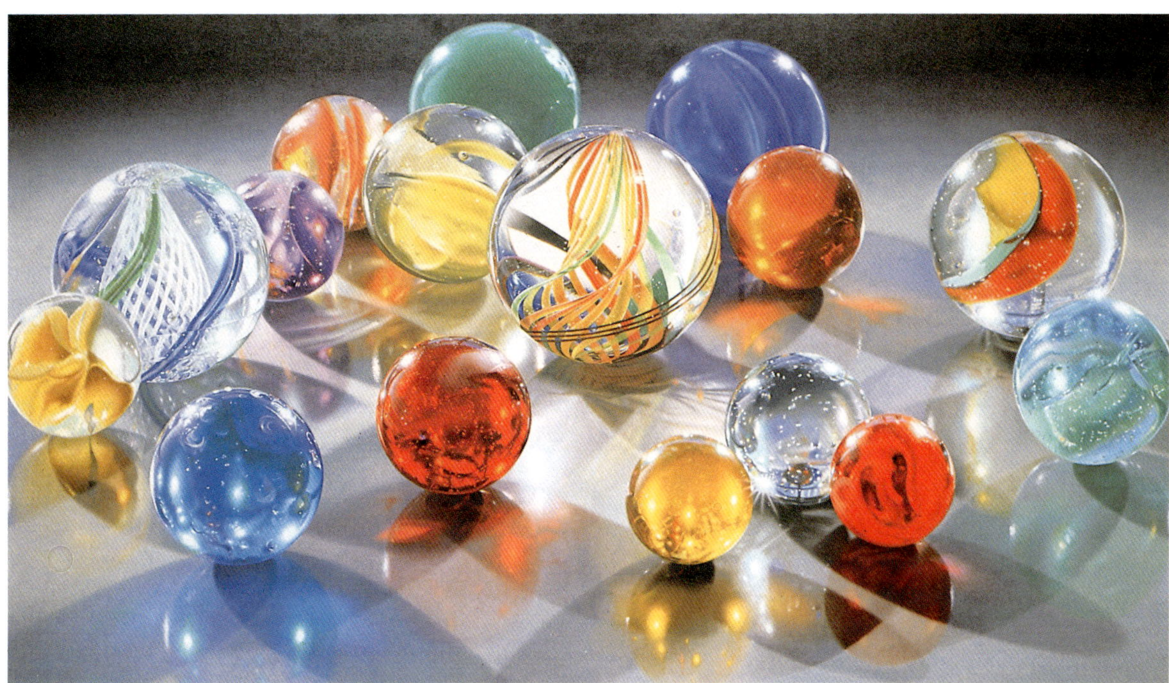

1

LOUIS K. MEISEL GALLERY

141 Prince Street
New York, NY 10012
212.677.1340
212.533.7340 FAX

Contact:
Louis K. Meisel
Diane Sena

Exhibiting:
Photo-Realist painting and
other technically skilled
contemporary disciplines

Charles Bell

1. *Sixteen Candles*
   1992, Oil on canvas,
   60" x 108"

2. *Majorette*
   1993, Oil on Linen,
   50" x 83.75"

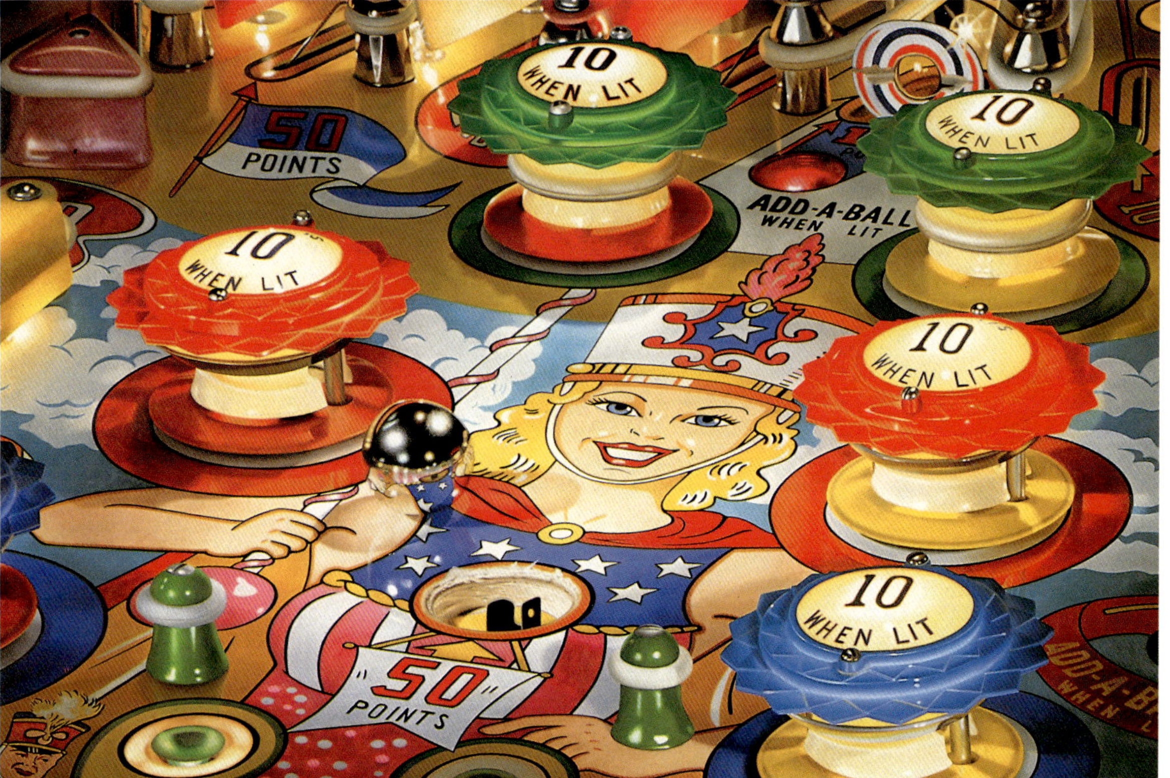

2

Selected Collections:

Solomon R.
Guggenheim Museum,
New York, NY;
Metropolitan Museum
of Art, New York, NY;
Akron Art Museum,
OH; Hiroshima City
Museum of
Contemporary Art,
Japan

KIYO HIGASHI GALLERY

8332 Melrose Avenue
Los Angeles, CA 90069
213.655.2482
213.655.7016 FAX

Contact:
Kiyo Higashi

Exhibiting:
Abstract-reductive work:
Paintings and sculpture

Larry Bell

WBKDEN 5
1993, Glass & black
denim,
53" x 53"

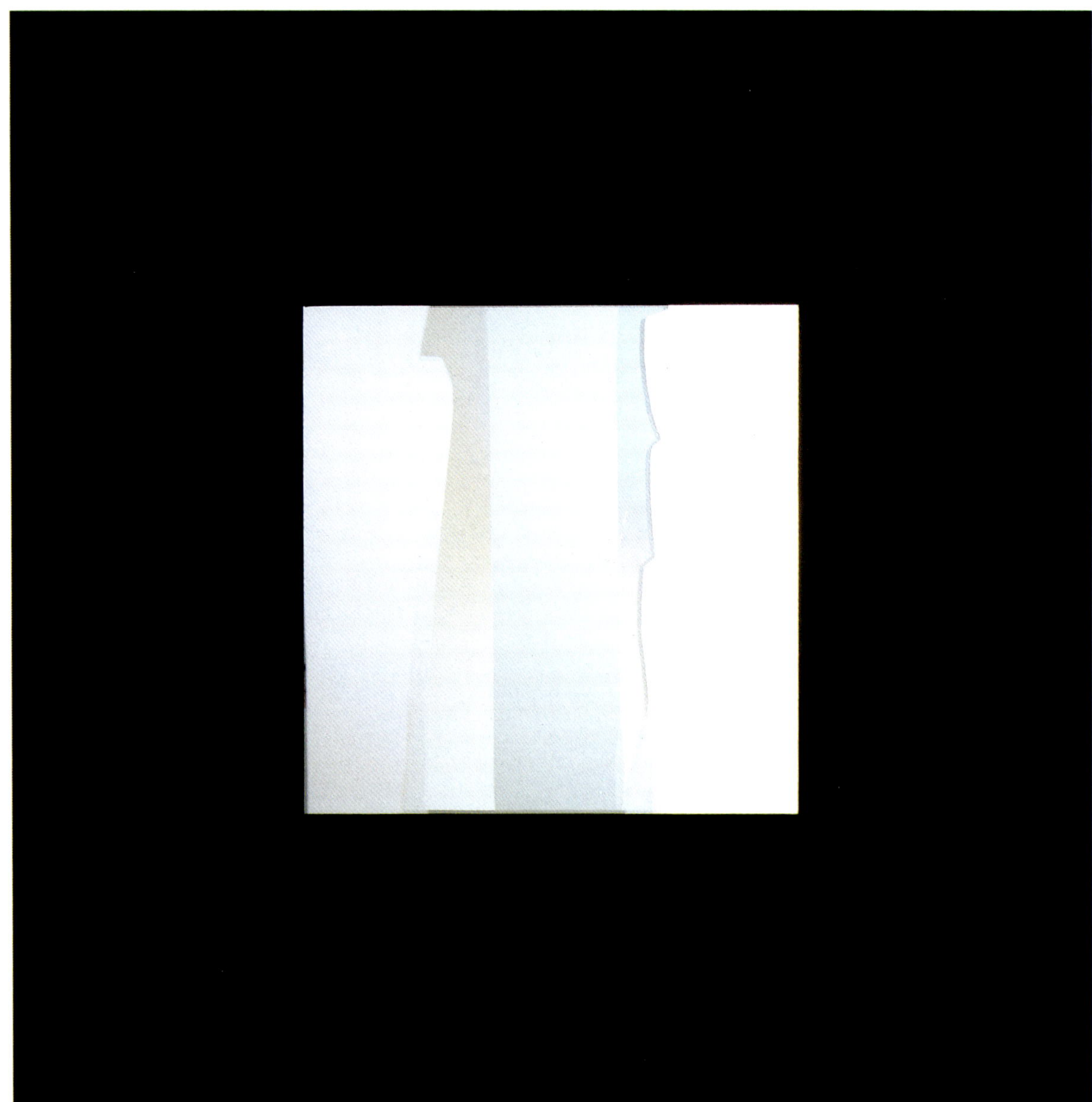

Selected biography:
1993 Newport Harbor Art
      Museum, Newport
      Beach, CA;
      Musee du Palais du
      Luxembourg, Paris,
      France
1992 Kiyo Higashi Gallery,
      Los Angeles, CA:
      Sculpture Project
      Arolsen, Germany;
1991 Tucson Museum of Art,
      Tucson, AZ; Tony
      Shafrazi Gallery, NY;
1990 Galerie Montenay,
      Paris; Galerie Rolf
      Ricke, Köln, Germany;
      Musee d'art
      Contemporain Lyon,
      Lyon, France

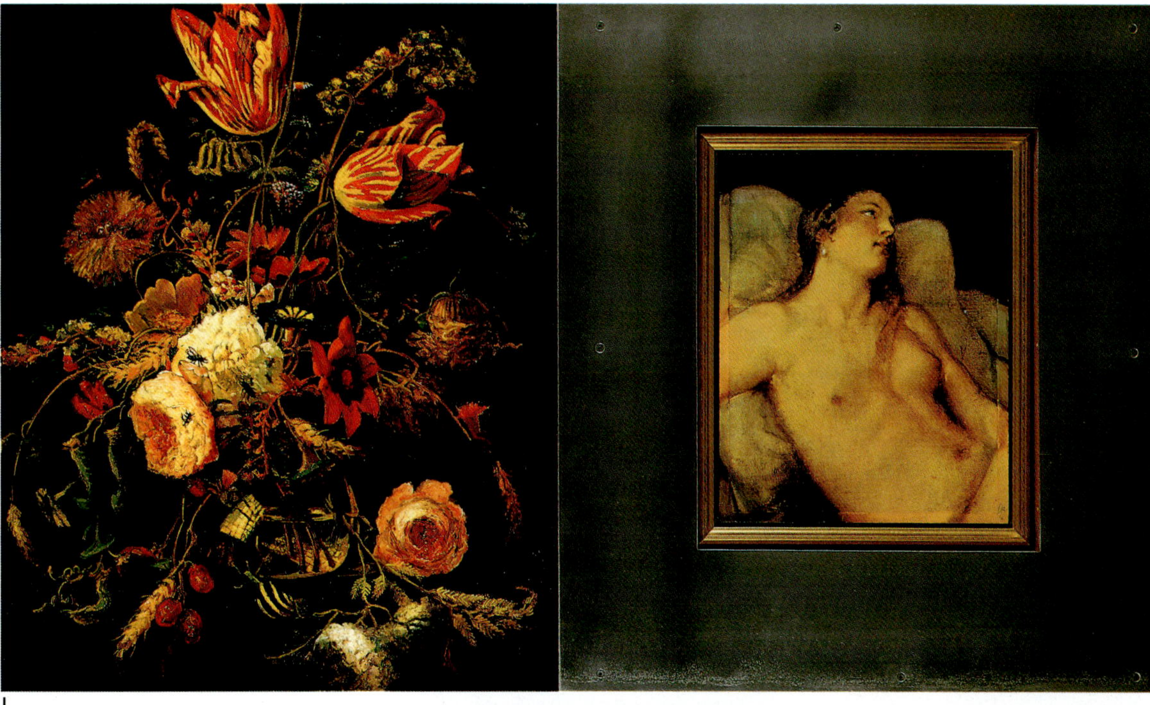

1

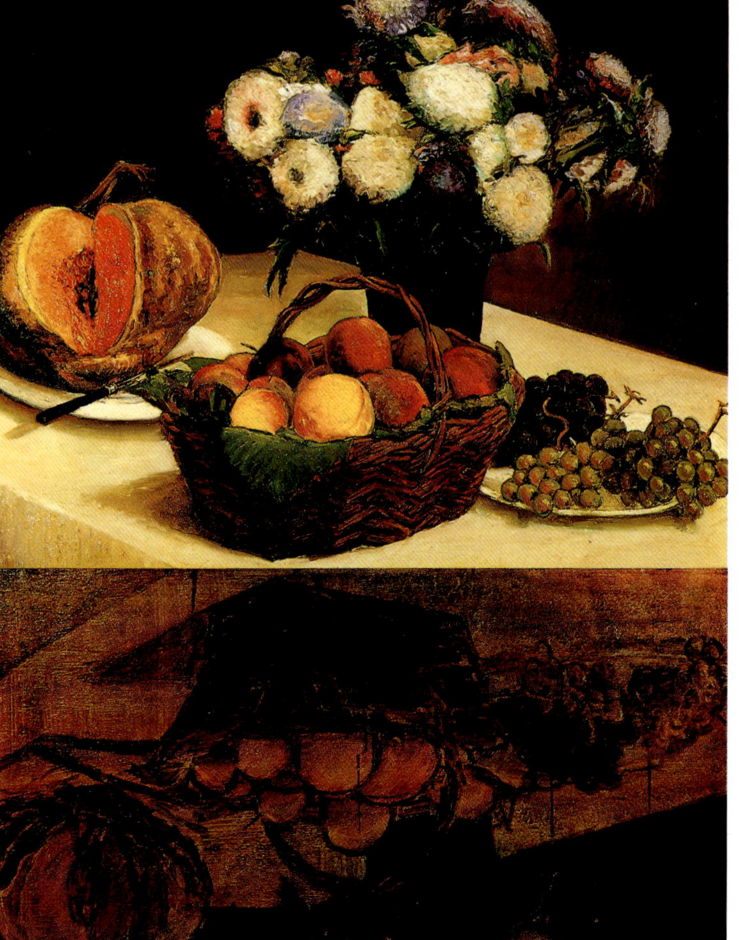

2

DIANE FARRIS GALLERY

1565 West 7th Avenue
Vancouver B.C. V6J 1S1
Canada
604.737.2629
604.737.2675 FAX

Contact:
Diane Farris, Director

Exhibiting:
Contemporary Canadian
and International Art

David Bierk

1. *A Eulogy to Art & Life:
   To Mignon & Titian*
   1994, Oil on canvas,
   oil on photo, steel
   construction, 38" x 60"

2. *Reflective Still life,
   China Asters & Fruit,
   to Favitin Latoue*
   1994, Oil on canvas,
   oil on gold left, 65" x 49"

Selected Biography:

1994 "Still Life", Solo Show,
   Diane Farris Gallery,
   Vancouver, BC;
   Leedy Voulkos Gallery,
   Kansas City, MO;
   Rodman Hall
   Arts Centre,
   St. Catherines, ON

1993 In the Absence of
   Pararlise, Dayton Art
   Centre, Dayton,OH;
   Adams Middleton
   Gallery, Dallas, TX;
   Diane Farris Gallery,
   Vancouver, BC

HART GALLERY

113 Upper St. Islington
London N1 1QN England
071.704.1131

23 Main St. Linby
Nottingham NG15 8AE
England
0602.638.707
0602.640.743 FAX

Contact:
John Hart, Director
Katherine Hart, Director
Jane Holt, Assoc. Director

Exhibiting:
Contemporary British art

David Blackburn

A Landscape Vision, No 7
1990, Pastel,
60" x 65"

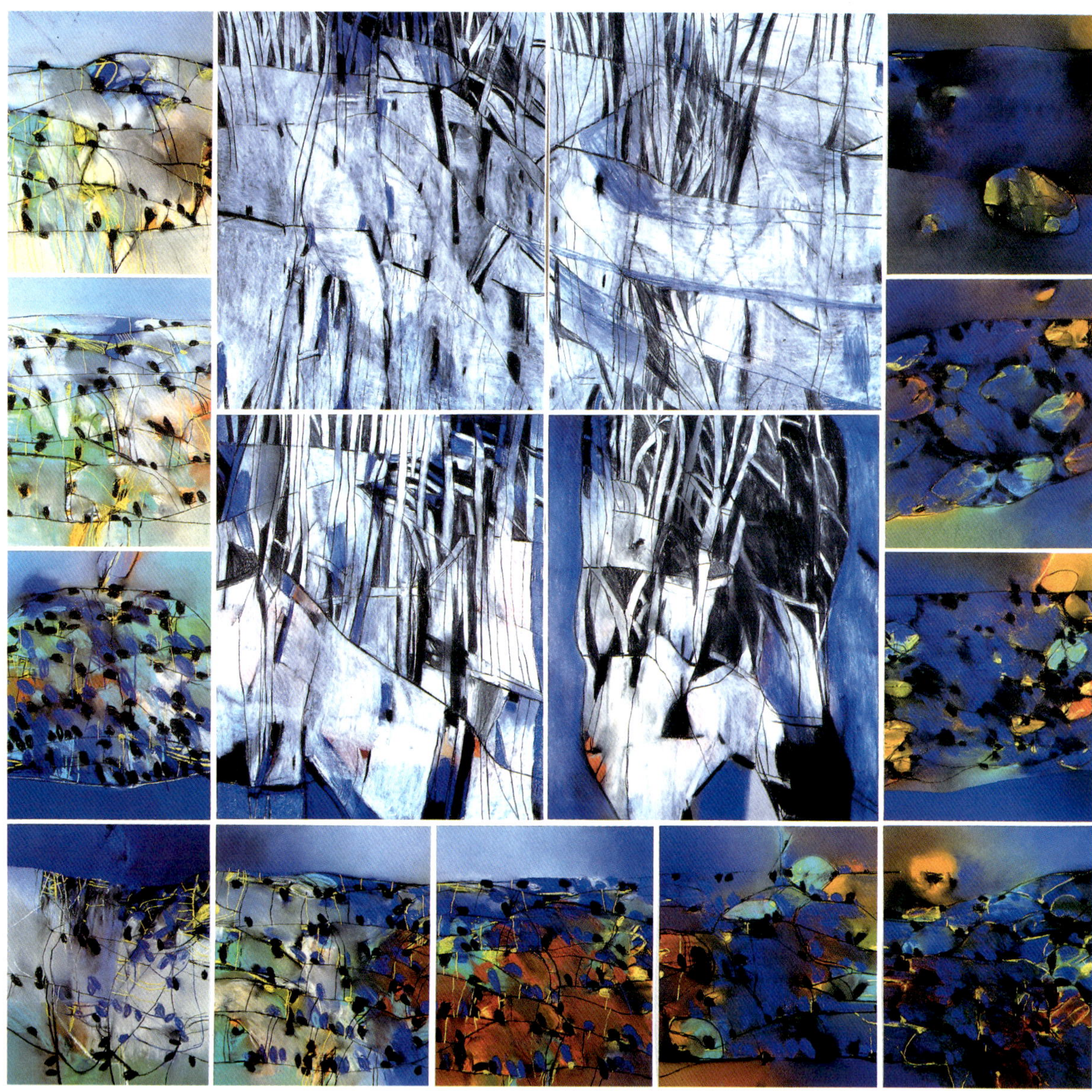

Selected Biography:

1989 Yale Center for British
Art, New Haven.
Catalogue written by
Peter Fuller

1986 Exhibition:
Dulwich Picture
Gallery, London

1965 First exhibition:
Melbourne, Australia

1939 Born:
Huddersfield, England

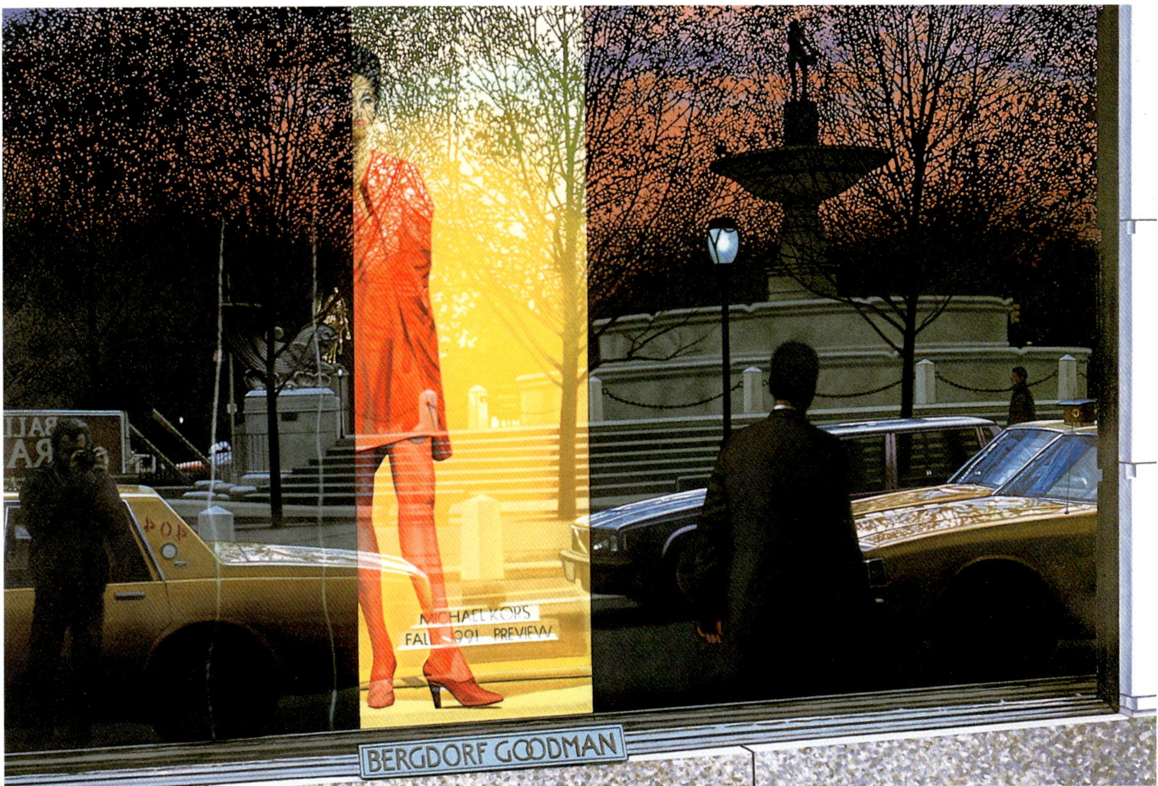

1

2

LOUIS K. MEISEL GALLERY

141 Prince Street
New York, NY 10012
212.677.1340
212.533.7340 FAX

Contact:
Louis K. Meisel
Diane Sena

Exhibiting:
Photo-Realist painting and
other technically skilled
contemporary disciplines

Tom Blackwell

1. *Bergdorf's at Dusk*
   1992, Oil on linen,
   48.25" x 72"

2. *Odalisque Express*
   1992-93, Oil on linen,
   61" x 93.63"

Selected Collections:

Museum of Modern
Art, New York, NY;
Solomon R.
Guggenheim Museum,
New York, NY;
Metropolitan Museum
of Art, New York, NY;
National Air &
Space Museum,
Washington, DC;
Detroit Institute
of Arts, MI;
Phoenix Museum
of Art, AZ

CARIB ART GALLERY

584 Broadway
New York, NY 10012
212.343.2539
212.343.2659 FAX

Contact:
Veronica Ortiz
Sully Saneaux

Exhibiting:
Contemporary art from
Latin America and the
Caribbean

Dionisio Blanco

1. *Sembradores:*
    Maquina de la Fautasia
    1994, Acrylic and oil on
    canvas, 40" x 50"

2. *Sembradores Miticos*
    1993, Acrylic on canvas,
    36" x 48"

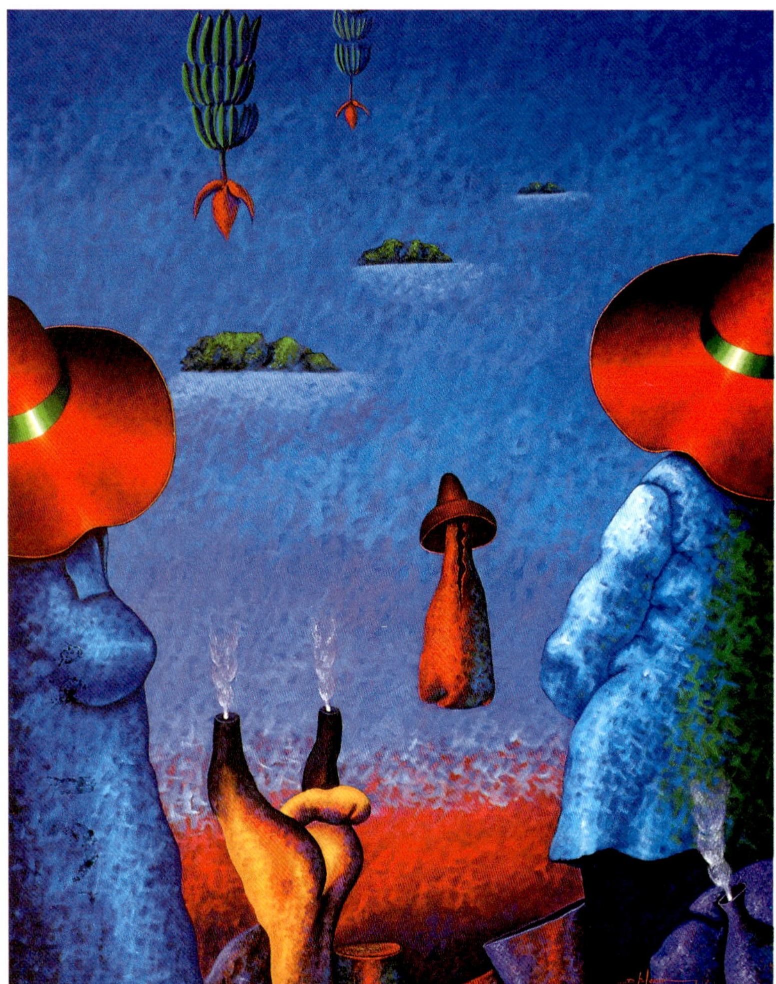

1

Selected Biography:

1994 International
      Miami Art Fair,
      Carib Art Gallery of
      New York
1992 National Museum of
      History and Geography,
      Dominican Republic;
      Contemporary
      Dominican Painting
      in Israel
1991 Museum of Modern
      Art, Dominican
      Republic
1984 Voluntariado del
      Museo de las Casas
      Reales, Casa de
      Bastidas, Santo
      Domingo

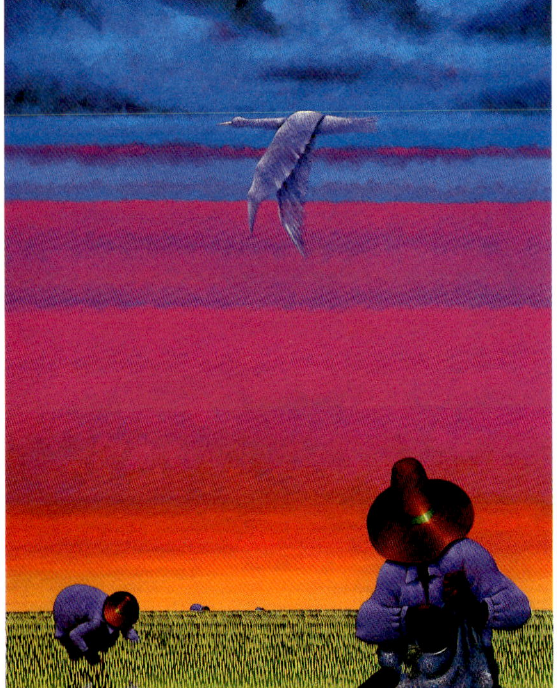

2

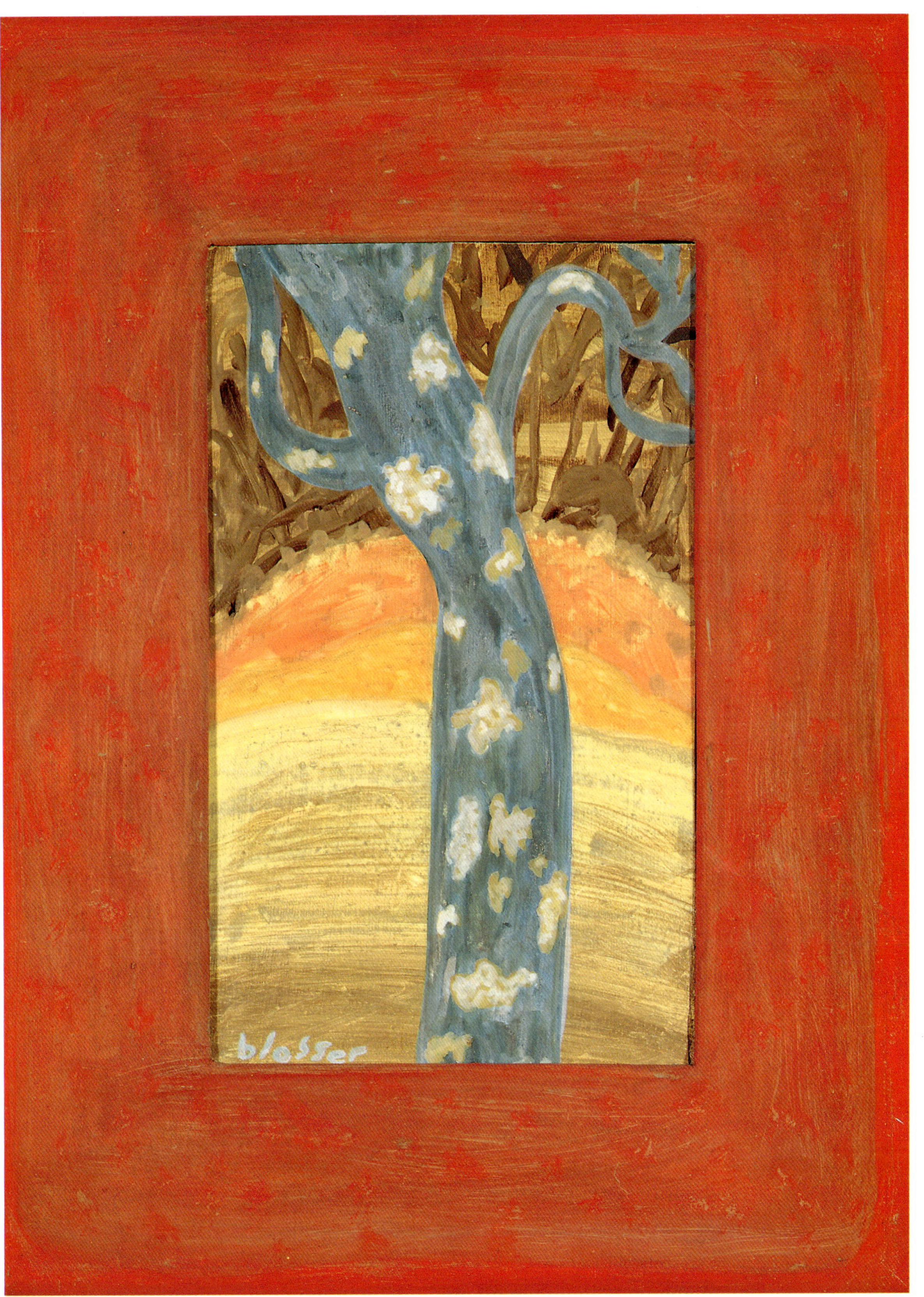

JAMISON THOMAS
GALLERY

1313 NW Glisan
Portland, OR 97209
503.222.0063
503.222.1167 FAX

Contact:
William Jamison
Charles Froelick

Exhibiting:
Contemporary and
Self-Taught; painting,
sculpture, drawings, prints
and photography

Nick Blosser

Spreading Lichen
1993,
egg tempera on wood,
17.5" x 13"
Photo Credit: Bill Bachhuber

Selected Biography:

1994 Jamison Thomas
Gallery, Portland, OR
(also 1993 & 1992)
1993 "New Regional Painting
II," University
of Alabama,
Tuscaloosa, AL
1992 National Endowment
for the Arts Fellowship
(also 1987);
"In/Outsiders from the
American South,"
Montgomery Museum
of Fine Arts,
Montgomery, AL
1984 Rome Prize Fellowship
in painting, American
Academy, Rome, Italy

DOHENY GALLERY

2199 Granville Street
Vancouver B.C. V6H 3E9
Canada
604.737.7537
604.736.8826 FAX

Contact:
Patrick Doheny,
Director

Exhibiting:
Important 20th century art

Bonifacho

Birth of Phoenix
1993, Oil on canvas,
57" x 57"

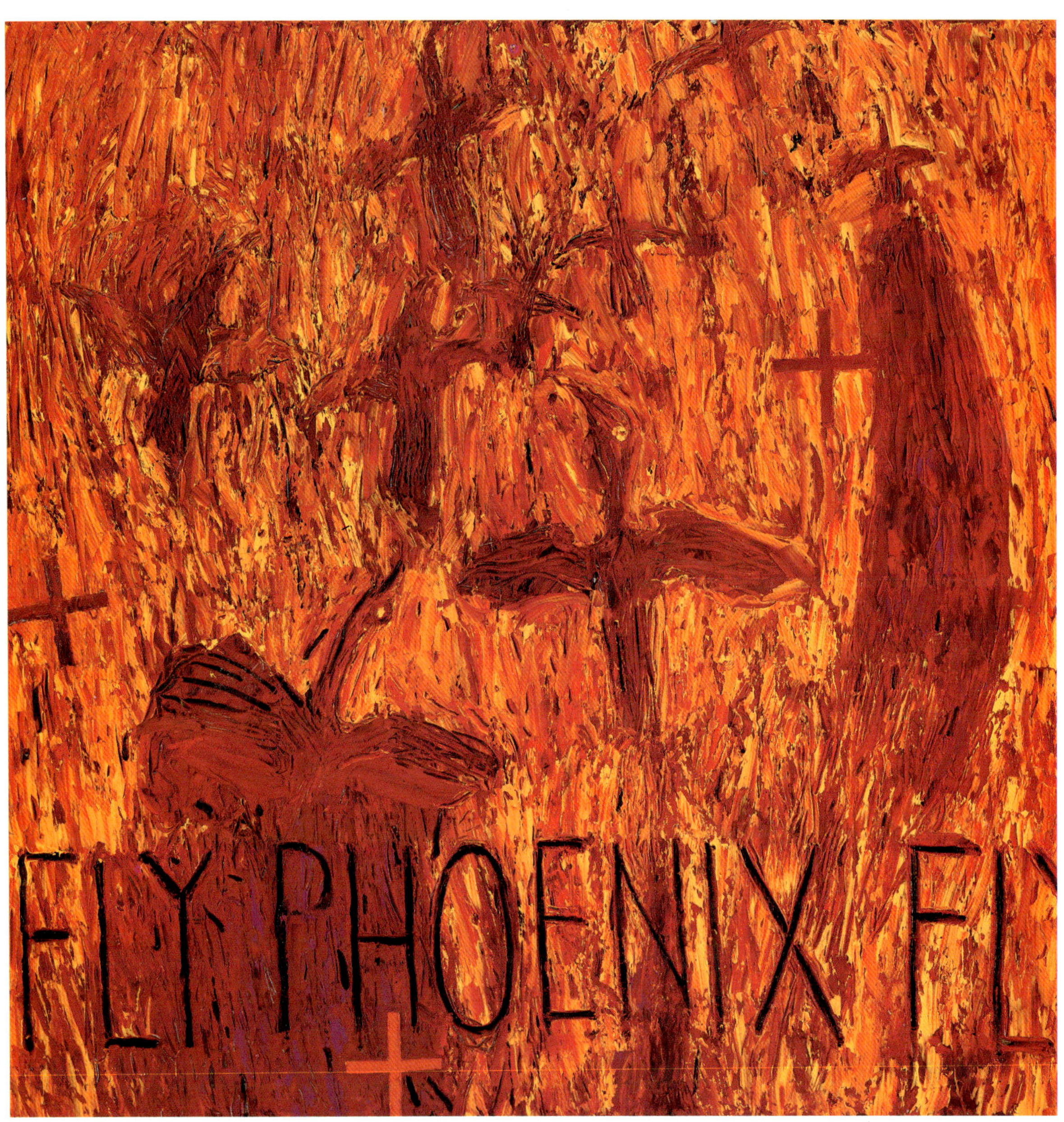

Selected Biography:

1994   Doheny Gallery,
       Vancouver, B.C.

1993   Threshold Gallery,
       Vancouver, B.C.
       Fran Willis,
       Victoria, B.C.
       Artropolis,
       Vancouver, B.C.
       Richmond Art Gallery,
       Richmond, B.C.

1993   Doheny Gallery,
       Vancouver, B.C
       Heffel Gallery,
       Vancouver, B.C

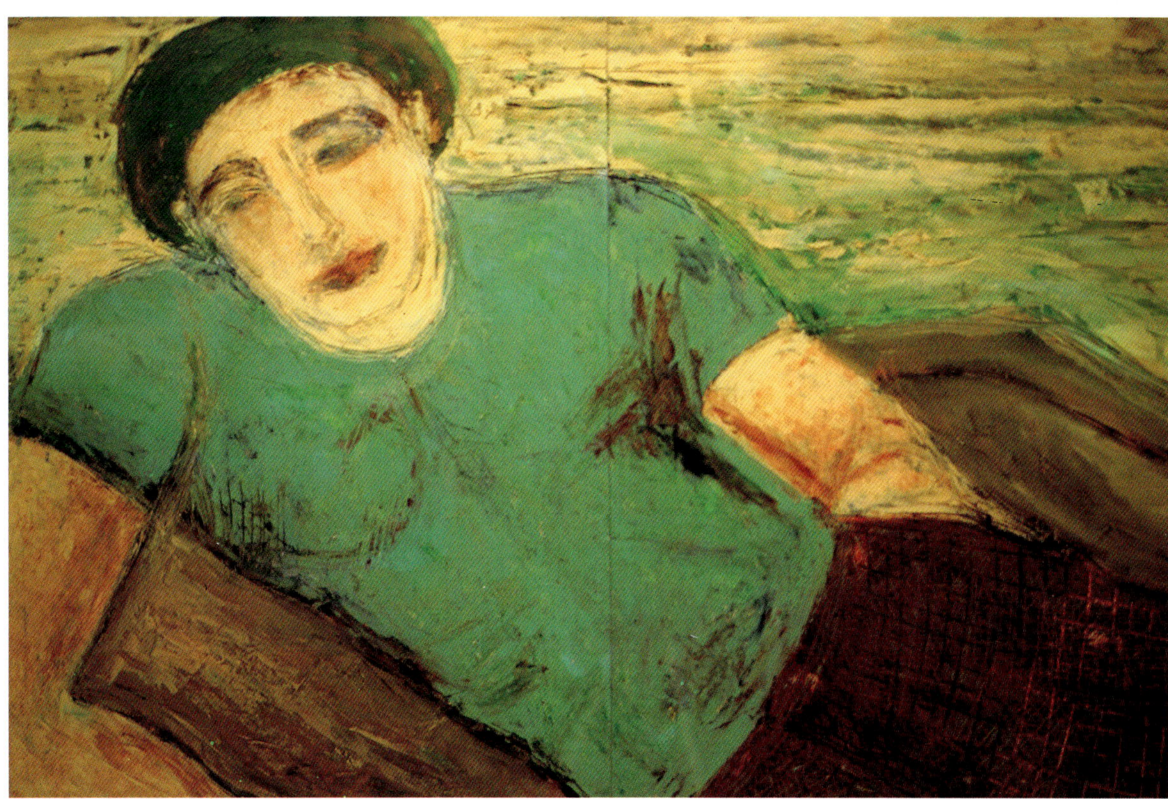

ALDO CASTILLO GALLERY

3513 N. Lincoln Ave. 2nd Fl.
Chicago, IL 60657
312.525.2536
312.525.2582 FAX

Contact:
Aldo Castillo, Director

Exhibiting:
Fine Latin American Art

Antonio Bou

Alzafat
1990, Oil on paper,
42" x 56"

Selected Biography:

Antonio Bou was Born in San Juan, Puerto Rico in 1944. He is a painter and writer of masterpieces who resides and exhibits mainly in his native island, Puerto Rico. As in much of Puerto Rican art today, Antonio Bou successfully combines cultural tradition with popular culture. In these remarkable works of oil on paper, he captures his country's national identity. He is rapidly becoming known abroad as an Artist who is representative of an exciting national art movement of his country.

NAN MILLER GALLERY

3450 Winton Place
Rochester, NY 14623
716.292.1430
716.292.1253 FAX

Contact:
Nan Miller

Exhibiting:
Graphics and originals by
Contemporary artists

Romero Britto

The Dancers
1993, Acrylic on canvas,
72" x 72"

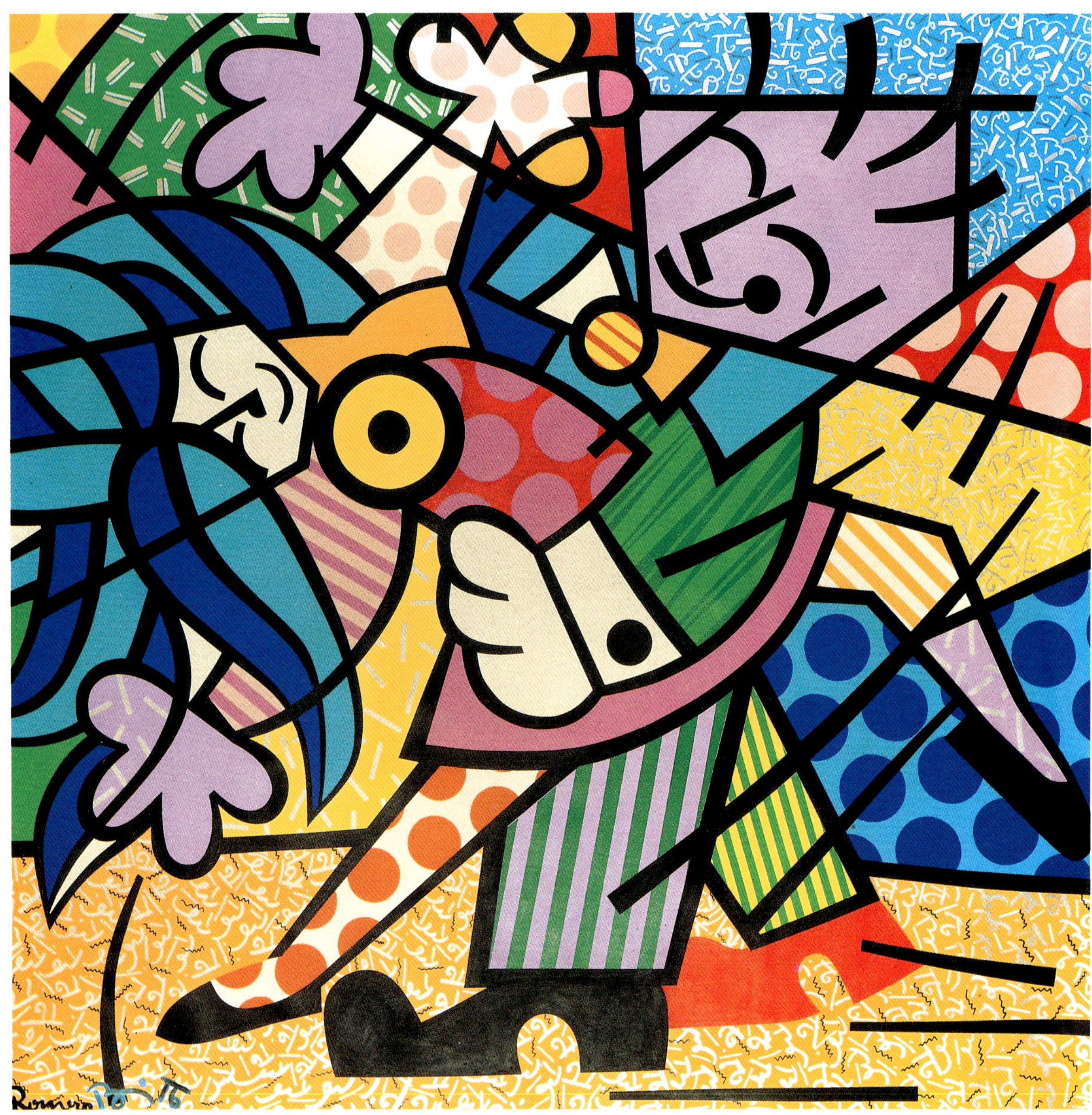

Selected biography:

1994 Art Fair, Art Miami,
Nan Miller Gallery

1993 Art Fair, LINEART,
Ghent

Art Fair, FIAC,
Paris, Frence

Solo Exhibition,
Harrington Fine Art,
Vancouver, British
Colombia

Solo Exhibition,
Kass/Meridian,
Chicago, IL

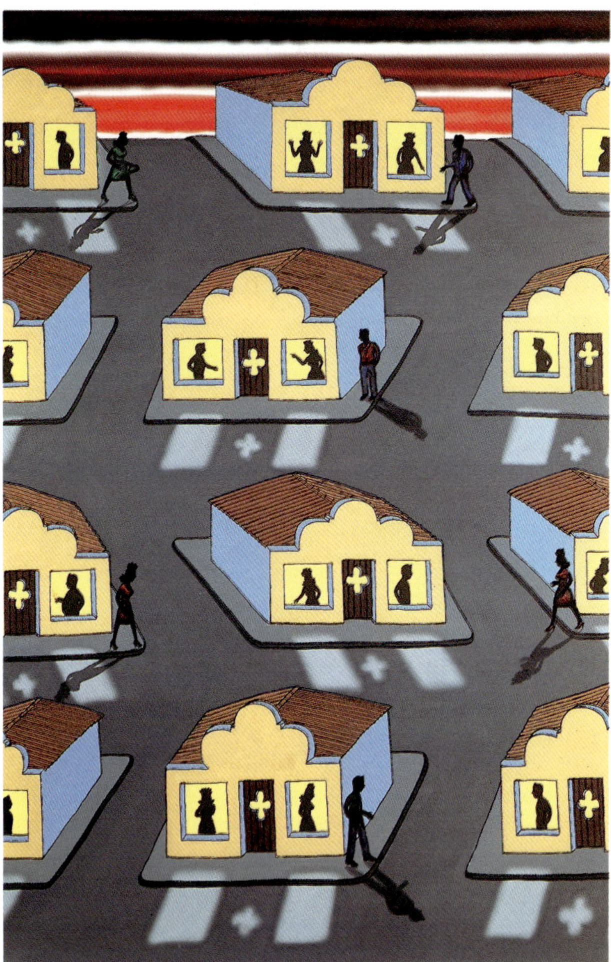

2

PHYLLIS KIND
GALLERY

313 West Superior
Chicago, IL 60610
312.642.6302
312.642.8502 FAX

136 Greene Street
New York, NY 10012
212.925.1200
212.941.7841 FAX

Contact:
Phyllis Kind

Exhibiting:
Contemporary
American, Soviet, Naive,
and Outsider art

Roger Brown

1. *In the Little Spanish Town*
    1993, Oil on canvas,
    72" x 48"

2. *The Rose Garden*
    1993, Oil on canvas,
    48" x 72"

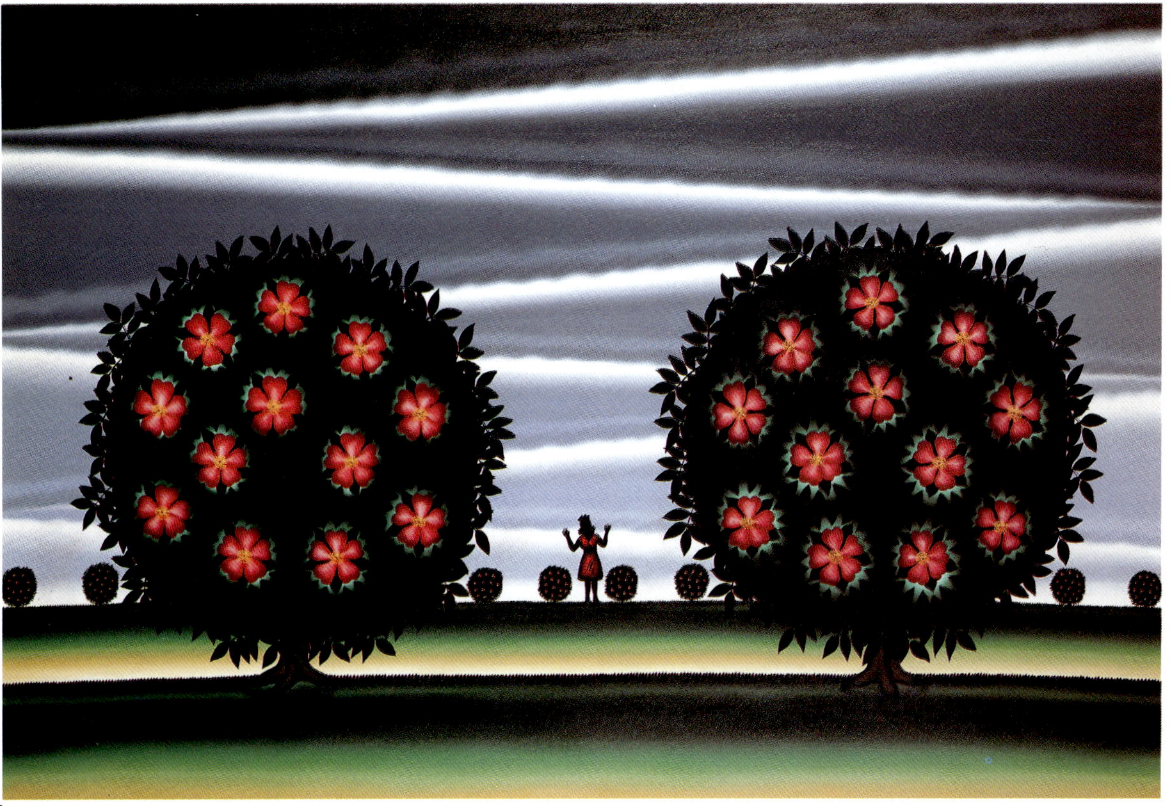

1

Selected Biography:

1994 Phyllis Kind Gallery,
        Chicago, IL

1992 Phyllis Kind Gallery,
        New York, NY

1987 Hirshorn Museum and
        Sculpture Garden,
        Washington, D.C.

HARMON-MEEK GALLERY

386 Broad Avenue South
Naples, FL 33940
813.261.2637
813.261.3804

4262 Gulfshore Blvd. N.
Naples, FL 33940
813.261.7775

Contact:
J. William Meek III,
Director-owner

Exhibiting:
20th Century American art

Colleen Browning

1. *Target*
   1991, Oil on canvas,
   59" x 59", (including
   painted frame)

2. *Fracture*
   1993, Oil on canvas,
   22 " x 31"

3. *Inside The Jumping Giraffe*
   1992, Oil on canvas,
   40" x 70 ¹/₂"

Selected Collections:
   Corcoran Gallery of
   Art, Washington, D.C.;
   Cleveland Museum of
   Art, OH; St. Louis Art
   Museum, MO; Detroit
   Institute of Arts, MI;
   Los Angeles County
   Museum of Art, CA;
   Philadelphia Museum
   of Art, PA
Solo exhibitions:
1994 Harmon-Meek Gallery,
   March 27 - 9 April;
   Nevada State Museum,
   Reno, Jan.-Feb.;
1993 Melvin Gallery,
   Florida Southern
   College, Lakeland

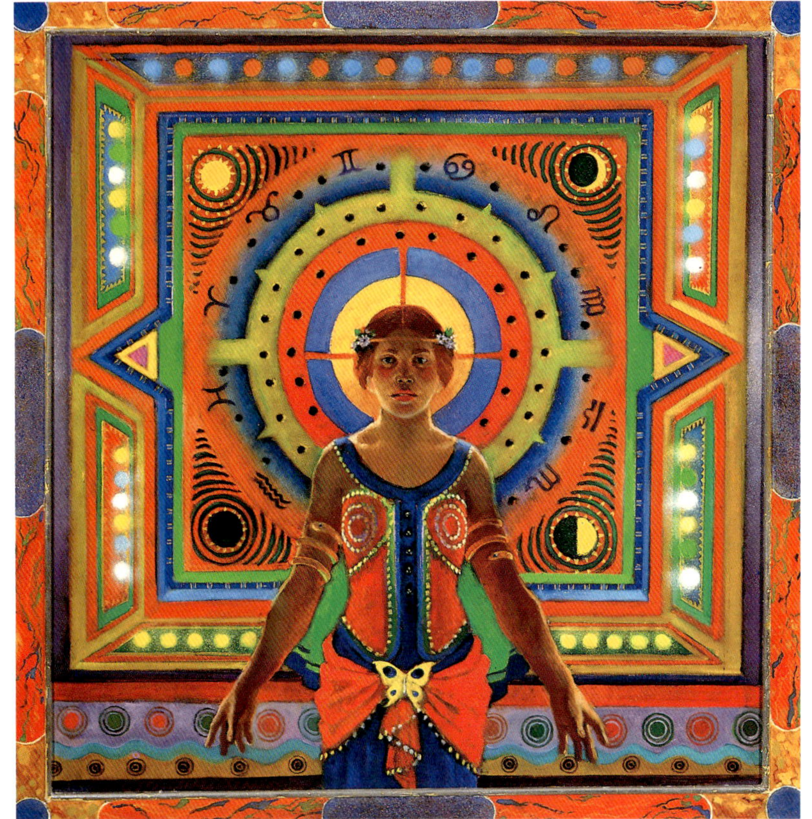

1

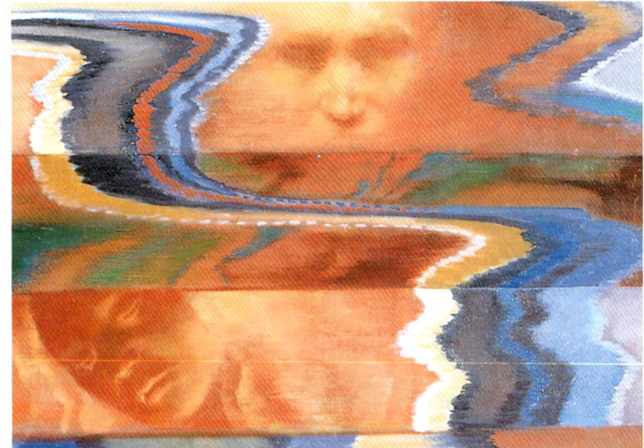

2

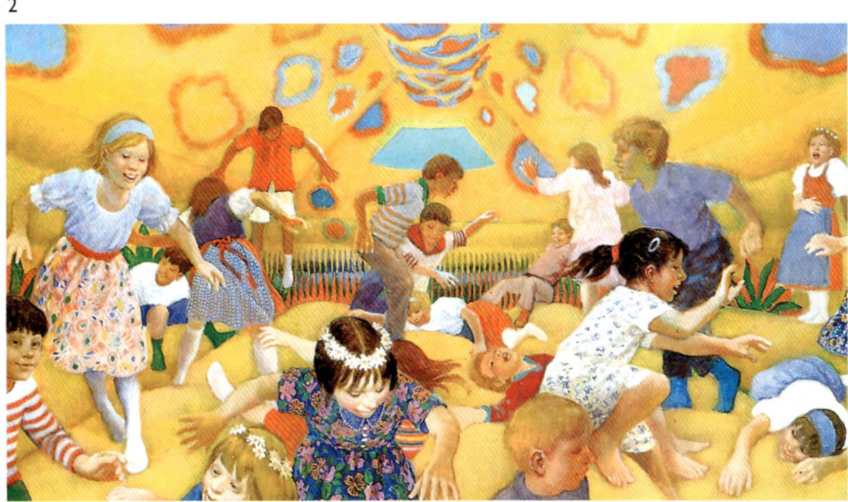

3

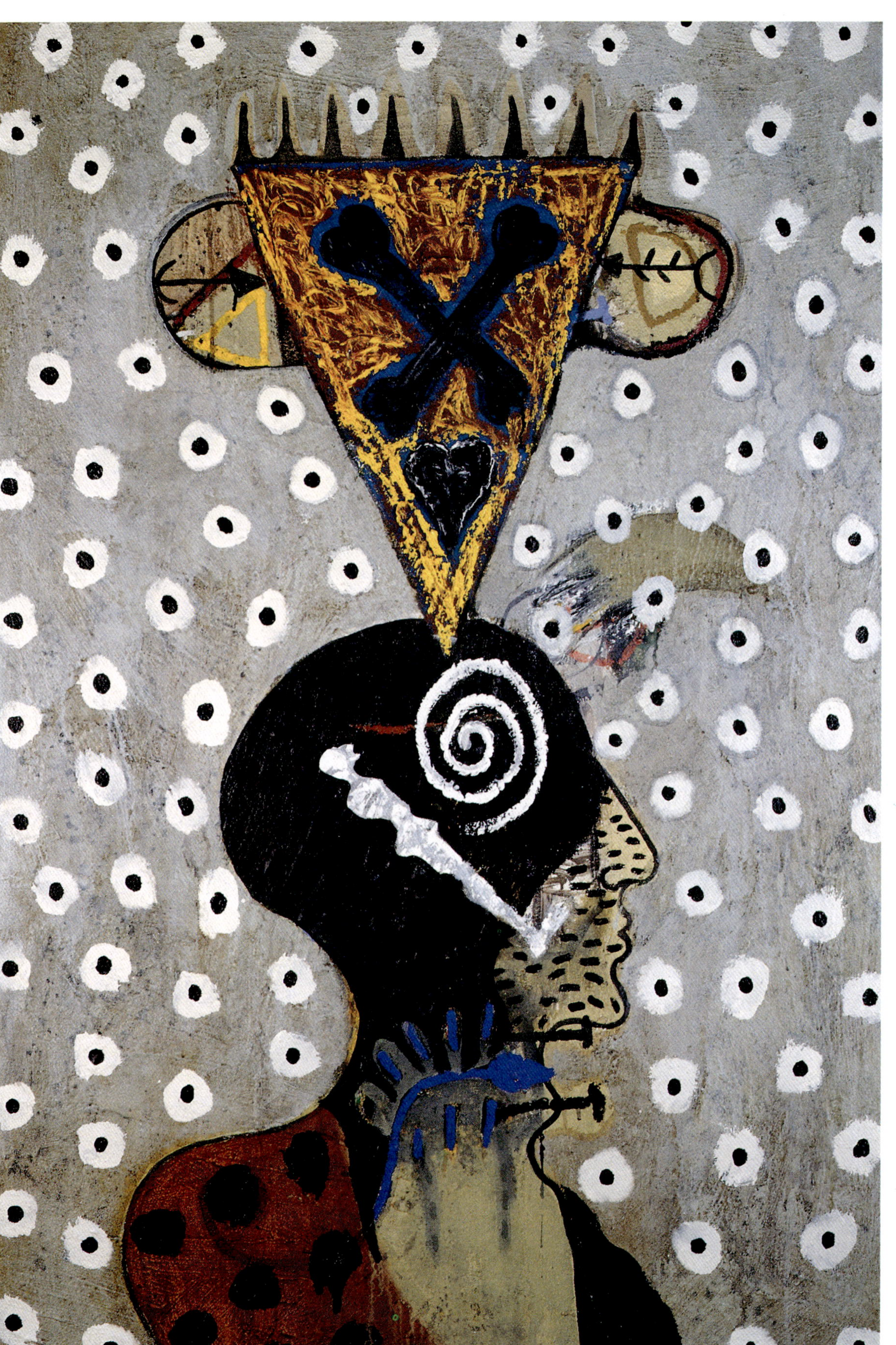

NADER ART GALLERY
Atarazana No. 9
Santo Domingo,
Dominican Republic
809.544.0878
809.565.6204 FAX

George Nader
Francisco Nader

NICOLAS ART GALLERY
2722 Ponce De Leon Blvd.
Coral Gables, FL 33134
305.446.5404
305.448.5993 FAX

George Nader
Patricia Nicolas

Exhibiting:
Latin American Art

Tony Capellan

Amuletos
1993, Oil on Canvas,
20" x 24"

Selected Biography:

1994 Art Miami 94, Miami, FL

1993 Nader Art Gallery,
Santo Domingo,
Dominican Republic

"Bastones de Mando",
Univeristy Museum,
UNAM

1992 "Mitos del Caribe",
History and Art Museum
of San Juan, Puerto Rico

"Al Encuentro con los
Otros", Kasel, Germany

"Una Nueva Mirada al
Caribe", Paris France

1991 X Bienal Internacional
de Valparaiso, Chile

PRAXIS
INTERNATIONAL
ART MEXICO

Arquimedes 175
Col Polanco
México, D.F. 11570
525.254.8813
525.255.5700
525.255.5690 FAX

Contact:
Alfredo Ginocchio
Doris Friedmann de Ginocchio

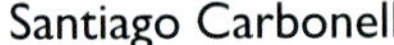

Santiago Carbonell

Paula
1993, Oil on Canvas,
110 cms. x 130 cms.

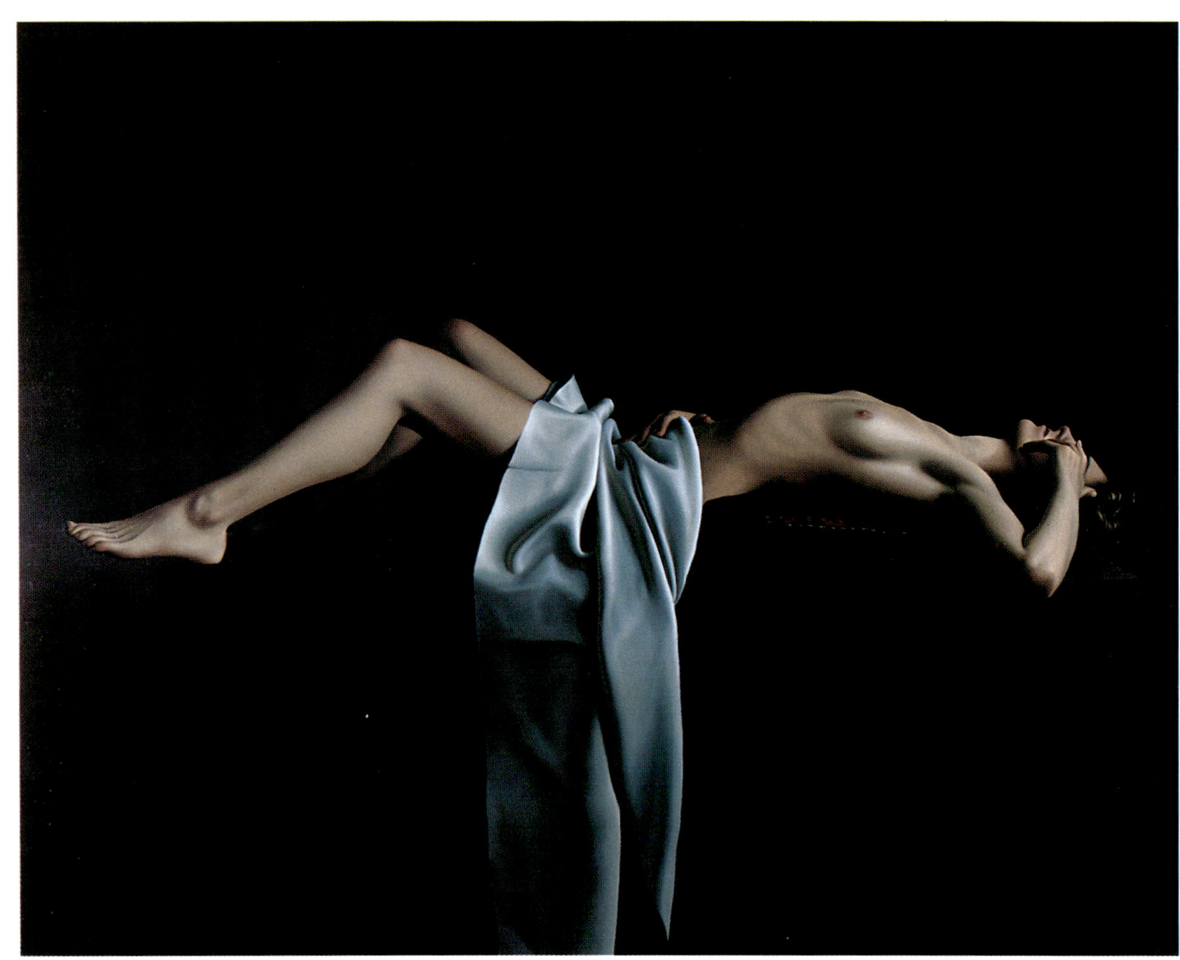

Selected Biography:

1994 Miami Art Expo '94
1993 Museo De Arte
      Moderno, Querétaro,
      México;
      Praxis Art Gallery,
      México, D.F.
      Miami Art Expo '93
1992 Miami Art Expo '92
1988 Dubose-Rein Gallery,
      Houston, TX

Auctions:

1993 Christie's, May 1993
1992 Christie's, November
      1992

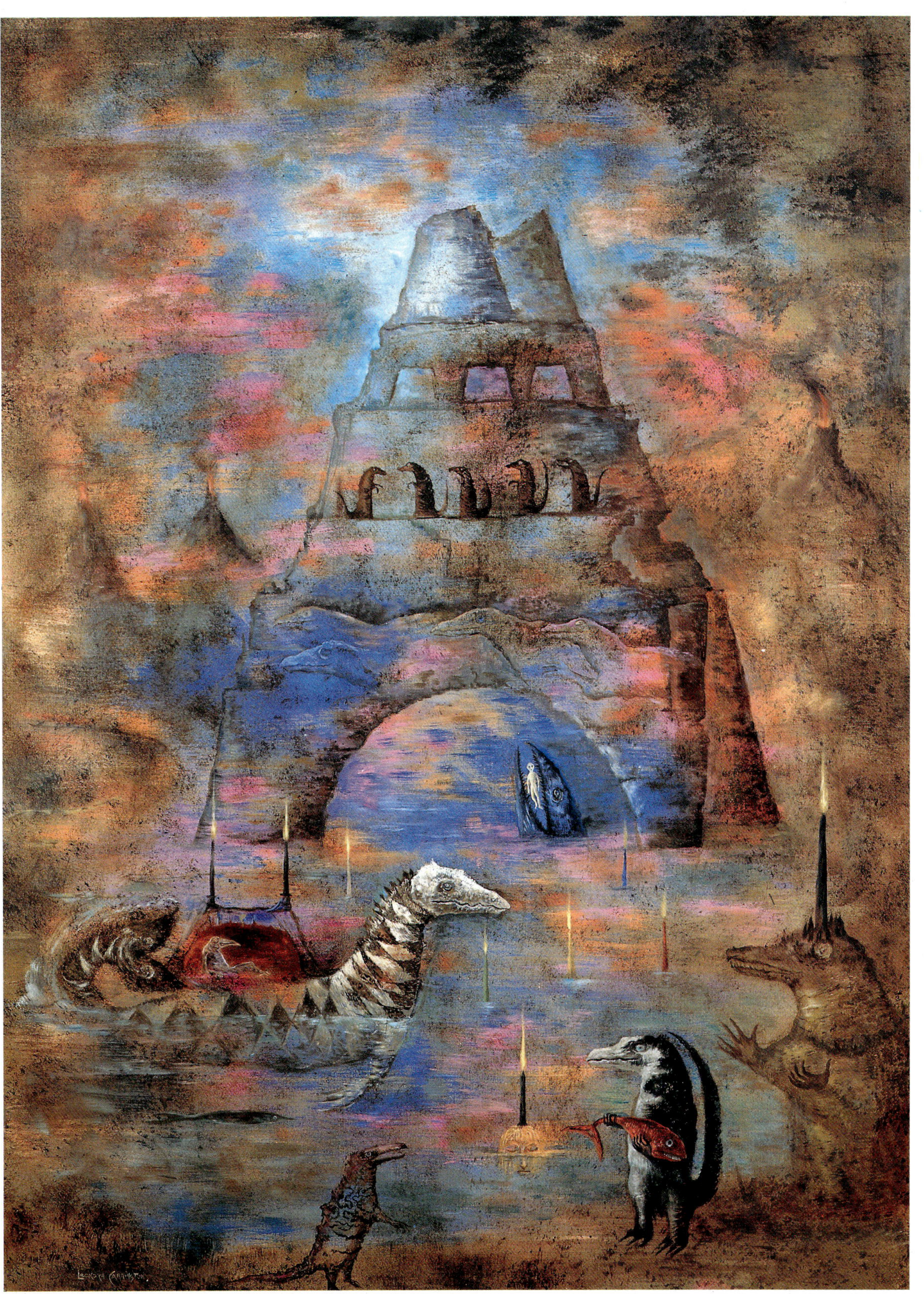

GALERIA DE ARTE MEXICANO

Rafael Rebollar #43,
Col. San Miguel
Chapultepec, Mexico 11850
525.272.5529
525.272.5583 FAX

Contact:
Ms. Mariana Perez Amor
Ms. Alejandra R de Yturbe

Exhibiting:
Contemporary Mexican art

Leonora Carrington

Tower of Nagas
1991, Oil on canvas,
112 x 81 cm.

RICHARD GRAY GALLERY

620 N. Michigan Ave.
Chicago, IL 60611
312.642.8877
312.642.8488 FAX

Contact:
Paul L. Gray

Luciano Castelli

1. *Alexandra Backside Nude*
   1991, Oil and
   pencil on paper,
   39" x 27½"

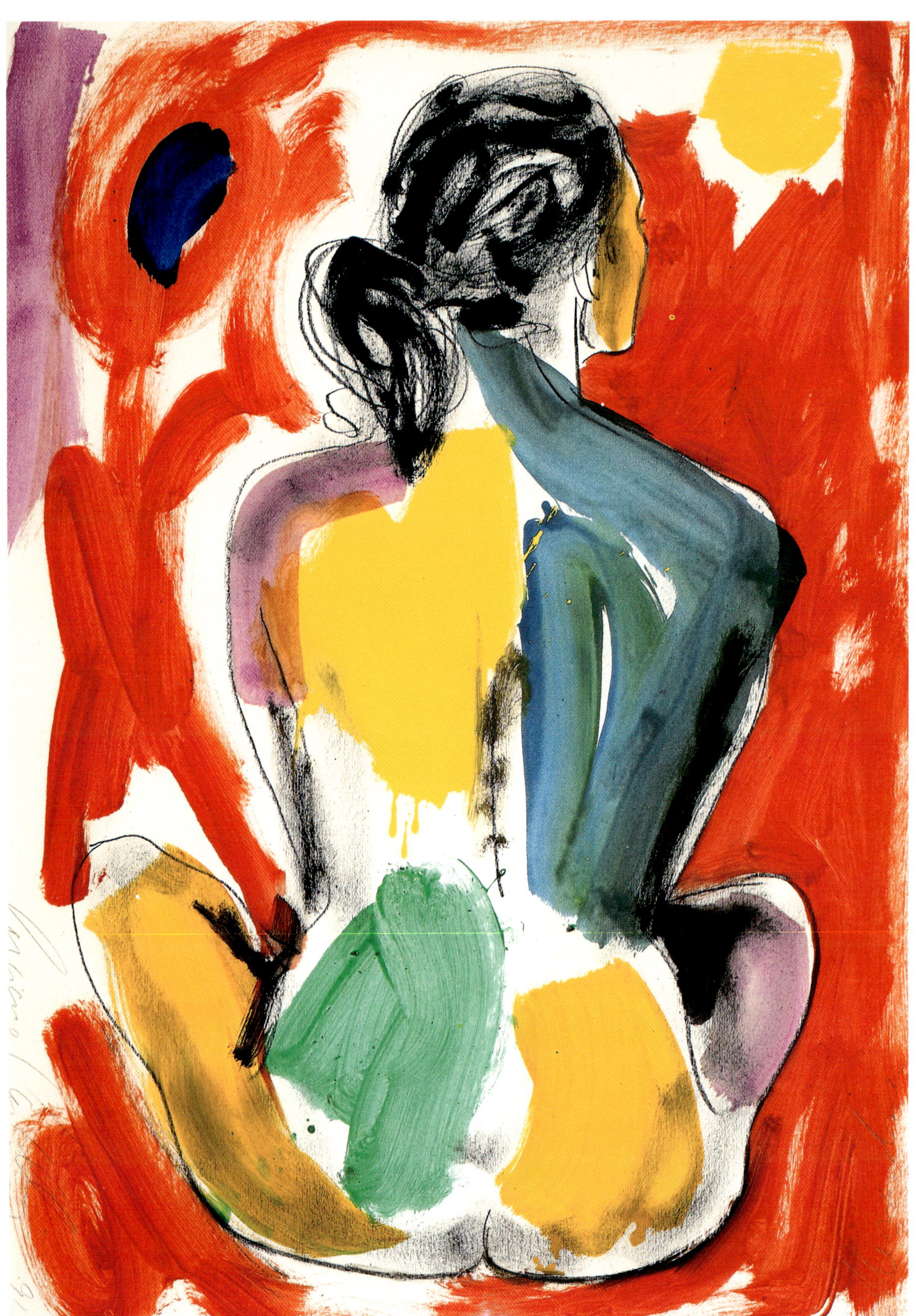

Selected Biography:

1990   Richard Gray Gallery,
       Chicago, IL

1989   Musee Cantonal
       Des Beaux Arts,
       Lausanne, Switzerland

1986   "Representation
       Abroad,"
       Hirshhorn Museum,
       Washington, DC

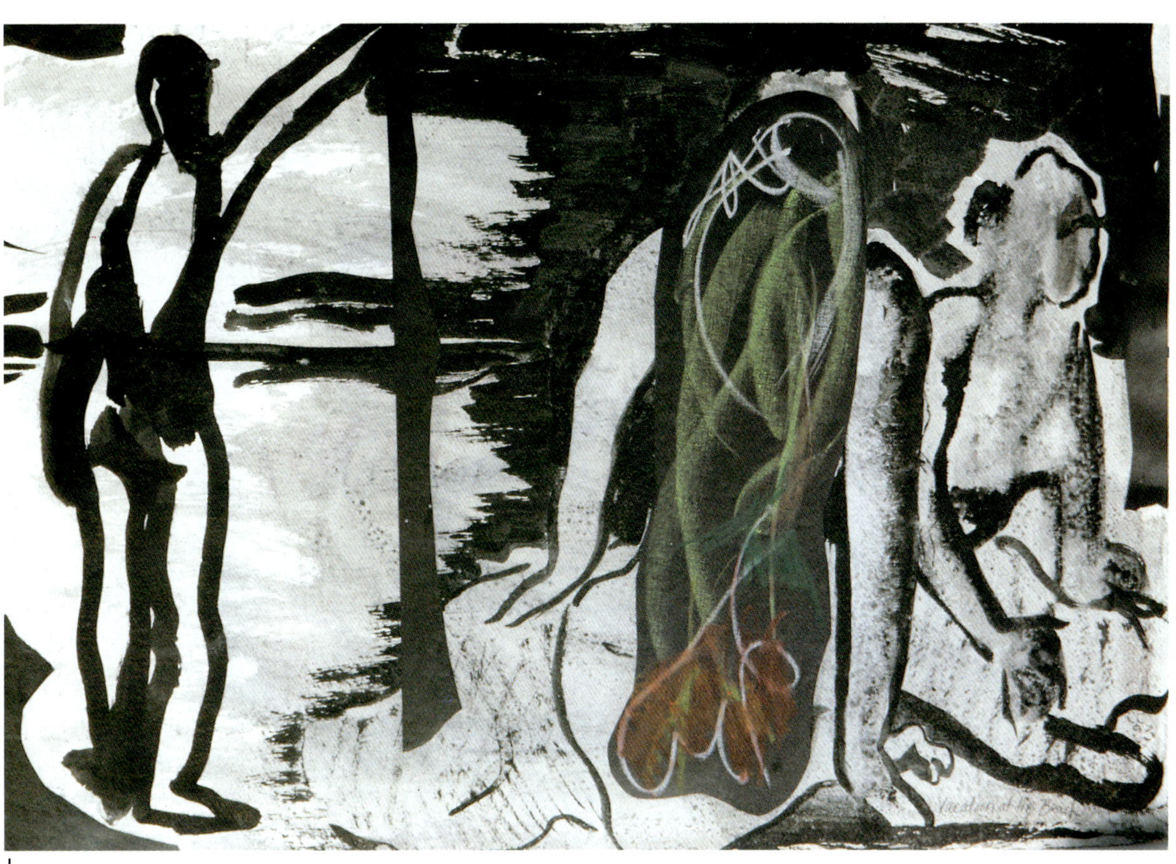

1

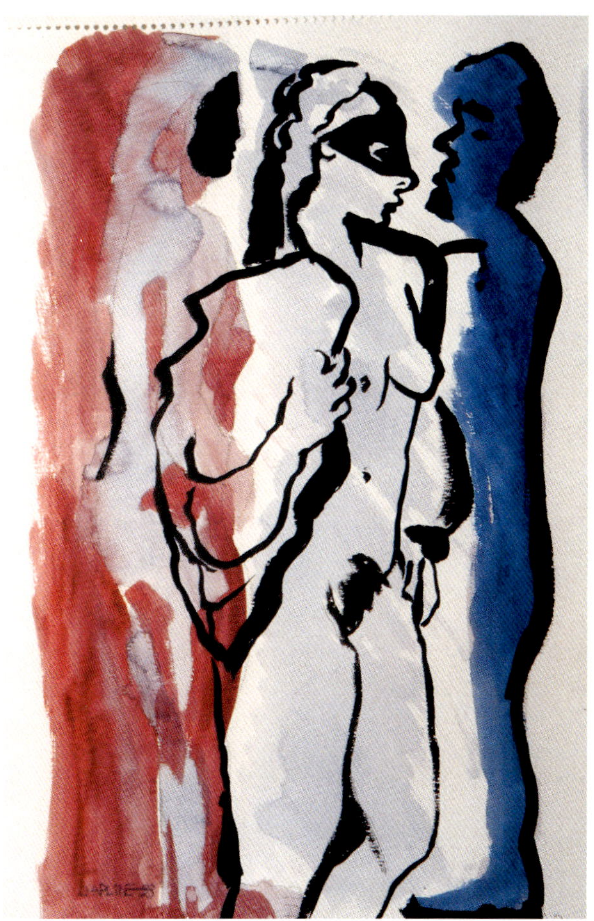

2

CLAUDIA CHAPLINE
GALLERY &
SCULPTURE GARDEN

3445 Shoreline Hwy.
P.O. Box 946
Stinson Beach, CA 94970
415.868.2308
415.868.9436 FAX

Contact:
Margot Merrill

Exhibiting:
Contemporary art

Claudia Chapline

1. *Vacation at the Beach*
   1993,
   Mixed media on paper,
   18" x 26"

2. *Backstage*
   1993, Watercolor,
   24" x 26"

STUART LEVY
FINE ART

588 Broadway, Suite 303
New York. NY 10012
212.941.0009
212.941.7987 FAX

Contact:
Stuart Levy, President
Michael Lederer,
Assoc. Director

Exhibiting:
Contemporary Russian,
European and American
Artists

Genia Chef

1. *The Birth of Myths*
   1993, Oil on board,
   39" x 59"

2. *The Autumn of Casanova*
   1991, Oil on wood,
   10.25" x 12.5"

3. *The Night Poet*
   with Lighting Hat
   1992-93, Oil and
   Chinese on board,
   6.25" x 9"

Selected Exhibitions:

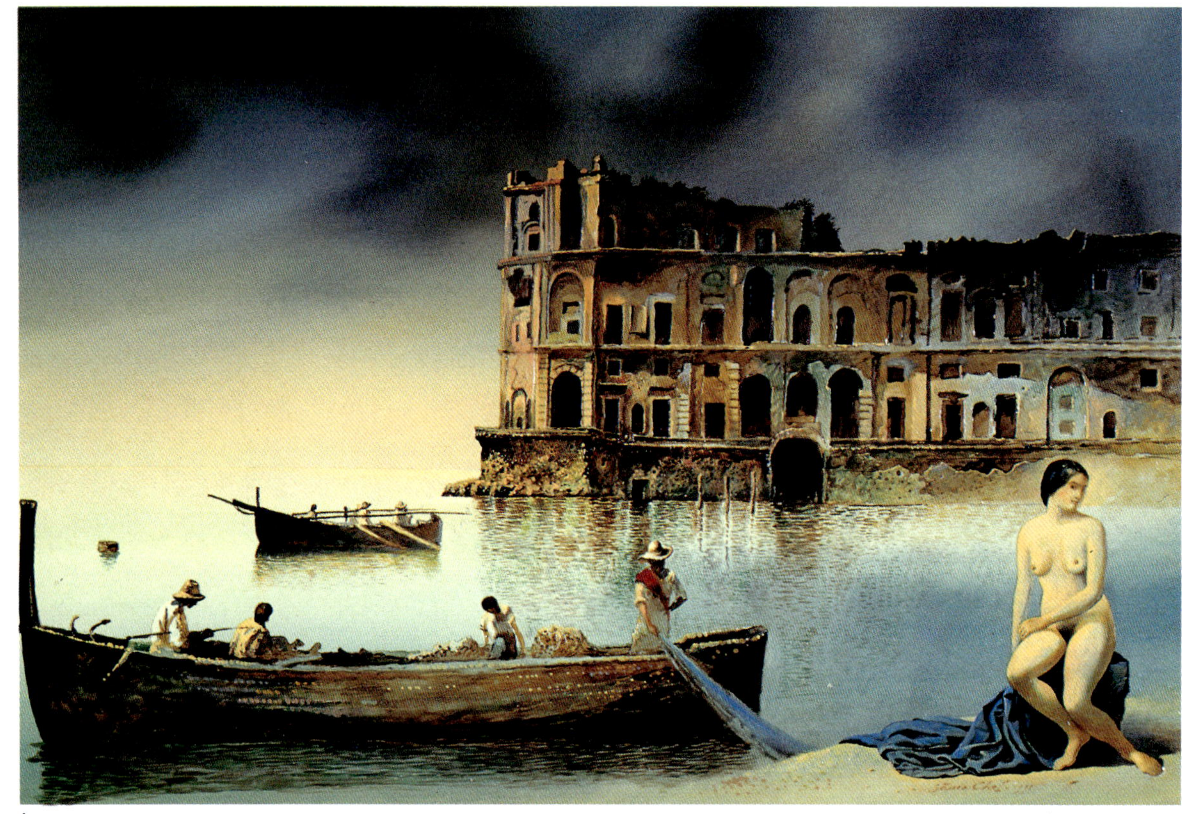

1

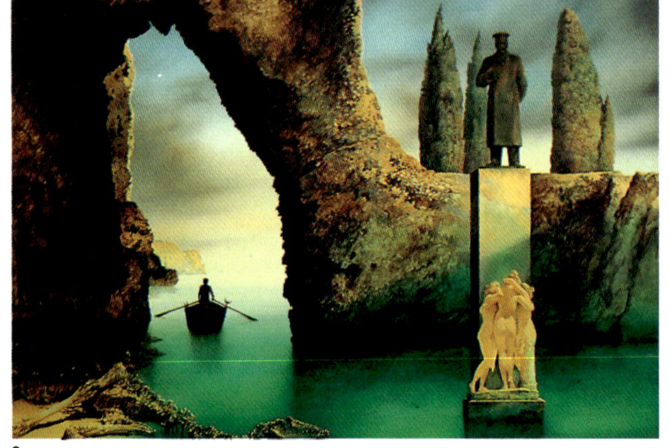

2

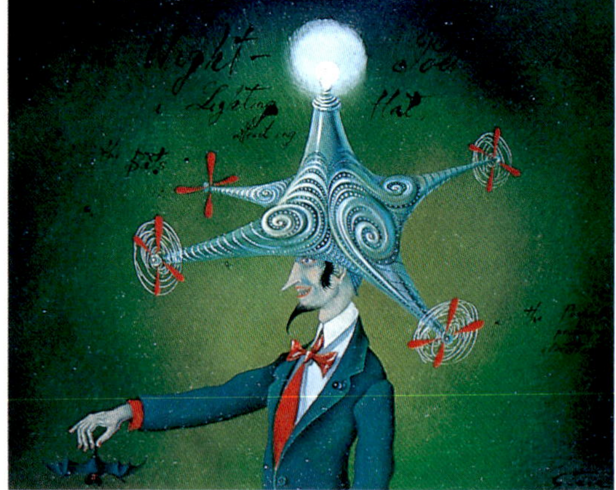

3

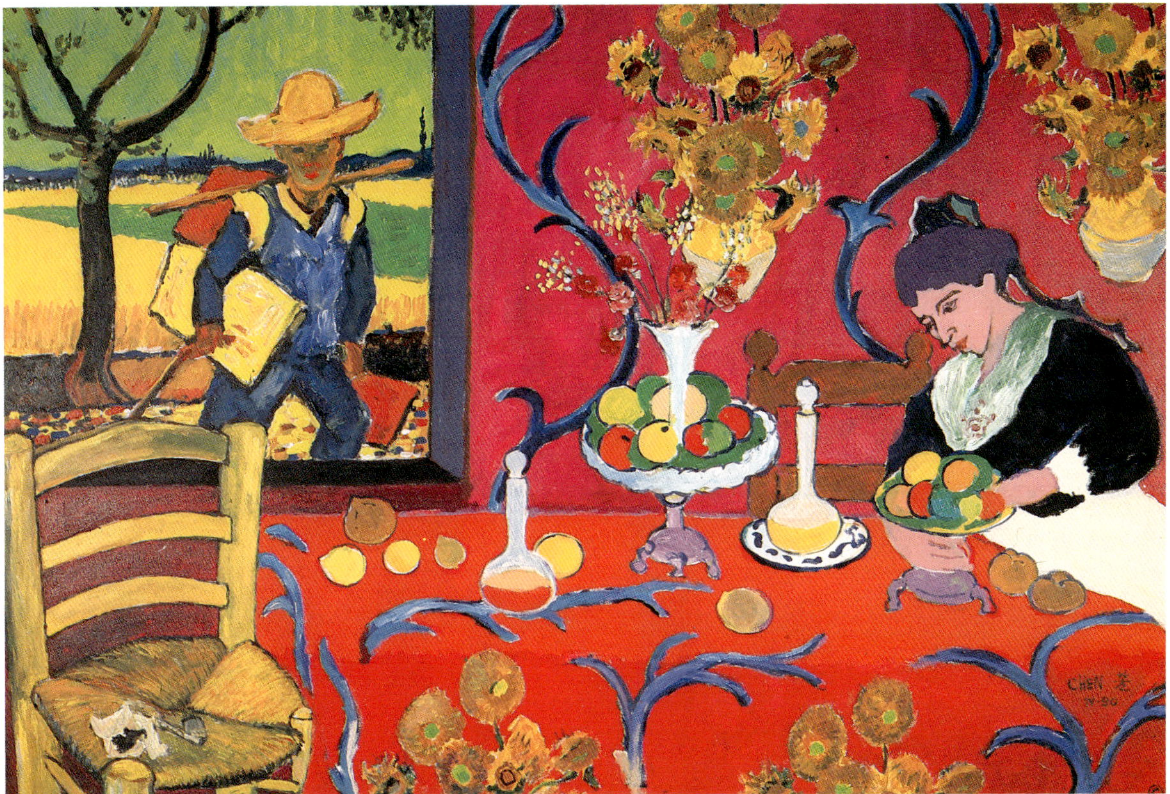

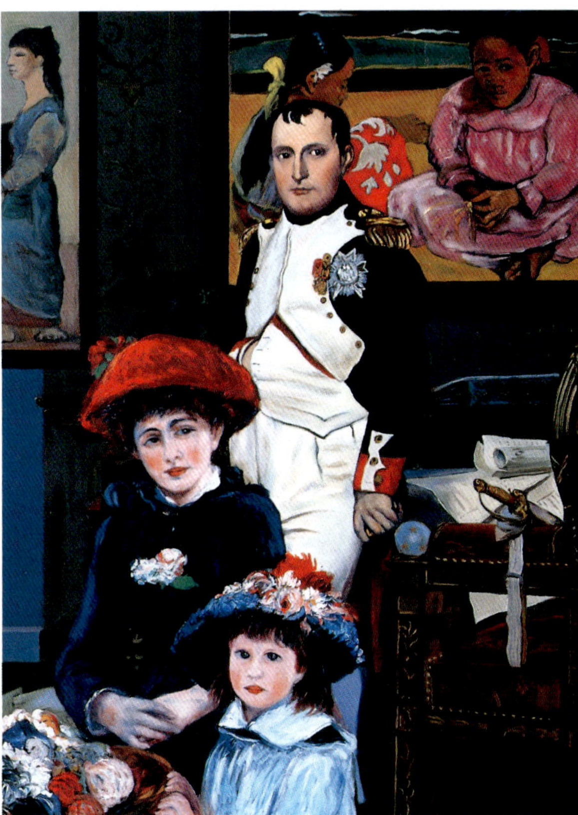

T. F. Chen

1. *Vincent Coming Home*
   1990, Acrylic on canvas,
   44" x 66"

2. *The Rich and the Poor*
   1976, Acrylic on canvas,
   72" x 50"

3. *Art-Loving Napoléon*
   1992, Oil on canvas,
   48" x 36"

Selected Biography:
1991-92
   One-year Art Tour to
   Taipei Fine Arts
   Museum and 19
   Cultural Centers in
   Taiwan

1990 Solo exhibition:
   "The Art of Dr. T.F.
   Chen: Neo-
   Iconography" at Taiwan
   Museum of Art

1978 Solo exhibition:
   The Art Alliance,
   Philadelphia, PA

ALFREDO MARTINEZ GALLERY

2311 Le Jeune Road
Coral Gables, Fl 33134
305.442.0808
305.442.0824 FAX

Contact:
Lawrence Casalins

Exhibiting:
Contemporary Art

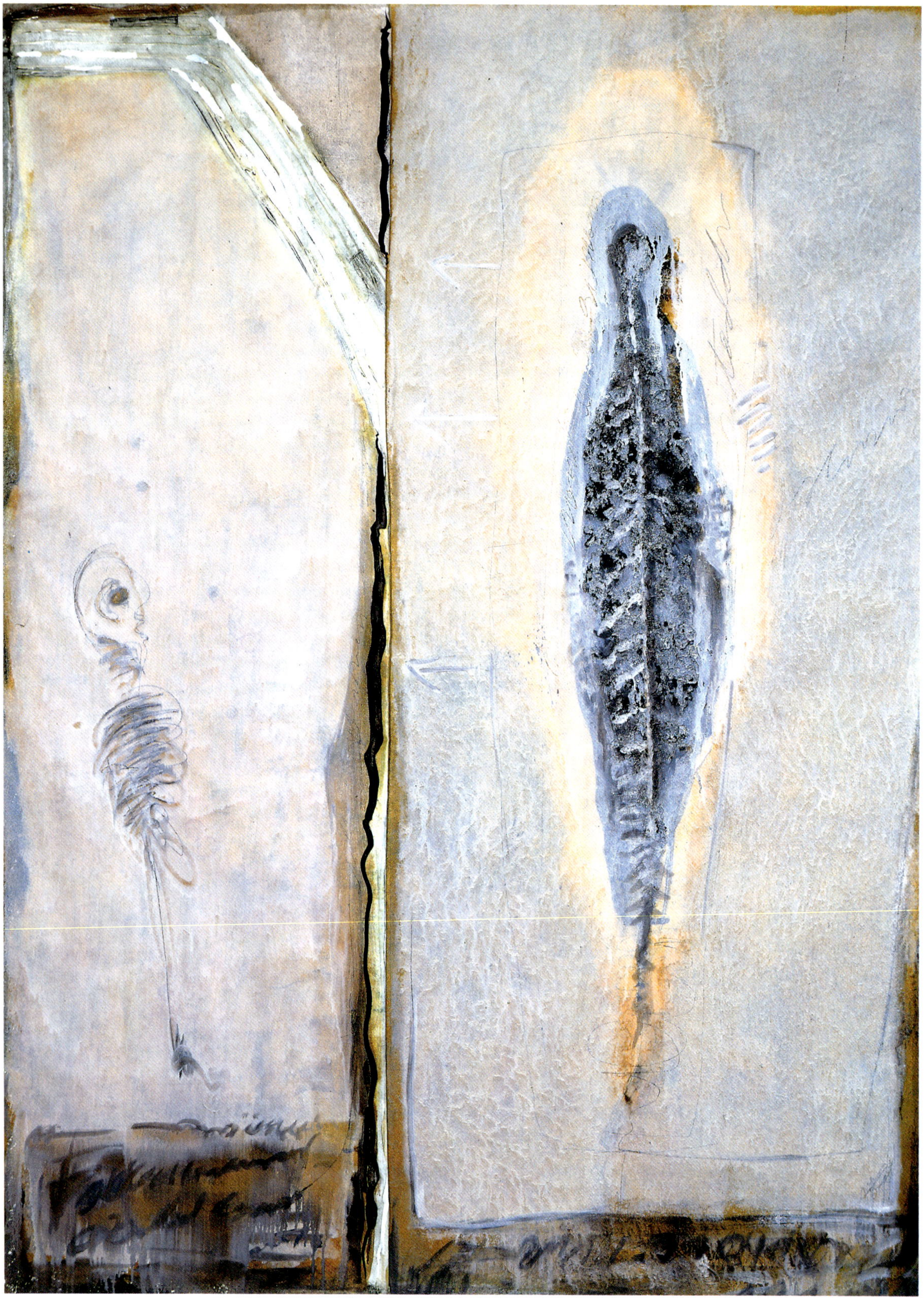

Marvin Chinchilla

Sancto
1993,
Mixed media on canvas,
72" x 53"

Selected Biography:

1994 Art Miami International
Exhibition

Diana Traficante
Gallery, Buenos Aires

1993 Solo exhibition, Alfredo
Martinez Gallery

Art Miami International
Exhibition

Participation in
numerous shows in
Argentina, Costa Rica,
Chile, Ecuador,
Panama, Peru and
Venezuela

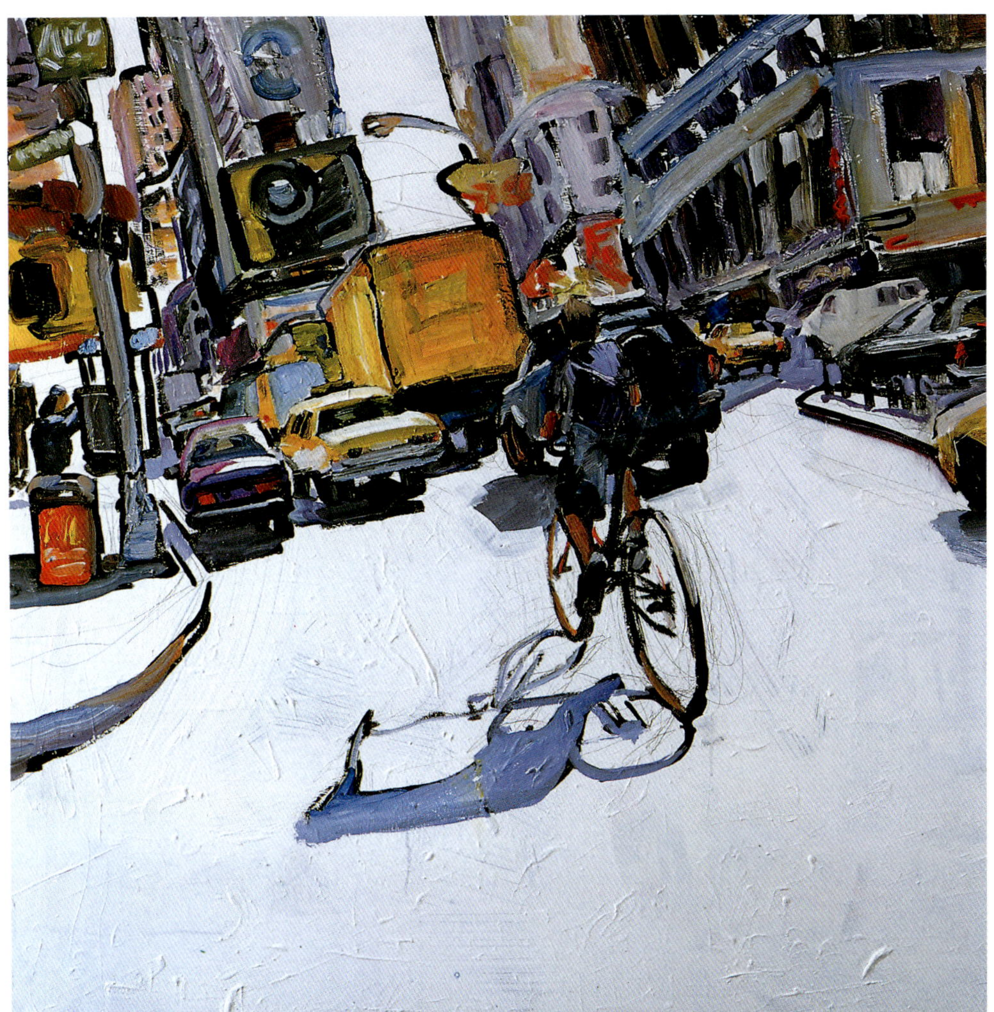

1

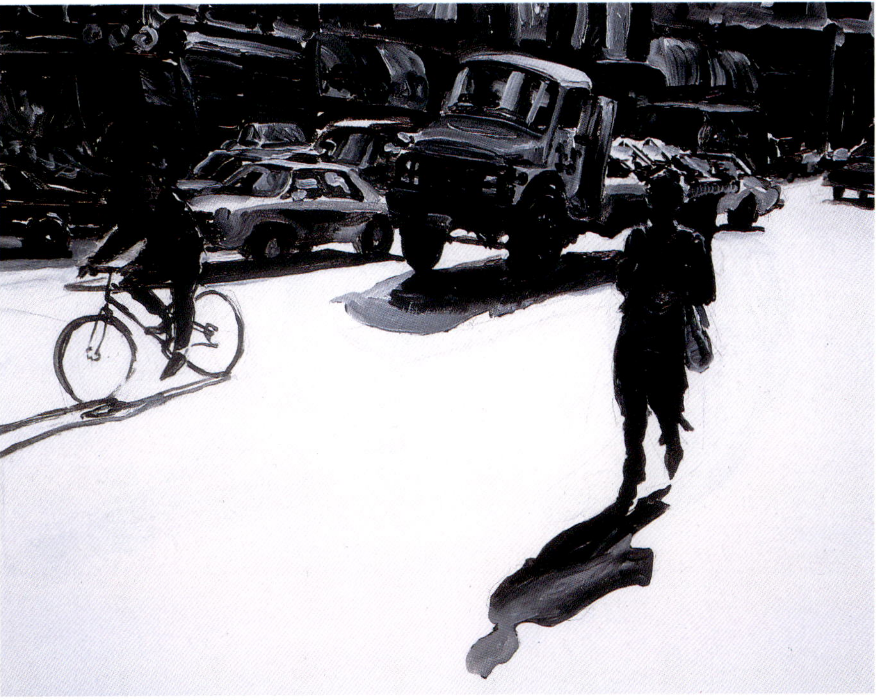

2

TAMENAGA GALLERY

982 Madison Avenue
New York, NY 10021
212.734.6789
212.734.9413 FAX

Contact:
Patrick O'Connor

Exhibiting:
Contemporary realist and
figurative painting

Tom Christopher

1. *Camera on Broadway*
   1993, Acrylic on canvas,
   46" x 46"

2. *Mid-Day Break*
   1993, Acrylic on canvas,
   30" x 40"

Selected Biography:

1994 Solo exhibition,
Tamenaga Gallery,
New York, NY

1993 Solo exhibition,
Tamenaga Gallery,
New York, NY

1992 "Modern Times,"
Katonah Museum of
Art, New York, NY;
Payton Rule Gallery,
Denver;
Socrates Sculpture
Park, New York

1991 Solo exhibition,
Richard Iri Gallery,
Los Angeles, CA

ALISAN FINE ARTS LTD.

315 Prince's Building
10 Chater Road
Central, Hong Kong
852.526.1091
852.845.3975 FAX

Contact:
Alice King, Director

Exhibiting:
Contemporary Chinese
artists.

Chao Chung-Hsiang

The Joys of Life
1988, Ink and acrylic on
paper,
123 x 91 cm.

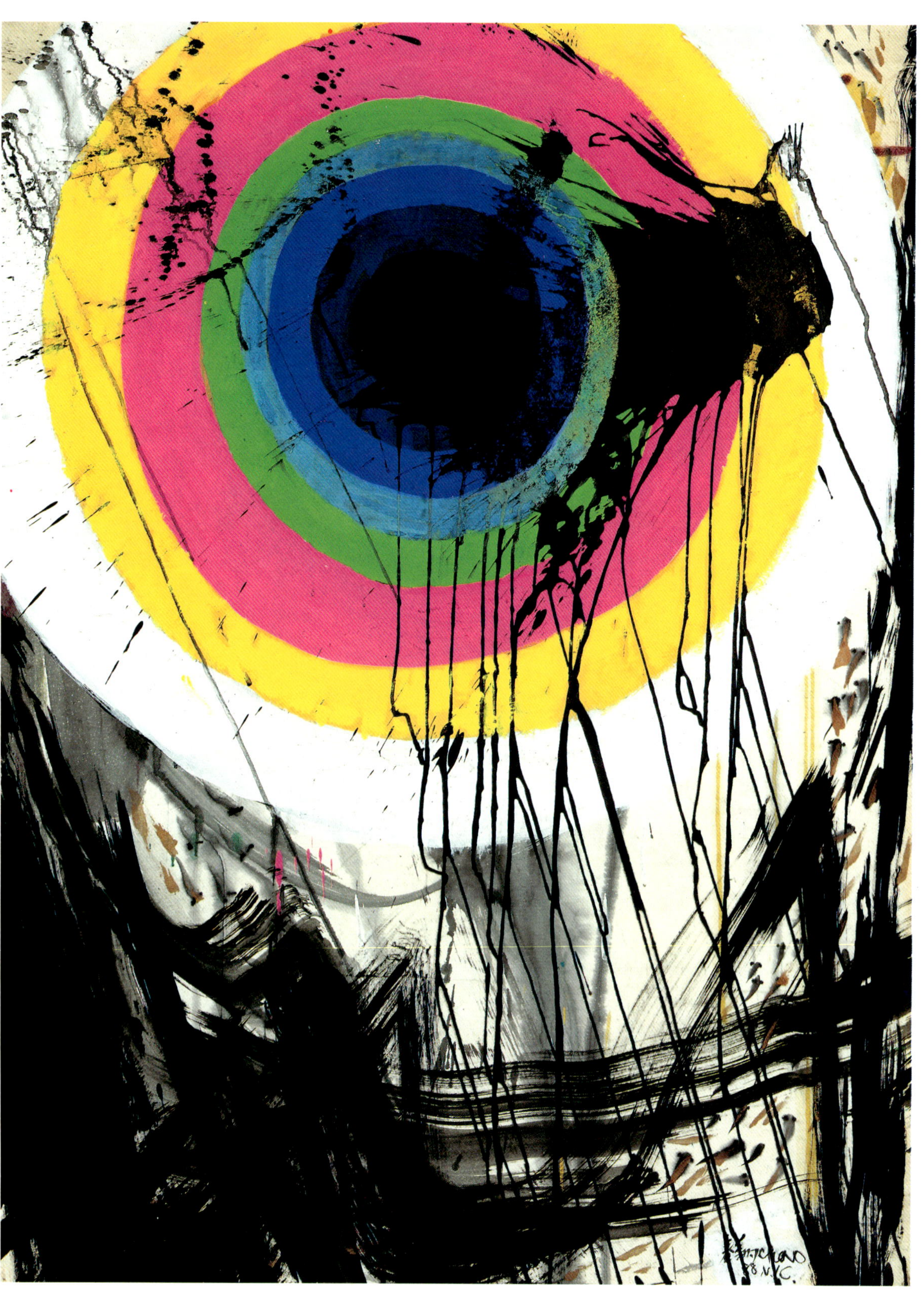

Selected Biography:
1991 Died in Miaoli, Taiwan
1980 Returned first time to
        exhibit in Taiwan since
        1965
1958 Moved to New York
        and stayed there until
        1984
1948 Left China for Taiwan
1935 Studied under Lin
        Fengmian
1913 Born in China
Selected Collections;
        Metropolitan Museum
        of Art, New York
        Columbia University,
        New York; Queens
        Museum, New York:
        New York University,
        New York

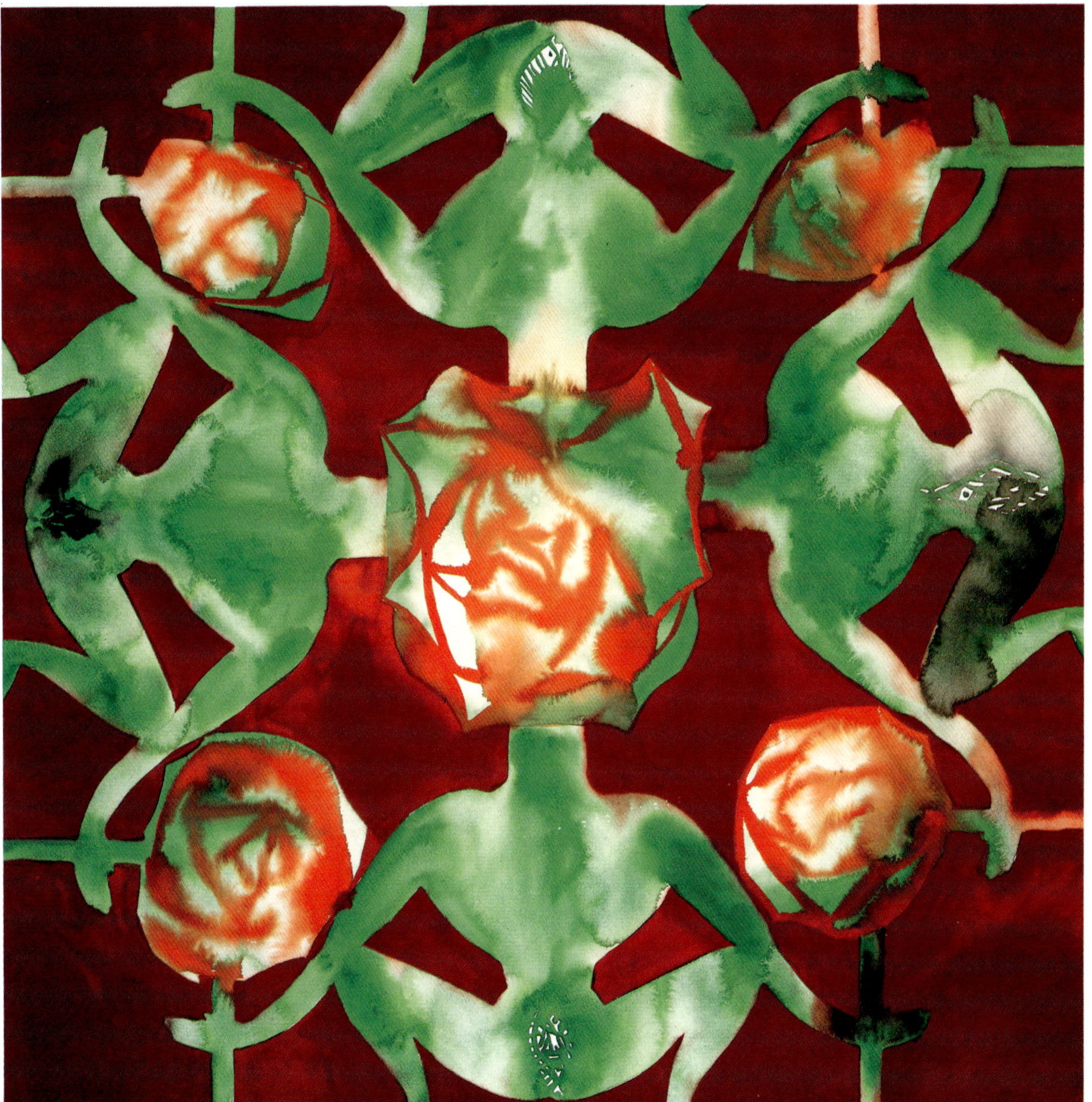

GAGOSIAN GALLERY

980 Madison Ave.
New York, NY 10021
212.744.2313
212.772.7962 FAX

136 Wooster Street
New York, NY 10012
212.228.2828
212.228.2878

Contact:
Melissa Lazarov, Director

Exhibiting:
20th-Century painting
and sculpture;
Abstract Expressionism,
Pop & Minimalism

Francesco Clemente

Untitled
(Amalfi Watercolors)
1992, Watercolor
on paper,
45" x 44 $^1/2$"

Selected Biography:
1993 Solo exhibition:
Anthony d'Offay
Gallery, London;
Group exhibition:
Akira Ikeda Gallery,
NY, NY; Sperone
Westwater, NY, NY
1992 Solo exhibition:
Gagosian Gallery,
Wooster Street, New
York, NY; Galerie
Bruno Bischofberger,
Zurich, Switzerland;
Group exhibition:
Musee d'Art Moderne
et D'Art Contemporain,
Nice, France; The
Museum of Modern
Art, New York, NY

THE PACE GALLERY

142 Greene Street
New York, NY 10012
212.431.9224
212.431.9280 FAX

32 East 57th Street
New York, NY 10022
212.421.3292
212.421.0835 FAX

Contact:
Marc Glimcher

Exhibiting:
20th-century paintings, drawings and sculpture

Chuck Close

April
1990-91, Oil on canvas,
100" x 84"

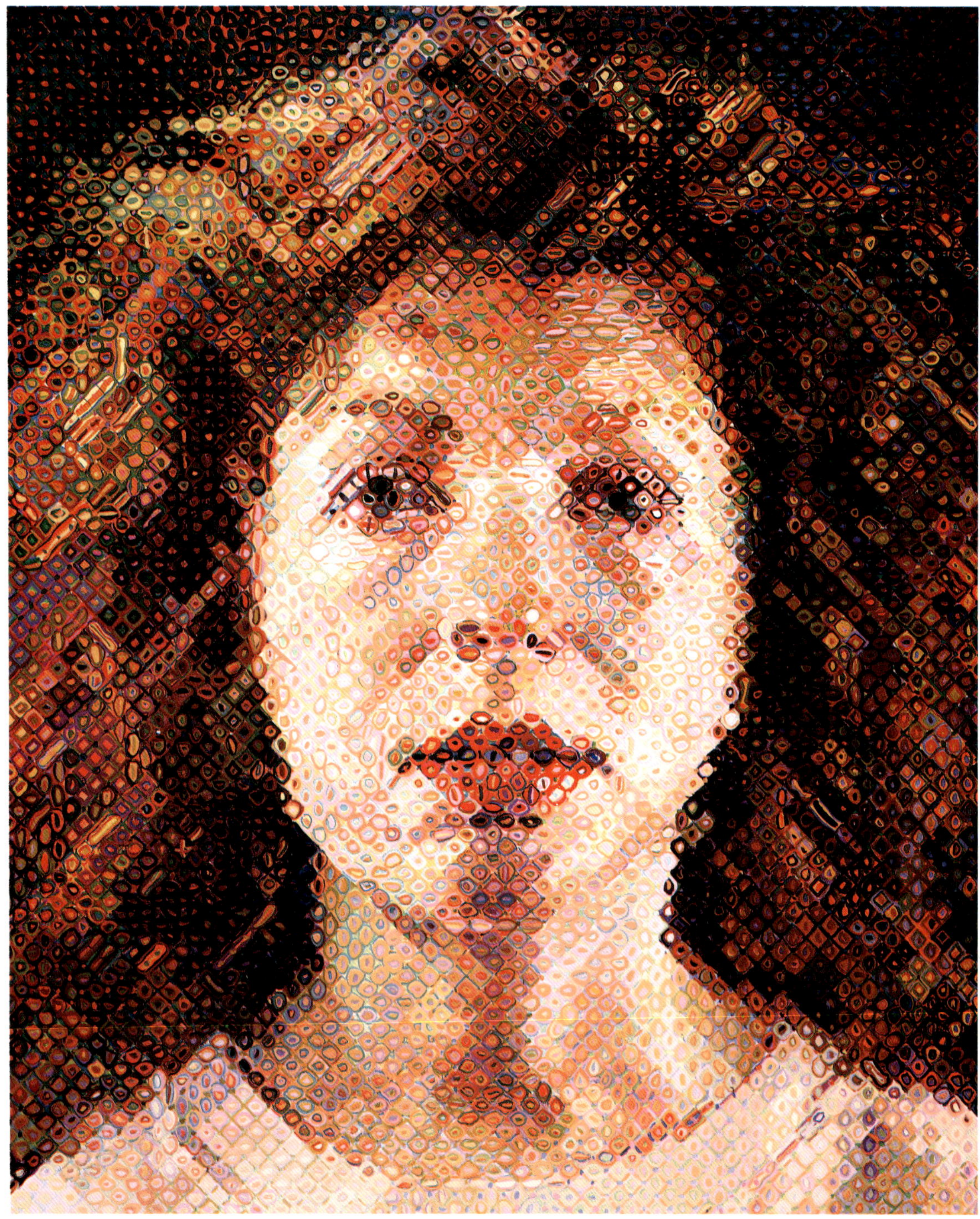

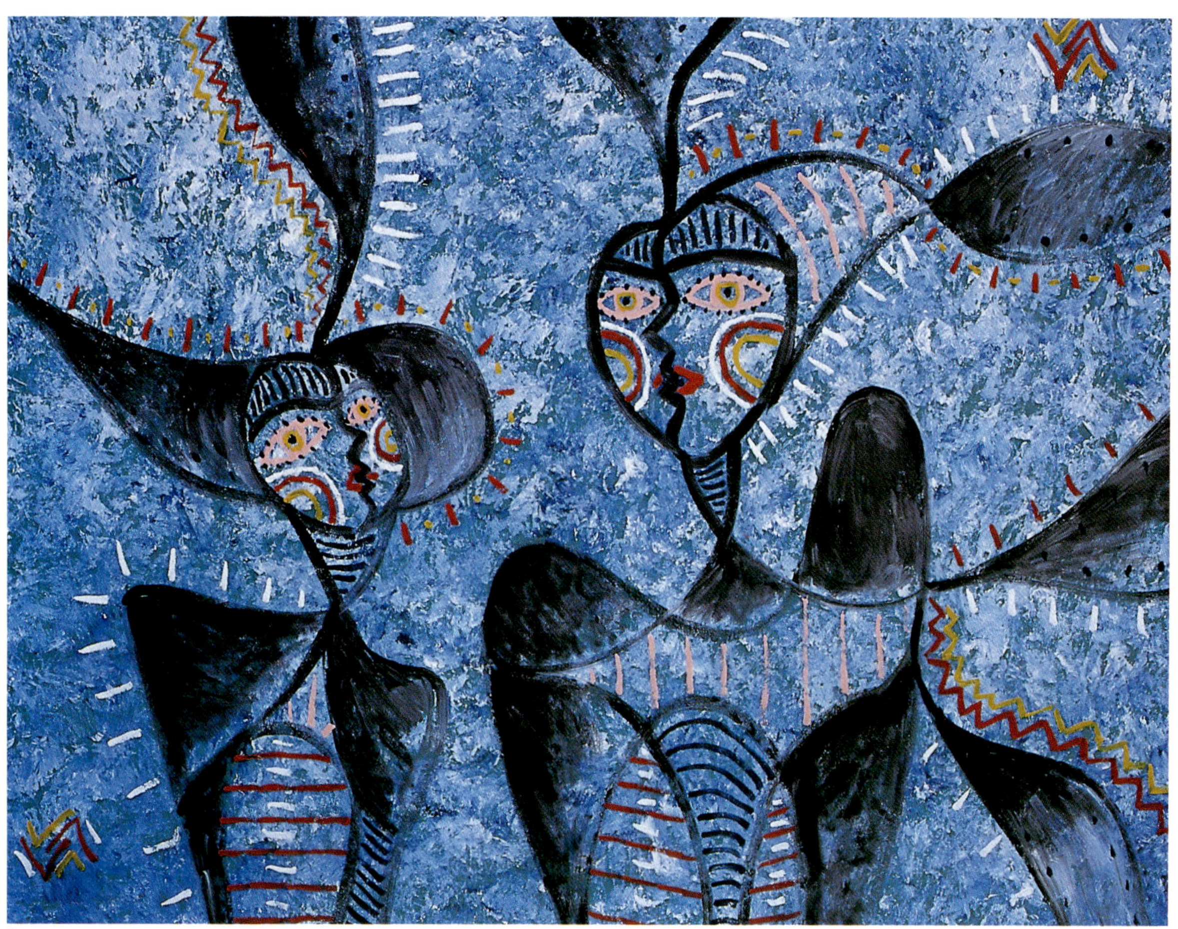

1

ROCFERN INTERNATIONAL GALLERIES, INC.

80 Carlauren Road Unit17
Woodbridge (Toronto),
Ontario L4L 7Z5 Canada
905.850.7647
905.850.8062 FAX

Contact:
Rocco Pannese
Fernando Rocco

Michael Close

1. *Untitled II*
   1993, Acrylic on canvas,
   48" x 60"

2. *Faces series 91-A*
   1991, Mixed media
   on paper, 11½" x 8"

3. *Faces series 91-B*
   1991, Mixed media
   on paper, 11½" x 8"

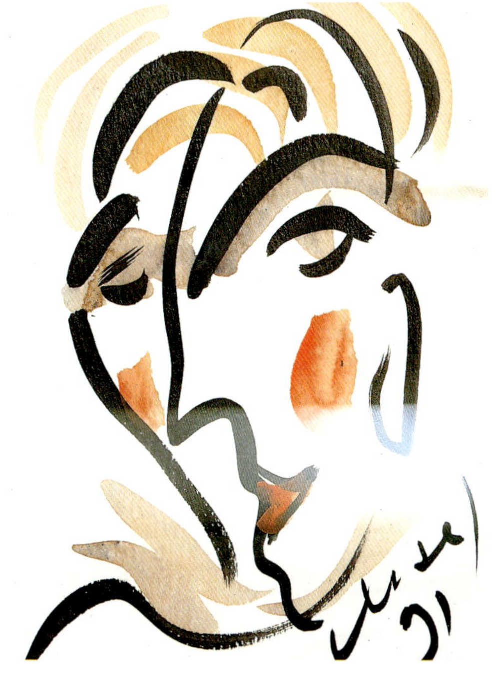

2

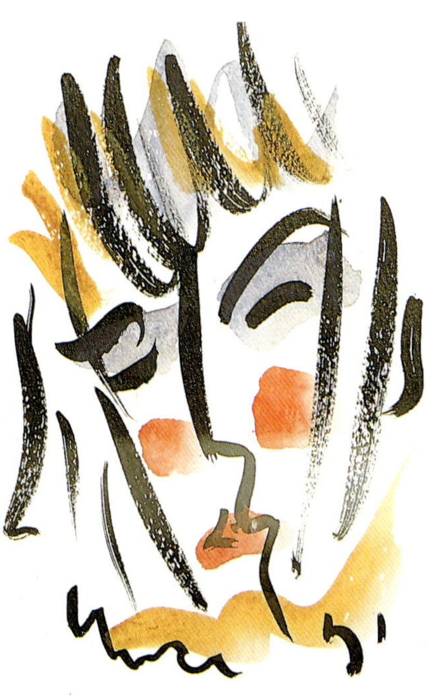

3

Selected Biography:

1994 Rocfern International
      Galleries, Woodbridge,
      Ontario, Canada

      Art Miami 94
      Miami, Florida

      Free & Free Gallery
      Boca Raton, Florida

      Lerner Gallery
      Beverly Hills, CA

1993 Biuro Wystaw Museum
      Poland

      Art Frankfurt
      Frankfurt, Germany

KIYO HIGASHI GALLERY

8332 Melrose Avenue
Los Angeles, CA 90069
213.655.2482
213.655.7016 FAX

Contact:
Kiyo Higashi

Exhibiting:
Abstract-reductive work:
Paintings and sculpture

Max Cole

Pale Horse
1993, Acrylic on linen,
52" x 62"

Selected biography:
1993 Museum of Art,
University of Arizona,
Tucson;
Kiyo Higashi Gallery,
Los Angeles, CA

1992 Kunstraum, Kassel,
Germany;
Galerie Schoppman,
Dusseldorf;
Museum Folkwang,
Graphics Kabinet,
Essen, Germany;

1991 Galerie Schlegl, Zurich

1990 Galerie Schroder,
Mönchengladbach,
Germany

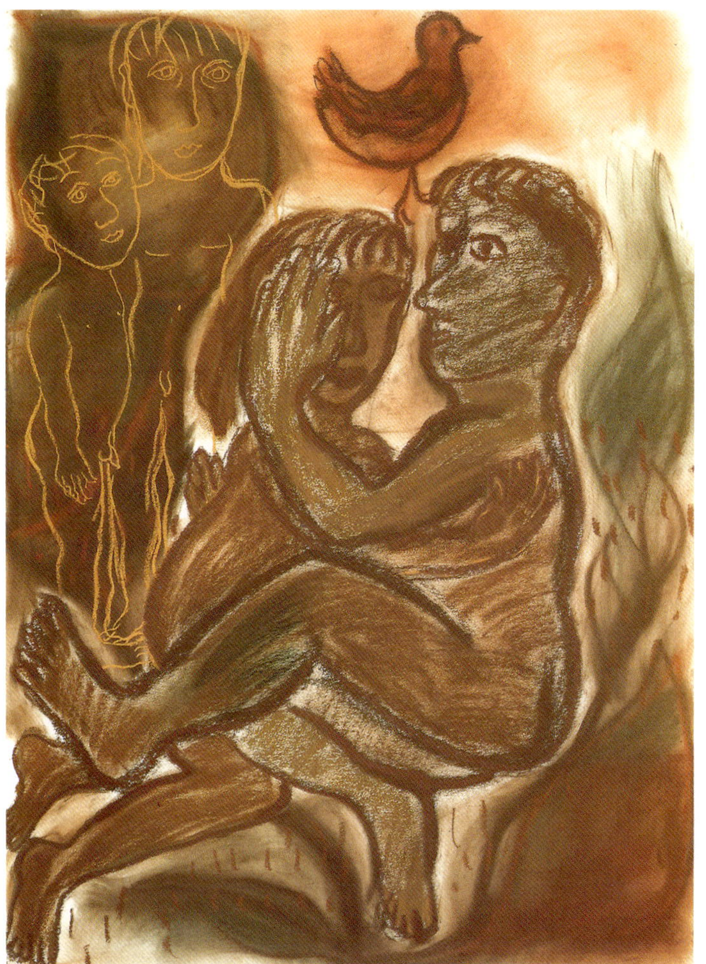

1

JASON & RHODES GALLERY

4 New Burlington Place
London, W1X 1SB
England
071.434.1768
071.287.8841 FAX

Contact:
Benjamin Rhodes, Director

Exhibiting:
British and international
contemporary art

Eileen Cooper

1. *Blissful*
   1992, Pastel on paper,
   40" x 30"

2. *Play Dead*
   1991, Oil on canvas,
   60" x 66"

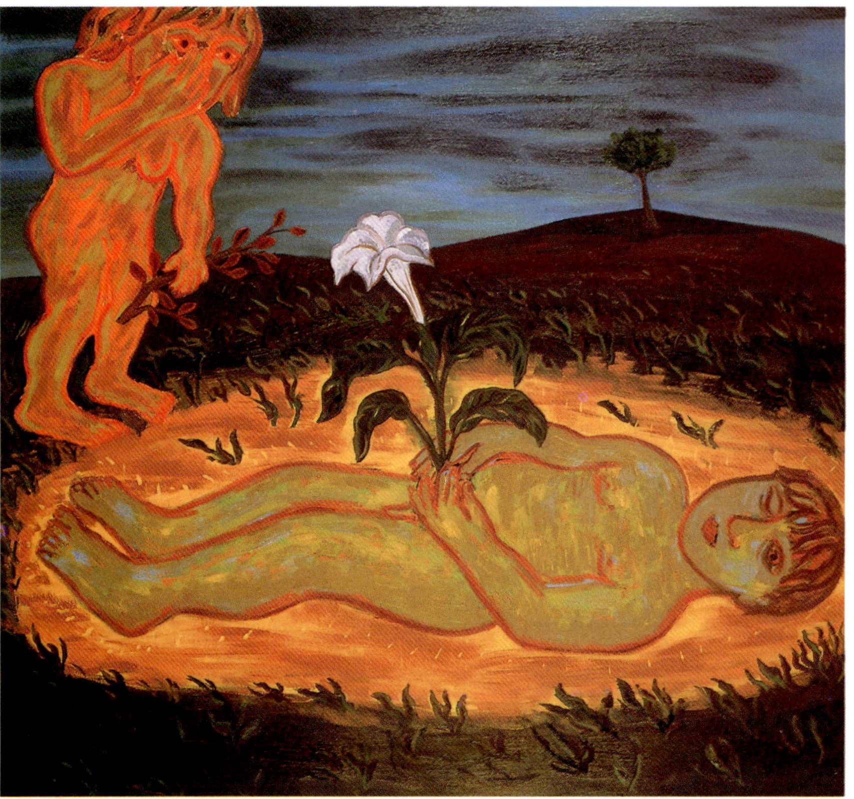

2

Selected Biography:

1993 One person show
touring British
museums

1992 "Innocence and
Experience" touring
show organized by the
South Bank Centre and
Manchester City
Artgallery

1991 "The Outsider: British
Figuration Now",
Palazzo Vecchio,
Florence, Italy

PRAXIS
INTERNATIONAL
ART MEXICO

Arquimedes 175
Col Polanco
México, D.F. 11570
525.254.8813
525.255.5700
525.255.5690 FAX

Contact:
Alfredo Ginocchio
Doris Friedmann de Ginocchio

Roberto Cortazar

1. *Numero 14*
   1993, Oil on Canvas,
   150 cms. x 100 cms.

Selected Biography:

1994 Praxis Art Gallery,
      México, D.F.;
      Museo Jose Luis
      Cuevas México, D.F.
1993 Europalia Ostende,
      Belgium; Monterrey
      Contemporary Art
      Museum, Monterrey,
      N.L. , México
1989 Museum of Modern Art,
      México, D.F.

Auctions:

1987 Christie's, November
      1987

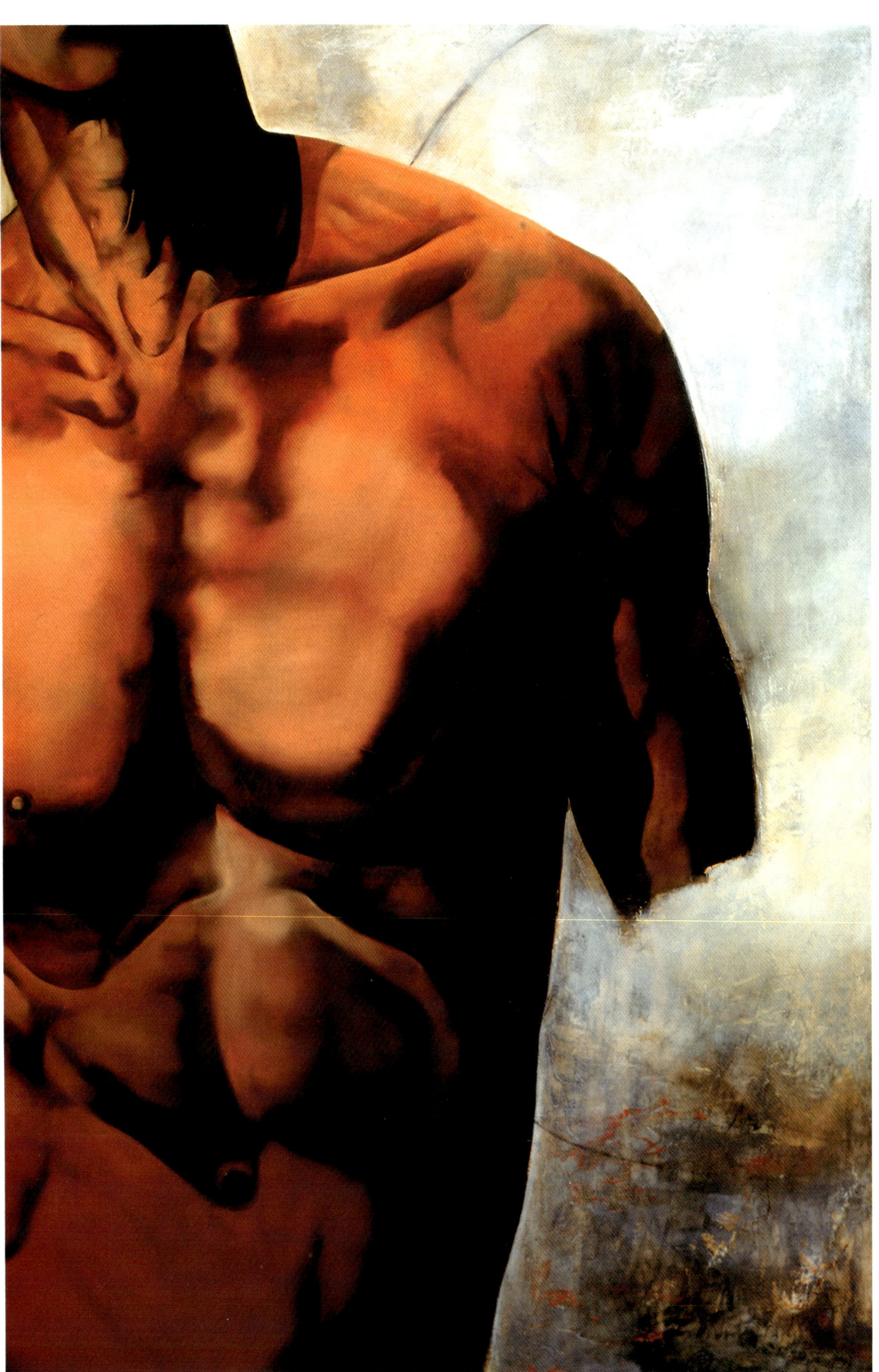

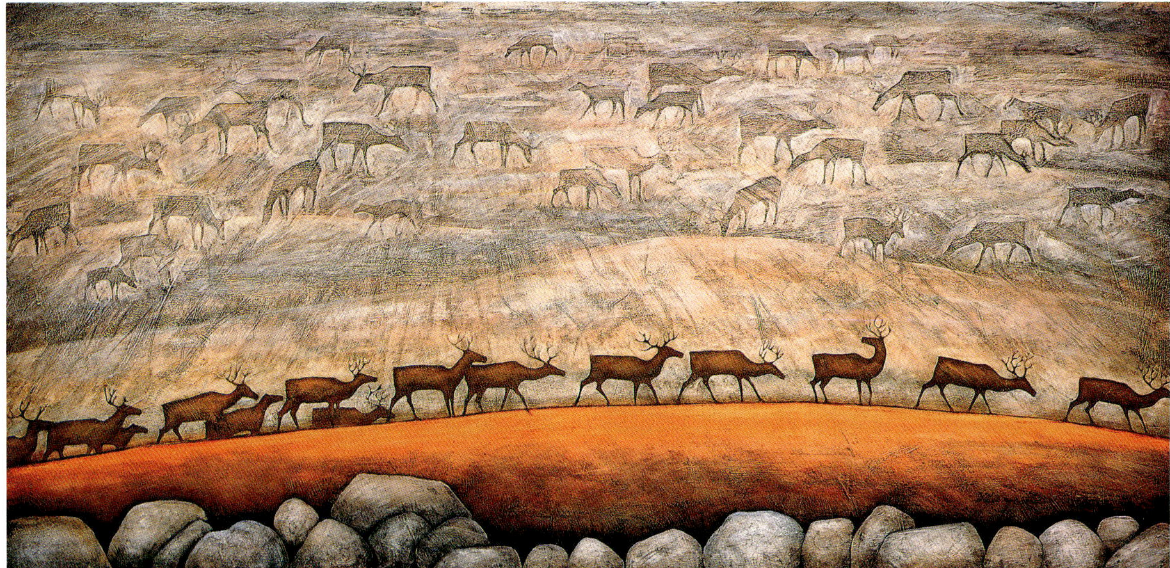

1

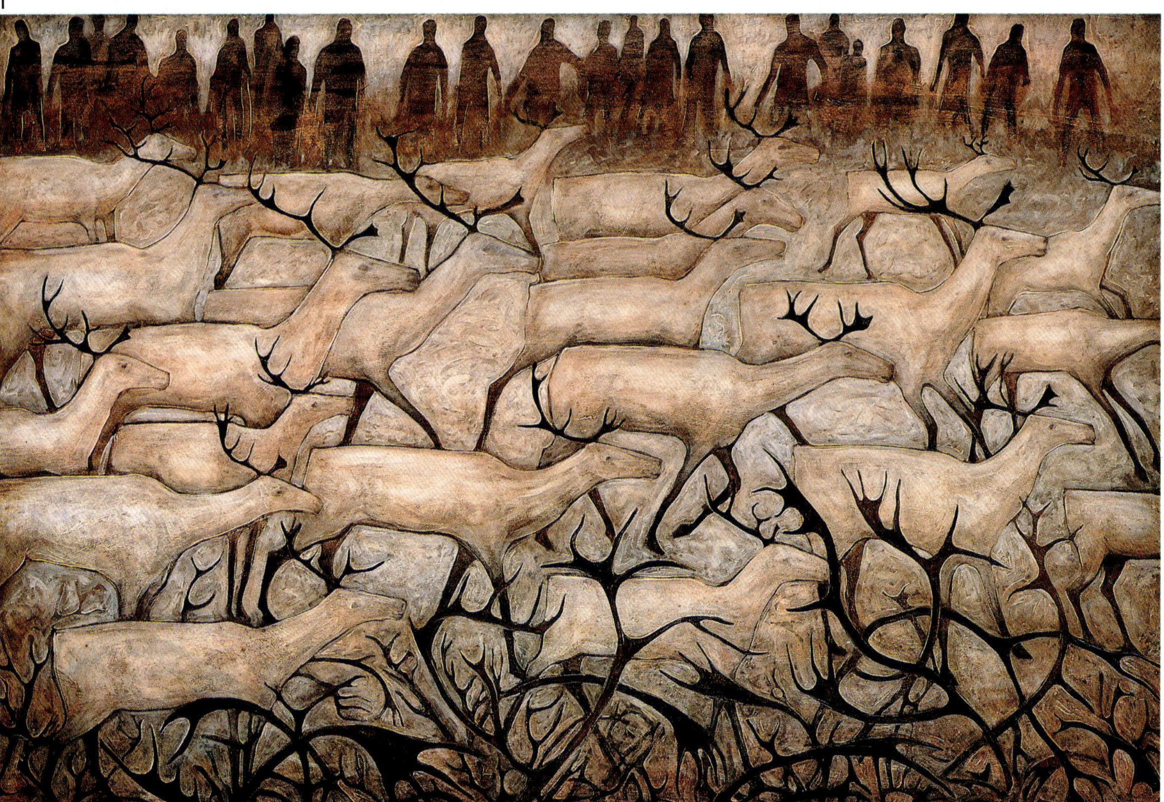

2

DIANE FARRIS GALLERY

1565 West 7th Avenue
Vancouver B.C. V6J 1S1
Canada
604.737.2629
604.737.2675 FAX

Contact:
Diane Farris, Director

Exhibiting:
Contemporary Canadian
and International Art

Judith Currelly

1. *Caribou Tracks*
   1993, Oil on panel,
   48" x 96"

2. *Phantom Herd*
   1993, Oil on panel,
   48" x 72"

Selected Biography:

1994 Solo show,
       Diane Farris Gallery,
       Vancouver, BC

1993 Solo show,
       Diane Farris Gallery,
       Vancouver, BC

1992 Solo show,
       Diane Farris Gallery,
       Vancouver, BC

       X- Changes Gallery,
       Victoria, BC

       Yukon College,
       Whitehorse, Yukon

MONTSERRAT GALLERY

584 Broadway
New York, NY 10012
212.941.8899
212.274.1717 FAX

Contact:
Marie Montserrat Coll,
Director

Exhibiting:
Contemporary European
and American art

De La Reina

1. *El abuelo*

2. *Bailarina*

3. *Untitled*

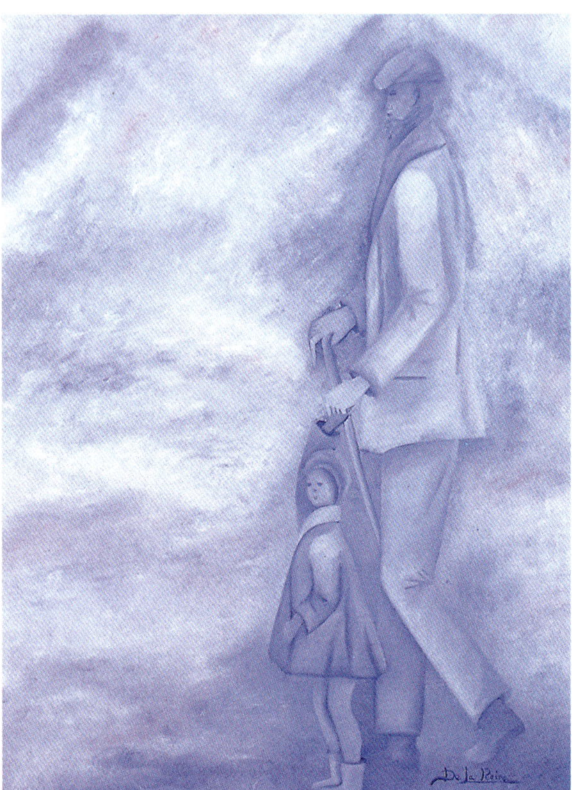

1

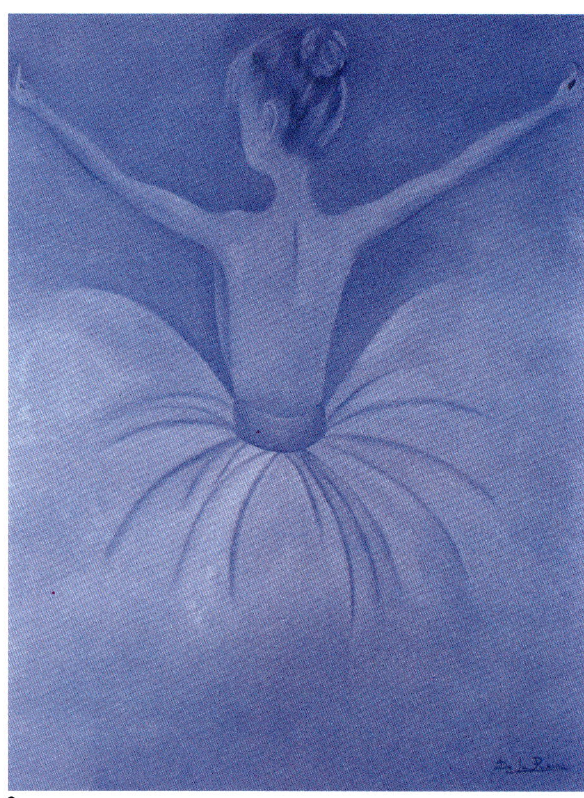

2

Artist Statement:

De La Reina blues are
quiet and serene as are
nature's elements....
the sky and sea.
Rarely does the artist
introduce a second or
third color; when she
does it is with purpose
and in absolute accord
with her prevailing
them of strength in
simplicity.
The underlying figure
renderings exemplify
her exceptional
talent and technical
proficiency

3

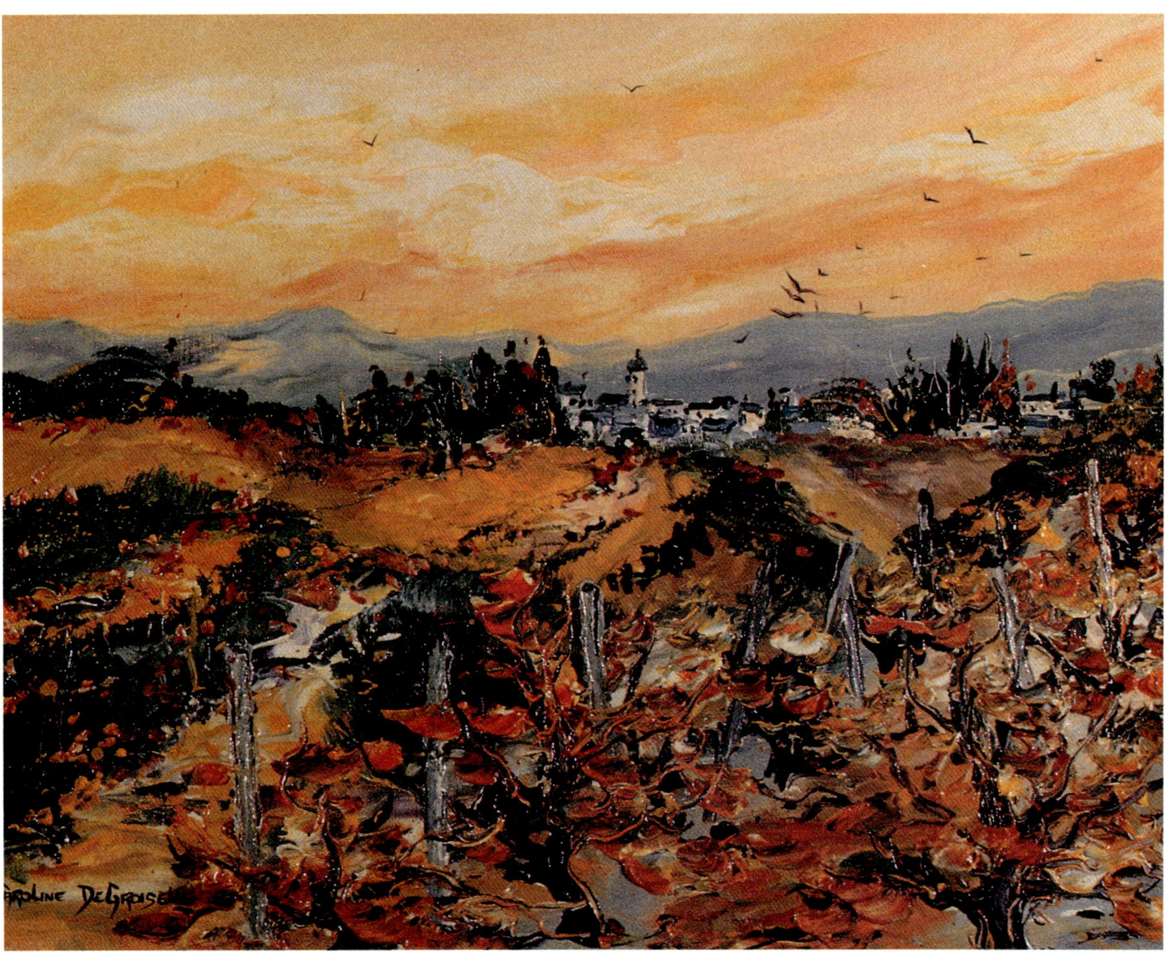

1

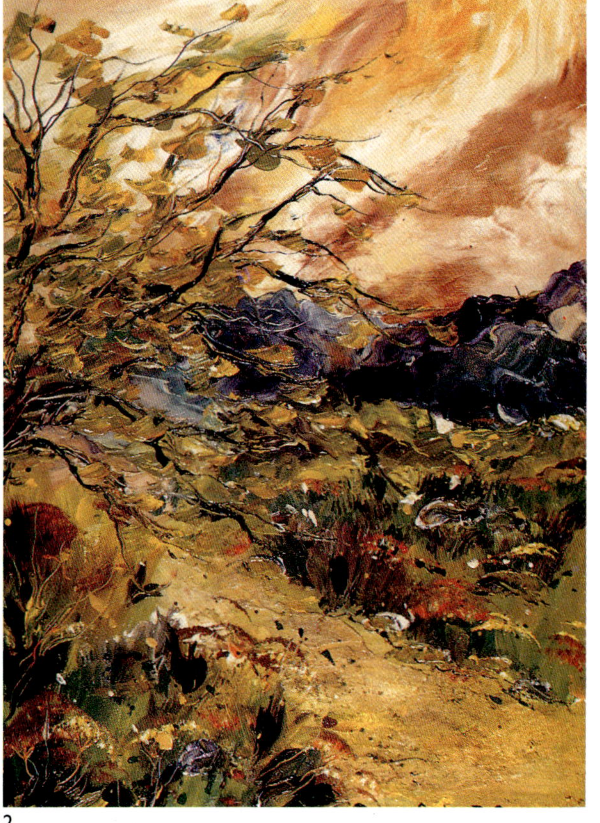

2

MONTSERRAT GALLERY

584 Broadway
New York, NY 10012
212.941.8899
212.274.1717 FAX

Contact:
Marie Montserrat Coll,
Director

Exhibiting:
Contemporary European
and American art

Caroline DeGroiselle

1. *Mes Vignes d'or*
   1992, Acrylique,
   20" x 26"

2. *Promenade Lumiere*
   1992, Acrylique,
   21" x 29"

Selected Biography:

1994 Montserrat Gallery,
New York, NY;
Galerie Herouet,
Paris

1992 Galerie I. Wingerter
Nancy, France;
Galerie Pons-
Debord Paris;
Novotel Surf Noumea,
Nouvelle Caledonia

1991 Galerie Reva-Reva
Papeete, Tahiti

1990 Alliance Francaise,
Sydney Australia

Adolf Dehn

1. *Good Americans All*
   1940, Watercolor,
   19 ¹/₂" x 29 ¹/₂"

2. *We The People*
   1950, Watercolor,
   20 ³/₄ " x 29"

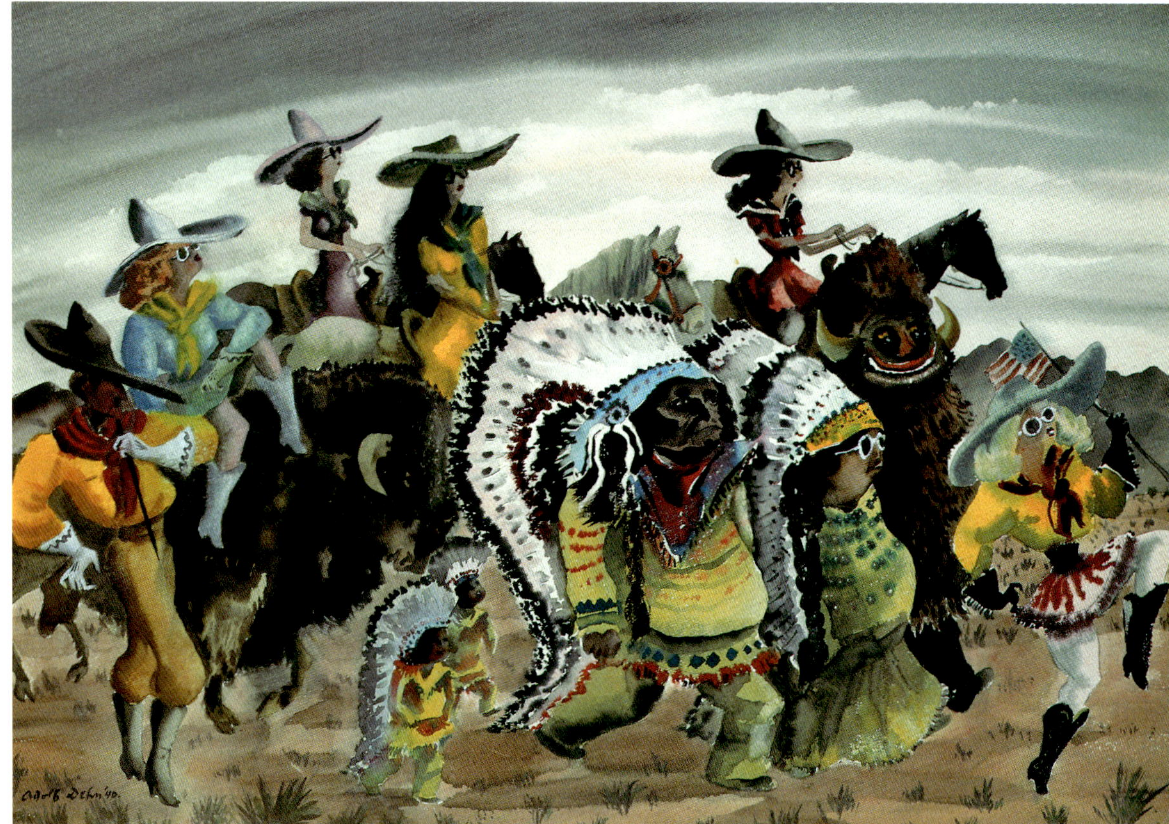

1

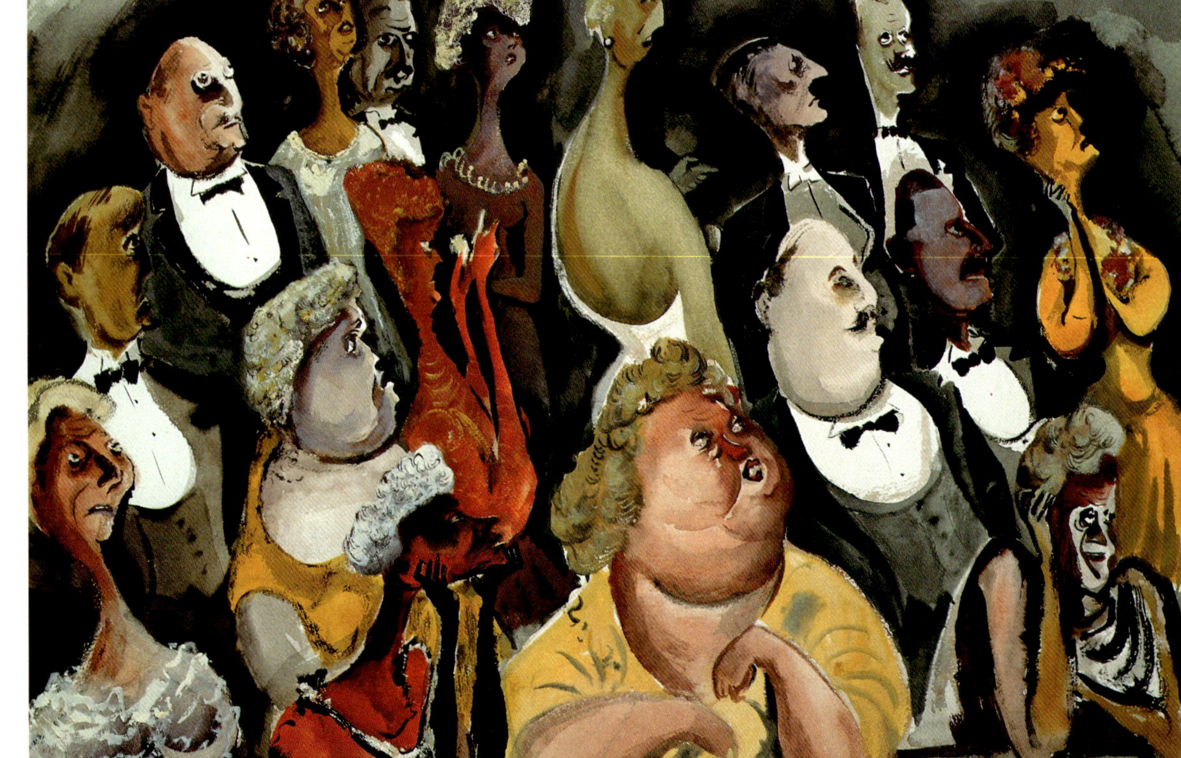

2

Selected Collections:
    Metropolitan Museum
of Art, NYC; Art
Institute of Chicago, IL;
Museum of Fine Arts,
Boston, MA; Whitney
Museum of American
Art, NYC; Museum of
Modern Art, NYC;
San Francisco Museum
of Modern Art, CA

Solo exhibitions:
1994 Harmon - Meek
Gallery, April 1-30
"Dehn's Funny People",
1992, 1985; Spiva Art
Center, Joplin, MO;
Butler Institute of
American Art, Salem
Branch, OH

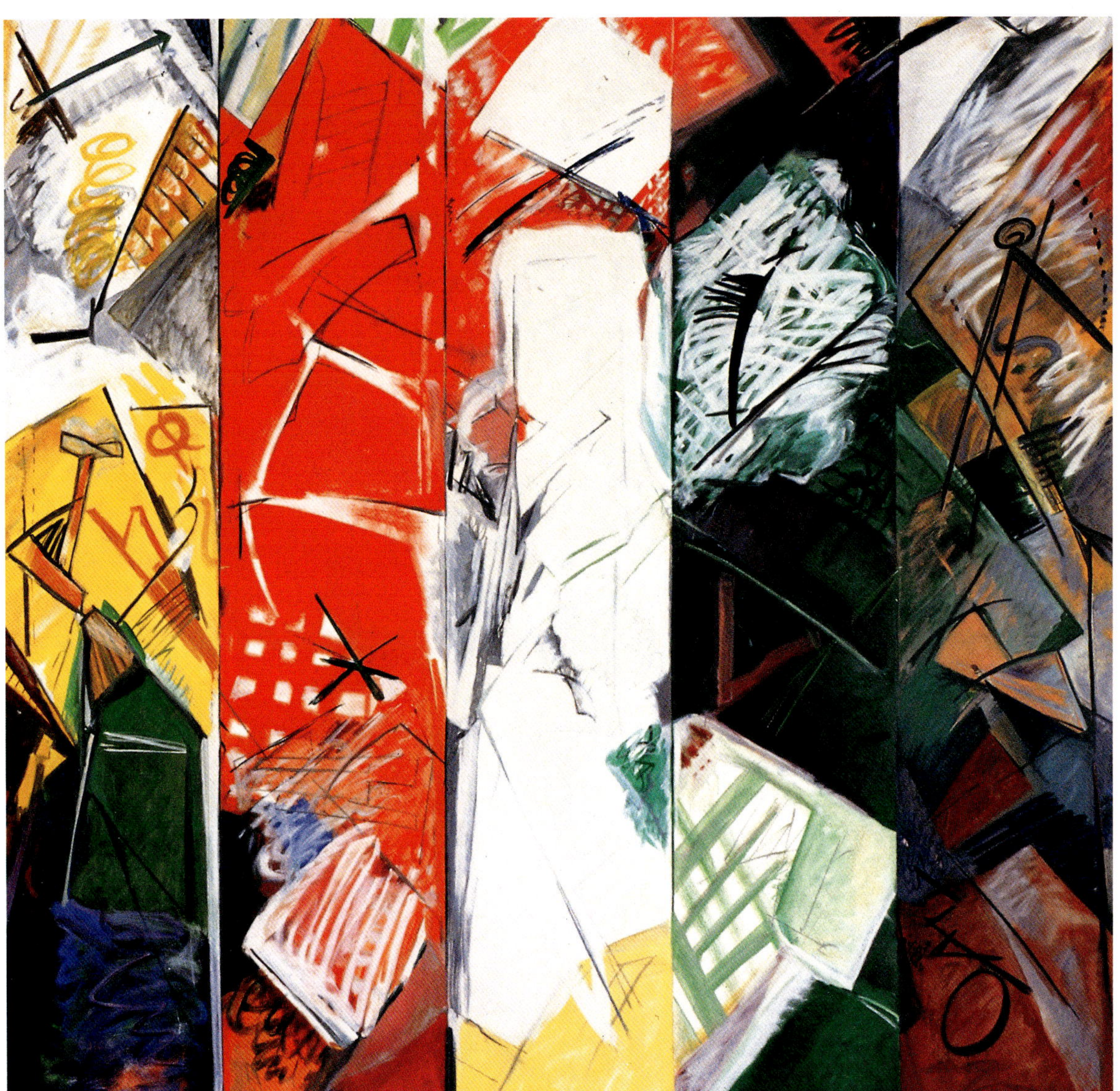

**CLAUDIA CHAPLINE
GALLERY &
SCULPTURE GARDEN**

3445 Shoreline Hwy.
P.O. Box 946
Stinson Beach, CA 94970
415.868.2308
415.868.9436 FAX

Contact:
Margot Merrill

Exhibiting:
Contemporary art

Etta Deikman

1. *Corona*
   1992, Oil on canvas,
   78" x 80"

ROCFERN
INTERNATIONAL
GALLERIES, INC.

80 Carlauren Road Unit17
Woodbridge (Toronto),
Ontario L4L 7Z5 Canada
905.850.7647
905.850.8062 FAX

Contact:
Rocco Pannese
Fernando Rocco

Daniel Diaz

1. *Sculptural Alpha*
   1992, Mixed media on
   canvas, 63" x 54"

2. *Untitled VI*
   1992, Mixed media on
   tar paper, 18⅛" x 15⅛"

3. *Untitled V*
   1993, Mixed media on
   tar paper, 24" x 17⅞"

Selected Biography:

1994 Rocfern International
      Galleries, Woodbridge,
      Ontario, Canada

      Lerner Gallery
      Beverly Hills, CA

      Free & Free Gallery
      Boca Raton, FL

1993 Art Frankfurt
      Frankfurt, Germany

      M & W Art Ltd.
      Hong Kong

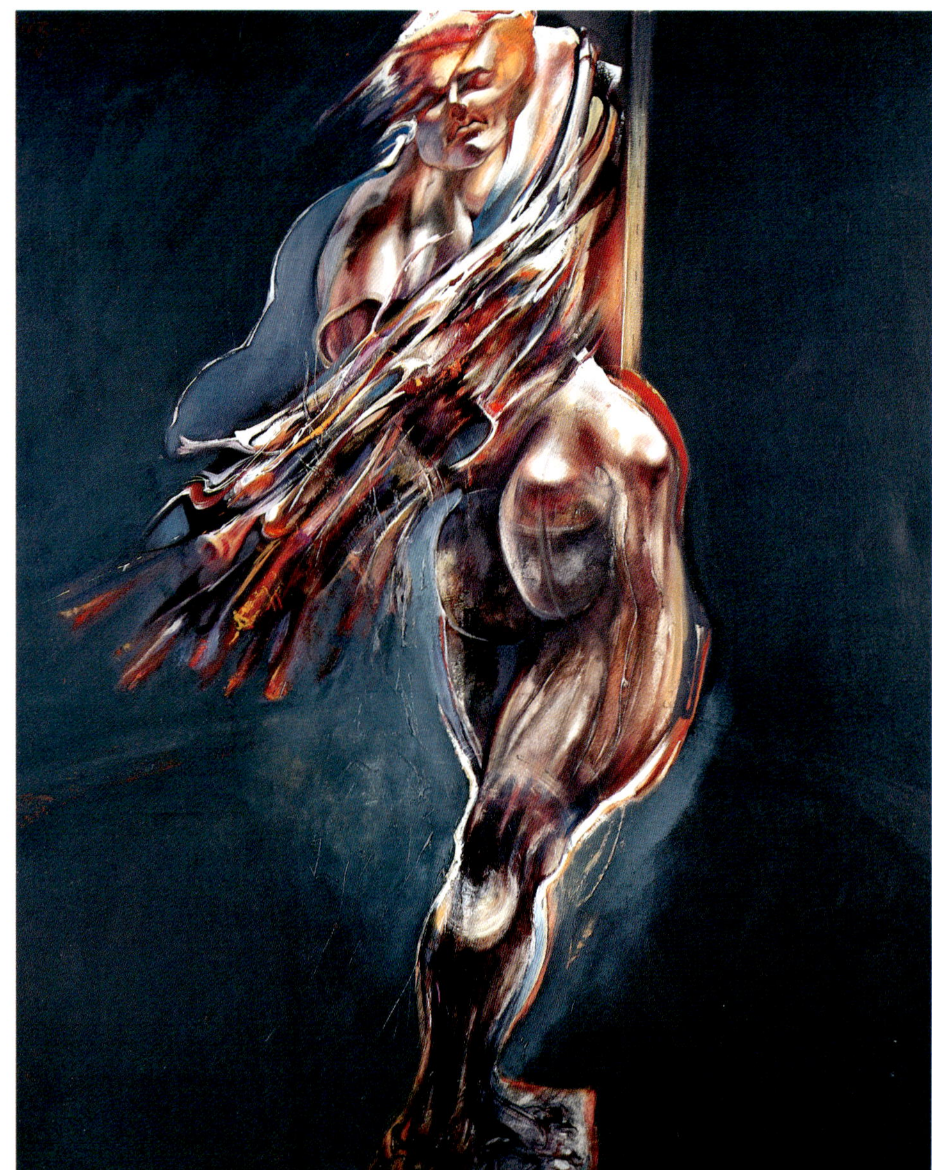

1

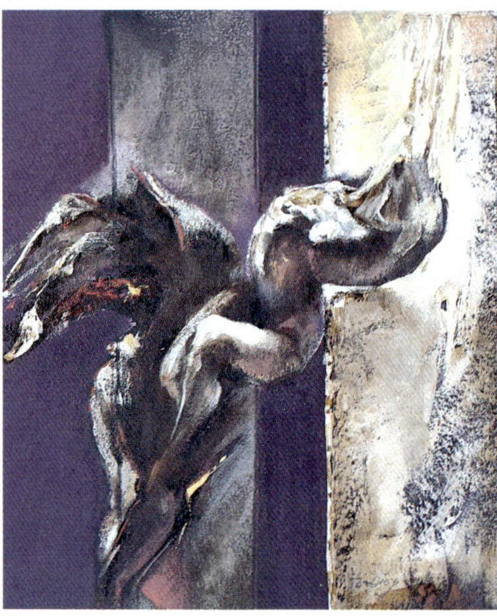

2

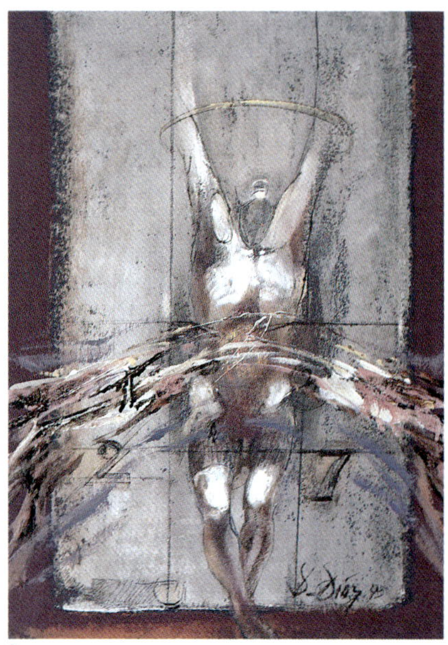

3

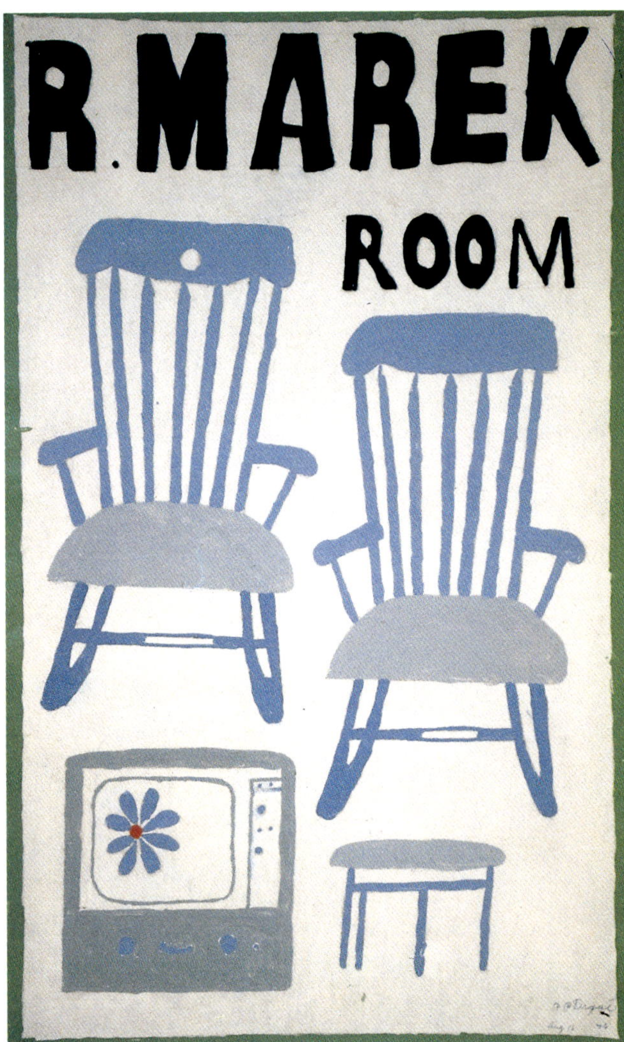

1

LESLIE MUTH
GALLERY

225 E. de Vargas
Santa Fe, NM 87501
505.989.4620
505.989.4937 FAX

Contact:
Leslie Muth, Director

Exhibiting:
Contemporary American
folk, self taught and
outsider art

"Uncle Pete" Drgac

1. *R. Marek Room*
   1976, Enamel on paper,
   20.5" x 12.75"

2. *Untitled*
   1971, Enamel on paper,
   16" x 12"

3. *Untitled*
   1972, Enamel on paper,
   12" x 12"

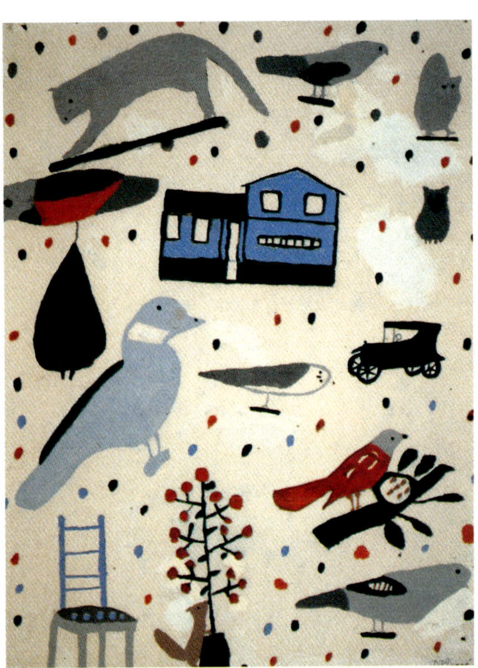

2

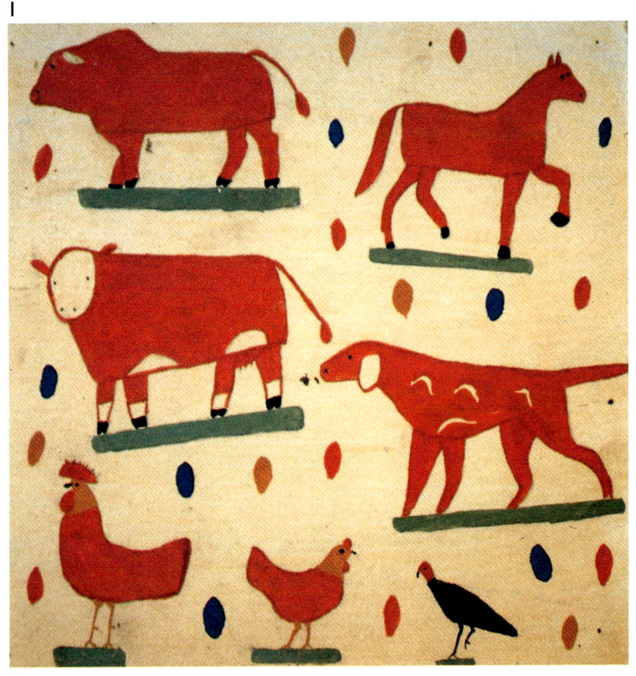

3

Selected Biography:

1994 "The Texas
      Connection",
      Leslie Muth Gallery

1993 "Contemporary
      American Folk Art",
      Museums of Abilene

1992 "Texas Folk Art",
      Sewell Gallery, Rice
      University

1991 "Two Texans and some
      Change", Leslie Muth
      Gallery

O. K. HARRIS
WORKS OF ART

383 West Broadway
New York, NY 10012
212.431.3600

Contact:
Ivan C. Karp

Exhibiting:
Contemporary American
And European painting,
sculpture, photography,
collectables and memorabilia

Leonard Dufresne

The Letter
1991, Acrylic on canvas,
14.25" x 18.25"

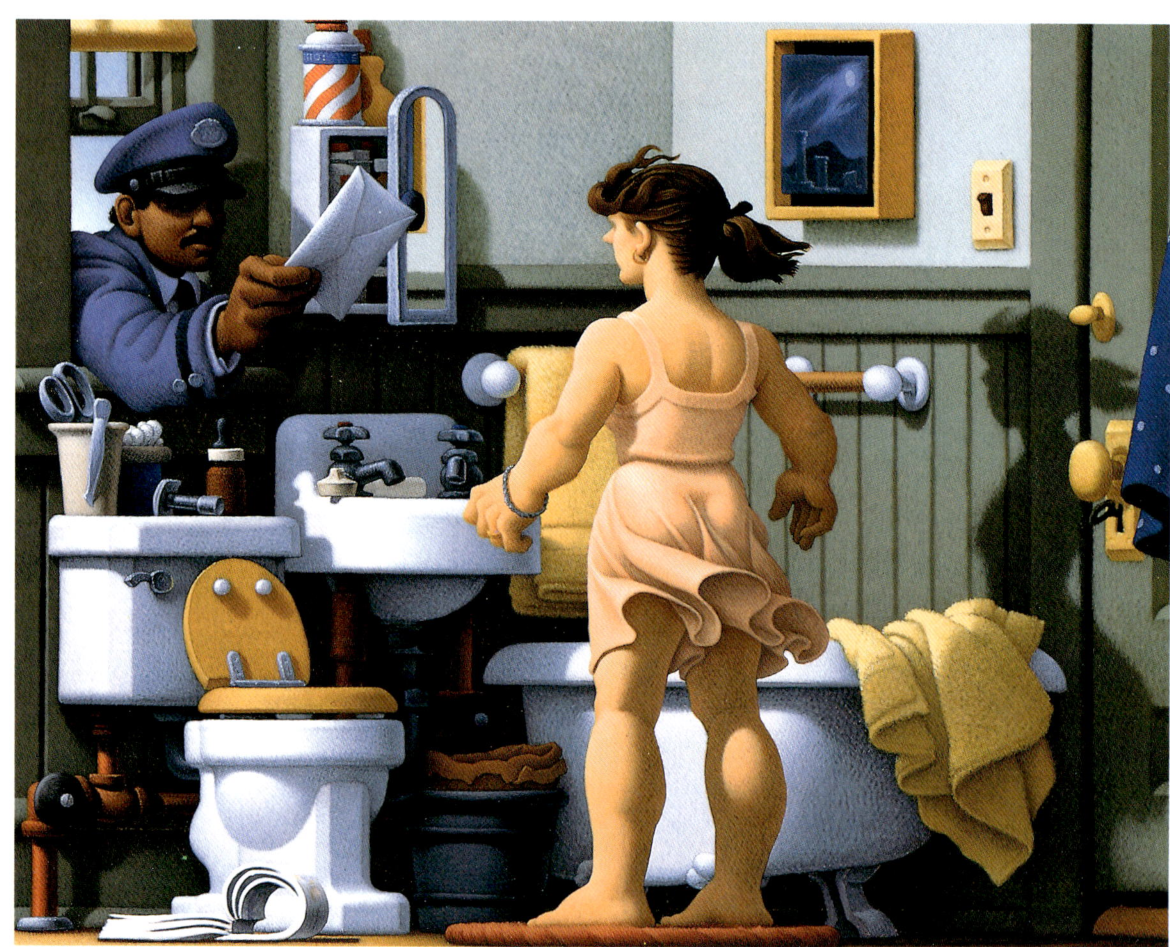

Selected Biography:

1995 O. K. Harris Works Of
Art, New York, NY

1993 "57th Annual National
Midyear Exhibition",
Butler Institute of
American Art,
Youngstown, OH

"Interiors",
Tortue Gallery,
Santa Monica, CA

1992 O. K. Harris Works Of
Art, New York, NY

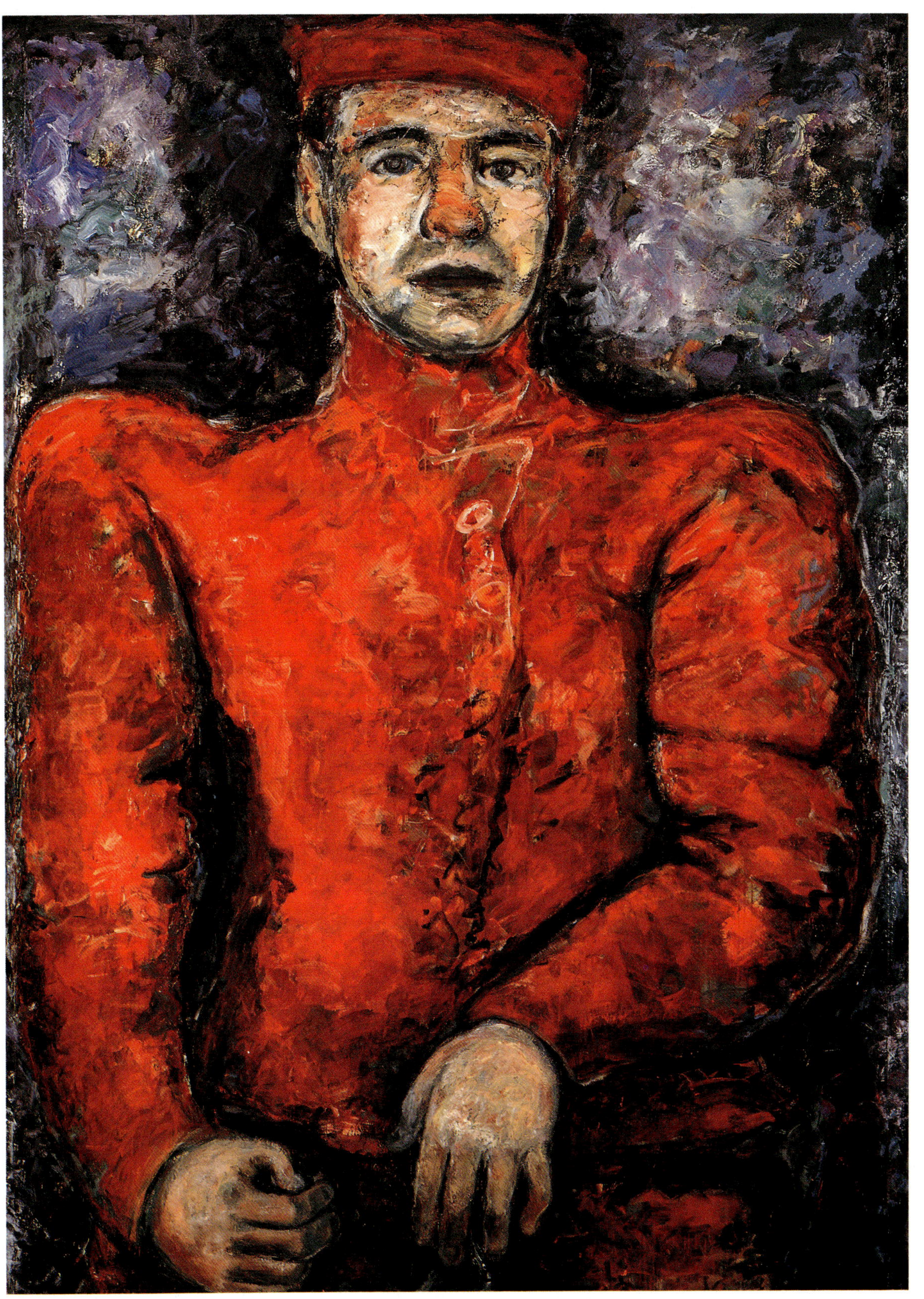

CENTRO DE ARTE EUROAMERICANO

Calle California, Las Mercedes
Caracas, D.F. 1060
Venezuela
58.2.921.204
58.2.915.401 FAX

AMBROSINO GALLERY

3155 Ponce De Leon Blvd.,
Coral Gables, FL 33134
305.445.2211
305.444.0101 FAX

Contact:
Rosanna De Ambrosino
Genaro Ambrosino
Richard Goihman

Exhibiting:
Latin American
contemporary art

Adonay Duque

*Self Portrait as Bellboy of
the Maxim, After Soutime*
1992, Acrylic on canvas,
245 x 180 cms.

Selected Biography:

1993 Selected solo
exhibitions: La Galeria,
Lima, Peru
Claudio Valansi Gallery,
Rio, Brazil
Arteconsult Gallery,
Panama City, Panama
Estudio Lisenberg,
Buenos Aires,
Argentina
1992 Selected solo
exhibitions:
Ambrosino Gallery,
Coral Gables, FL
Espacio Simonetti,
Valencia, Venezuela

THE LOWE GALLERY

75 Bennett St. Space A-Z
Atlanta, GA 30309
404.352.8114
404.352.0564 FAX

Contact:
Bill Lowe

Exhibiting:
Contemporary painting,
sculpture, and objects

Brad Durham

Edge of Promise
1994, Oil on canvas,
76" x 61"

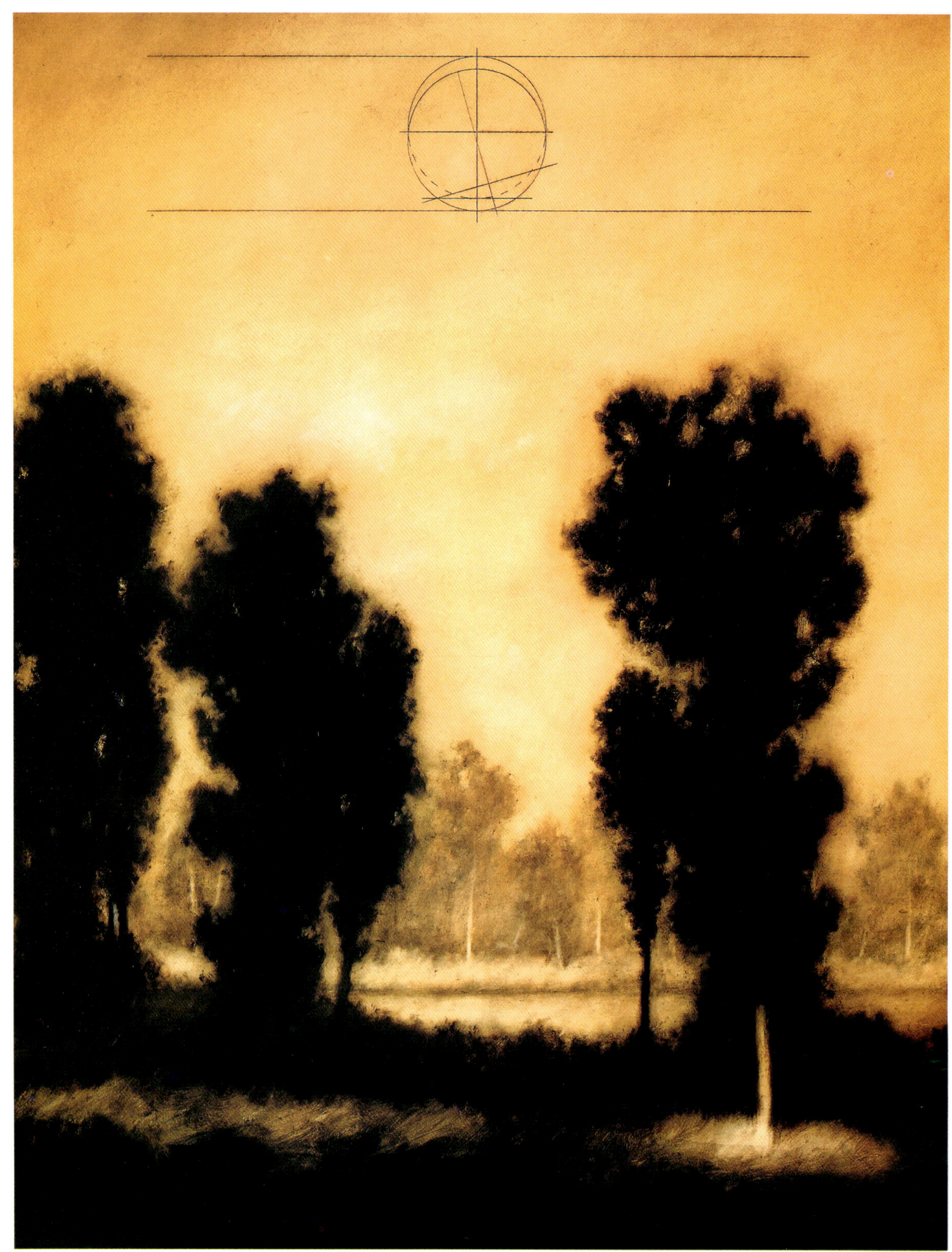

Selected Biography:

1994 Solo show,
      The Lowe Gallery,
      Atlanta, GA

1989 Solo show,
      Karl Bornstein Gallery,
      Santa Monica, CA

1987 Group show,
      Avant-Garde in the
      Eighties, LA County
      Museum, CA

1986 Group show,
      California exhibition,
      Laguna Art Museum,
      CA

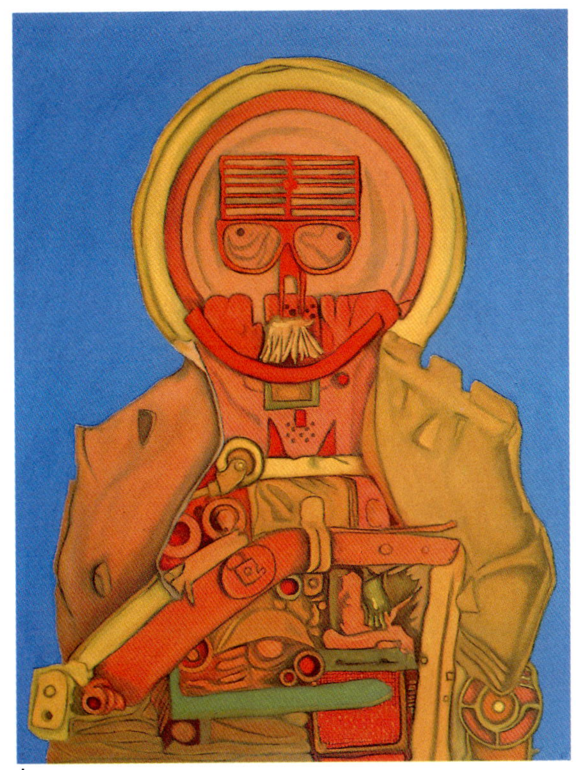

1

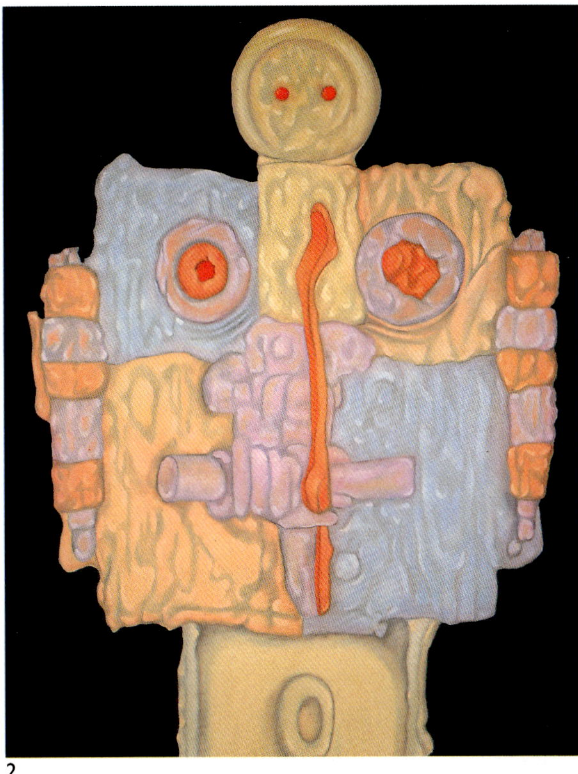

2

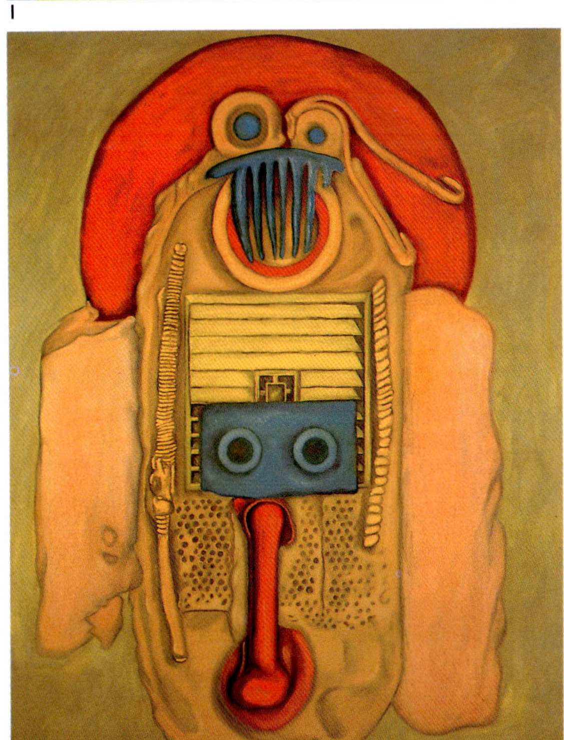

4

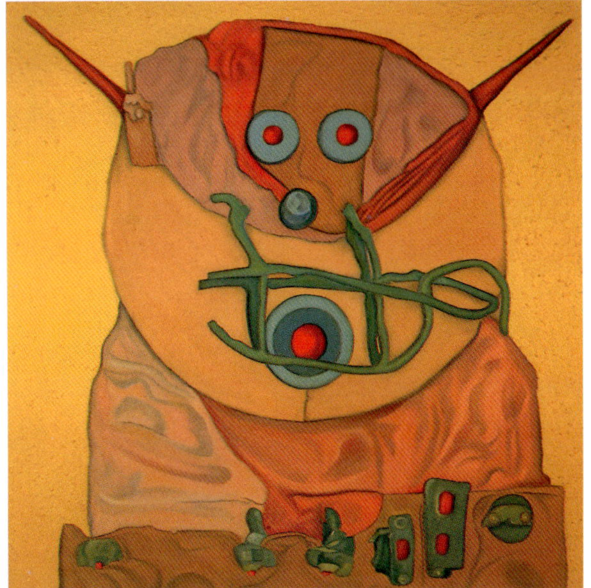

3

CAROLE JONES GALLERY

300 W. Superior Street
Chicago, IL 60610
312.587.8820
312.587.9859 FAX

Contact:
Carole Jones

Stan Edwards
3813 N. Oakley
Chicago, IL 60618
312.588.5538

Exhibiting:
Contemporary American
painting

Stan Edwards

1. *Smiling Saint # 1*
   1992, Oil & acrylic on
   canvas, 48" x 36"

2. *Jack of Tarts*
   1993, Oil & acrylic on
   canvas, 50" x 40"

3. *Guardian of the Truth*
   1994, Oil & acrylic on
   canvas, 52" x 42"

4. *Personnage in Helmet*
   1992, Oil & acrylic on
   canvas, 48" x 48"

Selected Exhibitions:

1994 One man show,
   Carole Jones Gallery,
   Chicago, IL
1993 Group exhibition, The
   Arts Club of Chicago,
   Chicago, IL
1991 Inaugural exhibition,
   Anderson Gallery,
   Buffalo, NY

Selected Collections:

National Museum of American
Art/Smithsonian,
Corcoran Gallery of Art,
Washington, D.C.
Walter Netsch Collection
Chicago, IL
American Embassy,
Oslo, Norway

MONTSERRAT GALLERY

584 Broadway
New York, NY 10012
212.941.8899
212.274.1717 FAX

Contact:
Marie Montserrat Coll,
Director

Exhibiting:
Contemporary European
and American art

Garcia Ergüin

1. *Golden Sky*
   Oil on canvas,
   45" x 58"

2. *Grey Sky*
   Oil on canvas,
   45" x 58"

Selected Biography:
1994 Galerie Egon
      von Kameke,
      Postdam, Germany;
      Debis Systemhaus DCS.
      Aachen, Germany;
1993 Solo Exhibition,
      Montserrat Gallery,
      New York, NY;
      Museo de Arte
      Contemporaneo,
      Bilbao
Museo de Arte
      Contemporaneo,
      Madrid,
      Museo de St. Paul,
      France;
      Spain Museum,
      Houston

1

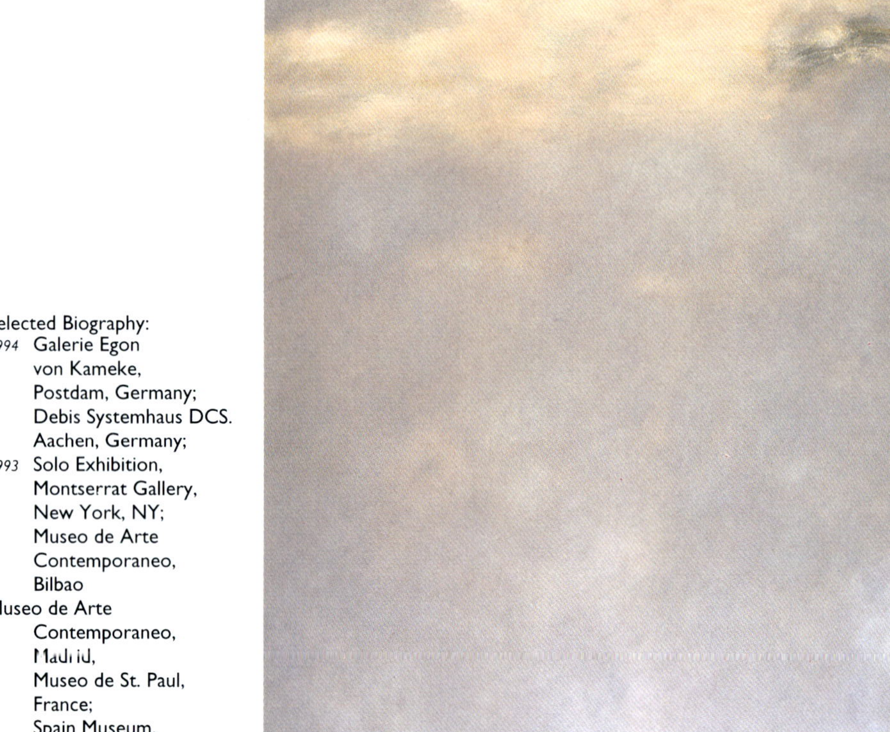

2

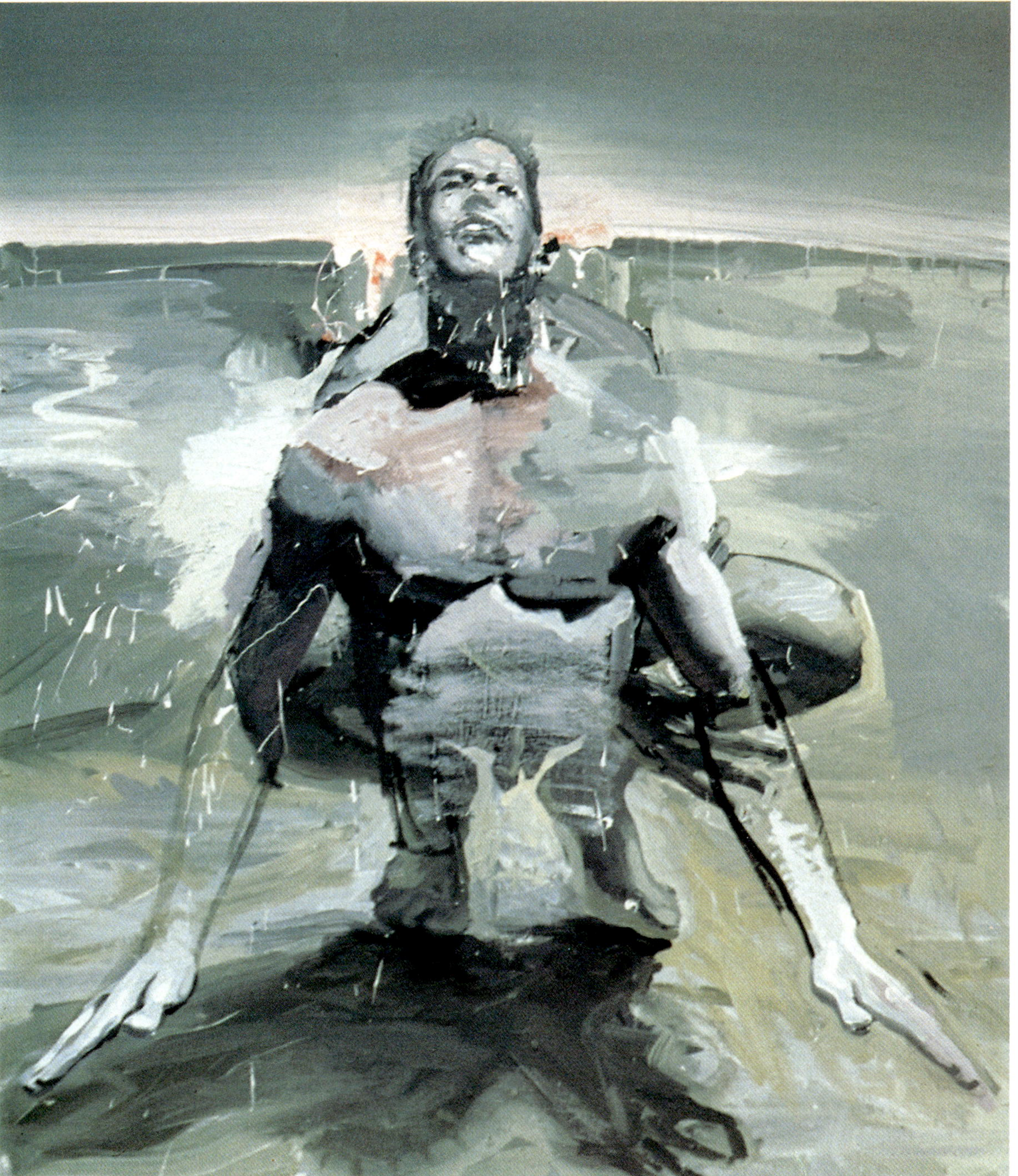

THE LOWE GALLERY

75 Bennett St. Space A-Z
Atlanta, GA 30309
404.352.8114
404.352.0564 FAX

Contact:
Bill Lowe

Exhibiting:
Contemporary painting,
sculpture, and objects

John Erickson

Home Improvement
1993, Acrylic on canvas,
48" x 48"

Selected Biography:

1994 Solo show,
The Lowe Gallery,
Atlanta, GA

1992 Solo show,
The Lowe Gallery,
Santa Monica, CA

1990 Utah Painting Show,
Museum of Fine Arts,
Salt Lake City, UT

1988 Group show,
Art Extra-Ordinary,
Springville Museum, UT

MICHAEL KIZHNER FINE ART

746 N. La Cienega Blvd.
Los Angeles, CA 90069
310.659.5222
310.659.0838 FAX

Contact:
Michael Kizhner

Exhibiting:
California Impressionism
1900 -1940 & Russian
Contemporary Art

Ilona Severovna Gansovskaya

1. *The Accident on the Lakes*
   1988, Oil on Canvas,
   21.5" x 31.75"

2. *Mirage on Ice*
   1988, Oil on Canvas,
   33" x 55"

3. *Estonian Shore, near Sweden*
   1988, Oil on Canvas,
   37" x 75"

Biography:

Born (1955) and lives in Moscow. Completed training/studies at Moscow SURIKOV School of Art in 1980, Faculty for Stage Art. Works as set painter at theatres in Moscow, in the Baltic Republics, in the Far East and is at present preparing a performance in Czechoslovakia. Furthermore, as painter-director, she is just completing work on the animated cartoon film, "The Rainy Story".

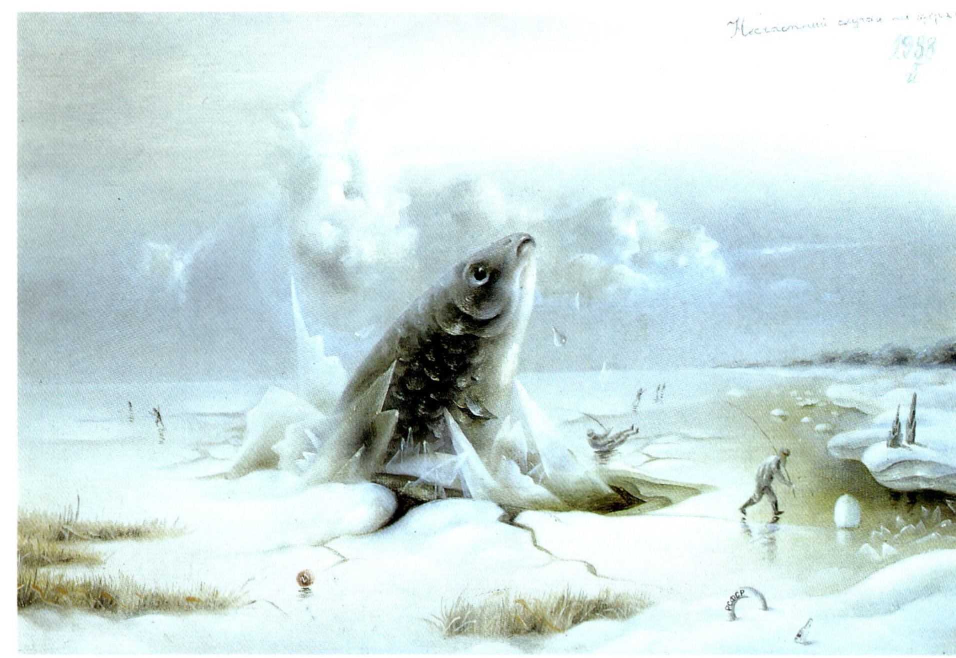

1

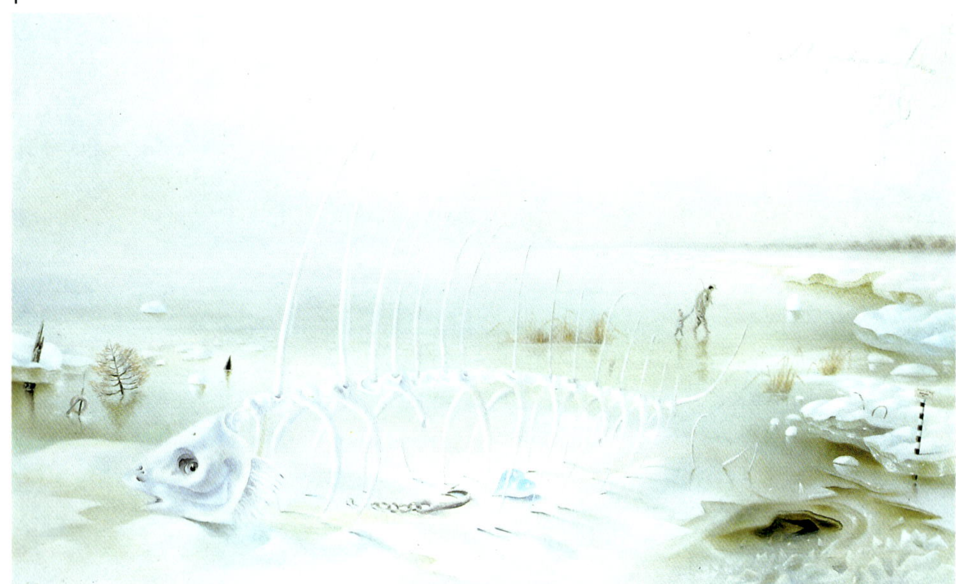

2

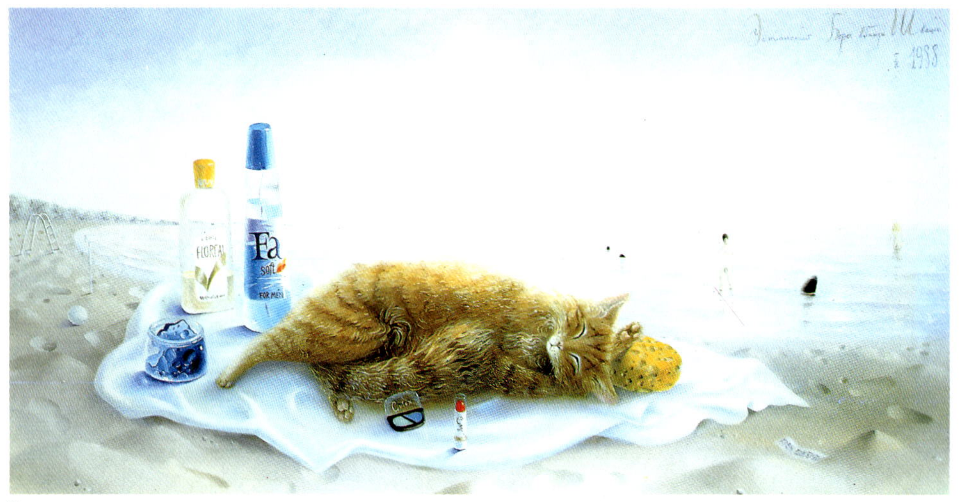

3

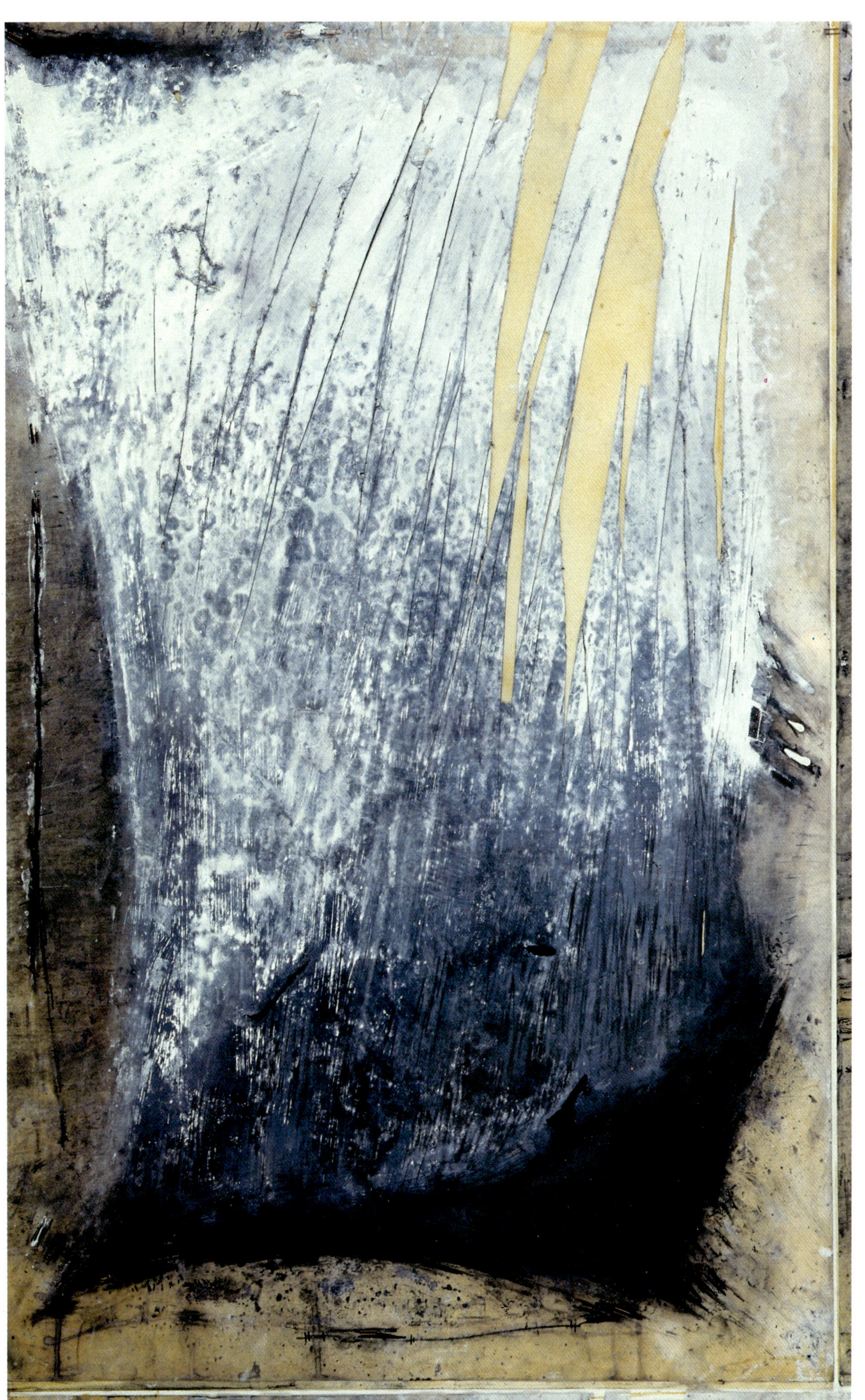

ALFREDO MARTINEZ GALLERY

2311 Le Jeune Road
Coral Gables, Fl 33134
305.442.0808
305.442.0824 FAX

Contact:
Lawrence Casalins

Exhibiting:
Contemporary Art

Ulrich Gehret

Untitled
1993, Mixed media on
paper, 102cm x 90cm

Selected Biography:

1994   Art Miami International
       Exhibition

       Museum am Ostwall,
       Dortmund

1993   Galerie M
       Bochum, Germany

1992   Art Basel, Art Cologne,
       Art Frankfurt, Galerie
       Bea, Voigt, Munich

1991   Municipal Gallery of
       Ostfildern

1988   Center of Modern Art
       Lisbon

LOUIS K. MEISEL GALLERY

141 Prince Street
New York, NY 10012
212.677.1340
212.533.7340 FAX

Contact:
Louis K. Meisel
Diane Sena

Exhibiting:
Photo-realist painting and
other technically skilled
contemporary disciplines

Paul Giovanopoulos

1. *The Bather "A" & "B"*
   1994, Acrylic on canvas,
   88" x 72"each

2. *Big Bug*
   1994, Acrylic on canvas,
   90" x 140"

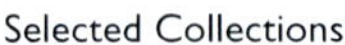

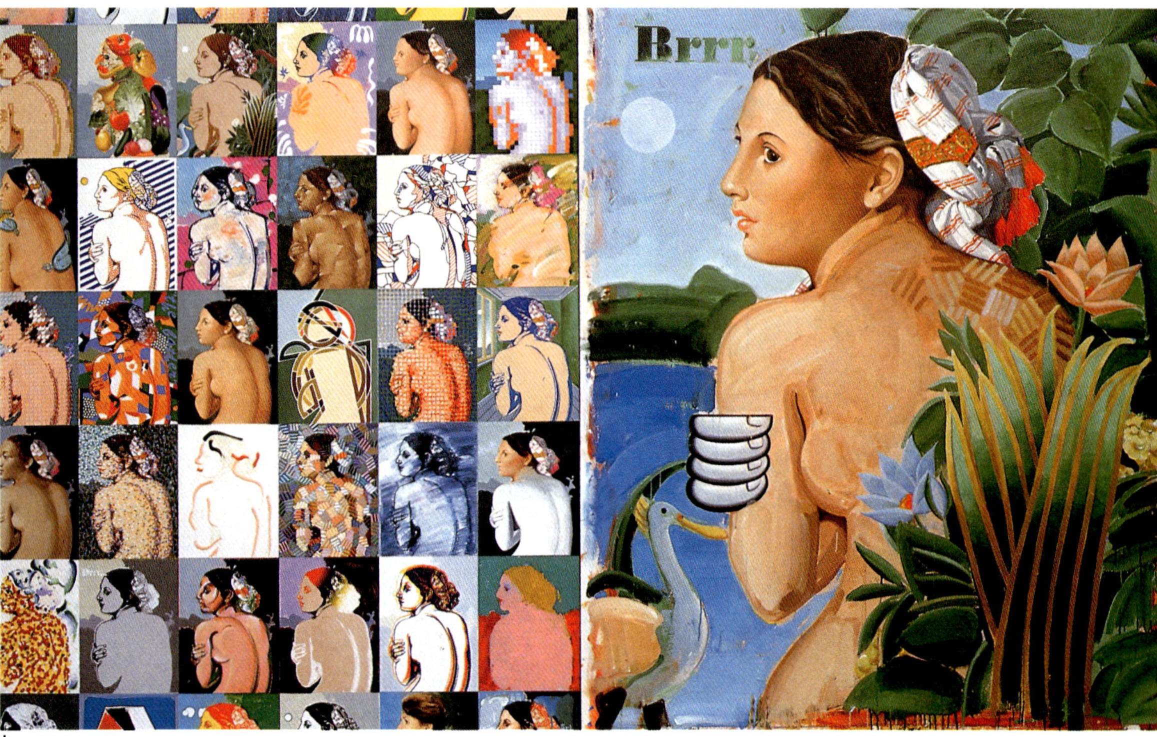

1

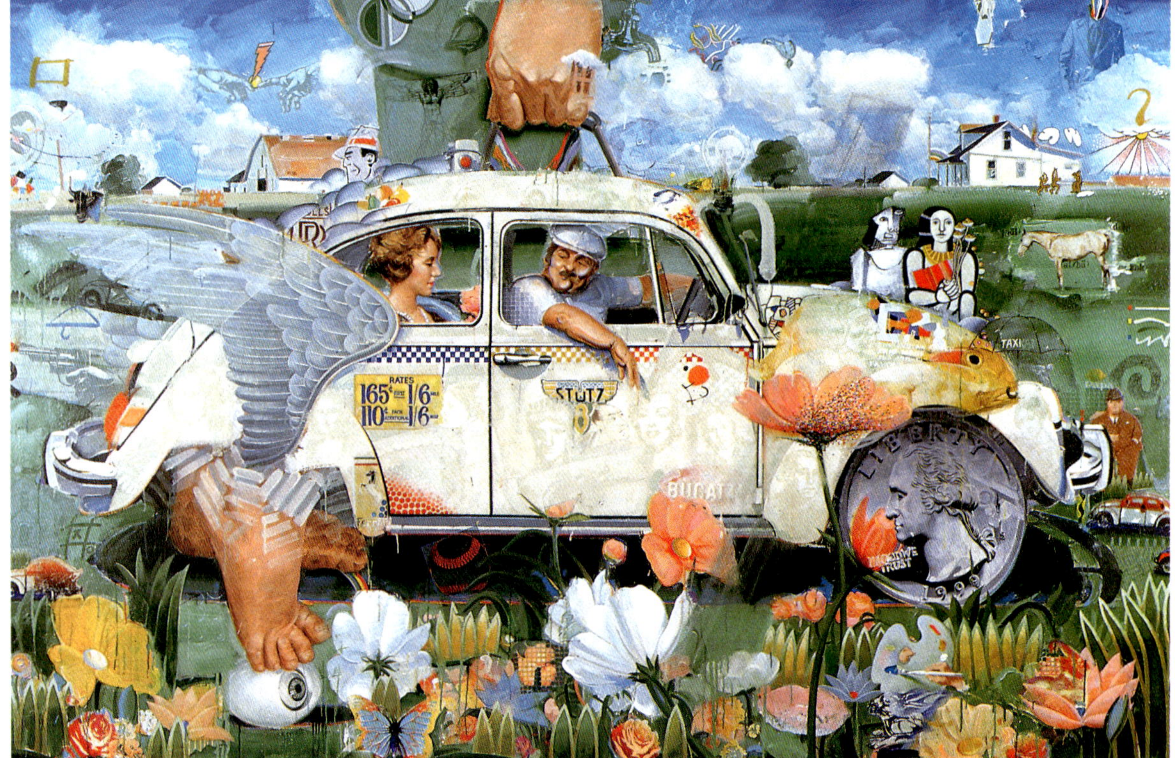

2

Selected Collections:

    The Butler institute
of American Art,
Youngstown, OH;
Museum of the City
of New York, NY;
Housatonic
Museum of Arts,
Bridgeport, CT;
Joslyn Art Museum,
Omaha, NE;
Guild Hall Museum,
East Hampton, NY;
Virlane Foundation,
New Orleans, LA

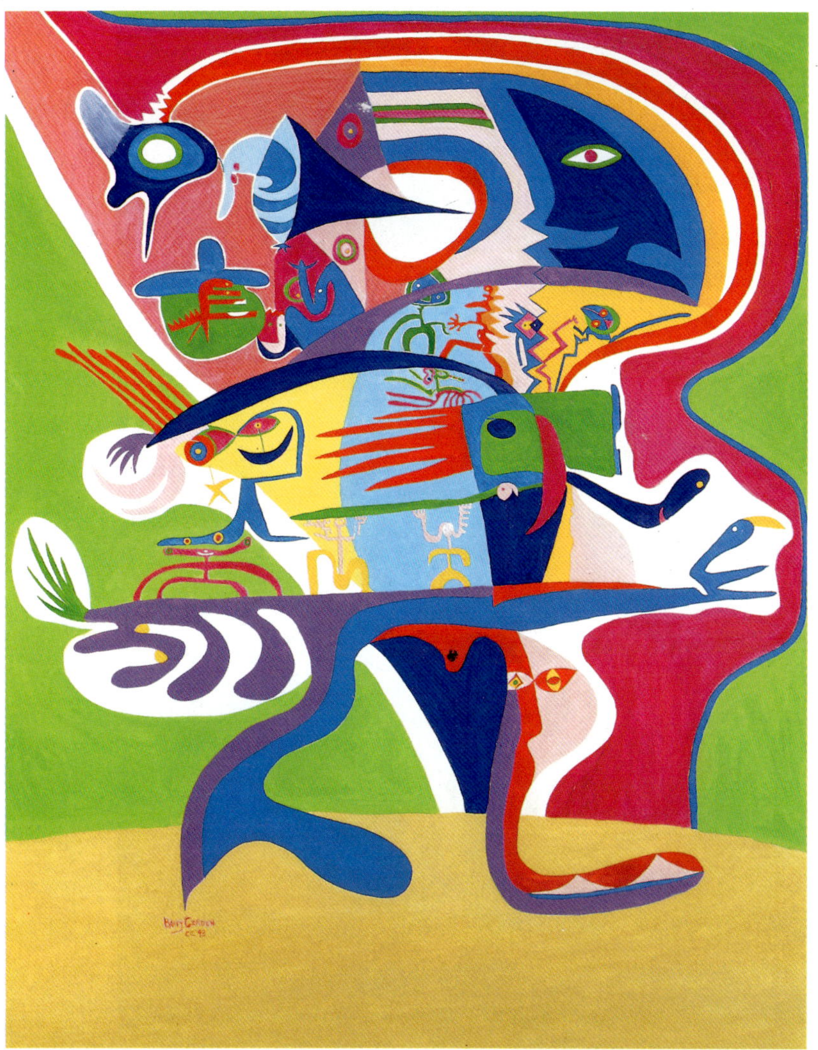

1

LANDAU/20TH CENTURY ART

1625 Thayer Ave
Los Angeles, CA 90024
310.474.5155
310.475.8212 FAX

Contact:
Jeffrey Landau
Mitzi Landau

Exhibiting:
20th century sculpture,
painting and photography

Barry Gordon

1. *Society: Stable Table and
   Other Life Patterns*
   1993, Oil on canvas,
   50" x 40"

2. *Melodramatic Landscape:
   The Act of Knowing*
   1993, Oil on canvas,
   36" x 48"

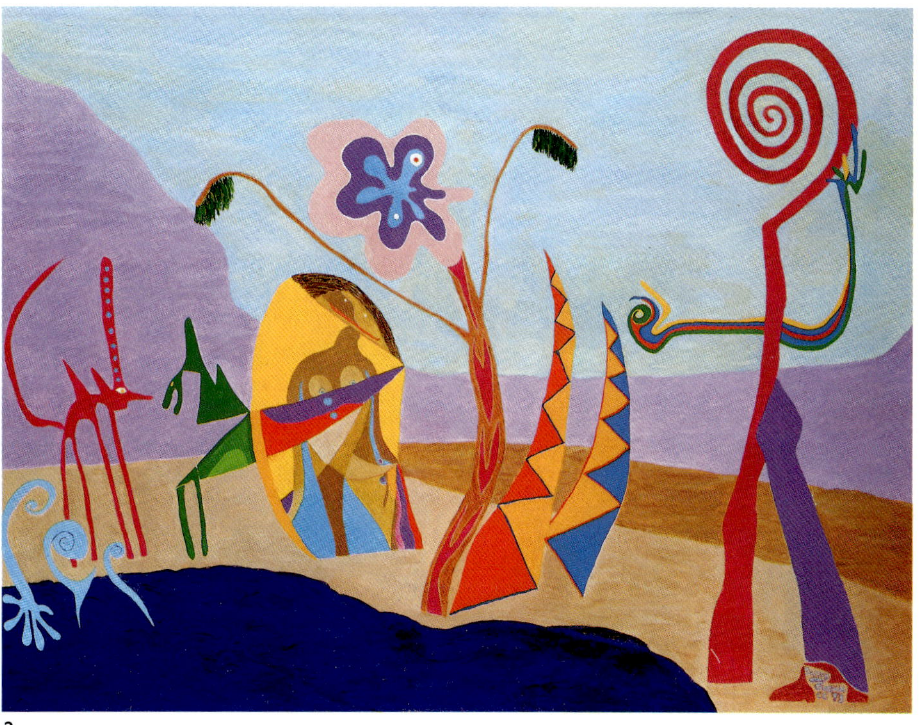

2

Selected Biography:

1993 Gübelin Gallery, Old
      Town Pasadena, CA

      Toepel Gallery,
      Seattle, WA

1987 Galeria Toulouse,
      Rio de Janeiro, Brazil

1985 Gallery K,
      Washington, D.C.

1965 Bognar Gallery,
      Los Angeles, CA

LOUIS K. MEISEL GALLERY

141 Prince Street
New York, NY 10012
212.677.1340
212.533.7340 FAX

Contact:
Louis K. Meisel
Diane Sena

Exhibiting:
Photo-Realist painting and
other technically skilled
contemporary disciplines

George D. Green

1. *Storyteller*
   1993, Acrylic & mixed
   Media on Wood,
   77.5" x 59"

2. *A Sequence of Events*
   1994, Acrylic & mixed
   Media on Wood,
   50" x 106.5"

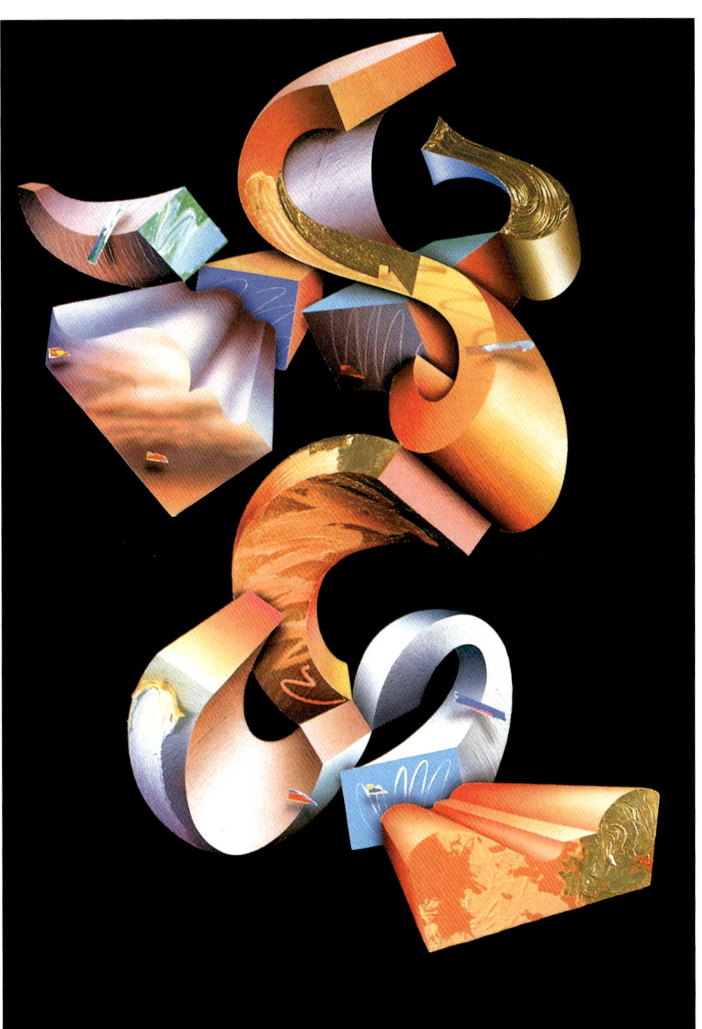

1

Selected Collections:

Solomon R.
Guggenheim Museum,
New York, NY;
Los Angeles County
Museum, CA;
Art Institute of
Chicago, IL;
Denver Art
Museum, CO;
Detroit Institute
of Art, MI;
Portland Art
Museum, OR;
Indianapolis Museum
of Art, IN;
Phoenix Art
Museum, AZ

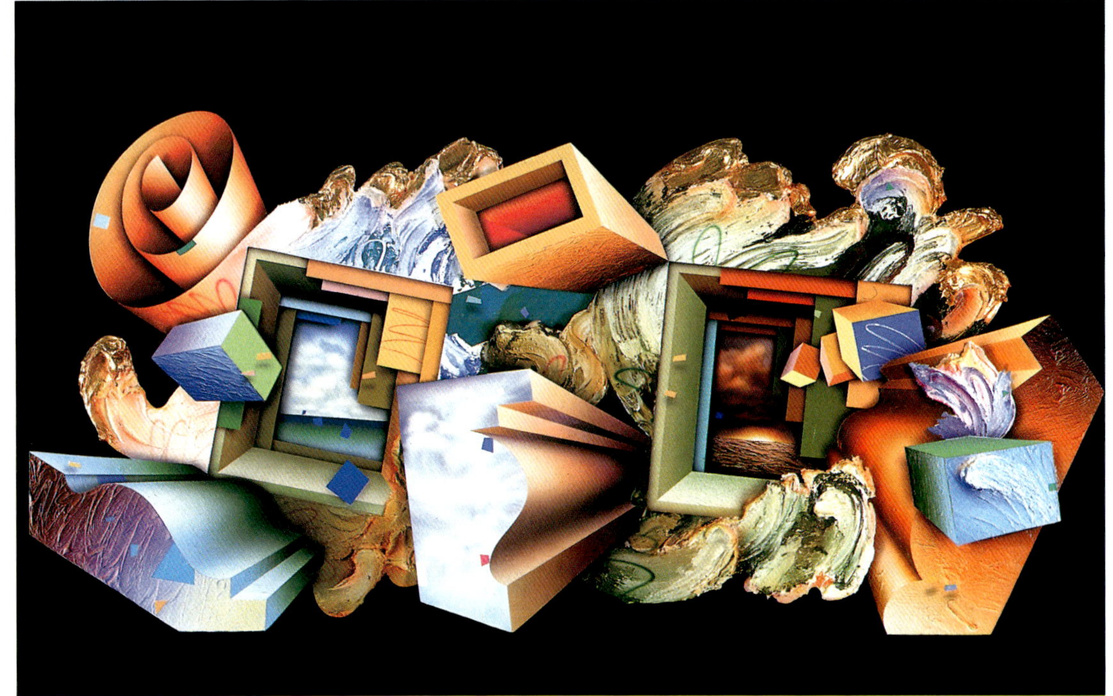

2

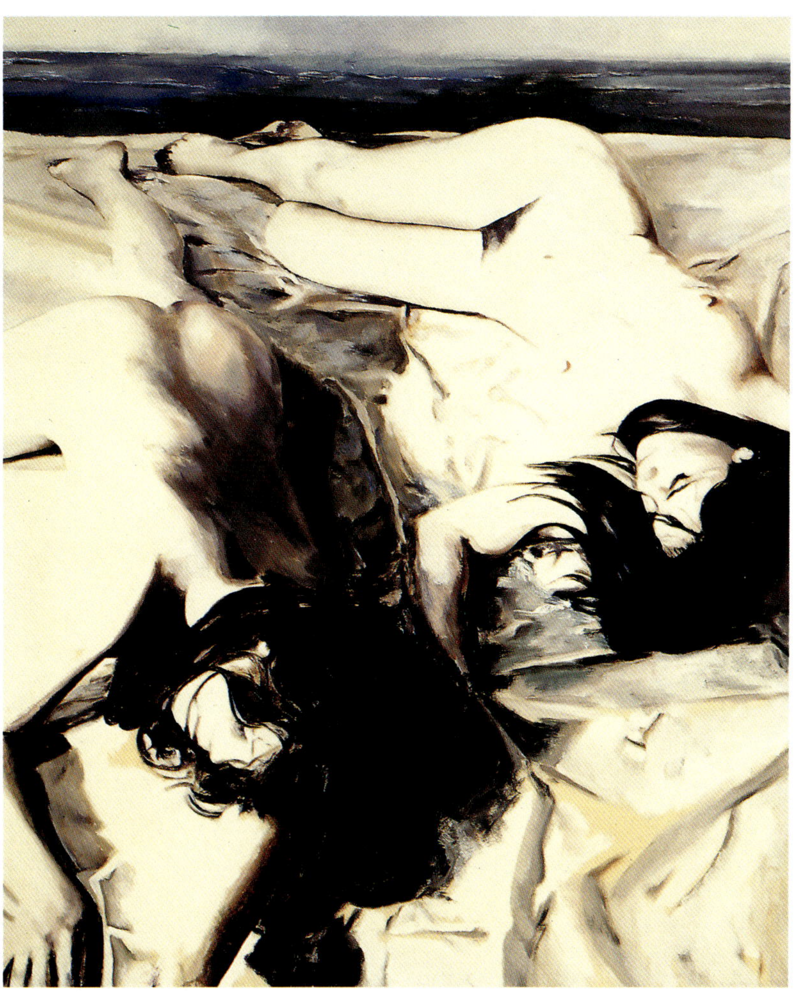

1

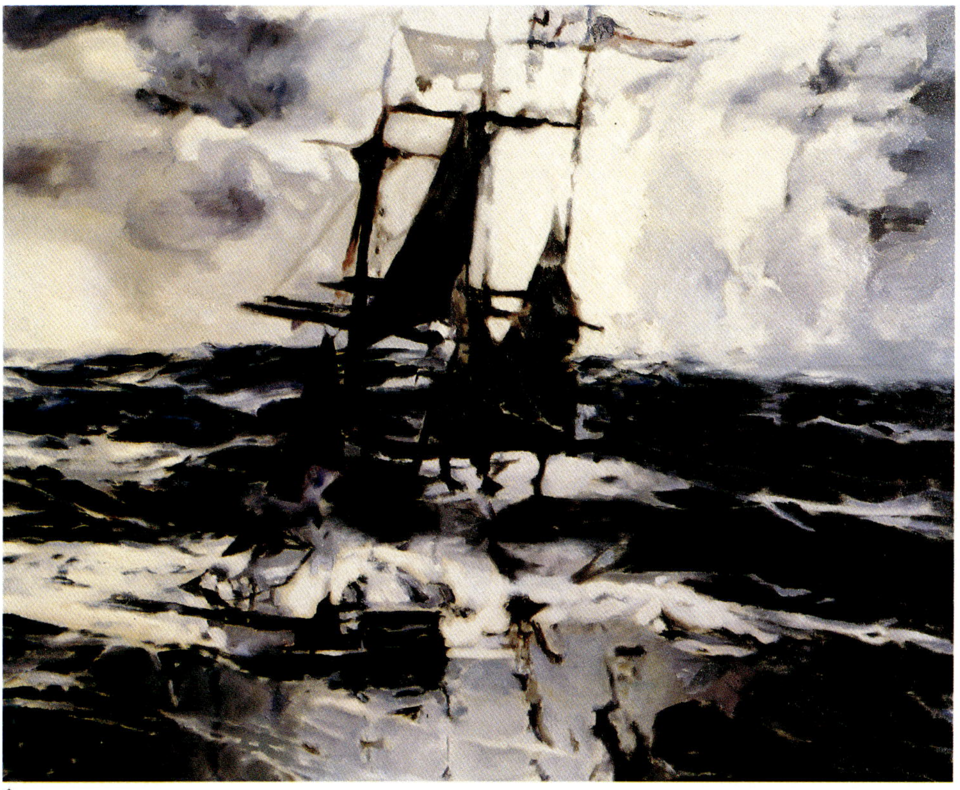

2

HARMON-MEEK GALLERY

386 Broad Avenue South
Naples, FL 33940
813.261.2637
813.261.3804

4262 Gulfshore Blvd. N.
Naples, FL 33940
813.261.7775

Contact:
J. William Meek III,
Director-owner

Exhibiting:
20th Century American art

Balcomb Greene

1. *Sleeping in the Sun*
   1970, Oil on canvas,
   56" x 46"

2. *Far From Land*
   1970, Oil on canvas,
   40 " x 50"

Selected Collections:
Metropolitan Museum
of Art, NYC;
Whitney Museum of
American Art, NYC;
Solomon R.
Guggenheim Museum,
NYC; Joseph H.
Hirshorn Museum,
Washington, D.C.; Art
Institute of Chicago, IL;
Museum of Modern
Art, NYC;
plus thirty others.

Solo exhibitions:
Harmon-Meek Gallery,
Feb. 27- Mar. 5, 1994,
also 1992, 1982, 1979,
1974-77

CHARLES
WHITCHURCH
GALLERY

5973 Engineer Drive
Huntington Beach, CA 92649
714.373.4459
714.373.4615 FAX

Contact:
Charles Whitchurch

Exhibiting:
Modern and contemporary
painting, graphic works and
sculpture

James Groff

Forest Light
1994, Acrylic on canvas,
48" x 36"

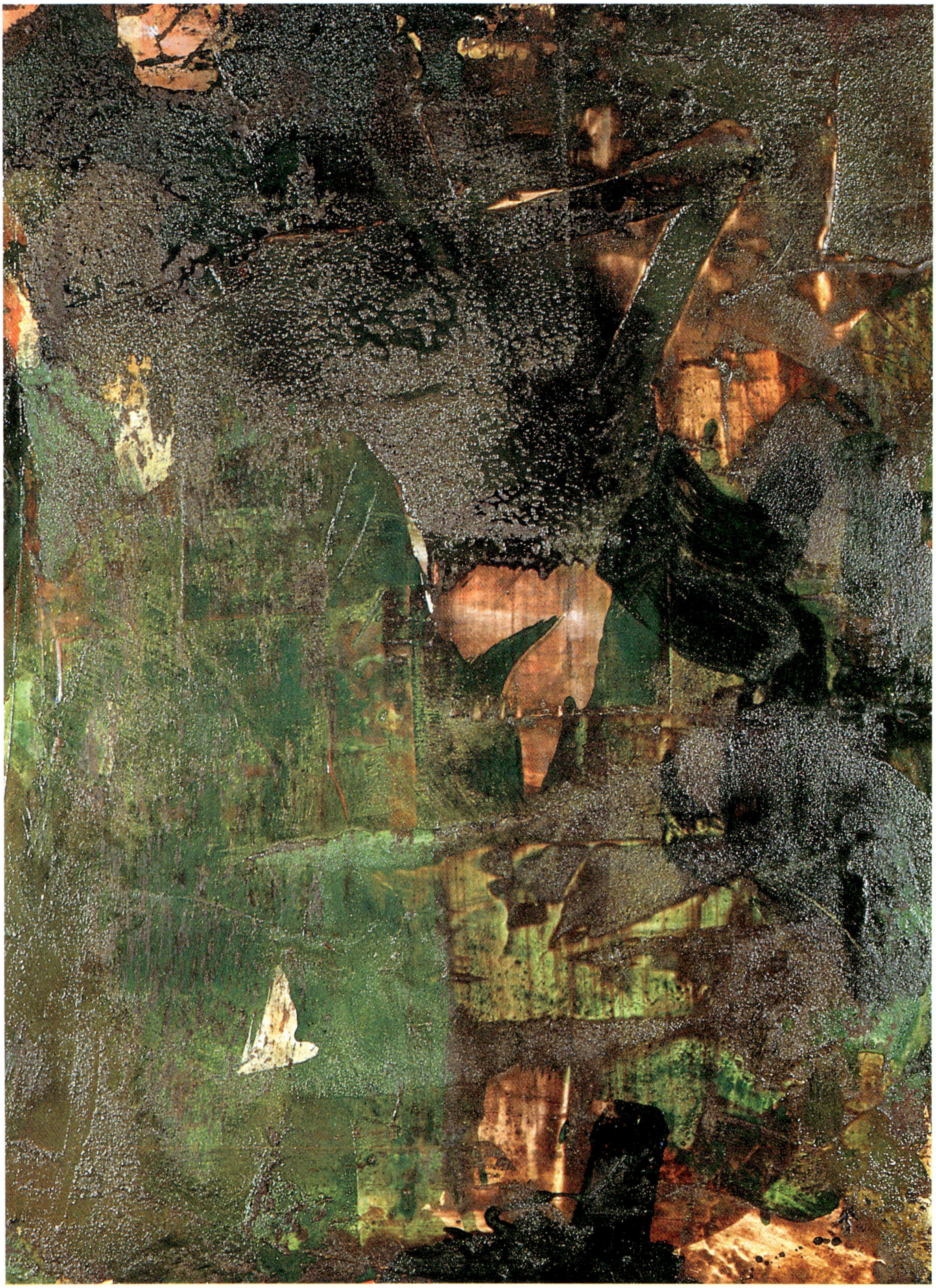

Selected Biography:

1992   Charles Whitchurch
Gallery, Art/LA92,
Los Angeles

1991   Van Straaten,
Chicago International
Art Exposition

1990   Solo exhibition,
Gremillion Fine Art,
Houston

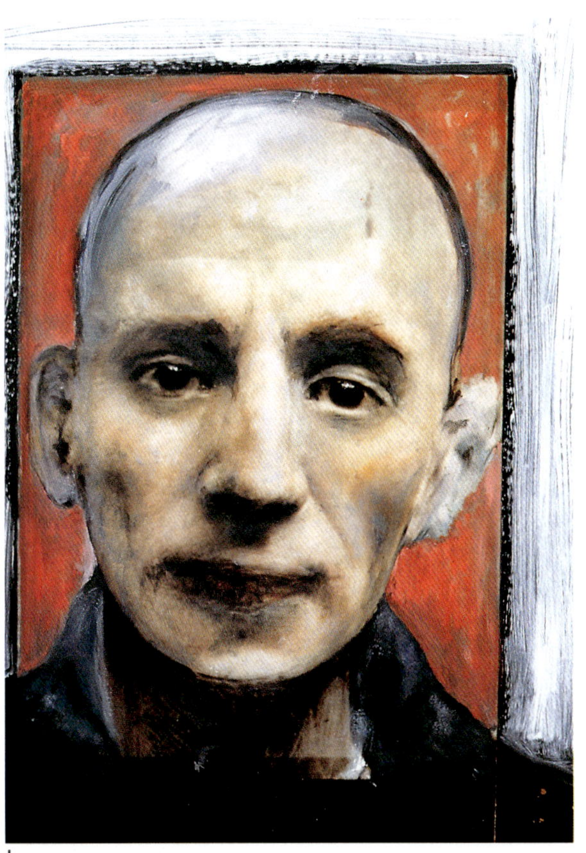

1

DIANE FARRIS GALLERY

1565 West 7th Avenue
Vancouver B.C. V6J 1S1
Canada
604.737.2629
604.737.2675 FAX

Contact:
Diane Farris, Director

Exhibiting:
Contemporary Canadian
and International Art

Angela Grossmann

1. *Untitled*
   1994, Oil on photo,
   48" x 36"

2. *Untitled*
   1992,
   Oil on photo/collage,
   63.5" x 33"

3. *Untitled*
   1991,
   Mixed media/collage,
   20" x 24"

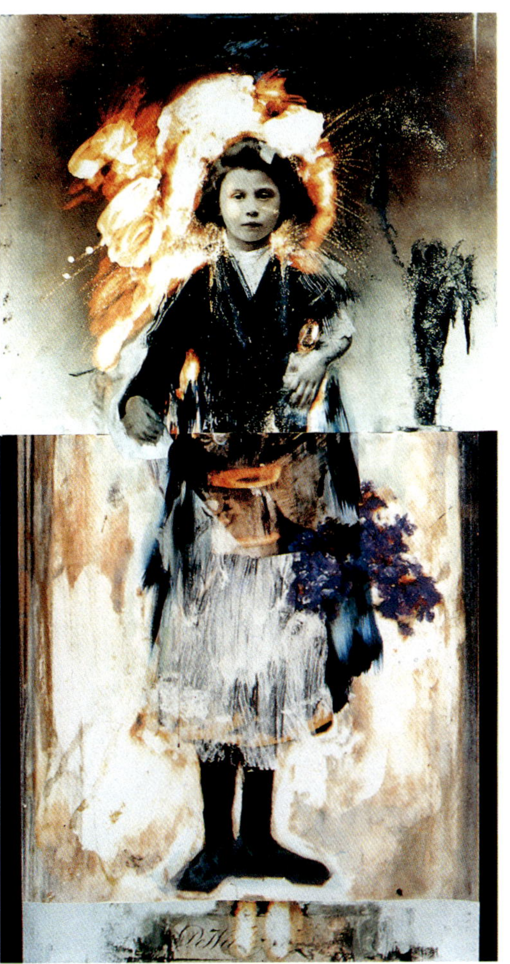

2

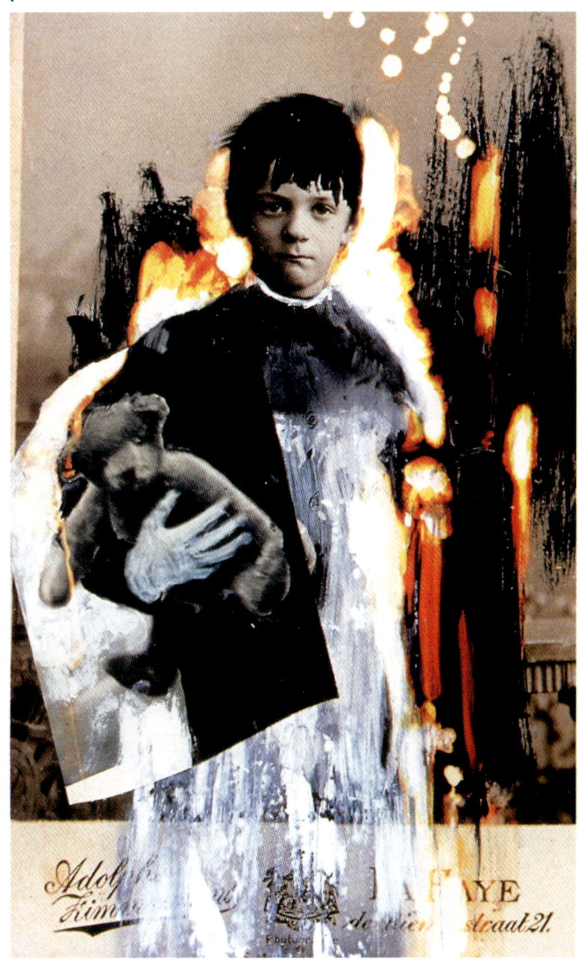

3

Selected Biography:

1994 Solo show,
Diane Farris Gallery,
Vancouver, BC;
Exposure Gallery,
Vancouver, BC

1993 Solo show,
Bourget Gallery,
Montreal, QUE;
MONTAGE 93:
International Festival
of the Image,
Rochester, NY

1992 Solo show,
Diane Farris Gallery,
Vancouver, BC

ZEE STONE GALLERY

No. 11, Forum,
Exchange Square
Central
Hong Kong
852.845.4476
852.877.2859 FAX

Contact:
Fong Yuk Yan, Director
Shaun Kelly, Director

Exhibiting:
Contemporary Chinese
painting, antique Chinese &
Tibetan carpets

Wu Guanzhong

1. *Tigers*
   1990, Ink & colour on
   paper, 68 x 137 cm.

2. *Rainbow Valley*
   1993, Oil on canvas,
   50 x 60 1/2 cm.

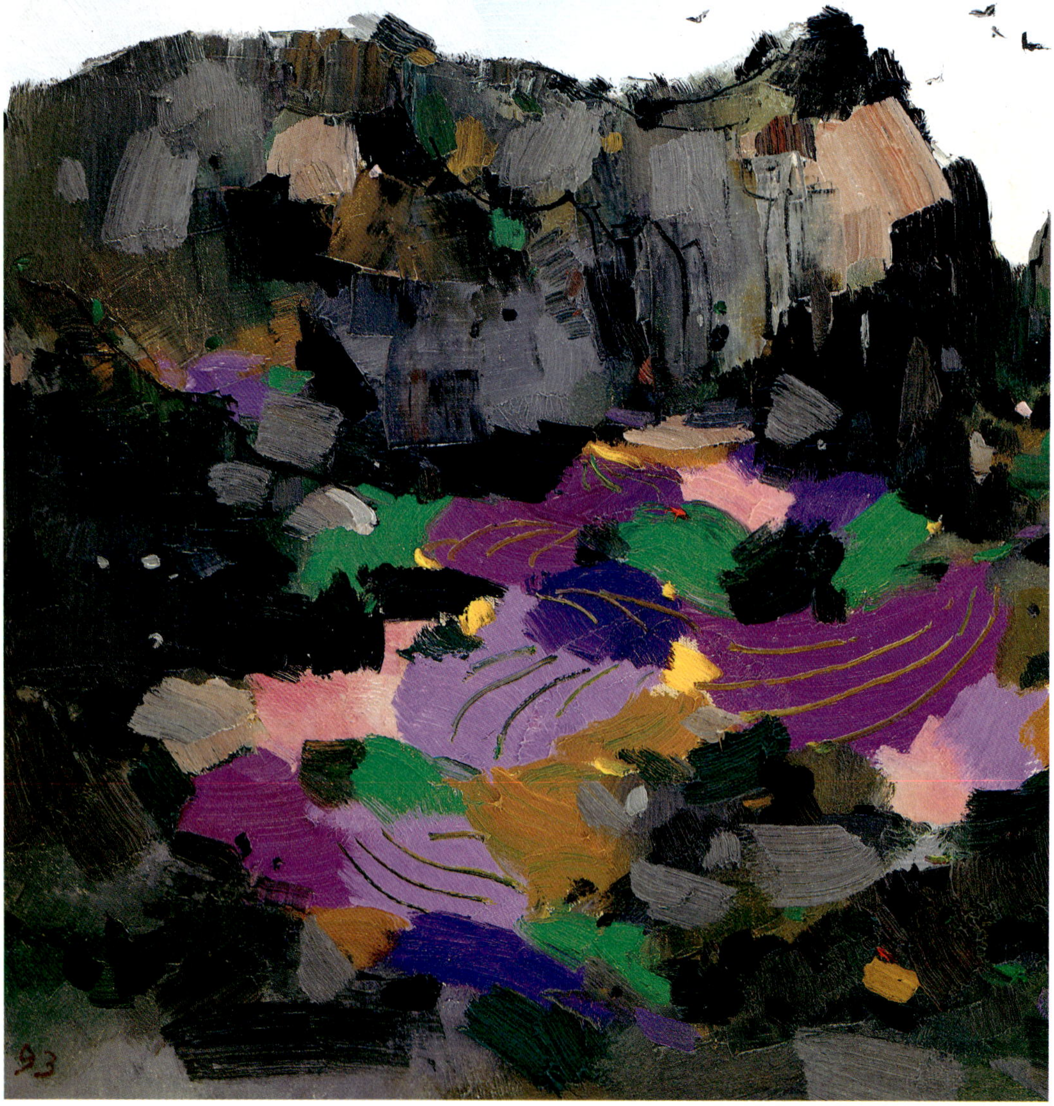

Selected Biography:
1993 Nov. 15, 1993 through
      Jan. 2, 1994; "Encres
      récentes de Wu
      Guanzhong, Peintre
      Chinois de notretemps
      Huiles et dessins,"
      Musee Cernuschi, Paris;
      ARTASIA, Hong Kong,
      Zee Stone Gallery,
      Soo Bin Art Gallery
1992 Wu Guanzhong - A
      20th Century Chinese
      painter, British
      Museum, London
1989 1990 Tour exhibition:
      Birmingham Museum of
      Art; Spencer Museum
      of Art, Kansas; Herbert
      F. Jonson Museum, N.Y.

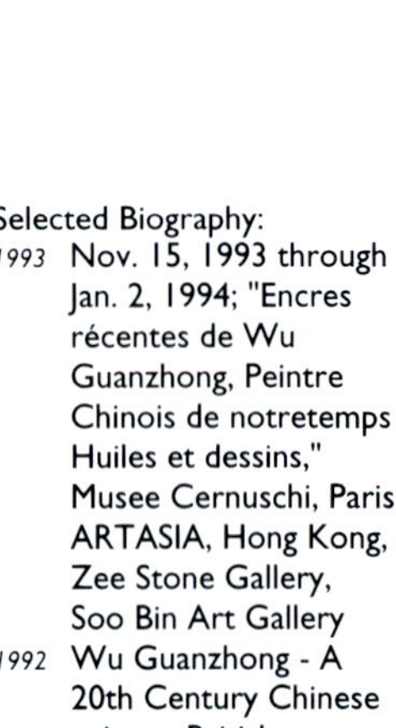

1

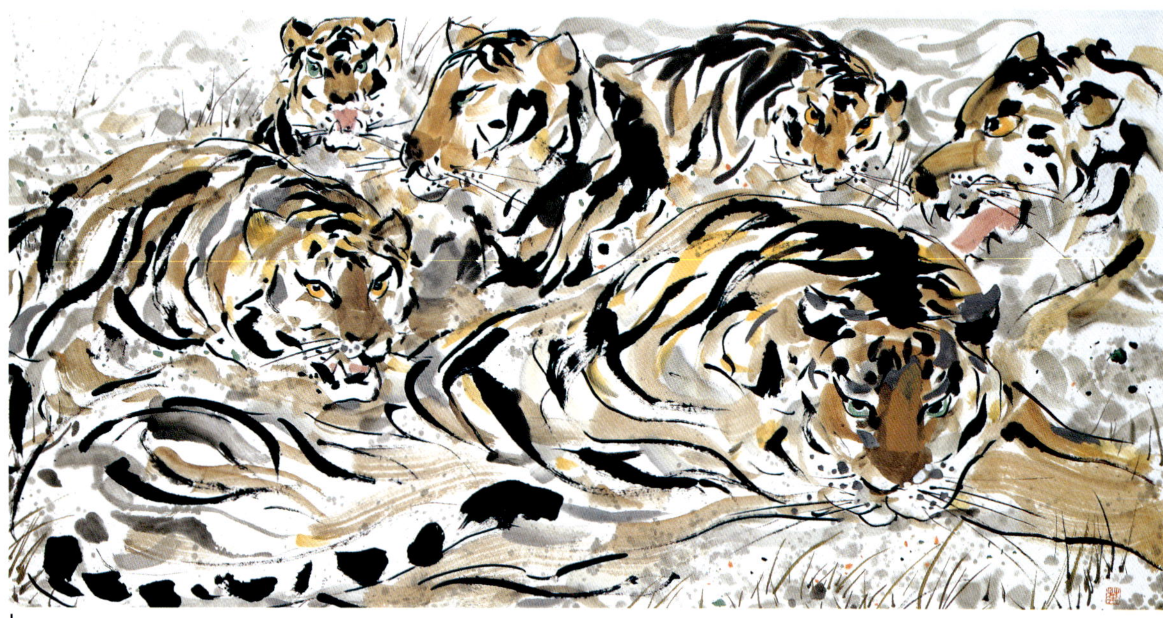

2

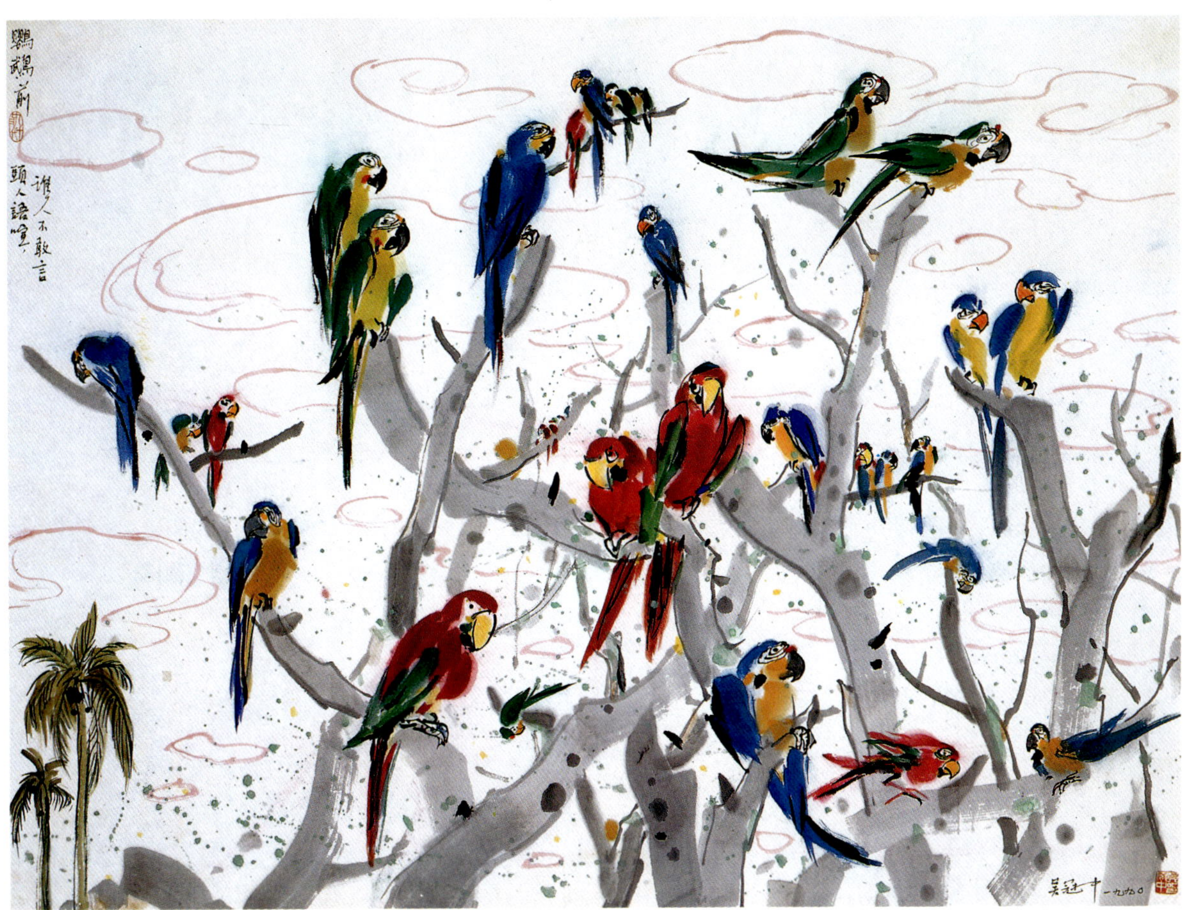

SOOBIN ART GALLERY PTE, LTD.

Office:
81 Oxley Road
Singapore 0923
65.7380488
65.7331294 FAX
Contact:
Chua Soo Bin
Gallery:
1 Empress Place
Empress Museum
#01-06, Singapore 0617
65.338.7677
65.338.6377 FAX

Exhibiting:
Fine contemporary ink and
oil paintings

Wu Guanzhong

Parrots
1990,
Ink and colour on paper,
96.5cm x 130.5cm

Selected Biography:

1993 Recent ink paintings,
      Musee Cernuschi, Paris

1992 "Wu Guanzhong- A
      20th century Chinese
      artist", The British
      Museum, England

1989 "Wu Guanzhong- A
      contemporary Chinese
      artist" 1989-1990
      San Francisco,
      California, Kansas,
      New York, Michigan

1985 "New works by Wu
      Guanzhong" China
      National Art Gallery

STROKOVICH FINE ART

40 NE 40th St.
Miami, FL 33137
305.576.6587
305.576.2011
305.534.0868 FAX

Contact:
Milan Strokovich
Eszter Gyory

Exhibiting:
Modernistic national and international art. Paintings, drawings, sculptures, installations, themes and exchange programs.

Eszter Gyory

Parallel Seclusion
1993, Acrylic, oil, natural pigment on canvas
87" x 50"

Selected Biography:
1993 Andres Art Gallery; Europ`art '93, Geneve; Palexpo, Geneve, Switzerland; Solo exhibition: The New England Fine Art Institute, Boston, MA
1992 Florida Museum of Hispanic and Latin American Art, Miami, FL
1991 Bacardi Art Gallery "I love America", Miami, FL; Art And Culture Center of Hollywood, Hollywood, FL
1990 Kecskeméti Keta'r Museum, Kecskemet, Hungary; Nicholas Roerich Museum, NY,

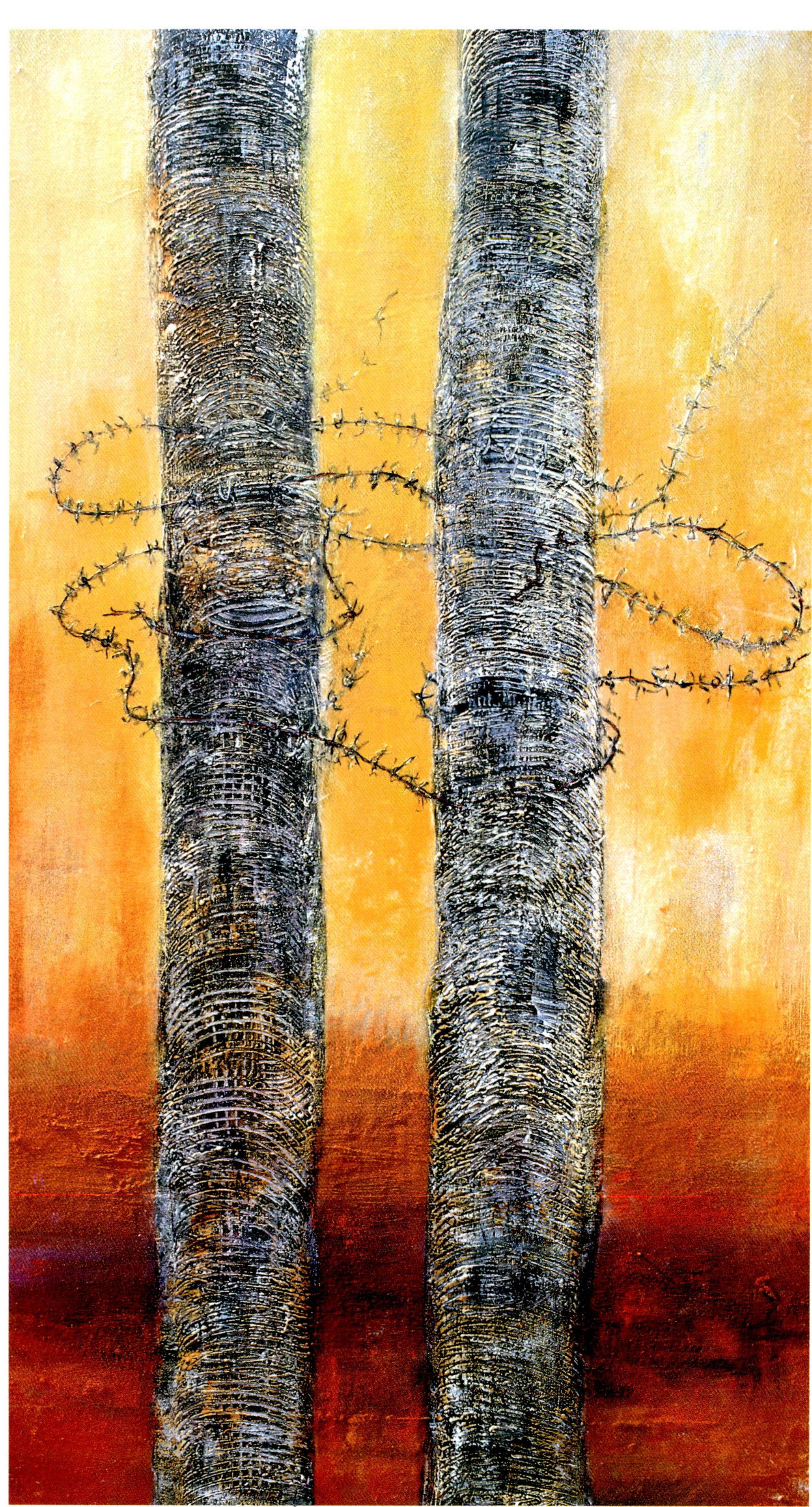

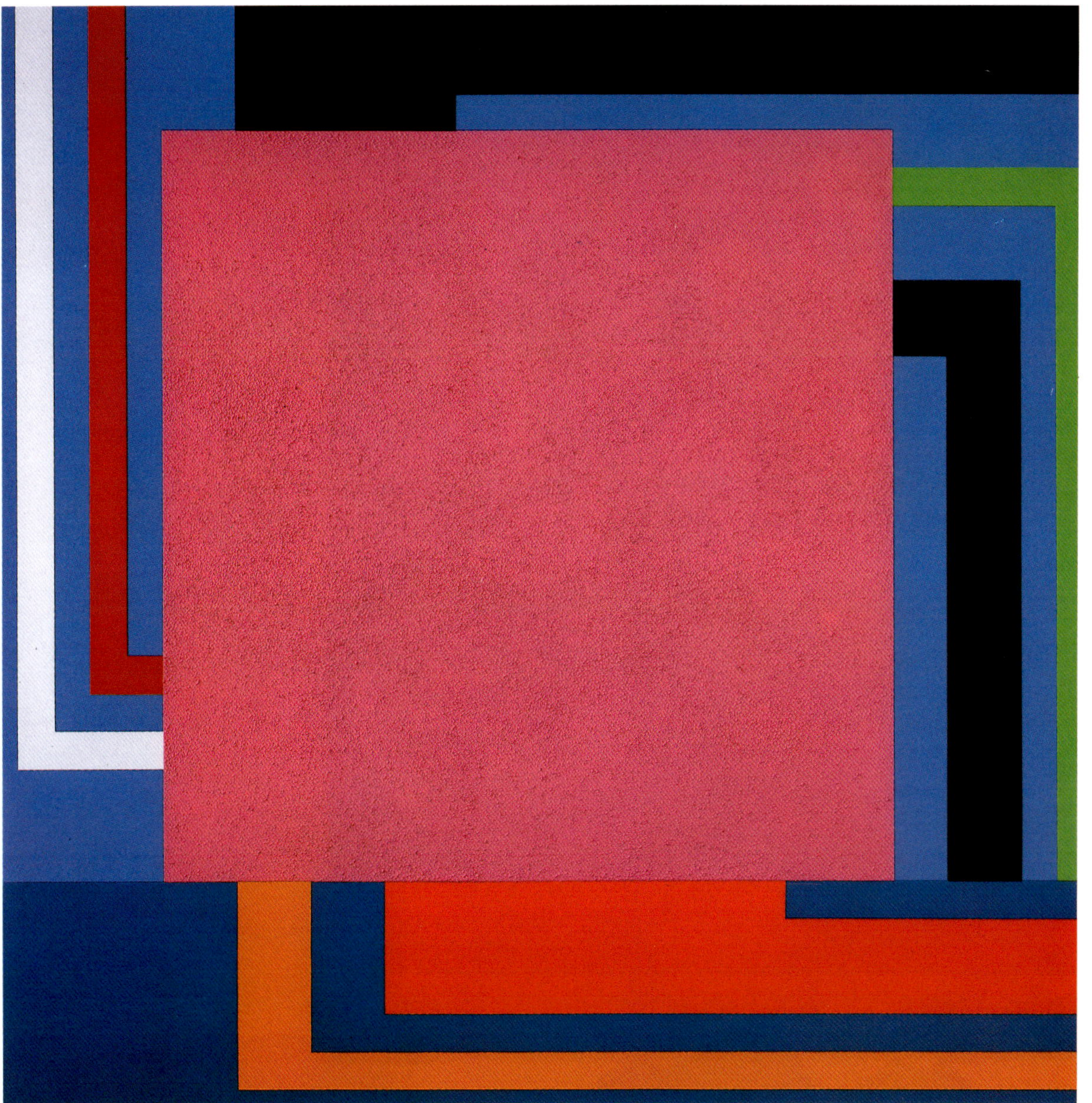

GAGOSIAN GALLERY

980 Madison Ave
New York, NY 10021
212.744.2313
212.772.7962 FAX

136 Wooster Street
New York, NY 10012
212.228.2828
212.228.2878 FAX

Contact:
Melissa Lazarov, Director

Exhibiting:
20th-Century painting
and sculpture;
Abstract Expressionism,
Pop & Minimalism

Peter Halley

Go
1993, Acrylic,
day-glo acrylic and
roll-a-tex on canvas,
93 3/4" x 93 3/4"

Selected Biography:
1993 Solo exhibition:
Eli Broad Foundation,
Santa Monica,
California; Art and
Public, Geneva;
Jablonka Galerie, Köln,
Germany;
Group exhibition:
Whitney Museum of
American Art,
New York, NY;
Museum of Fine Arts,
Boston, MA;
Thread Waxing Space,
New York, NY
1992 Solo exhibition:
Gagosian Gallery,
New York, NY; Galeria
Senda, Barcelona, Spain

ALBERS FINE ART GALLERY

1102 Brookfield Rd.
Memphis, TN 38119
901.683.2256

Contact:
Kathy Albers, Director

Exhibiting:
Contemporary painting,
sculpture, clay, glass, and
works on paper

Iris Harkavy

1. *The Renaissance Man Lives
   In A Timeless Space*
   1992, Mixed media
   on formed canvas,
   68" x 54" x 6"

2. *Family Prayer*
   1993, Mixed media
   on formed canvas,
   64" x 57" x 8"

3. *Looking forward/Thinking
   Behind*
   1992, Mixed media on
   formed canvas,
   66" x 47" x 7"

Selected Biography:
1993   Solo exhibition,
       Albers Fine Art Gallery,
       Memphis, TN

Collections:
1993   Memphis Cancer
       Center, Memphis, TN

       Tennessee State
       Museum, Nashville, TN

       Bauhaus, USA, Inc.,
       Tupelo, MS

1988   BFA Memphis College
       of Art

1938   Born, Louisville,
       Kentucky

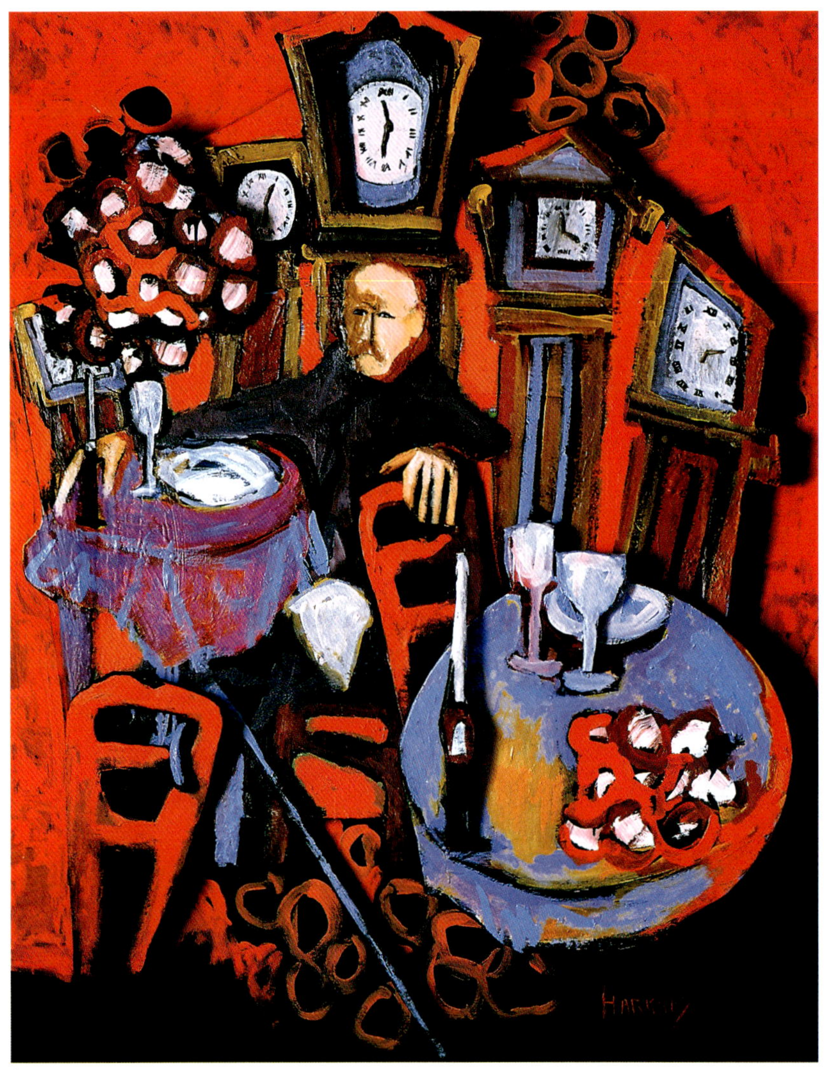

1

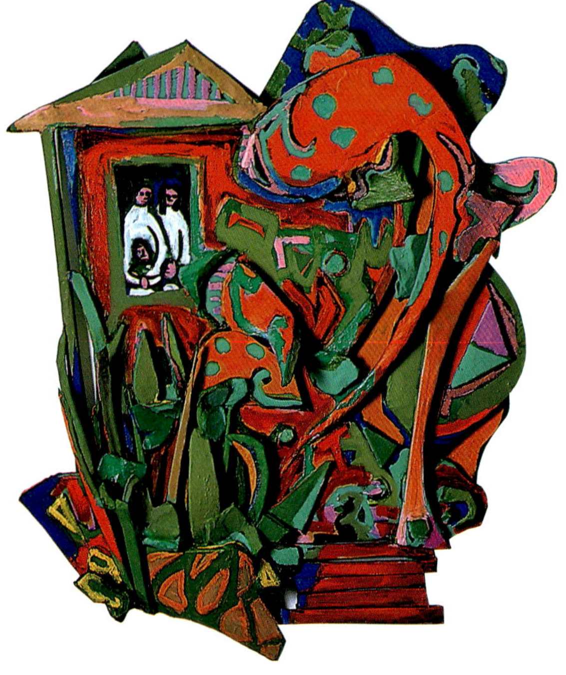

2

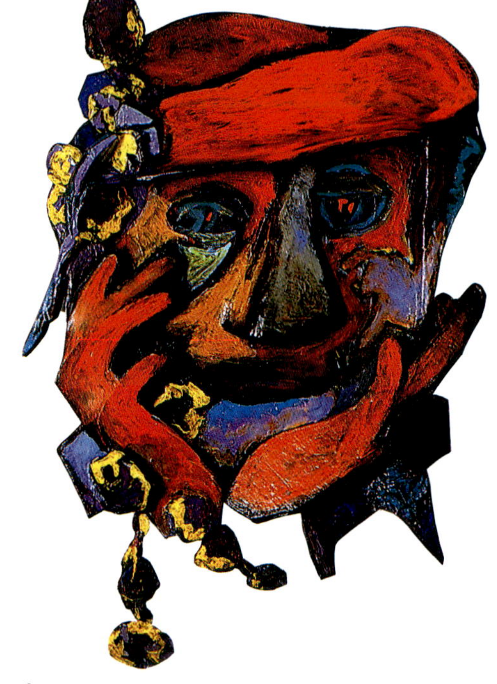

3

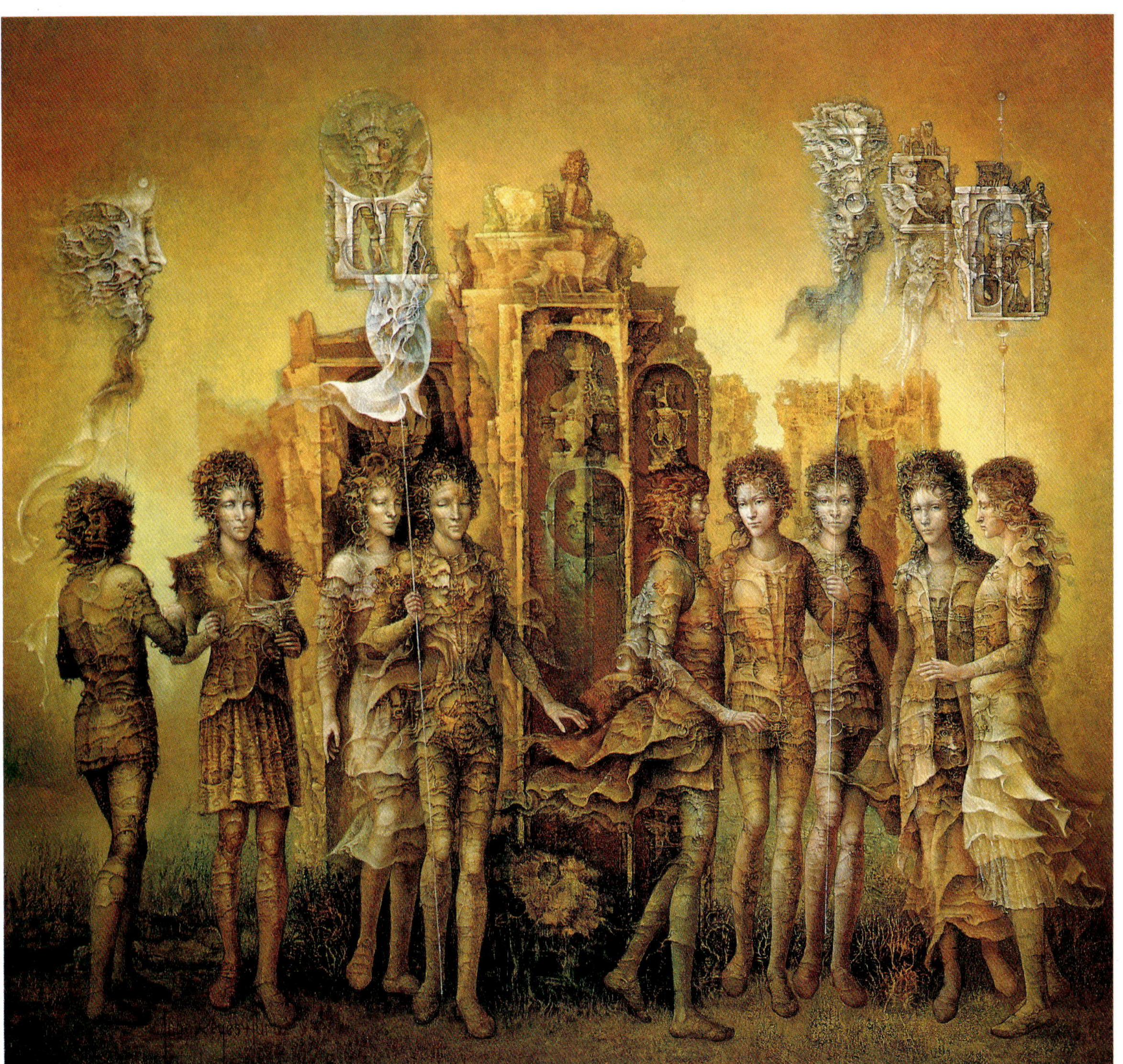

GALERIA MAREN

Hamburgo 175-A
Zona Rosa, D. F.
Mexico, 06600
525.208.0442
525.514.4341
525.533.3904 FAX

Contact:
Enrique Jimenez

Exhibiting:
Modern, contemporary and
Mexican art

Juan Reyes Haro

*Los Estandartes
(The Standards)*
1993, Oleo s/lona,
1.20 x 1.10 cms

Selected Exhibition:

1993 Art Miami 93
International Art
Exposition, Miami
1992 Art Asia Hong Kong
Convention Center
1968 Expsicion en la galeria
de la Escuela Nacional
de Artes Plasticas San
Carlos de la U.N.A.M.
1967 Exposicion, Concurso
en la Facultad de
Medicina de la
U.N.A.M. obteniendo
el 1er. lugar
1966 Expsicion en la galeria
de la Escuela Nacional
de Artes Plasticasde la
U.N.A.M.

CAROLE JONES GALLERY

300 W. Superior Street
Chicago, IL 60610
312.587.8820
312.587.9859 FAX

Contact:
Carole Jones

Exhibiting:
Contemporary International
Fine Art; Painting &
Sculpture

Eve Hennessa

1. *Dios III*
   1993,
   Acrylic & oil on canvas,
   64" x 52"

2. *Dios II*
   1993,
   Acrylic & oil on canvas,
   64" x 52"

3. *Dios I*
   1993,
   Acrylic & oil on canvas,
   64" x 52"

4. *Dios IV*
   1993,
   Acrylic & oil on canvas,
   64" x 52"

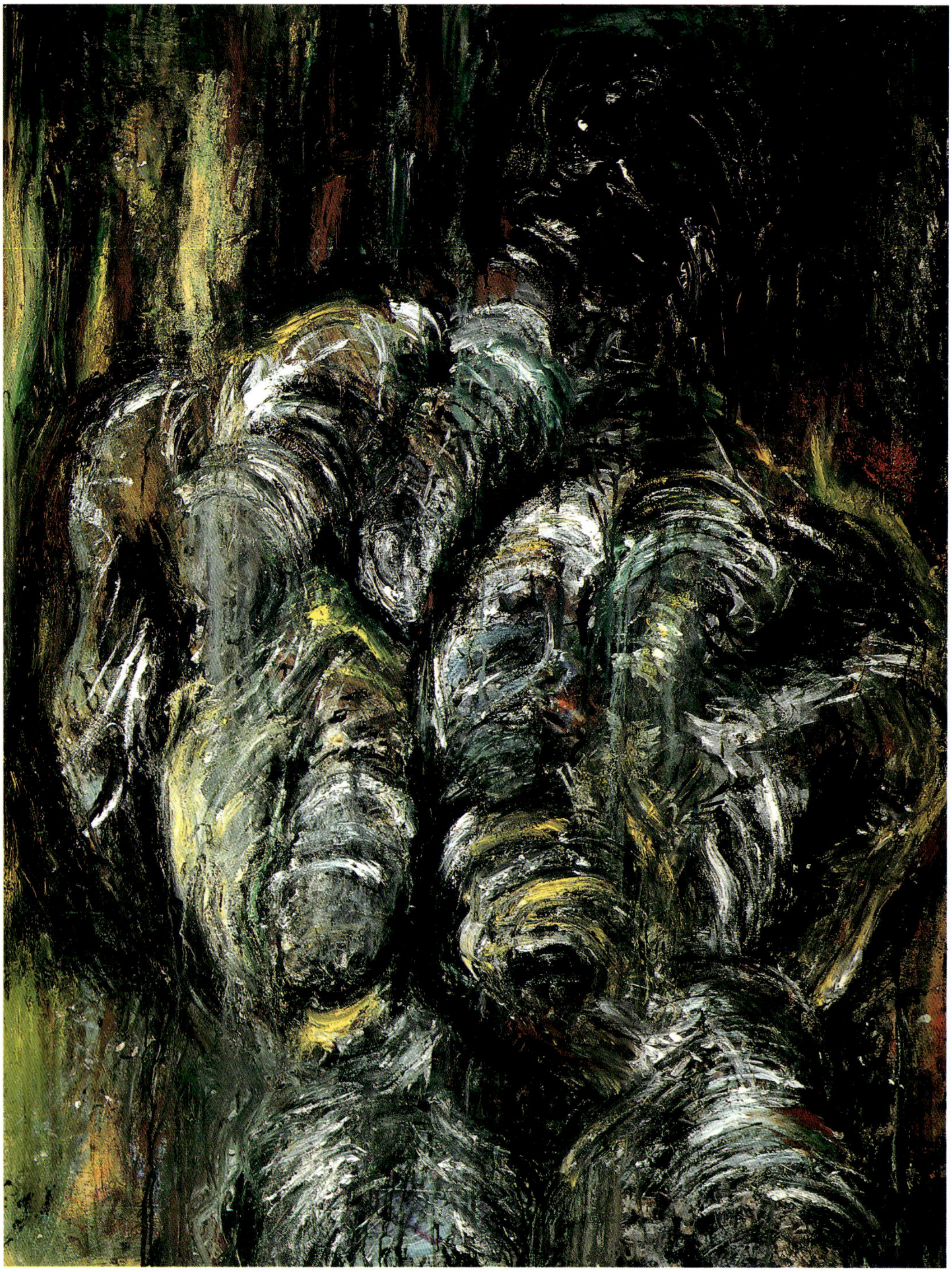

Selected Biography:

1994 Solo Exhibition:
      "Women Going To
      Drink Water",
      Carole Jones Gallery,
      Chicago, IL

1993 Exhibitions, Mexico,
      DF: Galeria del
      Colegio de Cristo,
      Salon Des Aztecas,
      Academia de
      San Carlos,
      Club Amistur

1

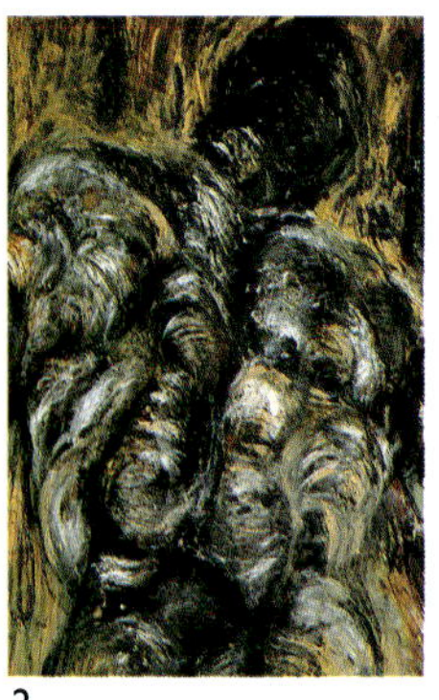

2

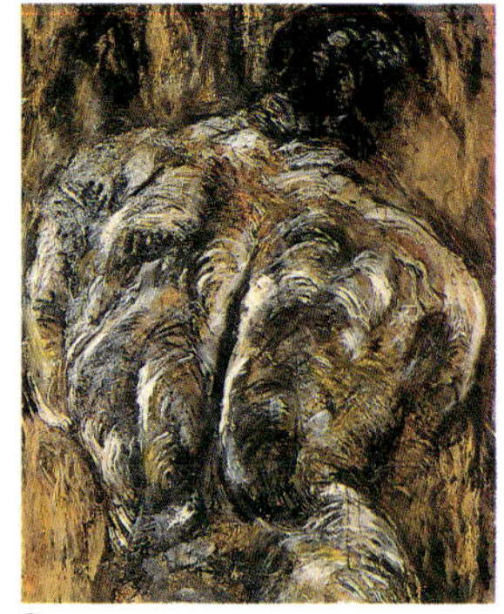

3

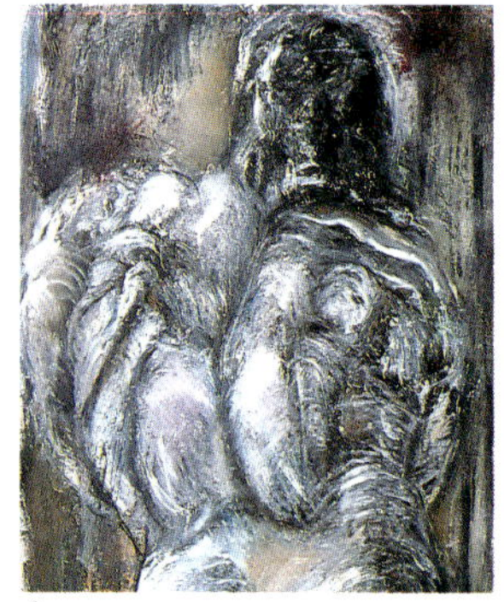

4

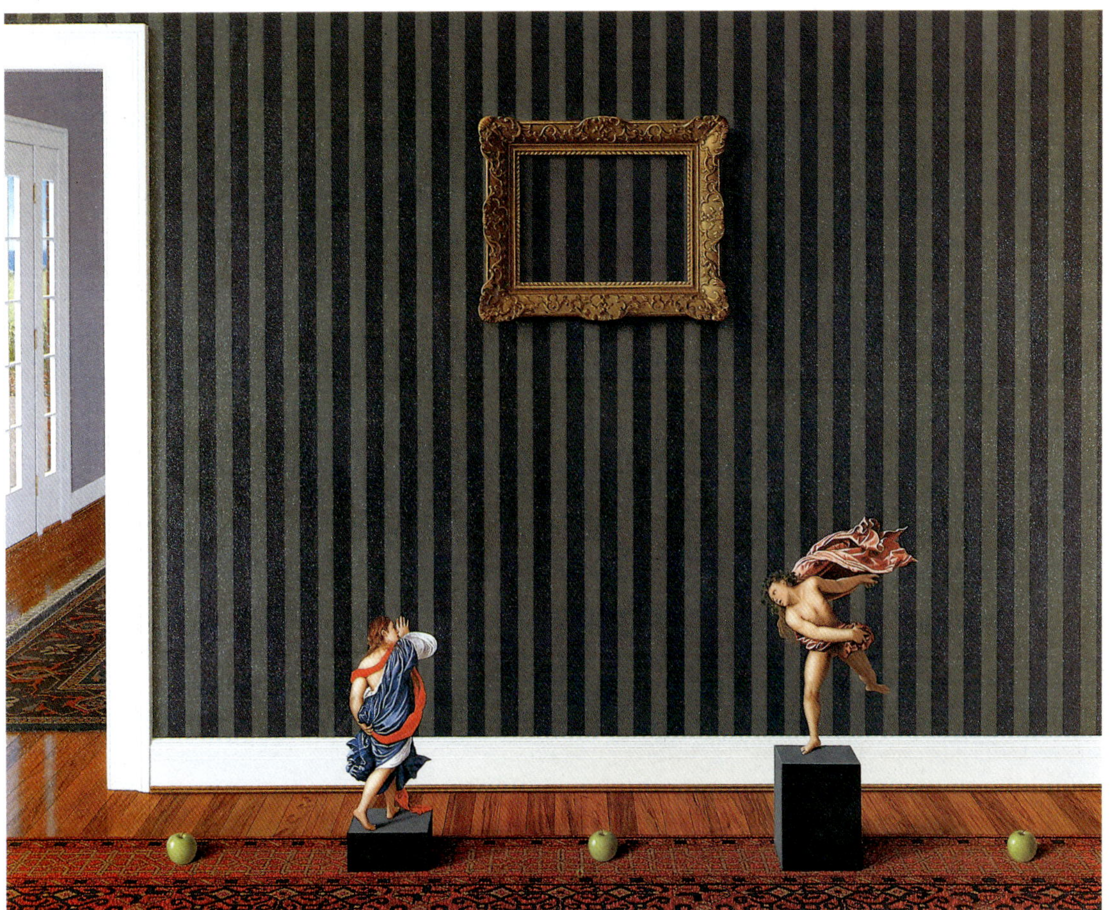

1

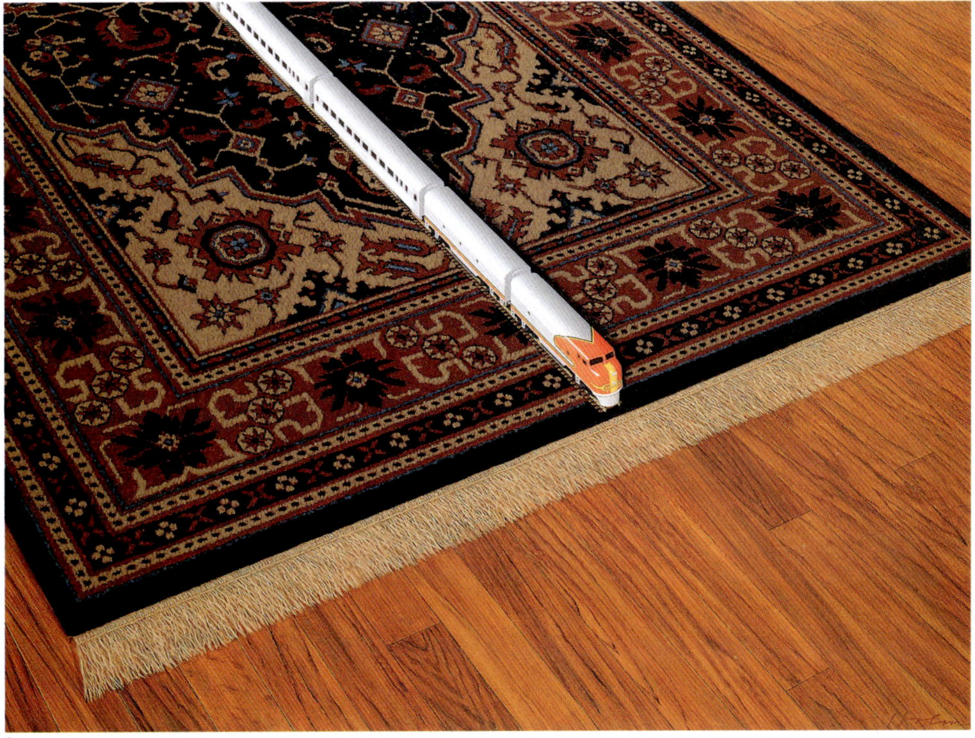

2

TAMENAGA GALLERY

982 Madison Avenue
New York, NY 10021
212.734.6789
212.734.9413 FAX

Contact:
Patrick O'Connor

Exhibiting:
Contemporary realist and
figurative painting

Frank Holmes

1. *Interior with Ariadne and Bacchus*
   1993, Oil on canvas,
   52" x 66"

2. *Little Super Chief*
   1992, Oil on canvas,
   36" x 50"

Selected Biography:

1994 Tamenaga Gallery,
New York, NY

1993 Solo Exhibition,
Delaware Art Center,
Narrowsburg, NY

1992 Tamenaga Gallery,
New York, NY

1991 Solo Exhibition,
Tamenaga Gallery,
New York, NY

1989 Solo exhibition,
Partner Gallery,
Bethesda, Maryland;
National Academy of
Engineering,
Washington, DC

ZAPLIN-LAMPERT
GALLERY

651 Canyon Road
Sante Fe, NM 87501
505.982.6100
505.988.2142 FAX

Contact:
Barbara Willette

Exhibiting:
Fine 19th & 20th Century
American Art

Lindsay Holt II

Tsikomo
1992,
Oil on stretched paper,
42" x 28"

Selected Biography:

1995 Exhibition, ABIQUIÚ
Ten Years After

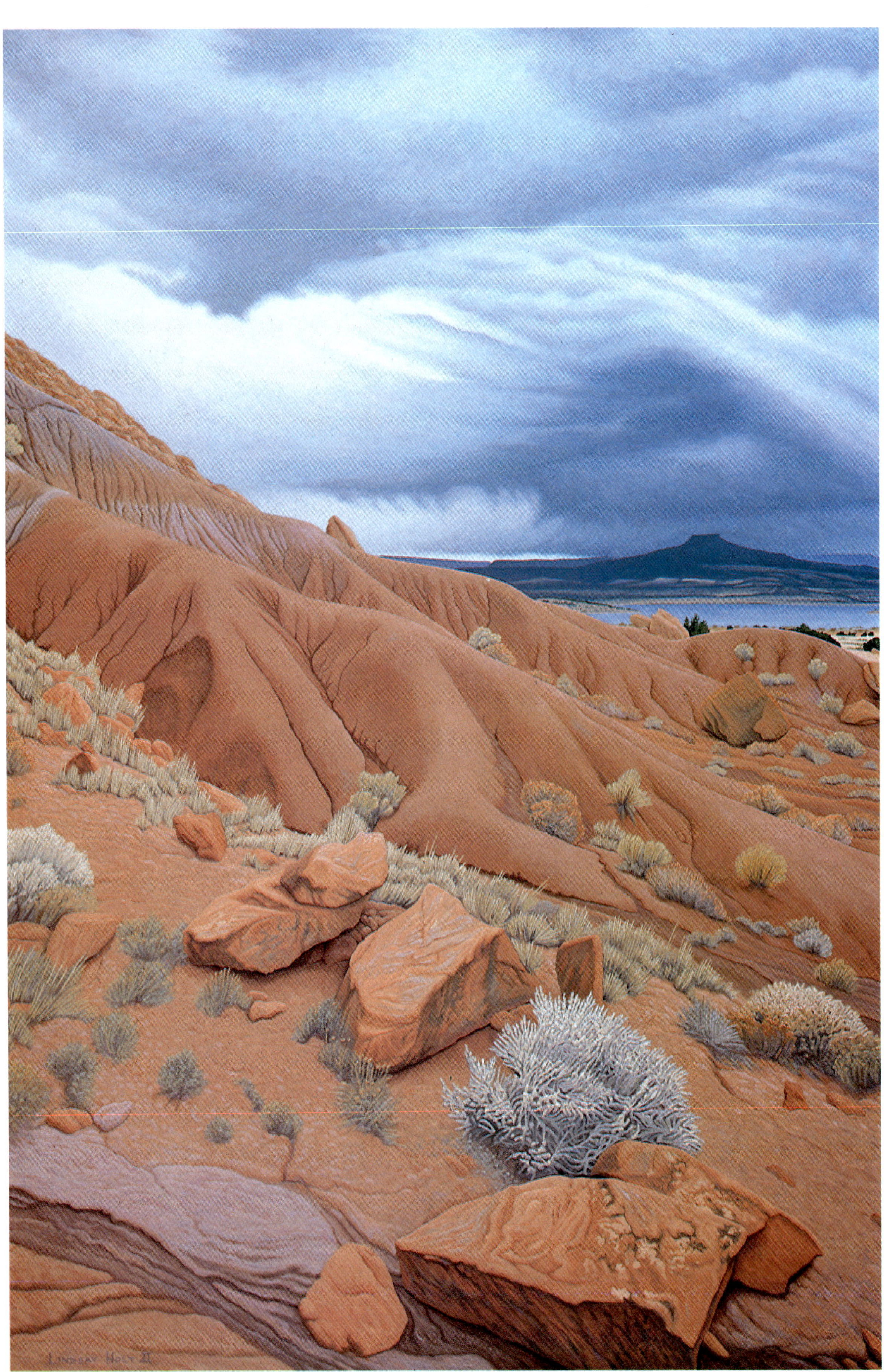

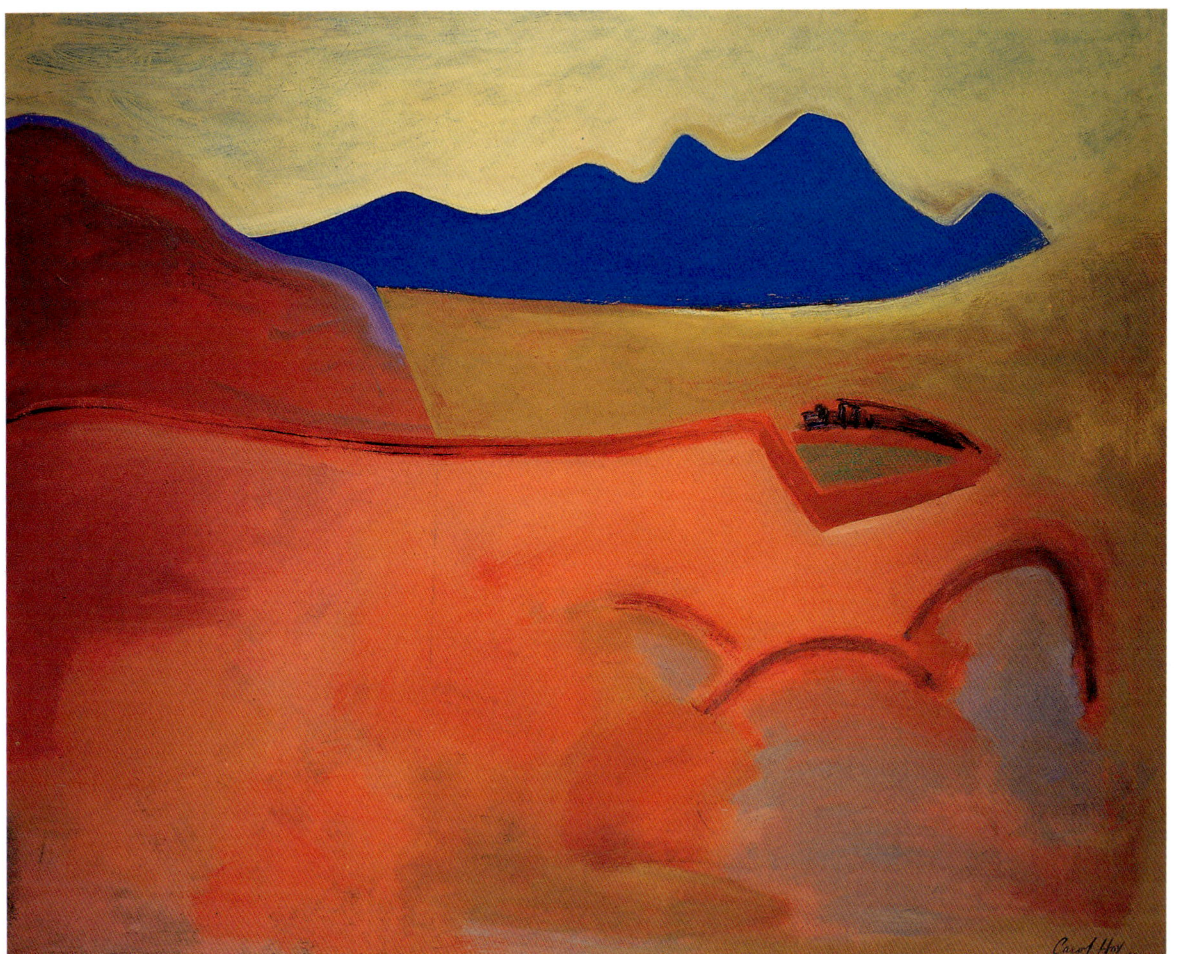

EDITH LAMBERT GALLERY

707 Canyon Rd.
Santa Fe, NM 87501
505.984.2783
800.594.9667
505.983.4494 FAX

Contact:
Edith Lambert, Owner
Anne Ward Burton,
Assoc. Director

Exhibiting:
Contemporary paintings,
drawings and sculpture

Carol Hoy

Sierra Azul
1993, Acrylic on linen,
34" x 42"

Selected Exhibitions:
1994 Edith Lambert Gallery,
Santa Fe, NM
1993 Edith Lambert Gallery,
Santa Fe, NM; B St.
Gallery, San Diego, CA
Publications:
Santa Fe, Art, Simone
Ellis, Random House;
The World & I,
Washington Times
Corp., Washington,
D.C., August 1993;
*Art From The Driver's
Seat: Americans and
Their Cars,* Herndon
Collection, Museum of
our National Heritage,
Lexington, MA

GALERIE PIERRE

12F, No. 19 Kuan Chien Rd.
Taichung, Taiwan 404
886.4.3224921
886.4.3224978 FAX

Contact:
Lily C. Li

Exhibiting:
Modern Art

Michell Hwang

Cat on the Garden
1991, Oil on canvas,
138cms x 180cms

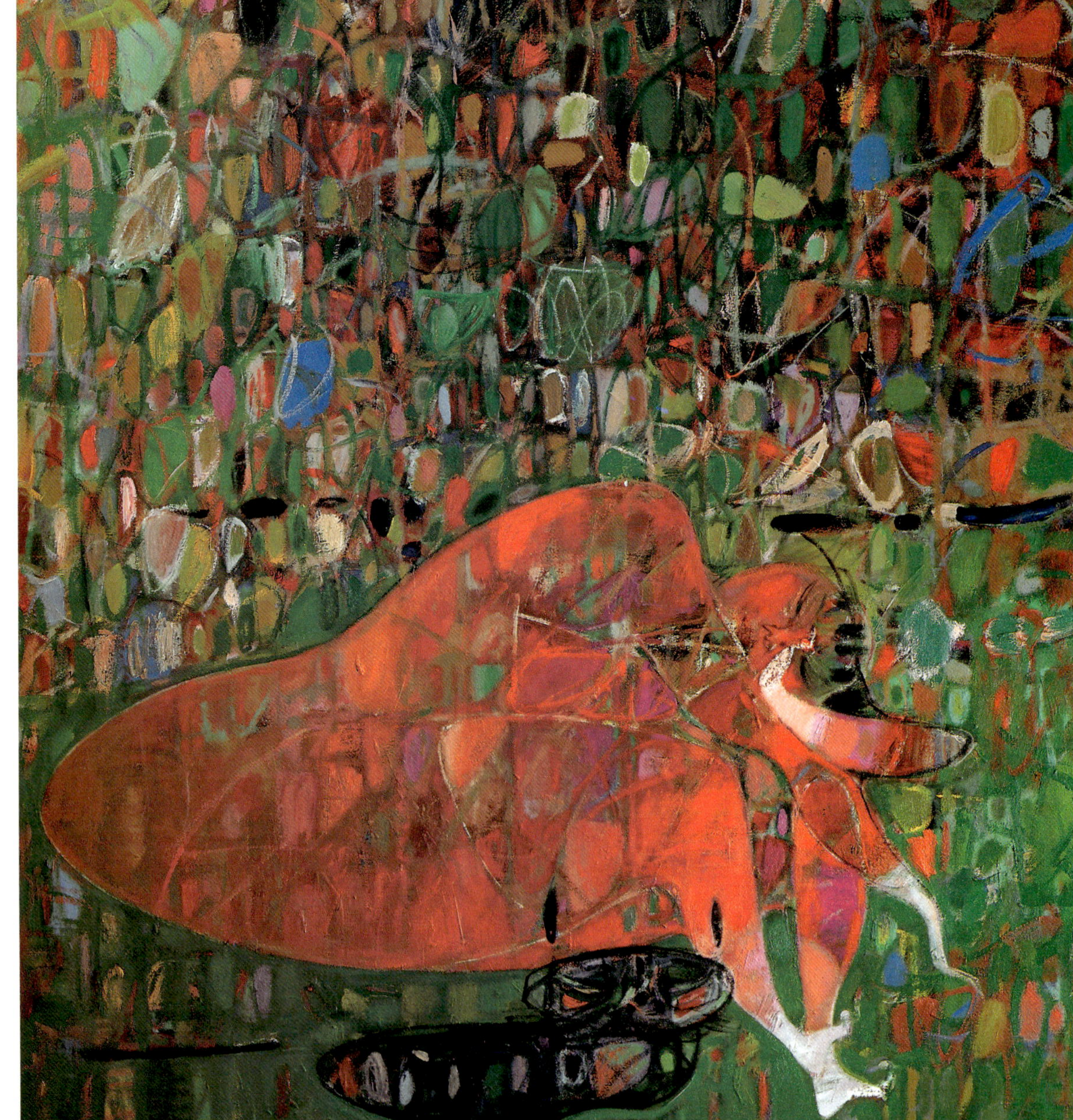

Selected Biography:

1993 Tokyo TIAS Art
Exposition,
Tokyo, Japan
Chicago International
Art Exposition,
Chicago, IL USA
Art Asia International
Hong Kong
1992 Solo show:
Galerie Perre,
Taiwan Museum of Art
Taichung, Taiwan
1991 Solo show:
Impression Gallery,
publishing Huang,
Ming-che Painting
Collection
1990 Established the Taipei
Respectful Artist Club

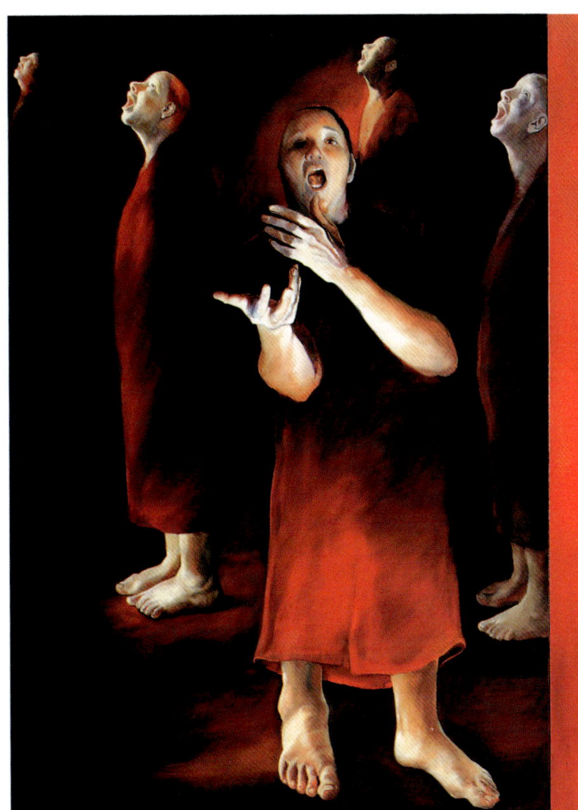

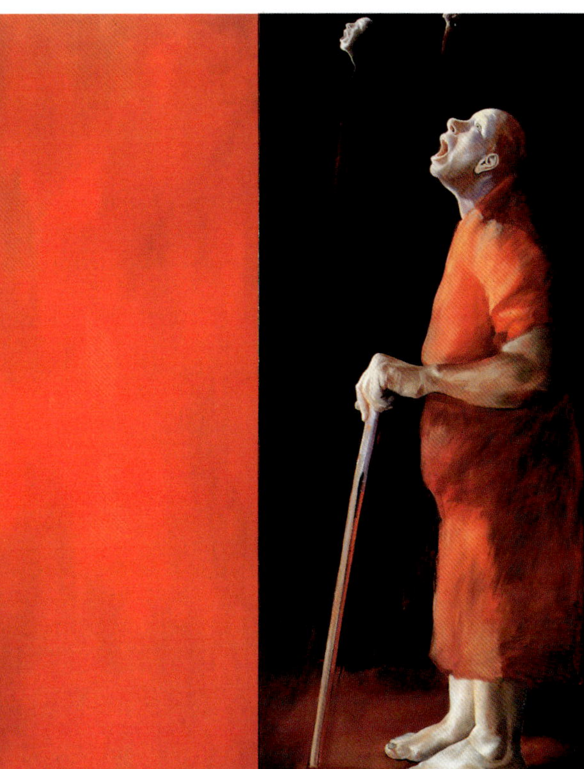

1

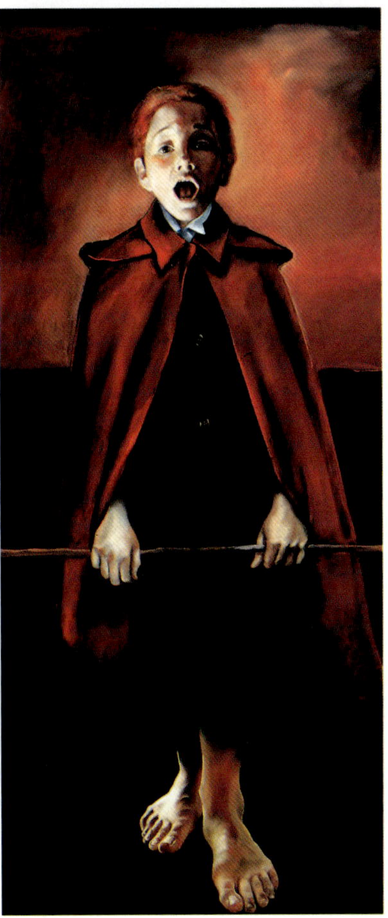

3

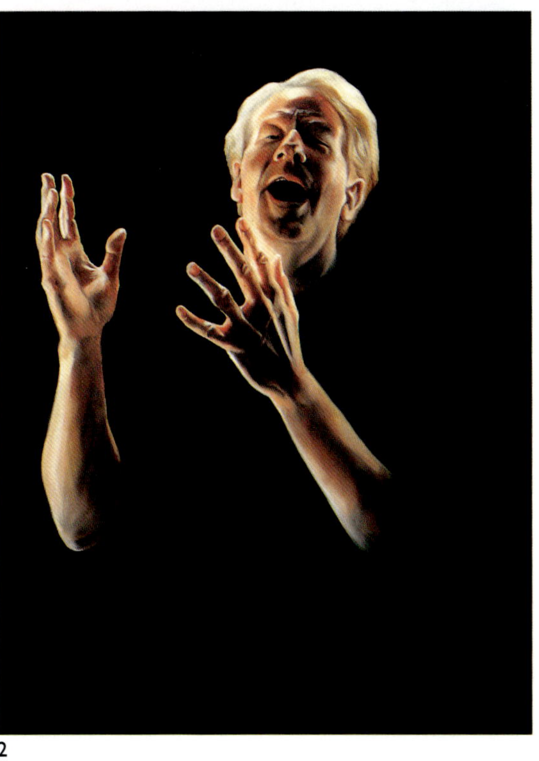

2

DIANE FARRIS GALLERY

1565 West 7th Avenue
Vancouver B.C. V6J 1S1
Canada
604.737.2629
604.737.2675 FAX

Contact:
Diane Farris, Director

Exhibiting:
Contemporary Canadian
and International Art

Kathryn Jacobi

1. *Diva in Extremis #17*
   1992, Oil on panel,
   triptych: 84" x 126"

2. *Mephistopheles*
   1993, Oil on panel,
   47" x 36"

3. *Boy' Choir
   Appearing at Dawn*
   1993, Oil on panel,
   88" x 126"
   (detail: 1 of 4 panels)

Selected Biography:

1994 "Ear to the Ground,
Nose to the Wind",
Solo show,
Fresno Art Museum,
Fresno, CA; travelling
"In Terms of Time",
Santa Barbara
Contemporary
Art Forum,
Santa Barbara, CA
1993 "Arias and Encores",
Solo show,
Diane Farris Gallery,
Vancouver, BC
"Paintings & Drawings",
Blue Point Gallery,
Berlin, Germany
Solo show, Paintings
Jan Baum Gallery,
Los Angeles, CA

ANITA SHAPOLSKY GALLERY

99 Spring St.
NY, NY 10012
212.334.9755
212.334.6817 FAX

Contact:
Anita Shapolsky, Director

Exhibiting:
Abstract painting and sculpture, first and second generation abstract expressionists

Buffie Johnson

The Eternal Present II
1963, Oil on canvas,
36" x 42"

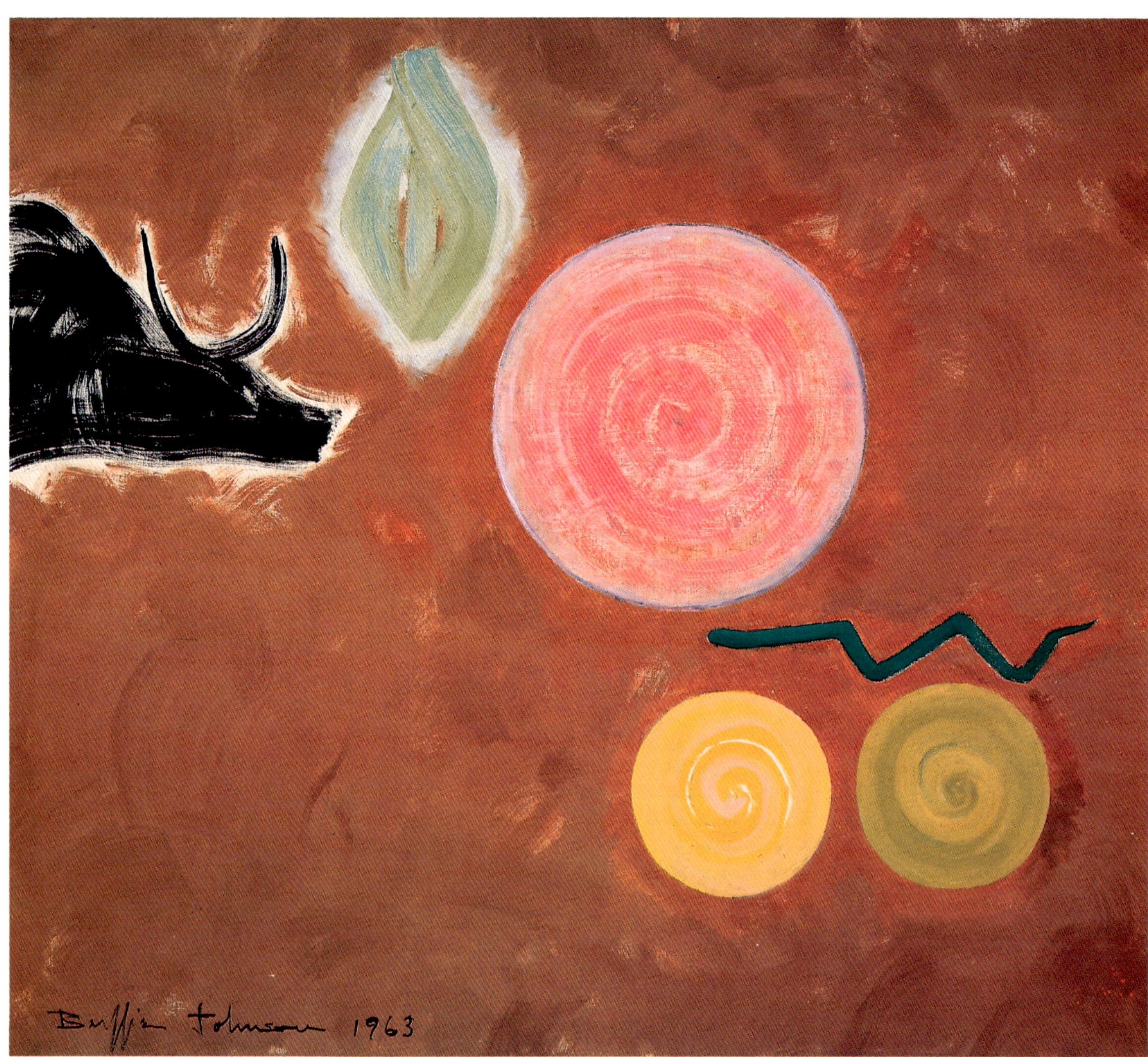

Selected Biography:
1990s "Paintings from the 40s and 90s," P.S. I Museum, Long Island City, NY; Anita Shapolsky Gallery, New York, NY
1970s Whitney Museum of American Art, Biennial, NY; The Hirshhorn Museum, Washington, D.C.
1950s Betty Parsons, NY; Brooklyn Museum, NY; Baltimore Museum, MD; The New School for Social Research, NY; The Parrish Museum, South Hampton, NY; Guild Hall, East Hampton, NY

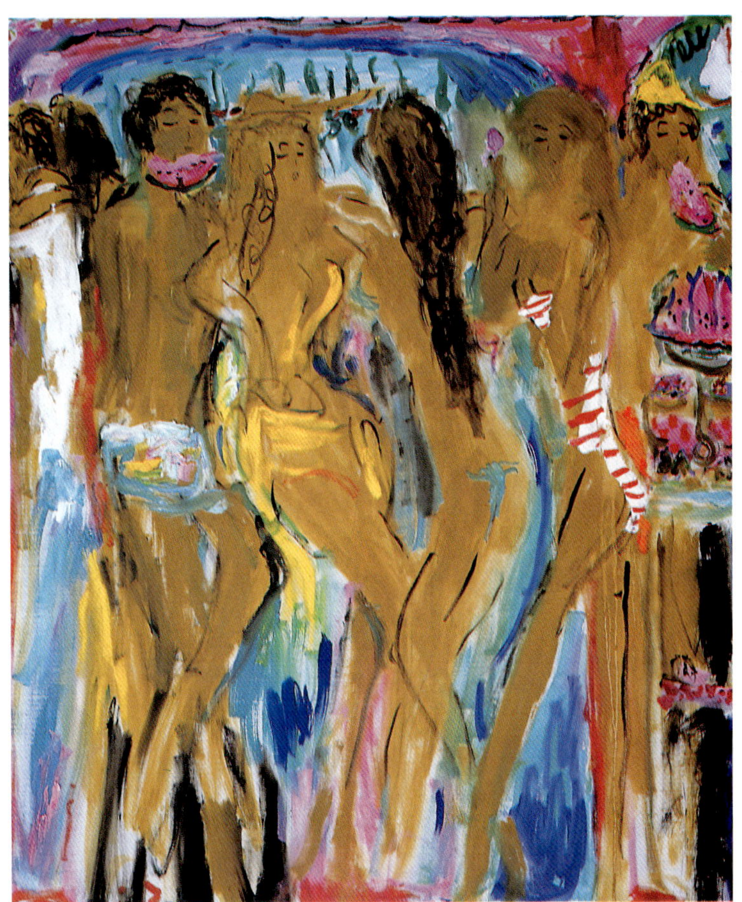

1

HARMON-MEEK GALLERY

386 Broad Avenue South
Naples, FL 33940
813.261.2637
813.261.3804

4262 Gulfshore Blvd. N.
Naples, FL 33940
813.261.7775

Contact:
J. William Meek III,
Director-owner

Exhibiting:
20th Century American art

Bob Kane

1. *Cocomer "Watermelon Eaters"*
   1992, Oil on canvas,
   60" x 50"

2. *Isola di Capri*
   1992-93, Oil on canvas,
   50 " x 60"

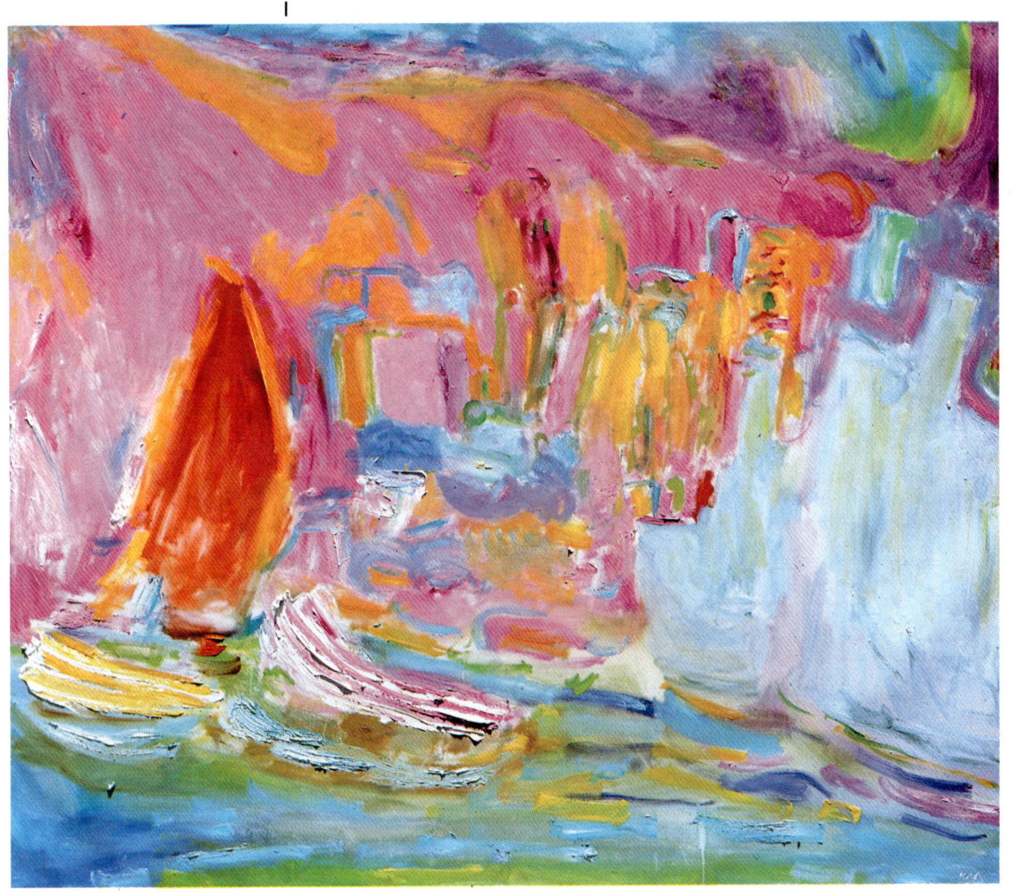

2

Selected Collections:
Joseph H. Hirshhorn Museum, Washington, D.C.; Pennsylvania Academy of the Fine Arts, Philadelphia, PA; Butler Institute of American Art, Youngstown, OH; Cincinnati Art Museum, Cincinnati, OH; Boca Raton Museum of Art, Boca Raton, FL

Solo exhibitions:
Harmon-Meek Gallery, Feb. 11- Mar. 9, 1994, 1989 - 93

INTERNATIONAL ART RESEARCH

140 Violet Avenue
Floral Park, NY 11001
516.352.7399
516.352.2156 FAX

Contact:
Lilo Kinne, Director

Exhibiting:
International contemporary, modern, impressionist art: paintings, works on paper, prints and installations

Lilo Kinne

1. *Past, Present, Future are Accessible to Us*
1992, Acrylic on linen, 63" × 78"

2. *Verschmelzung Meiner Existenzen - Multidimensionality*
1990, Acrylic on linen, 78" × 63"

3. *Other Dimensions Penetrating - Multidimensionality*
1990, Acrylic on linen, 67.5" × 55"

Selected Biography:
1992 Exhibitions, video, live
-93 performances and receptions for the international art community, 6 solo shows: "Sexual Freedom", "Thoughts I & II", "Once I was Black", "Existences", and "Death" series, Thomas Erben Gallery and artist's Studio, Soho, NY;
1991 Art LA '91; Art Miami '91
1990 Solo show: "Mind over Matter", Thomas Erben Gallery, Soho, NY; Art L. A. '90
1989 Solo show: "Louis XVI" Thomas Erben Gallery. Soho, NY
1984 "Transcendence of
-89 Matter", Paris, France

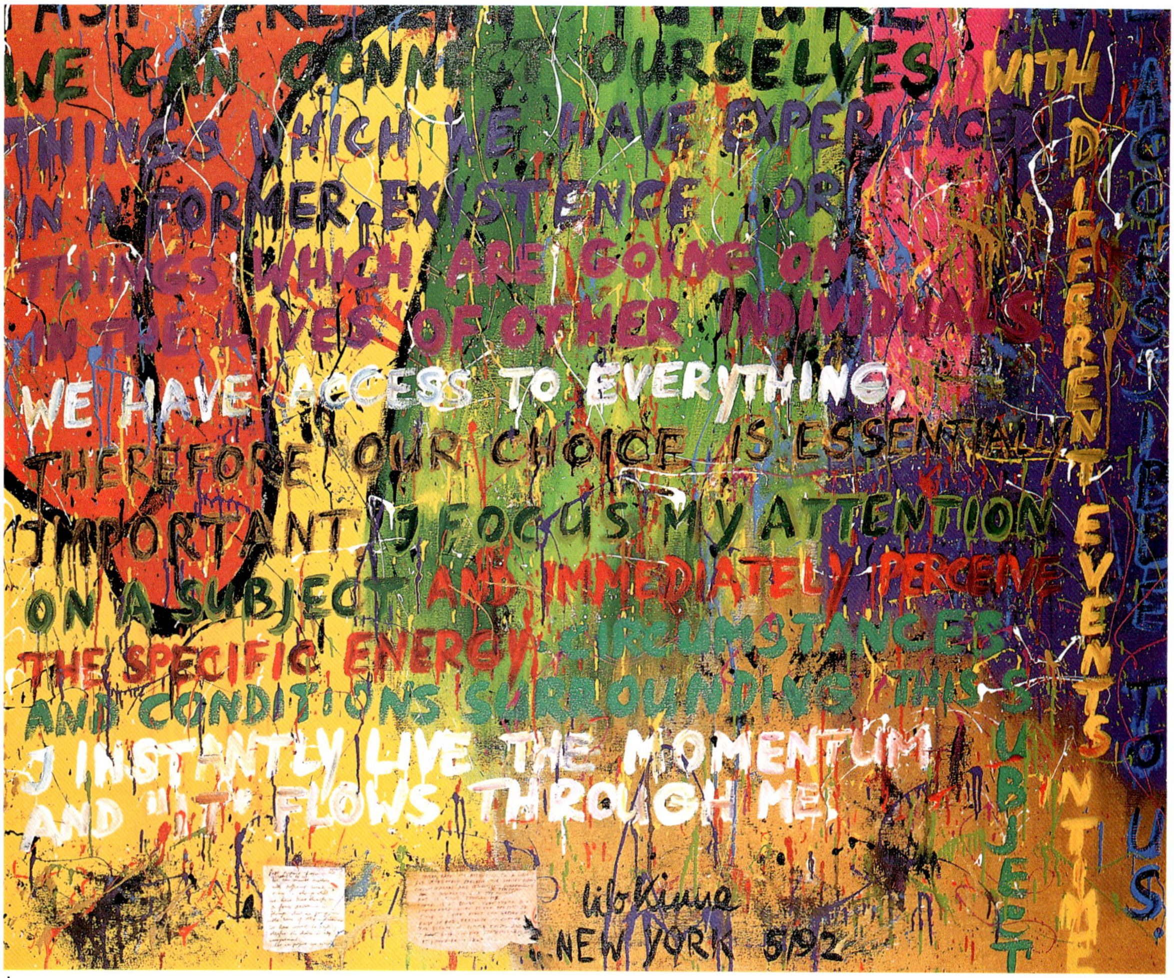

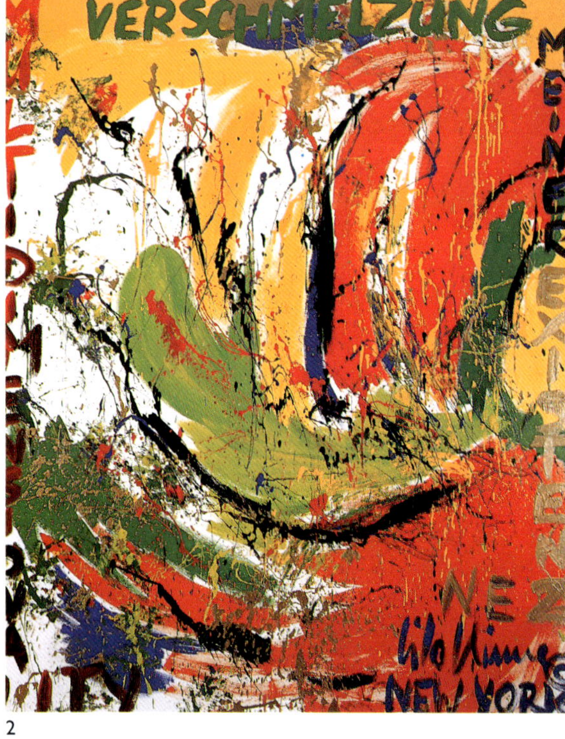

2

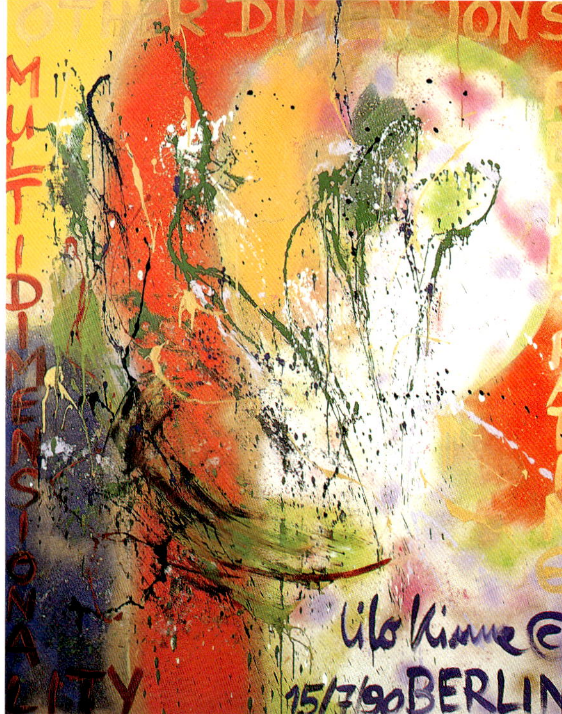

3

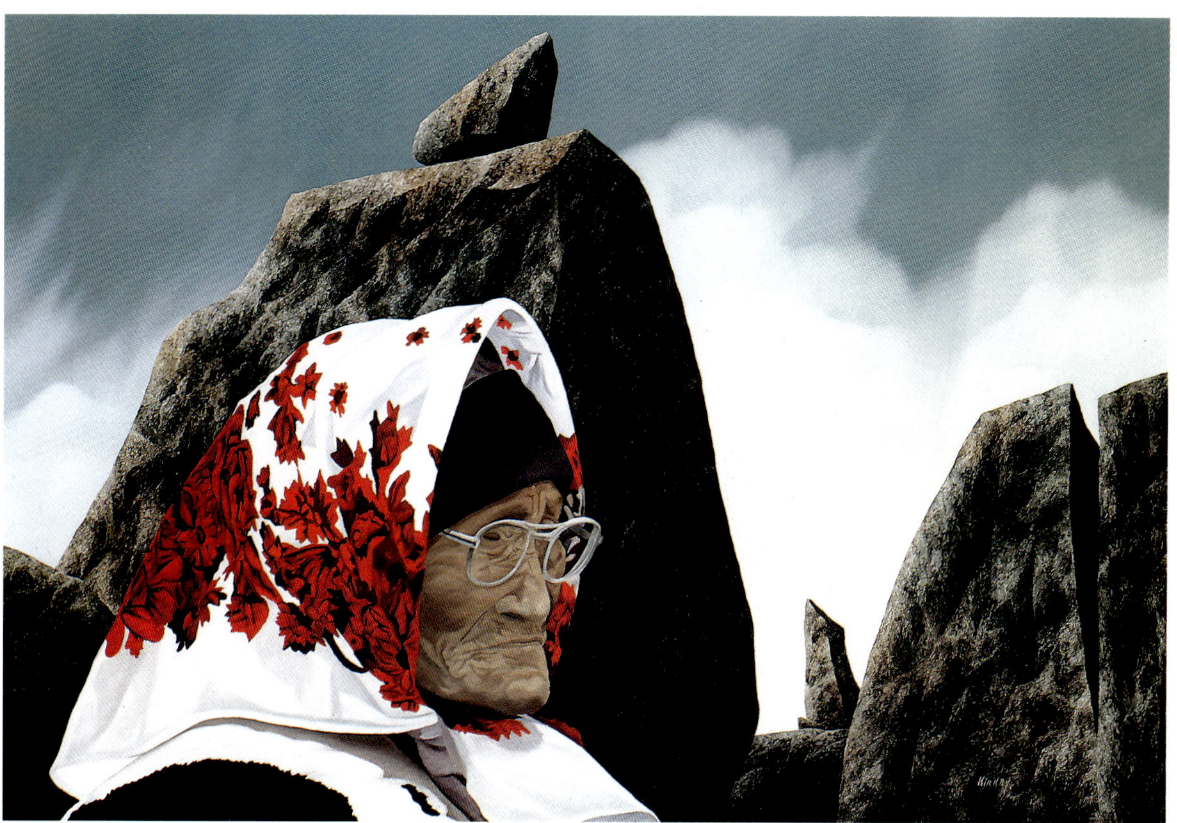

1

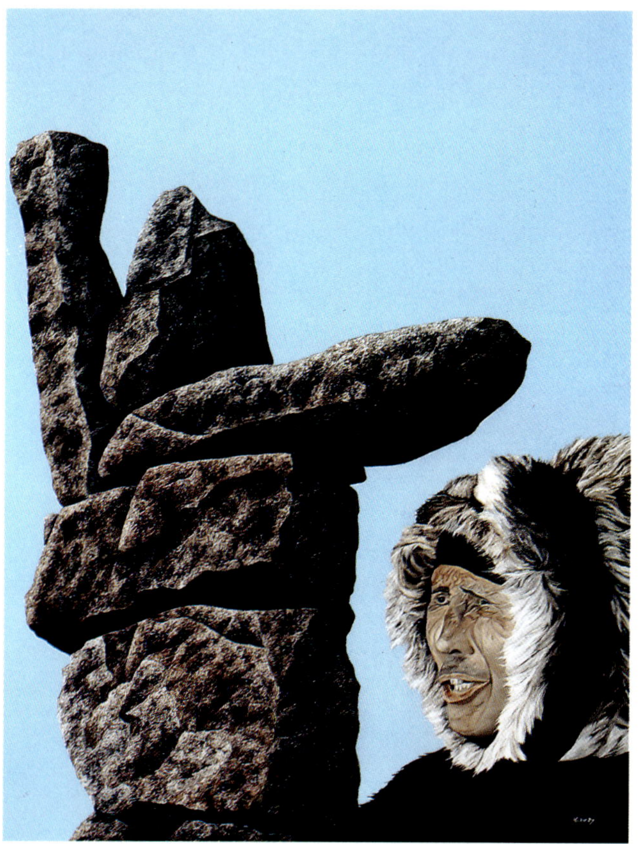

2

ROCFERN INTERNATIONAL GALLERIES, INC.

80 Carlauren Road Unit17
Woodbridge (Toronto),
Ontario L4L 7Z5 Canada
905.850.7647
905.850.8062 FAX

Contact:
Rocco Pannese
Fernando Rocco

Ken Kirkby

1. *Untitled*
   1990, Oil on canvas,
   40" x 60"

2. *Untitled*
   1989, Oil on canvas,
   48" x 36"

Selected Biography:

1994 Rocfern International
      Galleries, Woodbridge,
      Ontario, Canada

1993 Simon Fraser
      University Harbour
      Centre, Vancouver,
      British Columbia

      Ontario Place
      Toronto, Ontario

      Fine Art Warehouse
      Gallery, Vaughan,
      Ontario, Canada

      Art Expo
      New York, NY

MONTSERRAT GALLERY

584 Broadway
New York, NY 10012
212.941.8899
212.274.1717 FAX

Contact:
Marie Montserrat Coll,
Director

Exhibiting:
Contemporary European
and American art

Barbara Kirsch

1. *O.T.*
   1992, Mixed media on
   canvas, 65 x 55cm

2. *O.T.*
   1992, Mixed media on
   carton, 90 x 70cm

3. *O.T.*
   1992, Mixed media on
   canvas, 40 x 30cm

Selected Biography:

1994 Montserrat Gallery,
New York, NY

1992 Gallery Tullagasse
Breisach

1991 AEG
Frankfurt, Main

IBM AEG
Frankfurt, Main

Goedecke AG
Freiburg 1991

1

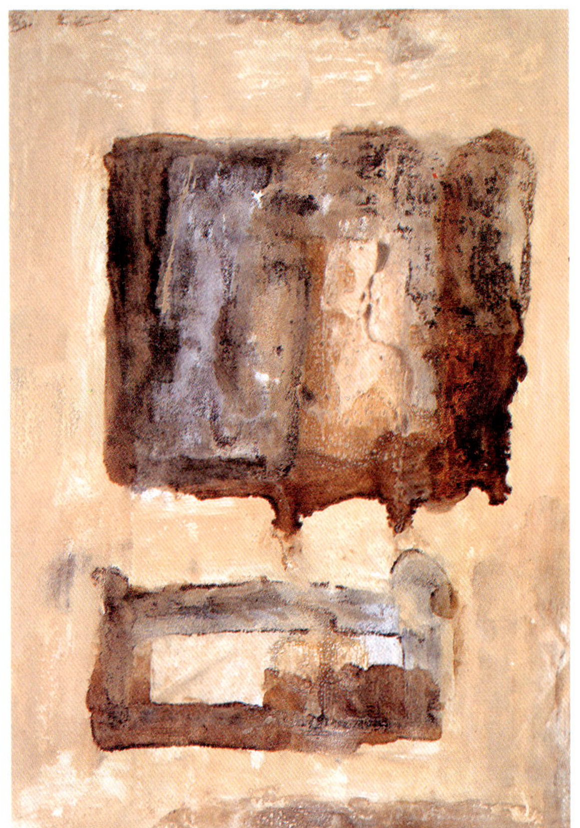

2

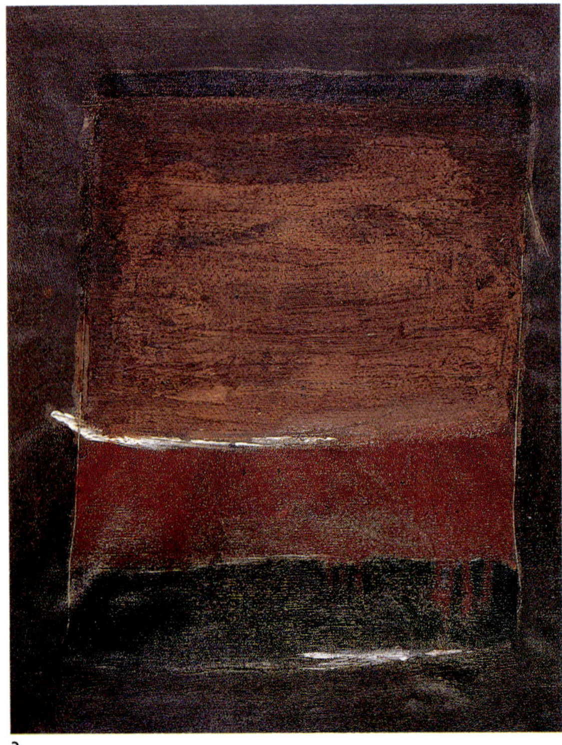

3

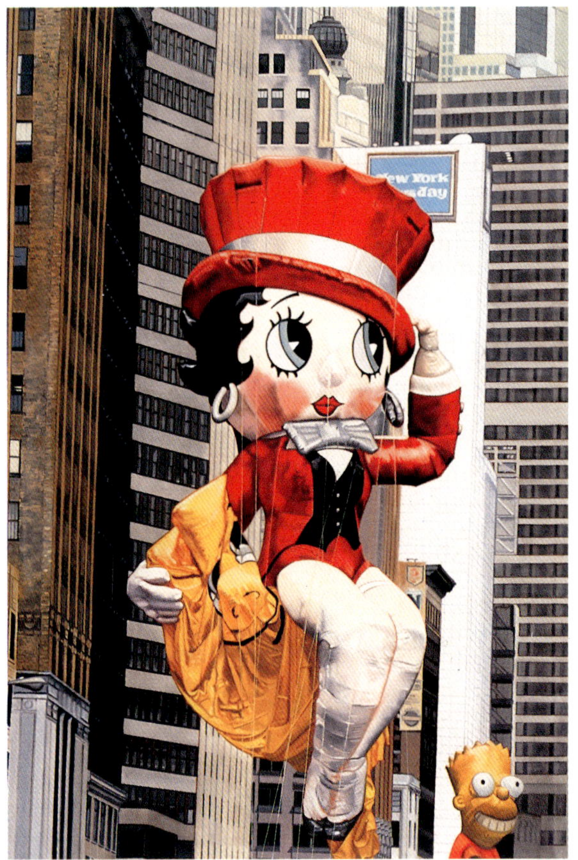

1

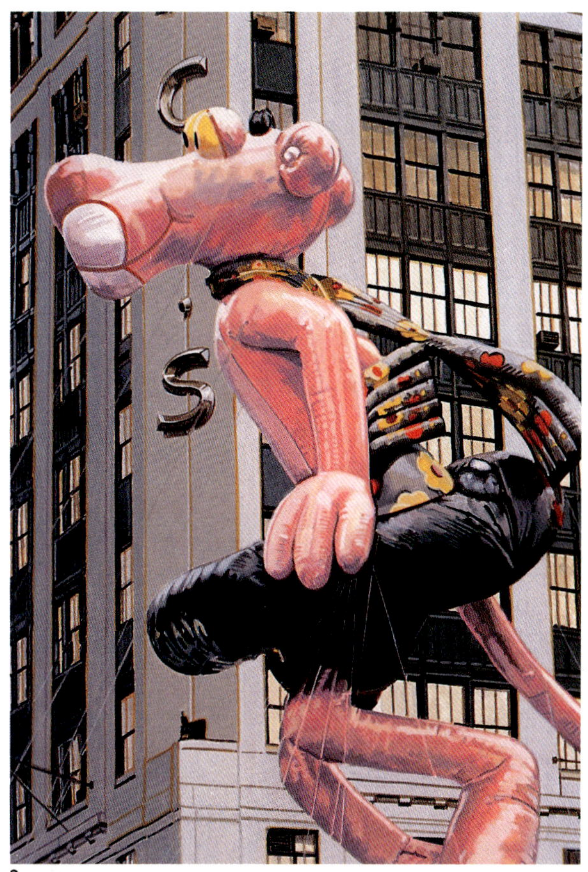

2

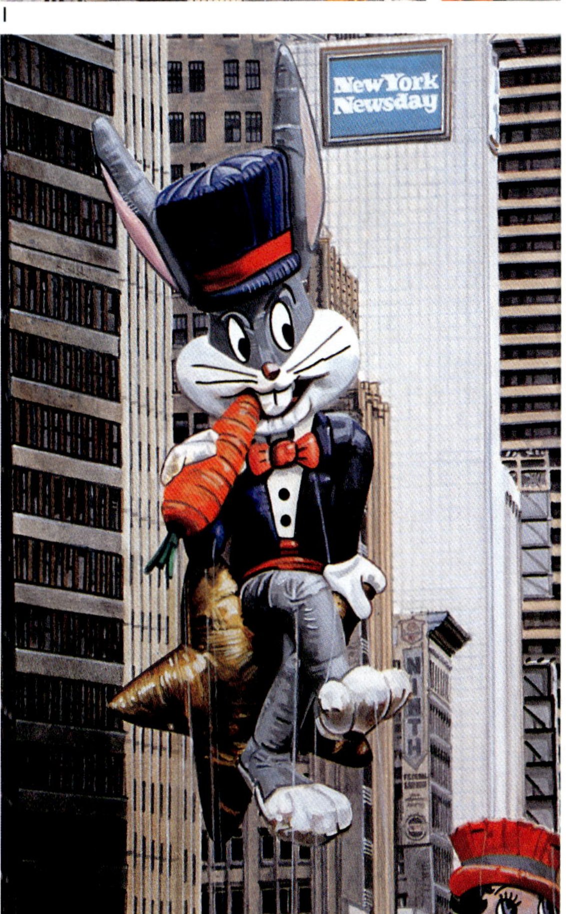

3

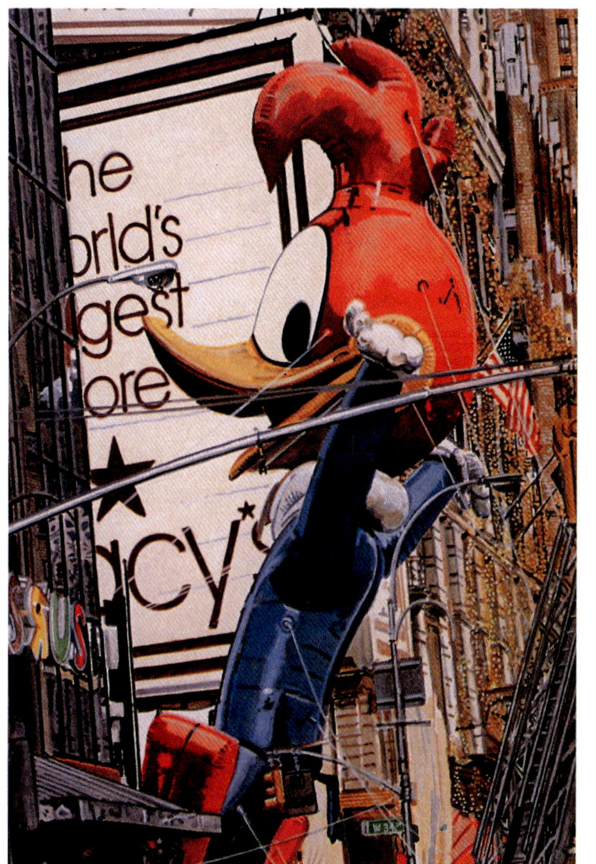

4

LOUIS K. MEISEL GALLERY

141 Prince Street
New York, NY 10012
212.677.1340
212.533.7340 FAX

Contact:
Louis K. Meisel
Diane Sena

Exhibiting:
Photo-Realist painting and
other technically skilled
contemporary disciplines

Ron Kleemann

1. *Boopsy*
   1993, Oil on linen,
   65" x 45"

2. *Panther Pass*
   1993, Acrylic on Board,
   16" x 10.75"

3. *Bugsy*
   1992, Acrylic on Board,
   16" x 10.5"

4. *Woody's Turn*
   1993, Acrylic on Board,
   17.75" x 11"

Selected Collections:

Museum of Modern
Art, New York, NY;
Solomon R.
Guggenhim Museum,
New York, NY;
Museum of
Contemporary Art,
Chicago, IL;
Indianapolis
Museum of Art, In;
National Air
& Space Museum,
Washington, DC

DIANE FARRIS
GALLERY

1565 West 7th Avenue
Vancouver B.C. V6J 1S1
Canada
604.737.2629
604.737.2675 FAX

Contact:
Diane Farris, Director

Exhibiting:
Contemporary Canadian
and International Art

John Koerner

1. *The Balcony (1)*
   1993, Acrylic on canvas,
   55" x 42"

2. *Hikaru (1)*
   1992, Acrylic on canvas,
   30" x 42"

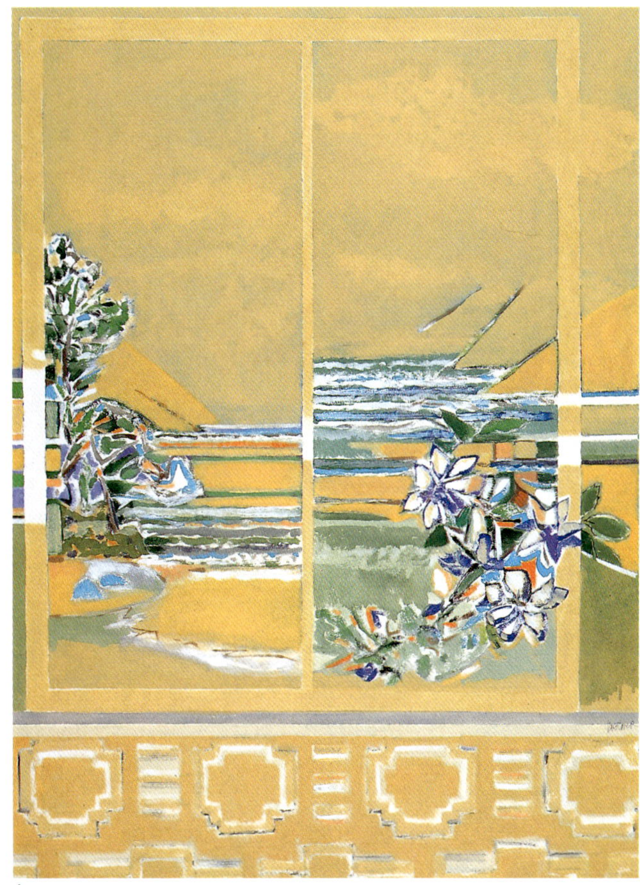

1

Selected Biography:

1994 "Variations on a
     Theme", Solo show,
     Diane Farris Gallery,
     Vancouver, BC

1993 Contemporary
     Canadian Art, Prague,
     Czech Republic;
     Solo show, Clare Hall,
     Cambridge University,
     Cambridge, GBR

1992 Retrospective, Art
     Gallery of Greater
     Victoria, Victoria, BC

1991 Diane Farris Gallery,
     Vancouver, BC

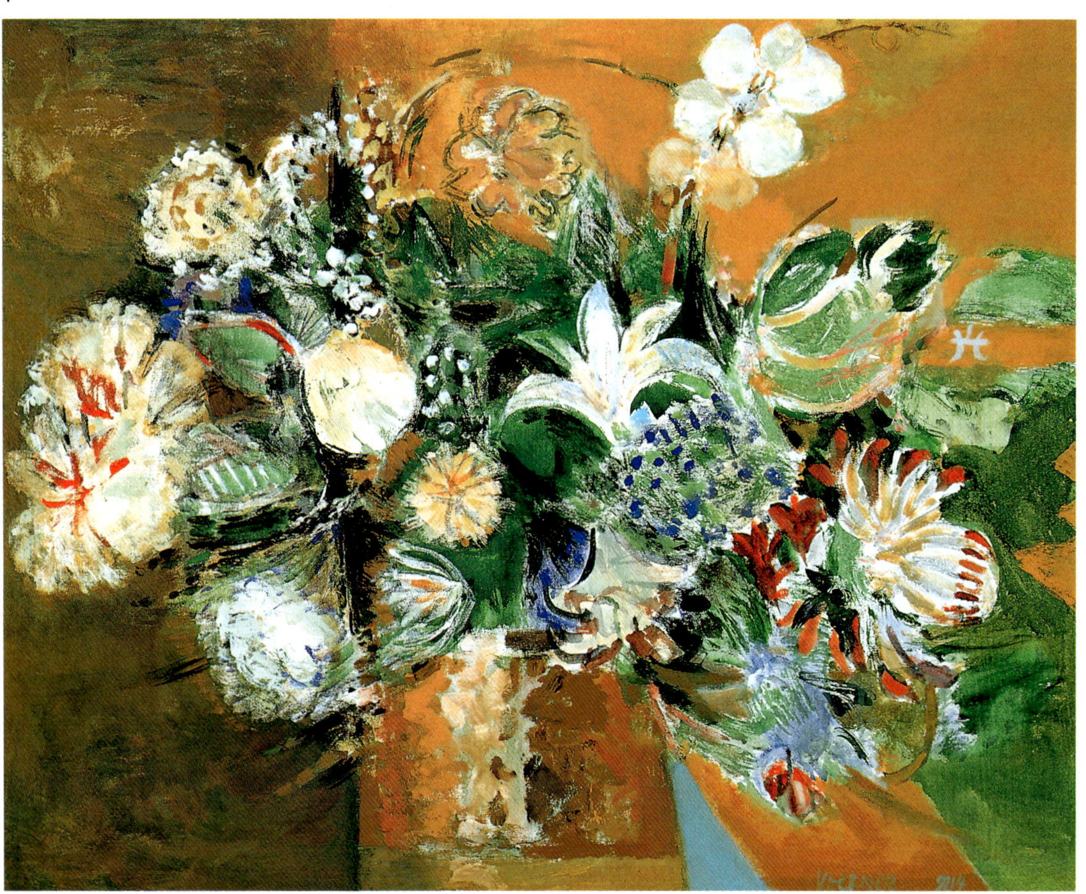

2

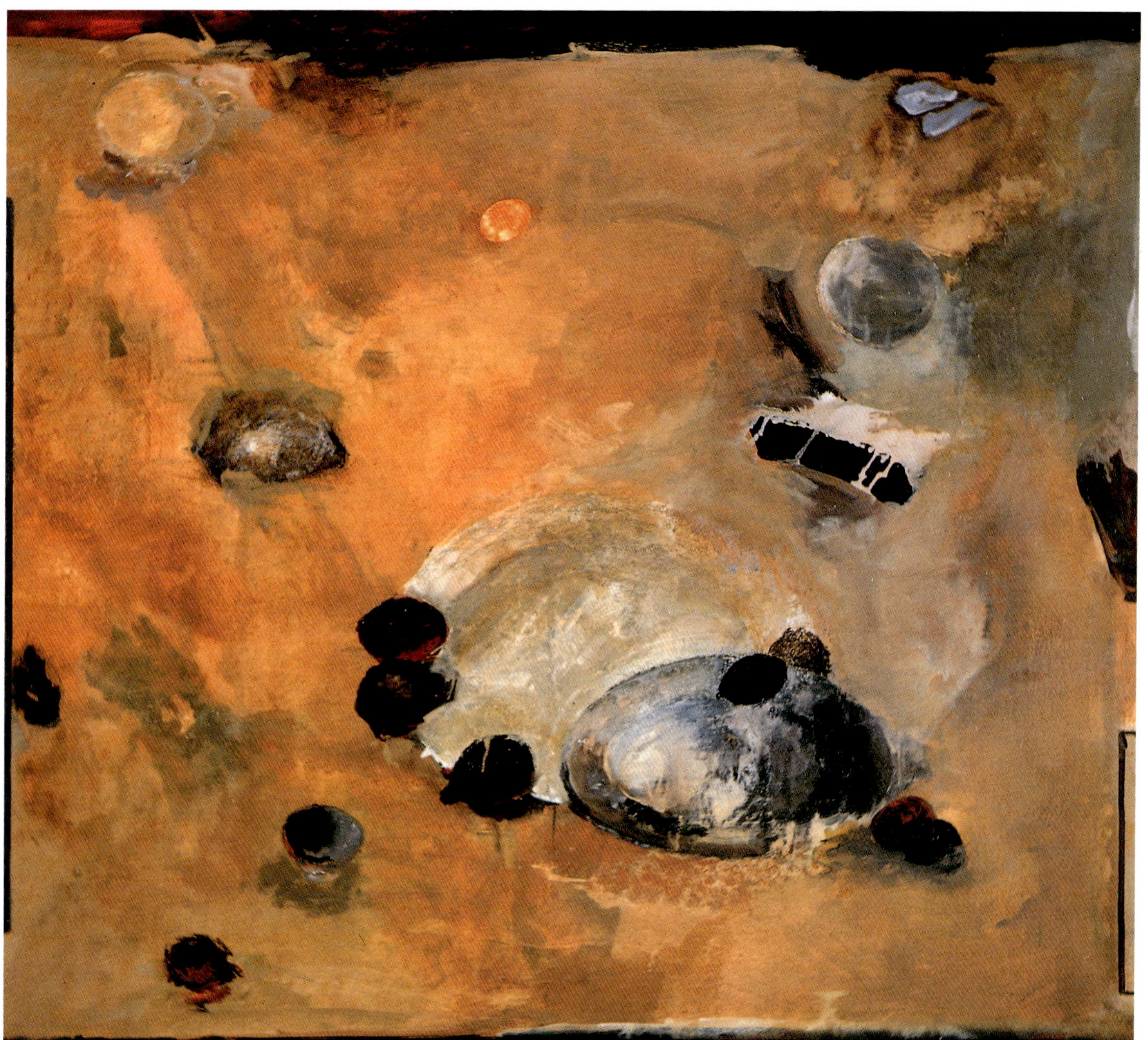

**HOWARD SCOTT
M-13 GALLERY**

72 Greene Street, 2nd Floor
New York, NY 10012
212.925.3007
212.925.3923 FAX

Contact:
Howard Scott

Exhibiting:
Contemporary art

Toon Kuijpers

Silver Plates
1992, Acrylic on canvas,
59" x 67"

Selected Biography:

1993 Howard Scott
M-13 Gallery,
New York, NY

DIANE FARRIS GALLERY

1565 West 7th Avenue
Vancouver B.C. V6J 1S1
Canada
604.737.2629
604.737.2675 FAX

Contact:
Diane Farris, Director

Exhibiting:
Contemporary Canadian
and International Art

Sam Lam

1. *Muse*
   1992-93,
   Acrylic on canvas,
   68" x 99"

2. *The Procession*
   1993, Acrylic on canvas,
   68" x 90"

Selected Biography:

1994 Solo show,
   Diane Farris Gallery,
   Vancouver, BC
1993 China Oil Painting
   Biannual Exhibition,
   National Gallery,
   Beijing, China
1992 Moos Gallery,
   Toronto, ON
1991 Solo show,
   Don Stewart Fine Art,
   Montreal, PQ;
   Echos After the Storm,
   Tiananmen Memorial
   Art Exhibition, travel-
   ling show; Toronto,
   Lincoln, Vancouver

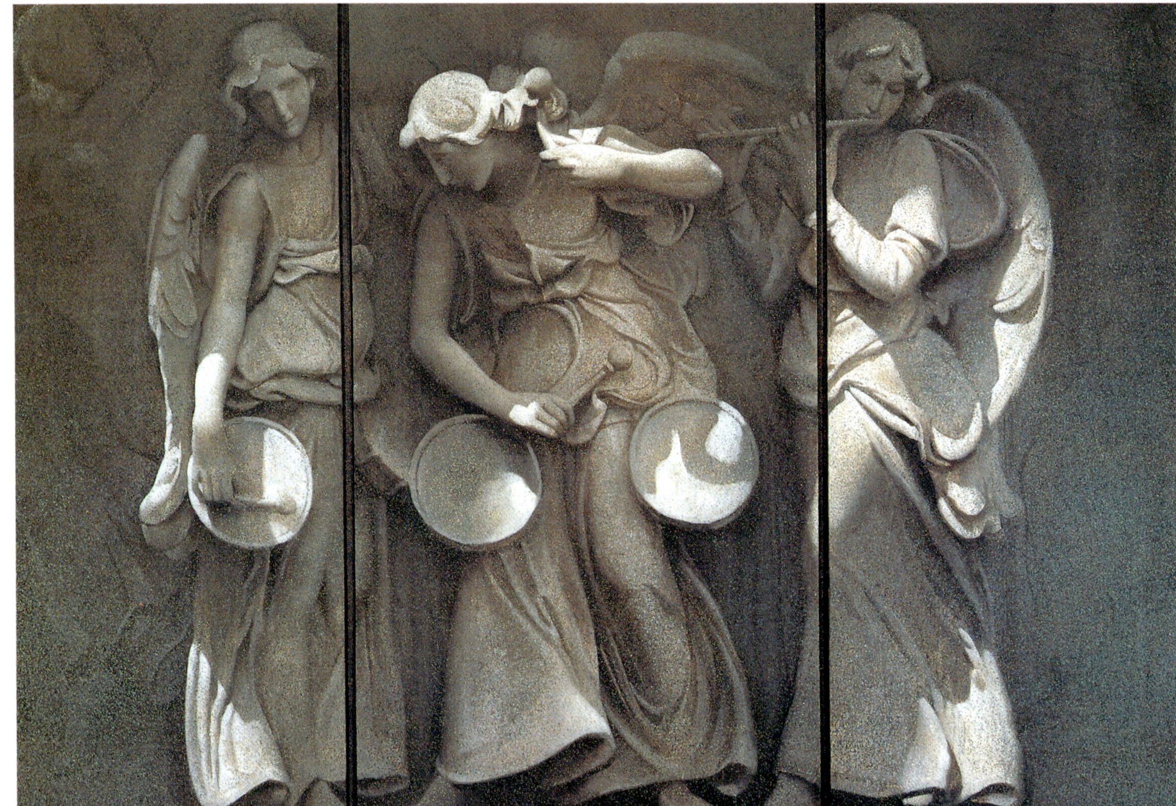

1

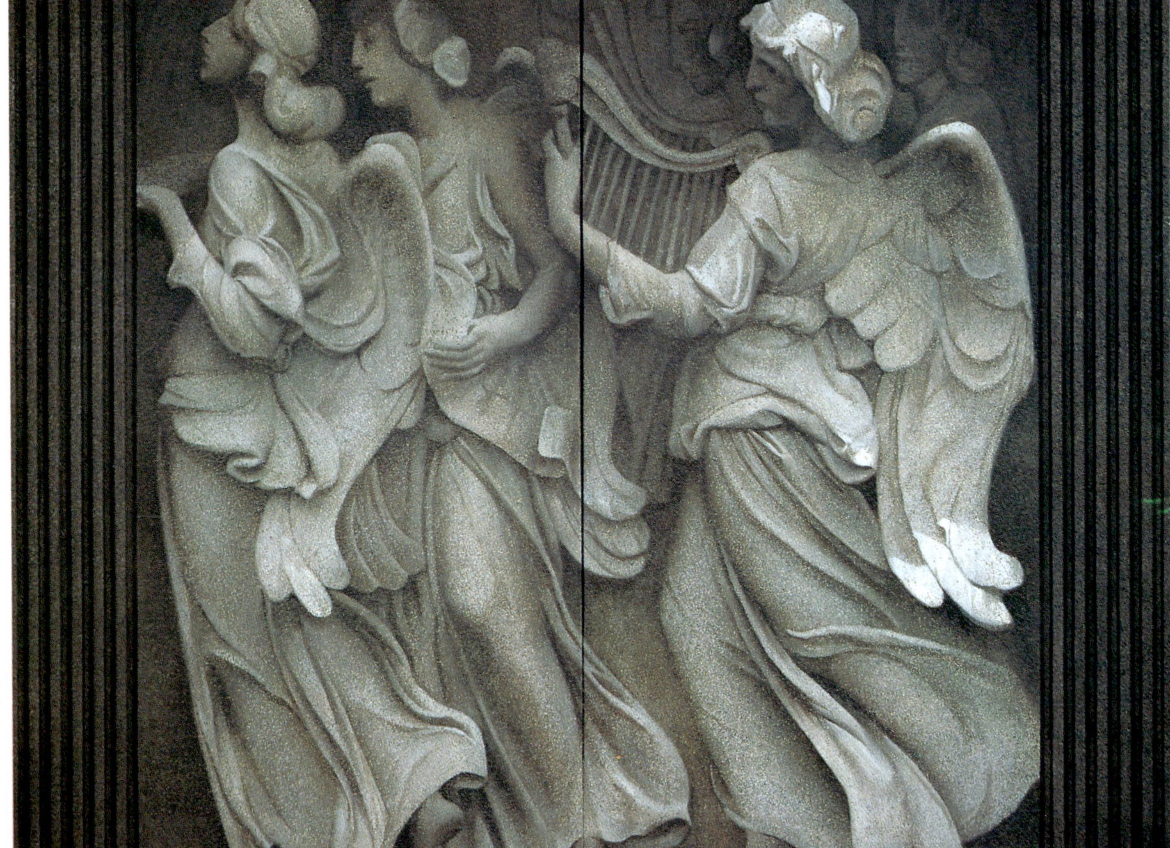

2

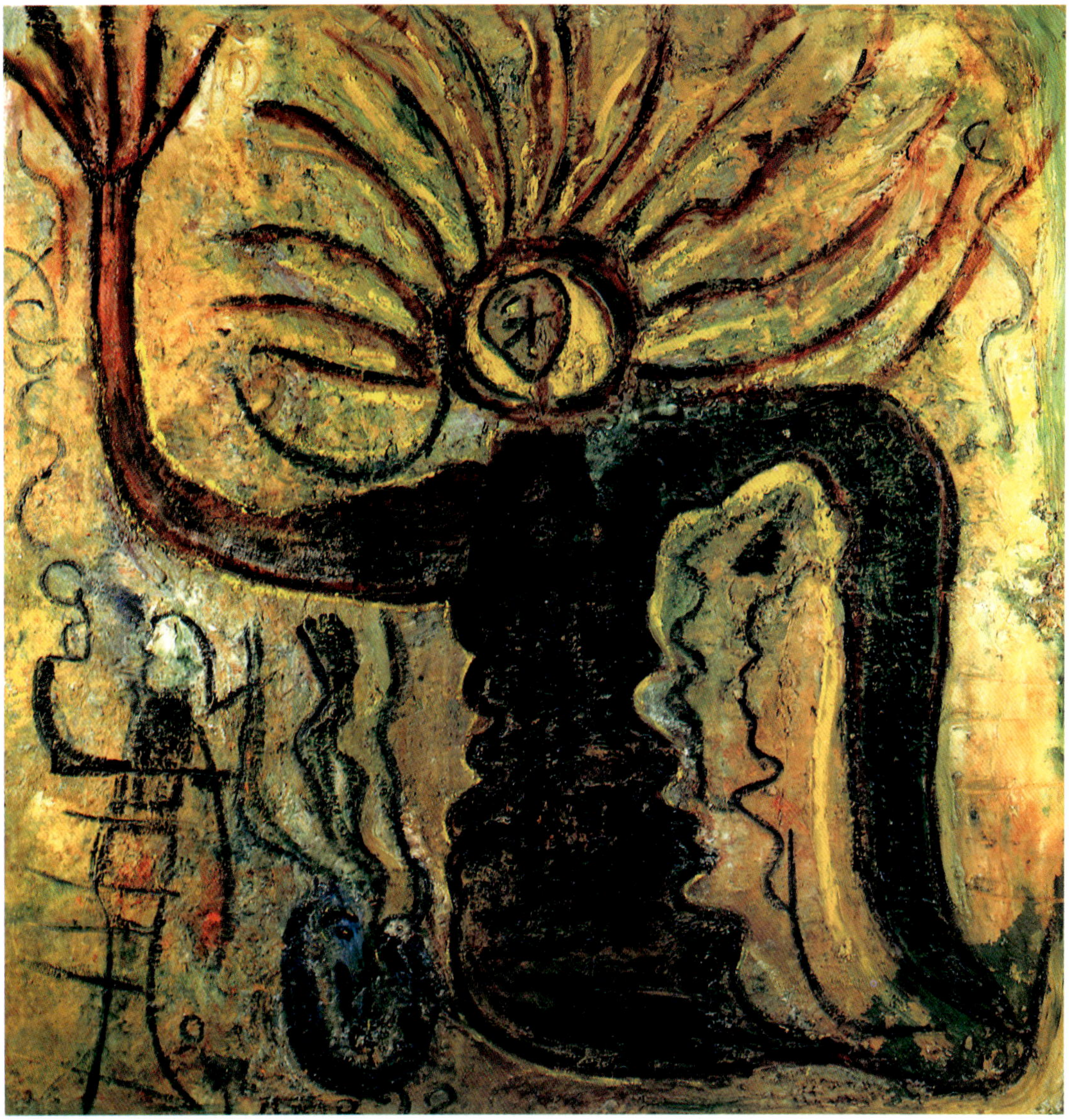

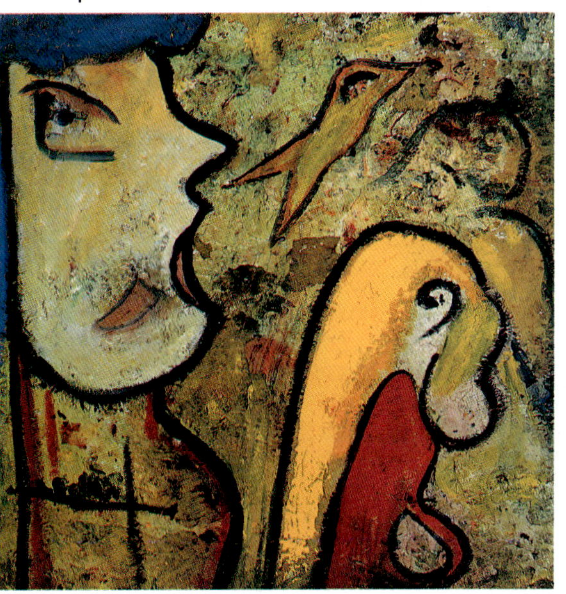

1

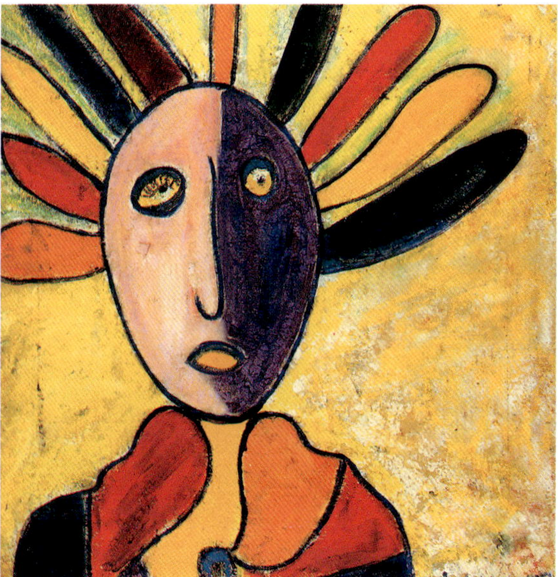

2   3

FASSBENDER ASSOCIATES

Representing Matt Lamb
Nationally & Internationally
415 N. Sangamon
Chicago, IL 60622
312.421.3600
312.733.6496 FAX
Contact:
Ingrid Fassbender

Carole Jones Gallery
Representing Matt Lamb in Chicago
300 W. Superior
Chicago, IL 60610
312.587.8820
312.587.9859 FAX
Contact:
Carole Jones

Matt Lamb

1. *Anchangel Series*
   1993, Mixed media
   concrete & plywood,
   96" x 96"

2. *Untitled*
   1992, Oil on canvas,
   24" x 24"

3. *Indian Series*
   1993, Oil on canvas,
   52" x 48"

Selected Biography:

1994   Modern Art Gallery,
   Vatican Museums,
   Rome, Italy

1993   Carol Jones Gallery,
   Chicago, IL

   Galleria Praxis, Mexico
   City, Mexico

1992   Galerie Berlin,
   Berlin, Germany

   Dolly Fiterman Fine Art
   Minneapolis, MN

UDITA LEBERG STUDIO

67-38 108 Street, Suite C-63
Forest Hills, NY 11375
718.261.0896
By Appointment only

Contact:
Israel Shapiro

Exhibiting:
Contemporary art from
Europe and America by
Udita Leberg

Udita Leberg

1. *The Village Dancers*
   1991, Oil on canvas,
   33" x 34"

2. *The Piano Bar*
   1977, Oil on canvas,
   24" x 31½"

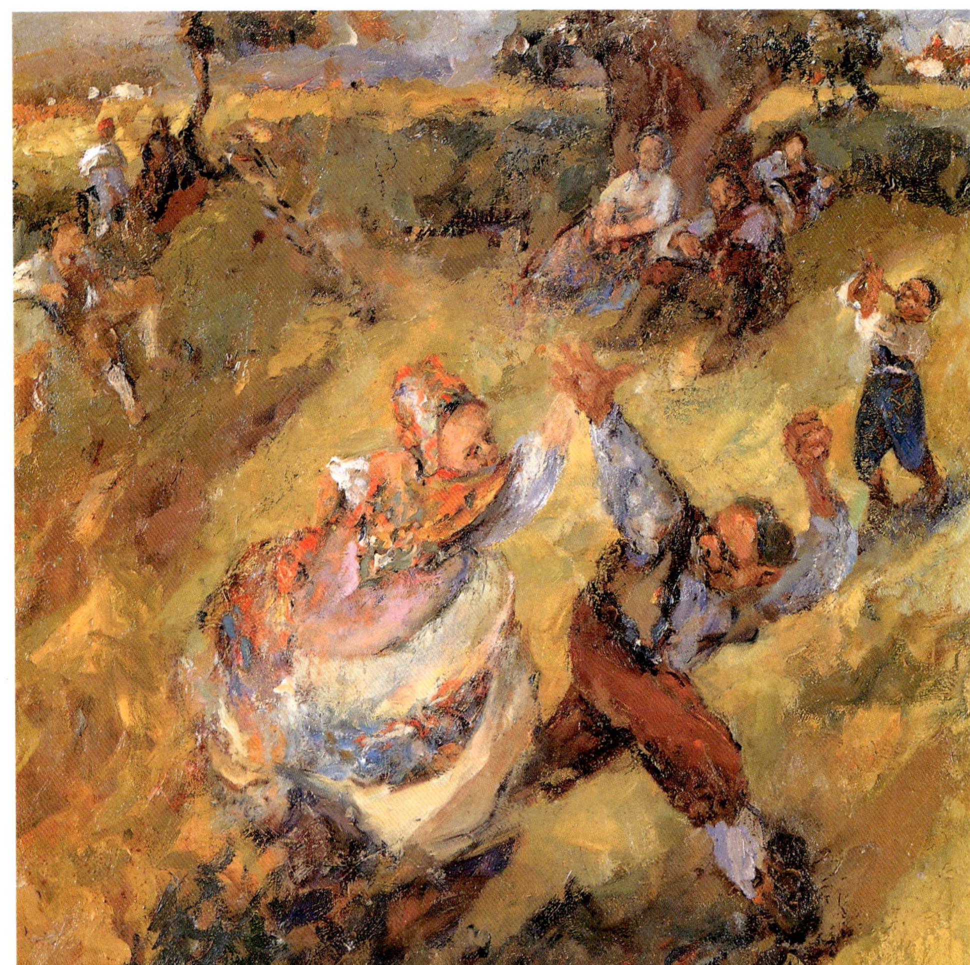

1

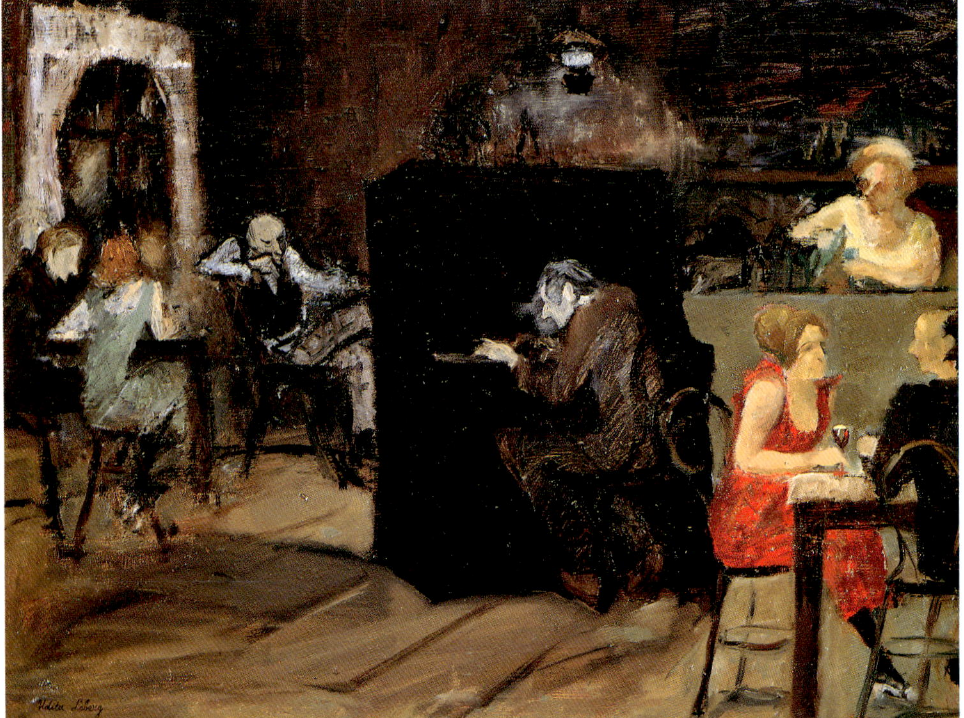

2

Selected Biography:

Born: 1955 in the
Carpathian Mountains.
At age 9 exhibited in
16 countries. The
Soviet government
organized her first
press conference and
exhibition at age 10,
produced two movies
about the child prodigy.
Government scholar-
ship in Moscow's elite
Academy of Fine Arts.
Studied: Budapest,
Jerusalem, Paris,
Honors scholarship
at prestigious New
York Studio School.

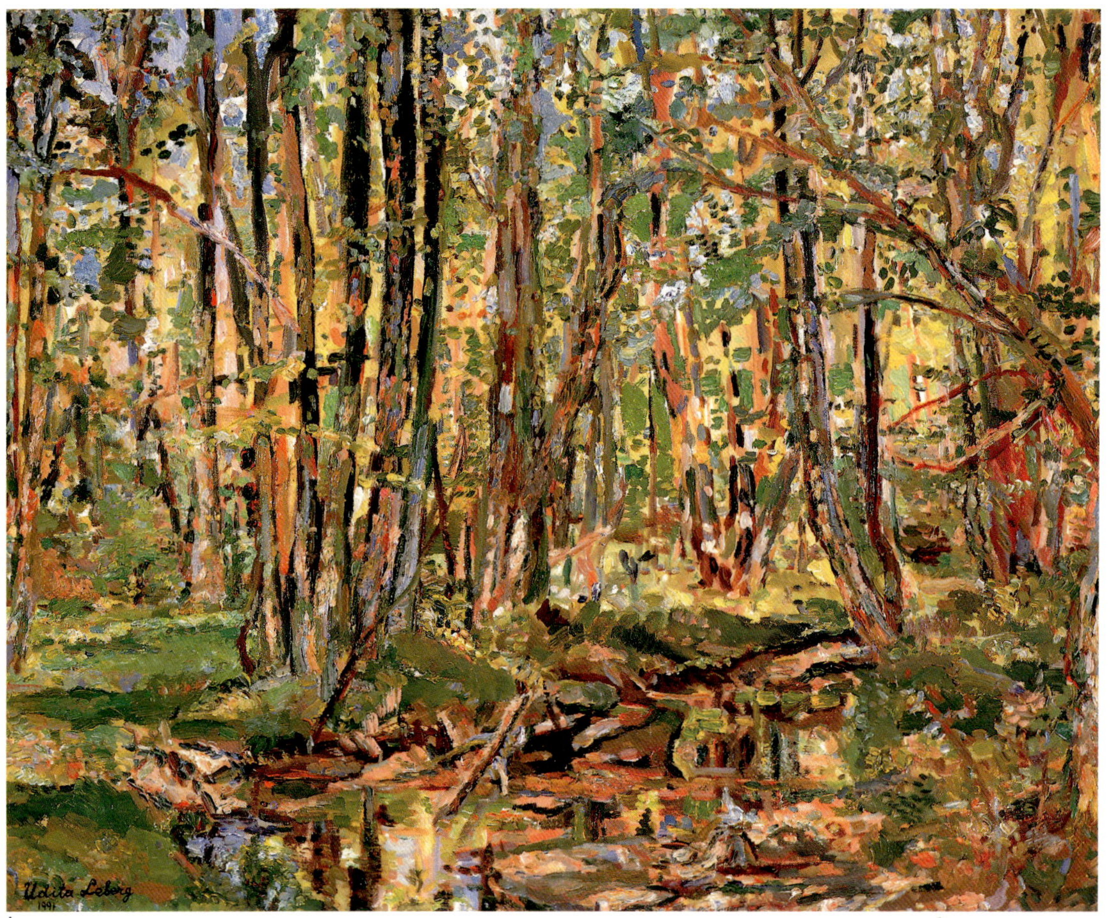

1

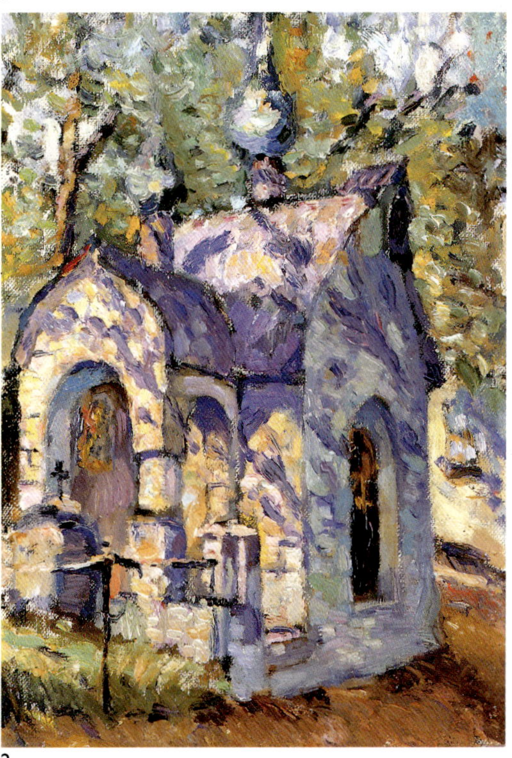

2

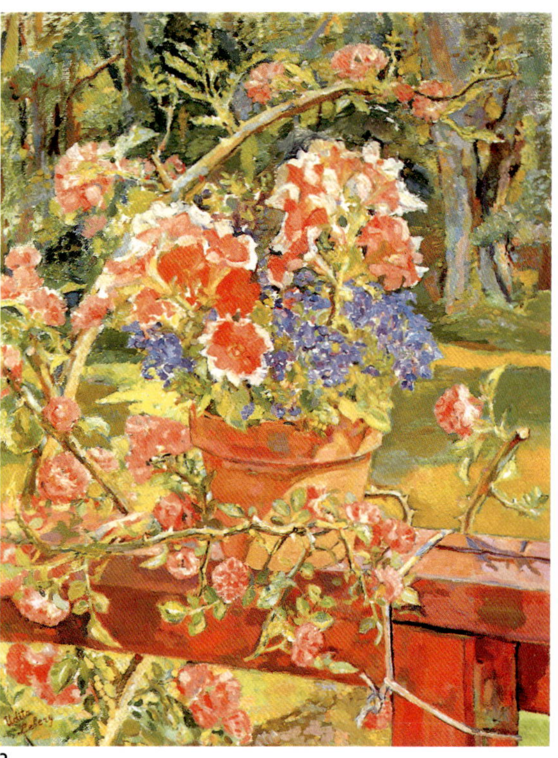

3

UDITA LEBERG STUDIO

67-38 108 Street, Suite C-63
Forest Hills, NY 11375
718.261.0896
By Appointment only

Contact:
Israel Shapiro

Exhibiting:
Contemporary art from
Europe and America by
Udita Leberg

Udita Leberg

1. *The Summer Forest*
   1992, Oil on canvas,
   24" × 30"

2. *An Old Russian Chapel*
   1973, Oil on canvas,
   20" × 14"

3. *Flowers in Clay Vase*
   1993, Oil on canvas,
   30" × 24"

Selected Biography:

Born: 1955 in the
Carpathian Mountains.
At age 9 exhibited in
16 countries. The
Soviet government
organized her first
press conference and
exhibition at age 10,
produced two movies
about the child prodigy.
Government scholar-
ship in Moscow's elite
Academy of Fine Arts.
Studied: Budapest,
Jerusalem, Paris,
Honors scholarship
at prestigious New
York Studio School.

UDITA LEBERG STUDIO

67-38 108 Street, Suite C-63
Forest Hills, NY 11375
718.261.0896
By Appointment only

Contact:
Israel Shapiro

Exhibiting:
Contemporary art from
Europe and America by
Udita Leberg

Udita Leberg

1. *Still Life with Peaches*
   1993, Oil on canvas,
   24" x 30"

2. *The Bolshoi - The Swan Lake*
   1971, Oil on canvas,
   28" x 22"

3. *The Matchmaker*
   1983, Oil on canvas,
   15" x 11"

Selected Biography:

Born: 1955 in the
Carpathian Mountains.
At age 9 exhibited in
16 countries. The
Soviet government
organized her first
press conference and
exhibition at age 10,
produced two movies
about the child prodigy.
Government scholar-
ship in Moscow's elite
Academy of Fine Arts.
Studied: Budapest,
Jerusalem, Paris,
Honors scholarship
at prestigious New
York Studio School.

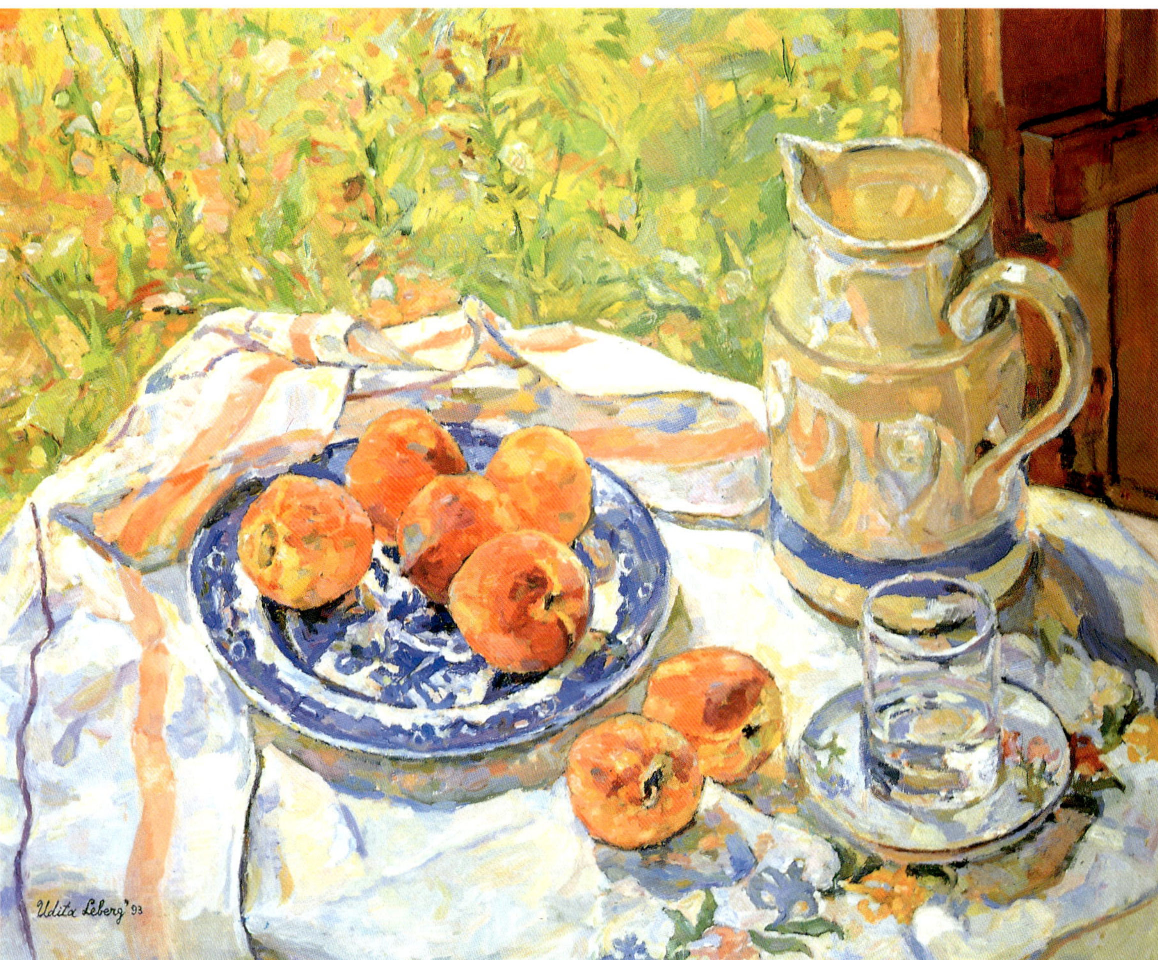

1

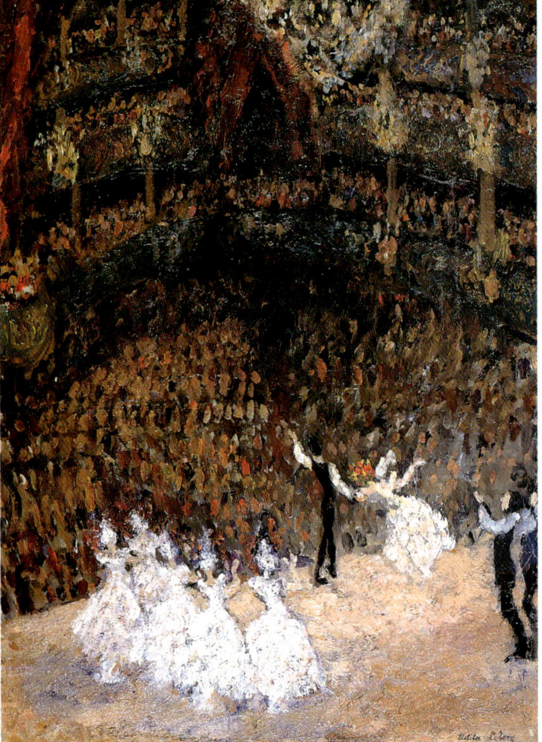

2

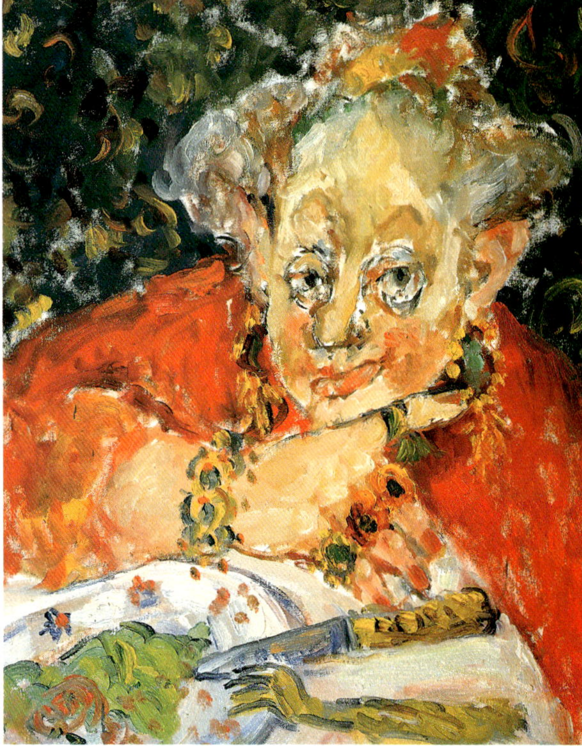

3

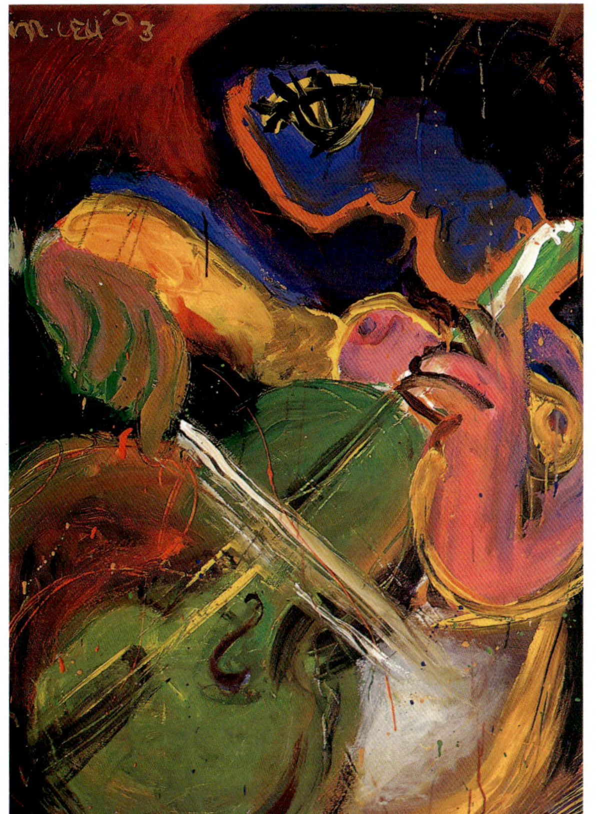

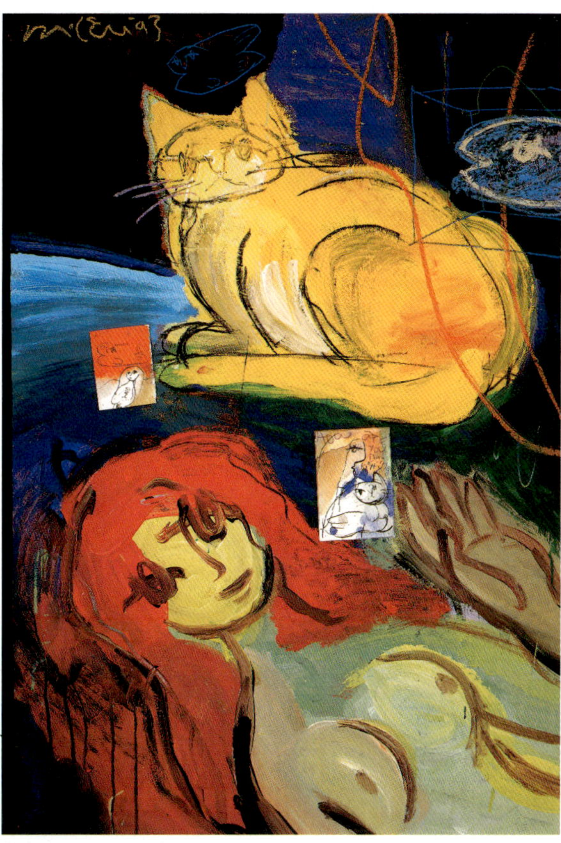

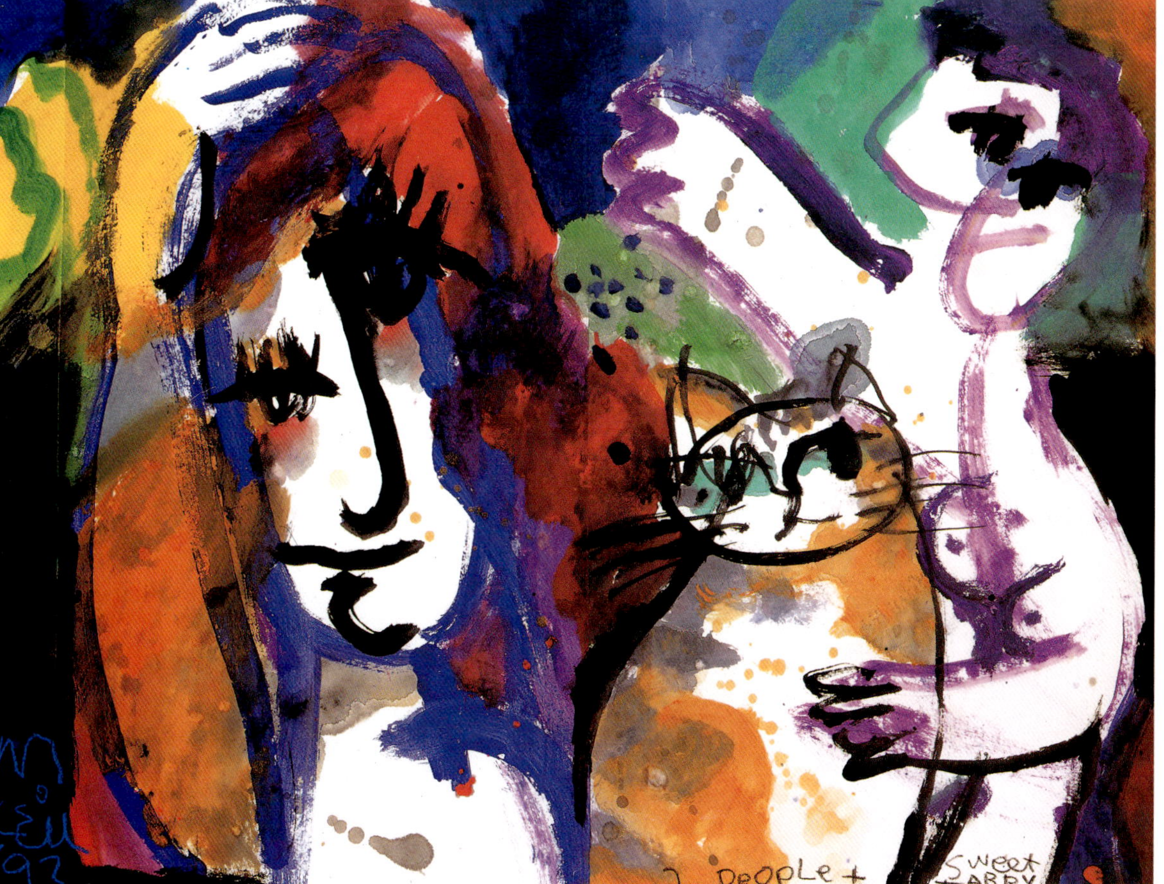

1

2

3

GALLERY LEU INC.

49 Pacheco Creek Dr.
Novato, CA 94949
414.382.9549
415.883.9714 FAX

Contact:
Rachel Leu, Manager

Exhibiting:
Contemporary paintings and prints

Michael Leu

1. *The Cellist*
   1993, Mixed,
   41" x 29.5"

2. *How Are You Doing ? Kitty*
   1993, Mixed,
   41" x 29.5"

3. *2 People + Sweet Tabby*
   1992, Mixed,
   18" x 24"

Selected Biography:

1993 Solo exhibition:
   Apollo Gallery, Taipei,
   Taiwan

   Solo exhibition:
   Genius Gallery, Kobe/
   Gallery Kishi, Osaka,
   Japan

   Frankfurt Art Fair,
   Germany

1992 Solo exhibition:
   The Gallery,
   Indianapolis, IN, USA

O. K. HARRIS
WORKS OF ART

383 West Broadway
New York, NY 10012
212.431.3600

Contact:
Ivan C. Karp

Exhibiting:
Contemporary American
And European painting,
sculpture, photography,
collectables and memorabilia

Josef Levi

*Still Life with Lichtenstein
and De La Tour*
1992, Acrylic and graphite
on canvas, 38" x 58.5"

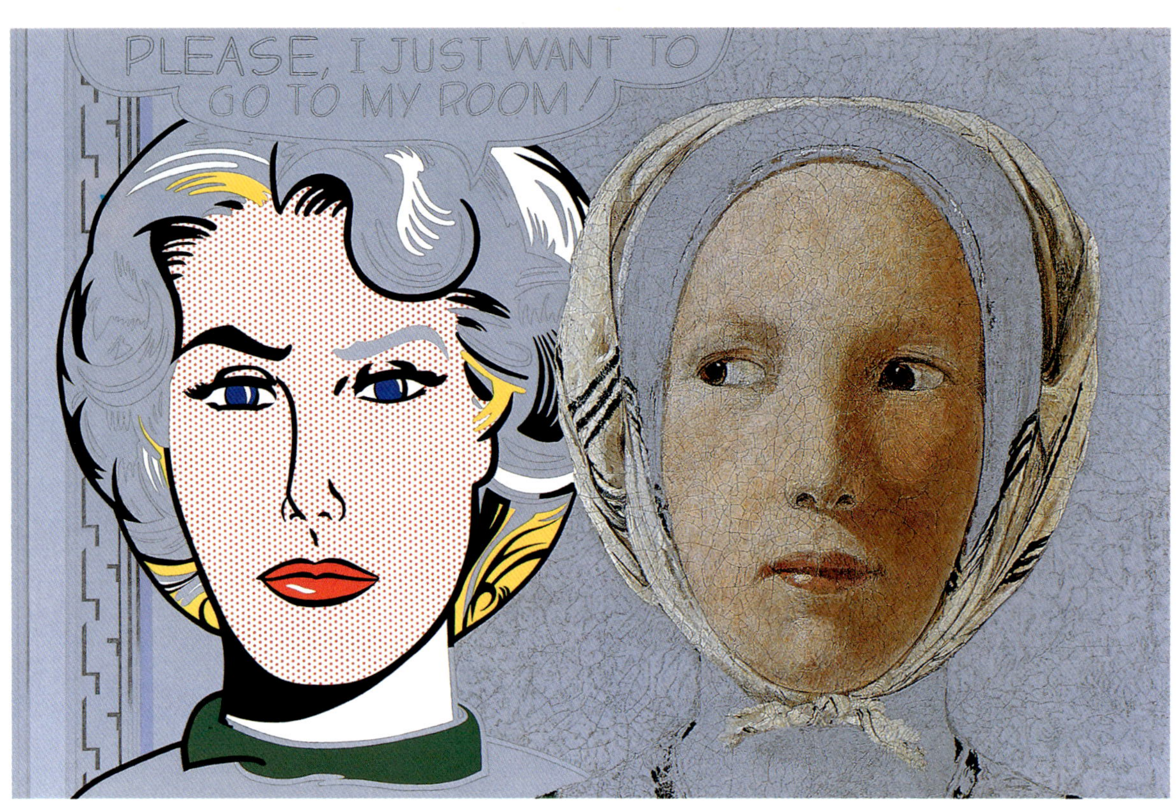

Selected Biography:

1994 O. K. Harris Works Of
Art, New York, NY
1993 "The Purloined Image",
Flint Institute of Arts,
Flint, MI
1992 O. K. Harris Works Of
Art, New York, NY
1990 "The Humanist Icon",
Bayly Art Museum,
University of Virginia,
Charlottesville, VA
1988 "Selections from
the Ellen and
Jerome Westheimer
Collection",
Oklahoma Art Center,
Oklahoma City, OK

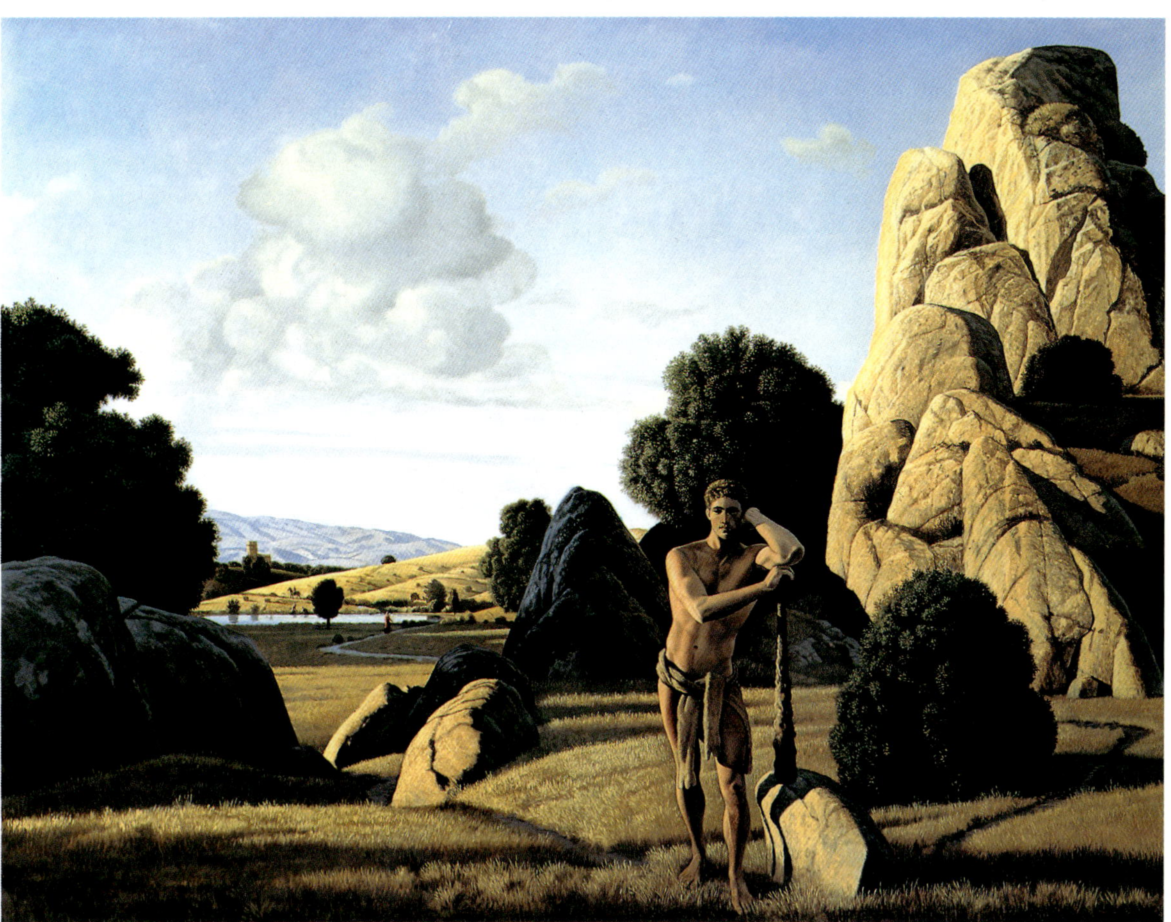

1

STIEBEL MODERN

32 E. 57th St. 6th Fl.
New York, NY 10022
212.759.5536
212.935.5736 FAX

Contact:
Deven Golden, Director

Exhibiting:
Contemporary
representational
painting and drawing

David Ligare

1. *Hercules at the Crossroads*
   1993, Oil on linen,
   60" x 78"
2. *Criteria: Nature, Thought,
   Action*
   1993, Oil on linen,
   16" x 12"

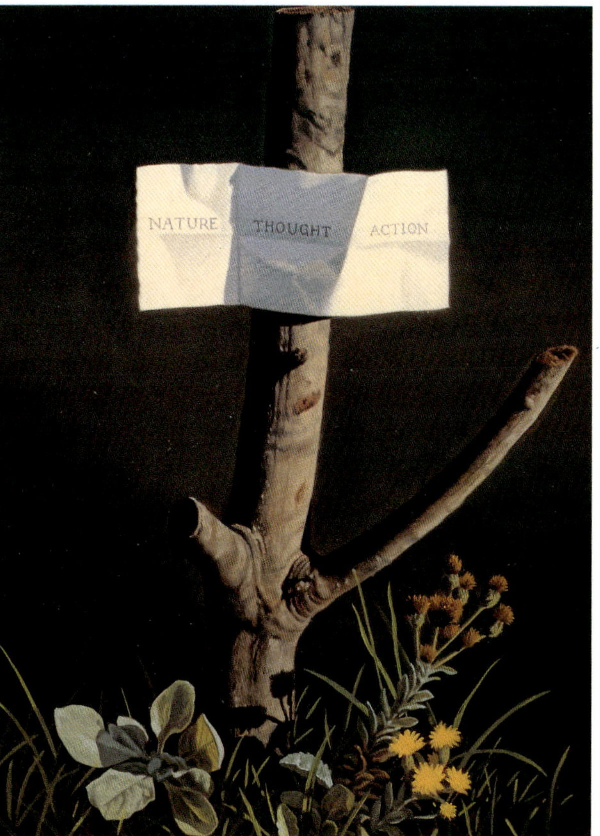

2

Selected Biography:

1993 "The Choice of
        Hercules",
        Stiebel Modern, NY

1992   Koplin Gallery,
        San Monica, CA

        "Stage for
        Contemplation",
        Fresno Museum,
        Fresno, CA

1990 Robert Schoelkopf
        Gallery, NY

C. G. REIN GALLERIES

949 Sibley Memorial Highway
St. Paul, MN 55118-3698
800.328.3158
612.455.7100
612.455.1211 FAX

Contact:
Sterling Blumstein

OTHER GALLERY LOCATIONS:
Minneapolis, MN
Sean Morton 612.927.4331
Scottsdale, AZ
Connie Calhoun 602.941.0900
Houston, TX
Jill Winspear 713.526.4916

Exhibiting:
Contemporary fine art and
sculpture; limited edition
reduction woodcuts, seri-
graphs and lithographs

Earl Linderman

1. *Ten Cents a Dance,*
   1993, Oil on canvas,
   60" x 72"

2. *Rhythm and Blues at the
   Stork Club,*
   1993, Oil on canvas,
   62" x 72"

The saga of Doktor Thrill
continues to flourish by way
of Earl Linderman's fantasies;
so does the dancing, the
wine and the romance. "I
think that DoktorThrill taps
into what everybody wants -
the good life," proclaims
Linderman. "He's the proper
vehicle for you and me to do
anything, limited only by
our imaginations."

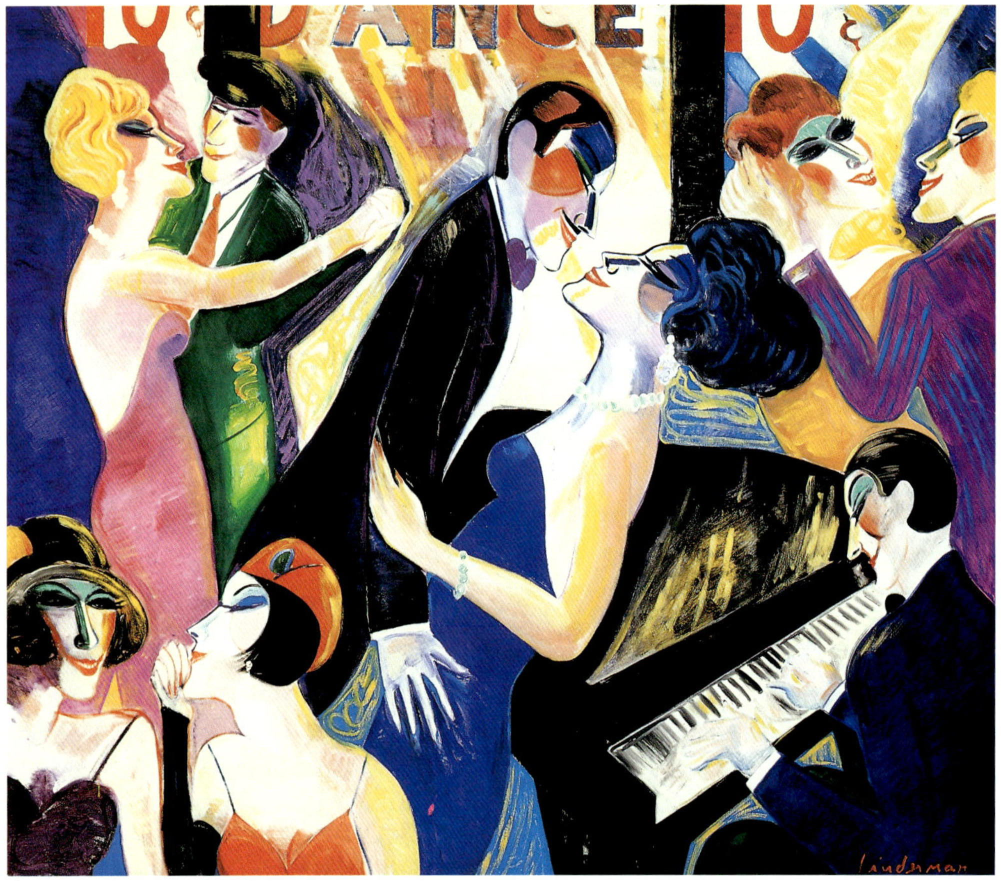

1

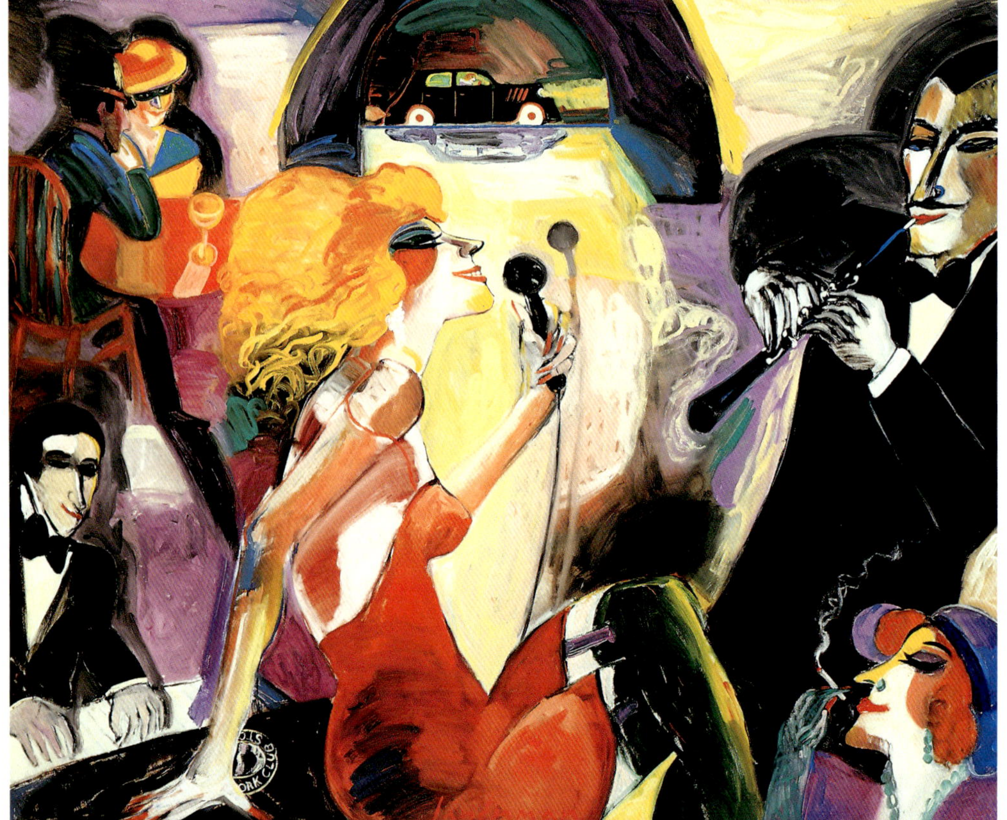

2

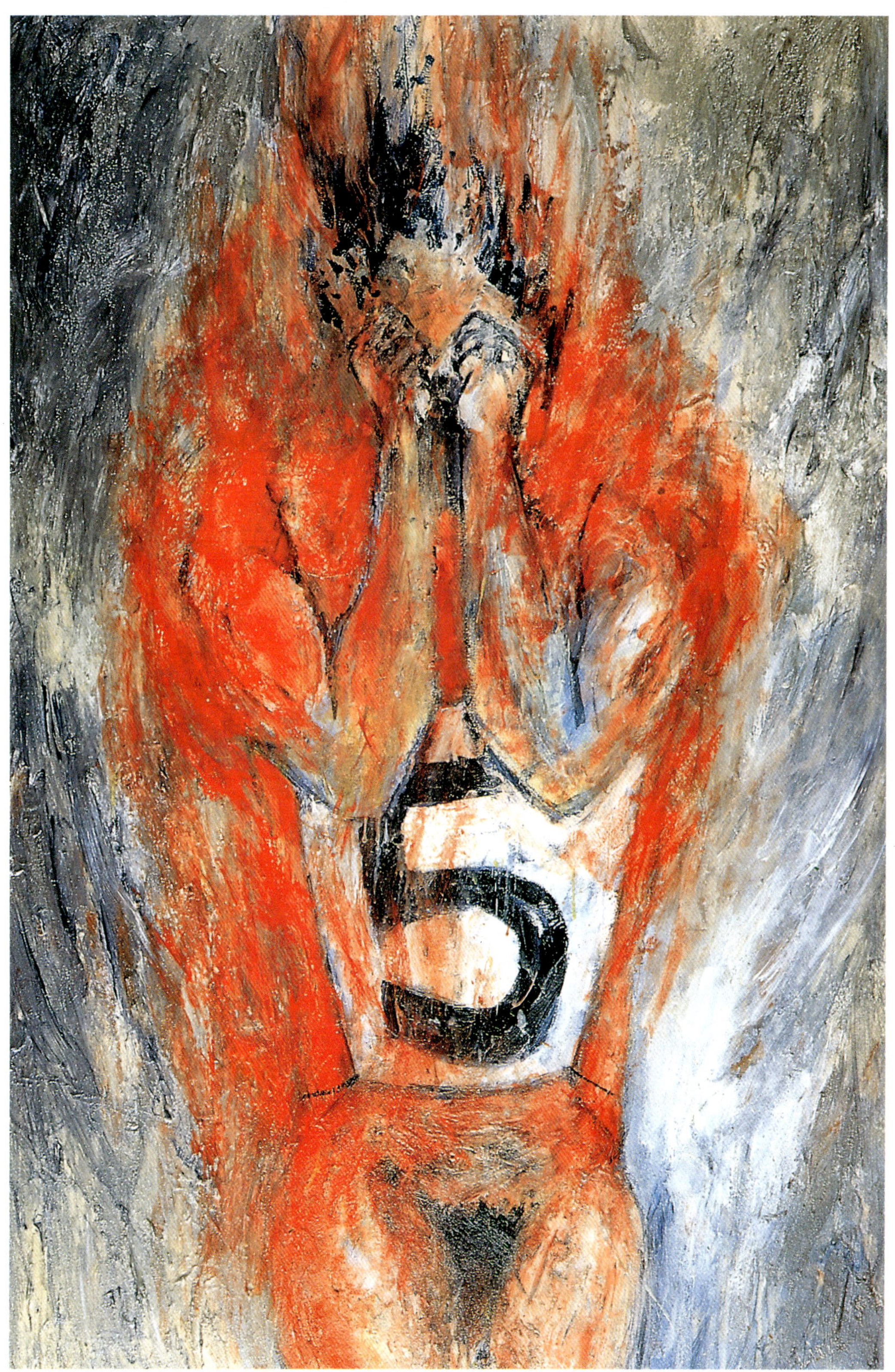

ENID OKLA HOMA

233 West Huron
Chicago, IL 60610
312.787.6011
312.787.6617 FAX

Contact:
Celeste Sotola, Director

Exhibiting:
Contemporary painting,
sculpture, and objects

Mike Linz

The Contestant
1994, Acrylic, 40" x 74"

ARTE NUCLEO GALERIA

Edgar Allan Poe 308,
Col. polanco
Mexico DF 11560
Mexico
525.254.3732
525.531.6875
525.531.2905
525.254.1942 FAX

Contact:
Diana Ripstein de Nankin,
Director

Exhibiting:
Classic and contemporary
Latin American art

Agueda Lozano

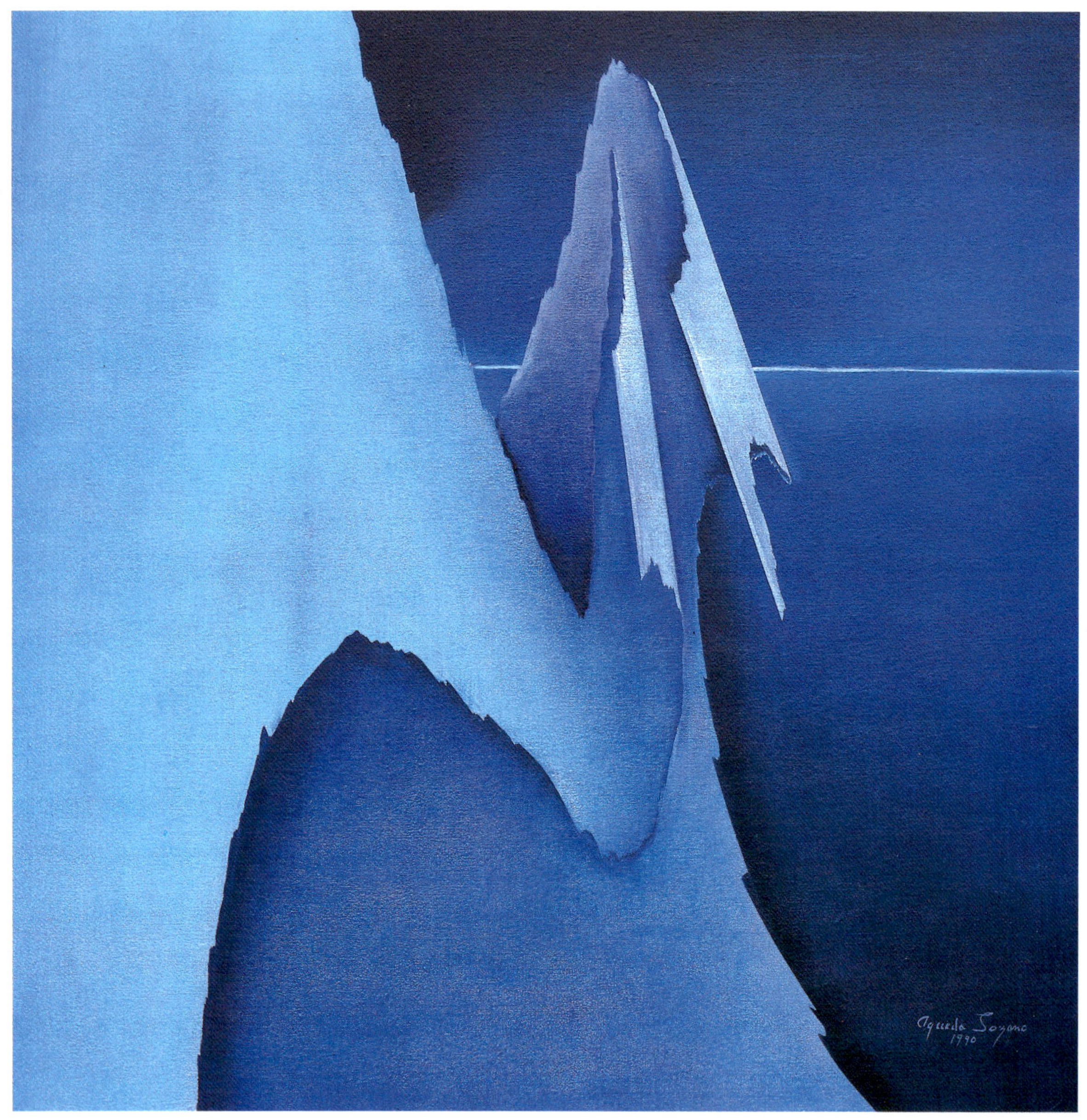

Una Ola En La Montaña
1990, Acrilico/Tela,
150 x 150 cms.
Photograph by
Manuel Zavala

Prizes:
1978 Special mention on "La
Biennial Ibero
Americana in Mexico"
1972-73
Obtains the prize in
the "Festival De
Cagnes/Mer"

Solo Exhibitions:
1993 Centre Culturelle du
Mexique, Paris, France;
Museo Biblioteca Pape,
Monclova, Coah.
1988 Inst. Cultural Mexicano,
San Antonio, Texas
1984 Instituto Nacional de
Bellas Artes, Mexico,
D.F., Mexico
1979 Centro de Bellas Artes,
Maraicaibo, Venezuela
1976 Museo Nacional de
Arte Moderno, Mexico,
D.F., Mexico

Selected Biography:
1944 Born in Cuauhtémoc,
Edo. de Chihuahua, MX

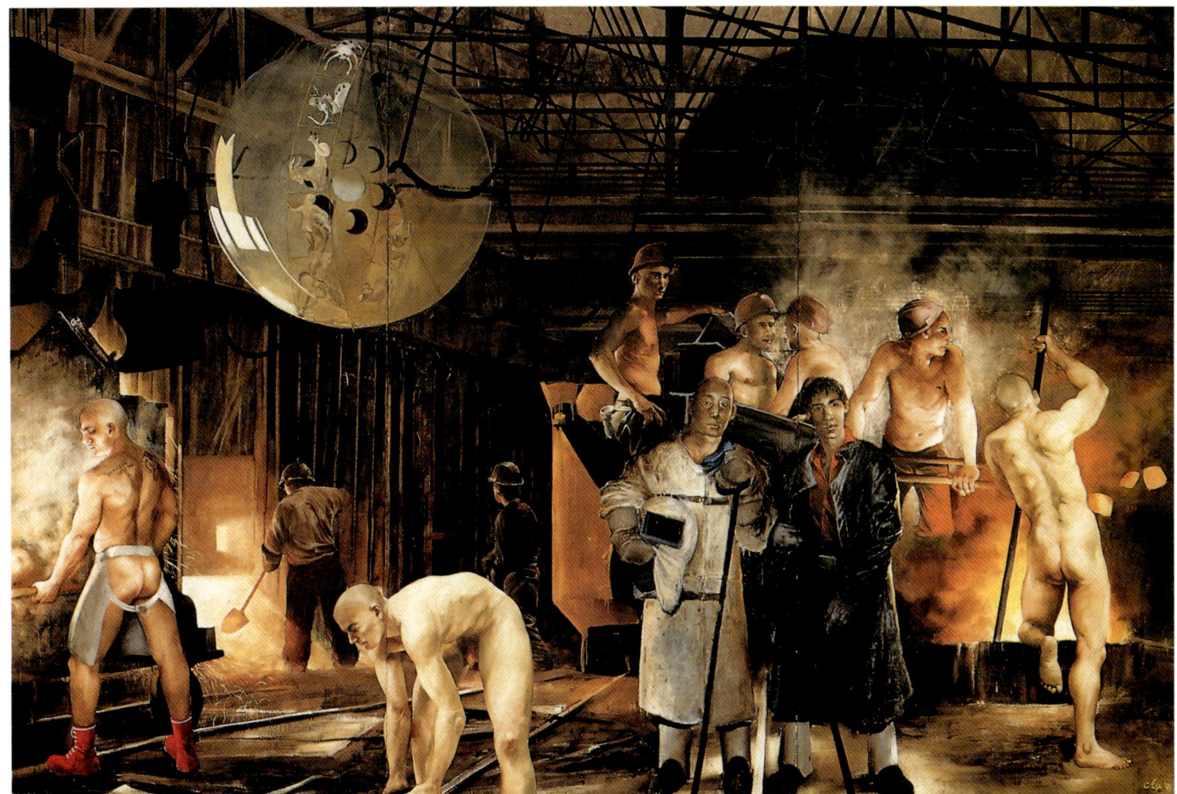

1

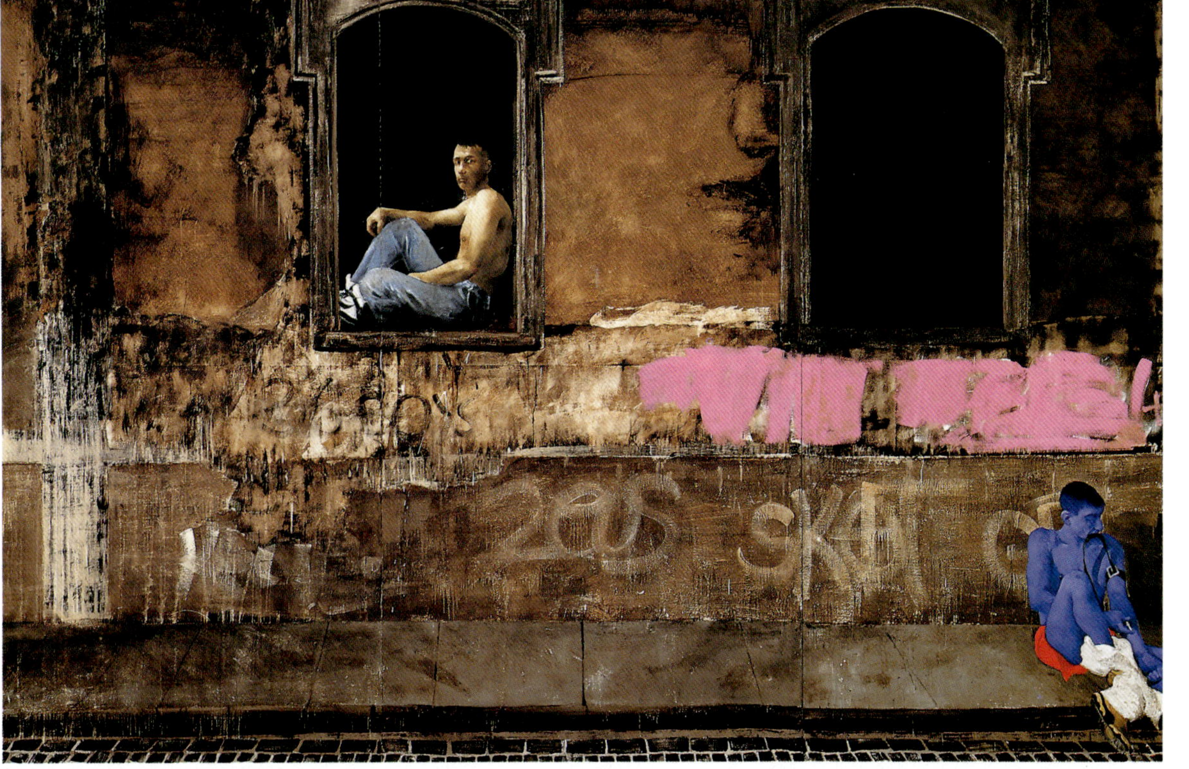

2

DIANE FARRIS GALLERY

1565 West 7th Avenue
Vancouver B.C. V6J 1S1
Canada
604.737.2629
604.737.2675 FAX

Contact:
Diane Farris, Director

Exhibiting:
Contemporary Canadian
and International Art

Attila Richard Lukacs

1. *Tomorrow and Tomorrow
   and Tomorrow*
   1991, Oil on canvas,
   154" x 240"

2. *Everybody Wants
   The Same Thing*
   1993, Oil on canvas,
   154" x 240"

Selected Biography:
1994 Ewerk, Musee
     d'Art Contemporain
     de Montreal,
     Montreal, Quebec
1993 The Anxious Salon,
     MIT list Visual
     Arts Centre,
     Cambridge, MA;
     Interferenzin-Kunst aus
     West Berlin 1960-90,
     Rige, USSR;
     St. Petersberg, USSR
     Seoul International
     Art Festival, The
     National Museum of
     Contemporary Art,
     Seoul, Korea
1992 Varieties of Love,
     Diane Farris Gallery,
     Vancouver, BC
     Documenta IX,
     Kassel, Germany

FENIX FINE ARTS

180 N.E. 40th St.
Miami, FL 33137
305.573.2727
305.542.8289
305.576.7707 FAX

Contact:
George Gandelman

Exhibiting:
Latin American Art

Mario Madrigal-Arcia

1. *Fruta-Ofrenda*
    1992, Oil on canvas,
    115 cms. x 100 cms.

2. *Frutas, Objetos con Paisaje Lacustre*
    1992, Oil on Canvas,
    120 cms. x 130 cms.

3. *Fruta, Objetos y Volcanto (Fruit, Objects & the Song of The Volcano)*
    1993, Oil on Canvas,
    123 cms. x 113 cms.

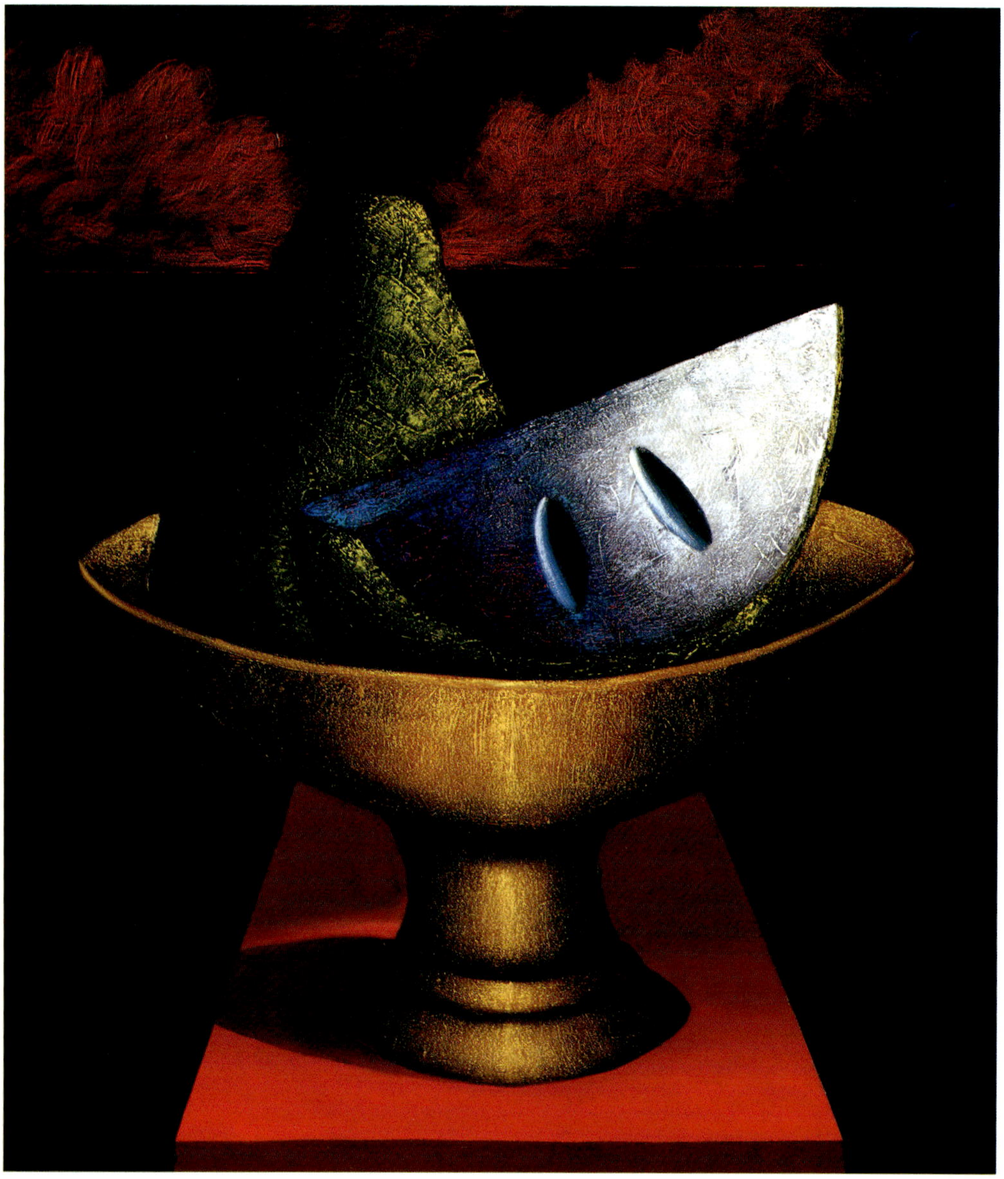

Selected Biography:

1994 Gandelman's "Fenix Six 1994", Miami, FL

1993 The Americas Gallery, "Casa Latina", New York, NY

The Florida Museum of Hispanic & Latin American Art, Spring International Competition, Second place winner, Miami, FL (With work shown above "Frutas-Ofrenda", image 1)

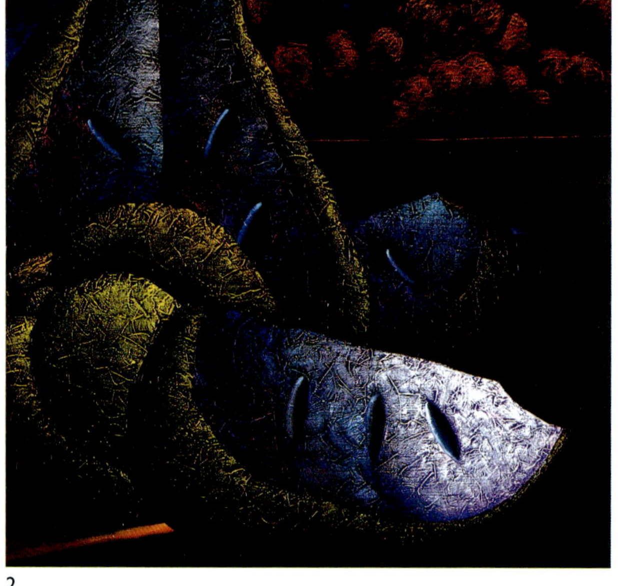

1

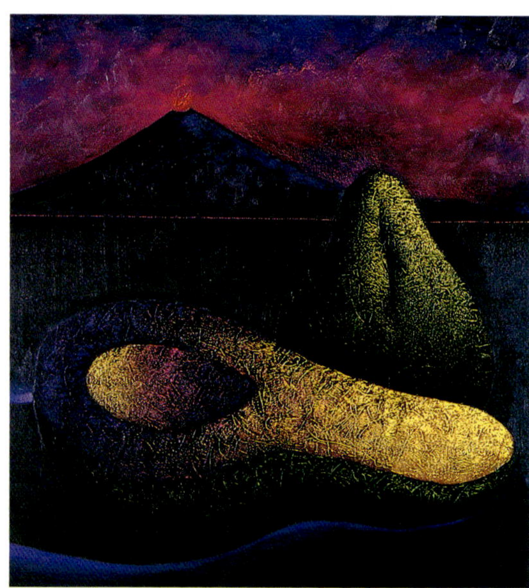

2

3

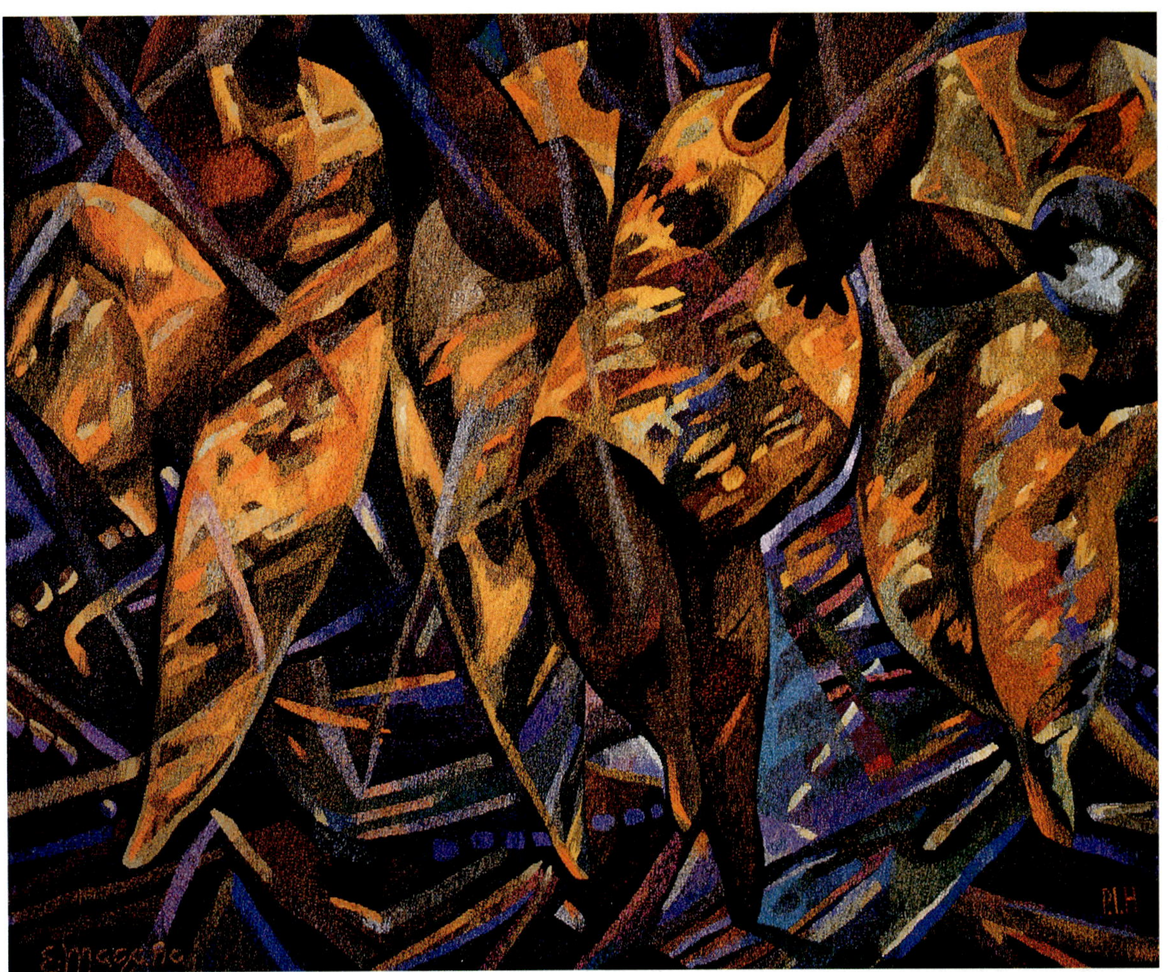

1

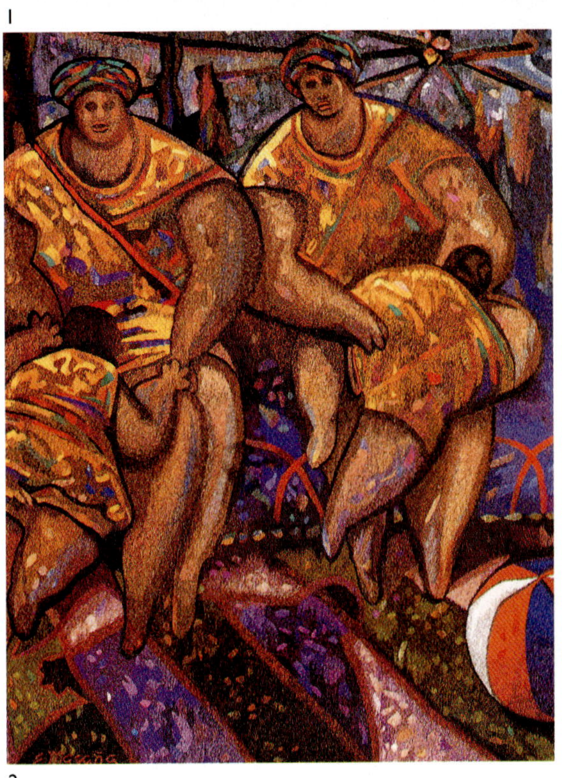

2

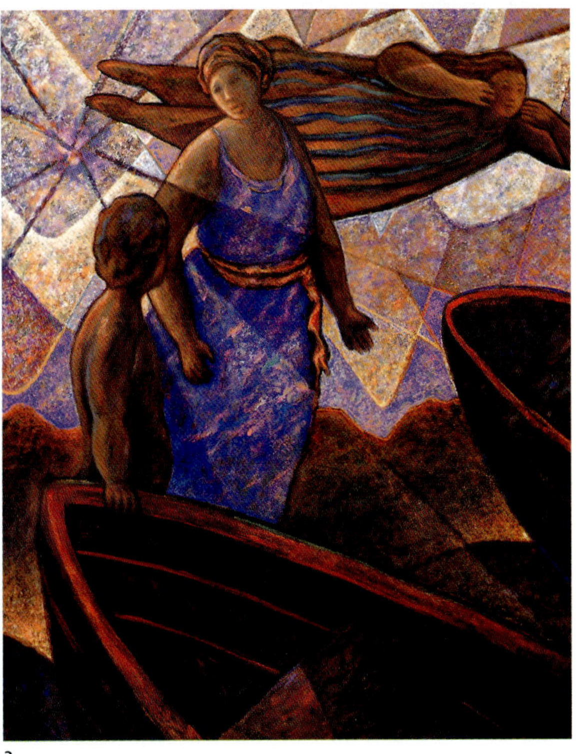

3

GALERIA VERTICE

Lopez Cotilla 2285
44120 Guadalajara, Jalisco,
Mexico
3.630.1330
3.630.1330 FAX

Contact:
Enrique Magaña, Director

Exhibiting:
Contemporary Mexican art

Enrique Magaña

1. *Fandango II*
   1993, Tapestry,
   84" x 96"

2. *La Sombra*
   1993, Tapestry,
   104.5" x 86.7"

3. *Presagio*
   1993, Acrylic on canvas,
   53" x 43.5"

Selected Biography:

1994   Miami Art Expo
       Chicago Int. Art Expo

1993   Miami Art Expo

1993-1984
       Solo exhibitions in
       Mexico

1966   Studies fine arts in
       Guadalajara, Mexico

1951   Born in Zamora,
       Mexico

ROCFERN
INTERNATIONAL
GALLERIES, INC.

80 Carlauren Road Unit17
Woodbridge (Toronto),
Ontario L4L 7Z5 Canada
905.850.7647
905.850.8062 FAX

Contact:
Rocco Pannese
Fernando Rocco

Ernesto Manera

1. *Microcosmos Hembra I*
   1993, Mixed media
   on burlap, 64" x 43"

2. *Matter I*
   1992, Mixed media
   on burlap, 43" x 38"

3. *Microcosmos IX*
   1992, Mixed media
   on tar paper, 23" x 17¼"

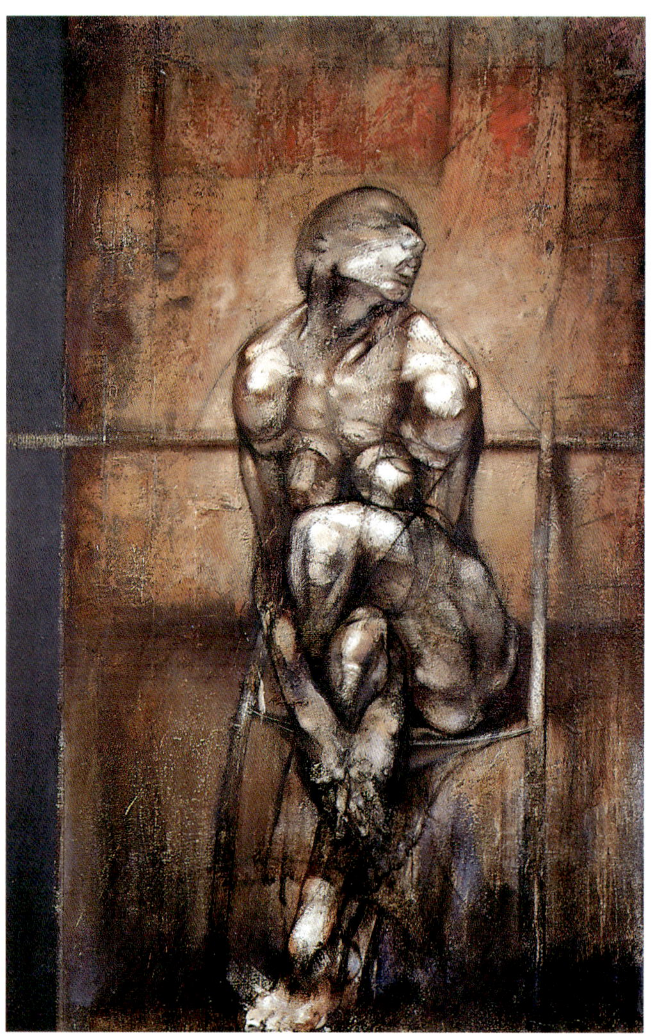

1

Selected Biography:

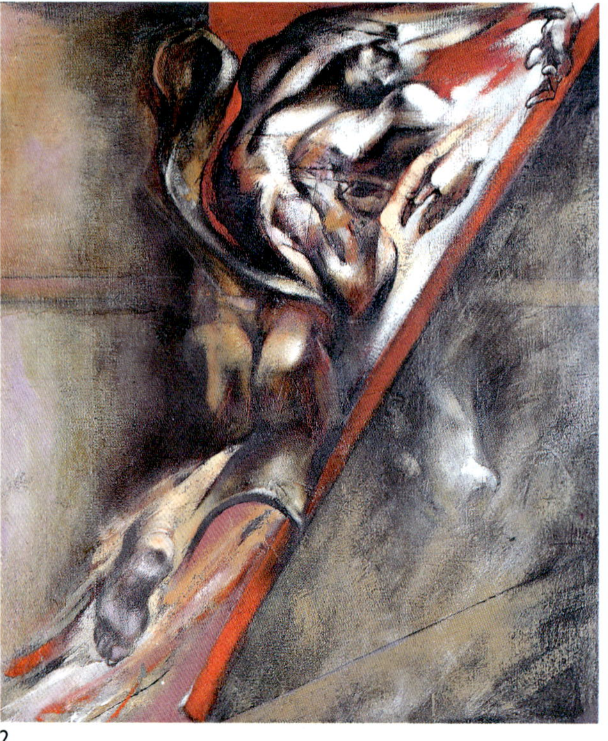

2

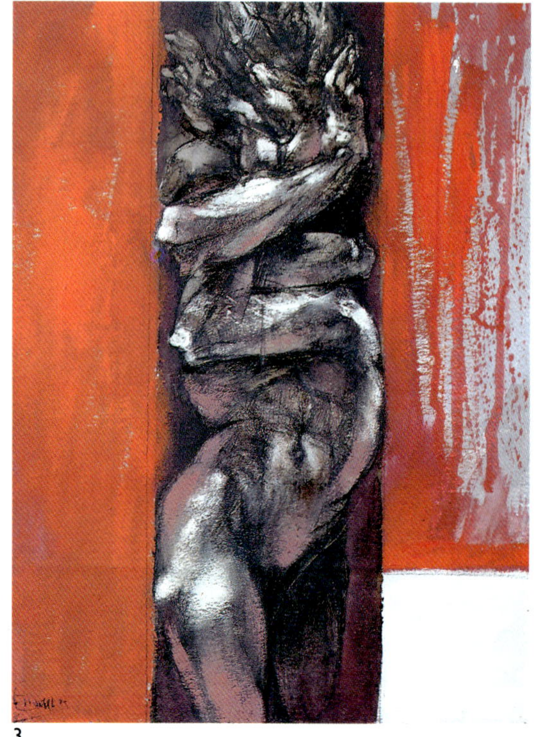

3

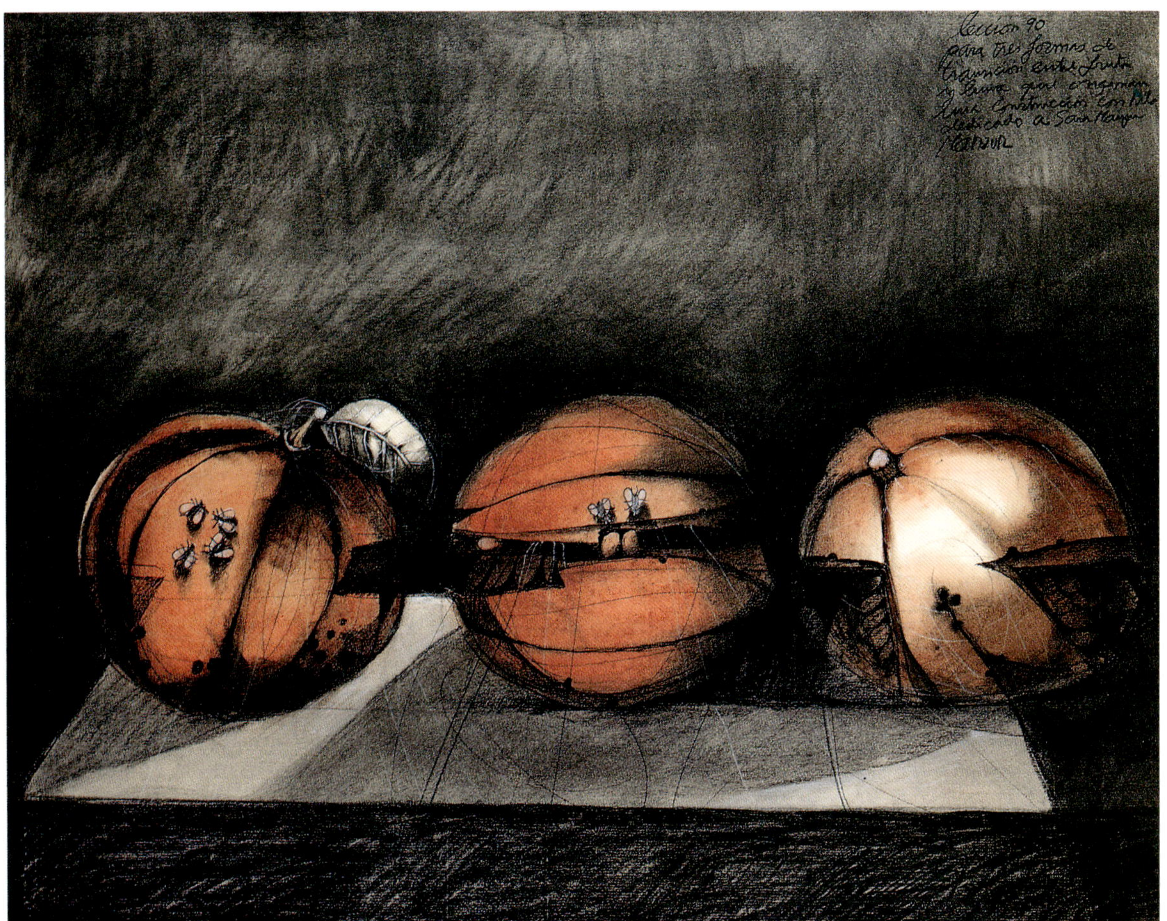

1

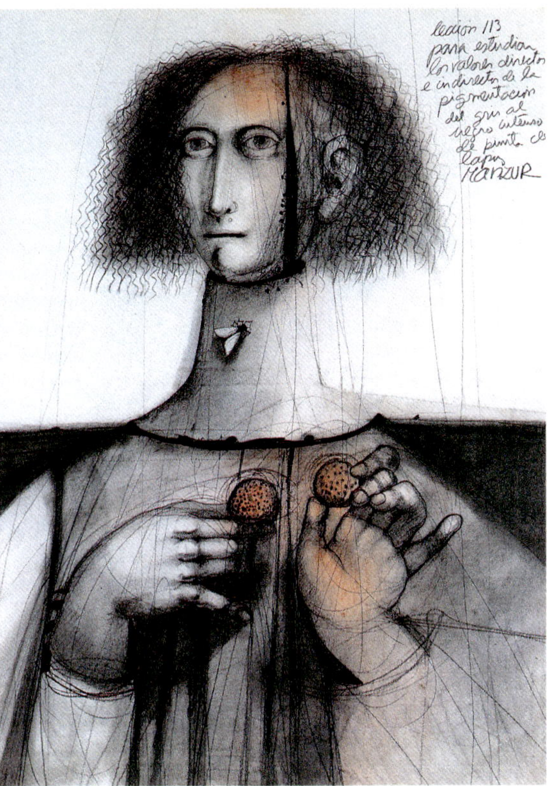

2

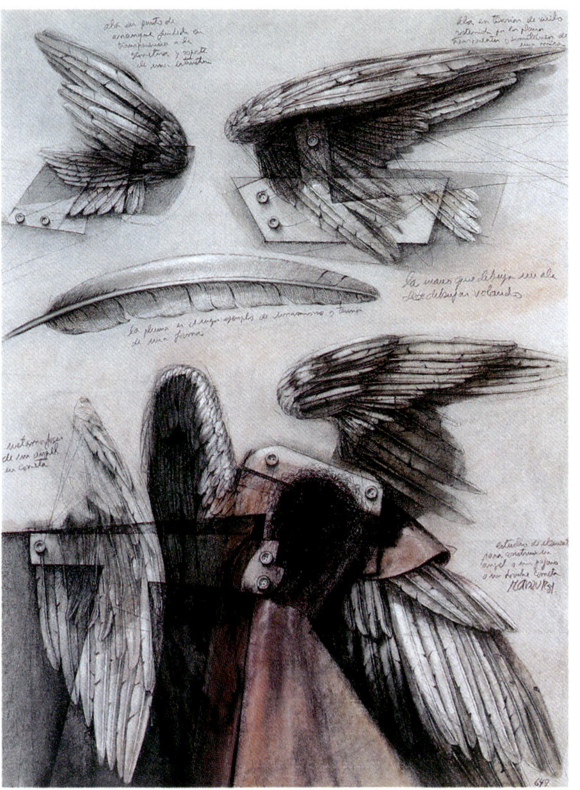

3

FENIX FINE ARTS

180 N.E. 40th St.
Miami, FL 33137
305.573.2727
305.542.8289
305.576.7707 FAX

Contact:
George Gandelman

Exhibiting:
Latin American Art

David Manzur

1. *Leccion 90, Para tres formas de transicion entre frutas y Luna...*
   Mixed media on Paper, 65 cms. x 50 cms.

2. *Leccion 113, Para estudiar los valores directos e indirectos de la pigmentacion del gris al negro en punta de lapiz*
   Mixed media on Paper, 65 cms. x 50 cms.

3. *Estudio de elementos para construir un angel o un pajaro o un hombre cometa*
   1981, Mixed media on Paper, 65 cms. x 50 cms.

Selected Biography:

1993 Gandelman's "The Best of Fenix 93", Fenix Fine Arts, Miami, FL

1992 Exposevilla, Seville, Spain

1991 Museum of Modern Art, Bogota, Colombia

ROCFERN
INTERNATIONAL
GALLERIES, INC.

80 Carlauren Road Unit17
Woodbridge (Toronto),
Ontario L4L 7Z5 Canada
905.850.7647
905.850.8062 FAX

Contact:
Rocco Pannese
Fernando Rocco

Michael Marchese

1. *Woman*
   1993, Acrylic and ink
   on paper, 22" x 22"

2. *Dove*
   1993, Acrylic and ink
   on paper, 22" x 22"

3. *Baby*
   1993, Acrylic and ink
   on paper, 22" x 22"

4. *Wine*
   1993, Acrylic and ink
   on paper, 22" x 22"

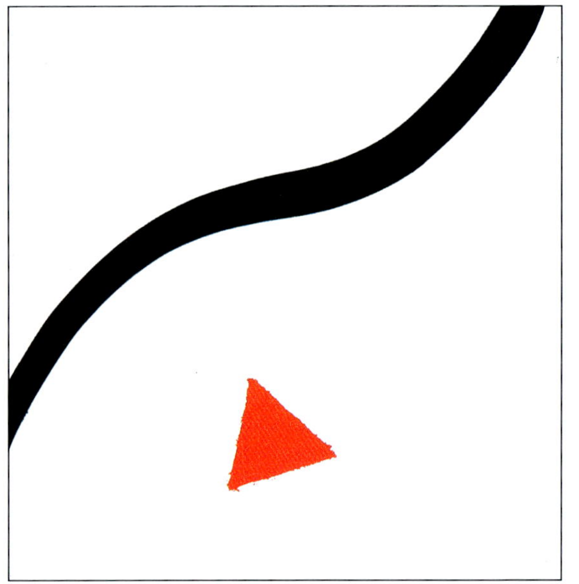

1

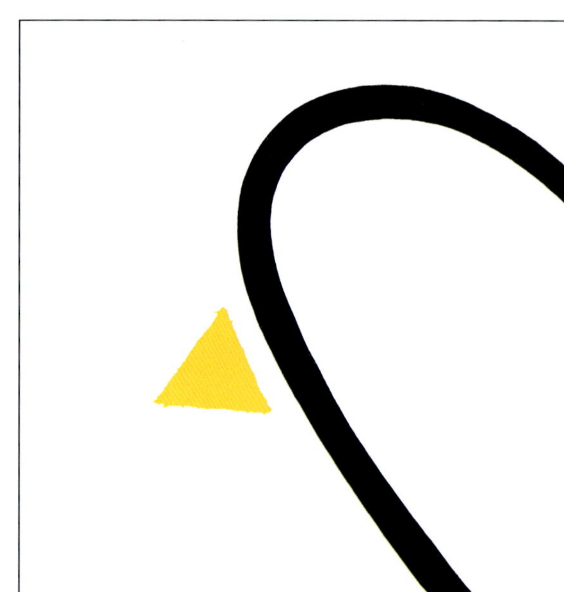

2

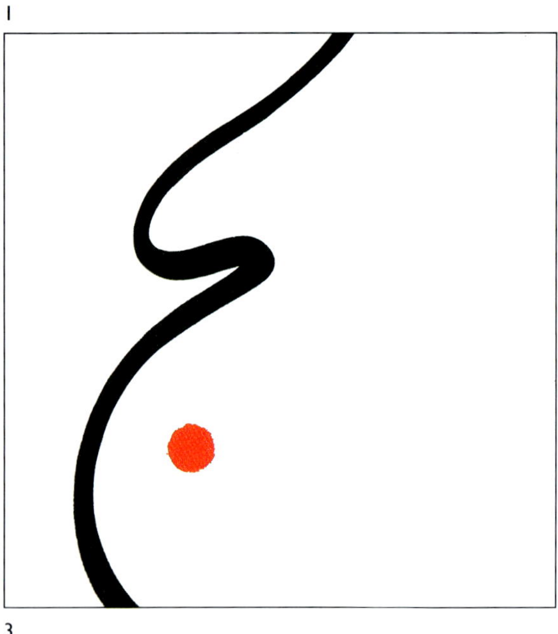

3

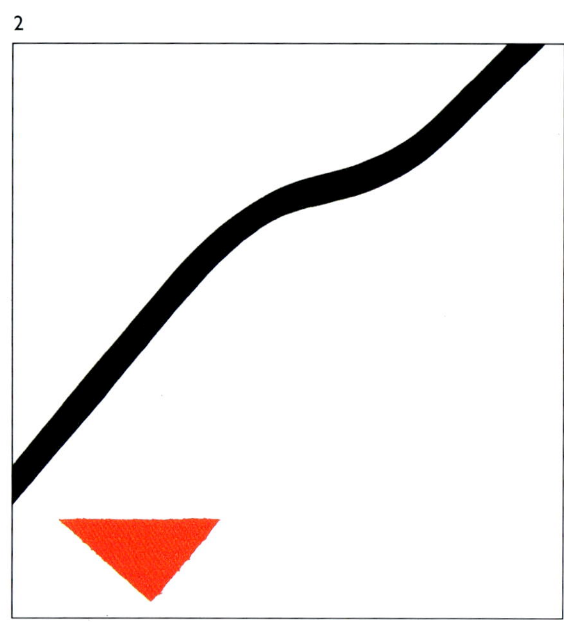

4

Selected Biography:

1994   Rocfern International
       Galleries, Woodbridge,
       Ontario, Canada

       Lerner Gallery
       Beverly Hills, CA

1993   Fine Art Warehouse
       Gallery, Vaughan,
       Ontario, Canada

       Fine Art Publishing Inc.
       Nobleton, Ontario,
       Canada

       Art Probe International
       Inc. , Etobicoke,
       Ontario, Canada

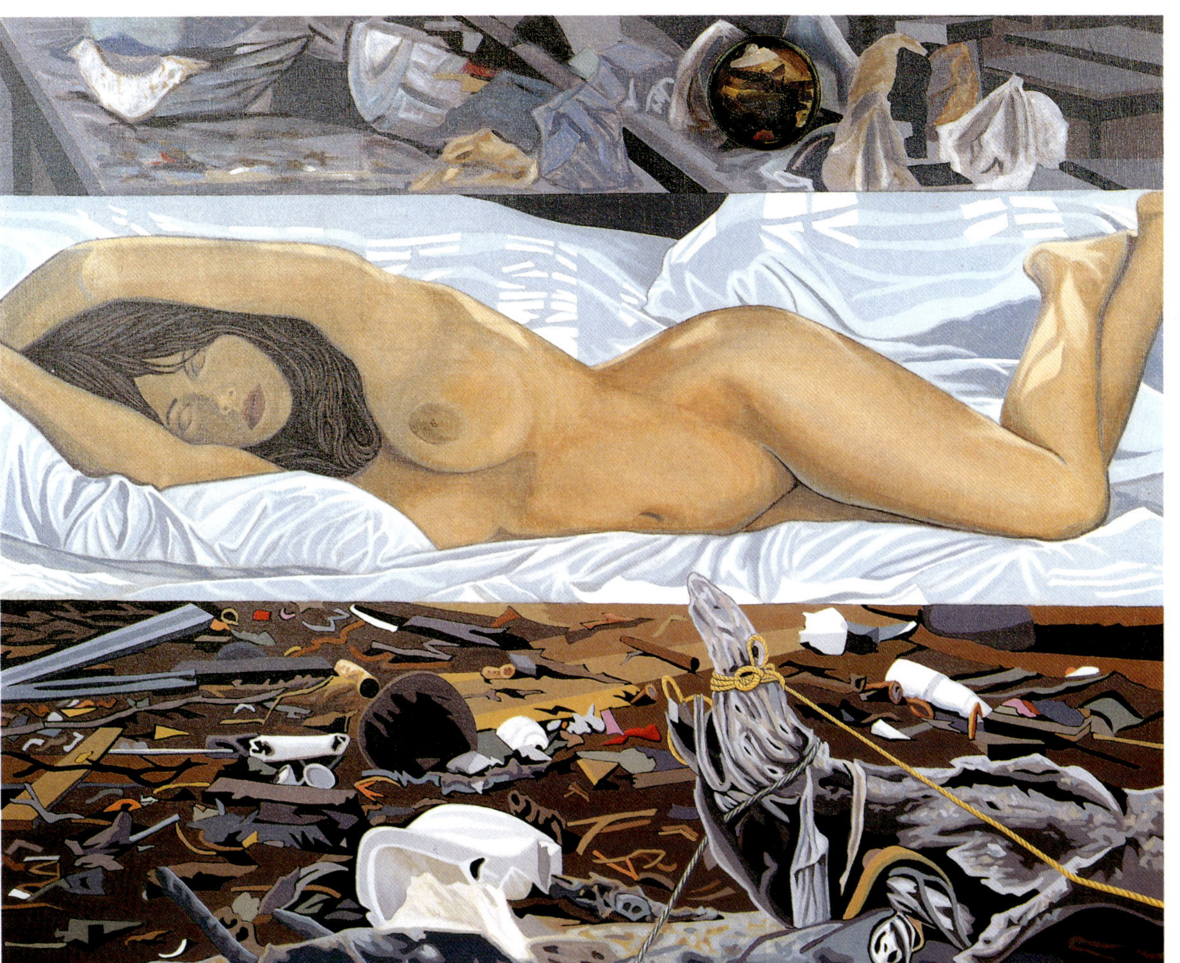

GALERIA NORMANDIE

Lobby Radisson
Normandie Hotel, Ave
Munoz Rivera
San Juan, Puerto Rico 00902
Puerto Rico
809.725.4252
809.729.3083 FAX

CONTACT:
Maria Elba Torres, Director

Exhibiting:
Puerto Rican contemporary
arts, sculptures, graphics,
ceramics and crafts

Carlos Marcial

Puerto de Luna
1993, Acrylic on canvas

Selected Biography:

1993 Puerto Rican National
Art Show, Puertorrican
Culture Institute,
San Juan, Puerto Rico

1992 Art from the Caribbean
Espace, Carpaux, Paris,
Francia

Images of the Land,
Puertorrican National
Pavillion, Expo 92,
Sevilla, Spain

MARSHA CHILD CONTEMPORARY

P.O. Box 364
Solebury, PA 18963
215.297.0414
215.297.0414 FAX

Contact:
Marsha Child

Exhibiting:
Contemporary European,
Eastern European and
American paintings, sculpture
and graphics

Georges Mazilu

1. *Trio*
   1991, Acrylic on canvas,
   35" x 46"

2. *Girl with Ribbon*
   1993, Acrylic on canvas,
   14" x 11"

3. *Six-fingered Magician*
   1993, Acrylic on canvas,
   29" x 36"

Selected Biography:

1994 "Mazilu: Under the
      Spell," Marsha Child
      Contemporary,
      Solebury, PA

1993 Solo exhibition, Galerie
      Schemes, Lille, France;
      "Mirror of the Mind,"
      101 Wooster Street
      Gallery, New York,
      NY; Galerie Nunki,
      Paris, France; Galerie
      Pieter Breughel,
      Amsterdam,
      Netherlands; Galerie
      Tempera, Brussels,
      Belgium

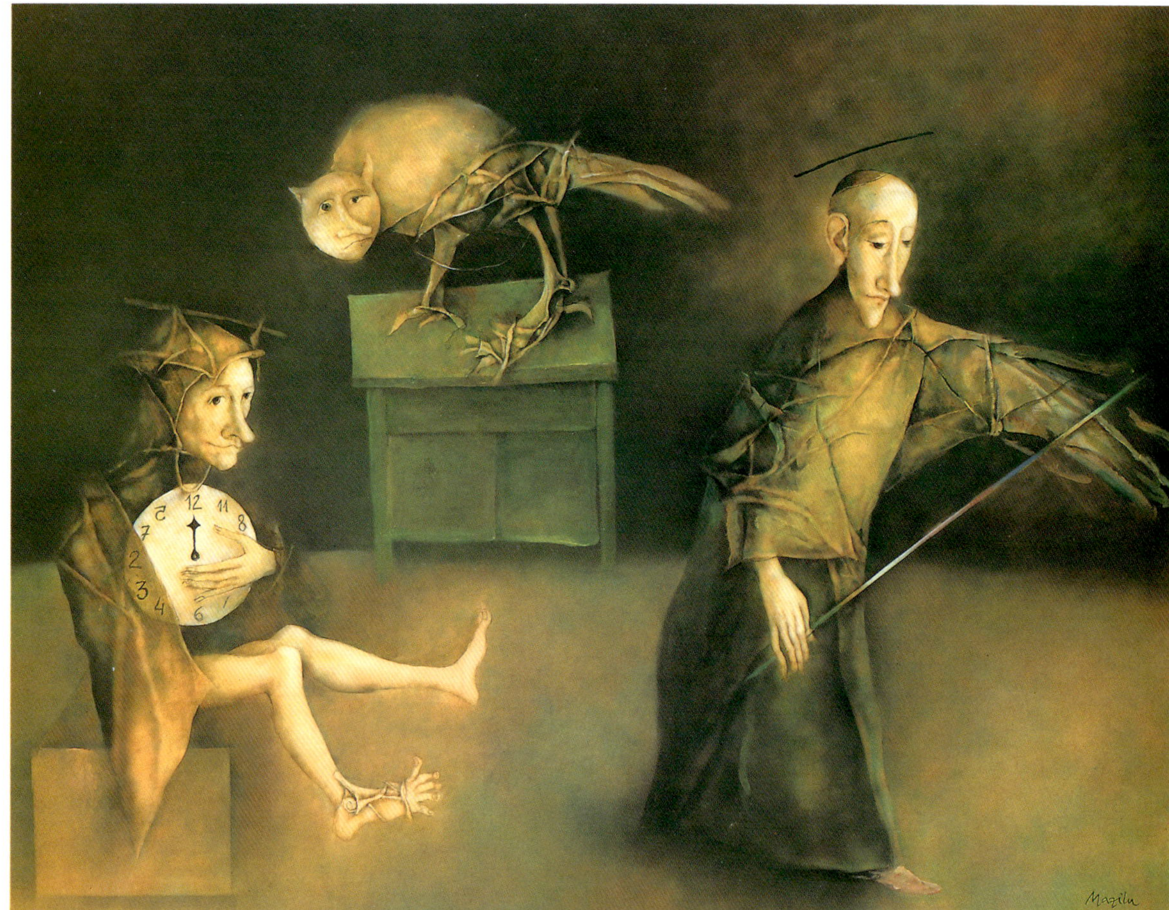

1

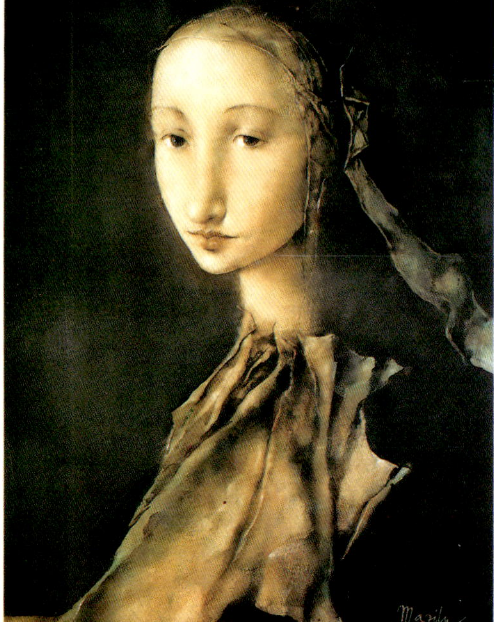

2

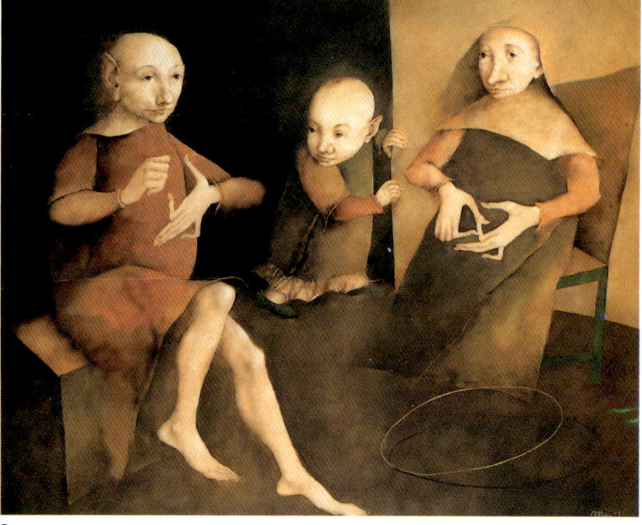

3

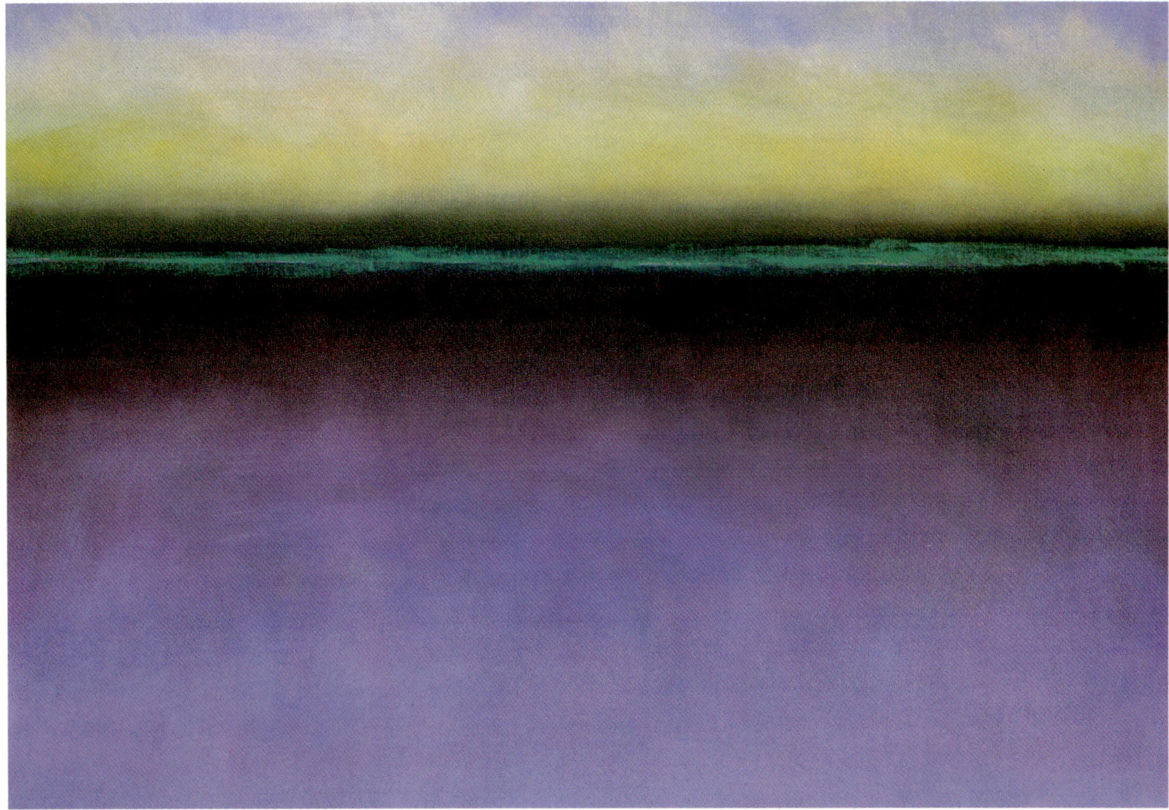

1

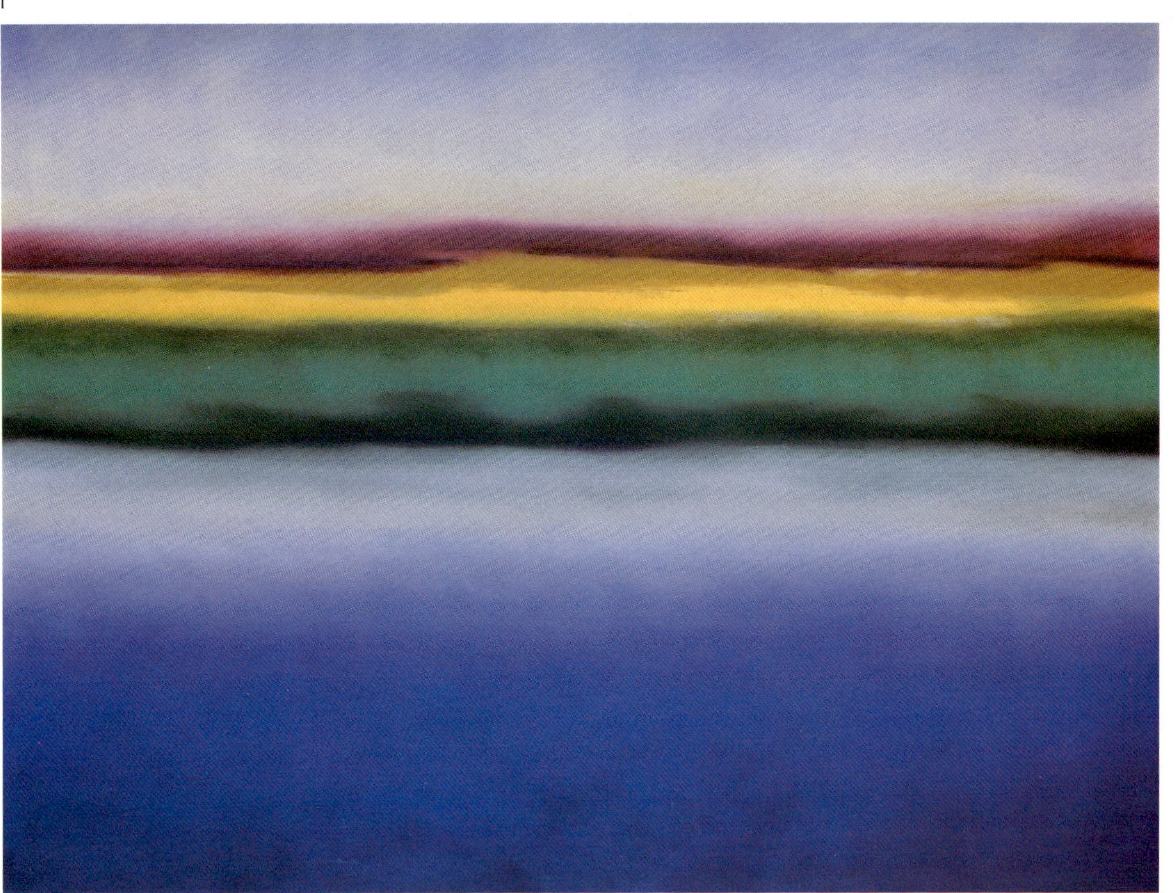

2

MONTSERRAT GALLERY

584 Broadway
New York, NY 10012
212.941.8899
212.274.1717 FAX

Contact:
Marie Montserrat Coll,
Director

Exhibiting:
Contemporary European
and American art

Victoria McClay

1. *Peace shall here remain*
   1993, Oil on canvas,
   24" x 36"

2. *Untitled*
   1993, Oil on canvas,
   30" x 36"

Selected Biography:

1993 Montserrat Gallery.
      New York, NY

1992 Montserrat Gallery.
      New York, NY

ARTE NUCLEO GALERIA

Edgar Allan Poe 308,
Col. polanco
Mexico DF 11560
Mexico
525.254.3732
525.531.6875
525.531.2905
525.254.1942 FAX

Contact:
Diana Ripstein de Nankin,
Director

Exhibiting:
Classic and contemporary
Latin American art

Guillermo Meza

La Ofrenda
1992, Oleo/Lino,
90 x 80 cms.
Photograph by
Manuel Zavala

Prizes:
1961 Honorific special
mention on "VI Biennial
de Tokio, Japon"
1954 1st prize, Instituto
Nacional De Bellas
Artes, Mexico, D.F.
1953 "Gran Premio Anual",
Instituto Nacional De
Bellas Artes, Mexico,
D.F.

Selected Exhibitions:
1978 I Biennial Latinoamericana
de Sao Paolo, Brasil;
Museo del Palacio de
Bellas Artes, INBA,
Mexico, D.F.
1968 Museo de la
Universidad de Puerto
Rico, Puerto Rico;
1948 Museo Regional
Michoacano, Morelia,
Mich.;
"Pintura Mexicana",
Feria Industrial de
Toronto, Canadá;

Selected Biography:
1917 Born in Mexico City,
Mexico

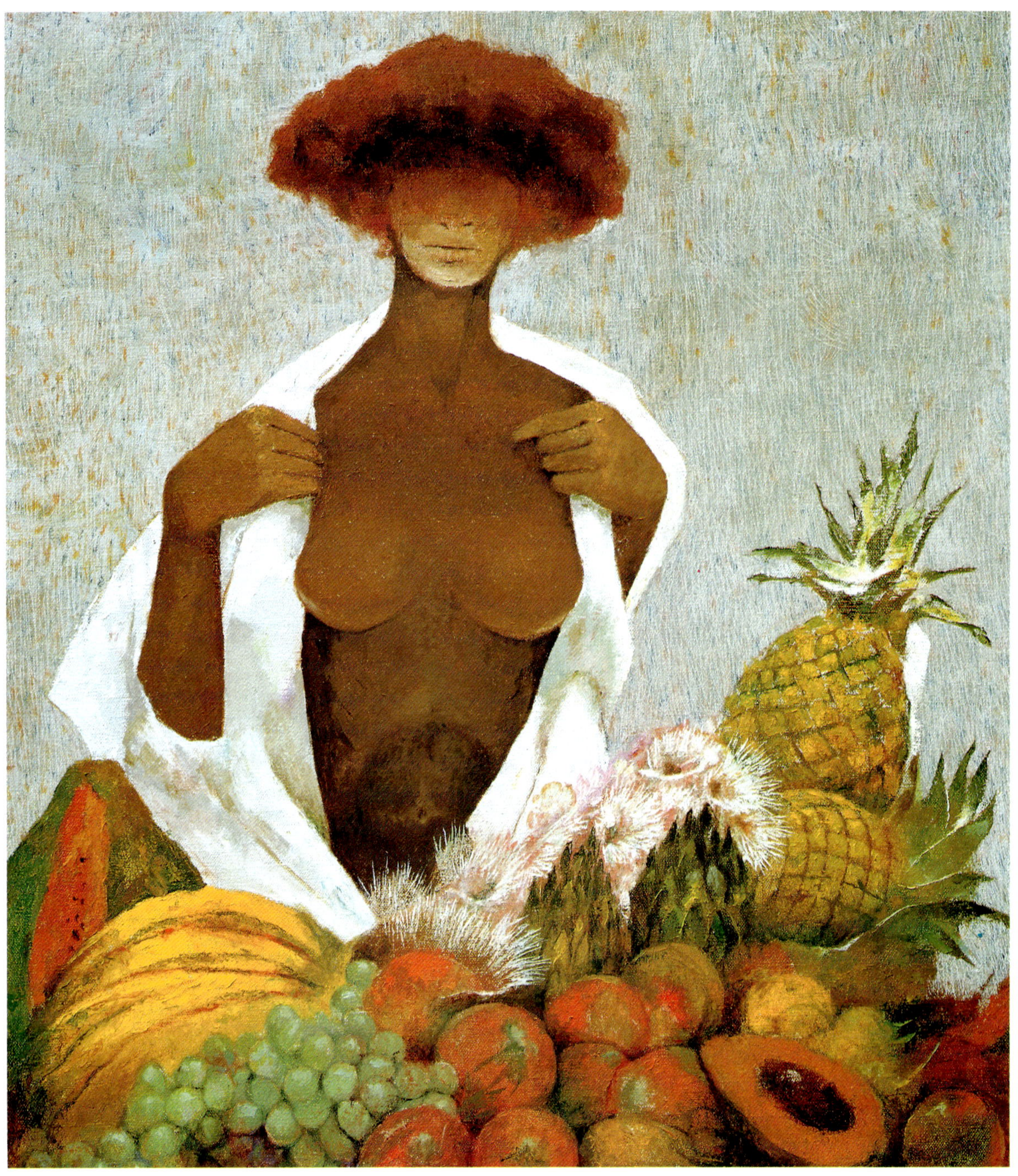

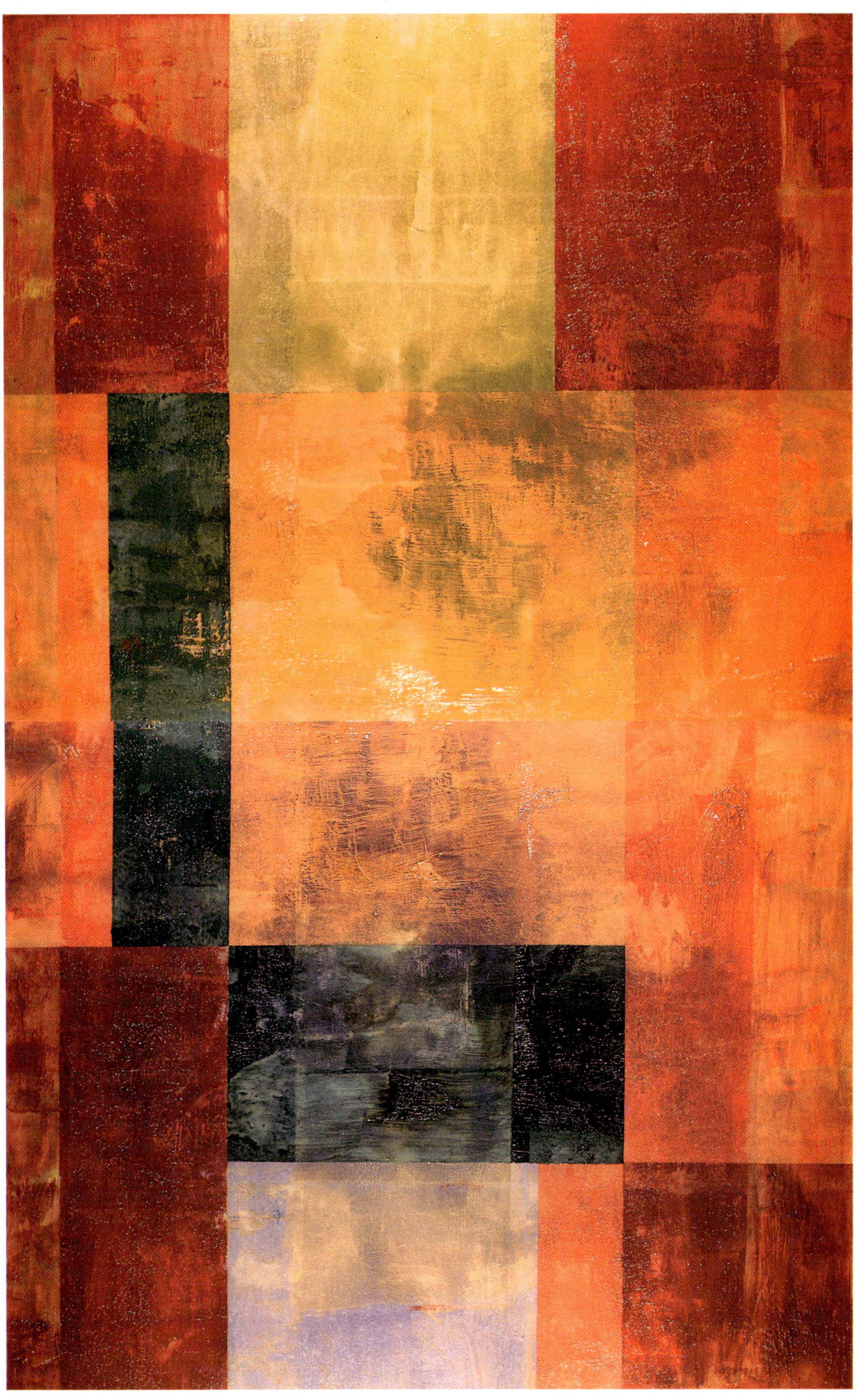

STUART LEVY
FINE ART

588 Broadway, Suite 303
New York. NY 10012
212.941.0009
212.941.7987 FAX

Contact:
Stuart Levy, President
Michael Lederer,
Assoc. Director

Exhibiting:
Contemporary Russian,
European and American
Artists

Ueli Michel

1. *156, (diptych)*
   1994, Oil on canvas,
   67" x 43.5" overall

Selected Solo Exhibitions:

1994 Magnus Akludh Gallery,
Lund and Stockholm

1993 Galerie Ludwig,
Krefeld; Janus Avivson
Gallery, London;
Galerie Axel Thieme,
Darmstadt

1992 Galerie Triebold, Basel;
Kunsthalle, Basel;
Galerie Bismarck,
Bremen

FENIX FINE ARTS

180 N.E. 40th St.
Miami, FL 33137
305.573.2727
305.542.8289
305.576.7707 FAX

Contact:
George Gandelman

Exhibiting:
Latin American Art

Roberto Milanes-Gala

1. *Litico Taino I*
   1993, Oil on canvas,
   198 cms. x 127 cms.

2. *Litico Maya I*
   1993, Oil and earth on
   linen, 152 cms. x 121 cms.

3. *Litico Taino III*
   1993, Oil and earth on
   linen, 152 cms. x 121 cms.

Selected Biography:

1994 Centro de Cultura de
      Yucatan, "Liticos
      Precolombinos",
      Mexico

1993 Susana Roth,
      Inversiones en Arte,
      Mexico City

      The Florida Museum of
      Hispanic & Latin
      American Art, Miami, FL

      "Metaforas Del
      Tiempo", Fenix Fine
      Arts, Miami, FL

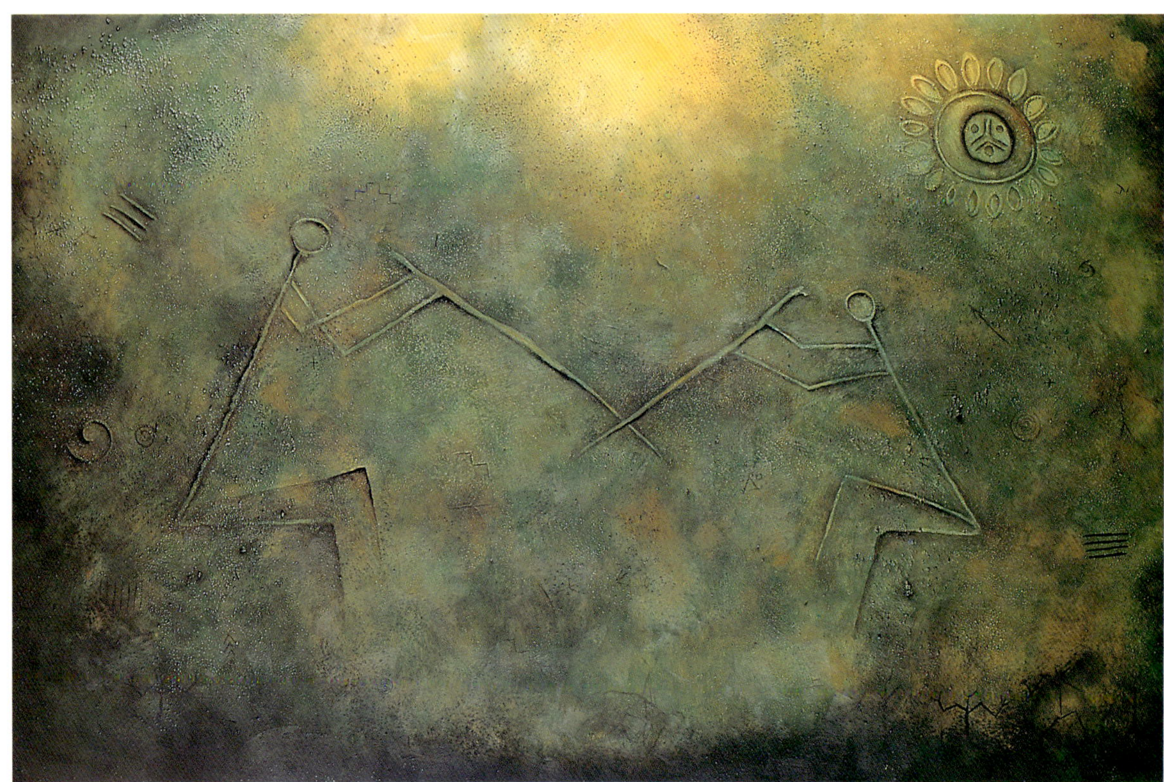

1

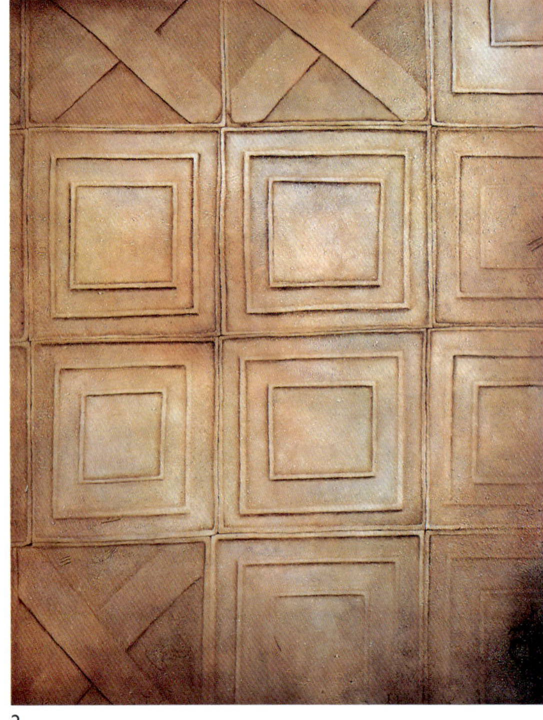

2

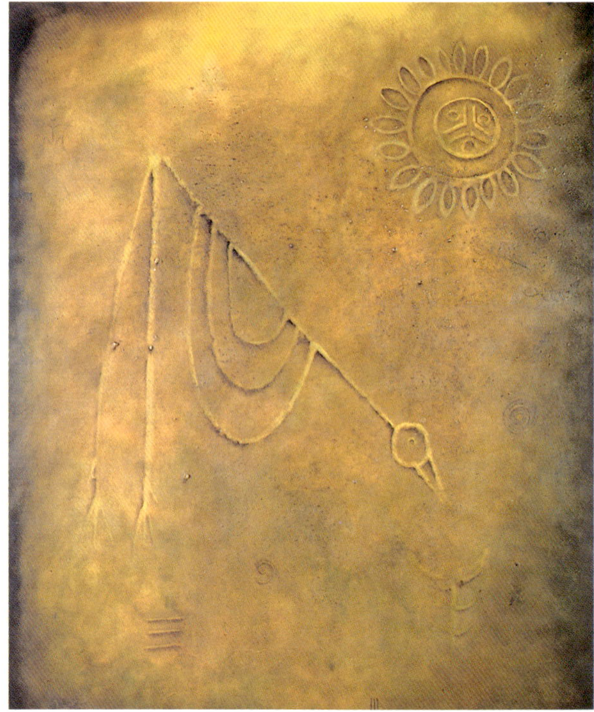

3

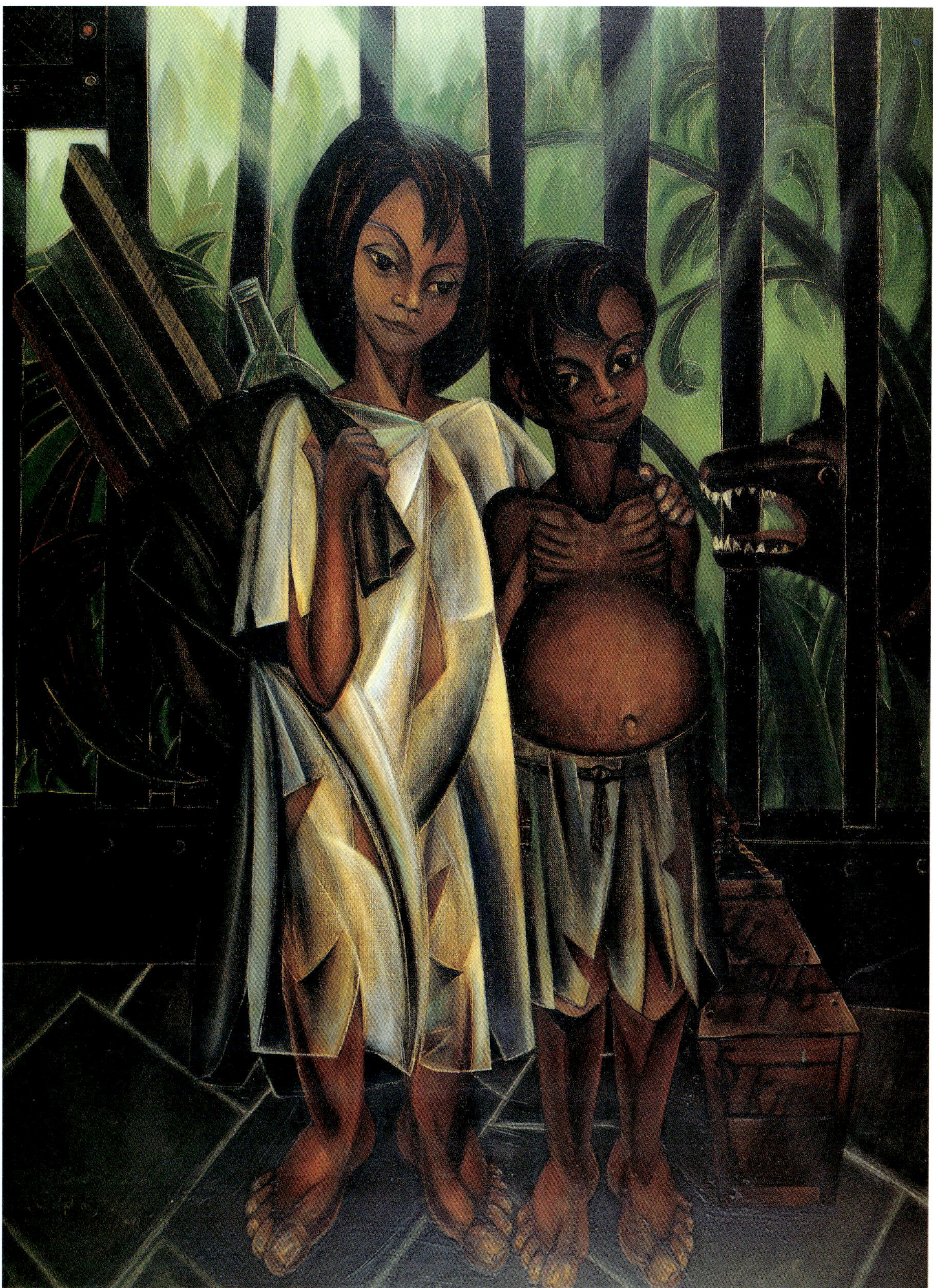

MARPAD ART GALLERY

393 Aragon Avenue
Coral Gables, Fl 33134
305.444.9360
305.888.2877 FAX

Contact:
Madelyn Padron

Exhibiting:
Cuban Masters &
Latin American Artists

Héctor Molné

*Ninos Latinoamericanos
(Felices)*
1992, Oil on canvas,
40" x 30"

Selected Biography:

1994-1993
Art Miami International
Exhibition

1976 Participated in
Contemporary Cuban
Art shows in Norway,
Sweden, Finland,
Denmark, Romania,
Hungary,
Czechoslovakia

Awarded scholarship to
study in Paris, France
Permanent collection,
Museo Nacional de
Bellas Artes, Havana,
Cuba

CHARLES WHITCHURCH GALLERY

5973 Engineer Drive
Huntington Beach, CA 92649
714.373.4459
714.373.4615 FAX

Contact:
Charles Whitchurch

Exhibiting:
Modern and contemporary
painting, graphic works and
sculpture

Karl Momen

Eclipse in Red
1990, Oil on canvas,
67" x 67"

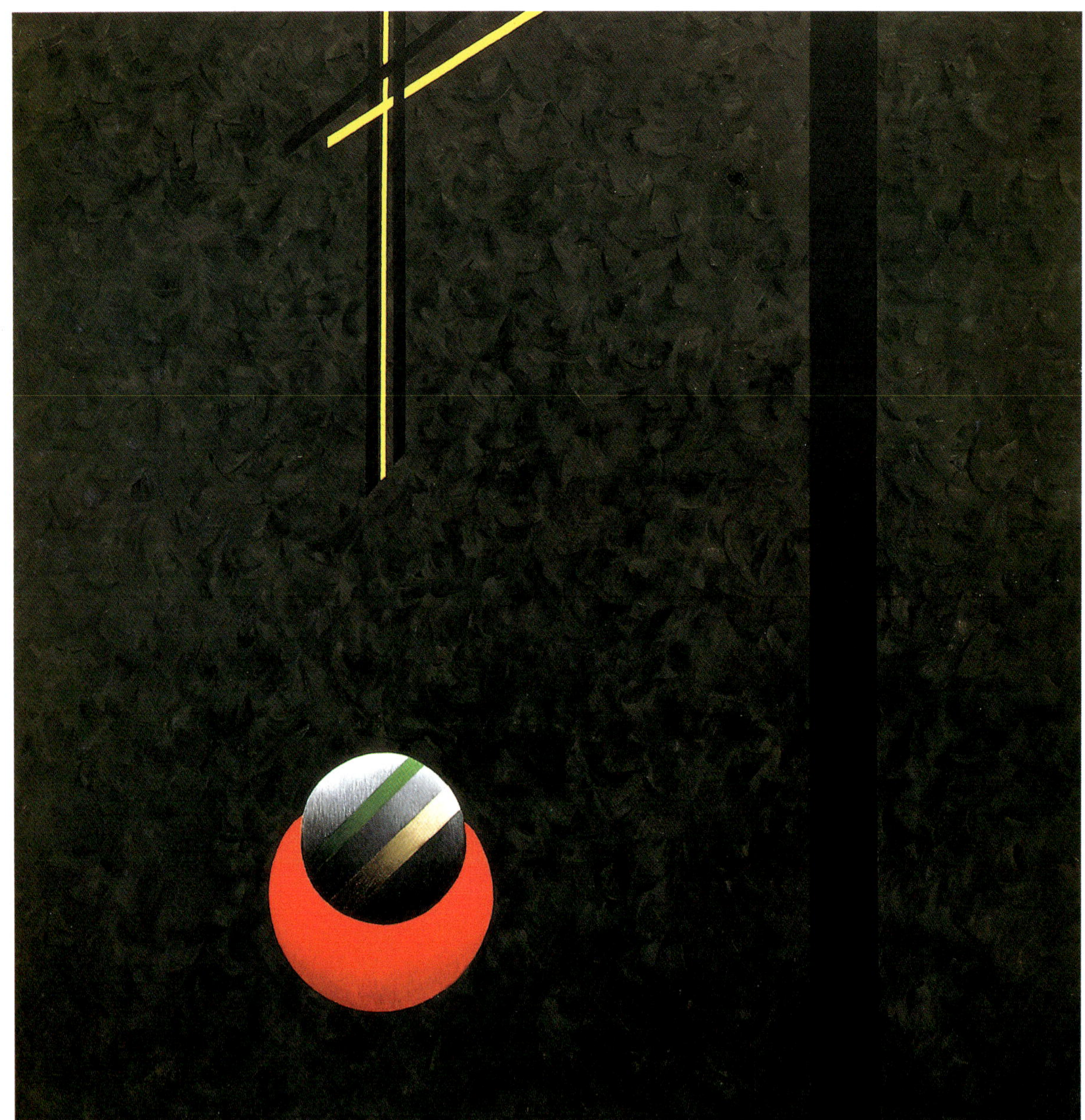

Selected Biography:

1994 Solo Exhibition,
Brigham Young
Museum, Utah

1989 Solo Exhibition,
Haus am Lützowplatz,
Cultural Center, Berlin

1985 Solo Exhibition,
Striped House
Museum, Tokyo

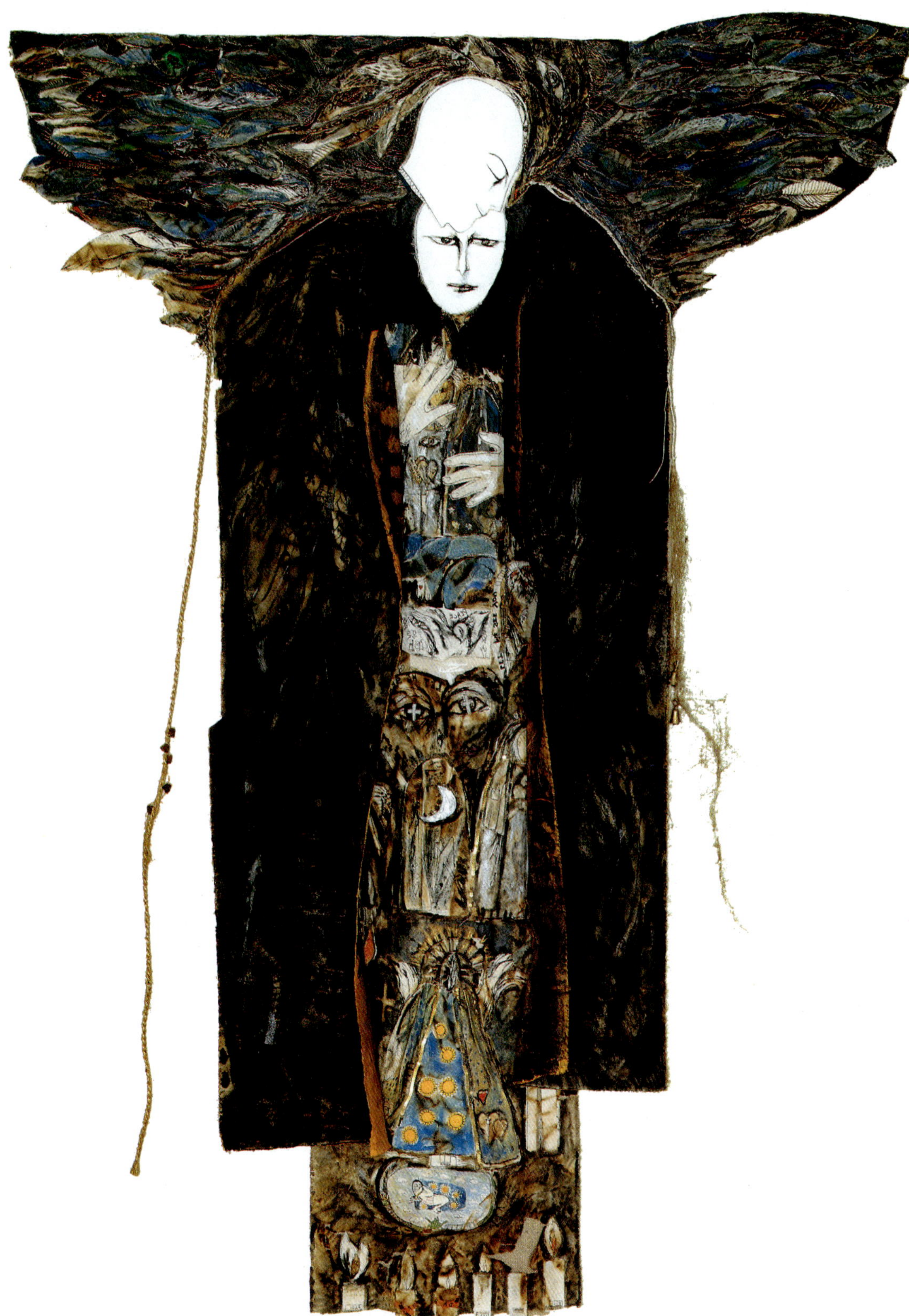

ALFREDO MARTINEZ GALLERY

2311 Le Jeune Road
Coral Gables, Fl 33134
305.442.0808
305.442.0824 FAX

Contact:
Lawrence Casalins

Exhibiting:
Contemporary Art

Clara Morera

Self Portrait
1993, Mixed media on
canvas with bells, rope
and tar, 90" x 79"

Selected Biography:

1994 Art Miami International
Exhibition

1993 Solo Show Alfredo
Martinez Gallery

1992 Symposium.
Baei- St. Paul,
Quebec, Canada

1989 Painting, Installation &
Performance,
Moscow, Russia.

Conference by Latin
American Specialist
Hermitage Museum,
St. Petersburg

LESLIE MUTH GALLERY

225 E. de Vargas
Santa Fe, NM 87501
505.989.4620
505.989.4937 FAX

Contact:
Leslie Muth, Director

Exhibiting:
Contemporary American folk, self taught and outsider art

Ike Morgan

George Washington Series,
1992, Pastel and India ink on paper, 32" x 24"

Selected Biography:

1994 "Outside In", Laguna Gloria Art Museum, Austin, TX
1993 "Made in the USA", Collection de l'art brut, Lausanne, Switzerland
1992 "Fresh Visions/New Voices: Emerging African-American Artists in Texas", Museum of Fine Arts Glassell School, Houston, TX
1990-92 "Cutting Edge", Museum of American Folk Art, NYC

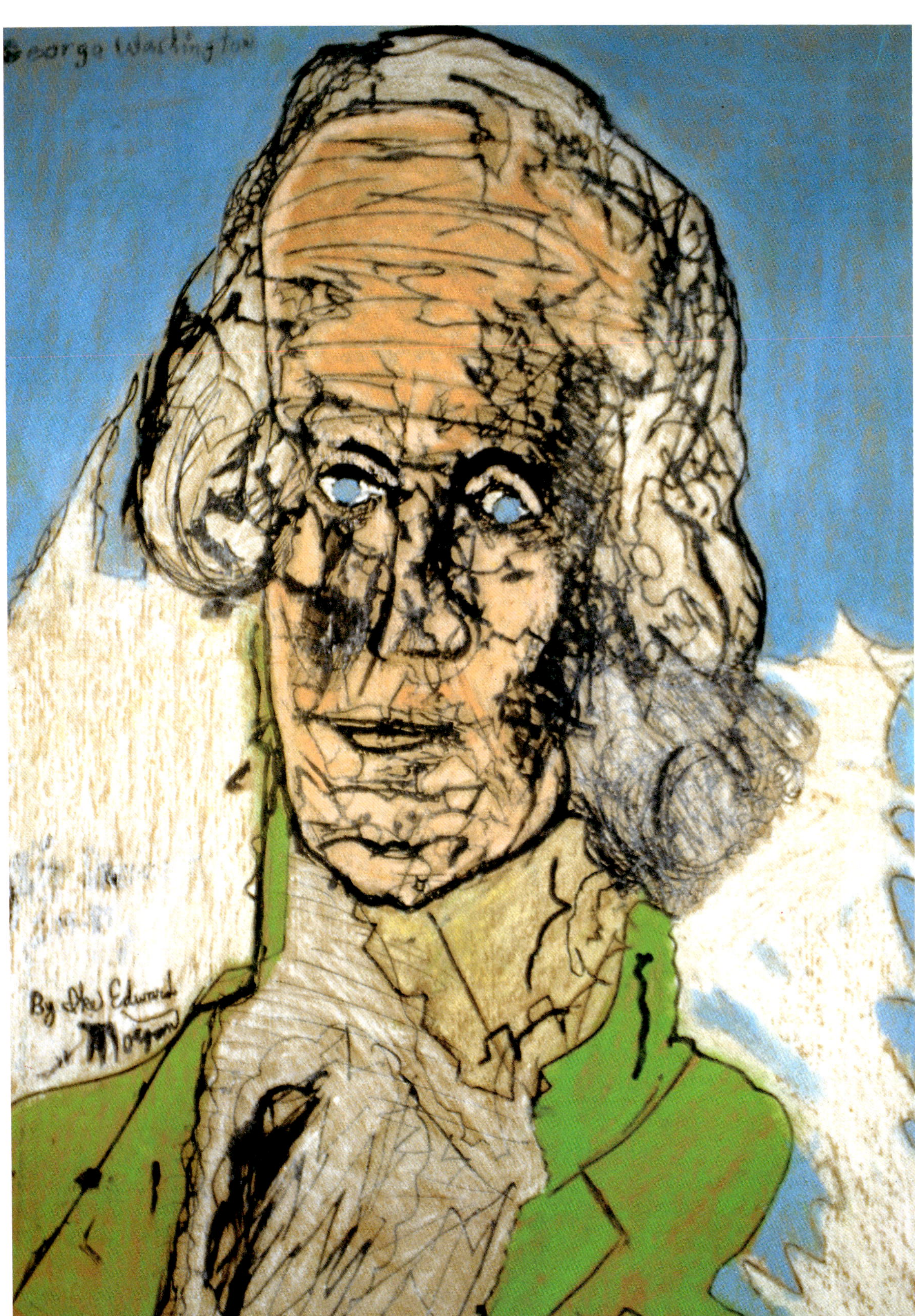

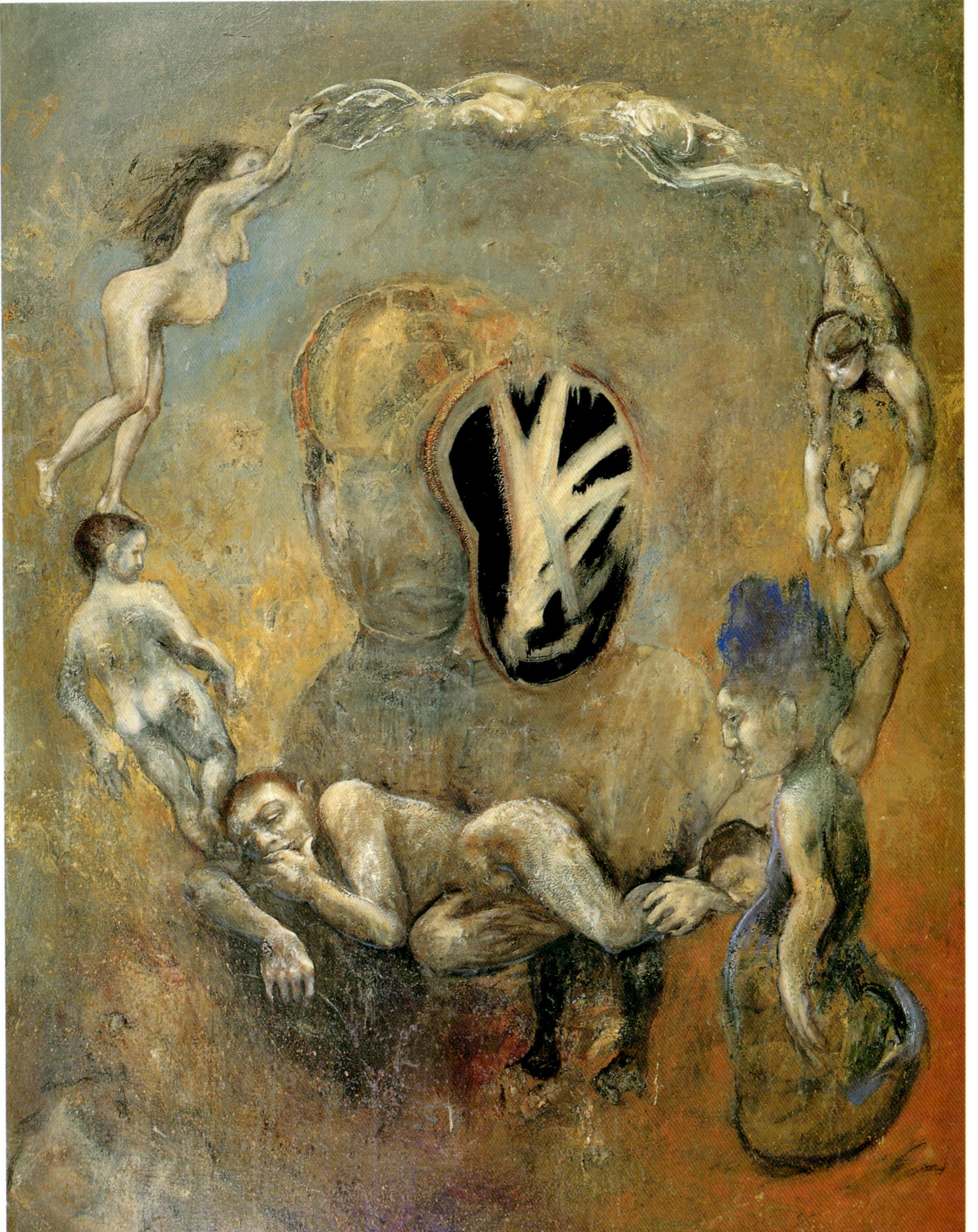

THE LOWE GALLERY

75 Bennett St. Space A-Z
Atlanta, GA 30309
404.352.8114
404.352.0564 FAX

Contact:
Bill Lowe

Exhibiting:
Contemporary painting,
sculpture, and objects

Kathleen Morris

Wheel
1993, Oil on linen,
90" x 72"

Selected Biography:

1992   Solo show,
       The Lowe Gallery,
       Santa Monica, CA

       Solo show,
       The Lowe Gallery,
       Atlanta, GA

1989   Solo show,
       Sena Galleries East,
       Santa Fe, NM

1984   Solo show,
       St. Marks Gallery,
       New York, NY

THE LOWE GALLERY

75 Bennett St. Space A-Z
Atlanta, GA 30309
404.352.8114
404.352.0564 FAX

Contact:
Bill Lowe

Exhibiting:
Contemporary painting,
sculpture, and objects

Todd Murphy

Untitled
1994, Painted Plexglass
over photo collage on
masonite with tar,
120" x 96"

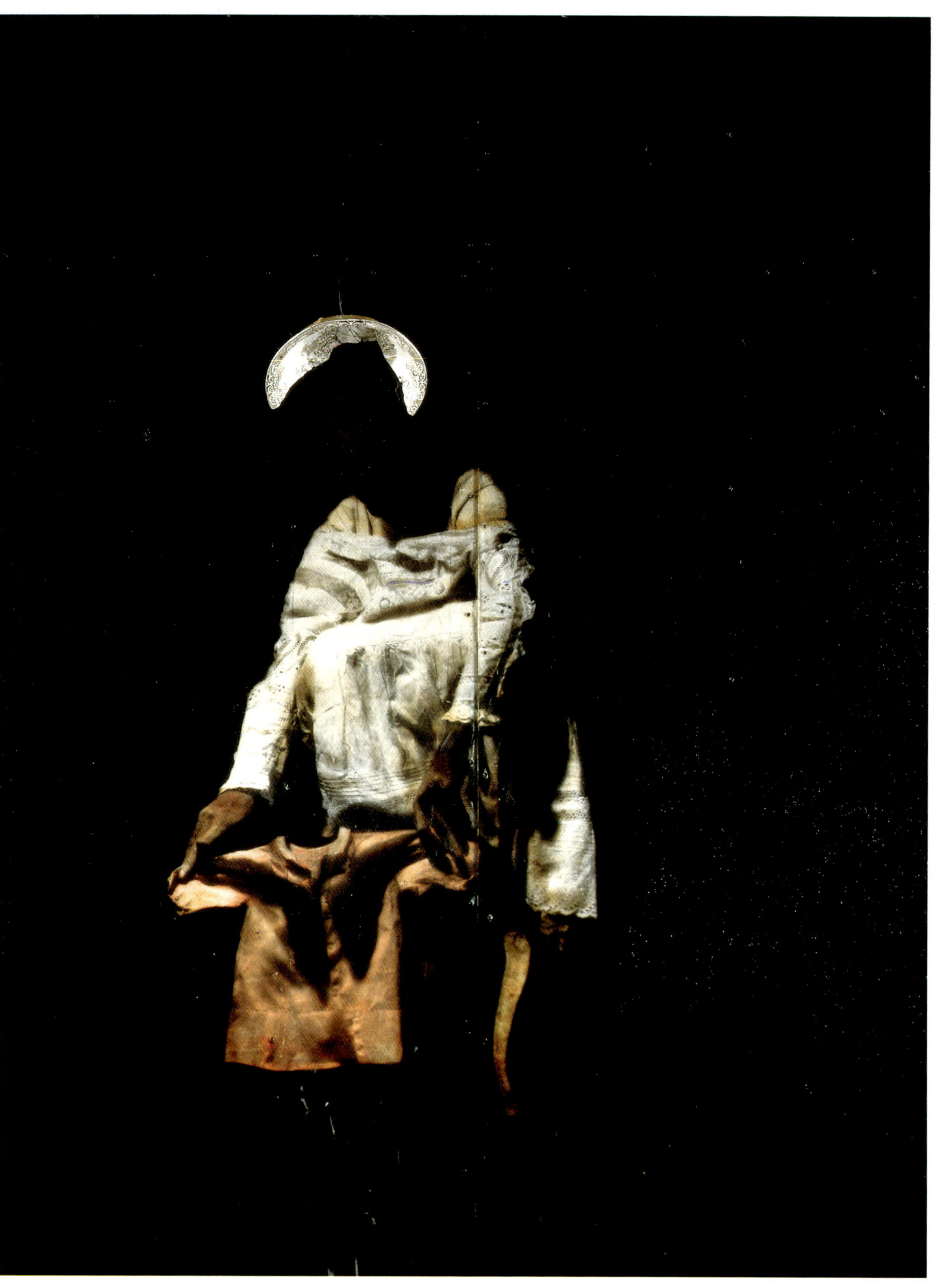

Selected Biography:

1994 Solo show,
       The Lowe Gallery,
       Atlanta, GA

1993 Solo show,
       The Lowe Gallery,
       Atlanta, GA

       Group show,
       "The Purloined Image",
       Flint Institute of Art, MI

       Group show,
       The Triton Museum,
       Santa Clara, CA

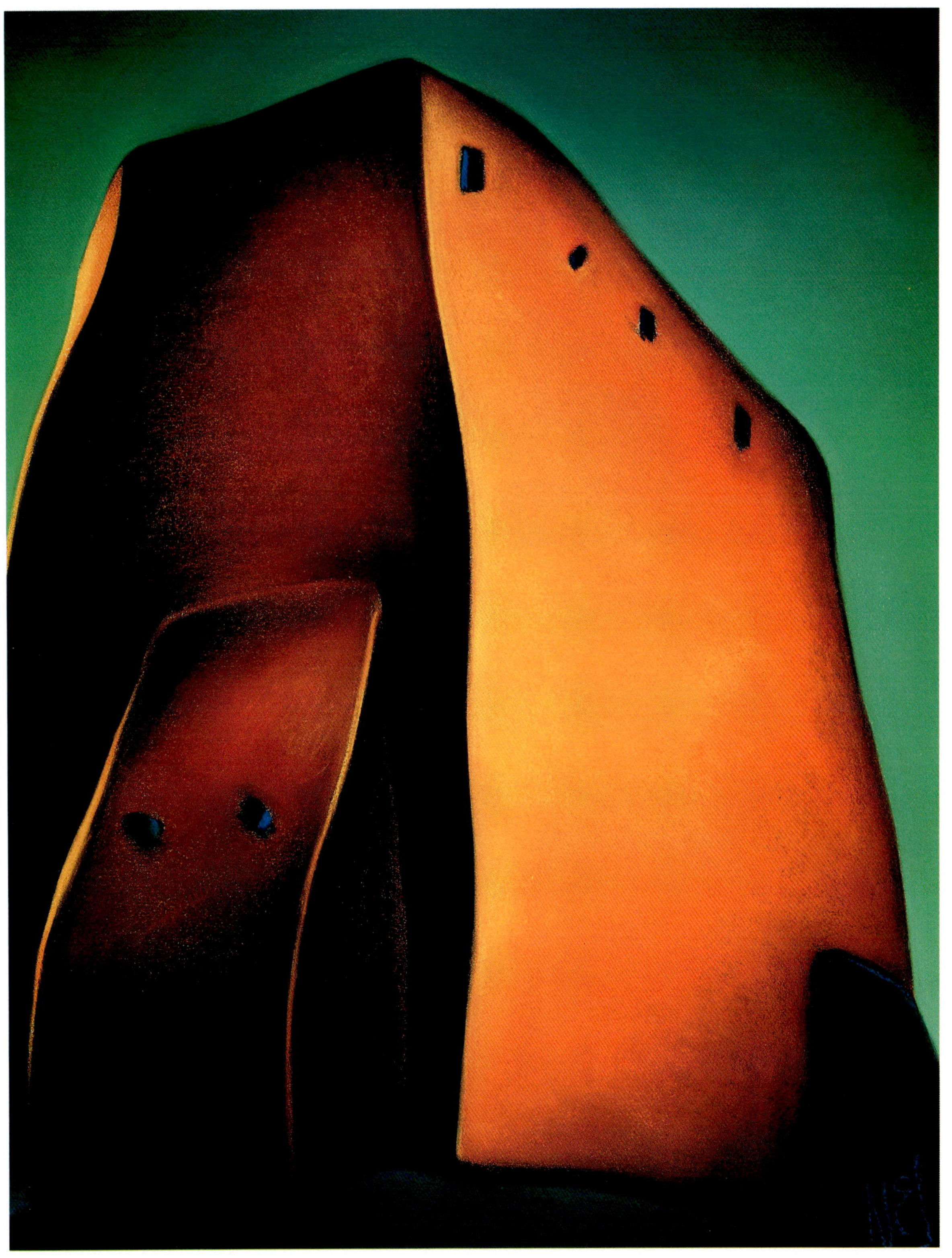

EDITH LAMBERT GALLERY

707 Canyon Rd.
Santa Fe, NM 87501
505.984.2783
800.594.9667
505.983.4494 FAX

Contact:
Edith Lambert, Owner
Anne Ward Burton,
Assoc. Director

Exhibiting:
Contemporary paintings,
drawings and sculpture

Margaret Nes

Mission Walls Like Africa,
1989, Pastel,
25 1/4" x 19 1/2"

Selected Exhibitions:
1994 Edith Lambert Gallery,
Santa Fe, NM

Selected Publications:
U.S. Art Magazine, 1989
Santa Fe, Art, Simone
Ellis, Random House,
Crescent Books, 1993;
Focus Magazine, 1993

Selected Collections:
Mount Sinai Medical
Center, New York, NY;
University of Texas
Law School, Austin,
TX; Mountain Bell
Telephone Co.,
Denver, CO; Mary
Cabot Enterprises,
Taos, NM

O. K. HARRIS
WORKS OF ART

383 West Broadway
New York, NY 10012
212.431.3600

Contact:
Ivan C. Karp

Exhibiting:
Contemporary American
And European painting,
sculpture, photography,
collectables and memorabilia

William Nichols

*Giverny, Garden and Water
Reflections*
1990, Oil on canvas,
45" x 80"

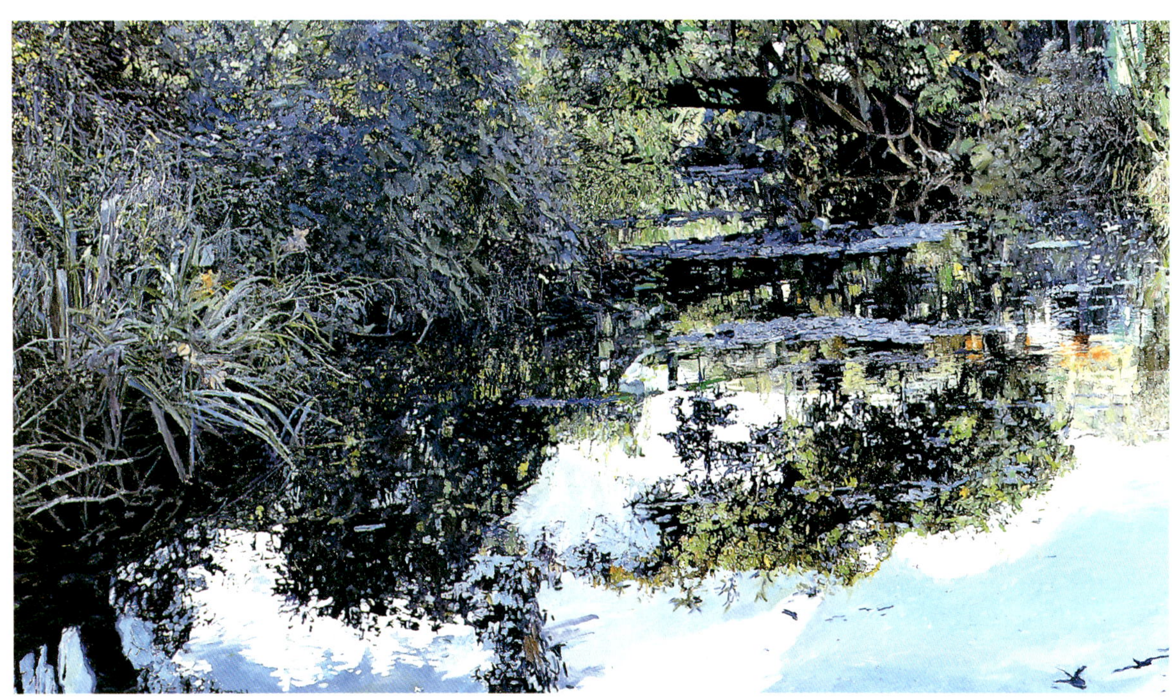

Selected Biography:

1994 O. K. Harris Works Of
Art, New York, NY

1993 "Nature's Territories/
Landscape Painting",
Tory Folliard Gallery,
Milwaukee, WI

1992 "A View From Here:
Heartland Landscape
Painters", McLean
County Arts Center,
Bloomington, IL

1990 "Contemporary
Landscapes"
Tortue Gallery,
Santa Monica, CA

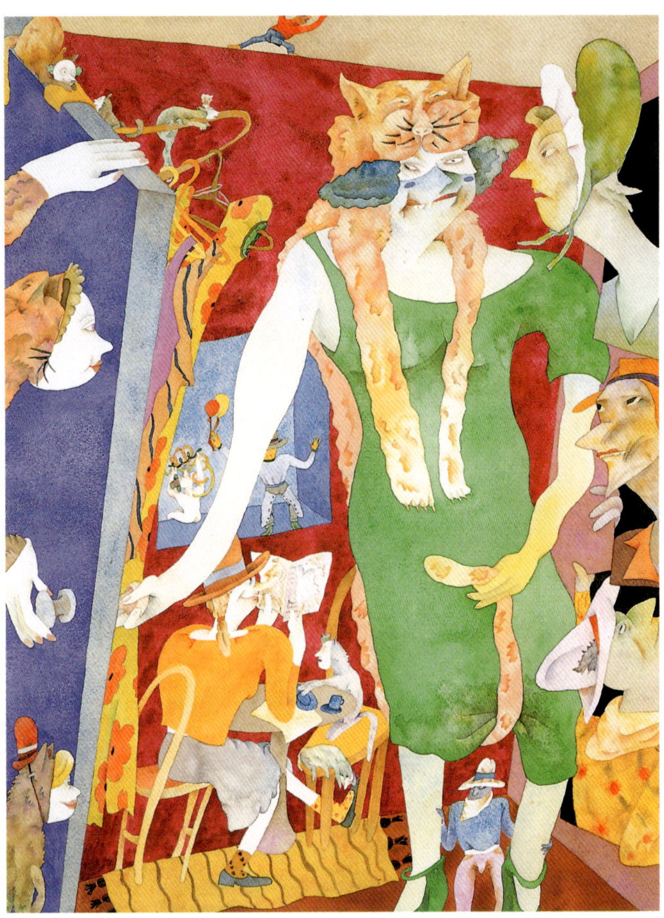

1.

PHYLLIS KIND
GALLERY

313 West Superior
Chicago, IL 60610
312.642.6302
312.642.8502 FAX

136 Greene Street
New York, NY 10012
212.925.1200
212.941.7841 FAX
Contact:
Phyllis Kind

Exhibiting:
Contemporary
American, Soviet, Naive,
and Outsider art

Gladys Nilsson

1. *Some Cats at Play*
   Sum Play at Cats
   1992,
   Watercolor on paper,
   $30\frac{1}{2}$" x $22\frac{1}{2}$"

2. *Some Kind of Girl Thing*
   1992,
   Watercolor on paper,
   $22\frac{5}{8}$" x $22\frac{1}{8}$"

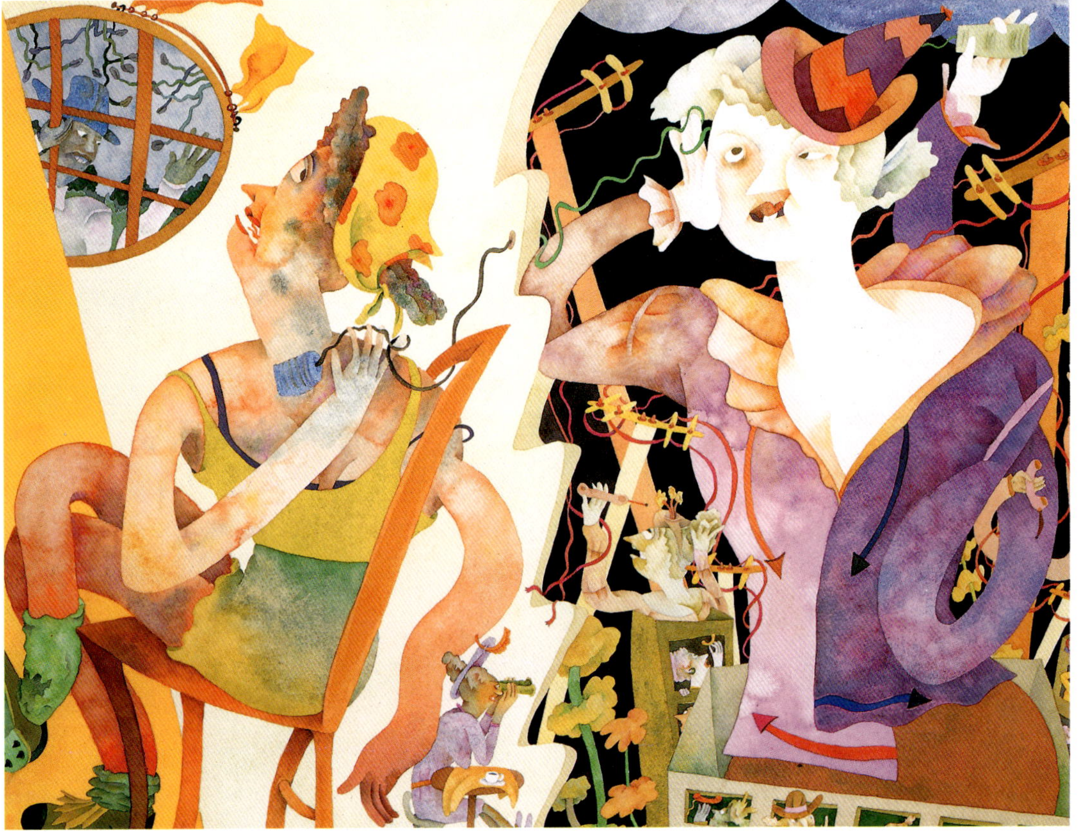

1.

Selected Biography:

1994 "Garden of Earthly
Delights," Phyllis Kind
Gallery, Chicago, IL

1992 "Personal Imagery,"
Phyllis Kind Gallery,
New York, NY

"Parallel Vision:
Modern Artists and
Outsider Art," Los
Angeles County
Museum and traveling
exhibition

LISA HARRIS GALLERY

1922 Pike Place
Seattle, WA 98101
206.443.3315

Contact:
Lisa Harris, Director

Gary Nisbet

1. *Spin*
   1993, Gold leaf
   collage, oil, oil pastel,
   37" x 34"

2. *Solar*
   1993, Gold leaf
   collage, oil, oil pastel,
   12 $^{1}/_{2}$" x 12 $^{1}/_{2}$"

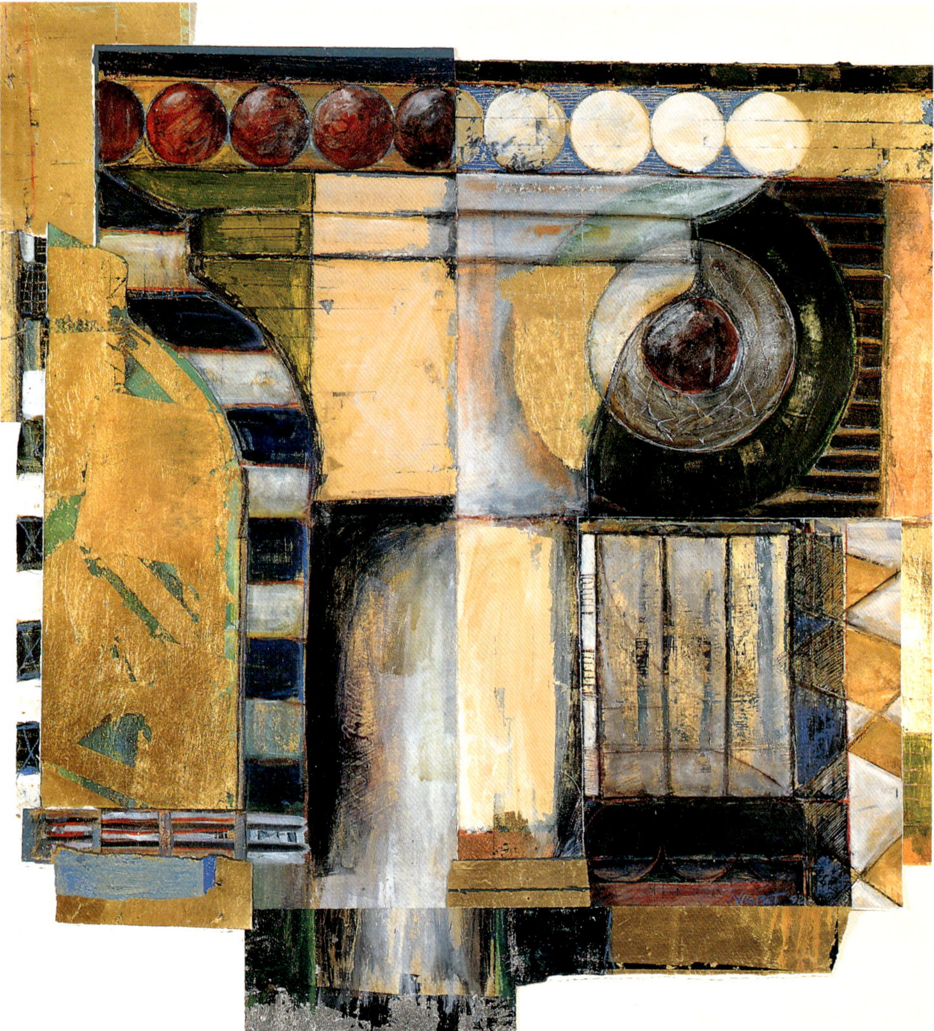

1

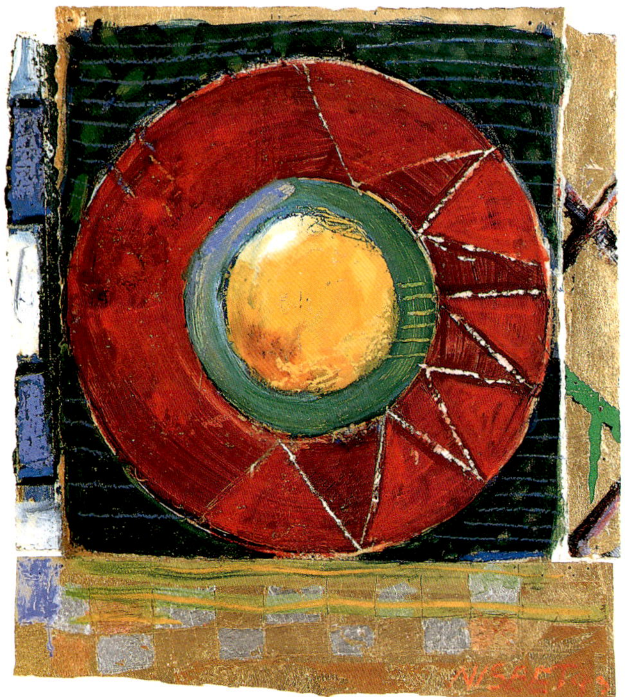

2

Selected Biography:

1993   Lisa Harris Gallery,
Seattle, WA

Harleen and Allen Fine
Art, San Francisco, CA

1992   Lisa Harris Gallery,
Seattle, WA

Whatcom County
Art Museum,
Bellingham, WA

Security Pacific Gallery,
Seattle, WA

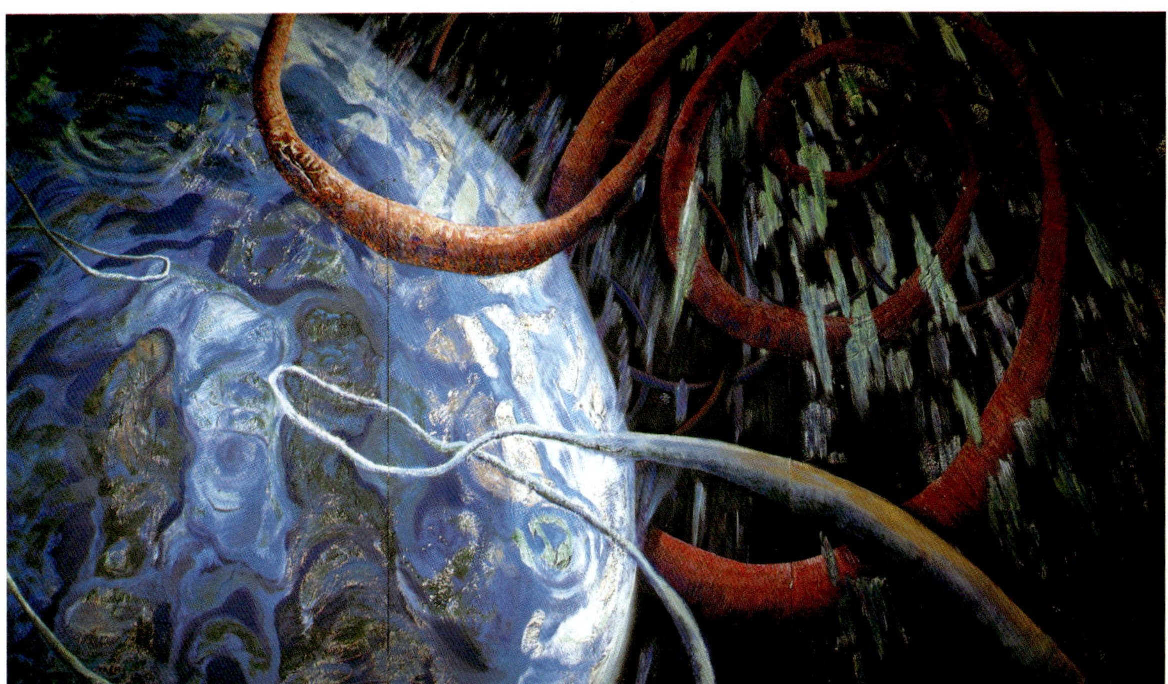

1

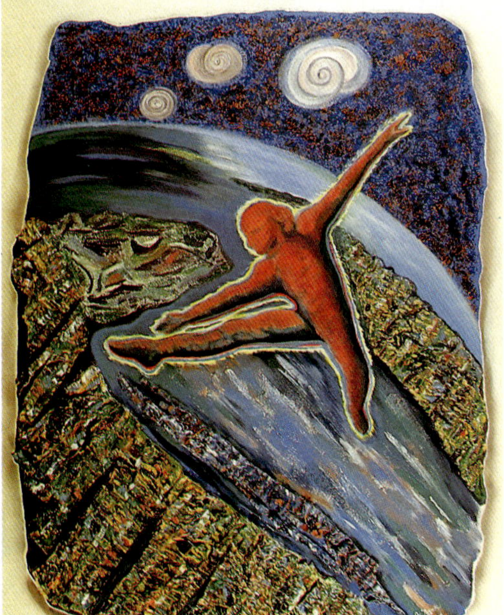

2

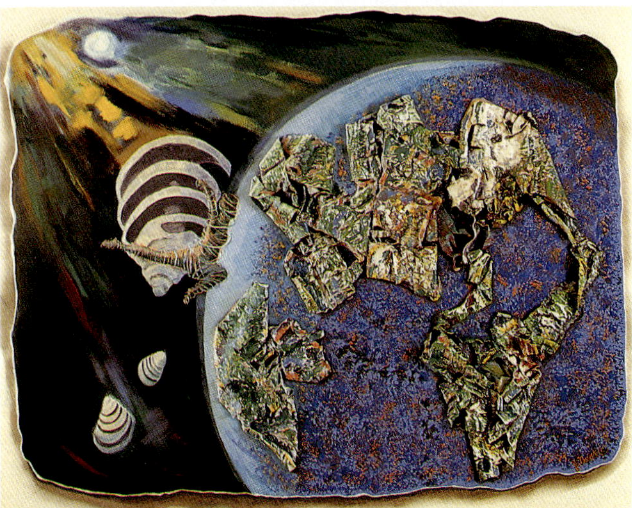

3

CAROLE JONES GALLERY

300 W. Superior Street
Chicago, IL 60610
312.587.8820
312.587.9859 FAX

Contact:
Carole Jones

Exhibiting:
Contemporary International
Fine Art; Painting &
Sculpture

Joyce Novak

1. *Journey Mural*
   1990, Mixed media on
   canvas, 84" x 144"

2. *Cosmic Leap*
   1992, Mixed media on
   canvas, 60" x 48"

3. *Parvati*
   1992, Mixed media on
   canvas, 48" x 60"

Selected Biography:

1994 "Patterns from Infinity",
      Carole Jones Gallery,
      Chicago, IL

      Group Show: Council
      for a Parliament of the
      World's Religious,
      Chicago, IL

1991 East West
      Contemporary
      Art Gallery,
      Chicago, IL

1989 Solo Show: People's
      Republic of China,
      Lecture/Exhibition
      Tour; Beijing, Shanghai
      Hangzhou

CAROLE JONES
GALLERY

300 W. Superior Street
Chicago, IL 60610
312.587.8820
312.587.9859 FAX

Contact:
Carole Jones

Exhibiting:
Contemporary International
Fine Art; Painting &
Sculpture

Tomas Ochoa

Temporal Transitions
1993, Acrylic on canvas,
64" x 52"

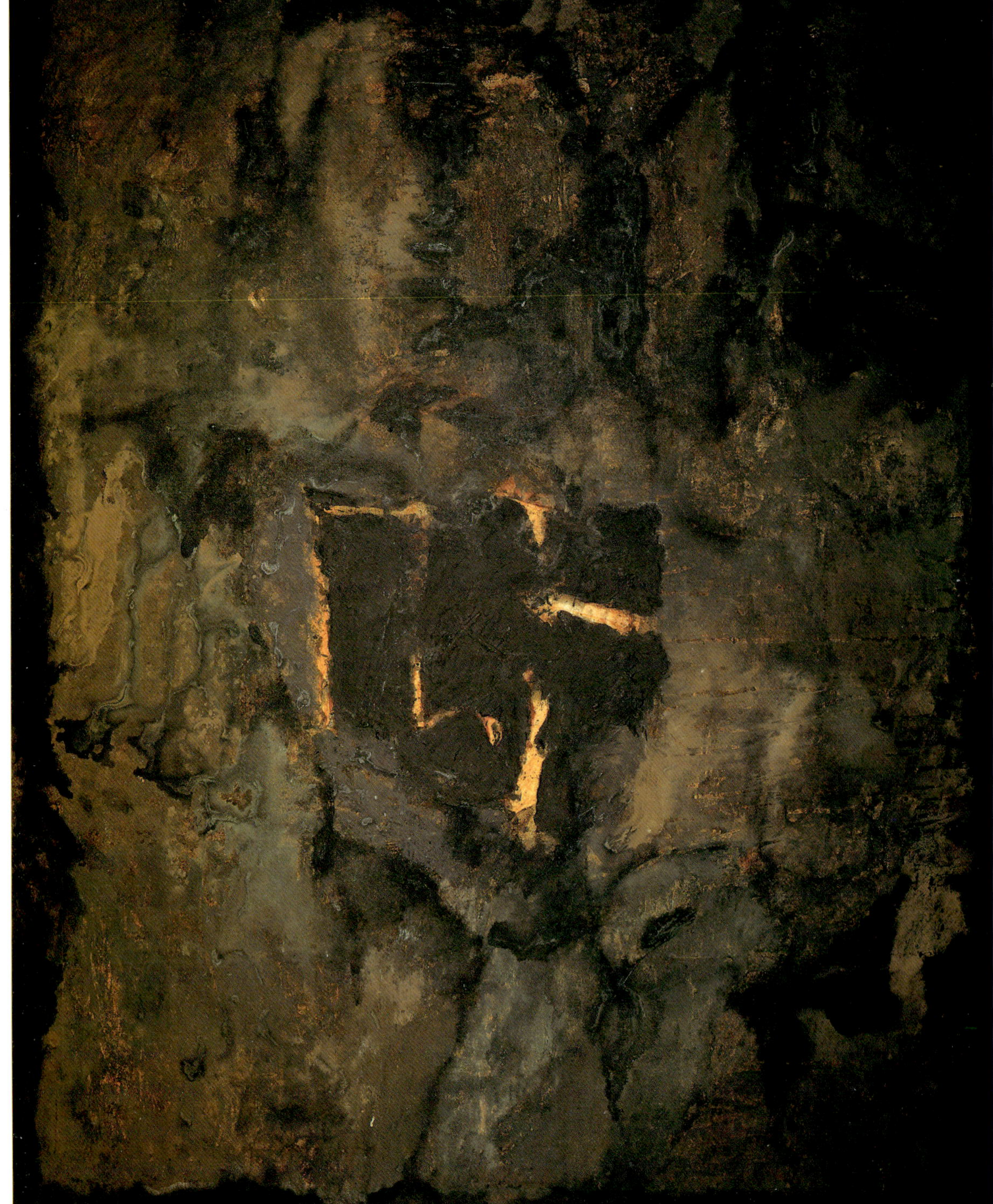

Selected Biography:

1993 "Landmark for a New
Generation",
Carole Jones Gallery,
Chicago, IL
1992 Grand Prize in
National Competition
"Exedra Fundation",
Quito, Ecuador
1991 Third Prize,
Contemporary
Latin American Art
Competition,
Piura, Peru;
Museo Del Banco
Central, Loja, Ecuador
1990 Third Prize
"Salon de Octubre",
Guayaquil, Ecuador

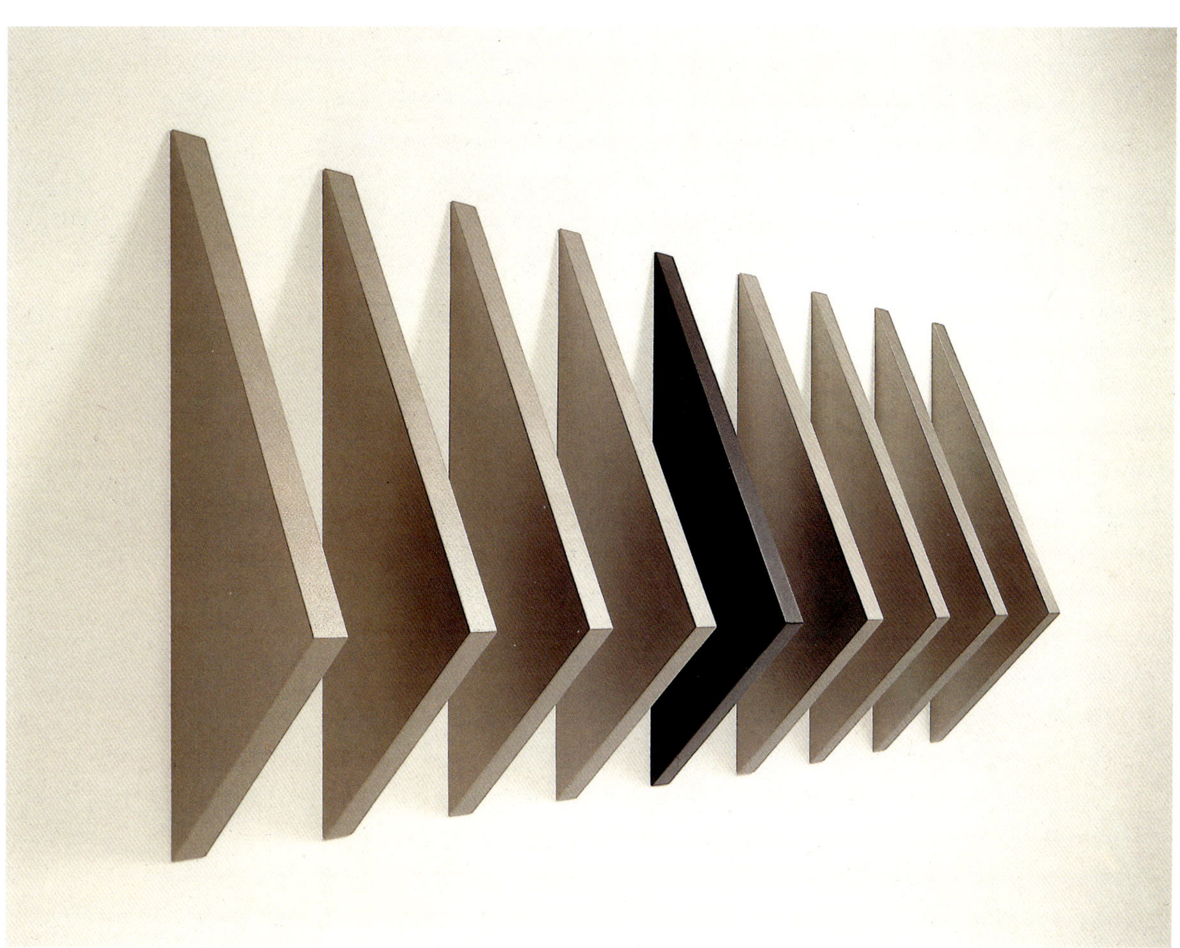

KIYO HIGASHI GALLERY

8332 Melrose Avenue
Los Angeles, CA 90069
213.655.2482
213.655.7016 FAX

Contact:
Kiyo Higashi

Exhibiting:
Abstract-reductive work:
Paintings and sculpture

Madeline O'Connor

Shrike
1993, Metallic powder,
acrylic on canvas,
44" x 98 1/2" x 14"

Selected biography:

1993 Kiyo Higashi Gallery,
Los Angeles, CA;
Center for
Contemporary Art,
Santa Fe, NM

1991 Moody Gallery,
Houston, TX

1988 Stamford Museum &
Nature Center,
Stamford, CT

1987 Project Gallery P.S.1,
Long Island City, NY

1986 101 Spring Street,
New York, NY

EUGENIA CUCALON GALLERY

145 East 72nd Street
New York, NY 10021
212.472.8741
212.472.8741 FAX

Contact:
Eugenia Cucalon
Marta Newman

Exhibiting:
Contemporary Art by
North and South American
and European Artists

Meret Oppenheim

HM-HM
1969, Acrylic on canvas,
wood and oil,
78¾" × 37½"

Selected Biography:

1994 Eugenia Cucalon
Gallery, Miami Art Fair
1993 Solo Show,
Rene Ziegler Gallery,
Zurich
1992 Group Show,
Eugenia Cucalon
Gallery,
New York
1990 Retrospective Show at
Palau de la Virreina
Museum, Barcelona
1989 Retrospective Show at
ICA, London
1987 Retrospective Show at
Kunst museum, Berna
Note: Besides the listed
exhibitions Meret Oppenheim
has had many more.

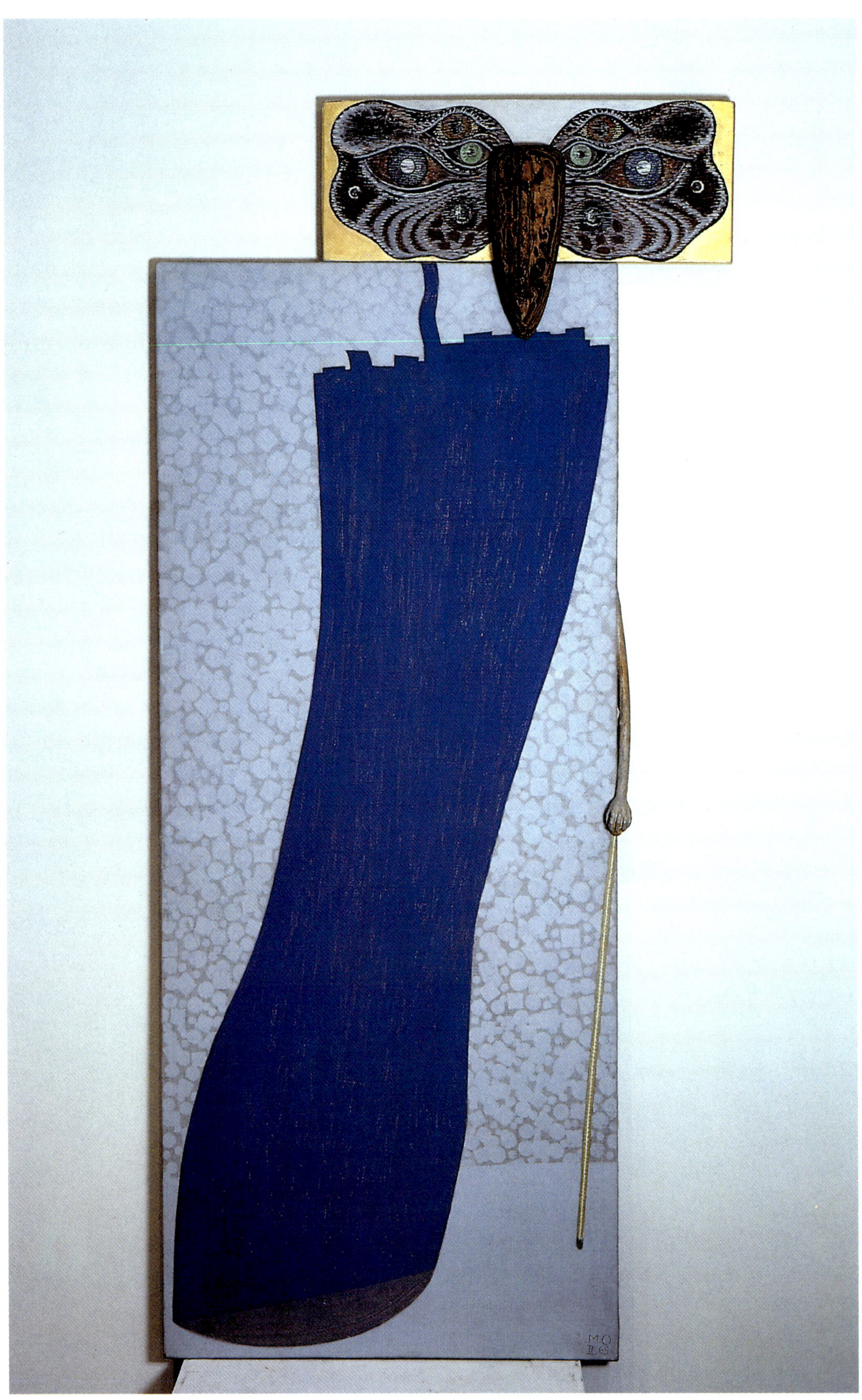

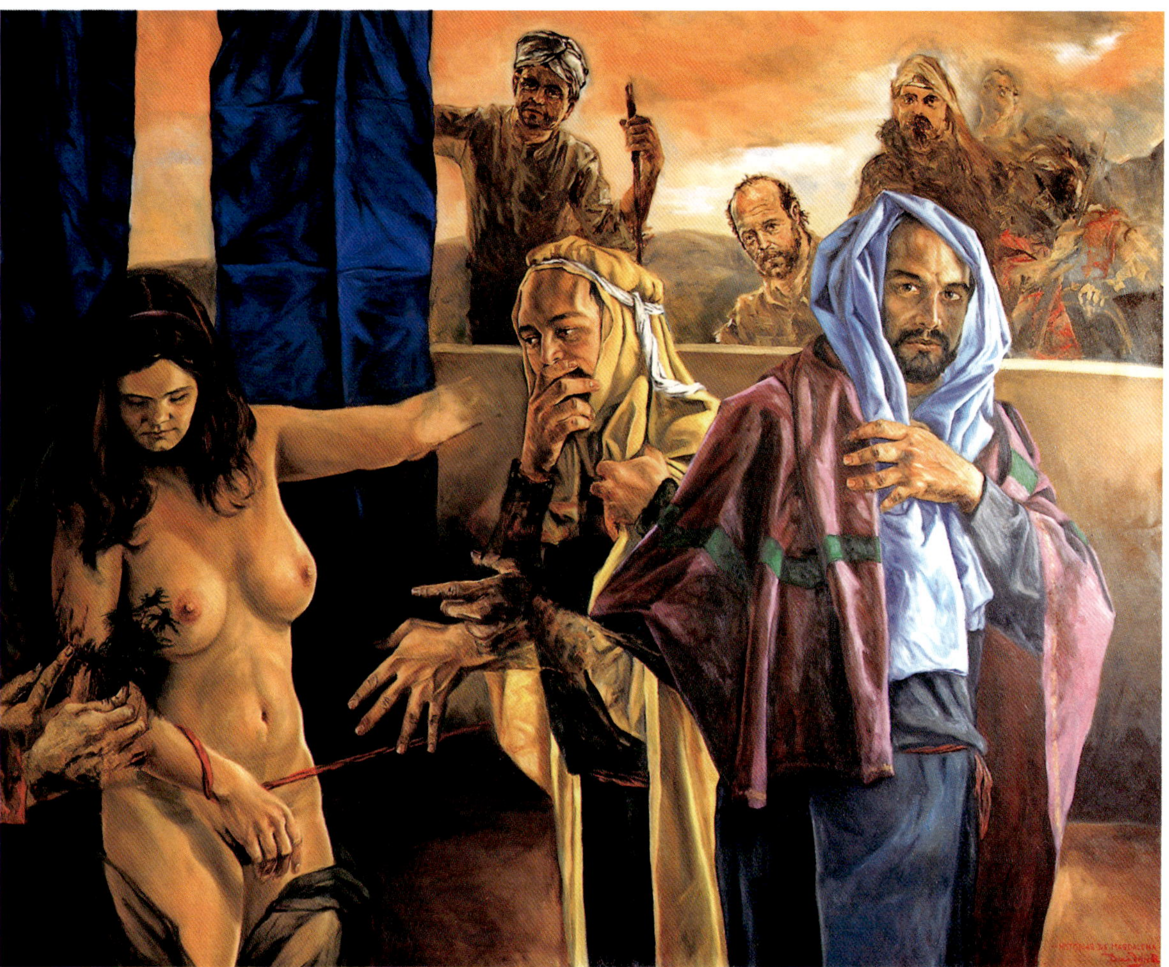

1

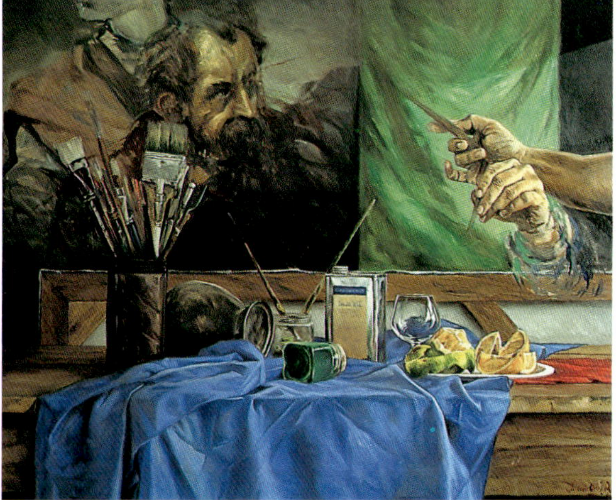

2

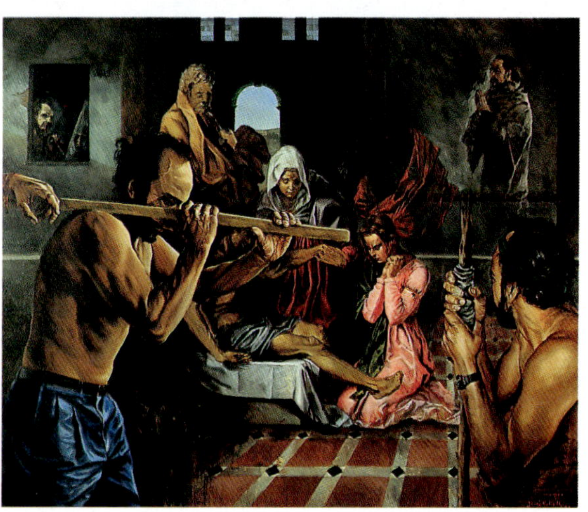

3

FENIX FINE ARTS

180 N.E. 40th St.
Miami, FL 33137
305.573.2727
305.542.8289
305.576.7707 FAX

Contact:
George Gandelman

Exhibiting:
Latin American Art

Dario Ortiz-Robledo

1. *Historias De Magdalena*
   ("Stories of Magdalena")
   ("Self Portrait")
   1993, Oil on Canvas,
   140 cms. x 170 cms.

2. *La Mesa En EL Taller*
   ("The Table At The Studio")
   1993, Oil on Canvas,
   85 cms. x 110 cms.

3. *Sobre Como Cargar Una*
   Cruz
   ("Of How To Carry A Cross")
   1993, Oil on Canvas,
   140 cms. x 170 cms.

Selected Biography:

1994 Gandelman's Fenix Six,
     Fenix Fine Arts,
     Miami, FL

1993 Galeria Duque-Arango,
     Medellin, Colombia

1991 Galerie Art-Vie,
     Paris, France

PRIOR EDITIONS

1049 Cambie St.
Vancouver, BC V6B 5L7
604.685.0535

Contact:
Nigel Harrison
Torrie Groening

Exhibiting:
Contemporary Canadian
and contemporary prints
and paperworks

David Ostrem

1. *Drunk Artist*
   1991, Acrylic on canvas,
   34" x 42"

2. *Always Trying to
   Understand Everything*
   1992, Acrylic on canvas,
   33" x 43"

Selected Biography:
1992 Solo show:
   Prior Editions
1991 Solo show:
   Prior Editions
1990 Solo show:
   Burnaby Public Art
   Gallery, Burnaby, BC

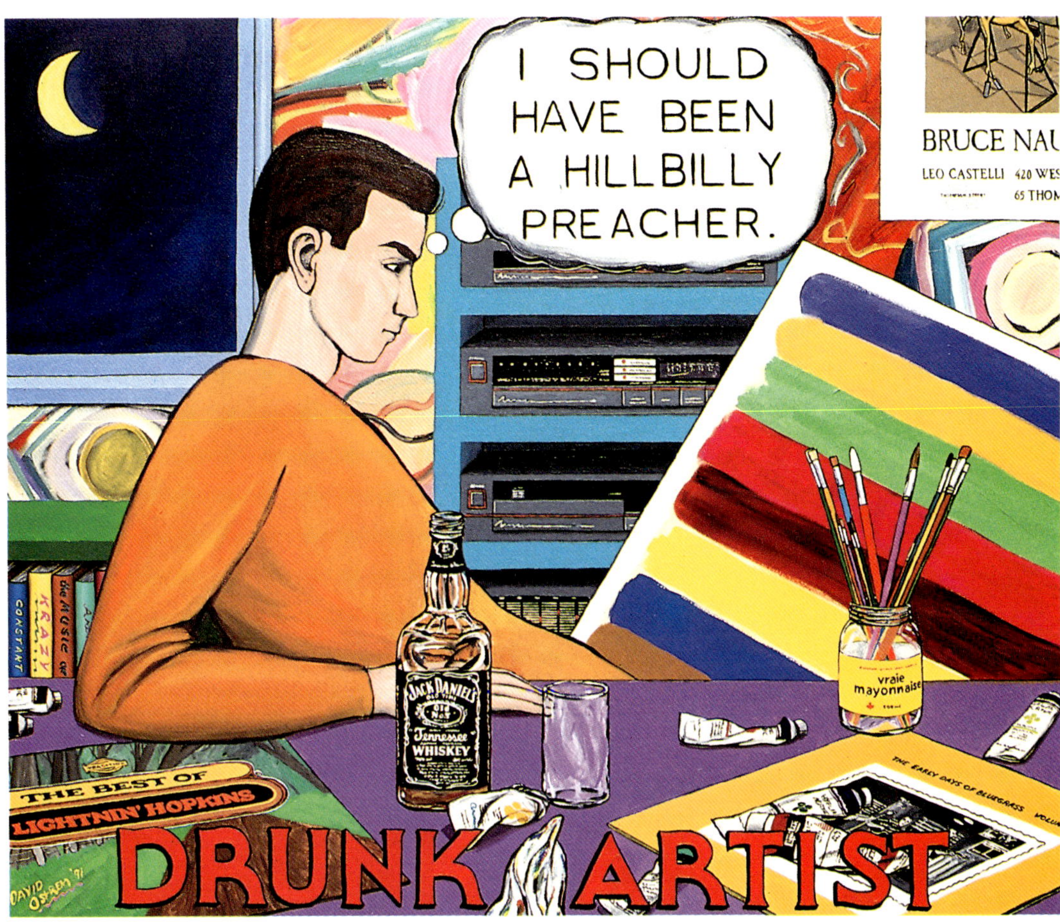

1

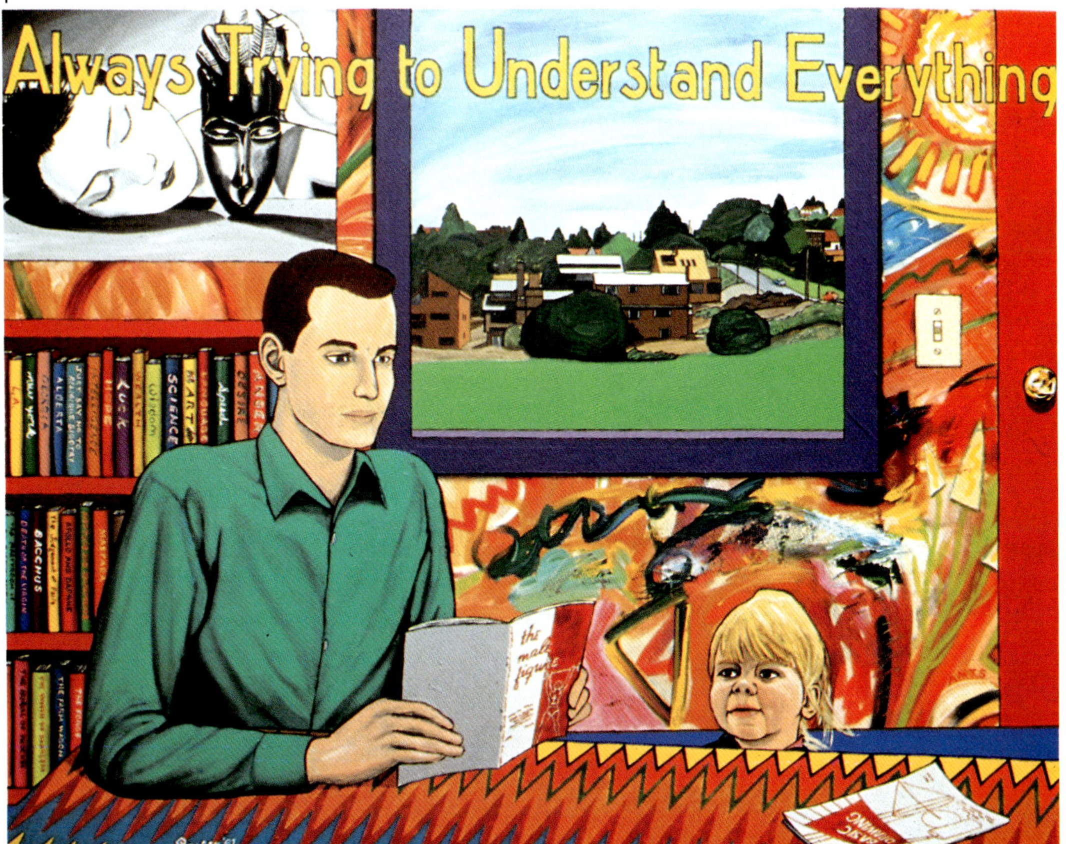

2

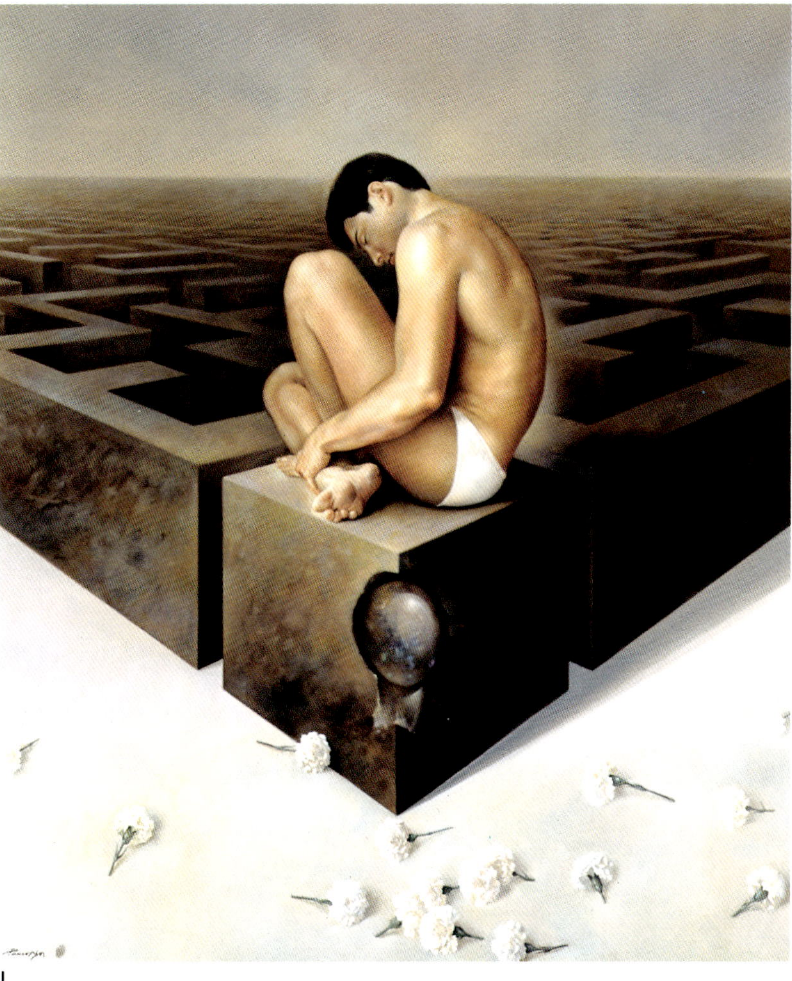

1

FENIX FINE ARTS

180 N.E. 40th St.
Miami, FL 33137
305.573.2727
305.542.8289
305.576.7707 FAX

Contact:
George Gandelman

Exhibiting:
Latin American Art

Alberto Pancorbo

1. *Laberintos Del Alma I*
   ("Mazes of The Soul I")
   1992, Oil on Linen,
   130 cms. x 114 cms.

2. *Alicia En La Ciudad*
   (From "In The City Series")
   1991, Lost wax bronze,
   Edition of 9,
   height 92.5 cms.

3. *January 15, 1991*
   (The Day The Gulf War
   Started)
   1991, Oil on Linen,
   146 cms. x 114 cms.

Selected Biography:

1993   The Americas Gallery,
       New York, NY

       Gandelman's Fenix Six,
       Fenix Fine Arts,
       Miami, FL

       1st Place Winner, The
       Spring Fine Arts
       Competition at the
       Florida Museum of
       Hispanic & Latin
       American Art, Miami, FL
       (With work shown
       above, "Laberintos Del
       Alma I", image 1)

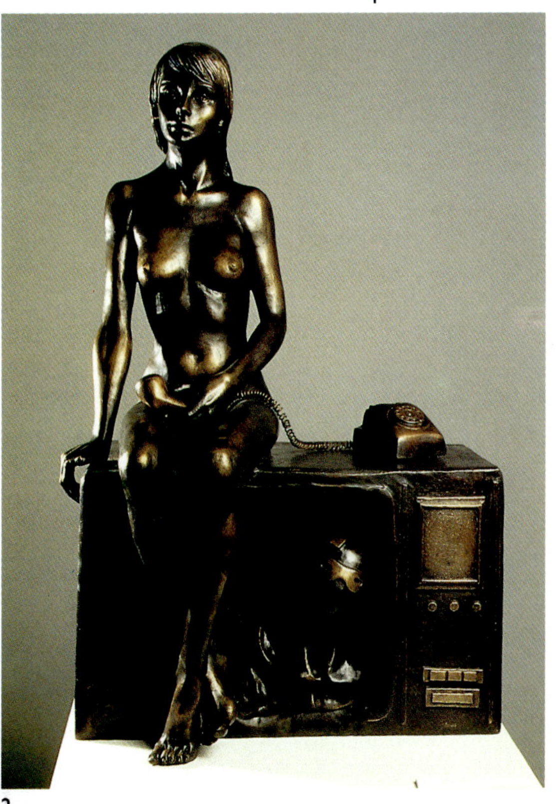

2

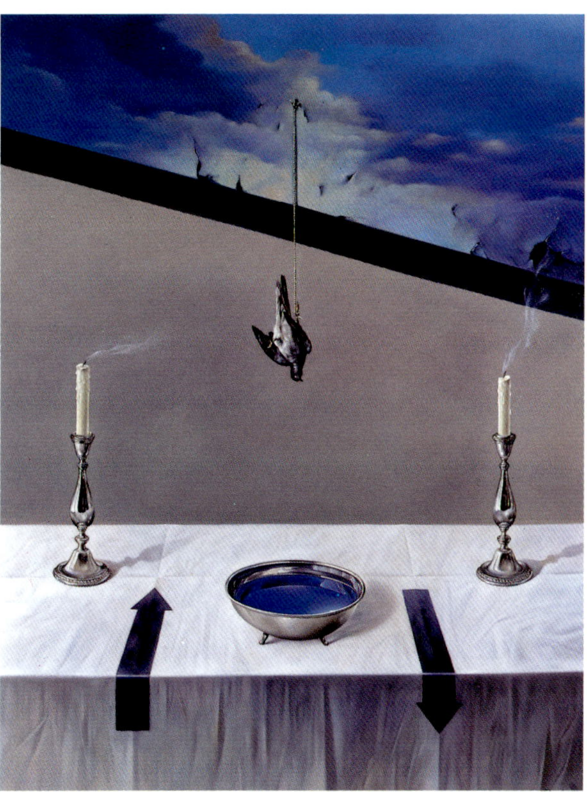

3

DIANE FARRIS GALLERY

1565 West 7th Avenue
Vancouver B.C. V6J 1S1
Canada
604.737.2629
604.737.2675 FAX

Contact:
Diane Farris, Director

Exhibiting:
Contemporary Canadian
and International Art

Laurie Papou

1. *Heaven & Earth*
   1993, Oil on panel;
   acrylic on metal,
   30.25" x 44"

2. *Check Mate*
   1991, Oil and wax on
   panel with wood &
   metal construction,
   72" x 120"

Selected Biography:

1994 Solo show,
   Diane Farris Gallery,
   Vancouver, BC

1993 Solo show,
   Diane Farris Gallery,
   Vancouver, BC

   London Life Young
   Contemporaries
   (National Touring
   Exhibition), London
   Regional Art Gallery,
   London, ONT

   Artropolis 93,
   Vancouver, BC

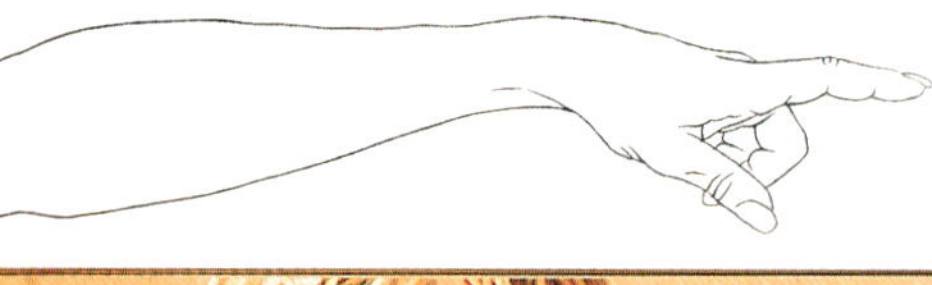
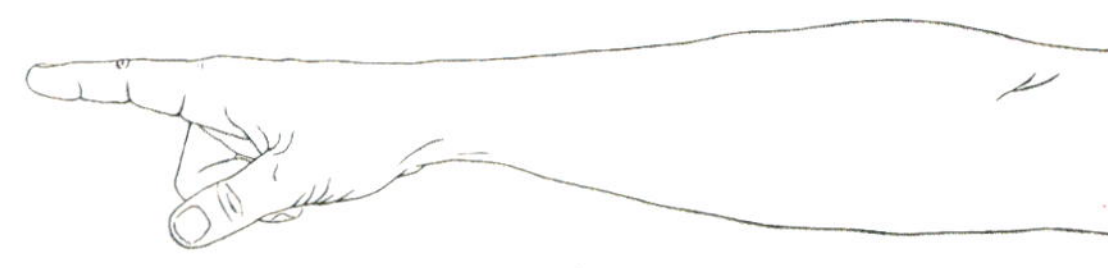
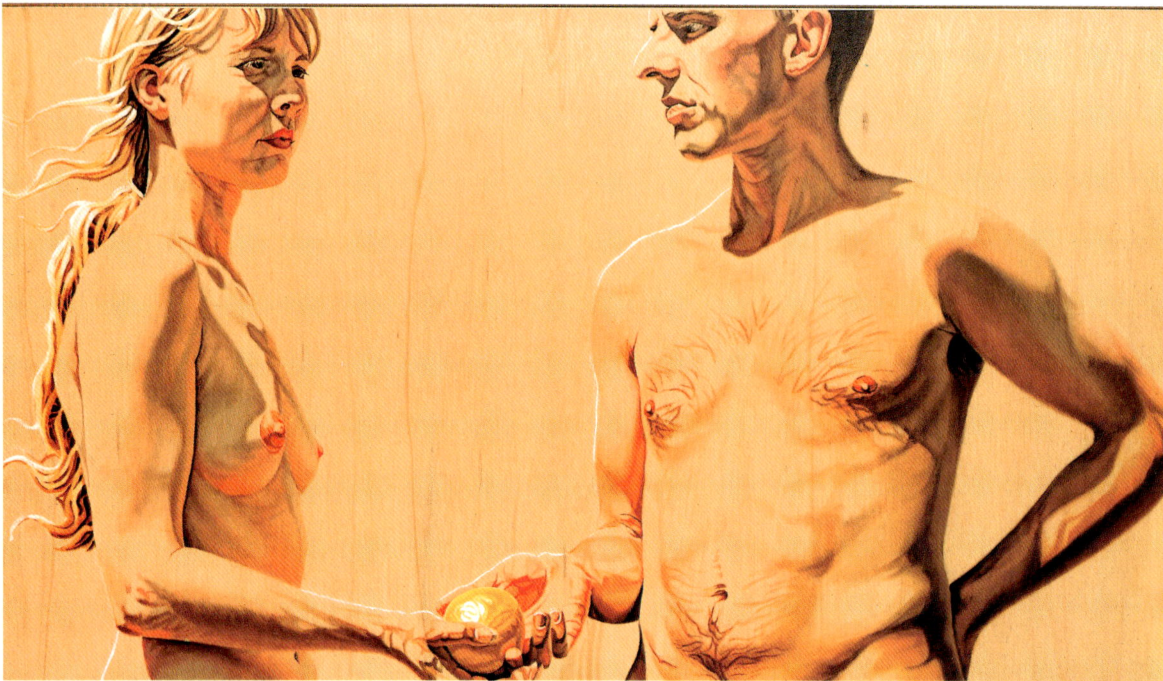

1

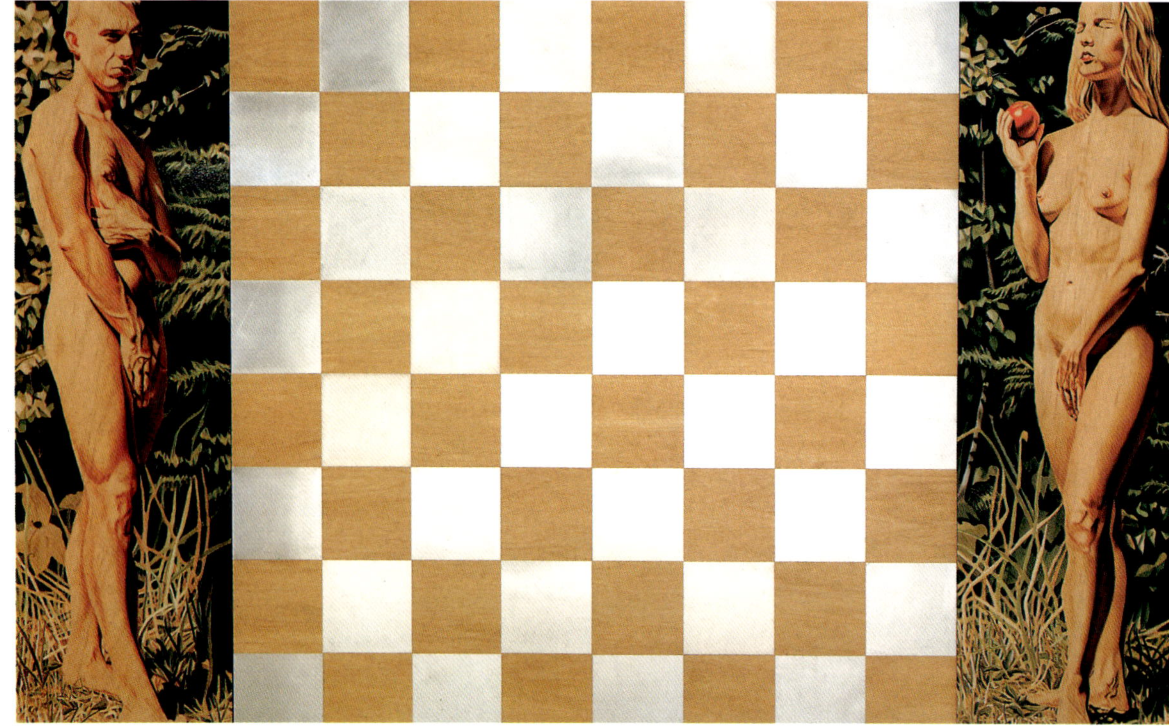

2

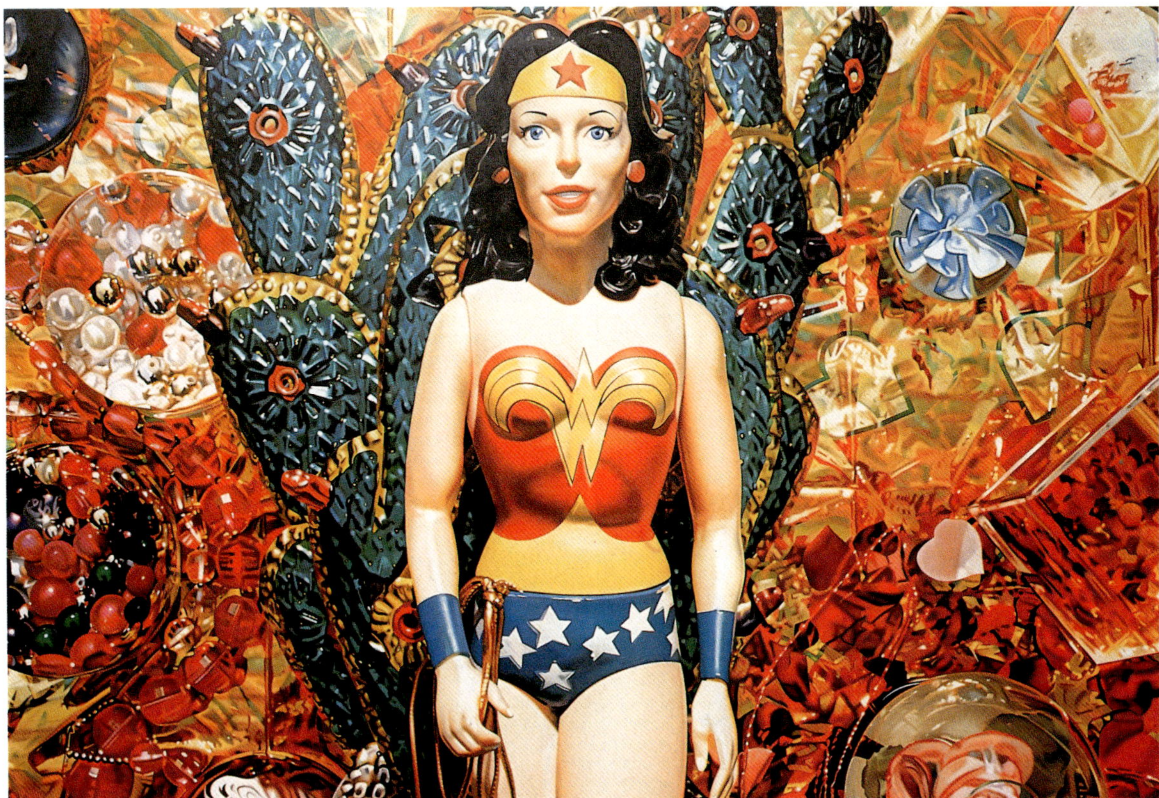

1.

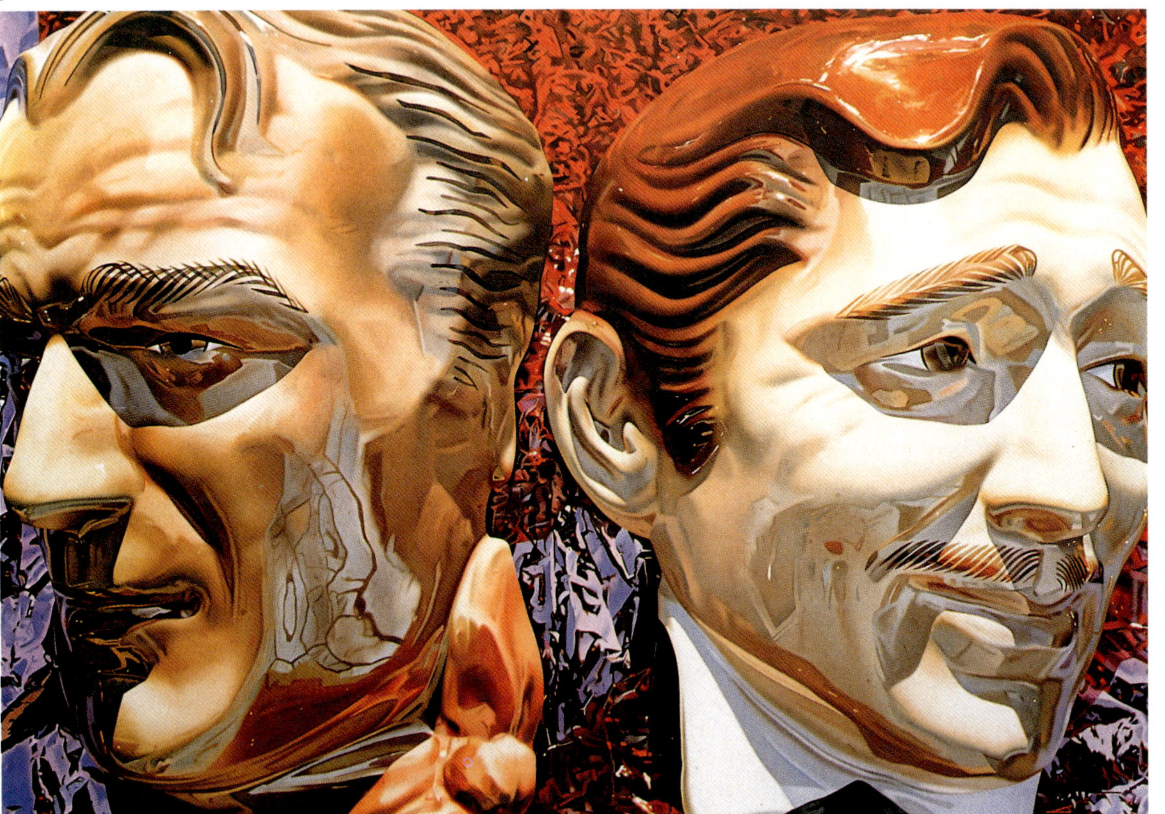

2.

LOUIS K. MEISEL GALLERY

141 Prince Street
New York, NY 10012
212.677.1340
212.533.7340 FAX

Contact:
Louis K. Meisel
Diane Sena

Exhibiting:
Photo-Realist painting and other technically skilled contemporary disciplines

David Parrish

1. *Wonder Woman*
   1993, Oil on canvas,
   67" x 100.5"

2. *The Duke and The King*
   1991, Oil on canvas,
   72" x 108"

Selected Collections:

Birmingham
Museum of Art, AL;
Montgomery Museum
of Fine Arts, AL;
Huntsville Museum
of Art, AL;
Greenville County
Museum of Art, SC;
Memphis Brooks
Museum of Art, TN;
Flint Institute
of Arts, MI;
Rose Art Museum,
Waltham, MA

PHYLLIS KIND
GALLERY

313 West Superior
Chicago, IL 60610
312.642.6302
312.642.8502 FAX

136 Greene Street
New York, NY 10012
212.925.1200
212.941.7841 FAX

Contact:
Phyllis Kind

Exhibiting:
Contemporary
American, Soviet, Naive,
and Outsider art

Ed Paschke

1. *Facade*
    1993, Oil on linen,
    40" x 36"

2. *Cineface*
    1993, Oil on linen,
    36" x 48"

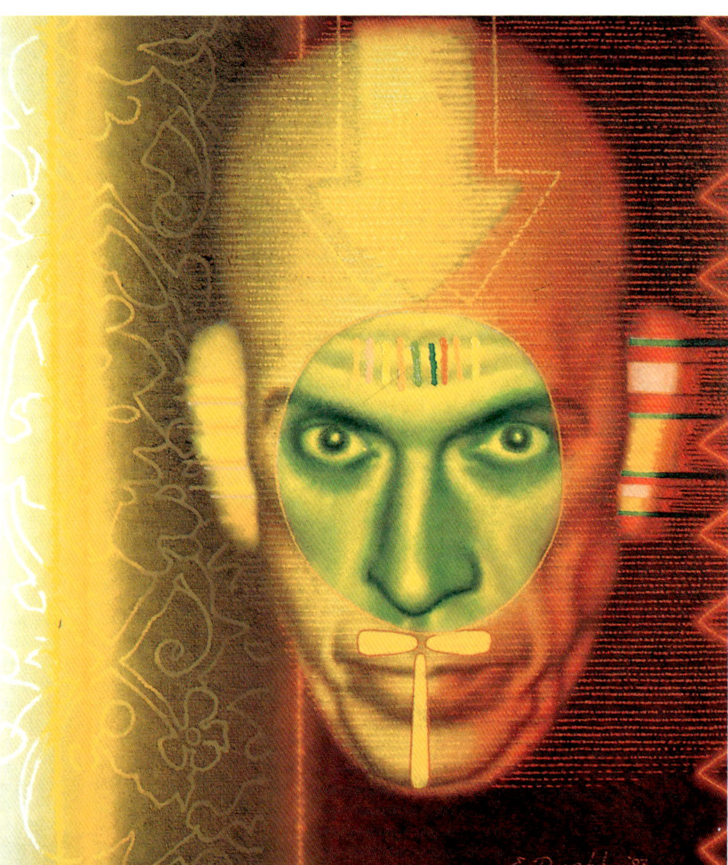

1

Selected Biography:

1993 Phyllis Kind Gallery,
       Chicago, IL

1992 Phyllis Kind Gallery,
       New York, NY

1989 Traveling exhibition:
       "Ed Paschke
       Retrospective",
       The Art Institute of
       Chicago; Musee
       National d'Art,
       Moderne, Paris;
       Dallas Art Museum,
       Dallas, TX

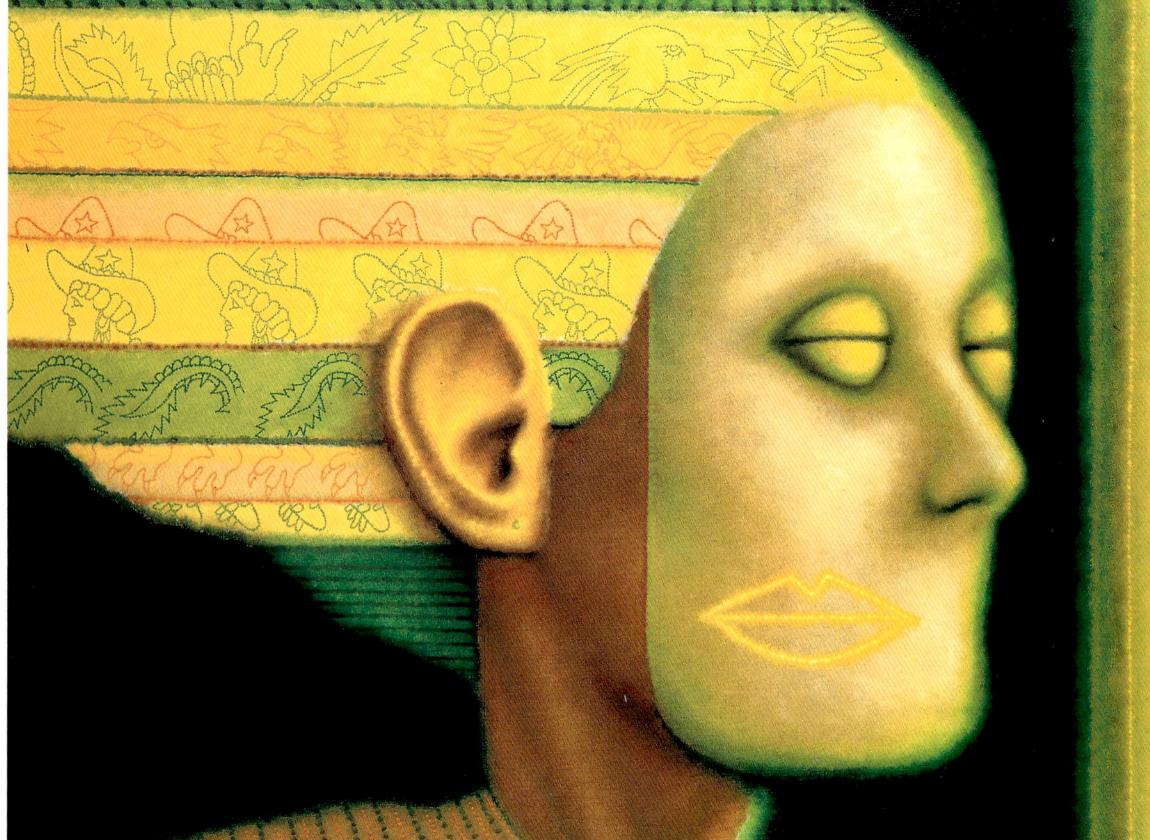

2

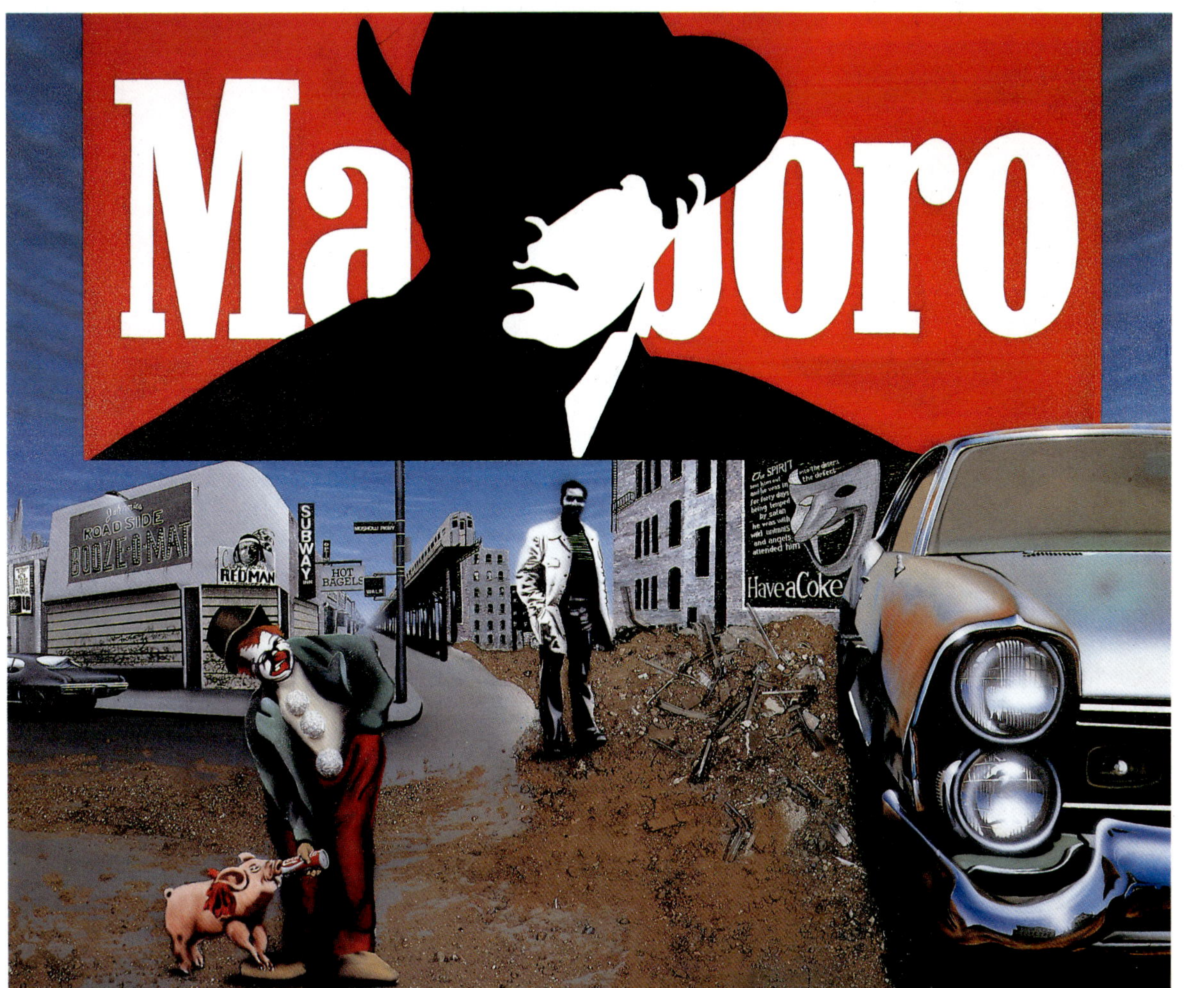

SARAH BAIN
GALLERY

1112 Brea
Brea, CA 92621
714.257.1440
714.257.0192 FAX

Contact:
Sally Waranch

Exhibiting:
Emerging & established
contemporary artists

Ron Pastucha

Badlands
1994,
Acrylic/dirt on canvas,
66" x 80"

Selected Biography:
1994 Solo exhibition;
       Sarah Bain Gallery,
       Brea, CA;
       New Trends Show'94,
       Hong Kong
1993 Solo exhibition;
       Sarah Bain Gallery,
       Brea, CA;
       Solo exhibition;
       Devorzon Gallery,
       Los Angeles, CA
1992 "Fat in the Fire: Fear
       and Loathing in L.A.",
       Ashley Craig Gallery,
       Venice, CA;
       Chicago International
       Art Expo;
       Art L.A. 92,
       Los Angeles, CA

CARIB ART GALLERY

584 Broadway
New York, NY 10012
212.343.2539
212.343.2659 FAX

Contact:
Veronica Ortiz
Sully Saneaux

Exhibiting:
Contemporary art from
Latin America and the
Caribbean

Guillo Perez

Homenaje a las Americas
1992, Oil on canvas,
45" x 50"

Selected Biography:

1992 Instituto Frances de
America Latina, Mexico
1990 Galeria de Arte
Moderno,
Santo Domingo,
Dominican Republic
1989 Centro de la Cultura,
Santiago, Dominican
Republic
1985 Casa de la Cultura,
Quito, Ecuador
1976 Palacio Nacional de
Bellas Artes,
Santo Domingo,
Dominican Republic

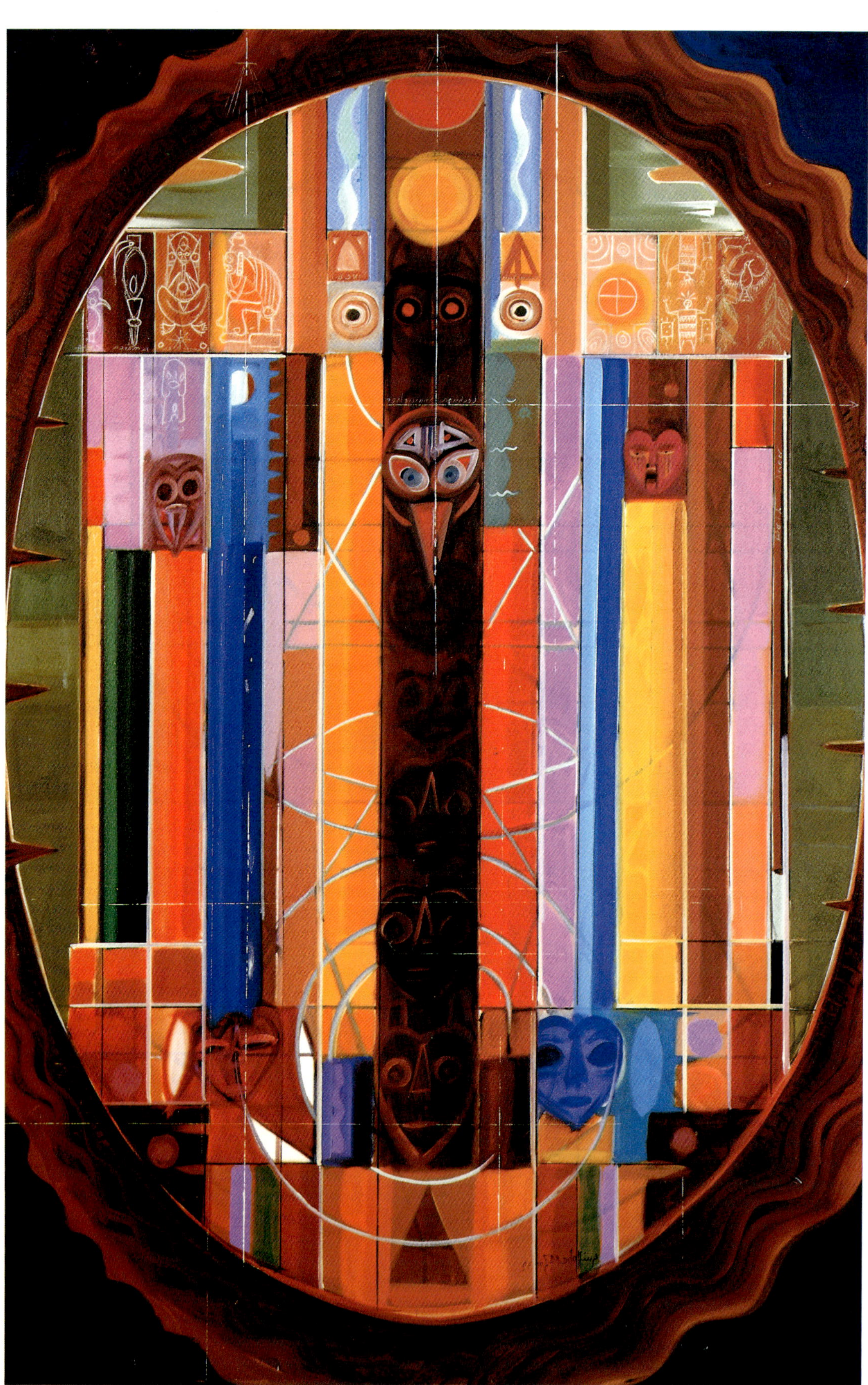

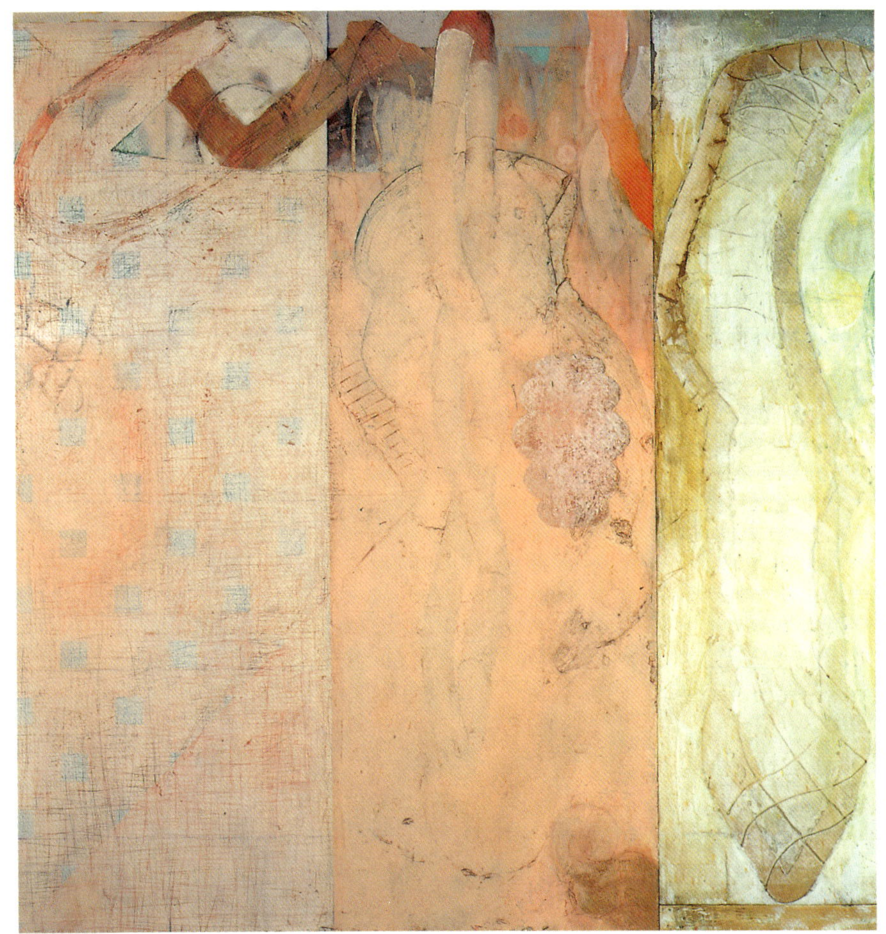

1

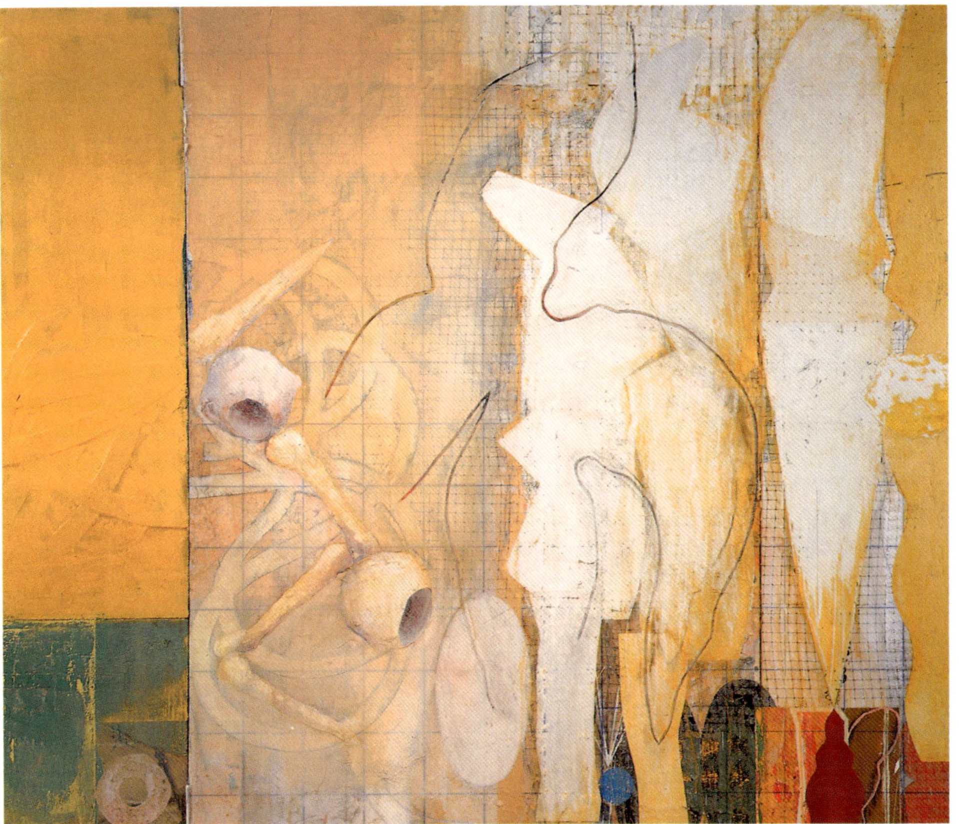

2

L.A. ARTCORE CENTER

420 East 3rd Street Ste. 110
Los Angeles, CA 90013
213.617.3274

Contact:
Lydia Takeshita, Director

Exhibiting:
Contemporary painting
and sculpture

Joseph Piasentin

1. *Pink Swirl*
   1993, Acrylic,
   oil, enamel on
   wood and canvas,
   68" x 66"

2. *Apparition*
   1992-93, Acrylic,
   oil, enamel on
   wood and canvas,
   70" x 84"

Selected Collections:

1993 Gallery Markant,
   Langelo (Norg),
   Netherlands;
   L.A. Artcore, L.A., CA;
   LACA Gallery, L.A., CA

1992 Shinsegae Dongbang
   Plaza Art Gallery,
   Seoul, Korea;
   L.A. Artcore, L.A., CA

1991 South Bay
   Contemporary,
   Torrance, CA;
   Korean Cultural
   Center, L.A., CA

ITURRALDE GALLERY

154 N. La Brea Avenue
Los Angeles CA 90036
213.937.4267
213.937.4269 FAX

Contact:
Teresa Iturralde
Ana Iturralde

Exhibiting:
Contemporary Latin
American Art

Rodrigo Pimentel

1. *Pandemia*
   1993, Gouache on paper
   12½" x 16"

2. *Tonantzin*
   1993 / 94, Oil on canvas,
   78¾" x 78¾"

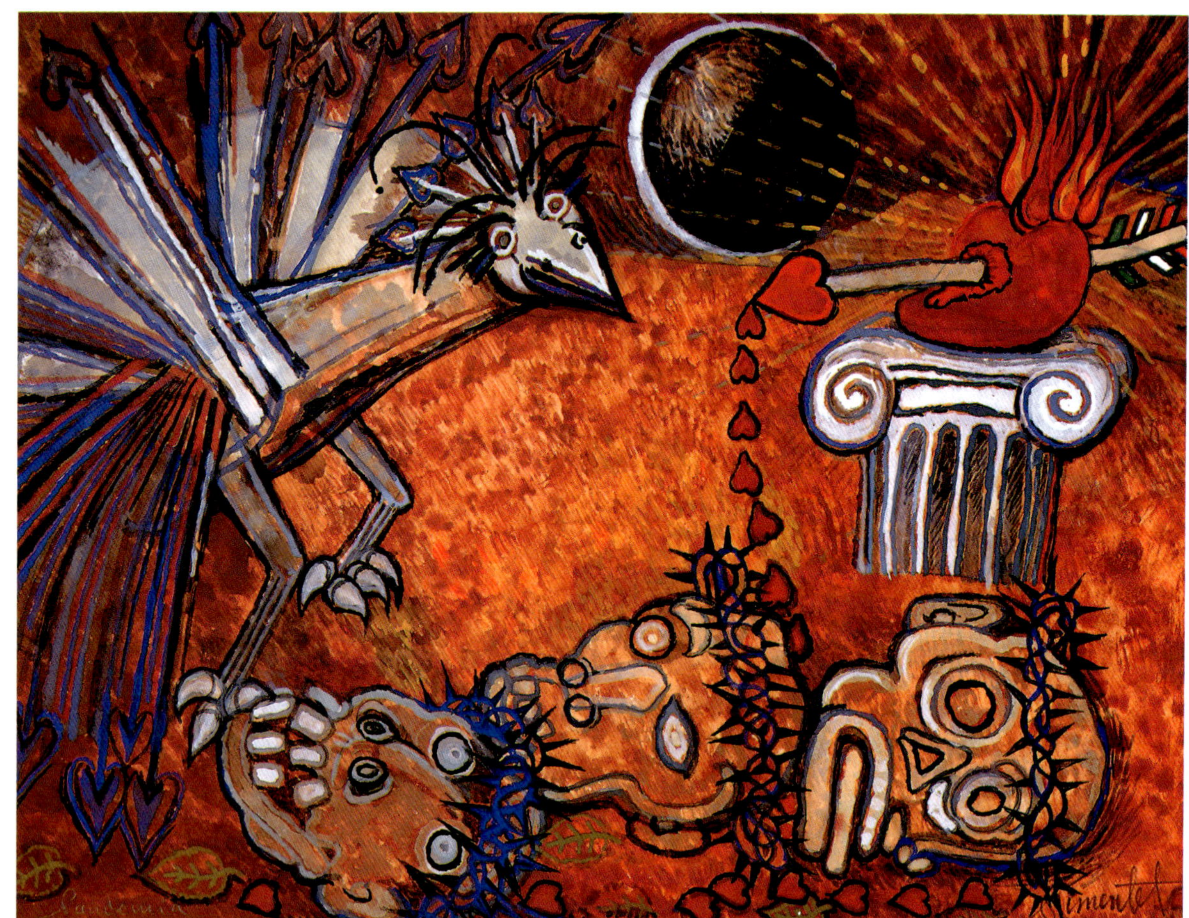

1

Selected Biography:

1994 Solo show,
   Iturralde Gallery,
   Los Angeles, CA

1993 Solo show,
   Elite Fine Art,
   Coral Gables, FL

1992 "Encuentros", Museo
   de Arte Moderno,
   Mexico City;
   Maison de L' Amerique
   Latine, Paris, France;
   Solo show,
   Iturralde Gallery,
   Los Angeles, CA

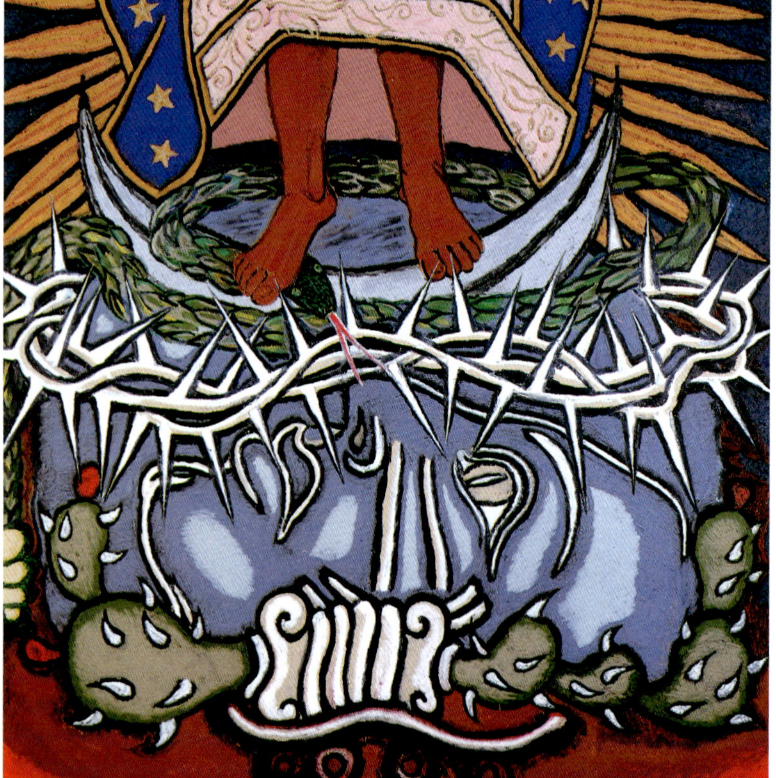

2

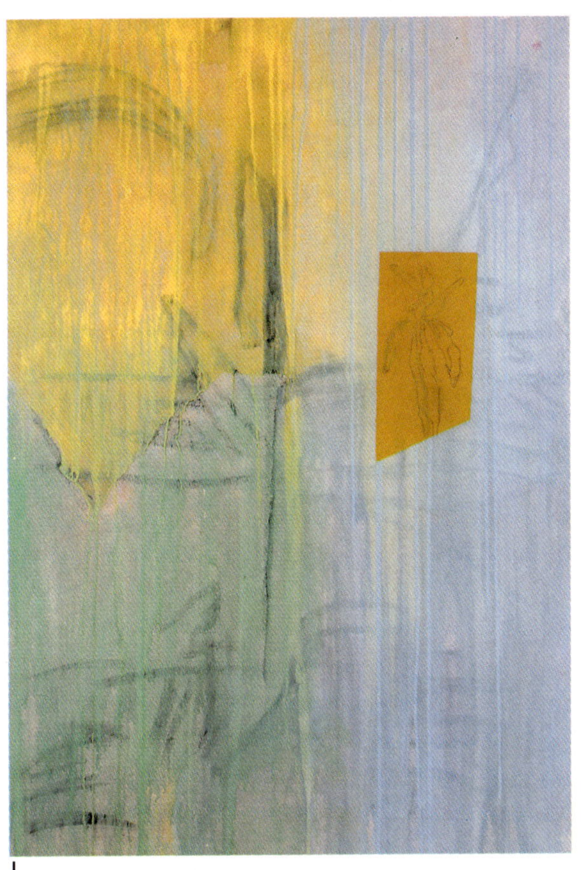

1

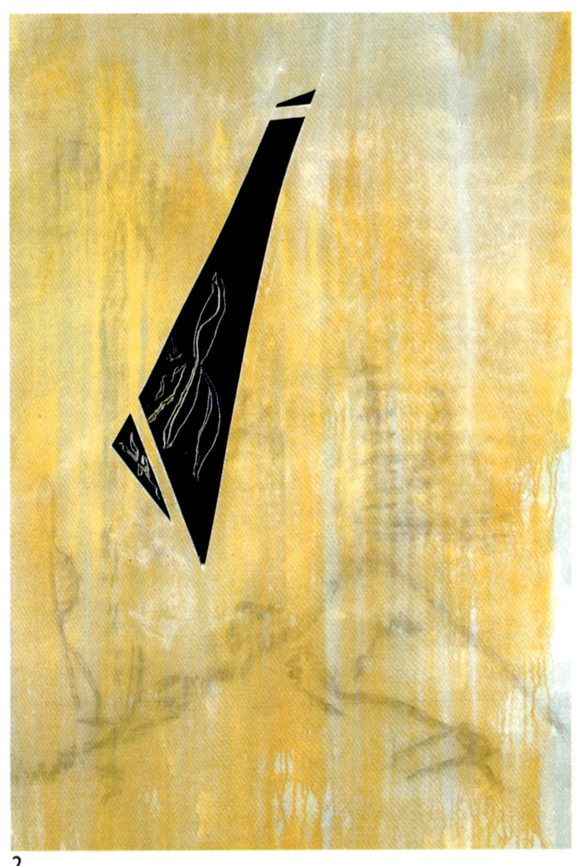

2

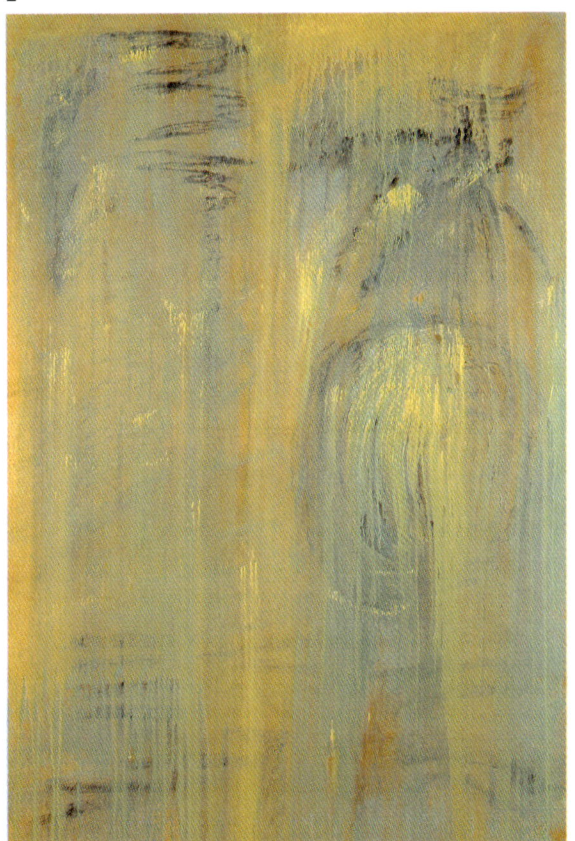

3

MONTSERRAT GALLERY

584 Broadway
New York, NY 10012
212.941.8899
212.274.1717 FAX

Contact:
Marie Montserrat Coll,
Director

Exhibiting:
Contemporary European
and American art

Kevin Pinkerton

1. *Formosan Landscape #3*
   23° x 120°
   1993, Acrylic, charcoal on
   canvas, 52" x 36"

2. *Formosan Landscape #8*
   1993, Acrylic, oil stick
   charcoal on canvas,
   52" x 38"

3. *Formosan Landscape #6*
   23° x 120°
   1993, Acrylic, charcoal
   on canvas,
   52" x 36"

Selected Biography:

1994 Montserrat Gallery,
        New York, NY

1993 Solo Exhibition Space II
        Taipei, Taiwan, R.O.C.

        New Phase Art Space,
        Tainan, Taiwan, R.O.C.

DIANE FARRIS GALLERY

1565 West 7th Avenue
Vancouver B.C. V6J 1S1
Canada
604.737.2629
604.737.2675 FAX

Contact:
Diane Farris, Director

Exhibiting:
Contemporary Canadian
and International Art

Taras Polataiko

1. *Photograph*
   1993, Acrylic on linen,
   78" x 78"

2. *You & the Artist*
   1993-94,
   Acrylic on canvas,
   65" x 130"

3. *You*
   1993, Acrylic on canvas,
   30" x 154"

Selected Biography:

1995 Solo show,
   Mendel Art Gallery,
   Saskatoon, SASK

1994 Solo show,
   Diane Farris Gallery,
   Vancouver, BC;
   Solo show,
   Rosemont Art Gallery,
   Regina, SASK;
   Solo show,
   MacKenzie Art Gallery,
   Regina, SASK

1989 Young Artist of the
   Soviet Union, National
   Gallery Manyezh,
   Moscow, U.S.S.R.

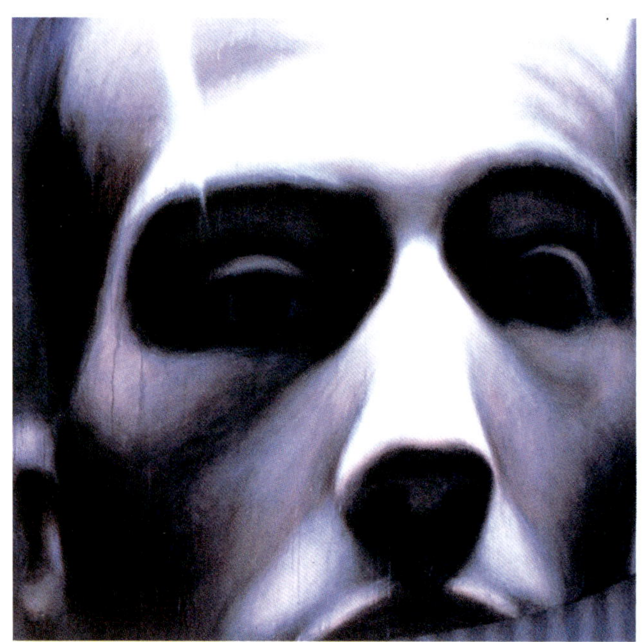

1

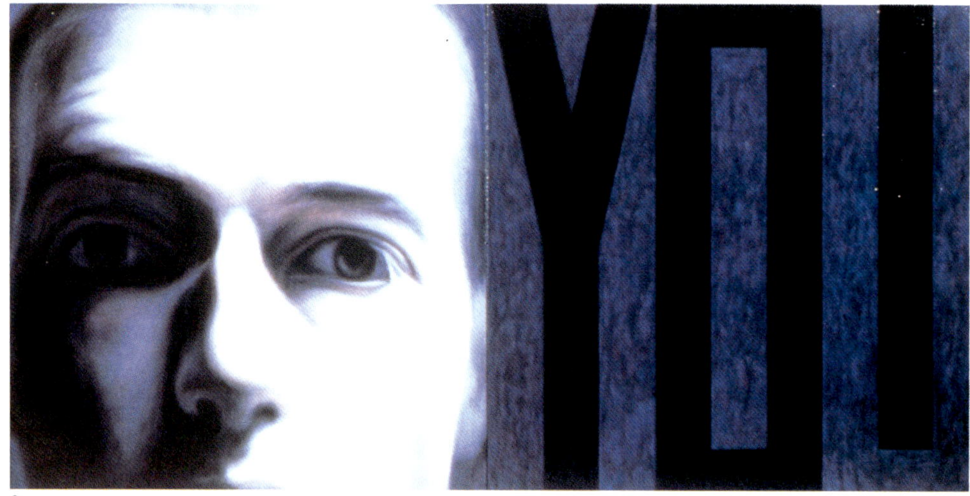

2

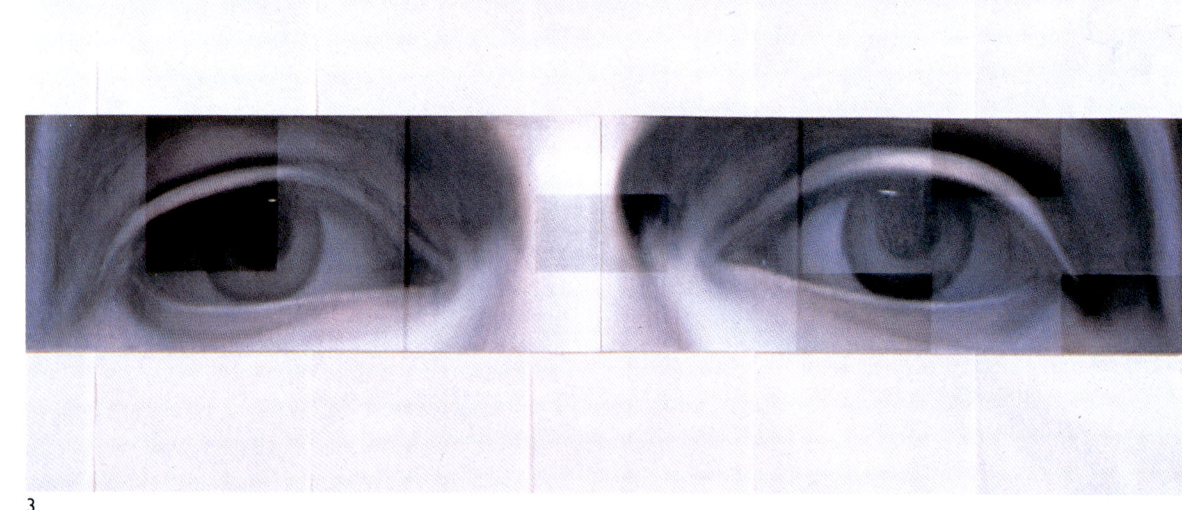

3

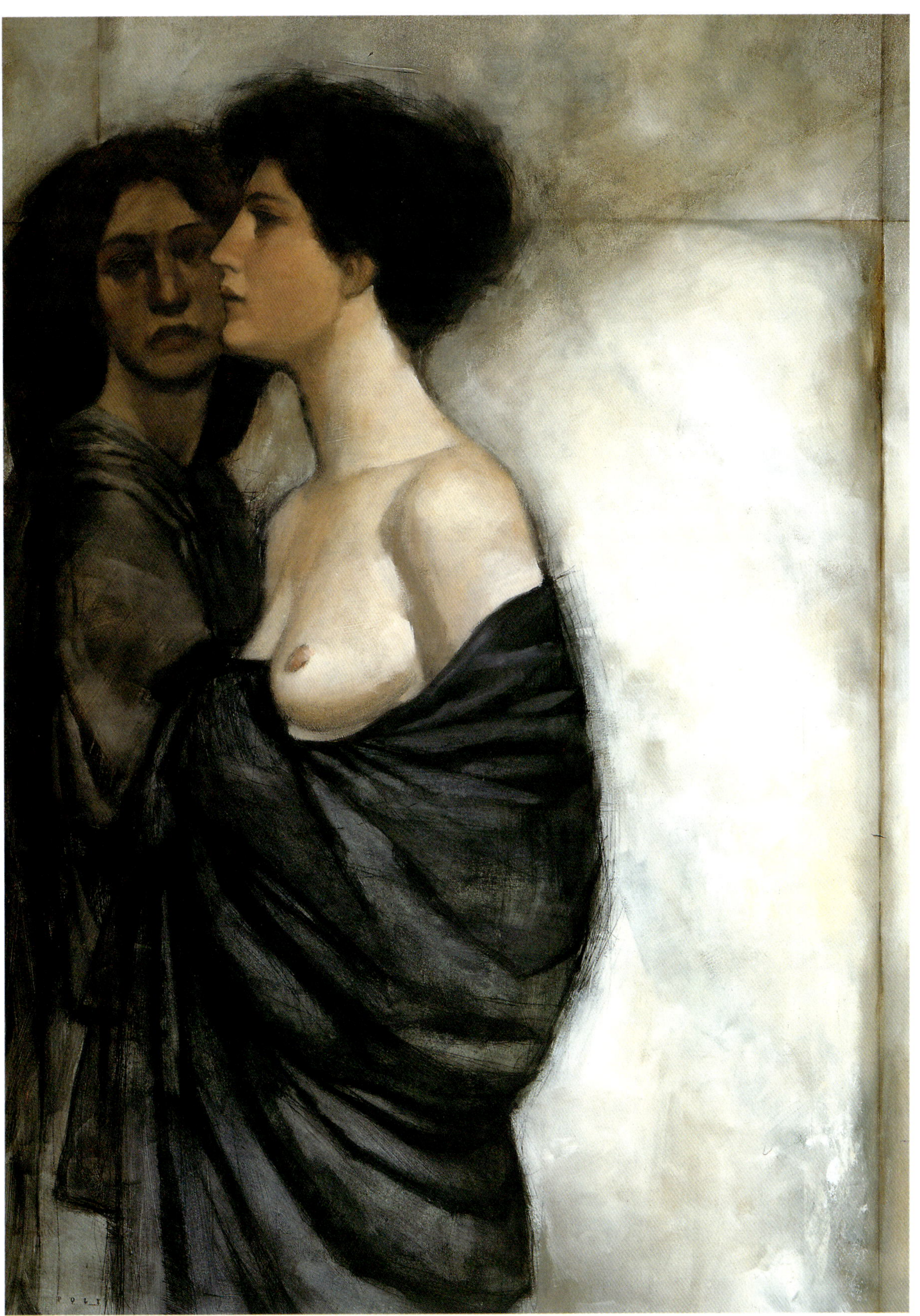

SARAH BAIN GALLERY

1112 Brea
Brea, CA 92621
714.257.1440
714.257.0192 FAX

Contact:
Sally Waranch

Exhibiting:
Emerging & established
contemporary artists

Poly

In Passing
1993, Acrylic on board,
30" x 40"

Selected Biography:

1995 Solo exhibition:
Gallery One,
Amsterdam, Holland

1994 New Trends 94,
Hong Kong

Solo exhibition:
Sarah Bain Gallery,
Brea, CA

Solo exhibition:
Kwai Fung Hin Gallery,
Hong Kong

MONTSERRAT GALLERY

584 Broadway
New York, NY 10012
212.941.8899
212.274.1717 FAX

Contact:
Marie Montserrat Coll,
Director

Exhibiting:
Contemporary European
and American art

Daniel Prieto

Viajes de Ulises
1989, Oil on canvas
68" x 57"

Works in museums:
Real Academia de
Bellas Artes, Spain;
Museo Santa Cruz de
Toledo, Spain;
Fondazione Carlo
Levi, Italy; Museo
Fader, Argentina;
Museo Jovellance,
Gijon, Spain;
Museo de Jaen, Spain;
Museo de la Rloja,
Spain; Museo Munioipal
de Santa Cruz de
Tenerite, Spain;
Biblioteca Nacional de
Espana, Spain; The
Florida Museum of
Hispanic and Latin
American Art

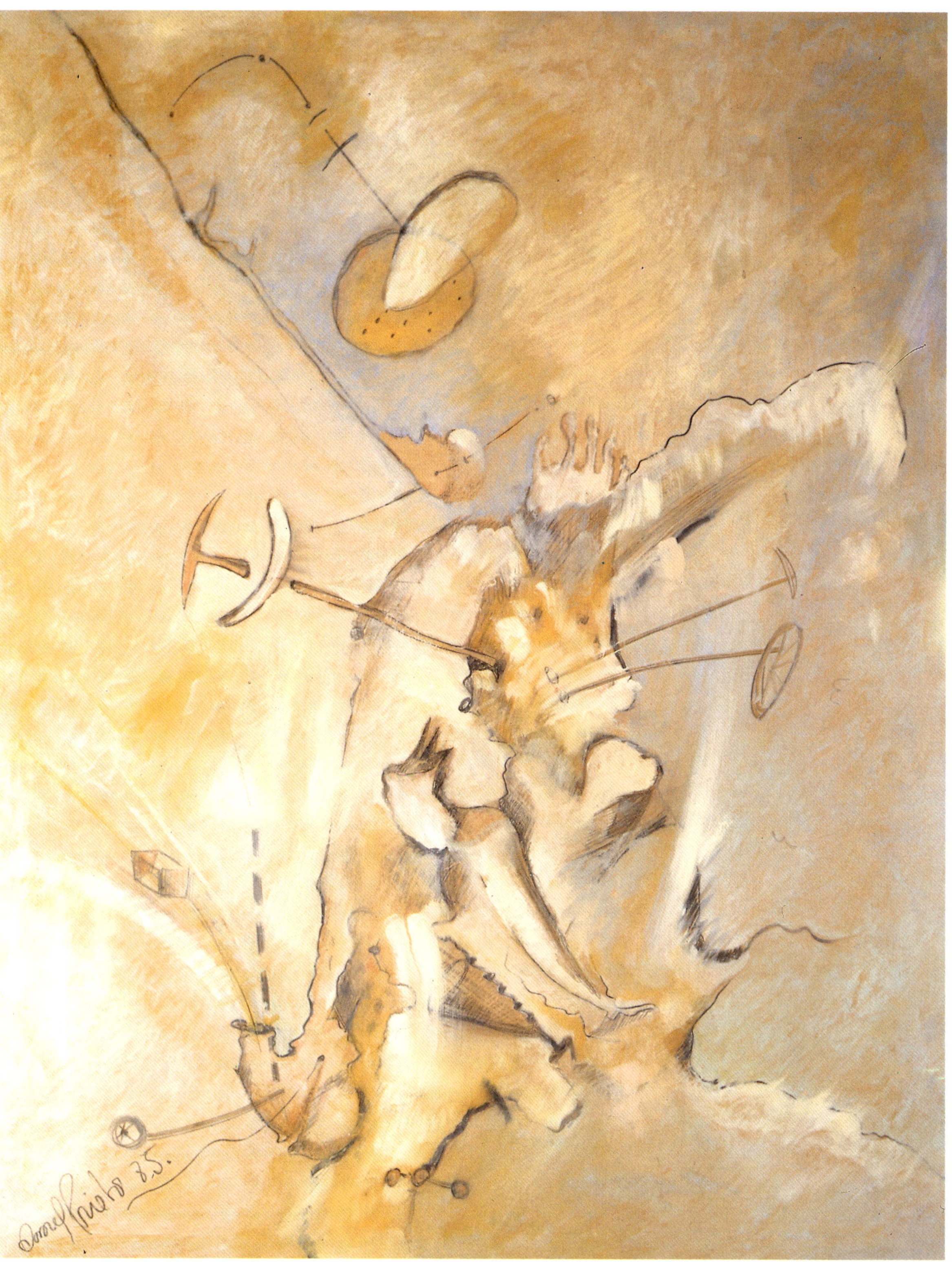

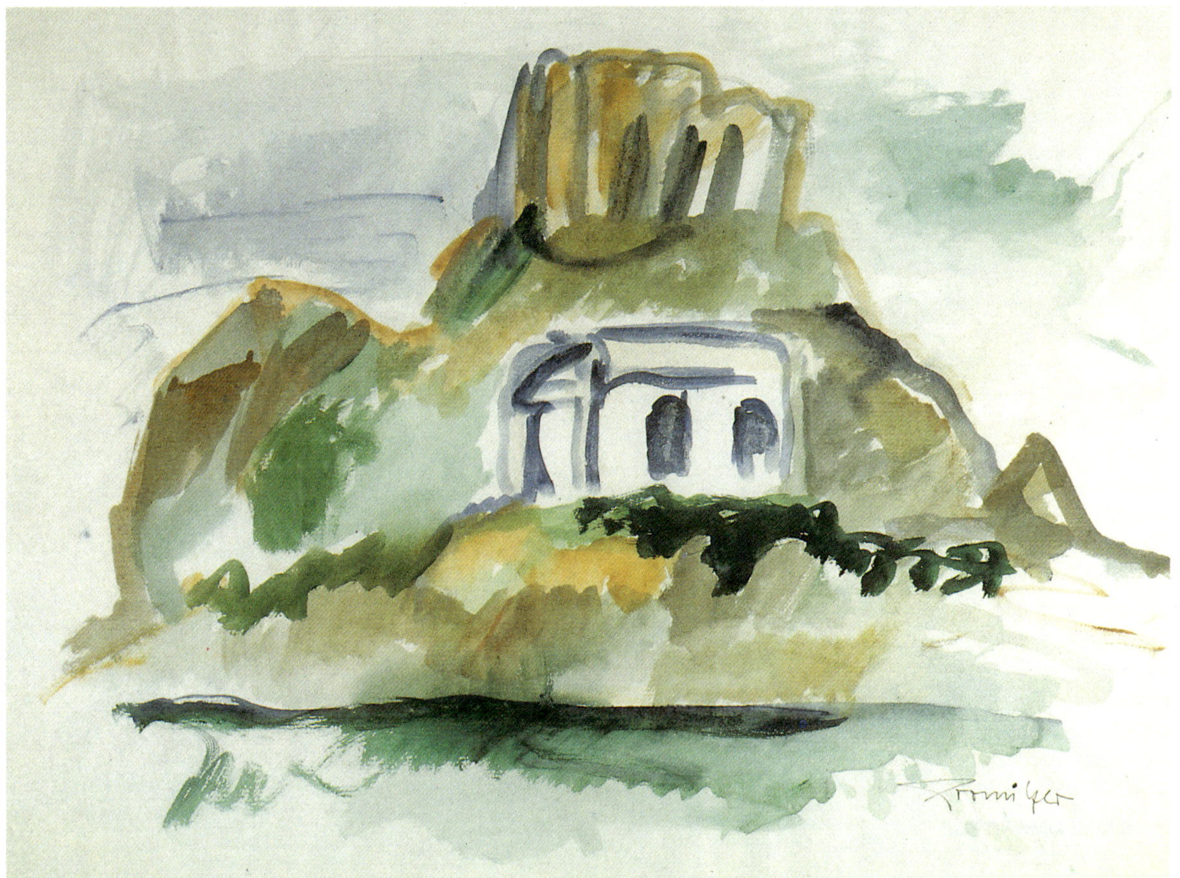

1

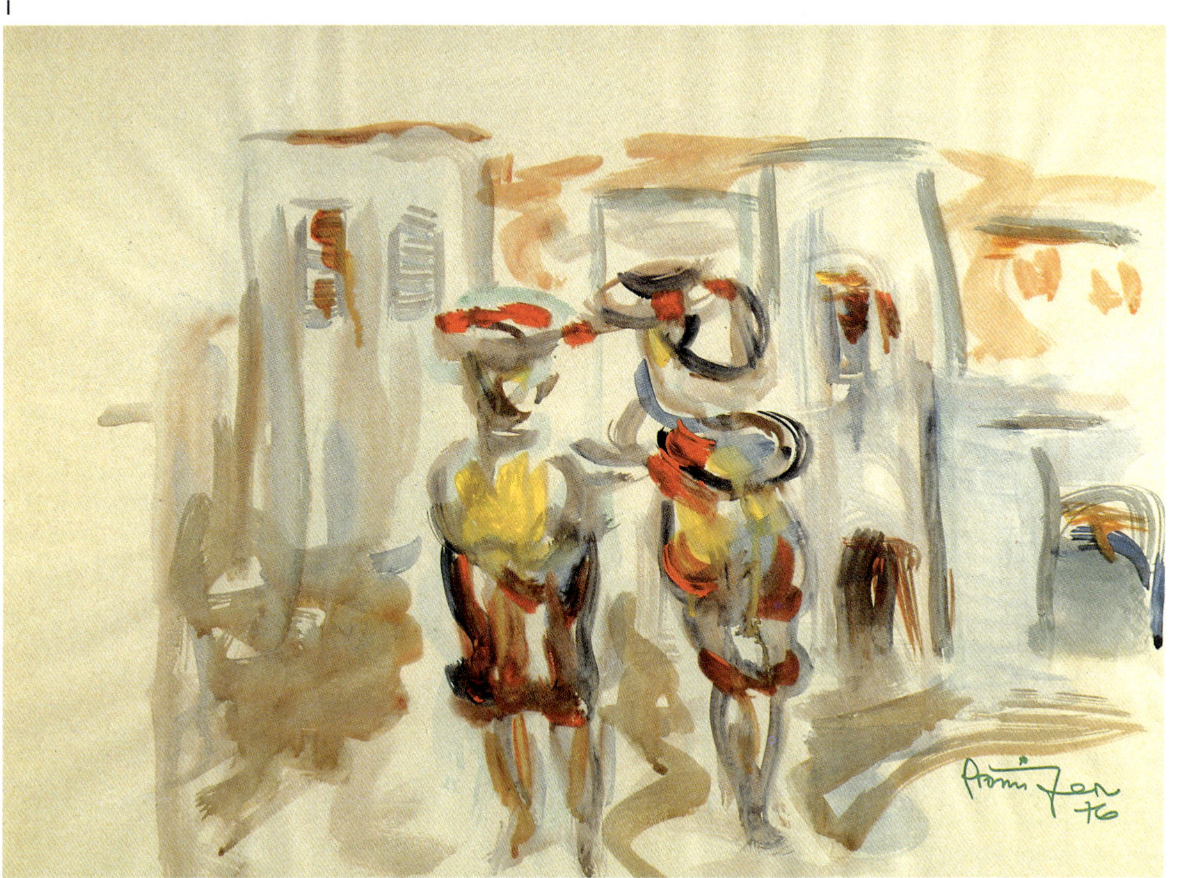

2

MONTSERRAT GALLERY

584 Broadway
New York, NY 10012
212.941.8899
212.274.1717 FAX

Contact:
Marie Montserrat Coll,
Director

Exhibiting:
Contemporary European
and American art

Gertrud Promitzer

1. *Kefalos*
   1992, Oil, 24" x 28"

2. *Fisherwomen Calabria Italy*

Selected Biography:

1993   Montserrat Gallery,
       New York, NY

1989   Galerie Der
       Bezirkshaupt
       Mannschaft, Melk

1987   Galerie Hofer Mit Josef
       E. Duvanel, Basel

1986   Kellergalerie Zurich

1985   Erte Spiga, Via Della
       Spiga Milano

       Schweizer
       Bankgesellschaft, Basel

CARIB ART GALLERY

584 Broadway
New York, NY 10012
212.343.2539
212.343.2659 FAX

Contact:
Veronica Ortiz
Sully Saneaux

Exhibiting:
Contemporary art from
Latin America and the
Caribbean

Andres Puig

*Dónde Estás ingenioso
Hidalgo?*
1994, Oil on canvas,
52" x 76"

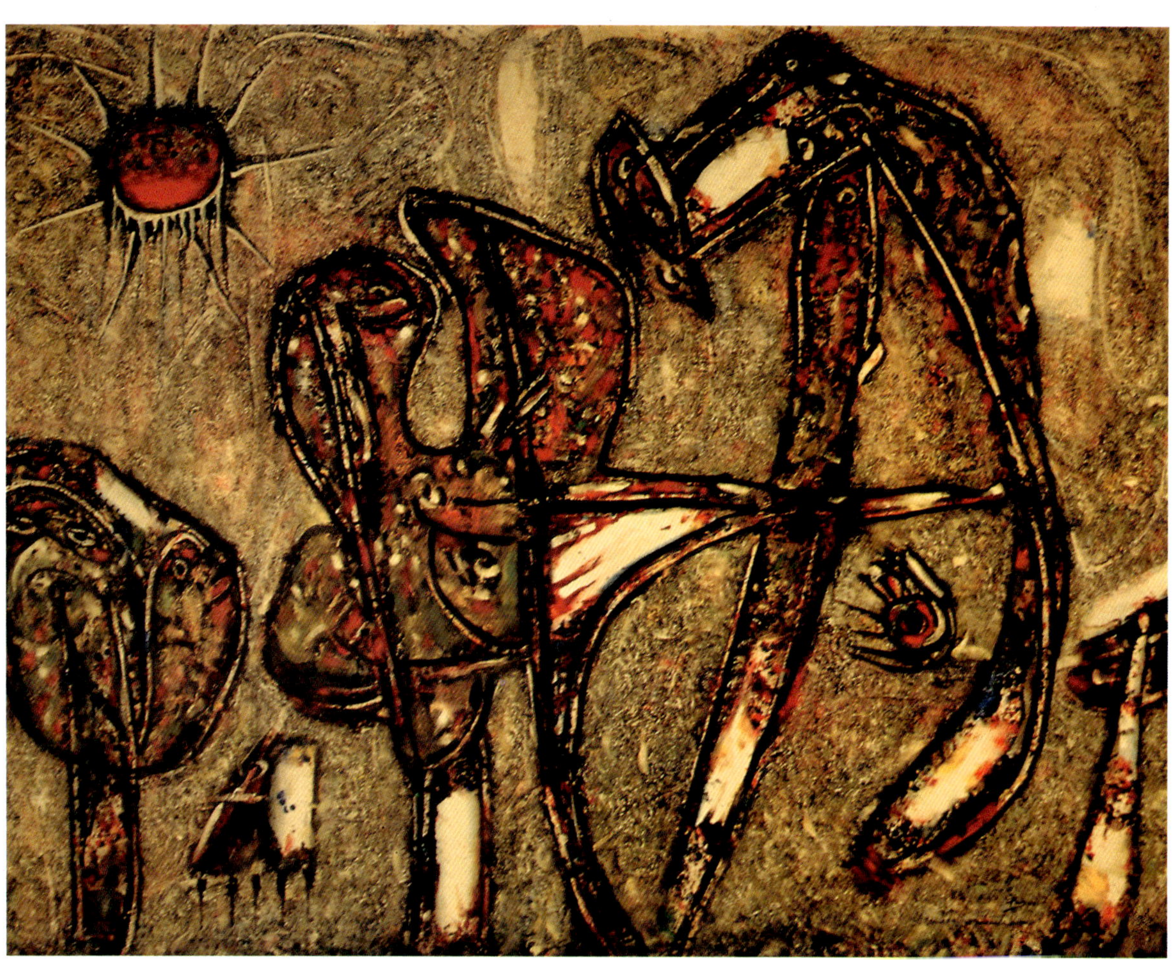

Selected Biography:

1993 From Cuba to Cuba:
Art as a Bridge,
Cuban Museum of Art
and Culture, Miami, FL;
Permanent Collection,
Carib Art Gallery,
New York, NY

1992 Something to Meditate,
Itinerant exhibition.
National Museum of
Fine Arts,
Santiago de Chile;
Cultural Center.
Buenos Aires,
Argentina;
Plastica
Latinoamericana,
Mexico City, Mexico

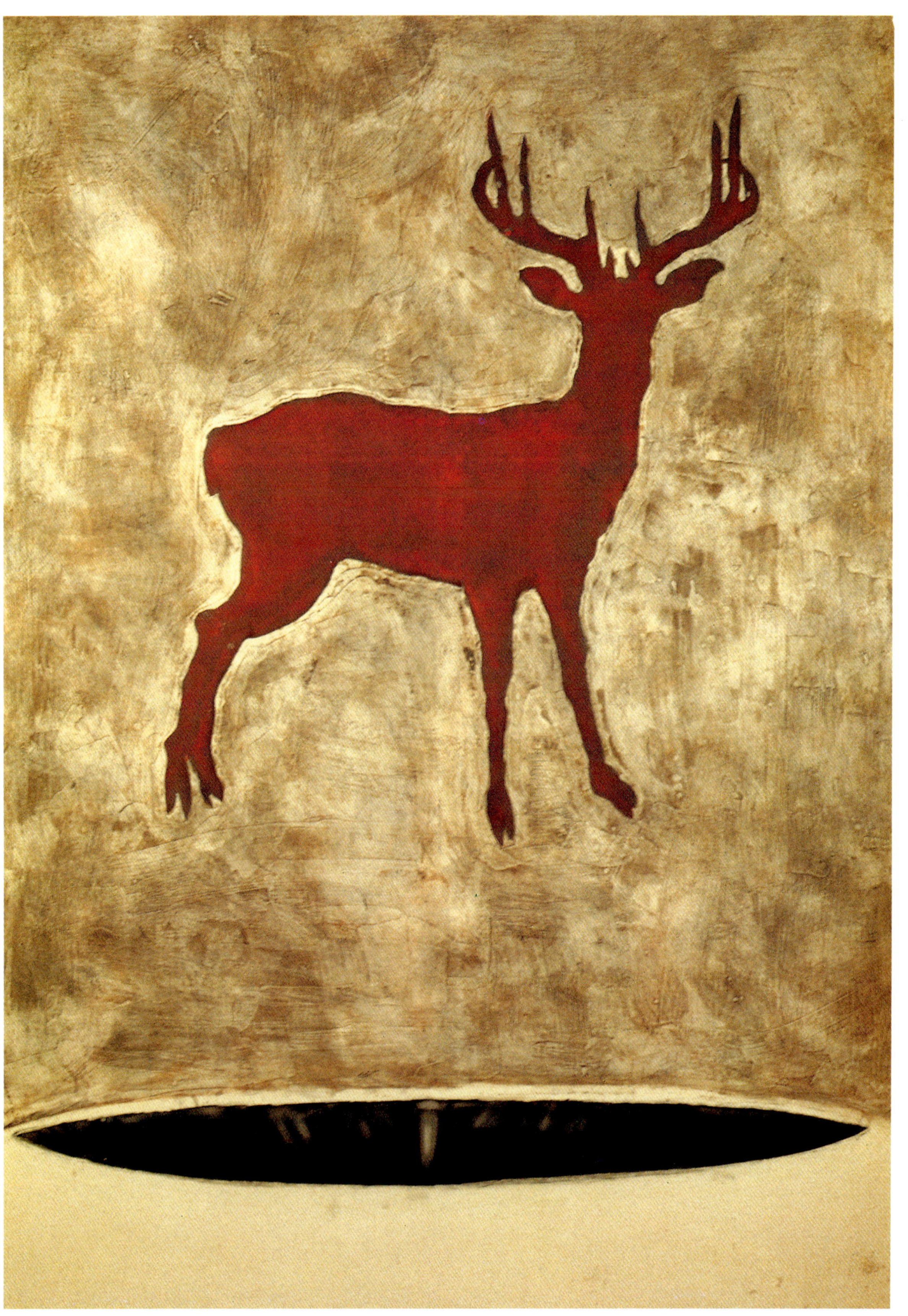

STUART LEVY
FINE ART

588 Broadway, Suite 303
New York. NY 10012
212.941.0009
212.941.7987 FAX

Contact:
Stuart Levy, President
Michael Lederer,
Assoc. Director

Exhibiting:
Contemporary Russian,
European and American
Artists

Osmo Rauhala

Early Morning I
1991,
Oil and wax on canvas,
96" x 66"

Selected Solo Exhibitions:

1994 "No Man's Land,"
Amos Anderson,
Helsinki, Finland

1993 Galleria Sculptor,
Helsinki; Institut
Finlandais, Paris

1992 Ratingen Stadt
Museum, Dusseldorf,
Germany; Crown
Gallery, Vancouver,
Canada; Nanky de
Vreeze Gallery,
Amsterdam; The Young
Artist of the Year 1992;
Tampere Art Museum,
Finland

KNOEDLER & COMPANY

19 E. 70 St.
New York, NY 10021
212.794.0550
212.772.6932 FAX

Contact:
Larry Rubin
Ann Freedman

Exhibiting:
Contemporary European
and American art

Robert Rauschenberg

Musical Sacks
1990, Acrylic on fabric,
61" x 64 1/8"

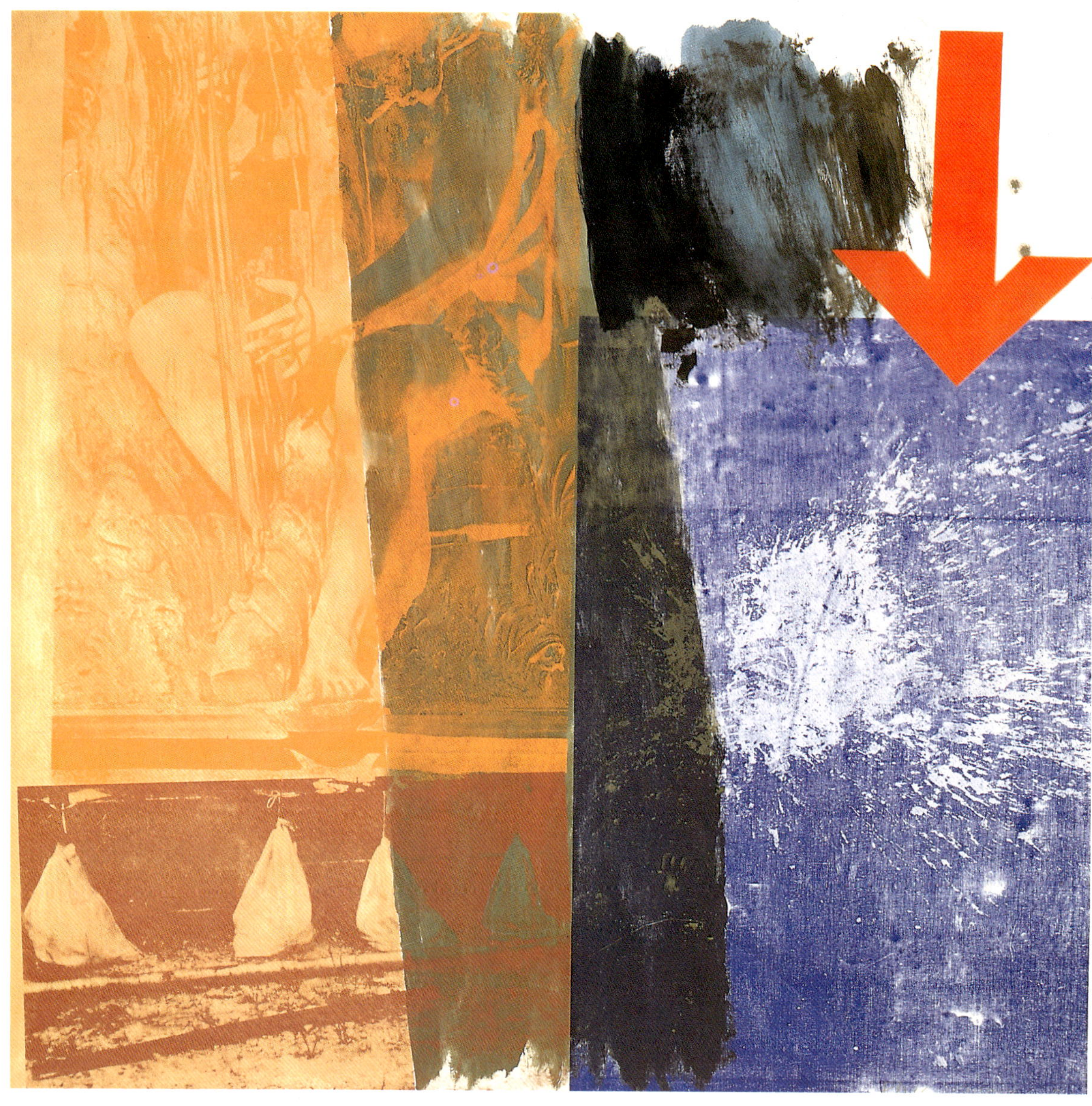

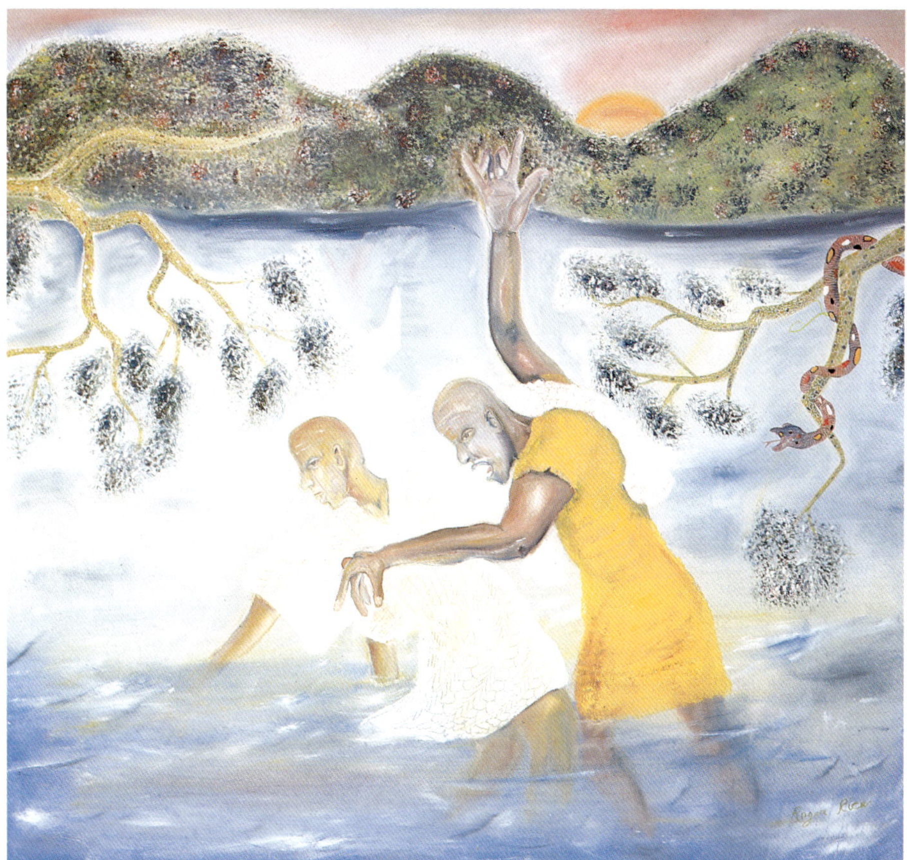

1

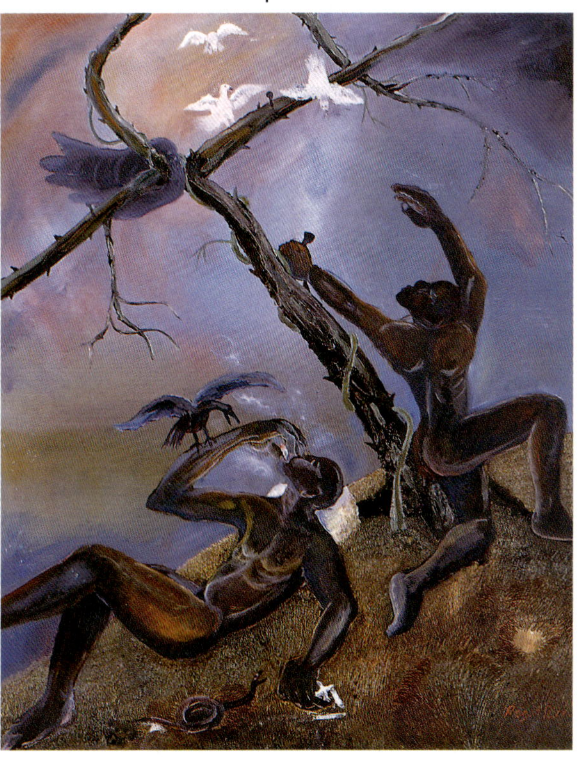

2

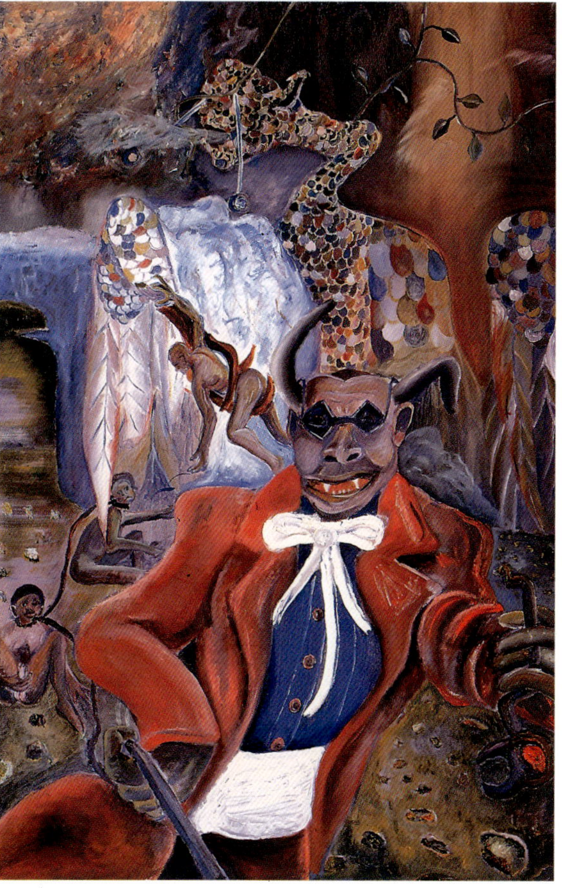

3

ROBERT CARGO FOLK ART GALLERY

2314 Sixth Street
Tuscaloosa, Alabama 35401
205.758.8884

Contact:
Robert Cargo, Owner

Exhibiting:
Contemporary folk art, antique quilts, African-American quilts. Haitian voodoo flags.

Roger Rice

1. *Christ Baptised*
   1988, Oil on canvas, 46" x 50"

2. *The Evil Ruler*
   1990, Oil on canvas, 36" x 24"

3. *Two Figures and Tree*
   1990, Oil on canvas, 30" x 24"

Selected Biography:

1993 "Unsigned, Unsung, Whereabouts Unknown," Florida State University Gallery and Museum, Tallahassee. Catalogue

1992 One-man show: Ferguson Gallery, The University of Alabama

1991 One-man show: Robert Cargo Folk Art Gallery

CONNAUGHT BROWN

2 Albemarle Street
London, W1X 3HF
England
4471.408.0362
4471.495.3137 FAX

Contact:
Anthony Brown,
Managing Director

Exhibiting:
Specializing in Post
Impressionist, Modern and
Contemporary works of art

Paul Richards

Milly
1993, Oil on canvas,
20³/₄" x 18¹/₄"
Signed on reverse

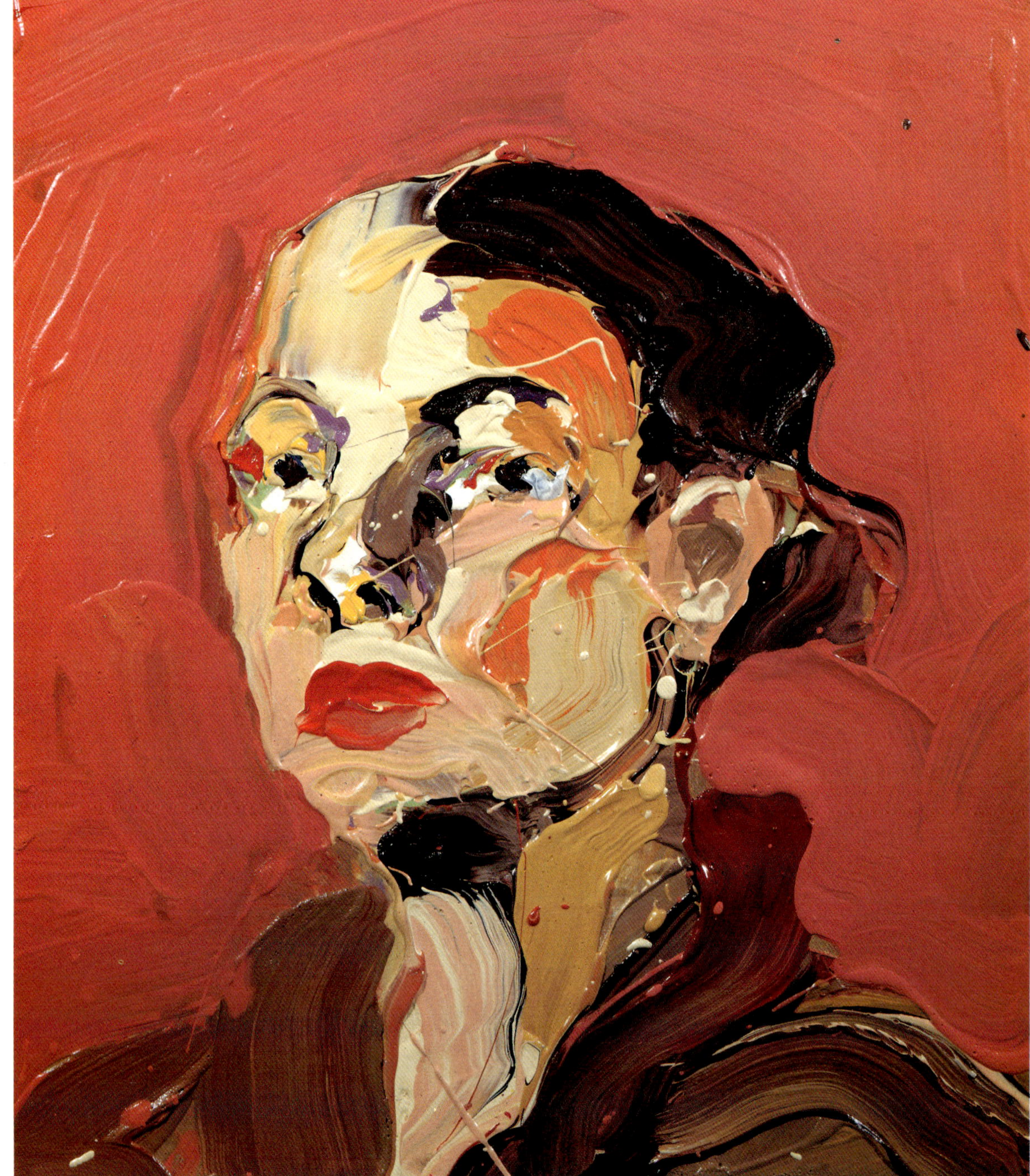

Selected Exhibitions:

1992   Solo exhibition:
Connaught Brown,
London, England

1991   Solo exhibition:
Dennis Hotz Fine Art,
Johannesburg,
South Africa

1985   Solo exhibition:
Connaught Brown,
London, England

1984   'Aperto '84'
Venice Biennale,
Venice, Italy

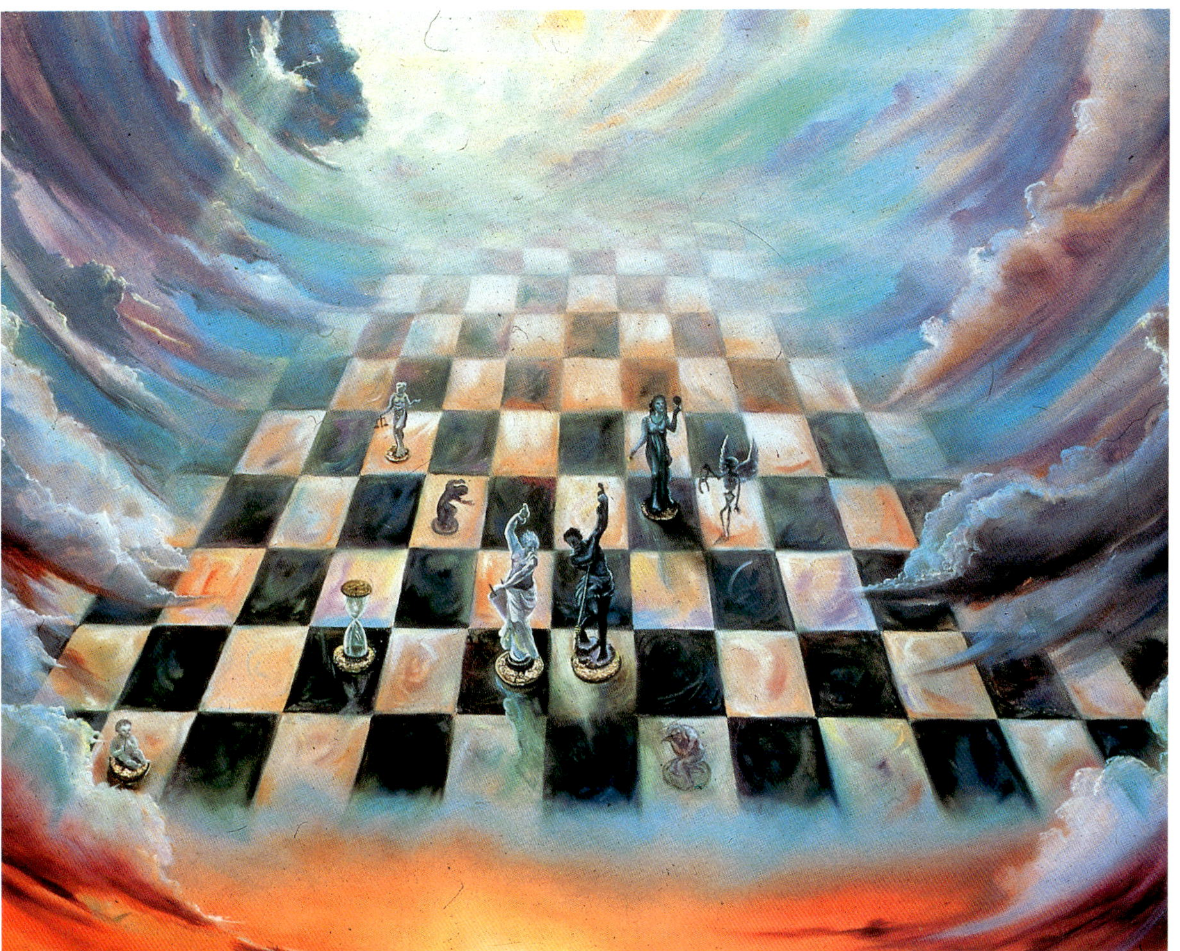

1

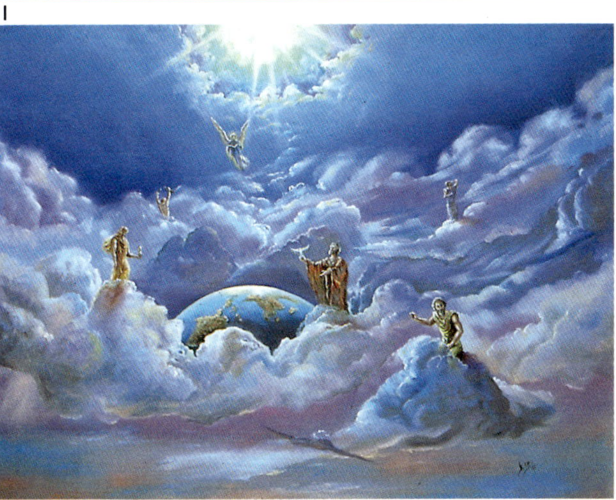

2

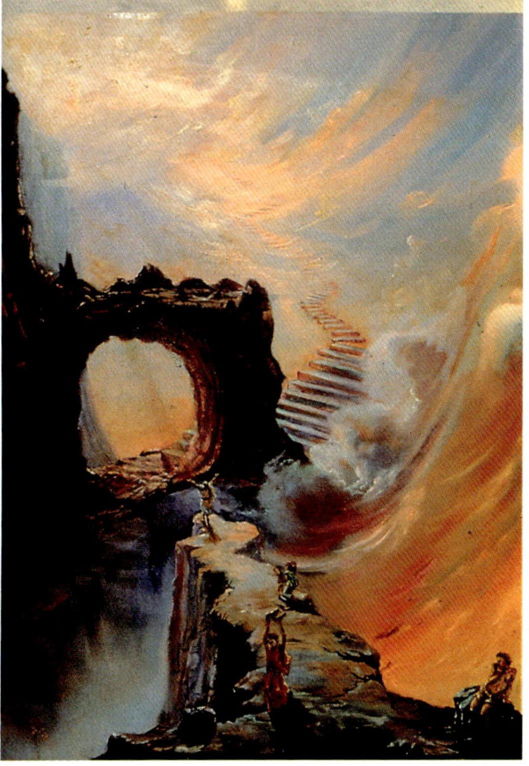

3

JACQUELINE RIPSTEIN

2800 Williams Island Blvd.
Williams Island, FL 33160
305.933.1410
525.202.8296

Contact:
Jacqueline Ripstein

Exhibiting:
Oil paintings, lithographs, and a unique, new, invisible technique developed by the artist.

Jacqueline Ripstein

1. *Cosmic Chess Game,*
   1992, Oil on canvas,
   70 x 90 cm
   © by Jacqueline Ripstein

2. *The Garden of the Prophets*
   1982, Oil on canvas,
   70 x 90 cm

3. *The Sacred Journey,*
   1988, Oil on canvas,
   70 x 90 cm

Selected Collections:

1991 Tecnologico Museum,
      Mexico

1990 St. Carmen Museum,
      Mexico

1980 MGM Grand Gallery,
      Las Vegas, Nev.

1978 Cúermuaca Library´
      Museum, Mexico

1972 Jewish Sport Center,
      Mexico

CLAUDIA CHAPLINE
GALLERY &
SCULPTURE GARDEN

3445 Shoreline Hwy.
P.O. Box 946
Stinson Beach, CA 94970
415.868.2308
415.868.9436 FAX

Contact:
Margot Merrill

Exhibiting:
Contemporary art

Sally Robertson

1. *Pacific Coast Iris*
   1994,
   Watercolor on paper,
   22" x 30"

2. *Iris Chinese Treasure*
   1992,
   Watercolor on paper,
   30" x 18"

3. *Cymbidium Erythrostylm*
   1993,
   Watercolor on paper,
   22" x 30"

Selected Biography:

1994   Orchids in Art, World
       Financial Center,
       New York, NY

1993   "Flower Paintings",
       Claudia Chapline
       Gallery,
       Stinson Beach, CA

1992   California Arts
       Council Gallery,
       Sacramento, CA

1991   "In the Garden",
       Bolinas Museum

1990   "Watercolor Inspired
       by the Garden",
       Thackrey & Robertson

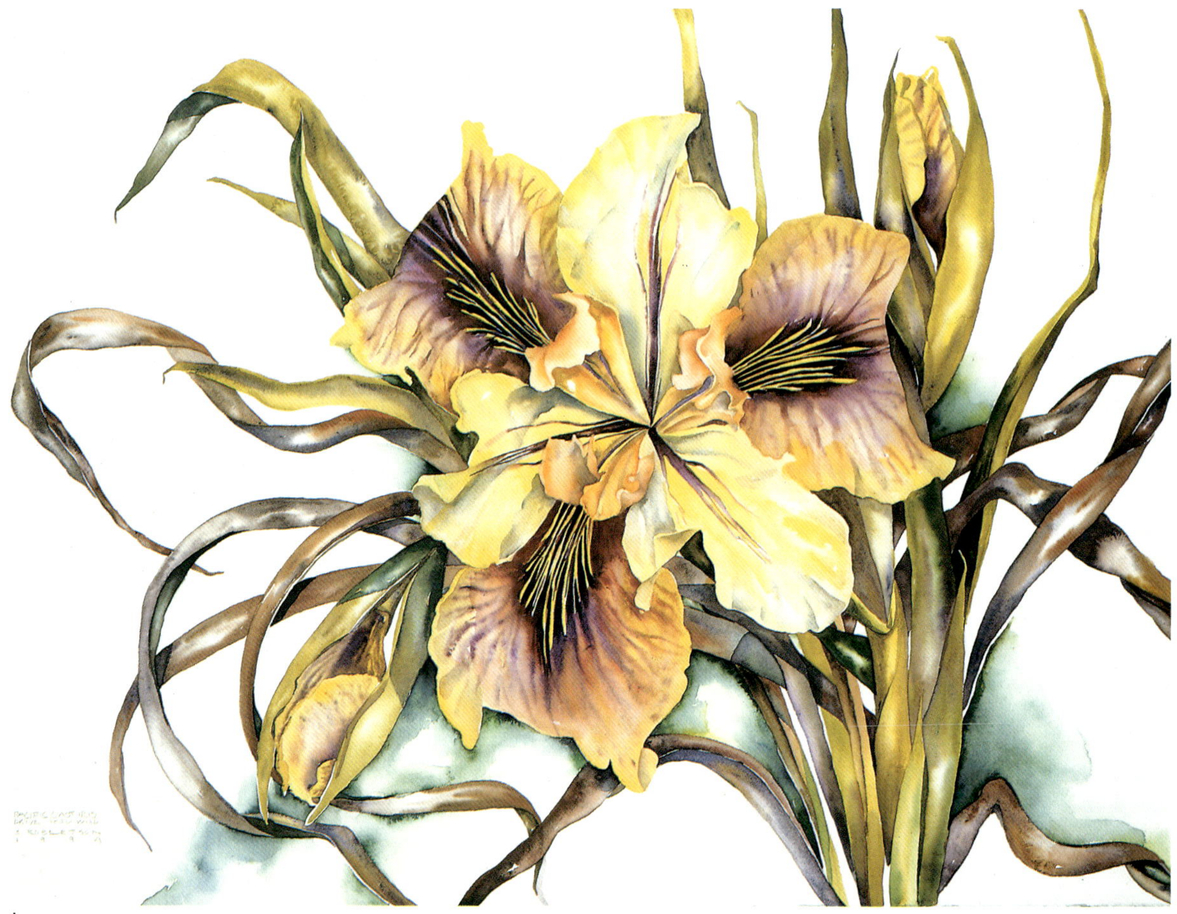

1

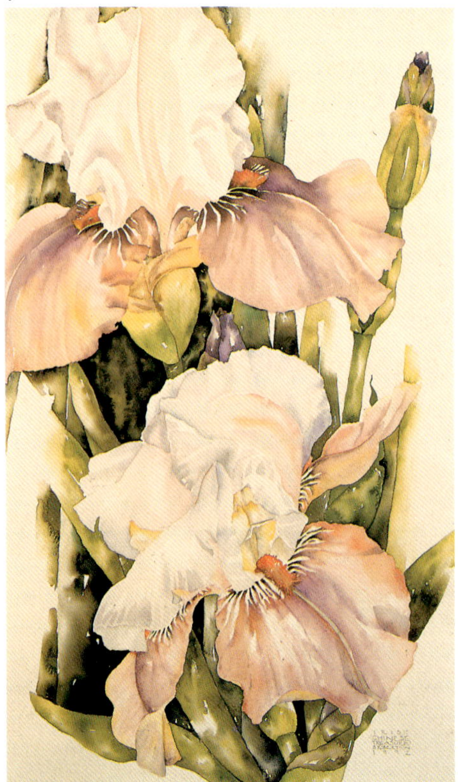

2

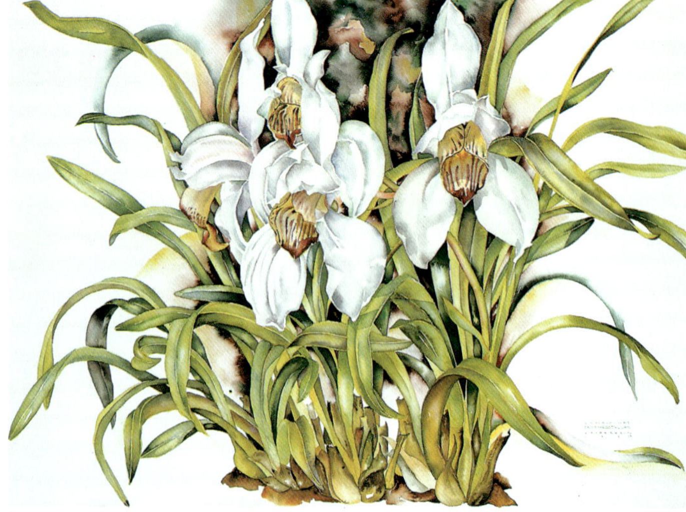

3

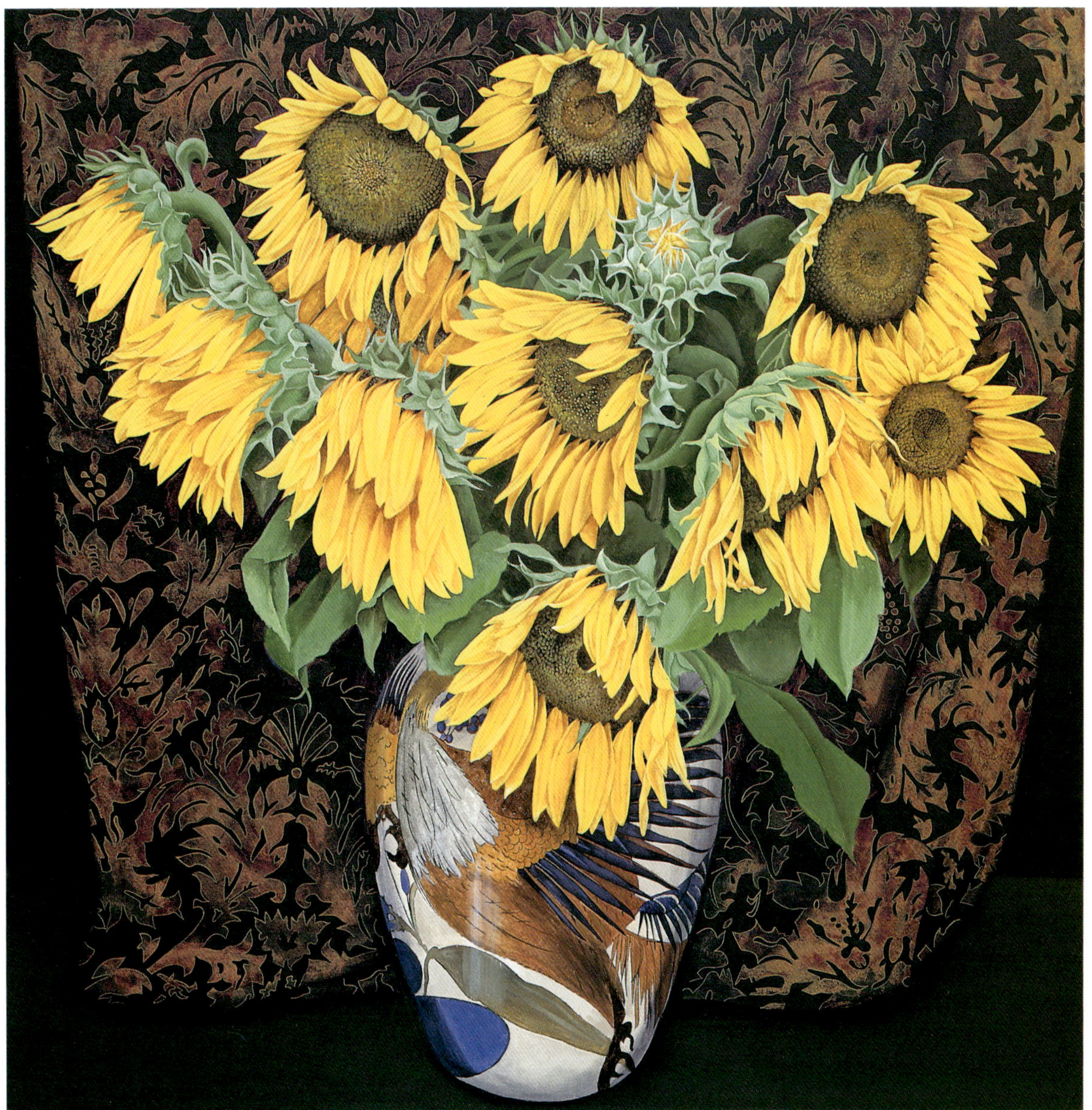

ARTE NUCLEO GALERIA

Edgar Allan Poe 308,
Col. polanco
Mexico DF 11560
Mexico
525.254.3732
525.531.6875
525.531.2905
525.254.1942 FAX

Contact:
Diana Ripstein de Nankin,
Director

Exhibiting:
Classic and contemporary
Latin American art

Oris Robertson

Girasoles
1993, Acrilico/ Tela,
105 x 105 cms.
Photograph by
Manuel Zavala

Prizes:
1967 1st place, Artist Guild
      of Houston, Houston,
      Texas, USA
      2nd place, University
      of Houston and the
      Texas Chapter of ASID
      1st place, Dallas-Fort
      Worth Art Directors
      Club, Dallas, Texas
1966 1st place, Harvest,
      University of Houston,
      Houston Texas,USA

Selected Exhibitions:
1992 II Biennial Museo de
      Monterrey, Monterrey,
      N.L.
1988 VI Biennial Iberoamericana
      de Arte, Palacio de
      Bellas Artes, Mexico, D.F.
1987 Los Angeles Art Expo,
      Los Angeles, CA
1986 Art Expo New York,
      New York City, NY
1971 Brownsville Art League
      Museum, Texas
1968 University of Houston,
      Texas, USA

Selected Biography:
1970 Since 1970 he resides
      in Mexico
1939 Born in Texas, USA

DIANE FARRIS GALLERY

1565 West 7th Avenue
Vancouver B.C. V6J 1S1
Canada
604.737.2629
604.737.2675 FAX

Contact:
Diane Farris, Director

Exhibiting:
Contemporary Canadian
and International Art

Hanneline Røgeberg

1. *Untitled*
   1992-93, Oil on canvas,
   78" x 96"

2. *Untitled*
   1991, Oil on canvas,
   36" x 72"

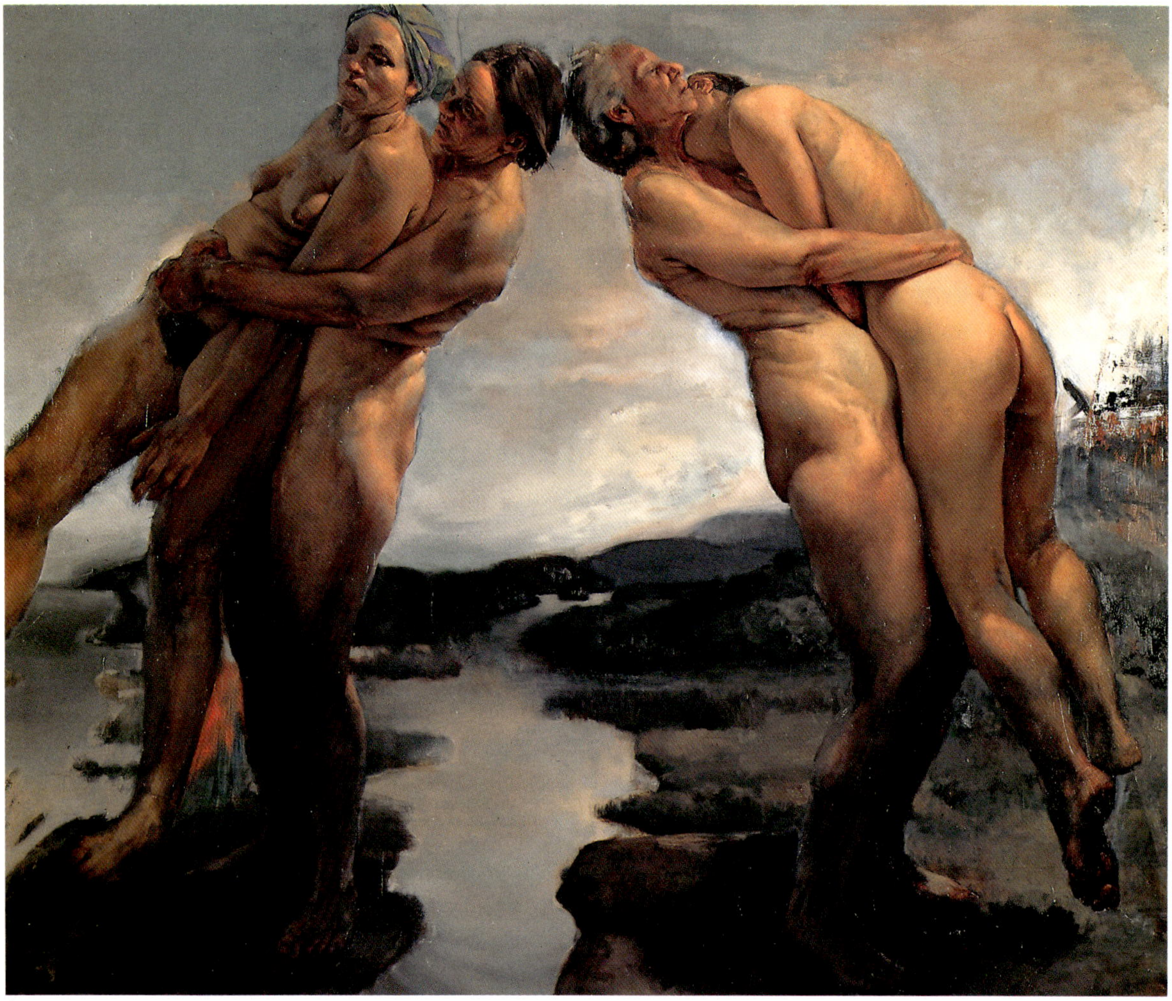

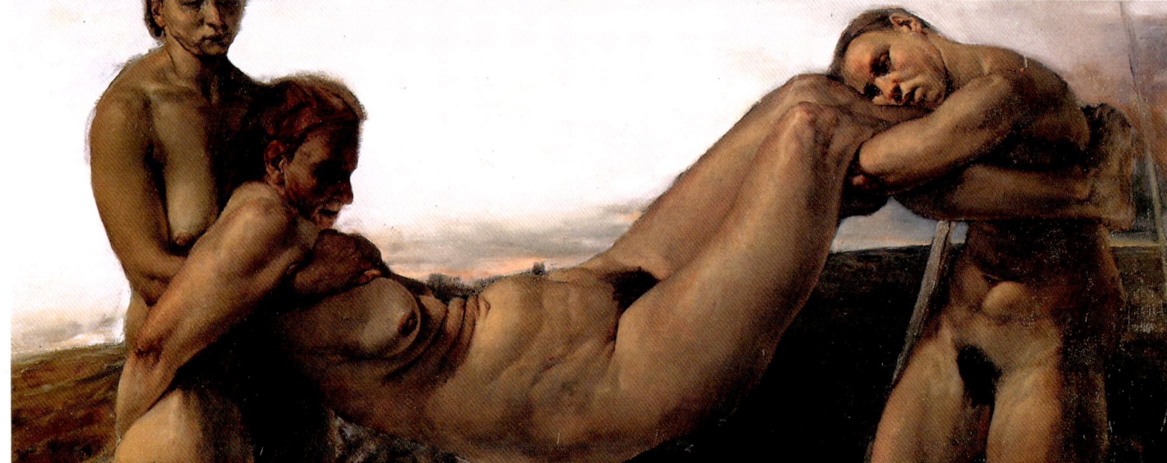

1

2

Selected Biography:

1994 Gallery Artists:
Figurative Work,
Diane Farris Gallery,
Vancouver, BC
1993 The Anxious Salon,
MIT List Visual Arts
Centre, Boston, MA;
Reciprocity: Artists
Choose Artists,
Baxter Gallery, Maine
College of Art,
Portland, ME
1992 American Prints:
Travelling to Art Space,
Sarornon, GAllery-OH,
Gallery-M (Millhouse,
ZF), Aich., Japan

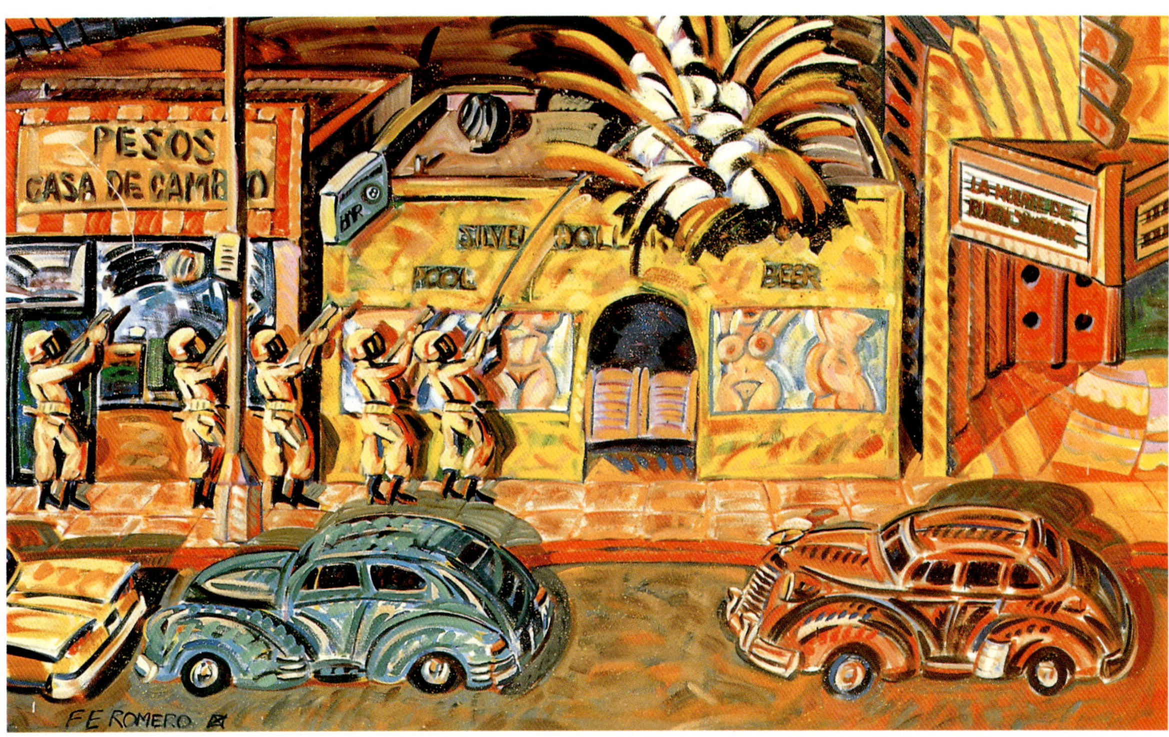

1

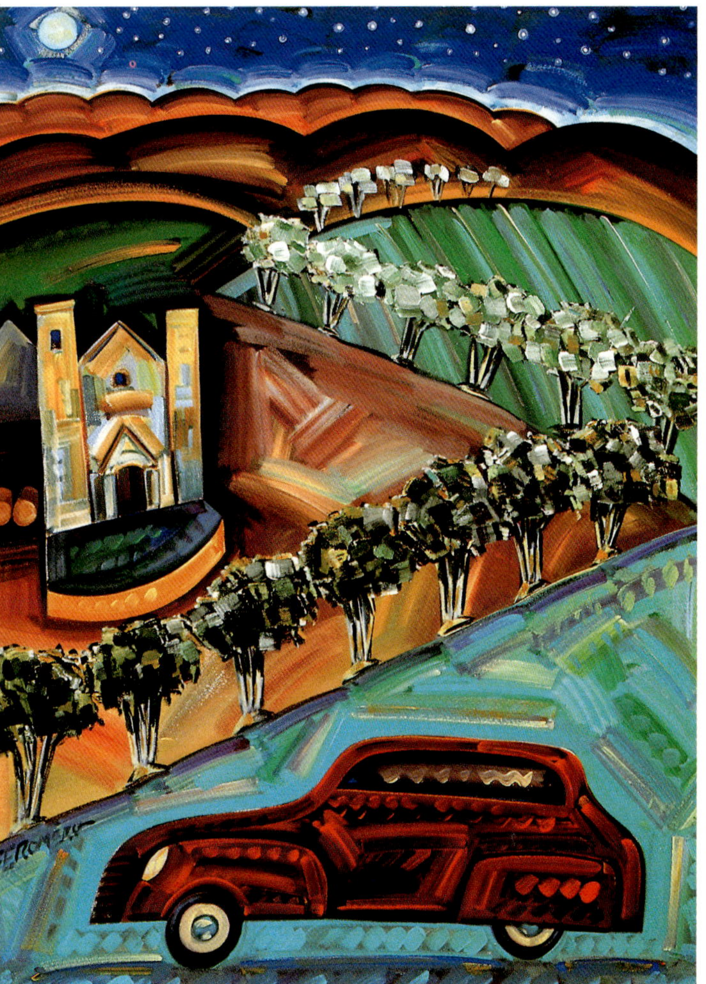

2

ROBERT BERMAN GALLERY

2044 Broadway
Santa Monica, CA 90404
310.453.9195
310.453.2383 FAX

Contact:
Robert Berman
Gabriela Trench

Exhibiting:
Contemporary, modern and American-Latin Art in all medium

Frank Romero

1. *Death of Rubén Salazar*
   1985-86, Oil on canvas,
   72" x 120"
   Collection of National Museum of American Art/Smithsonian Institution

2. *La Cresta*
   1990, Oil on canvas,
   48" x 36"

Selected Biography:

1993 "Paintings", Robert Berman Gallery, Santa Monica

1990 "Chicago Art Resistance & Affirmation", UCLA Wright Gallery, Los Angeles and tour

1989 "Le Demon des Angles", Halle Du Croc, Nantes, France; Barcelon, Spain; Lund, Sweden; Brussels, Belgium

MONTSERRAT
GALLERY

584 Broadway
New York, NY 10012
212.941.8899
212.274.1717 FAX

Contact:
Marie Montserrat Coll,
Director

Exhibiting:
Contemporary European
and American art

Amalia Ronzoni

The Chant of the Sun
1993, Oil, 42" x 28"

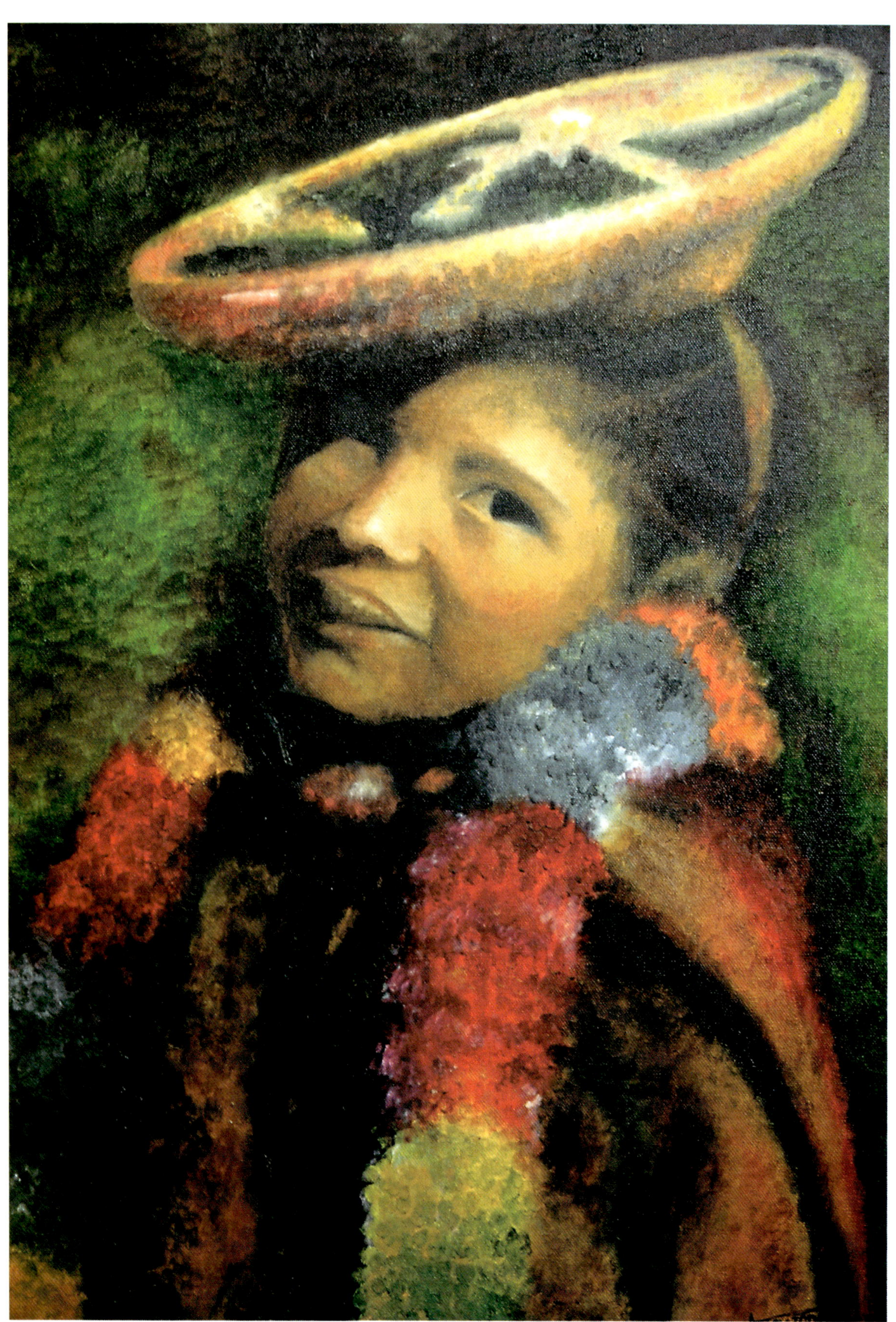

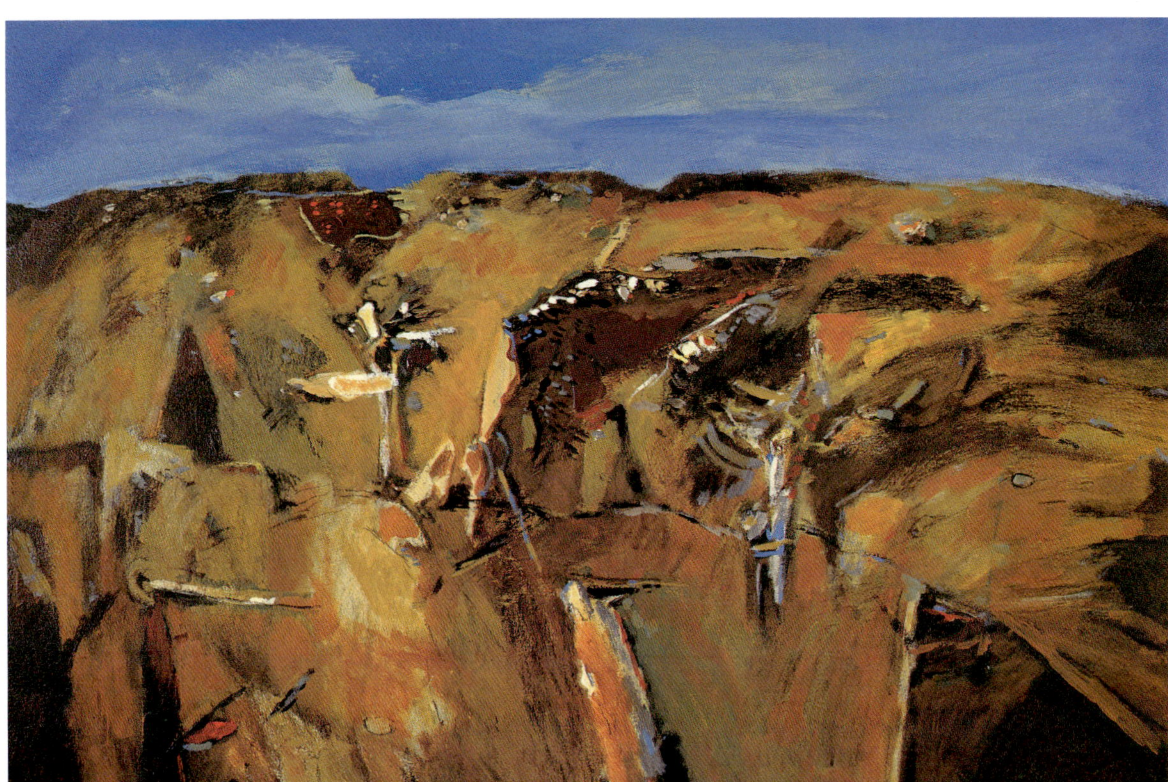

1

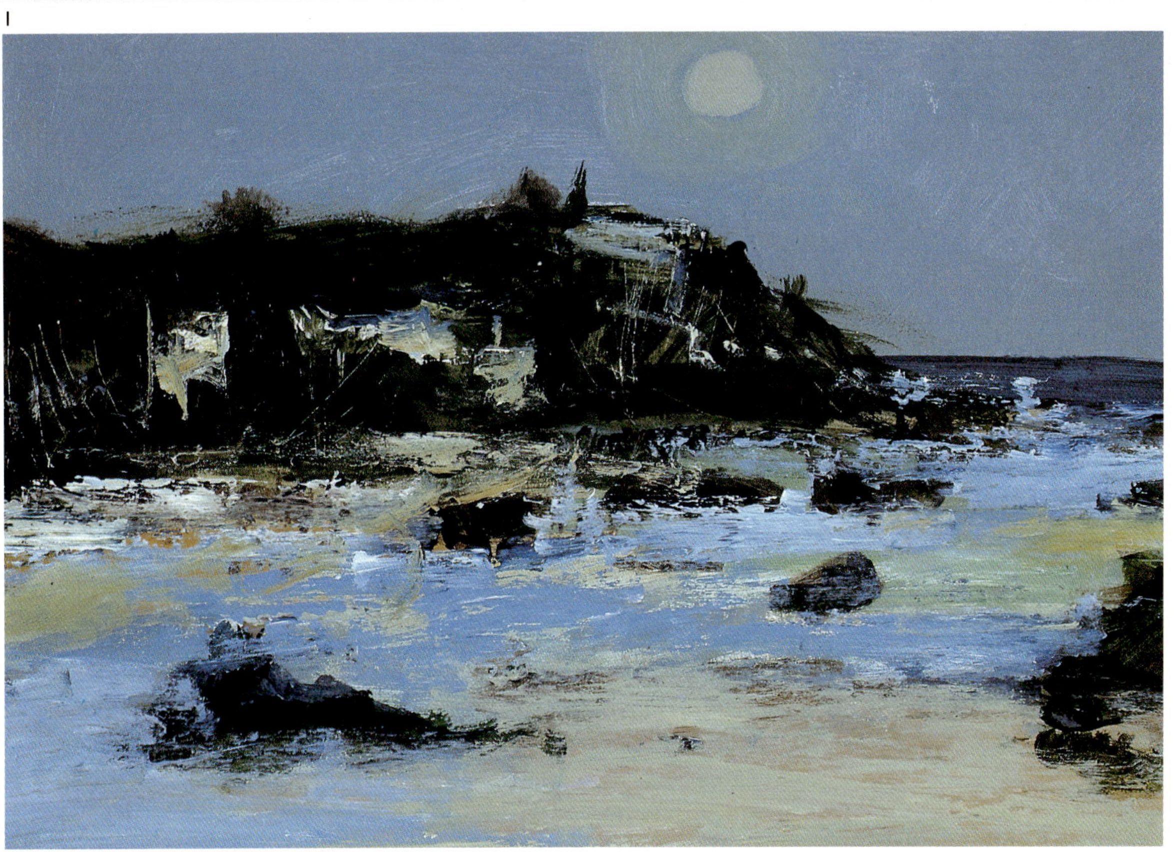

2

FRIEDLAND ART INC.

18181 NE 31st Ct., Ste.1106
N. Miami Beach, Fl 33160
305.935.7544
305.935.3780 FAX

Contact:
Lara Block

Specialty:
Supplies leading art dealers
with available works

Nico Roos

1. *On the Border of the Desert*
   1991, Acrylic on canvas,
   24" × 36"

2. *The Coast at Glenmore,*
   1992, Acrylic on paper,
   9" × 13 1/2"

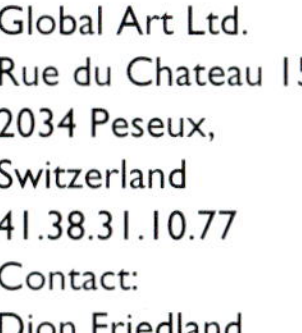

Global Art Ltd.
Rue du Chateau 15
2034 Peseux,
Switzerland
41.38.31.10.77
Contact:
Dion Friedland

Philip Samuels Fine Art
8112 Mayland Ave.
St. Louis, MO 63105
314.727.2444
314.727.6084 FAX
Contact:
Philip Samuels

Selected Collections:
Price Forbes Group,
London, UK

State Collection
of South African Art,
Bonn, Germany

Pretoria Art Museum,
South Africa

Government of
Namibia Collection,
Windhoek

**HOWARD SCOTT
M-13 GALLERY**

72 Greene Street, 2nd Floor
New York, NY 10012
212.925.3007
212.925.3923 FAX

Contact:
Howard Scott

Exhibiting:
Contemporary art

Robin Rose

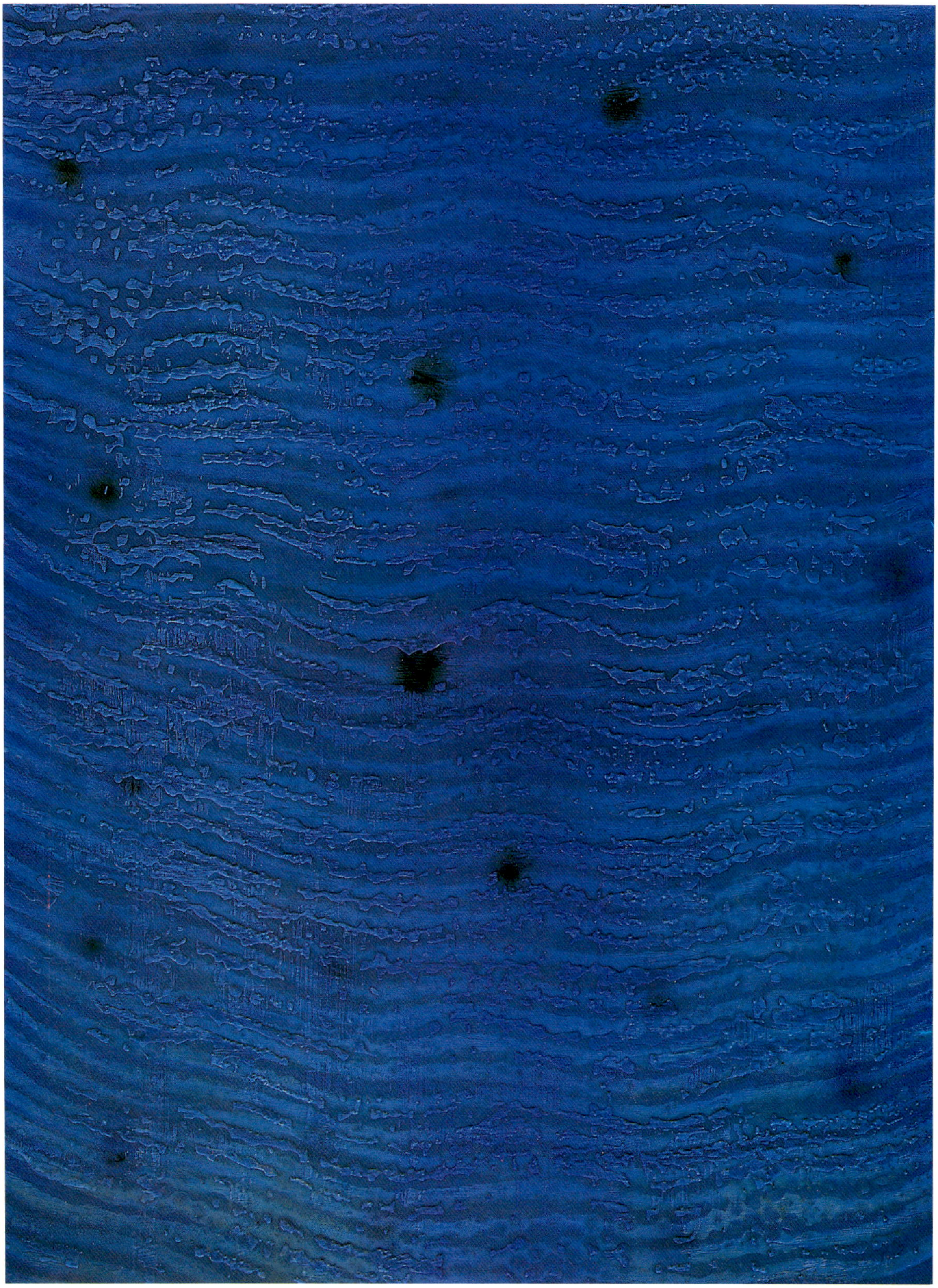

Safe Haven
1992, Encaustic on Linen
on hexcel panel,
24" x 18"

Selected Biography:

1993 M-13
      Howard Scott Gallery,
      New York, NY

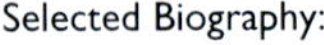

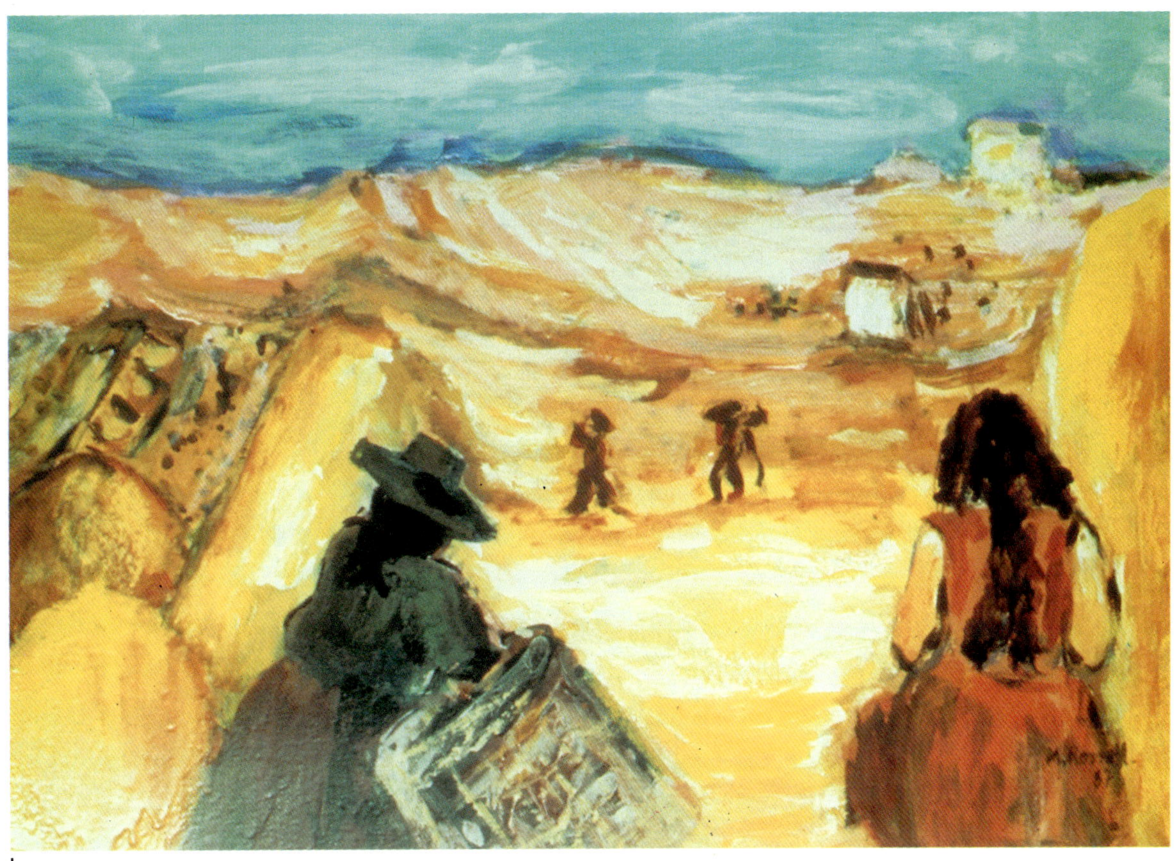

1

MONTSERRAT GALLERY

584 Broadway
New York, NY 10012
212.941.8899
212.274.1717 FAX

Contact:
Marie Montserrat Coll,
Director

Exhibiting:
Contemporary European
and American art

Mercedes Rossell

1. *La Triga*
   1992, Oil on canvas,
   28" x 25"

2. *Castilla*
   1992, Oil on canvas,
   28" x 20"

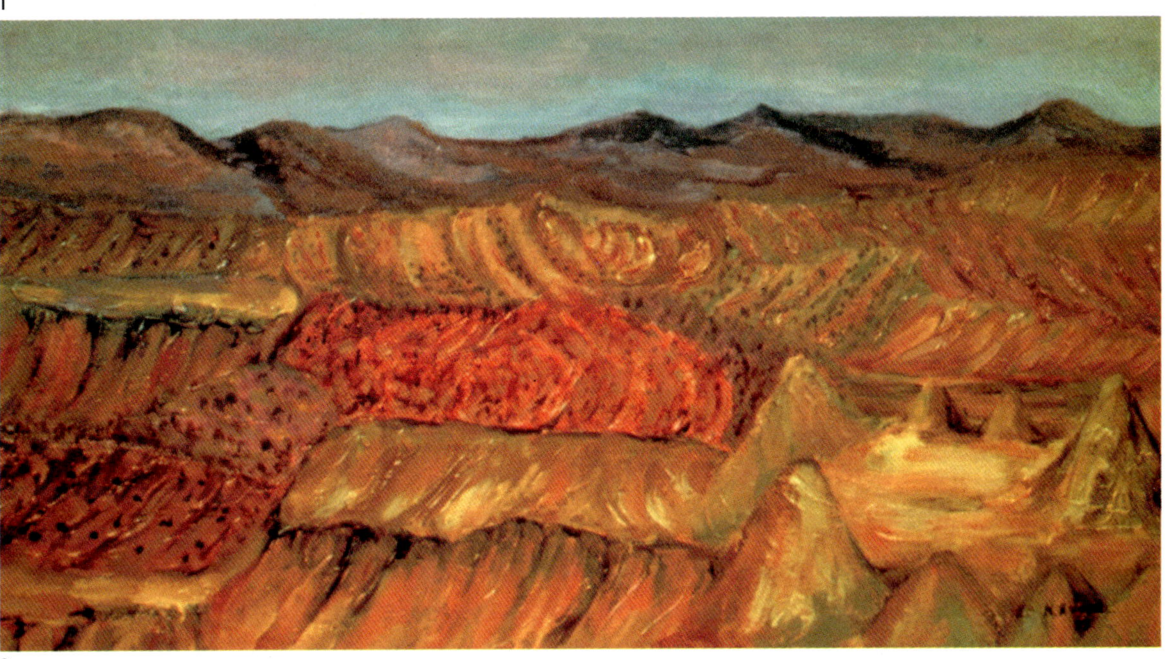

2

Selected Biography:

1993 Montserrat Gallery,
New York, NY

Galeria Torres Vegui
Madrid

Centro Nicolas
Almezo

Pozuelo casa de la
Cultura

Circulo de Bellas
Artes de Madrid

LEO CASTELLI

420 W. Broadway
New York, NY 10012
212.431.5160
212.431.5361 FAX

Contact:
Susan Brundage, Director

James Rosenquist

1. *Gift Wrapped Doll #13*
   1992, Oil on canvas,
   60" x 60"

2. *Fleurs De Tabac*
   1990, Oil on canvas,
   96" x 64"

3. *E.E.E.*
   (Eclipse, Elapse, Elipse)
   1990, Oil on canvas,
   81" x 144" (2 panels)

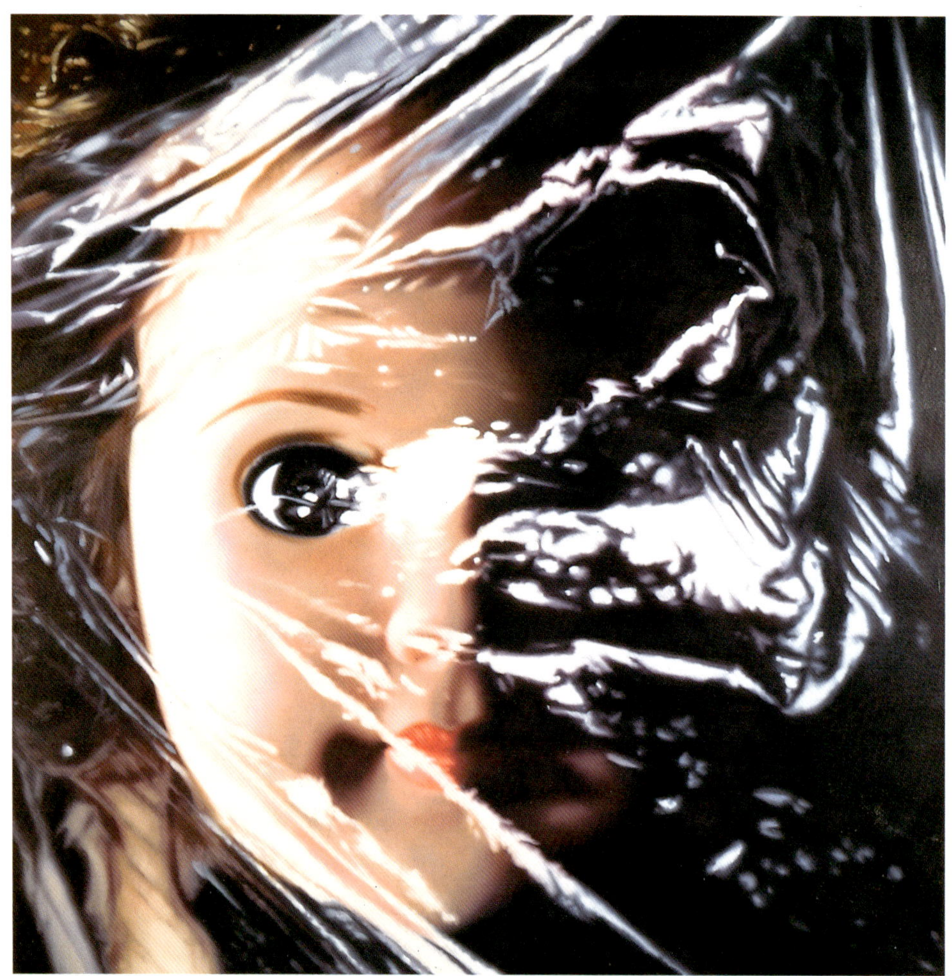

1

Selected Biography:

1993 Solo exhibitions:
"James Rosenquist",
Leo Castelli Gallery,
420 W. Broadway,
New York, NY,
March 20 - April 17

"James Rosenquist,
Time Dust - The
Complete Graphics
1962 - 1992,"
Walker Arts Center,
Minneapolis, MN
March 7 - May 9

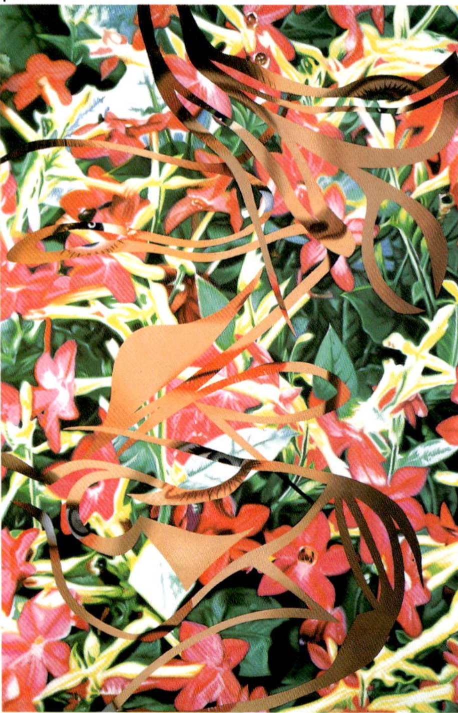

2

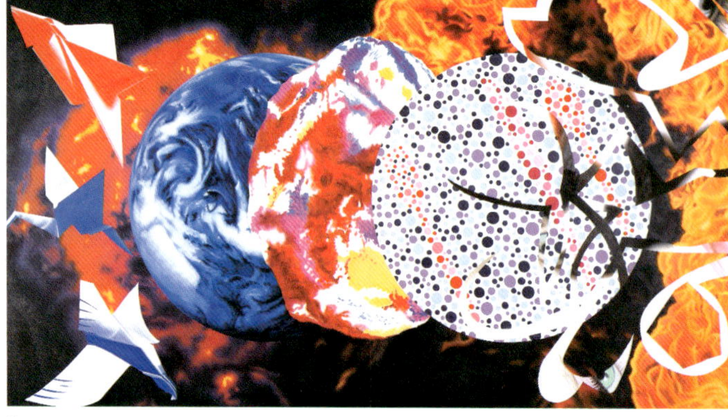

3

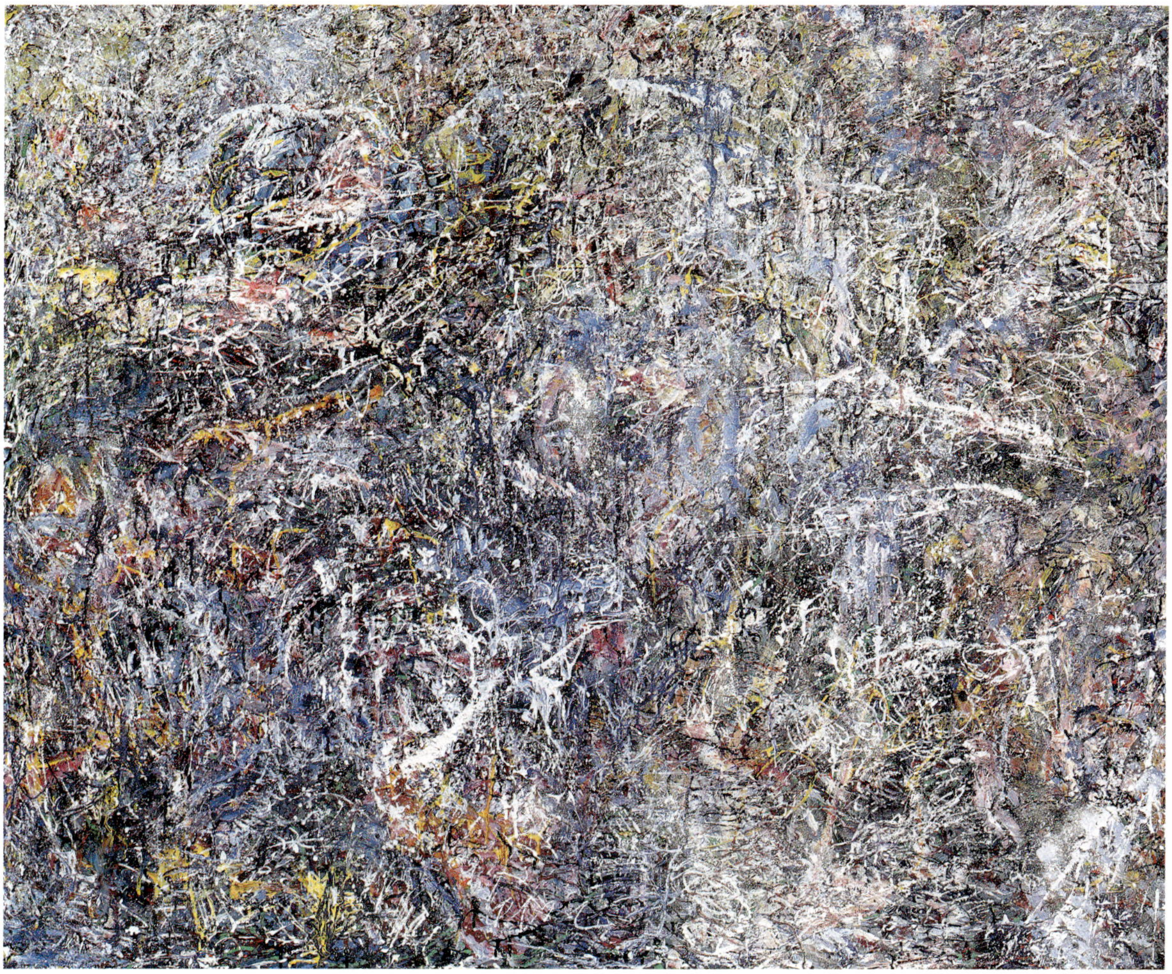

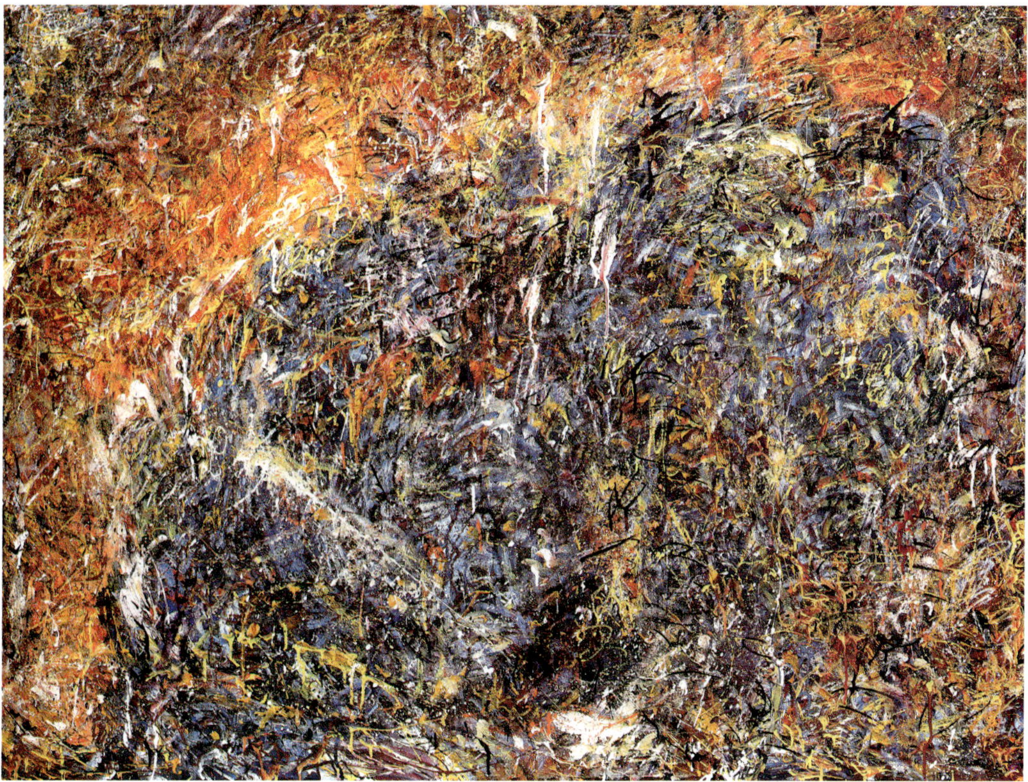

PHILIP SAMUELS
FINE ART

8112 Maryland Ave. Ste. 200
St Louis, MO 63105
314.727.2444
314.727.6084 FAX

Contact:
Philip Samuels

Exhibiting:
Contemporary paintings
and sculpture

Michael Rubin

1. *Water Reflection #5*
   (Flora Series)
   1993, Acrylic on linen,
   54" × 66"

2. *Aurora II*
   (Flora Series)
   1992, Acrylic on linen,
   48" × 66"

Friedland Art Inc.
18181 NE 31st Ct.
N. Miami Beach, Fl
33160
305.935.7544
305.935.3780 FAX
Contact:
Lara Block

Global Art Ltd.
Rue du Chateau 15
2034 Peseux,
Switzerland
41.38.31.10.77
Contact:
Dion Friedland

Selected Collections:
    Metropolitan
    Museum of Art, NY

    Vincent Melzac
    Collection
    Washington,D.C.

    IBM

**CHARLES
WHITCHURCH
GALLERY**

5973 Engineer Drive
Huntington Beach, CA 92649
714.373.4459
714.373.4615 FAX

Contact:
Charles Whitchurch

Exhibiting:
Modern and contemporary
painting, graphic works and
sculpture

Michael Rubin

Gold's Vein (Paradise Series)
1991, Acrylic on linen,
54" x 42"

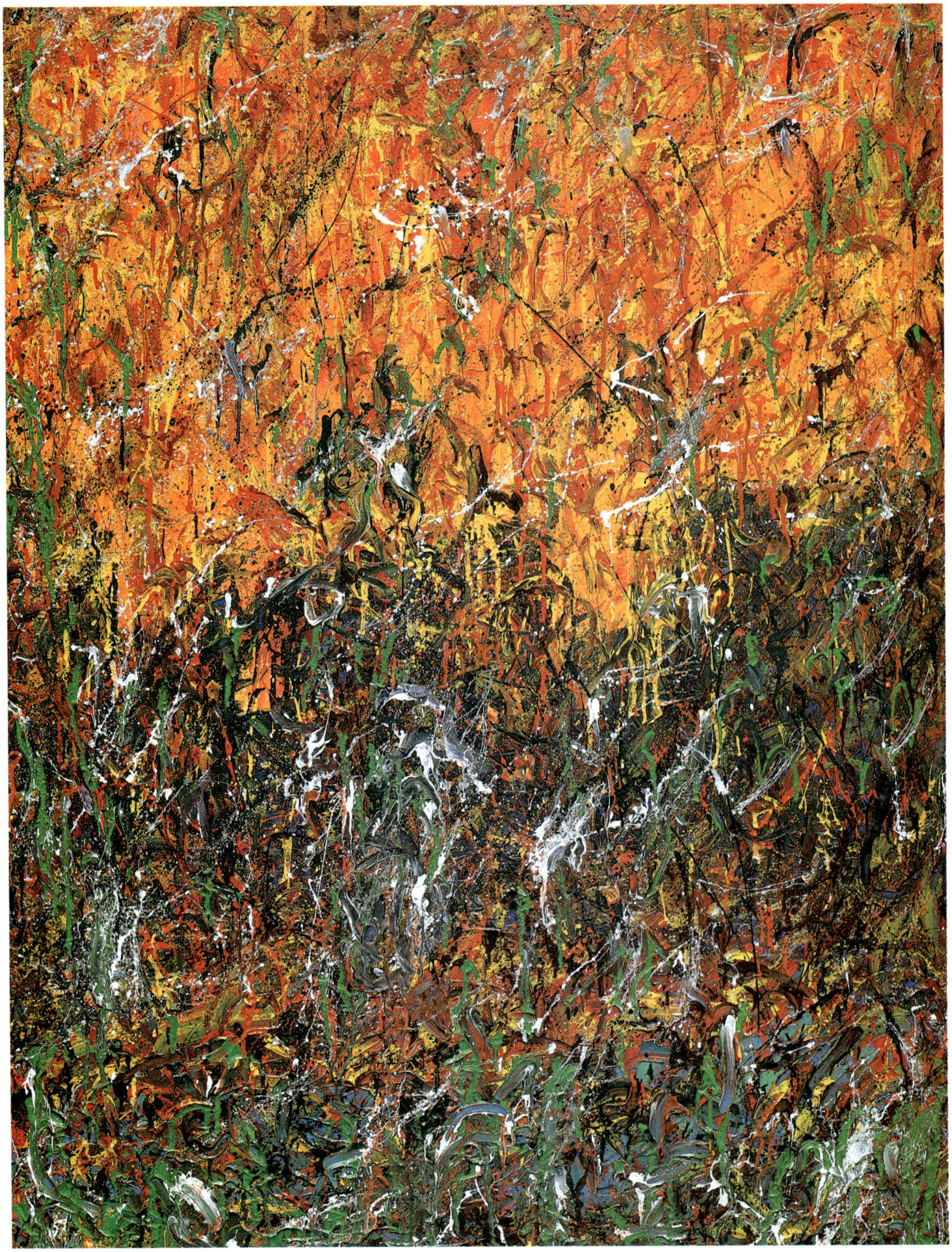

Selected Biography:

1994 Solo Exhibition,
Galerie Kaj Forsblom,
Helsinki

1993 Solo Exhibition,
Robert Stein Fine Art,
St. Louis

1992 Solo Exhibition,
LACA Gallery,
Los Angeles

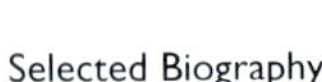

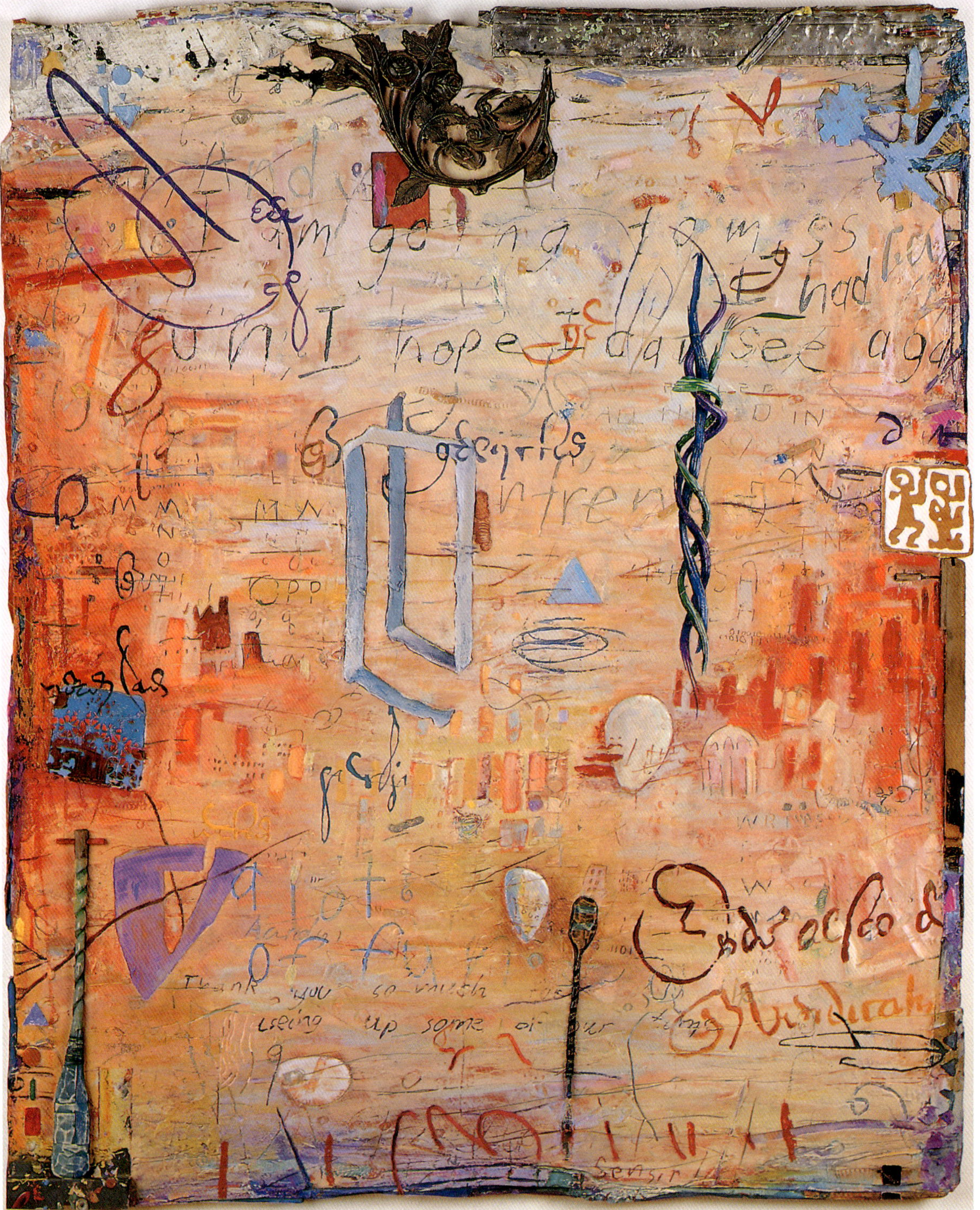

THE LOWE GALLERY

75 Bennett St. Space A-Z
Atlanta, GA 30309
404.352.8114
404.352.0564 FAX

Contact:
Bill Lowe

Exhibiting:
Contemporary painting,
sculpture, and objects

Andrew Saftel

Good Words
1994,
Mixed media on wood,
60" x 50"

Selected Biography:

1994 Solo show,
Knoxville Museum of
Art, Knoxville, TN

1993 Solo show,
The Lowe Gallery,
Atlanta, GA

1992 Solo show,
The Lowe Gallery,
Atlanta, GA

1990 Solo show,
Kyle Belding Gallery,
Denver, CO

GAGOSIAN GALLERY

980 Madison Ave
New York, NY 10021
212.744.2313
212.772.7962 FAX

136 Wooster Street
New York, NY 10012
212.228.2828
212.228.2878 FAX

Contact:
Melissa Lazarov, Director

Exhibiting:
20th-Century painting
and sculpture;
Abstract Expressionism,
Pop & Minimalism

David Salle

Picture Builder
1993, Oil and
acrylic on canvas,
84" x 114"

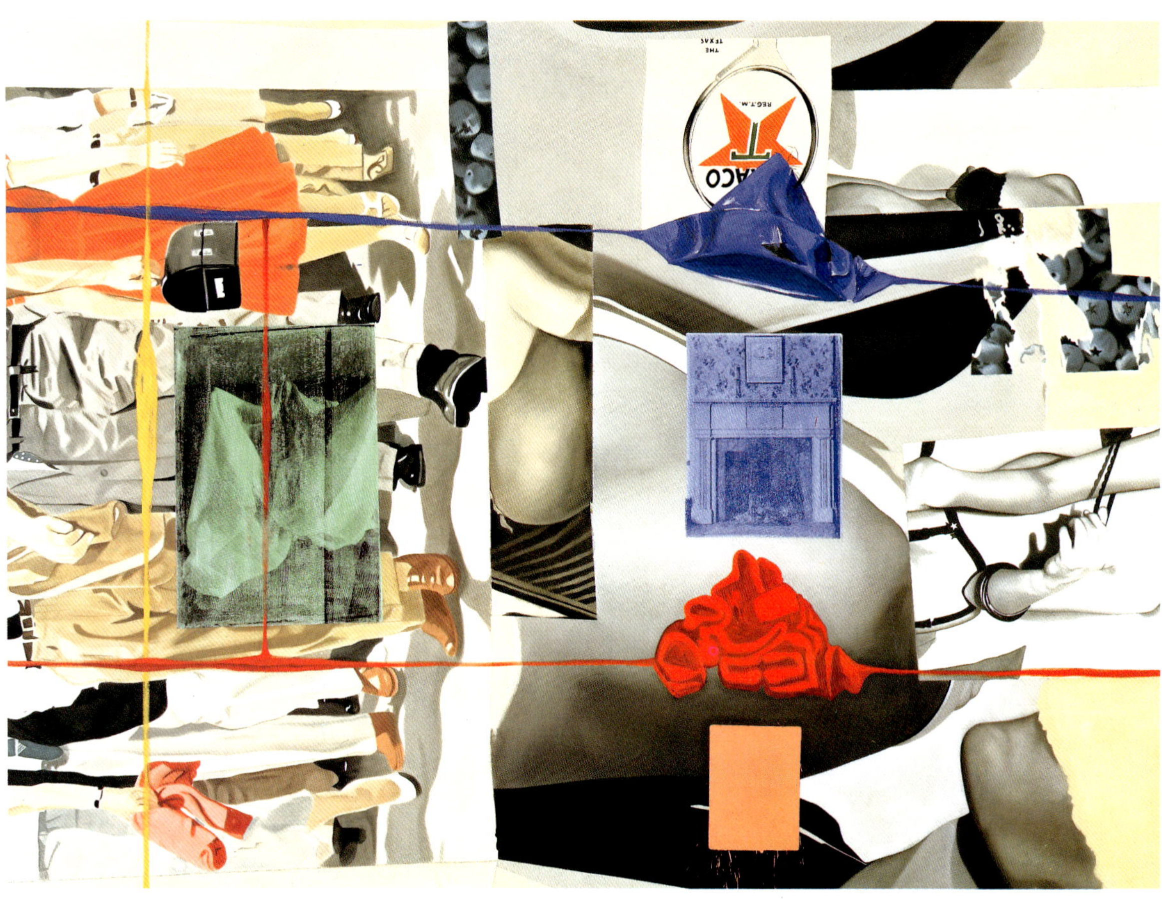

Selected Biography:
1993 Solo exhibition:
Jason Rubell Gallery,
Miami; Galerie Bruno
Bischofberger, Zurich
Group exhibition:
Galerie Beyeler, Basel
1992 Solo exhibition:
Haags Gemeente-muse-
um, The Hague;
Gagosian Gallery,
New York, NY;
Galeria Soledad
Lorenzo, Madrid
Group exhibition:
Museum of Modern
Art, New York, NY;
Musee D'Art Moderne
et D'Art Contemporain,
Nice, France

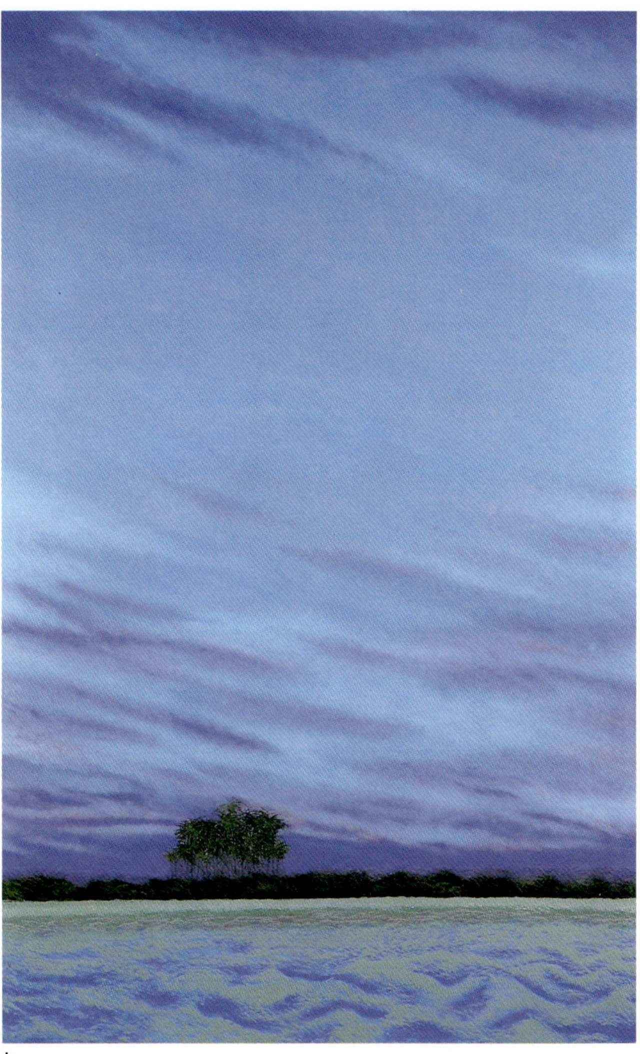

1

FENIX FINE ARTS

180 N.E. 40th St.
Miami, FL 33137
305.573.2727
305.542.8289
305.576.7707 FAX

Contact:
George Gandelman

Exhibiting:
Latin American Art

Ivan Santos

1. *...Y El Mar, Se Vistio de Verde*
   ("...And the Sea, Dressed in Green")
   1993, Oil on Canvas,
   198 cms. x 127 cms.

2. *Desde El Caribe II*
   ("From The Caribe II")
   1993, Oil on Canvas,
   127 cms. x 162 cms.

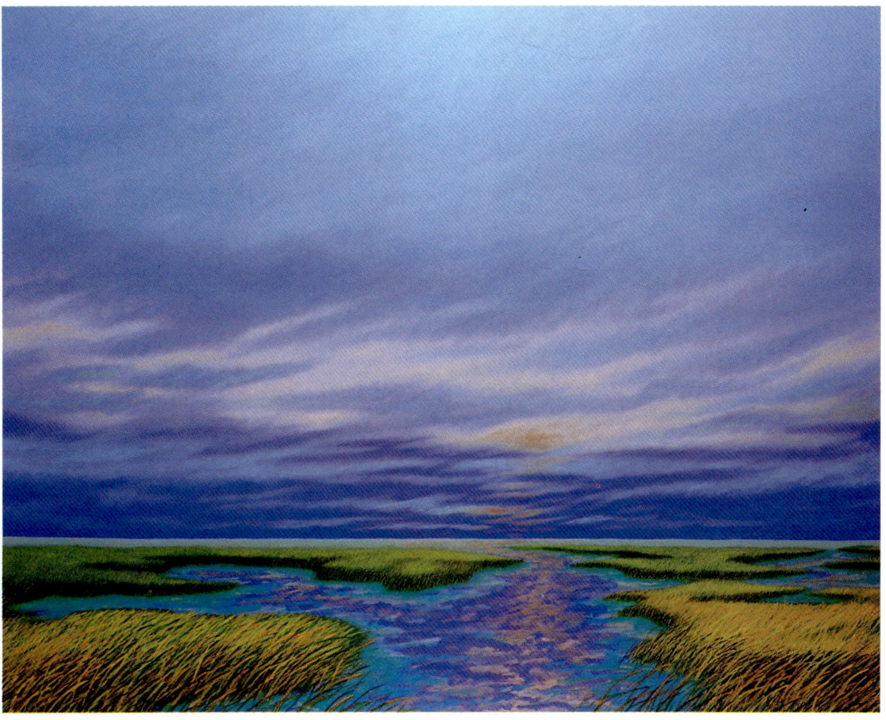

2

Selected Biography:

1993 Galeria Espacio,
El Salvador

Gandelman's Fenix Six,
Fenix Fine Arts, Miami FL

Best Graphic Work
Award at the Florida
Society of Fine Arts,
The Florida Museum of
Hispanic and Latin
American Art, Miami, FL

GALERIE ARIADNE

1010 Wien,
Beckerstrasse 6
Vienna 1010, Austria
1.512.9479
1.512.4296 FAX

Contact:
Ferdinand Netusil

Exhibiting:
Contemporary art

Horacio Sapere

1. *Gran Hoja Que Transporta
   A Personaje Dormido*
   180 x 50 cm.

2. *Gran Hojo Con
   Ciudad Y Huesos*
   180 x 50 cm.

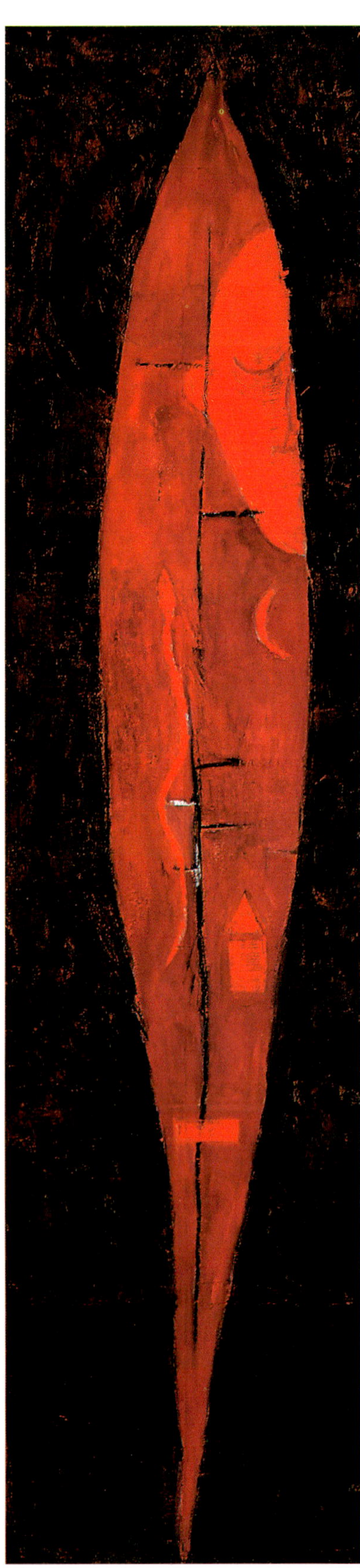

1

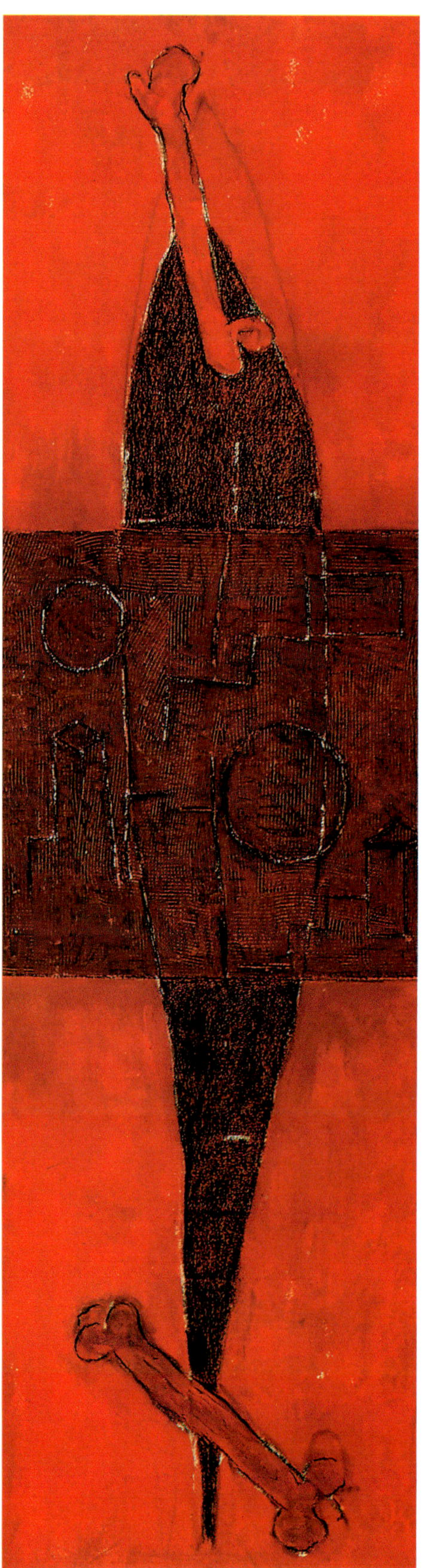

2

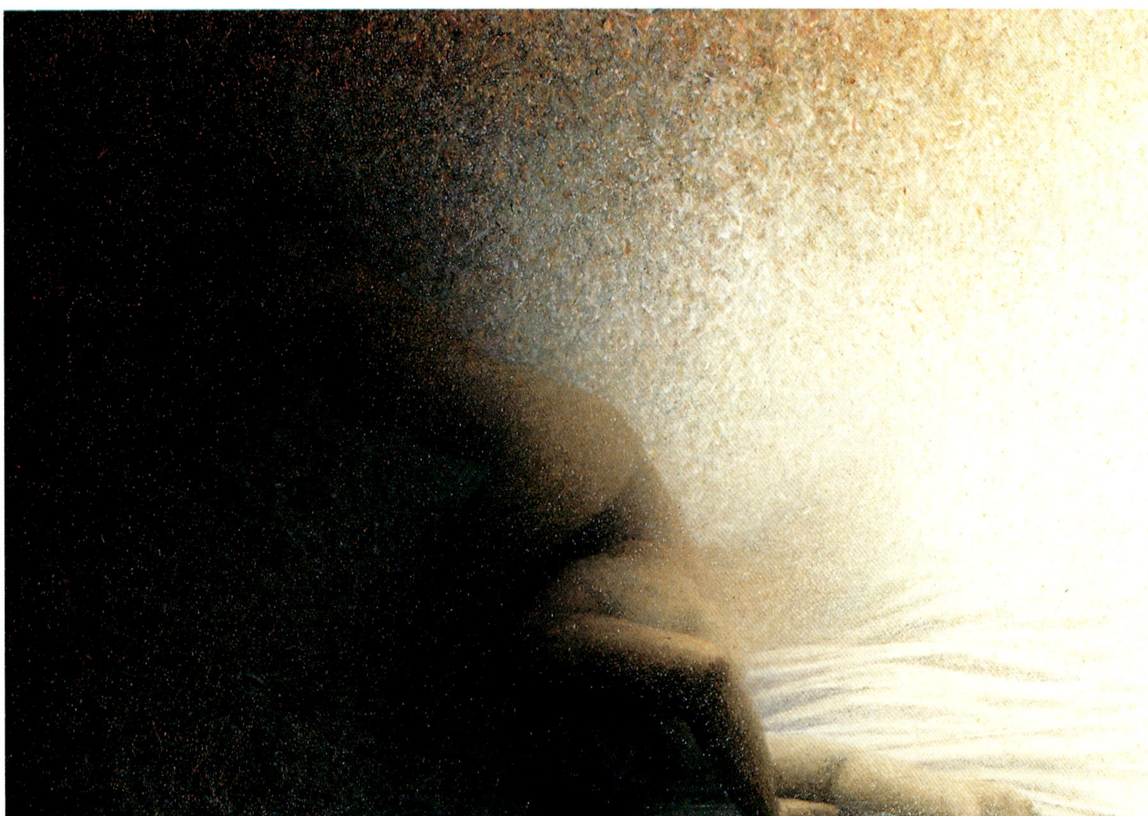

1

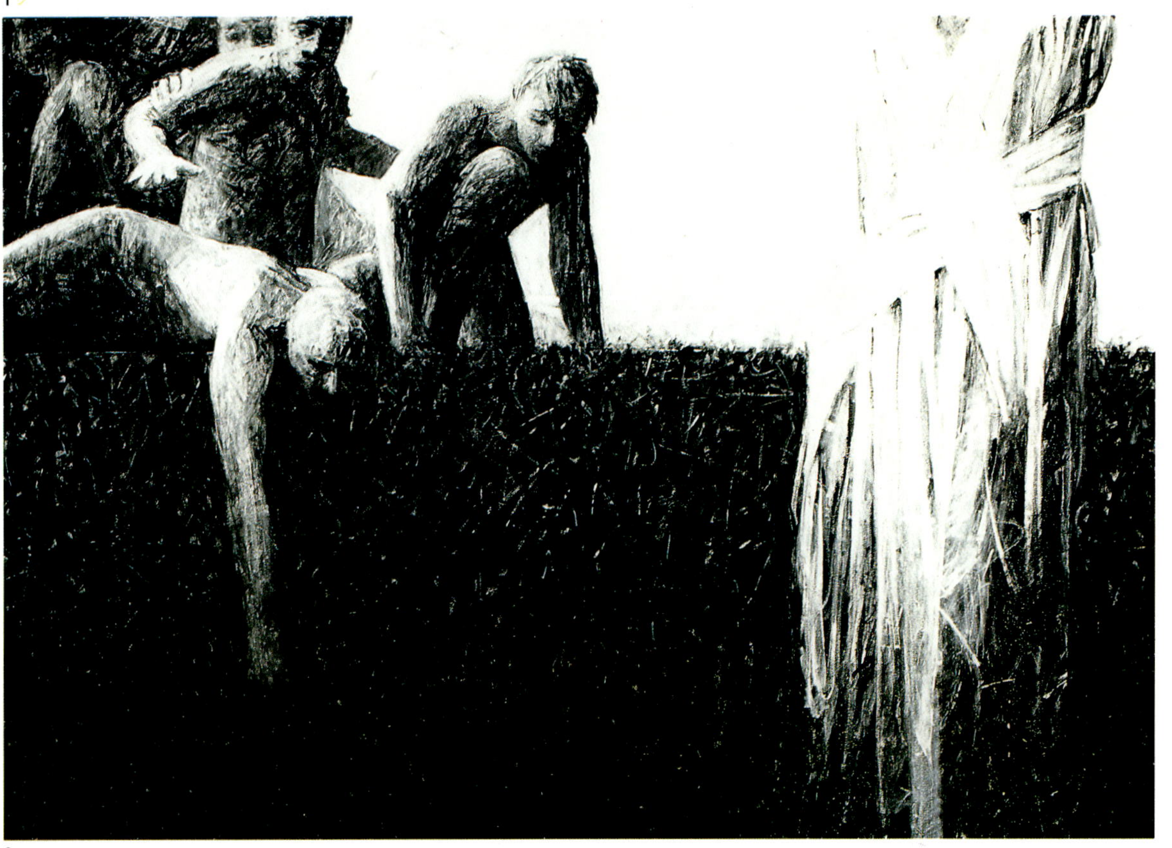

2

THE LOWE GALLERY

75 Bennett St. Space A-Z
Atlanta, GA 30309
404.352.8114
404.352.0564 FAX

Contact:
Bill Lowe

Exhibiting:
Contemporary painting,
sculpture, and objects

Stephen Schultz

1. *Detail of Creation:Materialism*
   1993, Oil on canvas,
   80" x 96"

2. *Agape series: Materialism*
   1993, Acrylic on canvas,
   90" x 120"

Selected Biography:

1994 Solo show,
The Lowe Gallery,
Atlanta, GA

1992 Solo show,
The Lowe Gallery,
Atlanta, GA

1991 Solo show,
Ovsey Gallery,
Los Angeles, CA

1986 Solo show,
Sid Devtsch Gallery,
New York, NY

CAROLE JONES GALLERY

300 W. Superior Street
Chicago, IL 60610
312.587.8820
312.587.9859 FAX

Contact:
Carole Jones

Exhibiting:
Contemporary International
Fine Art; Painting &
Sculpture

Charlotte Segal

1. *Firebird no.1*
   1992, Oil on canvas,
   76" x 76"

2. *Arbor*
   1993, Oil on canvas,
   46" x 44"

3. *At Liberty*
   1994, Oil on canvas,
   46" x 46"

Selected Biography:

1994 Retrospective'75 to '93
     Carole Jones Gallery,
     Chicago, IL
1993 ARC Gallery, 20th
     Anniversary Exhibition,
     Chicago, IL;
     "Genesis",
     R.H. Love Gallery,
     Chicago, IL;
     Solo Show,
     Carole Jones Gallery,
     Chicago, IL;
     Bower Cultural
     Arts Museum,
     Santa Ana, CA
1992 Solo Show,
     Carole Jones Gallery,
     Chicago, IL

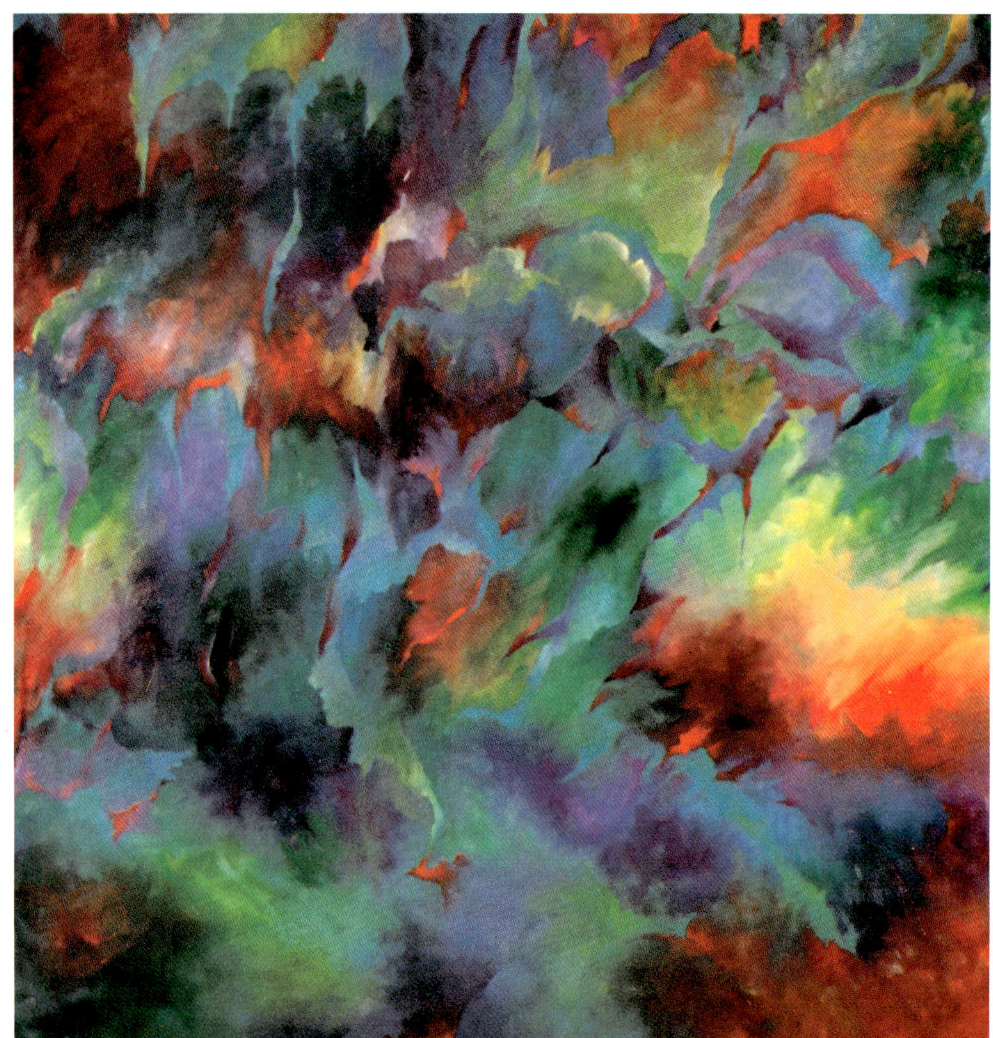

1

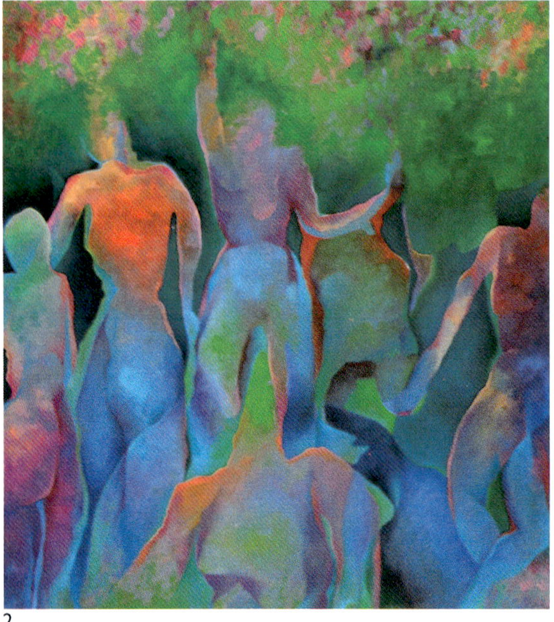

2

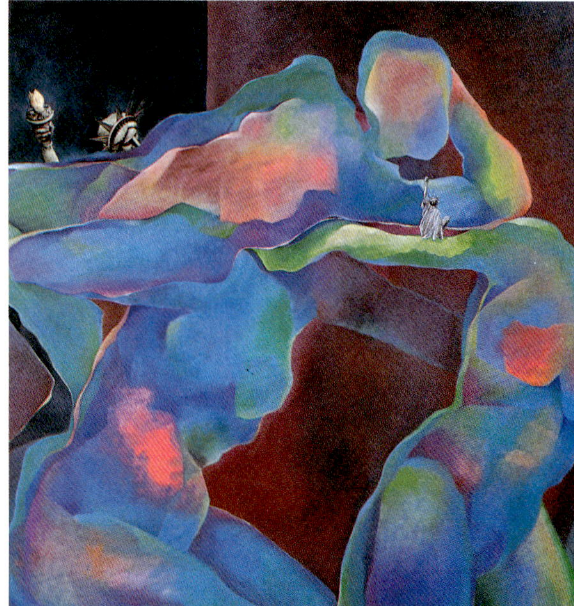

3

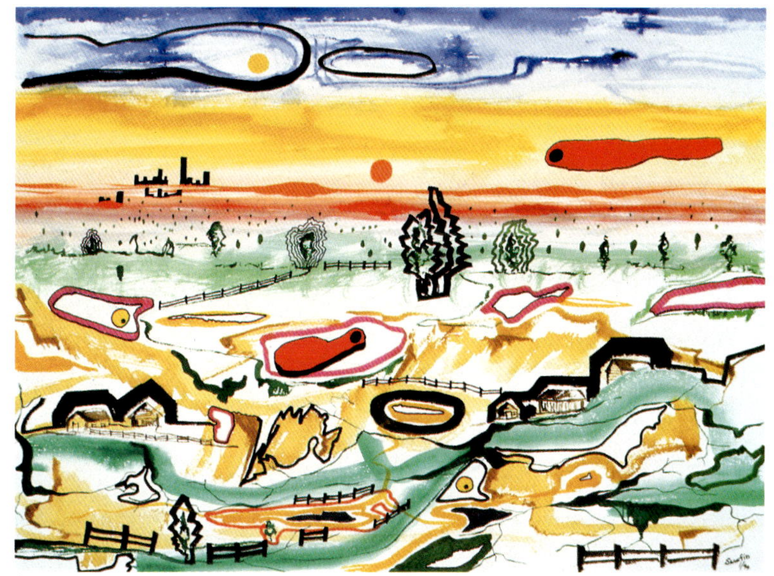

1

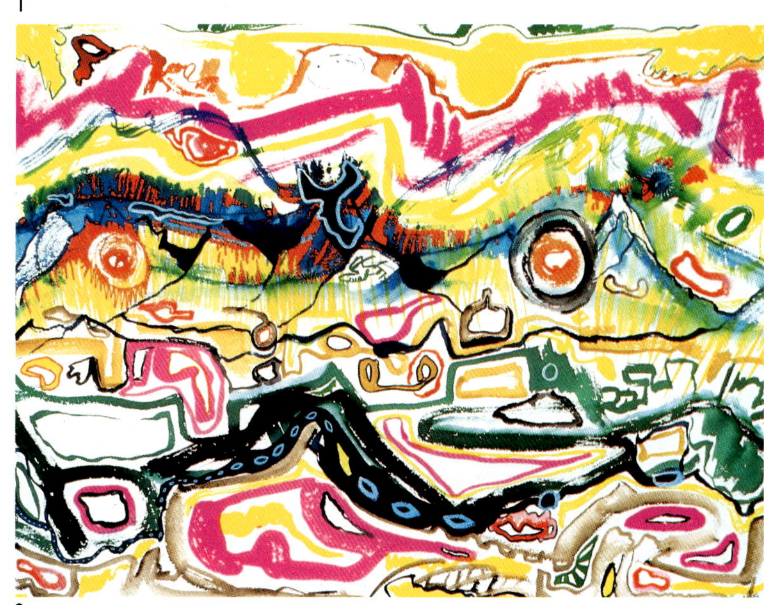

2

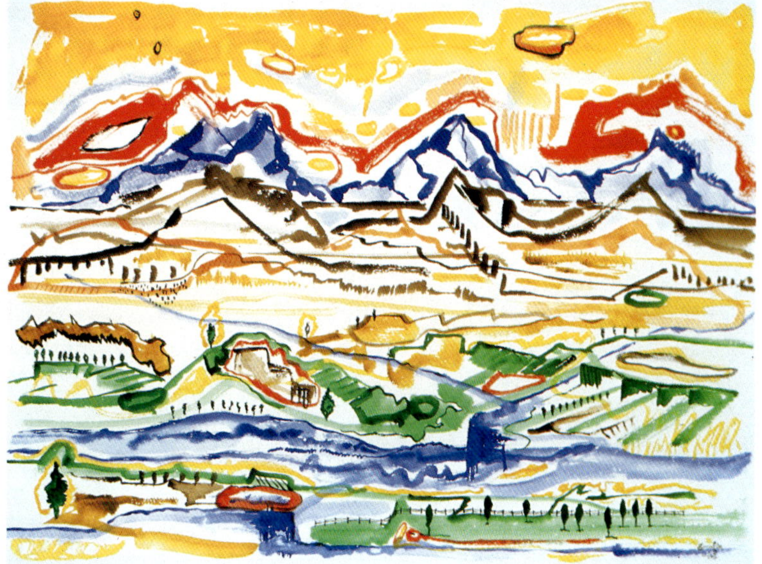

3

MONTSERRAT GALLERY

584 Broadway
New York, NY 10012
212.941.8899
212.274.1717 FAX

Contact:
Marie Montserrat Coll,
Director

Exhibiting:
Contemporary European
and American art

John Serafin

1. *City Ranch*
   1994, Watercolor,
   22" x 30"

2. *Understanding
   Nature's Forces*
   1994, Watercolor,
   22" x 30"

3. *Riverbrook Falls*
   1994, Watercolor,
   22" x 30"

Selected Biography:

1994 Montserrat Gallery,
New York, NY
1993 "Highlights '93" Group
Show, Limner Gallery
New York, NY;
Edgewood Gallery,
Dewitt, NY
1992-1990
Syracuse Stage Gallery,
Syracuse, NY
1991 Cooperstown
National Show,
Cooperstown, NY
1986 Everson
Museum of Art,
Syracuse, NY

C. GRIMALDIS GALLERY

523 N. CHARLES ST.
BALTIMORE, MD 21201
401.539.1080
401.539.2229 FAX

Contact:
Constantine Grimaldis

Exhibiting:
Contemporary sculpture
and painting

Mary Shaffer

1. *Point-of-View*
   1993, Installation glass,
   fiber optics,
   12' x 42' x 40'
   American Craft Museum

2. *Fragment*
   1993, Metal & Brick
   8' x 12' x 3'
   Muriel & Philip Berman Workshop

Selected Biography:

1994 "Transparenscene",
Palm Beach, CC
Museum of Art, FL

1993 "Saxe Collection",
The Toledo Museum
of Art, OH

1992 The Ruffino Tamayo
Museum, Mexico City,
Mexico

1991 Hakone Open-Air
Museum, Tokyo, Japan

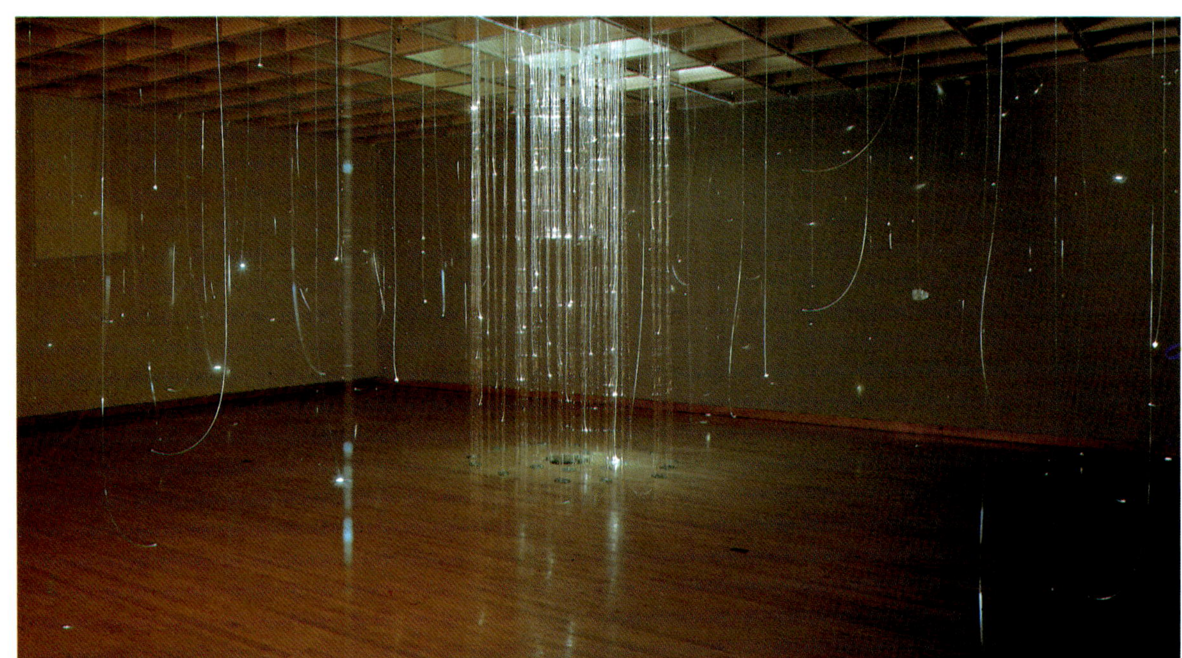

1

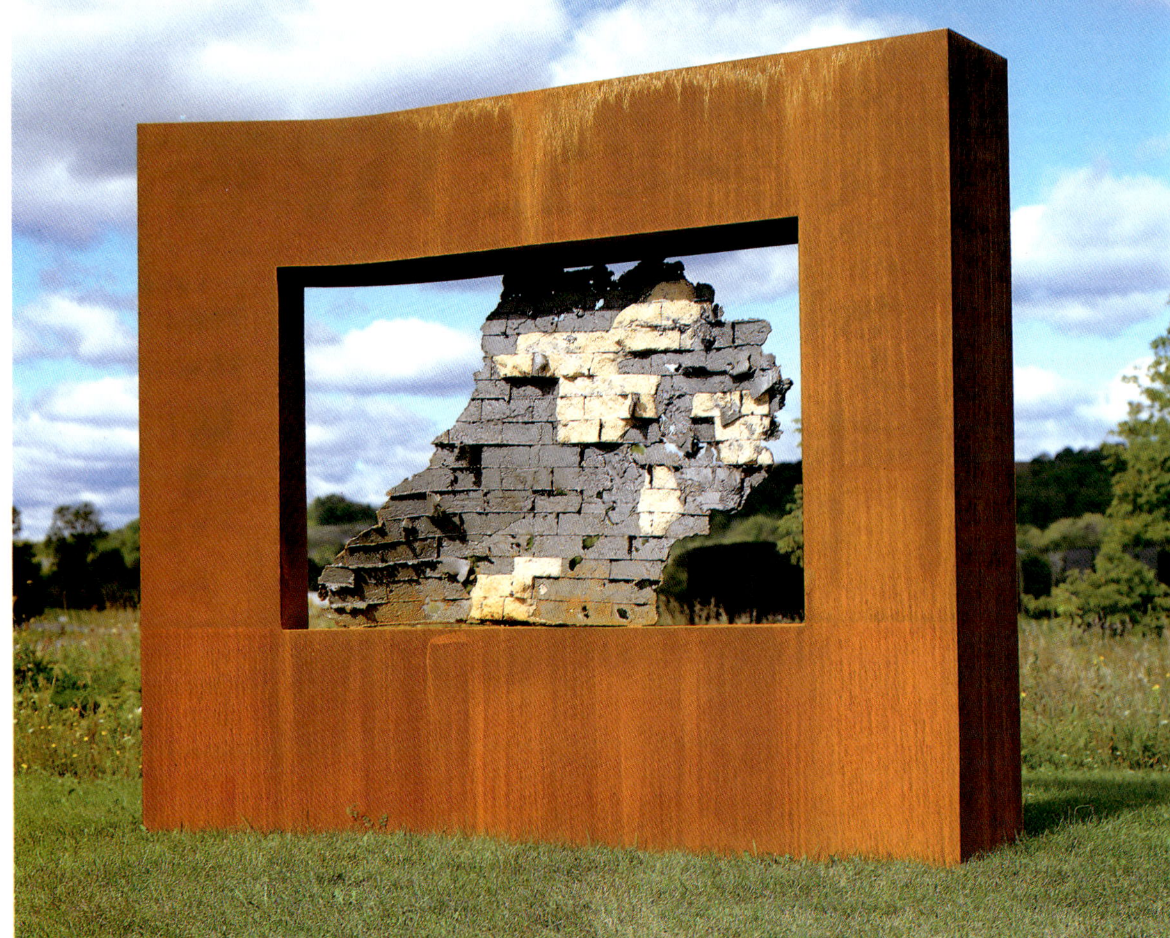

2

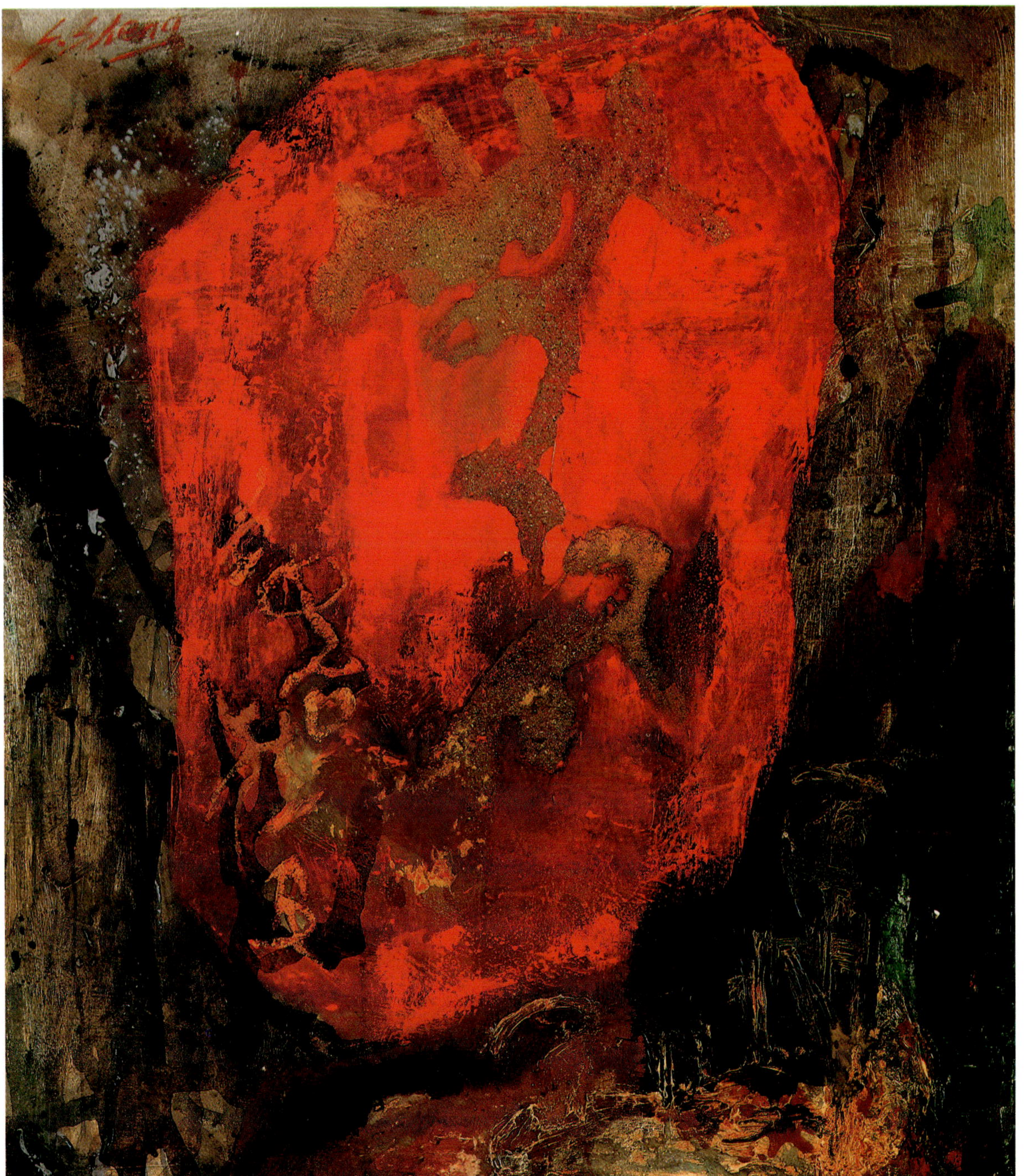

EAST WEST FINE ART

7 Hallam St. #2C
San Francisco, CA 94103
415.863.3078
408.739.9683 FAX

Exhibiting:
Contemporary Asian and
American Art

Shan-Shan Sheng

Calligraphy Forest
1992, Oil and mixed
media on canvas,
47" x 40"

Selected Biography:

1993 Solo show:
Art Miami International
Art Expo

1992 Solo show:
Art Asia - Hong Kong

Collection of Central
Plaza, Hong Kong

1987 Artist in Residence at
Harvard University,
Cambridge, MA

JOAN SHERMAN STUDIO

135 Greene Street
New York, NY 10012
212.387.0866
212.505.8550 FAX

Contact:
Joan Sherman, Director

Joan Sherman

1. *Fire*
   1993, Encaustic,
   18" x 24"

2. *Lotus*
   1993, Pastel,
   17¹/₂" x 25"

Selected Biography:

1992   Tribeca Gallery,
       New York, NY

1988   Solo exhibition:
       The Evansville Museum
       of Arts and Science,
       Indiana, IN

1985   Concord Gallery,
       New York, NY

1984   Solo exhibition:
       City Center Theater,
       New York, NY

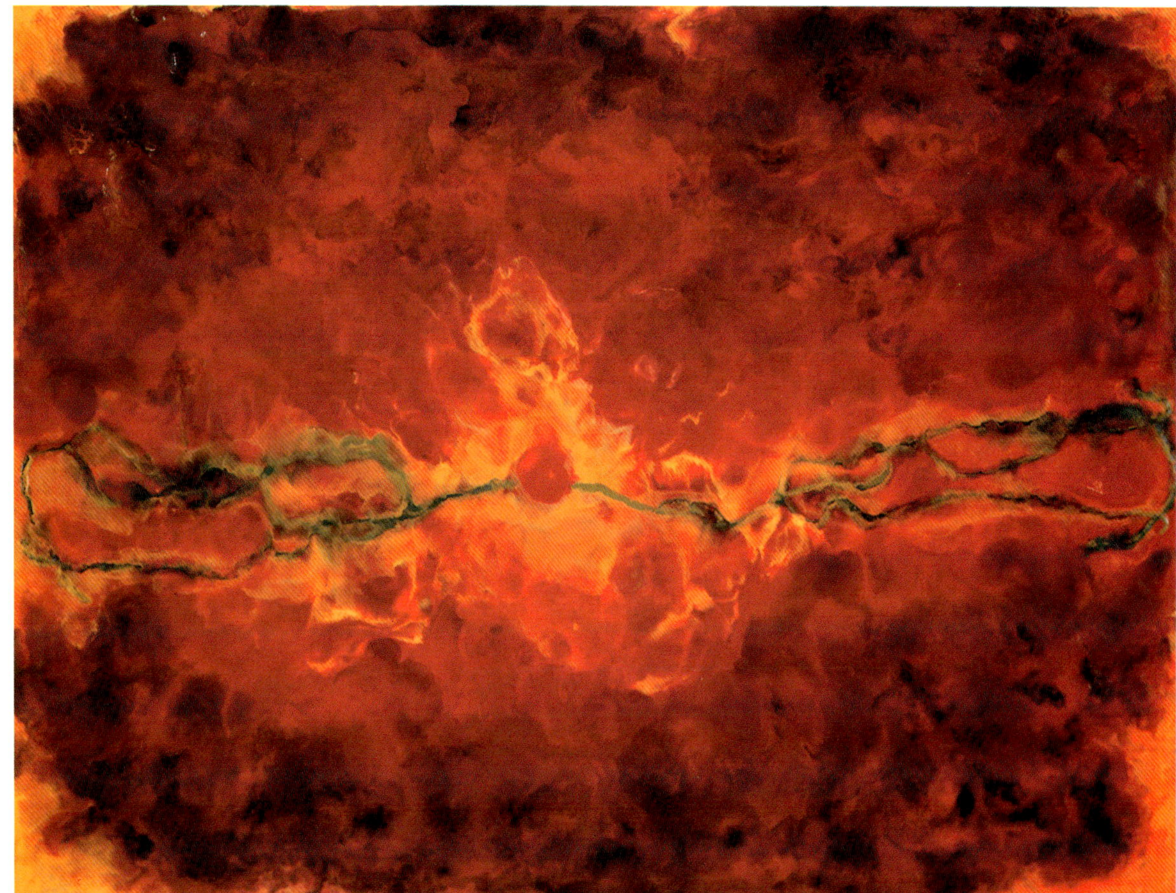

1

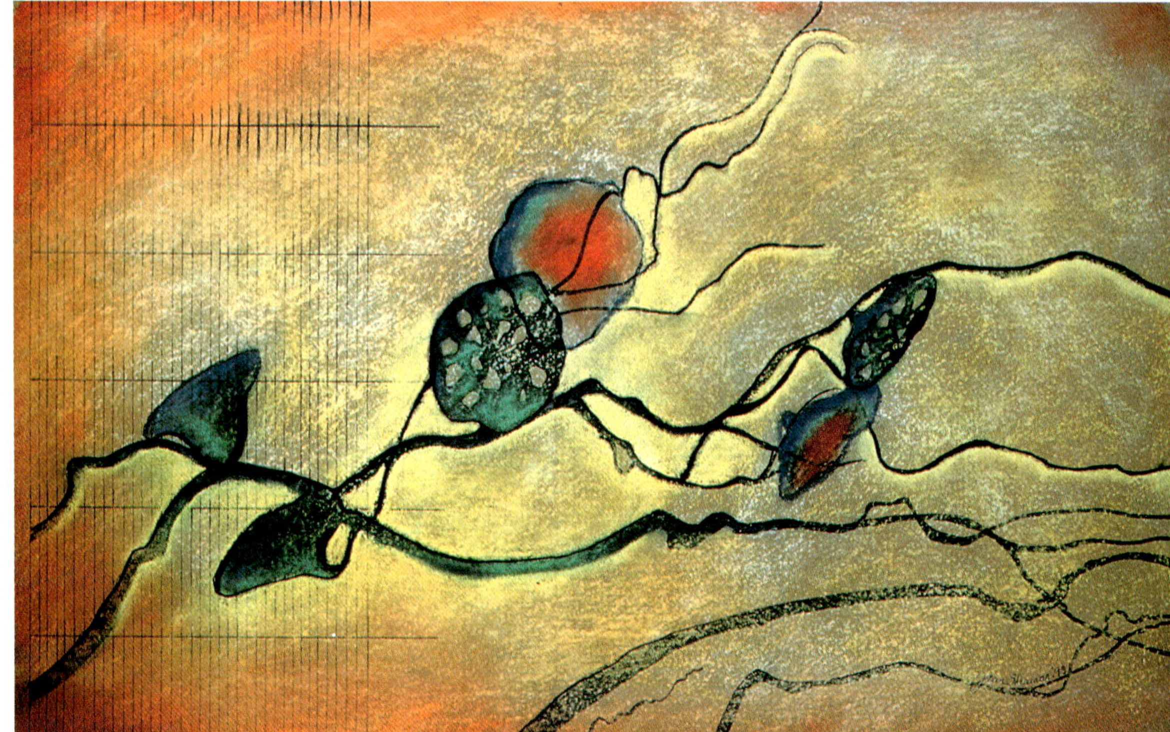

2

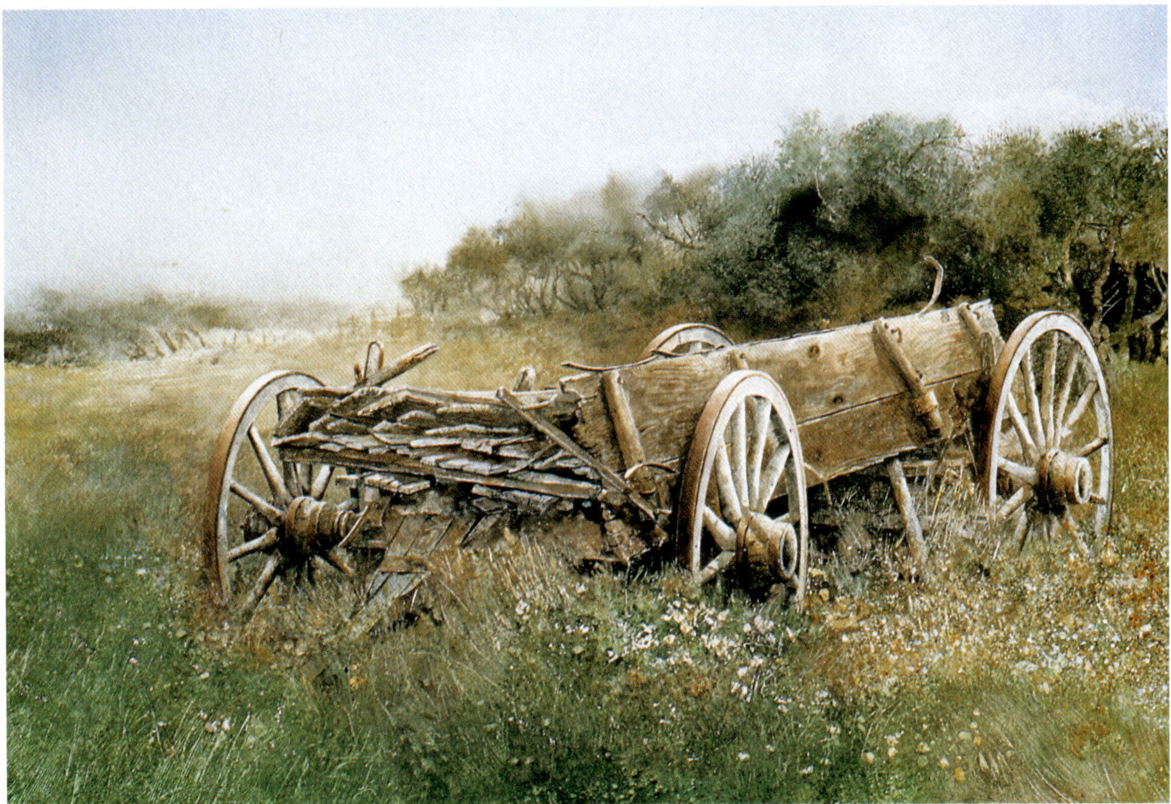

1

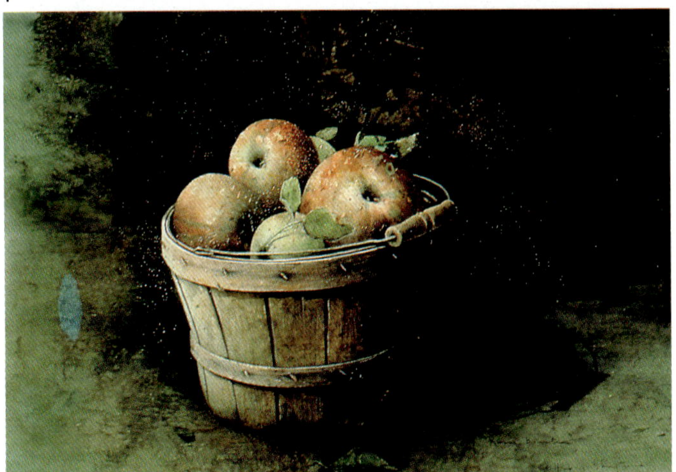

2

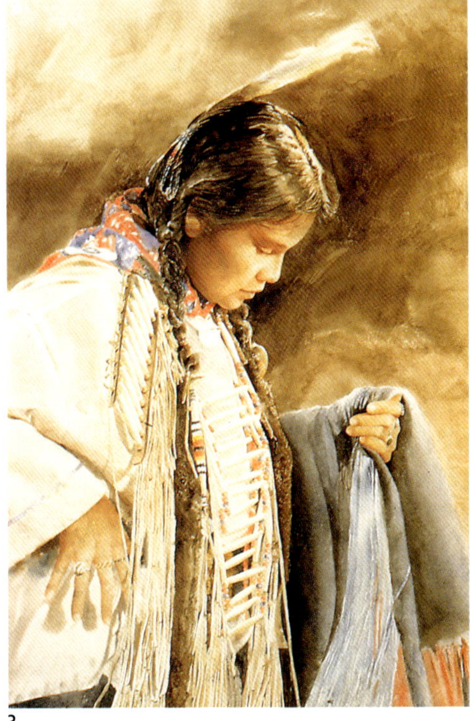

3

ROSENTHAL FINE ART, INC.

640 N. La Salle St. suite 582
Chicago, IL 60610
312.642.2966
312.642.5169 FAX

Contact:
Dennis Rosenthal

Exhibiting:
20th century modern and
contemporary international
uniques and multiples

Hubert Shuptrine

1. *April Morning*
   1985, Watercolor,
   17½" x 27¾"

2. *Rome Beauties*
   1976, Watercolor,
   17⅛" x 22"

3. *Festival Dancer*
   1988,
   Drybrush watercolor,
   29¾" x 22⅛"

GALLERY REVEL

96 Spring Street
New York, NY, 10012
212.925.0600
212.431.6270 FAX

Contact:
Marvin Carson
Gregory Carson

Exhibiting:
Contemporary paintings,
sculpture and prints by international artists

Victor Shvaiko

White Porch
1993, Oil on canvas,
14" x 11"

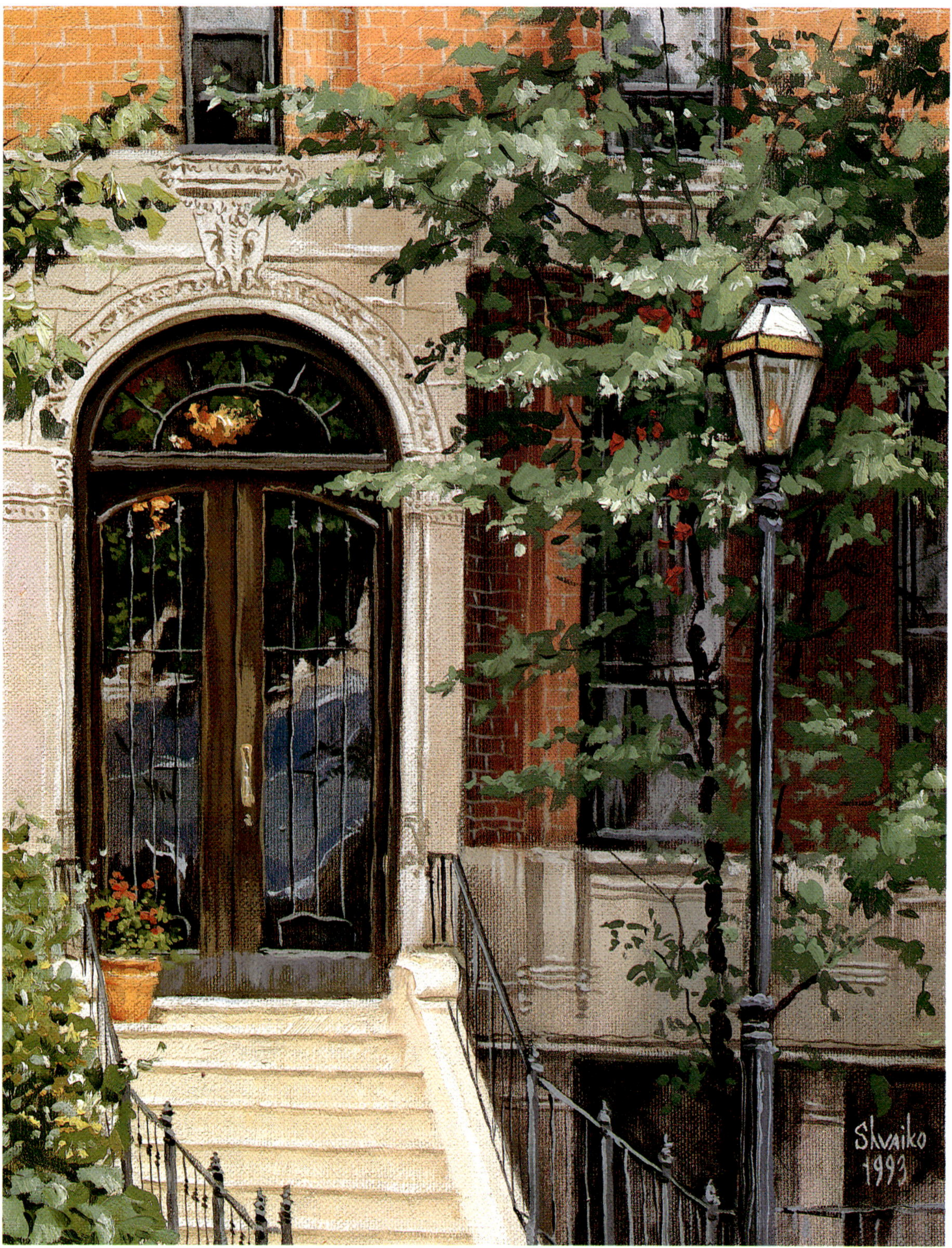

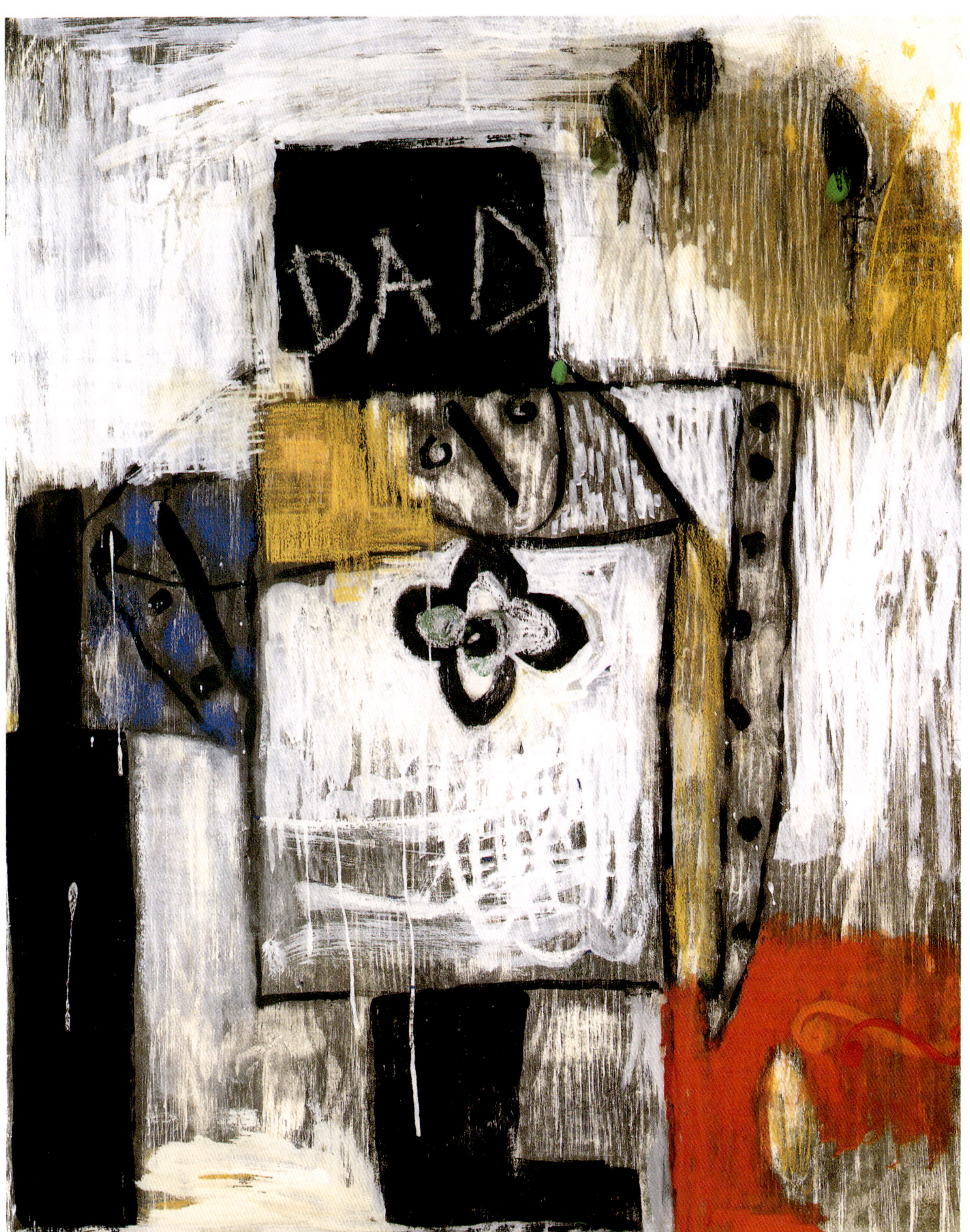

SPACE GALLERY

1945 West North Avenue
Chicago, IL 60622
312.276.5146
312.226.5587 FAX

Contact:
Fitz Gerald

Exhibiting:
Emerging contemporary
paintings, sculpture and
photography

Adam Siegel

Dad
1993, Mixed media,
30" x 42"

MARSHA CHILD CONTEMPORARY

P.O. Box 364
Solebury, PA 18963
215.297.0414
215.297.0414 FAX

Contact:
Marsha Child

Exhibiting:
Contemporary European,
Eastern European and
American paintings, sculpture
and graphics

Valerij Skrypka

1. *Riders*
   1990,
   Watercolor on paper,
   14" x 18"

2. *Two Solitudes*
   1993,
   Watercolor on paper,
   23" x 17"

3. *Faith and Hope*
   1993, Oil on canvas,
   21" x 28"

Selected Biography:

1994 Solo exhibition,
      Chryzanta Gallery,
      New York, NY

Group exhibitions:
1993 "Myth in Modern
      Times," Marsha Child
      Contemporary,
      Solebury, PA
1991 Ukrainian Gallery,
      Munich, Germany;
      Roxolana Gallery,
      Chicago, IL
1990 Galerie Marie-Therese
      Cochin, Paris, France;
      Shepmanshorden
      Gallery, Stockholm,
      Sweden

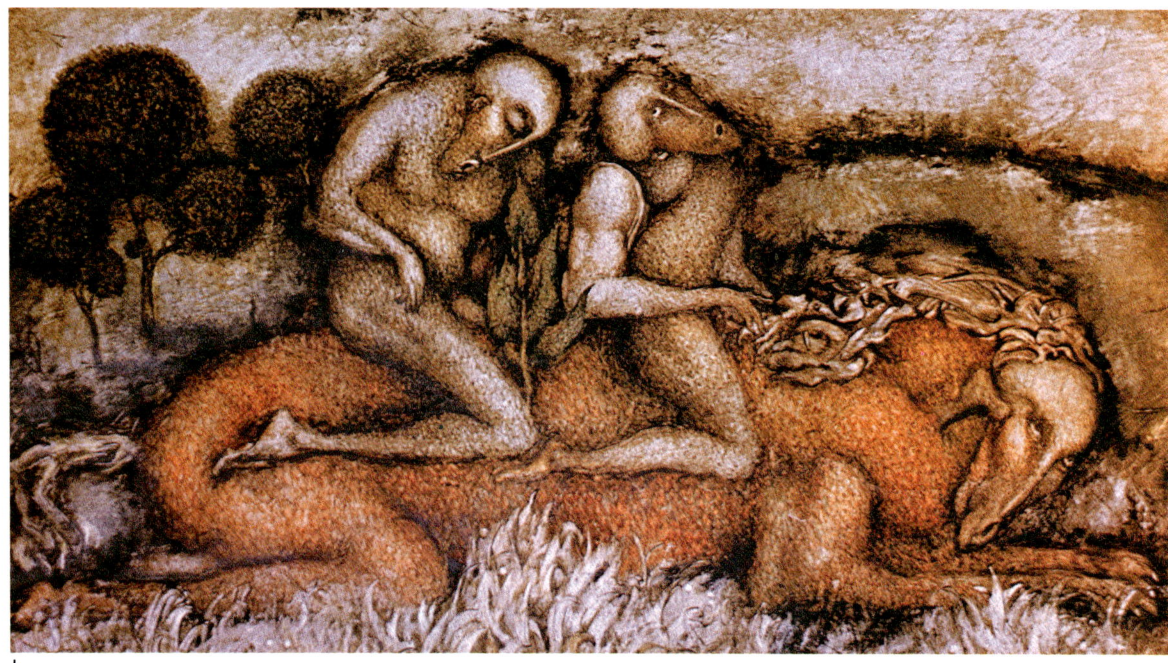

1

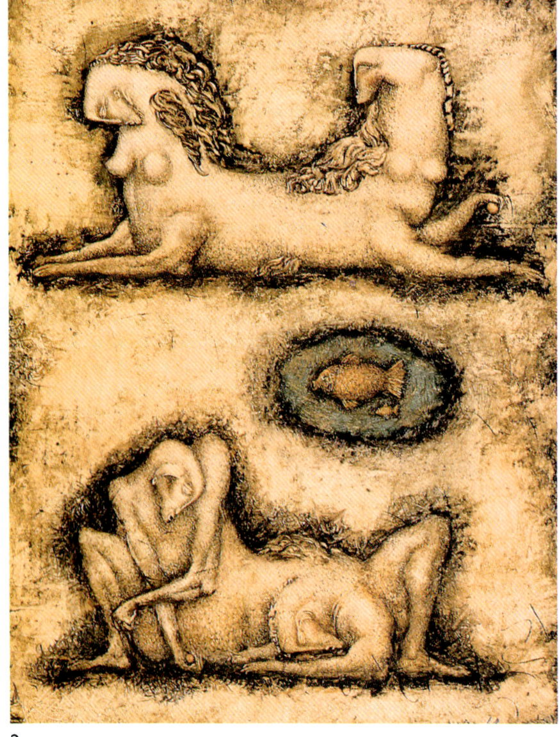

2

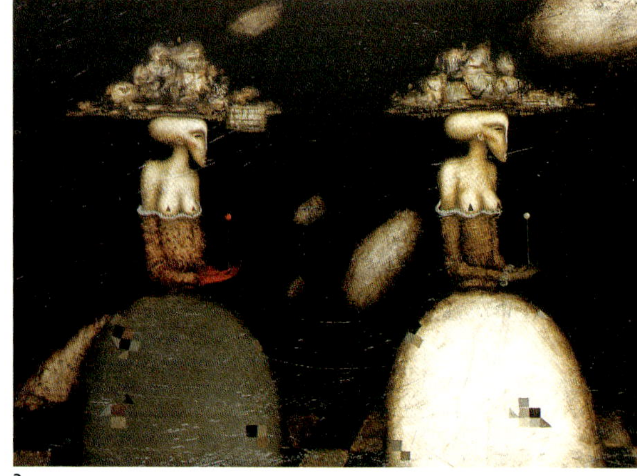

3

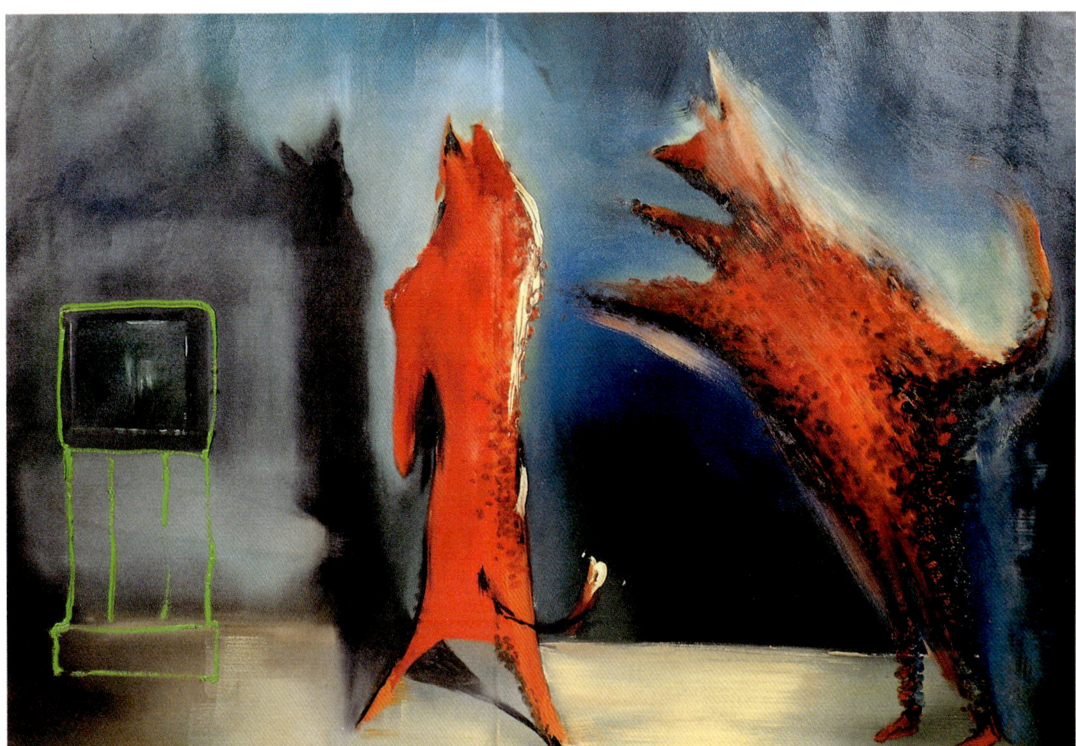

1

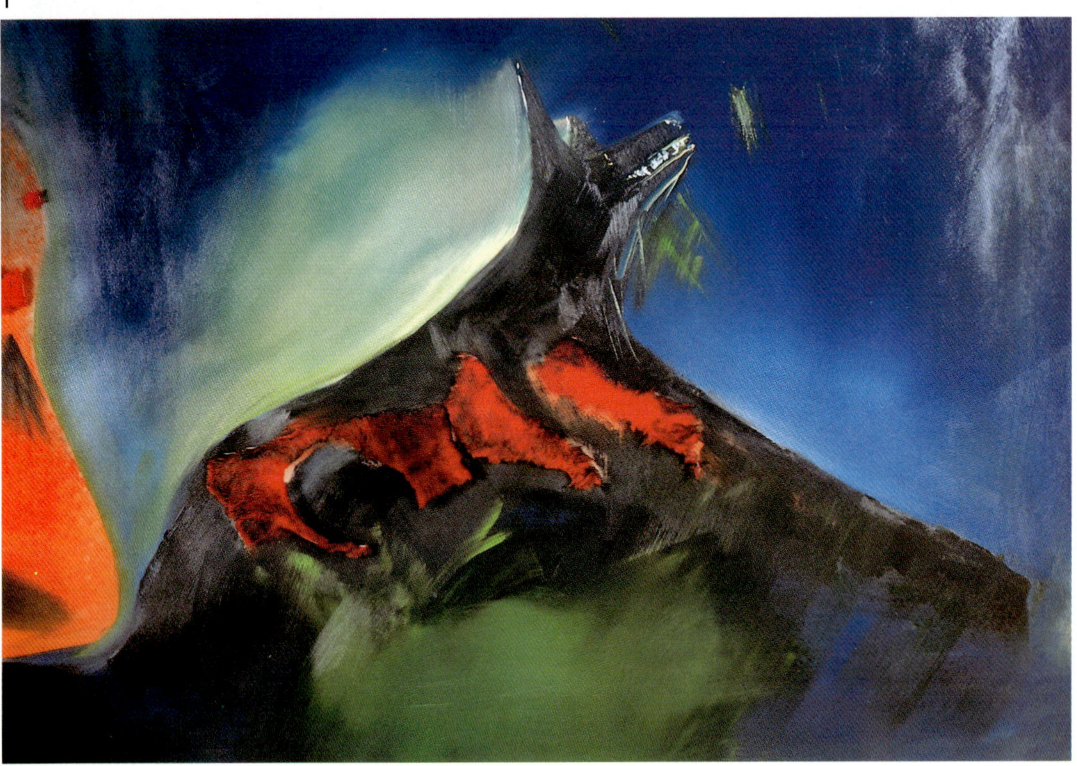

2

ENID OKLA HOMA

233 West Huron
Chicago, IL 60610
312.787.6011
312.787.6617 FAX

Contact:
Celeste Sotola, Director

Exhibiting:
Contemporary painting,
sculpture, and objects

Celeste Sotola

1. *The Explanation of Truth*
   1993, Oil, 48" x 72"

2. *Wolf in Sheep's Clothing*
   1993, Oil, 48" x 72"

L.A. ARTCORE CENTER

420 East 3rd Street Ste.110
Los Angeles, CA 90013
213.617.3274

Contact:
Lydia Takeshita, Director

Exhibiting:
Contemporary painting and
sculpture

Daniel Storozynsky

Winds
1992, Acrylic on canvas,
72" x 72"

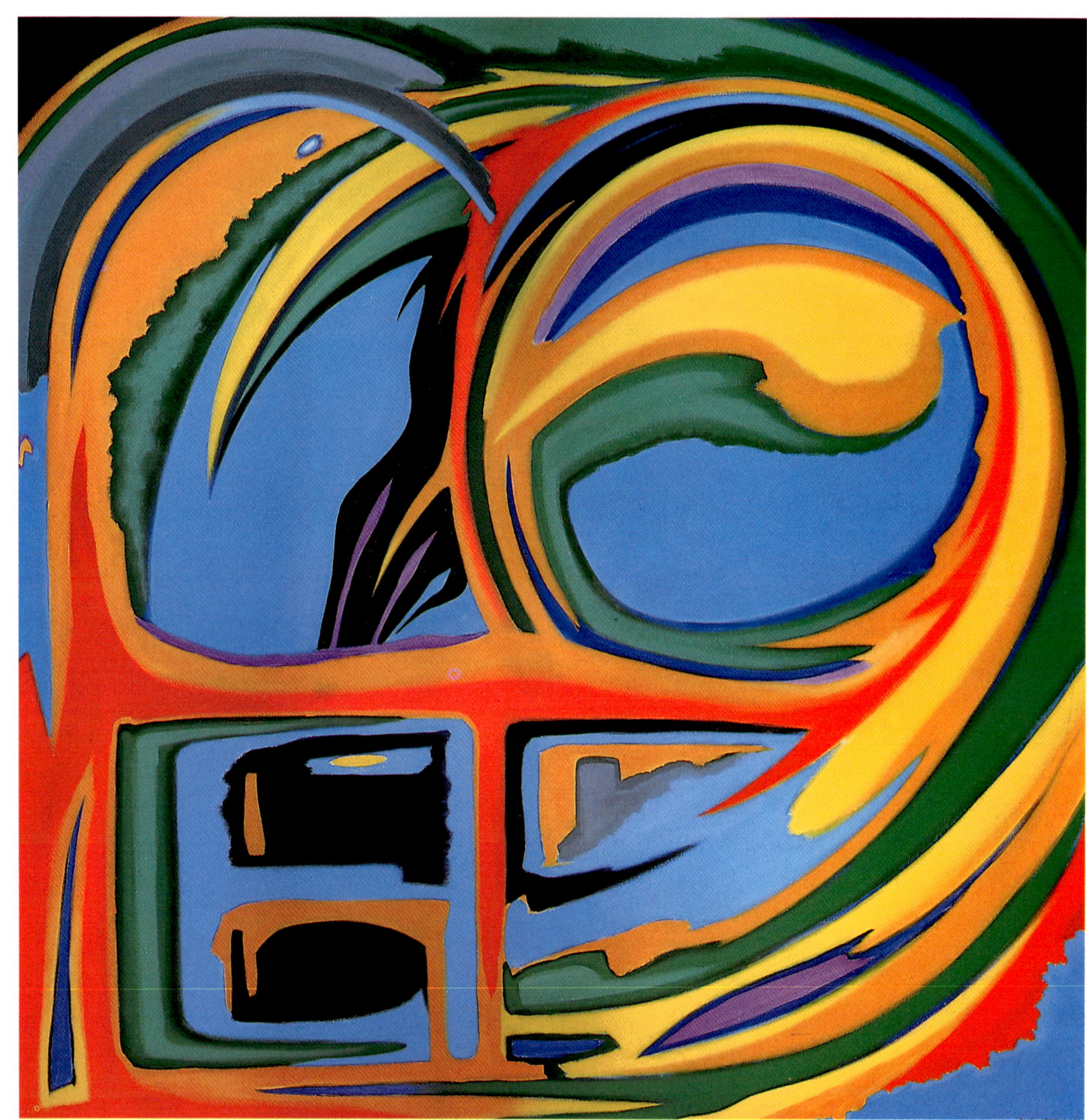

Selected Biography:

1994 Solo exhibition:
"Flesh and Bone"
L.A. Artcore, L.A., CA
1993 Group exhibition:
"Healing Power of Art"
L.A. Artcore, L.A., CA
1992 Group exhibition:
"Energy-Interaction of
Contrast", L.A.
Artcore-South Bay
Contemporary
Museum, L.A., CA
1991 Solo exhibition:
Boritzer-Gray,
Venice, CA
Solo exhibition:
"Forgotten Myth", L.A.
Artcore, L.A., CA

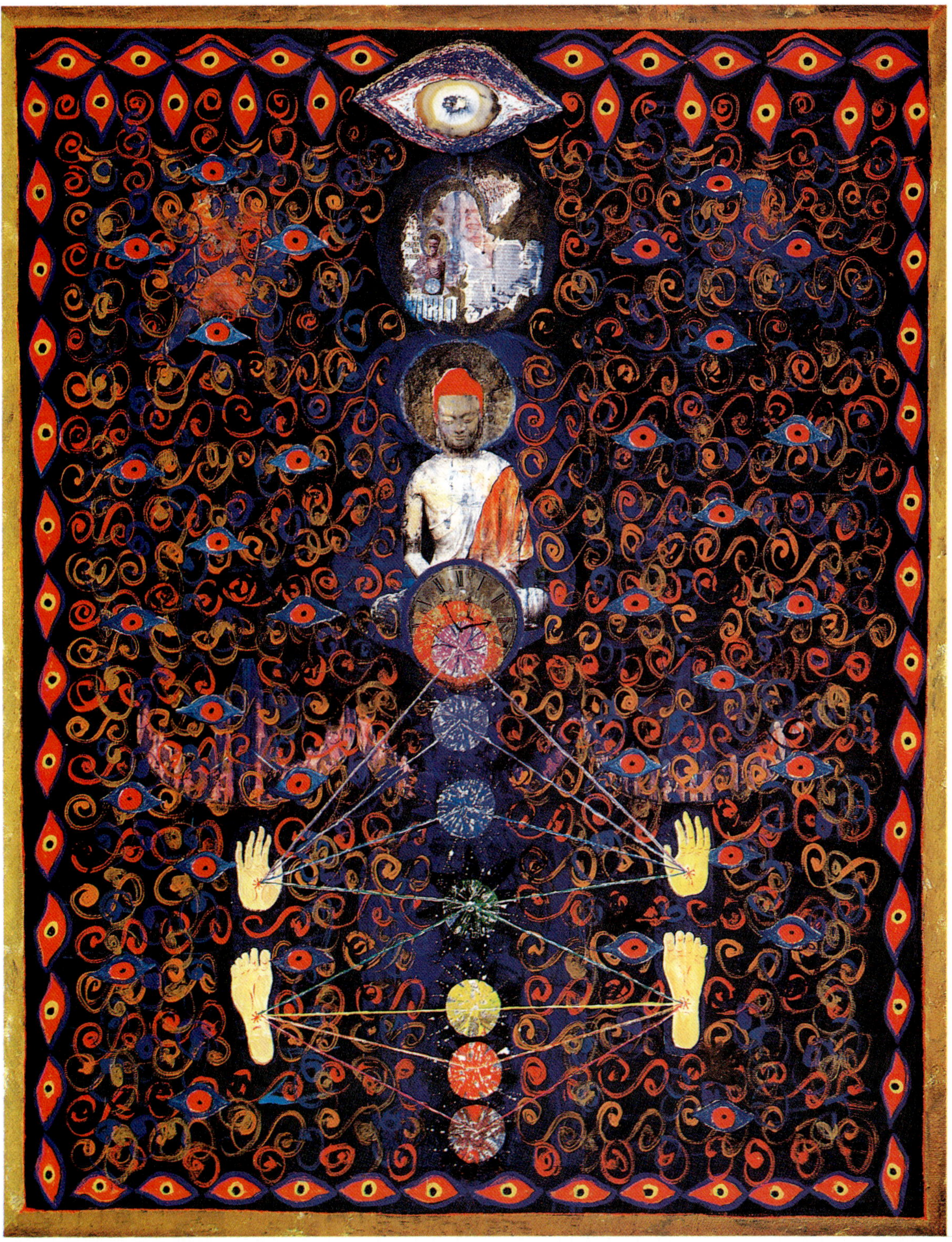

E. M. DONAHUE
GALLERY

560 Broadway #304
New York, NY 10012
212.226.1111
212.982.5579 FAX

Contact:
Ronald Sosinski

Exhibiting:
Contemporary painting,
brokerage; Impressionist and
Modern painting

Beth Ames Swartz

*The Return: Charging the
Species at the Eleventh Hour,*
Mixed media on canvas,
60" x 48"

GAGOSIAN GALLERY

980 Madison Ave
New York, NY 10021
212.744.2313
212.772.7962 FAX

136 Wooster Street
New York, NY 10012
212.228.2828
212.228.2878 FAX

Contact:
Melissa Lazarov, Director

Exhibiting:
20th-Century painting
and sculpture;
Abstract Expressionism,
Pop & Minimalism

David Salle

North African Strip
1993, Mixed
media on canvas,
113 1/2" x 114"

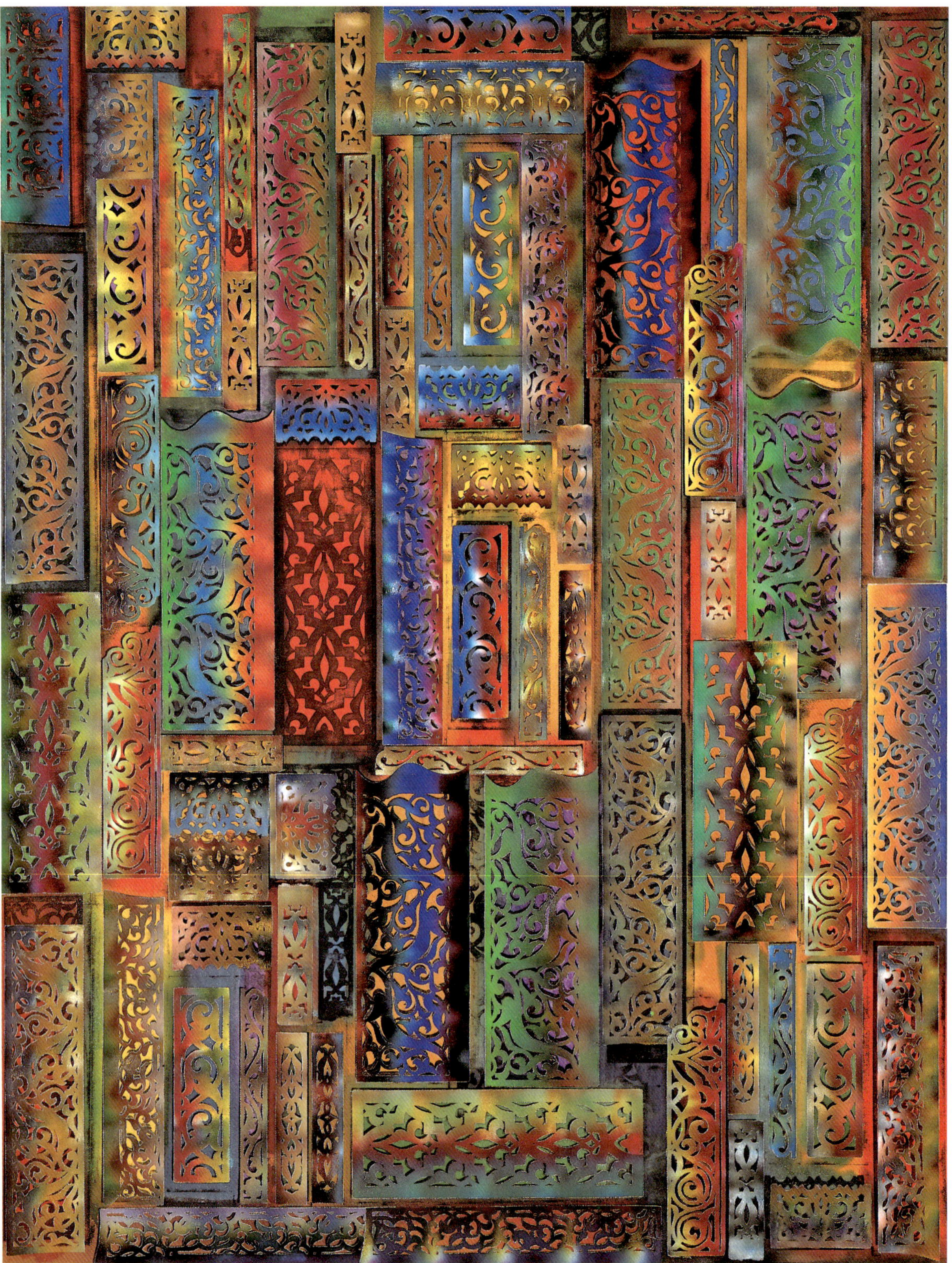

Selected Biography:
1993 Solo exhibition:
Center for the Fine
Arts, Miami;
Kunsthalle Wien, Wien;
Group exhibition:
Sidney Janis Gallery,
New York, NY
Galerie Beyeler, Basel
1992 Group exhibition:
Haywood Gallery,
London; Aldrich
Museum of
Contemporary Art,
Ridgefield, CT
1991 Solo exhibition:
Galerie Max Hetzler,
Cologne; Gagosian
Gallery, New York, NY

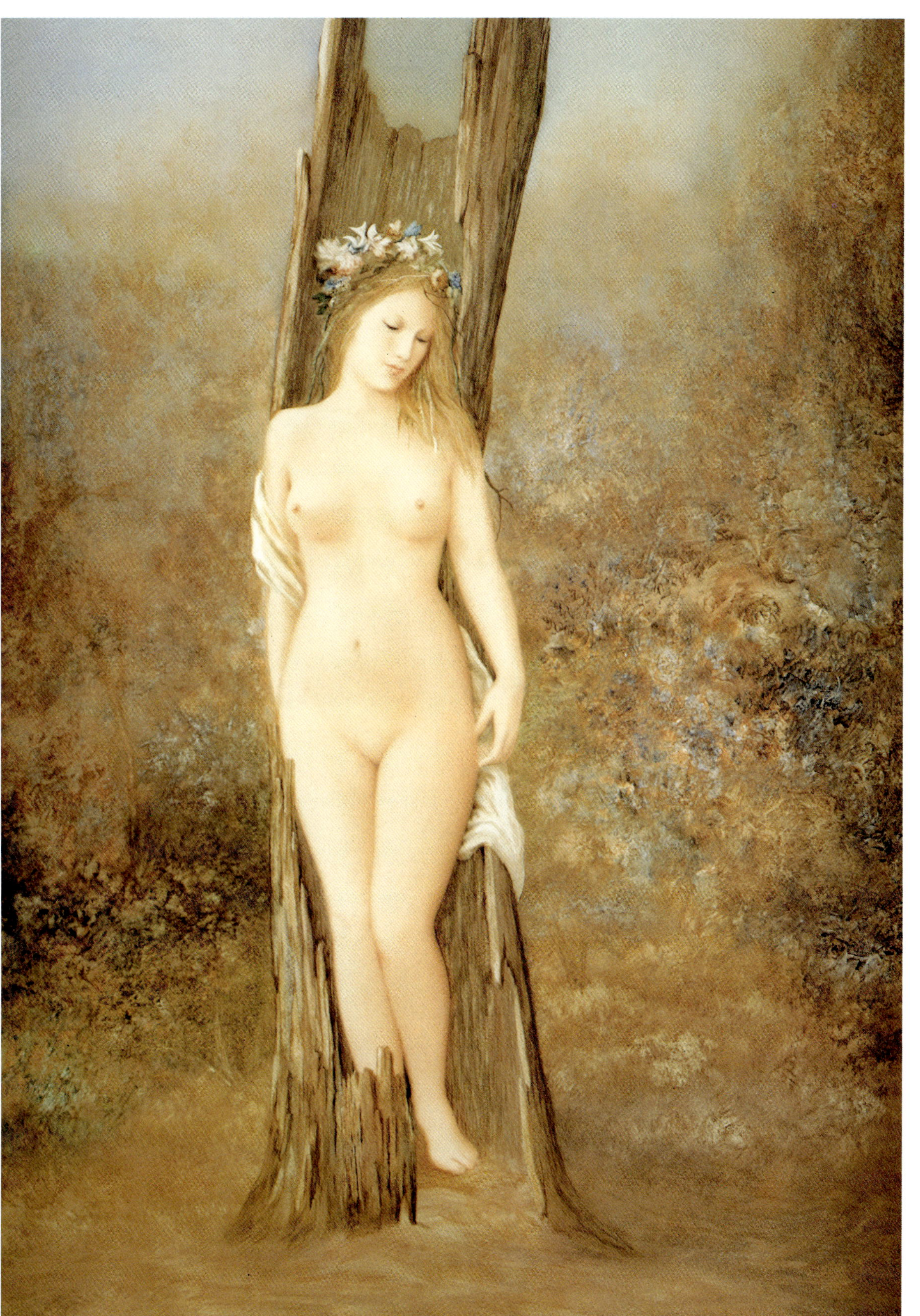

GALERIA MAREN

Hamburgo 175-A
Zona Rosa, D. F.
Mexico, 06600
525.208.0442
525.514.4341
525.533.3904 FAX

Contact:
Enrique Jimenez

Exhibiting:
Modern, contemporary and
Mexican art

Adrian Tavera

Otono (Fall)
1992, Oleo s/masonite,
1.00 x 70 cms

Selected Exhibition:

1993 Art Miami 93
International Art
Exposition,
Miami Beach
1992 Hotel Nikko Les
Celebrites Mexico, D.F.
Art Asia Hong Kong
Convention Center.
Jacob K. Javits
Convention Center,
New York.
1991 Galeria Maren
Individual, Mexico, D.F.
Mundo Oniricos
1990 VIII Clasico Miguel
Aleman, Club de Golf
los Encinos, individual,
Mexico, D.F.

**MONTSERRAT
GALLERY**

584 Broadway
New York, NY 10012
212.941.8899
212.274.1717 FAX

Contact:
Marie Montserrat Coll,
Director

Exhibiting:
Contemporary European
and American art

Francisco Torregrosa

1.   Mixed medium,
     1992, 40" x 40"

2.   Mixed medium,
     1992, 40" x 40"

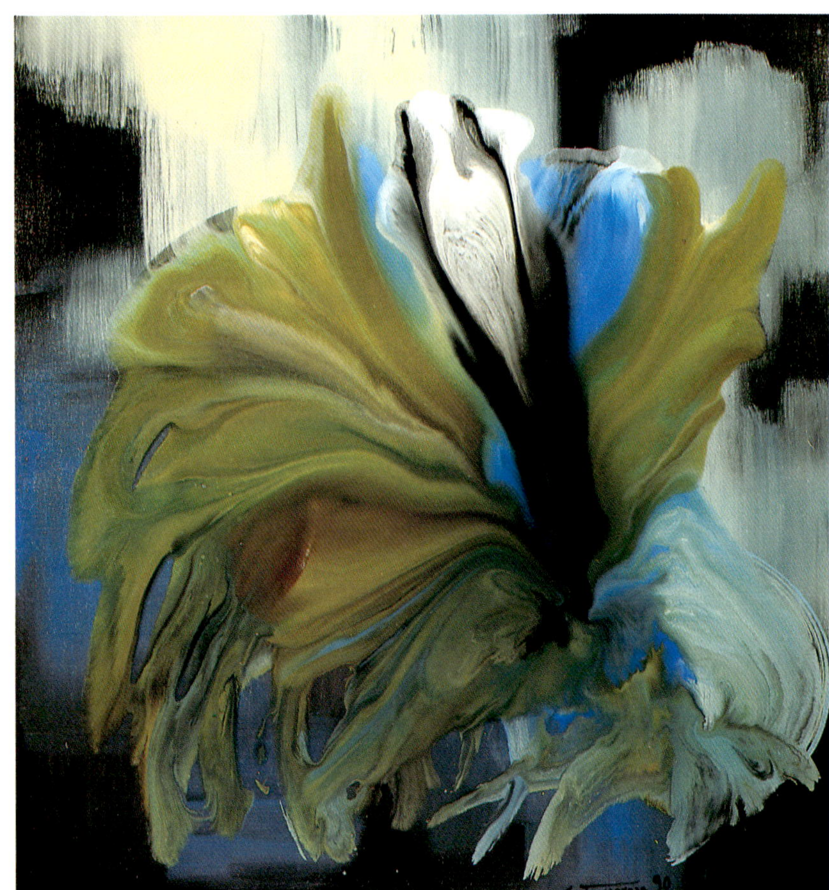

1

Selected Biography:

1993 Euro art Group,
      Italy;
      Arte Fiera,
      Bologna, Italy

1992 Reflejos Gallery,
      Quito;
      Medulio Gallery,
      Barcelona

1991 Milano Parco
      Novegreno, Italy;
      Gabernia Gallery,
      Valencia;
      Montserrat Gallery,
      New York, NY

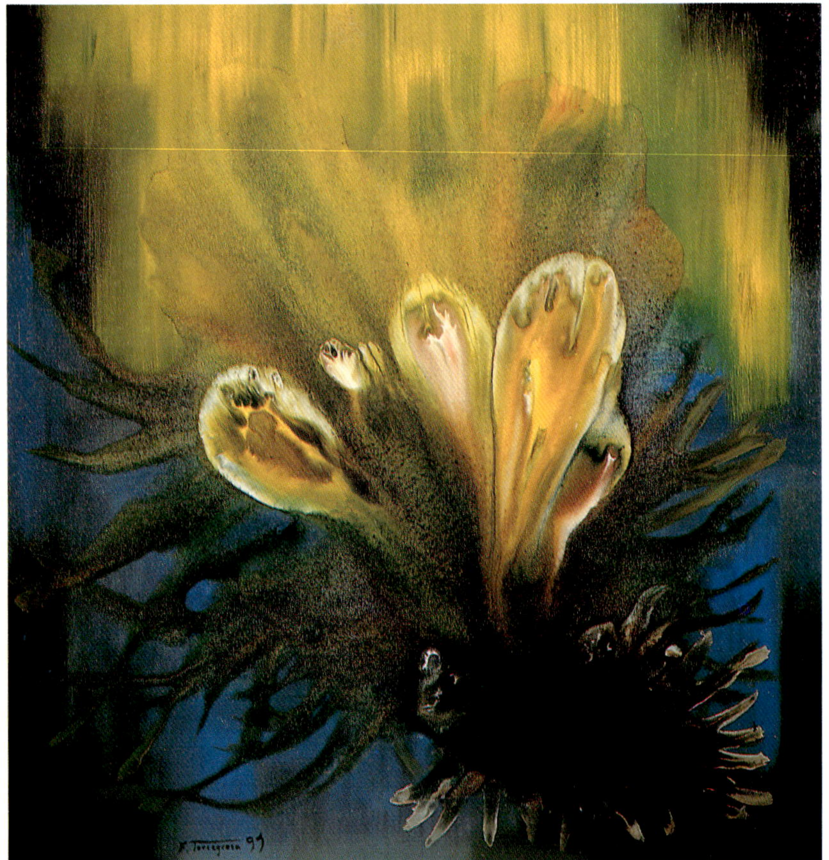

2

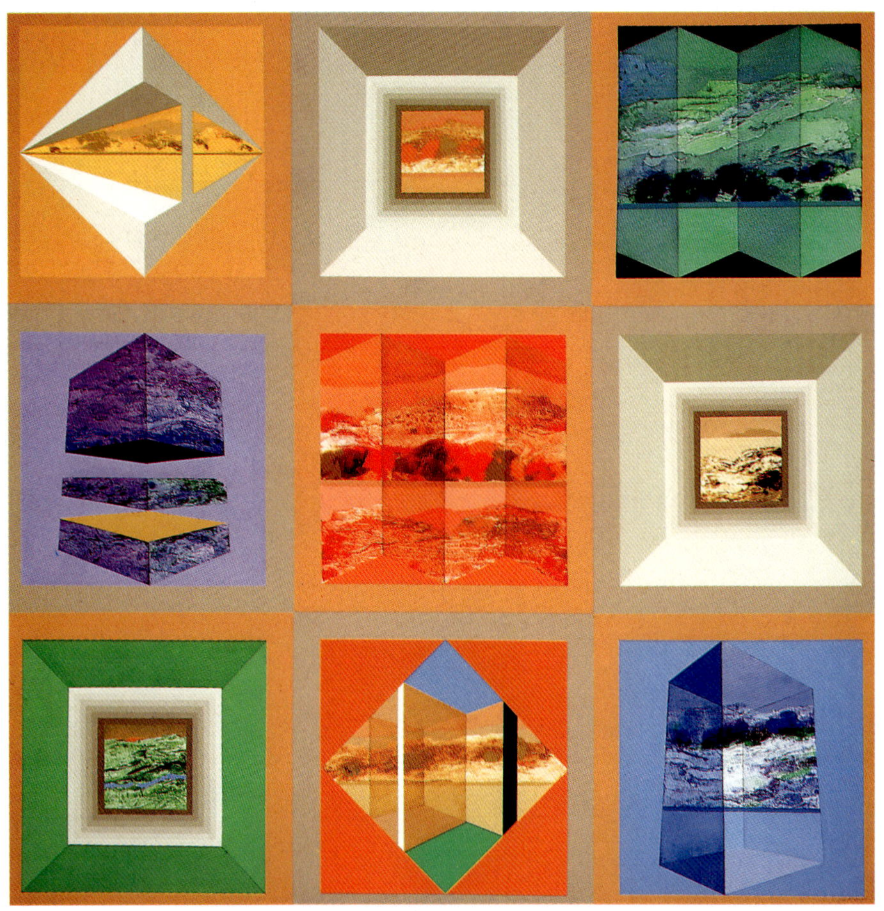

1

HARMON-MEEK GALLERY

386 Broad Avenue South
Naples, FL 33940
813.261.2637
813.261.3804

4262 Gulfshore Blvd. N.
Naples, FL 33940
813.261.7775

Contact:
J. William Meek III,
Director-owner

Exhibiting:
20th Century American art

James Twitty

1. *Smorgasbord*
   1991, Acrylic on linen,
   60" x 60"

2. *Blue Water*
   1988, Acrylic on linen,
   72 " x 72"

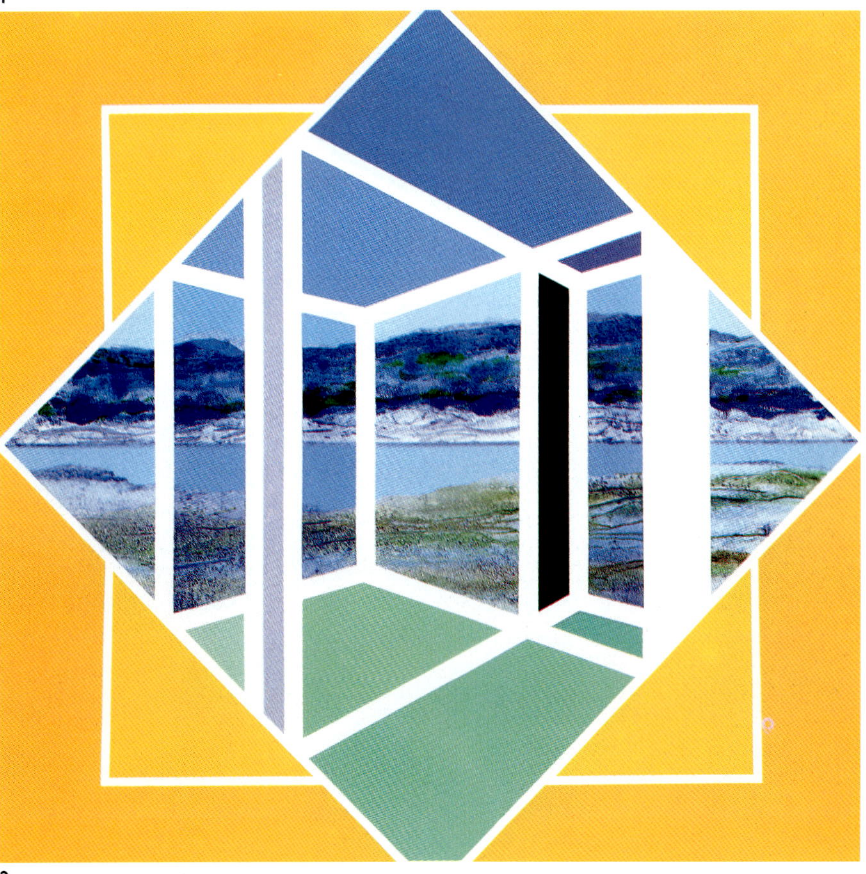

2

Selected Collections:
National Gallery of Art,
Wash., D.C.; Corcoran
Gallery of Art,
Washington, D.C.;
Butler Institute
of American Art,
Youngstown, OH;
Dallas Museum of Art,
TX; Houston Museum
of Fine Art, TX;
High Museum of Art,
Atlanta, GA;

Solo exhibitions:
1994 Harmon-Meek Gallery,
March 11 - April 9,
1992 Harmon-Meek Gallery
1991 Hickory Museum
of Art, NC
1990 Harmon-Meek Gallery

CORINNE TIMSIT INTERNATIONAL GALLERIES Inc.

81, rue Lepic
75018 Paris, France
33.1.4255.7682
33.1.4252.4868 FAX

Calle San José 104
Viejo San Juan
00901 Puerto Rico
809.724.1039
809.721.4174 FAX

Contact:
Jaime Otero
Marisa Guevara

Exhibiting:
Latin American and
European art

Fernando Varela

1. *Calis and Ciborium*
   1993, Mixed
   technique on paper,
   32" x 40"

2. *Chant to Spain*
   1993, Mixed
   technique on paper,
   31" x 32"

Selected Biography:

1994 Solo exhibitions:
O.E.A. Washington

1993 Solo exhibitions:
25e Festival Cagnes-sur-
Mer, Retrospective des
Lauréats

Art Miami '93
Corinne Timsit
International Galleries

Salon de la Jeune
Peinture
Grand Palais

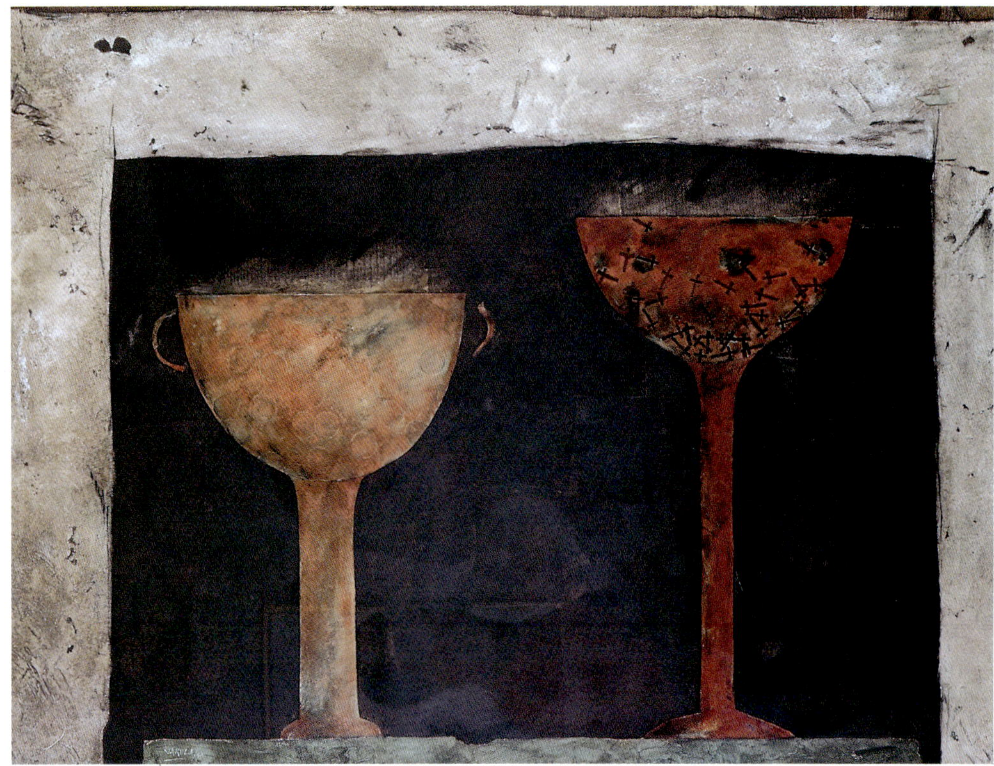

1

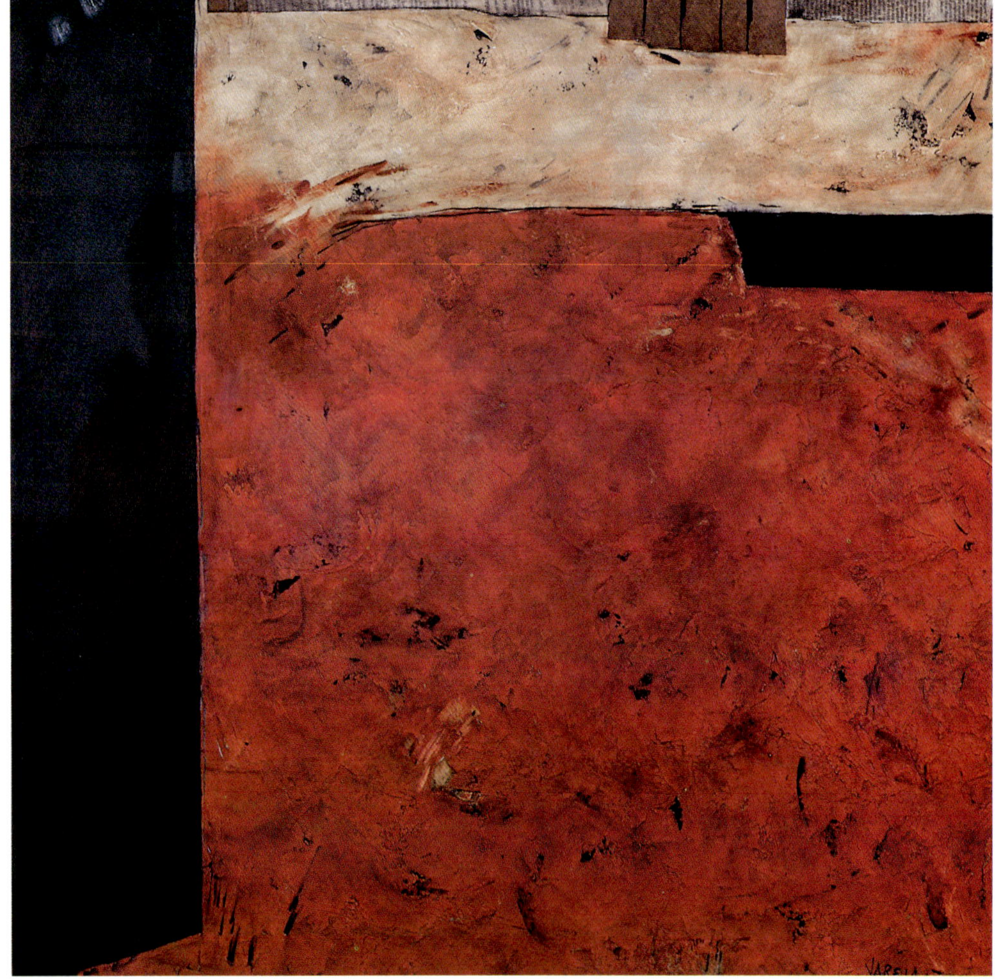

2

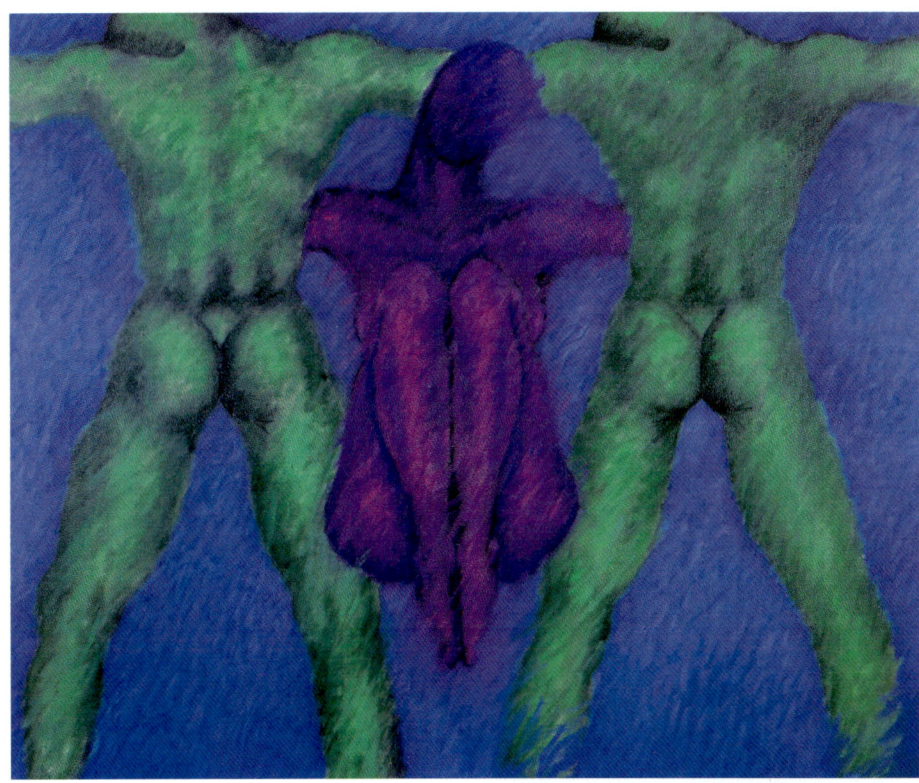

1

FENIX FINE ARTS

180 N.E. 40th St.
Miami, FL 33137
305.573.2727
305.542.8289
305.576.7707 FAX

Contact:
George Gandelman

Exhibiting:
Latin American Art

Lina Velazquez

1. *Corpus Delicti De Mi Amar*
   1993, Oil on Yute,
   165 cms. x 203 cms.

2. *Mi Ultimo Aliento*
   1993, Oil on Yute,
   152 cms. x 73 cms.

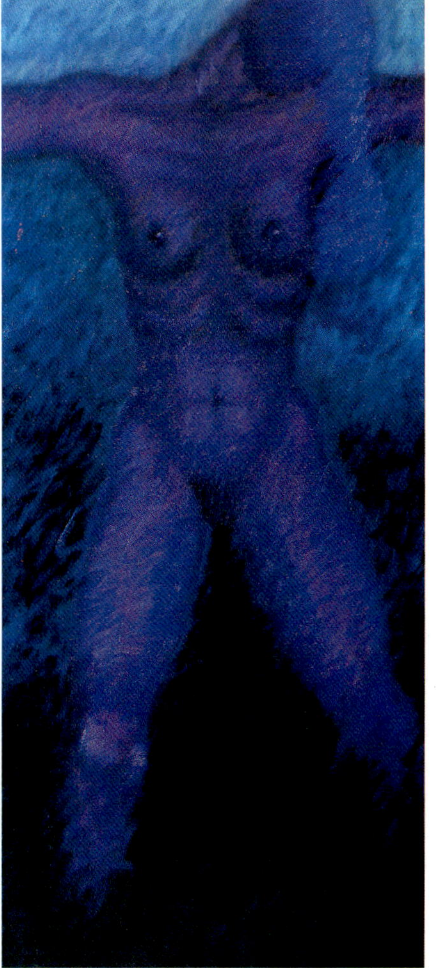

2

Selected Biography:

1993 Gandelman's Fenix Fine
Arts, "Visions of The
Andes I", Miami, FL

"7 Mujeres de 7 Paises"
("7 Women from 7
Countries"),
The Florida Museum of
Hispanic & Latin
American Art,
Miami, FL

1991 Museum of Modern
Art, Pereira, Colomba

FENIX FINE ARTS

180 N.E. 40th St.
Miami, FL 33137
305.573.2727
305.542.8289
305.576.7707 FAX

Contact:
George Gandelman

Exhibiting:
Latin American Art

Maria Victoria Velez

1. *Giran Memorias*
   ("Memories Swivel")
   From the Travels Thru
   the Desert series,
   1993, Oil on Canvas,
   130 cms. x 130 cms.

2. *Nido Flotante, autorretrato*
   ("Floating Nest") a self por-
   trait
   From the Travels Thru
   the Desert series,
   1993, Oil on Canvas,
   150 cms. x 170 cms.

Selected Biography:

1993 Gandelman's Fenix Fine
Arts, "Visions of The
Andes I", Miami, FL

1992 ARTFI, International
Exposition of Galleries,
Bogota, Colombia

1986 Museum of Modern Art
of Latin America OEA,
Washington, D.C.

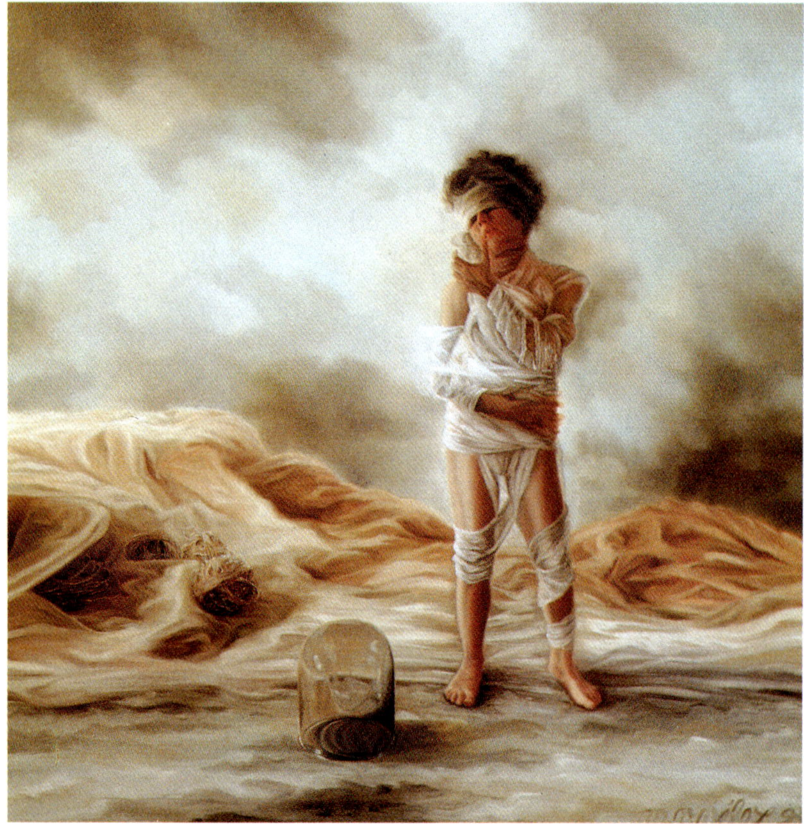

1

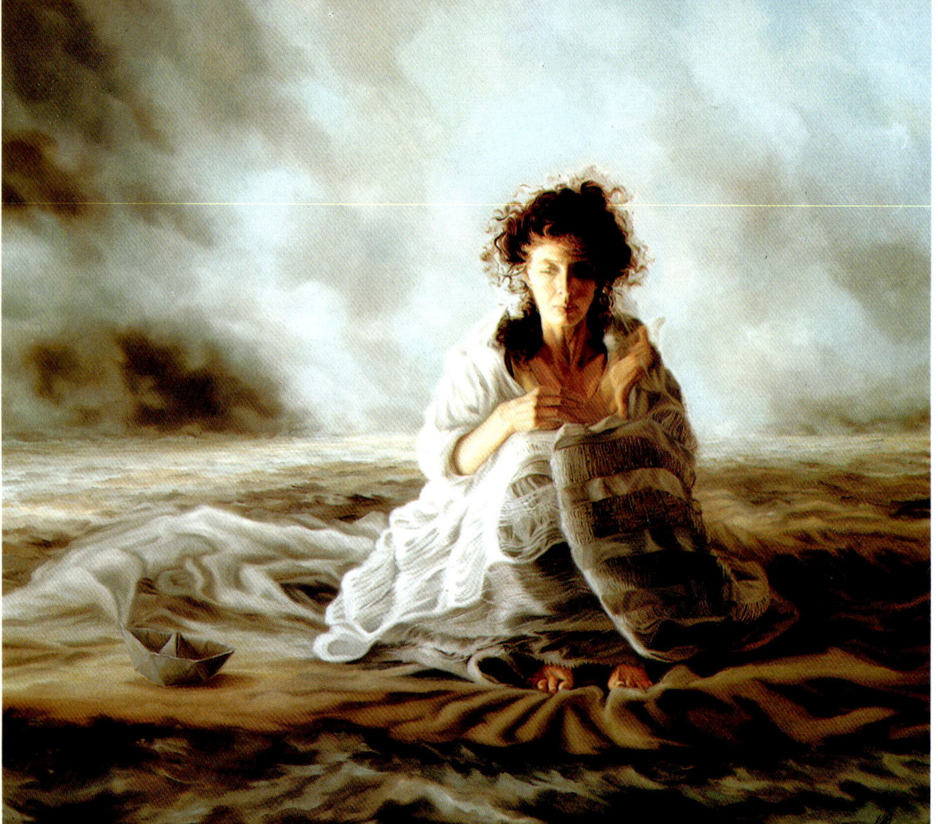

2

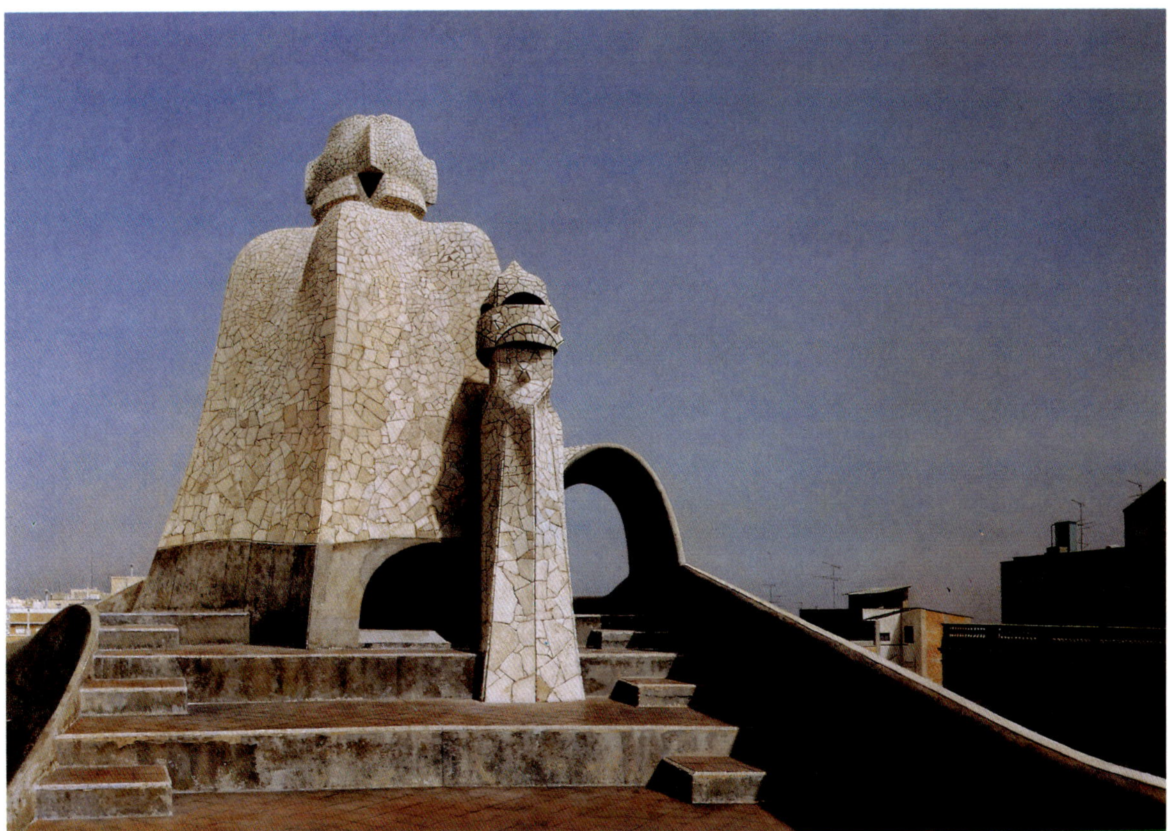

1

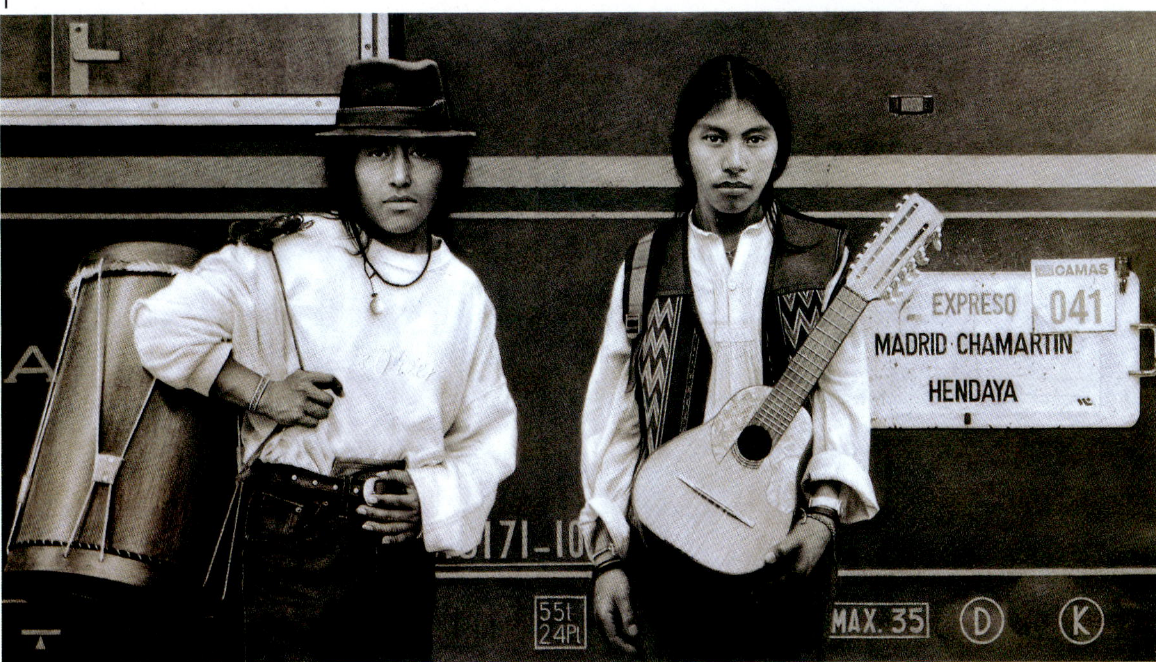

2

ANSORENA

Alcalá 54
Madrid 28014
Spain
1.521.5278
1.522.01.58 FAX

Contact:
Jaime Mato Ansorena
Pilar De La Puente

Exhibiting:
Spanish Contemporary
Realism

Muñoz Vera

1. *La Pedrera*
   1992, Oil on
   canvas on wood,
   106 x 155 cms.

2. *Peruvians in Chamartin
   Station*
   1992, Pencil and
   black crayon on
   paper on wood,
   74 x 138 cms.

Selected Biography:

1993 Solo Show: Ansorena,
      Madrid, Spain
      "Spanish Realism,"
      Gallery Tamenaga,
      New York, NY
      ARCO 93, Madrid,
      Spain
1992 "Tierra de Nadie,"
      Itinerary exhibition on
      realism throughout
      Spain
      "Chilean Painters in
      Spain," Council of
      Santiago, Chile
      "Latinamerican Painters
      in Spain," Caixagalicia
      Foundation, Santiago de
      Compostela, Spain

SPECIAL THINGS GALLERY

1407 Greenleaf
Evanston, IL 60202
708.869.8887
708.869.8909 FAX

Contact:
Michael W. Phillips

Exhibiting:
Art of emerging artist, ethnic art, fine art reproductions & framing

Zhao-Yu Wan

1. *Royal Ride*
   1986, Water color & ink on rice paper, 19.5" x 27"

2. *Buddha Scripture*
   1990, Water color & ink on rice paper, 16" x 17"

3. *Skyline*
   1991, Acrylic on canvas, 40" x 40"

Selected Solo Exhibitions:
1994 Shanghai-Chicago, Gallery at Work East & West, Chicago, IL
1991 Galerie Redies, La Mostra International d'Arte, Basel, Switzerland,
1990 Galerie Redies, Calligraphy Paintings, Dusseldorf, Germany; Chicago International Art Exposition, Chicago

Selected Biography:
Born 1957, in Shanghai, People's Republic of China, studied under Han Tienheng, 1982-1987, in Shanghai; graduated 1983, from Shanghai Conservatory of Music; Immigrated to the US, 1987; obtained American citizenship, 1991. The leading young contemporary artist of the Shanghai School.

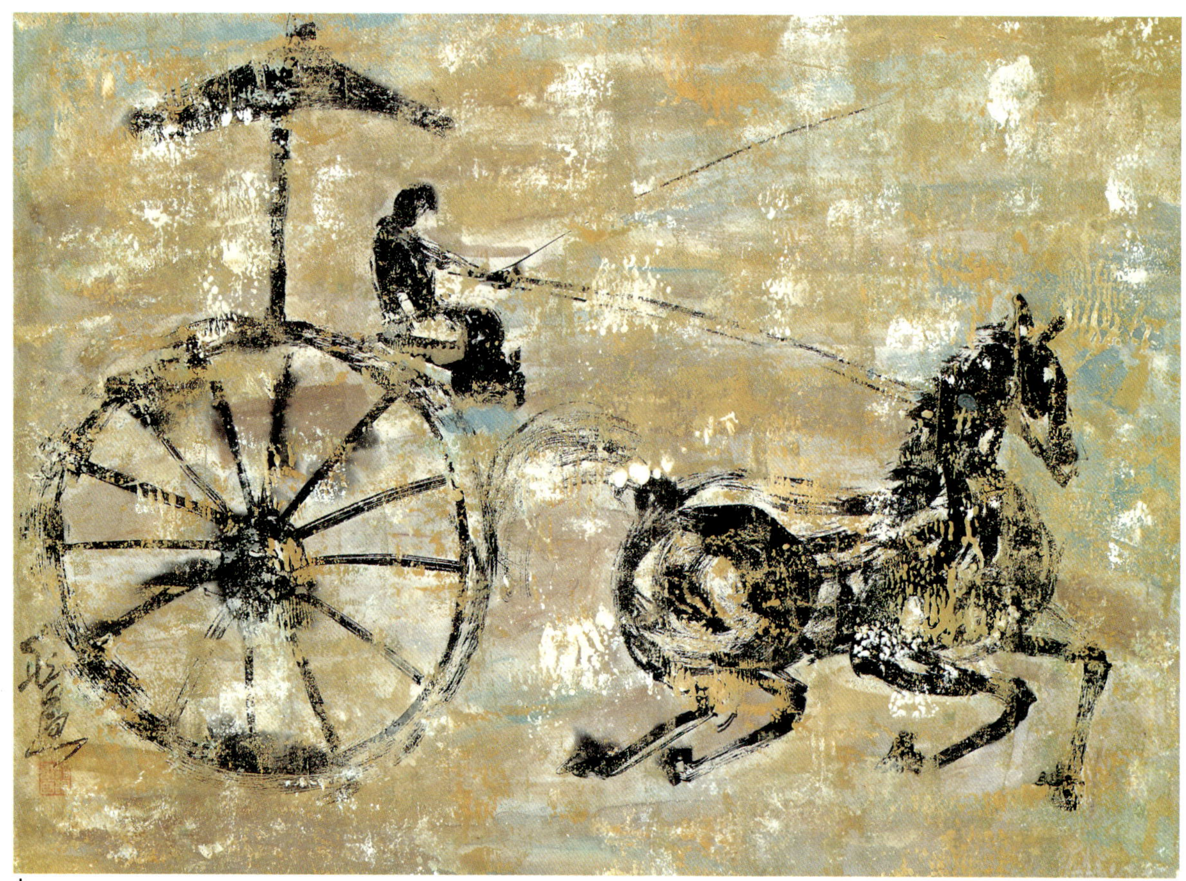

1

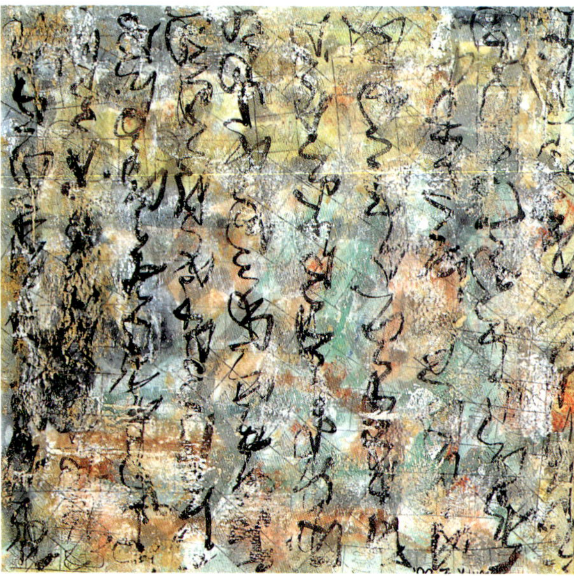

2

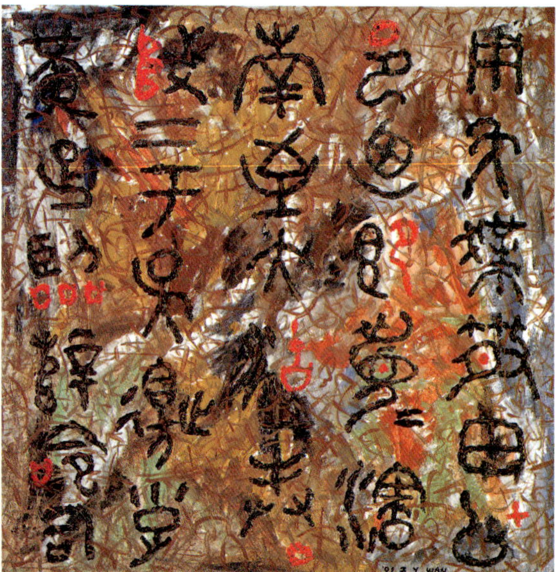

3

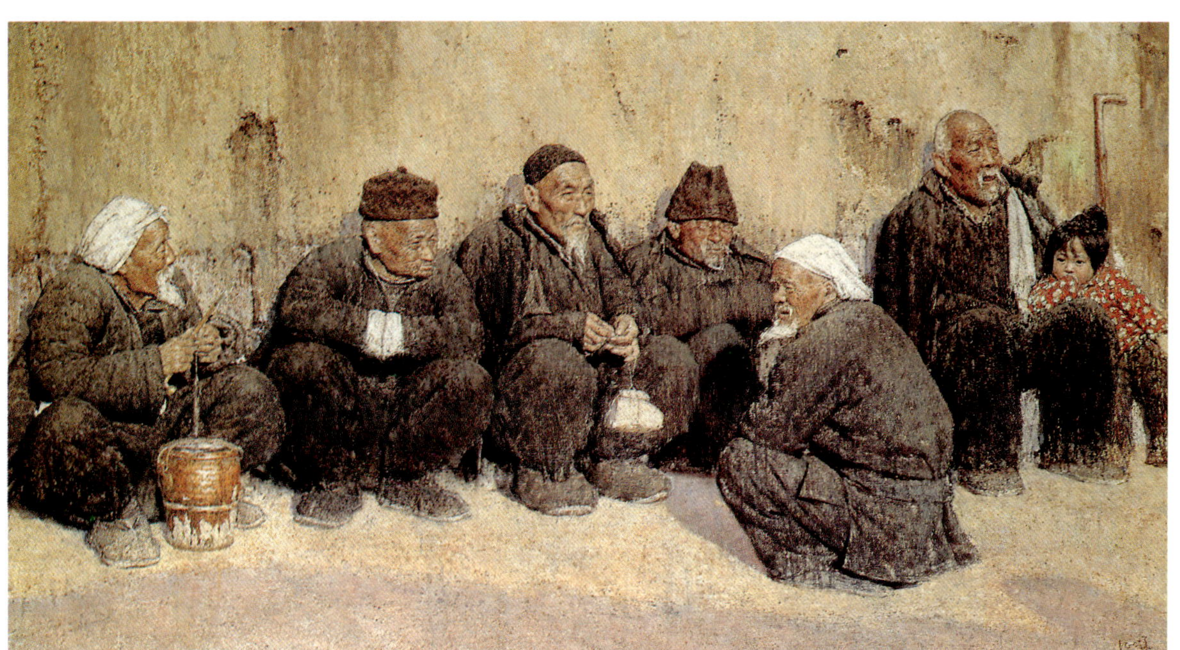

EAST WEST FINE ART

7 Hallam St. #2C
San Francisco, CA 94103
415.863.3078
408.739.9683 FAX

Exhibiting:
Contemporary Asian and
American Art

Zheng Hua Wang

The Remaining Years
1987, Oil on canvas,
73" x 39"

Selected Biography:

1992 Art Asia - Hong Kong,
Group show -
East West Fine Art

1988 Group Show;
Hefner Gallery,
New York

1982 Winning "David Di
Michelangelo Award",
by the Casarico Art
League, Italy

CLAUDIA CHAPLINE
GALLERY &
SCULPTURE GARDEN

3445 Shoreline Hwy.
P.O. Box 946
Stinson Beach, CA 94970
415.868.2308
415.868.9436 FAX

Contact:
Margot Merrill

Exhibiting:
Contemporary art

Ann Weber

1. *Winter at 3140 San Pablo*
   1993, Bronze,
   9" x 10" x 11"

2. *Gold Egg*
   1993, Charcoal, glue,
   pigment on paper,
   46" x 55"

Selected Biography:

1994 Claudia Chapline
      Gallery,
      Stinson Beach, CA

1993 Joan Roebuck Gallery,
      Lafayette, CA

      Pro-Art,
      Oakland, CA

1991 Periscope Gallery,
      Oakland, CA

      Crocker Art Museum,
      Sacramento, CA

1990 Berkeley Art Center,
      Berkeley, CA

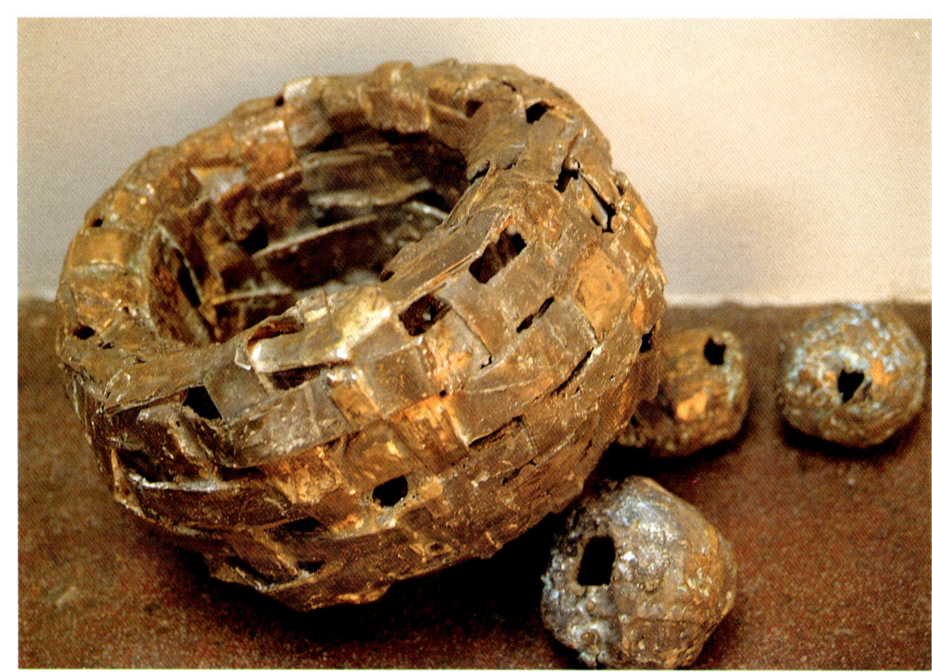

1

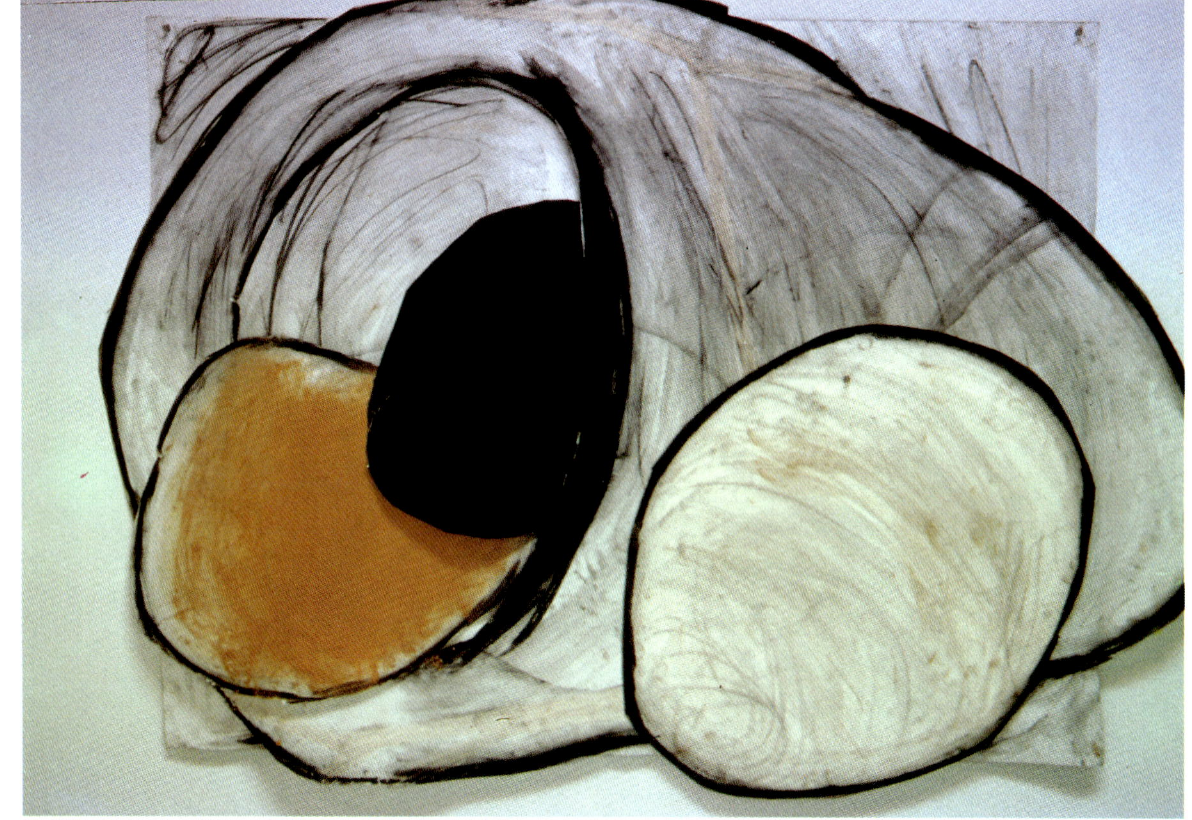

2

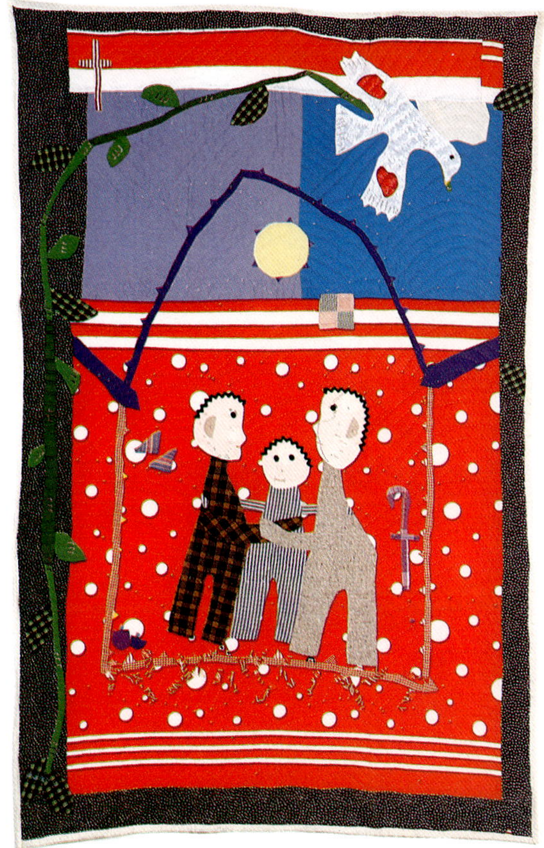

3

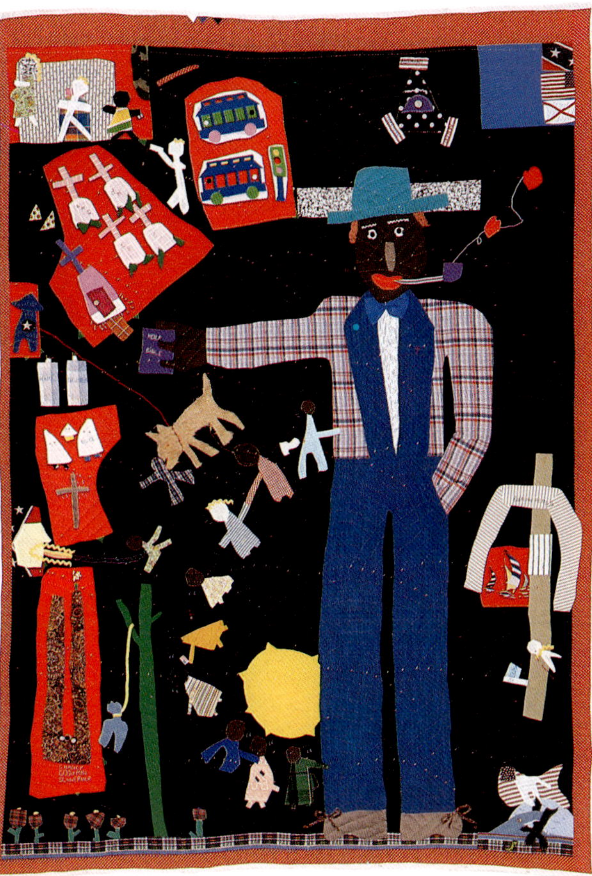

1

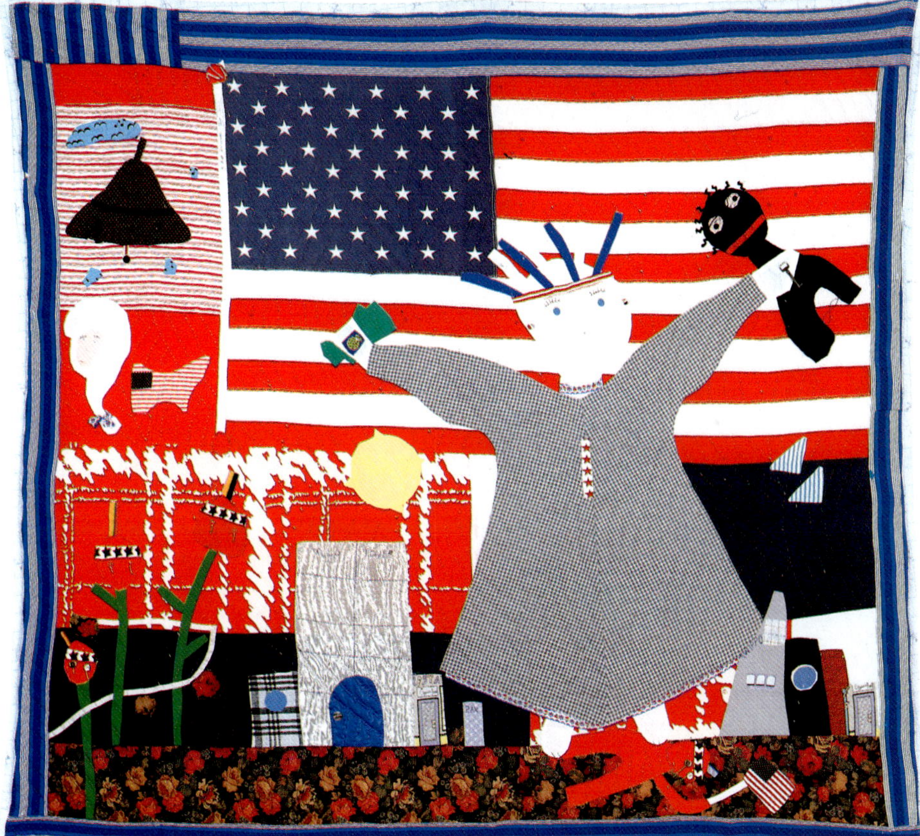

2

ROBERT CARGO FOLK ART GALLERY

2314 Sixth Street
Tuscaloosa, Alabama 35401
205.758.8884

Contact:
Robert Cargo, Owner

Exhibiting:
Contemporary folk art,
antique quilts, African-
American quilts. Haitian
voodoo flags.

Yvonne Wells

1. *Portrait of a King*
   1991-92, Cottons and
   cotton blends,
   107" x 74"

2. *Being in Total Contral of
   Herself*
   1990, Cottons, cotton
   blends, and various found
   objects, 71.5" x 81.5"

3. *The Fiery Furnace*
   1991, Cottons and cotton
   blends, 89" x 57"

Selected Exhibitions:
1993 "Signs and Symbols:
   African Images in Quilts
   from the Rural South,"
   Museum of American
   Folk Art/Great
   American Quilt Festival
   IV, New York.
1992 "Louisville Celebrates
   the American Quilt:
   Narrations."
1991 "Quilts of Conscience,"
   Museum of American
   Folk Art/Great
   American Quilt Festival
   III, New York;
   "For John Cox'
   Daughter," John Paul
   Slusser Gallery, The
   University of Michigan

MONTSERRAT GALLERY

584 Broadway
New York, NY 10012
212.941.8899
212.274.1717 FAX

Contact:
Marie Montserrat Coll,
Director

Exhibiting:
Contemporary European
and American art

Susan Dorothea White

*The Seven Deadly Sins of
Modern Times*
1993,
Acrylic painting on
round wooden table top,
diameter 48 inches. The
traditional sins have been
reversed.

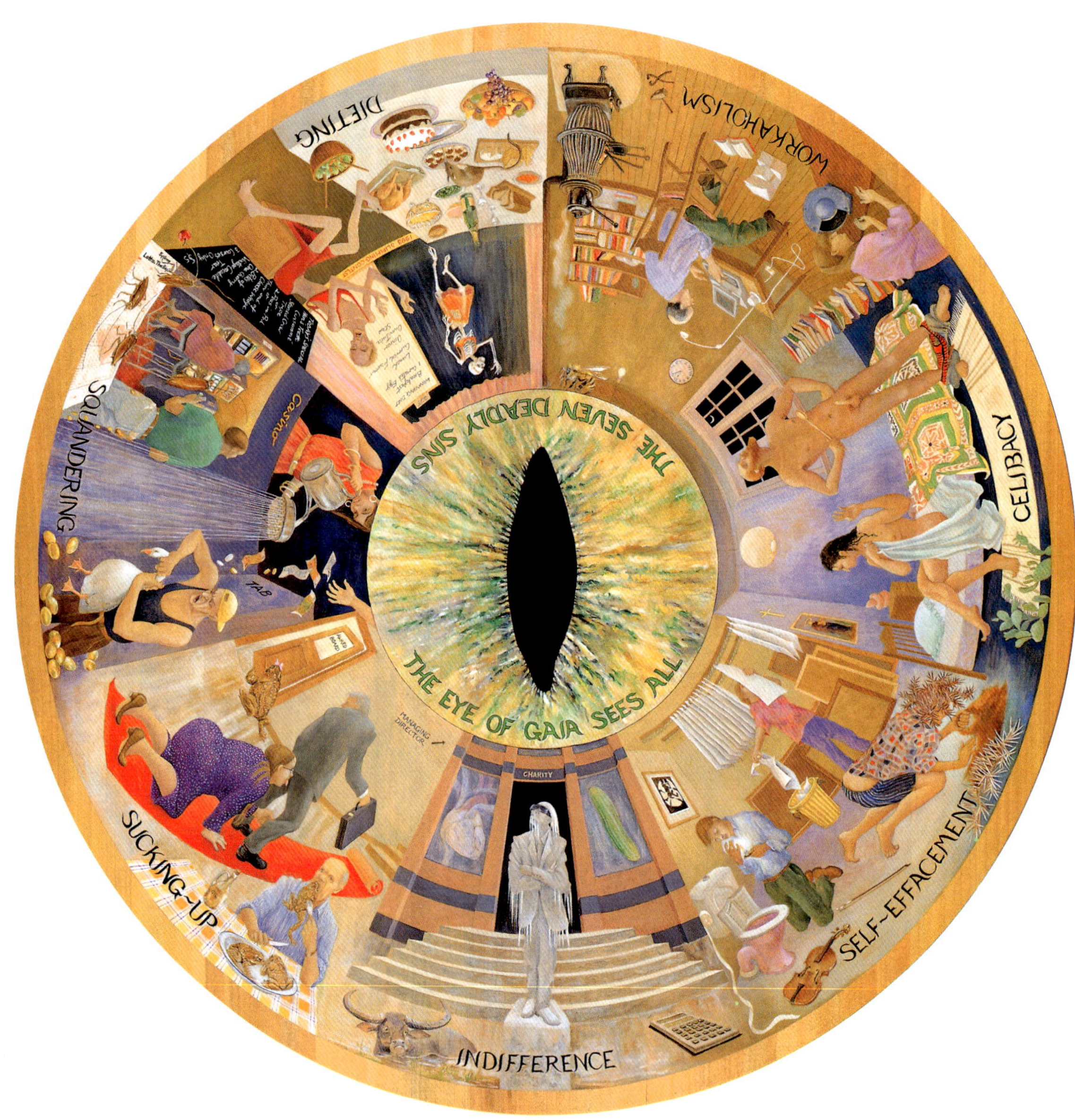

Selected Biography:

1994 Montserrat Gallery,
New York, NY

1991-1993
Group exhibitions,
Kyoto Impact Art
Festival, Kyoto Museum

1991 Solo exhibition,
Galerie am Buttermarkt
Cologne

1990 Solo exhibition,
Galerie Art &
Architecture,
Amsterdam

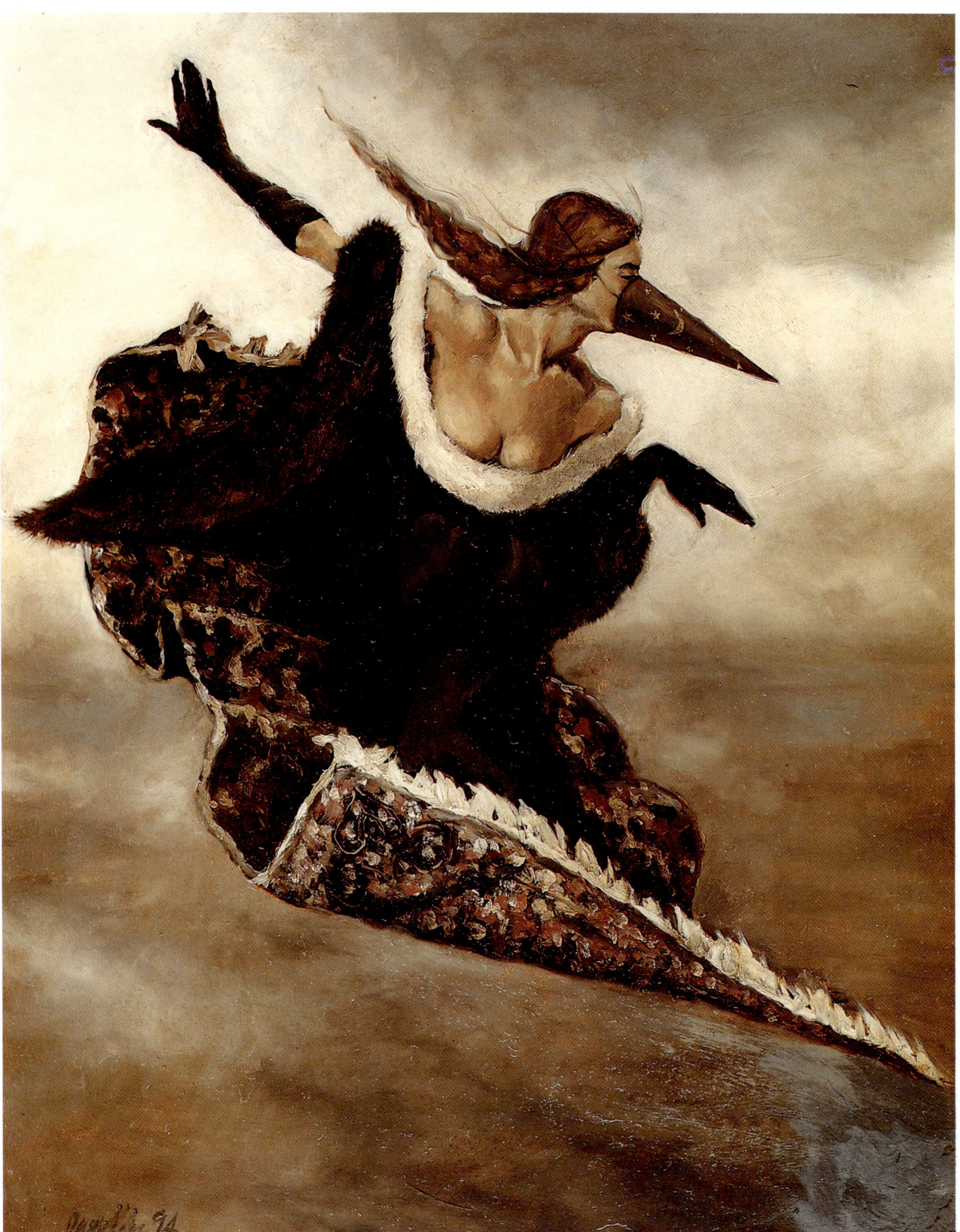

STUART KATZ GALLERY

1914 Upper Rim Rock
Laguna Beach CA 92651
714.497.1098
714.497.2569 FAX

Contact:
Stuart Katz
Niraj Katz

Exhibiting:
Contemporary painting,
drawing and sculpture

Exclusive representation of
Pamela Wilson

Pamela Wilson

When Wishes Work
1994, Oil on panel,
48" x 36"

Selected Biography:

1994 Art Miami,
Miami, FL;
Contemporary
Art Forum,
Santa Barbara, CA;
Koplin Gallery,
Santa Monica, CA;
Sarah Bain Gallery,
Brea, CA

1993 South Bay
Contemporary
Museum,
Long Beach, CA;
Maya Polsky Gallery,
Chicago, IL

PHYLLIS KIND GALLERY

313 West Superior
Chicago, IL 60610
312.642.6302
312.642.8502 FAX

136 Greene Street
New York, NY 10012
212.925.1200
212.941.7841 FAX

Contact:
Phyllis Kind

Exhibiting:
Contemporary
American, Soviet, Naive,
and Outsider art

Karl Wirsum

1. *Fig. Cure 88 Sneeze*
   1993, Acrylic on wood,
   49¼" x 34"x 1½"

2. *Mr. Answer Pants*
   1991, Acrylic on wood,
   49½" x 36"x 9"

3. *Jerry Cool Lollipop*
   1993, Acrylic on wood,
   58" x 48"x 13"

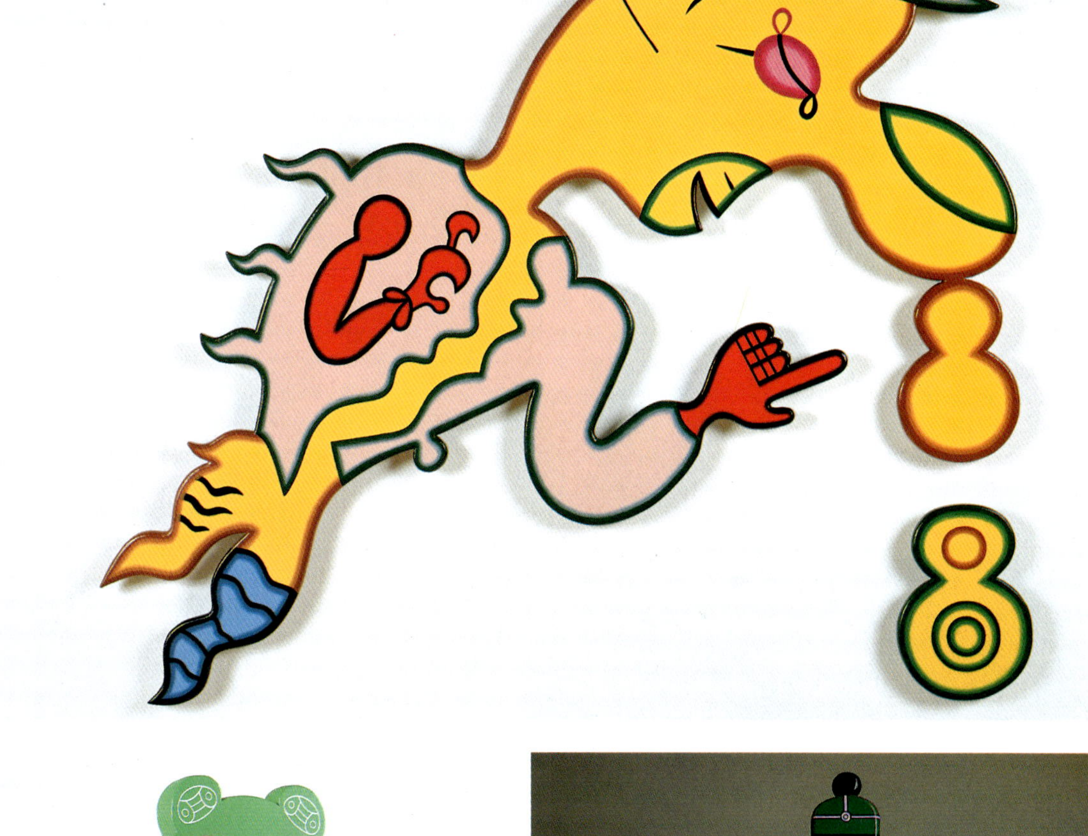

1

Selected Biography:

1992 Phyllis Kind Gallery,
      Chicago, IL

1988 Phyllis Kind Gallery,
      New York, NY

1981 " Hare Toddy Kong
      Tamari", Museum of
      Contemporary Art,
      Chicago, IL

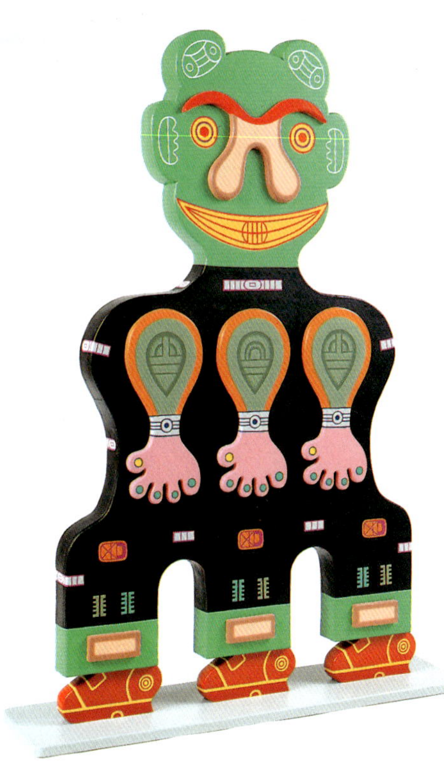

2

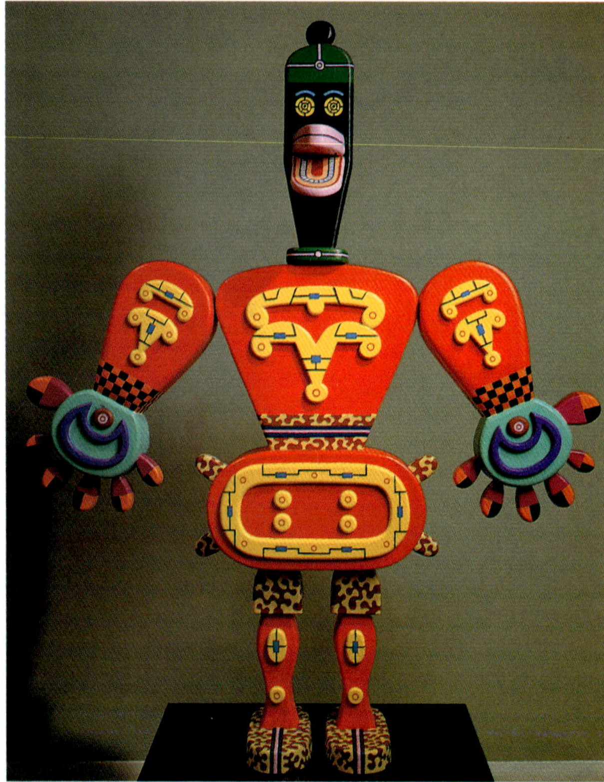

3

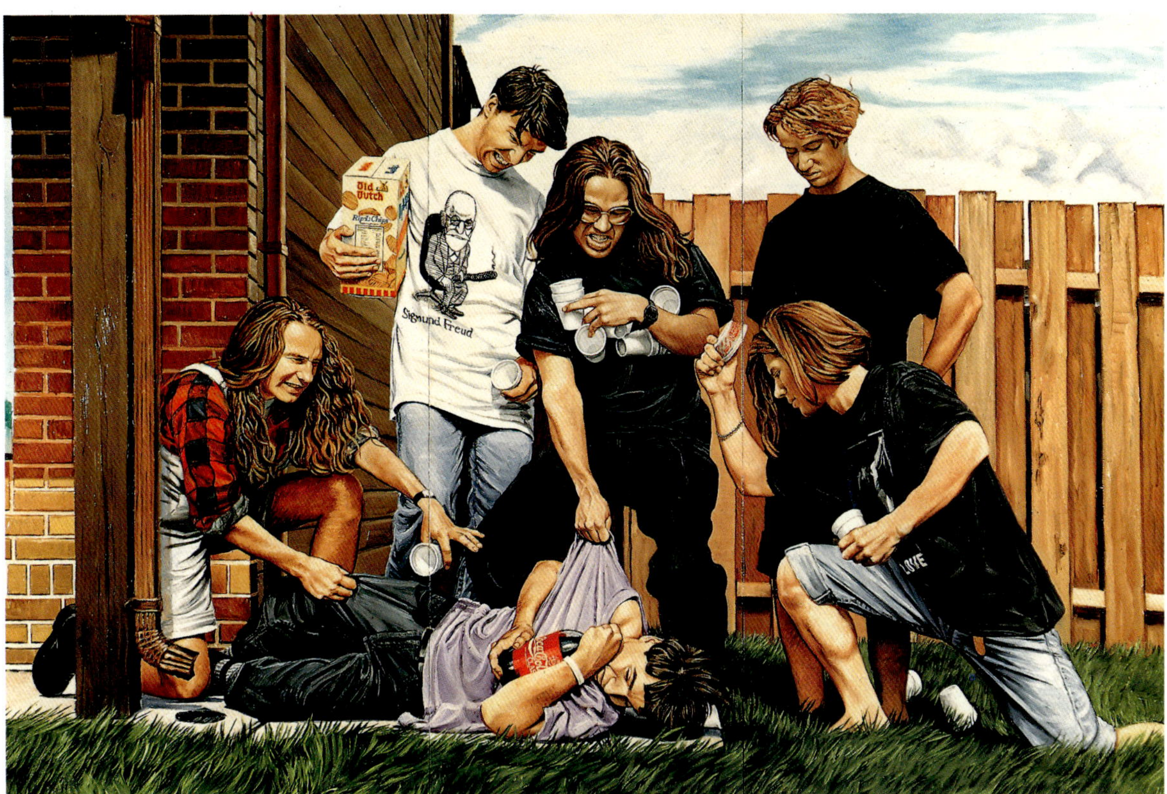

1

DIANE FARRIS GALLERY

1565 West 7th Avenue
Vancouver B.C. V6J 1S1
Canada
604.737.2629
604.737.2675 FAX

Contact:
Diane Farris, Director

Exhibiting:
Contemporary Canadian
and International Art

Chris Woods

1. *Wrath of the Devourers*
   1992, Oil on canvas,
   68" x 103"

2. *The Reverent Mid II*
   1992, Oil on canvas,
   72" x 48"

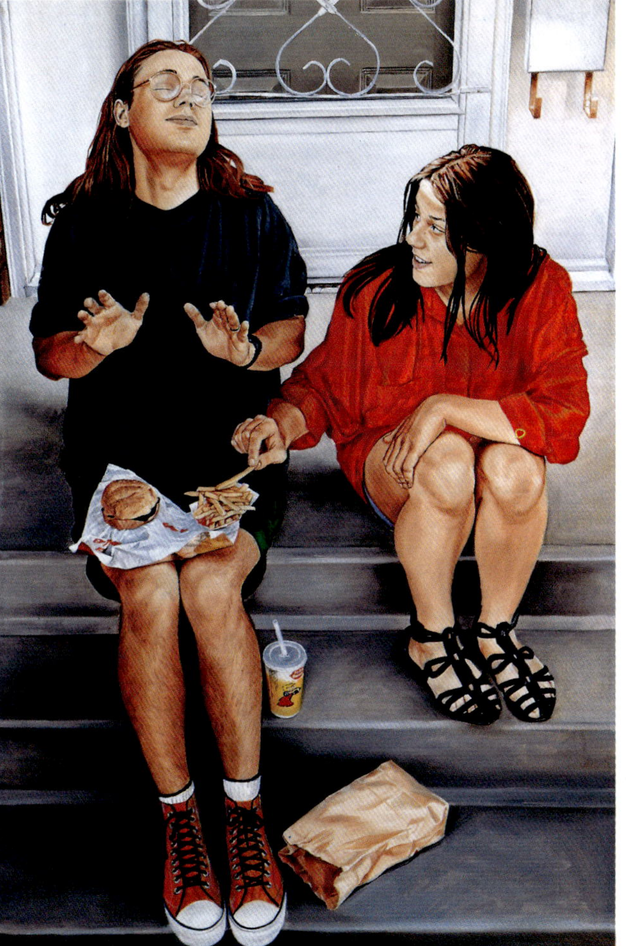

2

Selected Biography:

1994 Solo show,
      Diane Farris Gallery,
      Vancouver, BC

1993 Solo show,
      Diane Farris Gallery,
      Vancouver, BC

      London Life Young
      Contemporaries
      (National Touring
      Exhibition), London
      Regional Art Gallery,
      London, ON

      Artropolis 93,
      Vancouver, BC

JANET FLEISHER GALLERY

211 S. 17th Street
Philadelphia, PA 19103
215.545.7562
215.545.6140 FAX

Contact:
John Ollman, Director
Nancy Yecies, Asst. Director

Exhibiting:
Contemporary American Art
Self-taught and visionary
artist

Purvis Young

Miles Davis
1988, Paint on wood,
50" x 30"

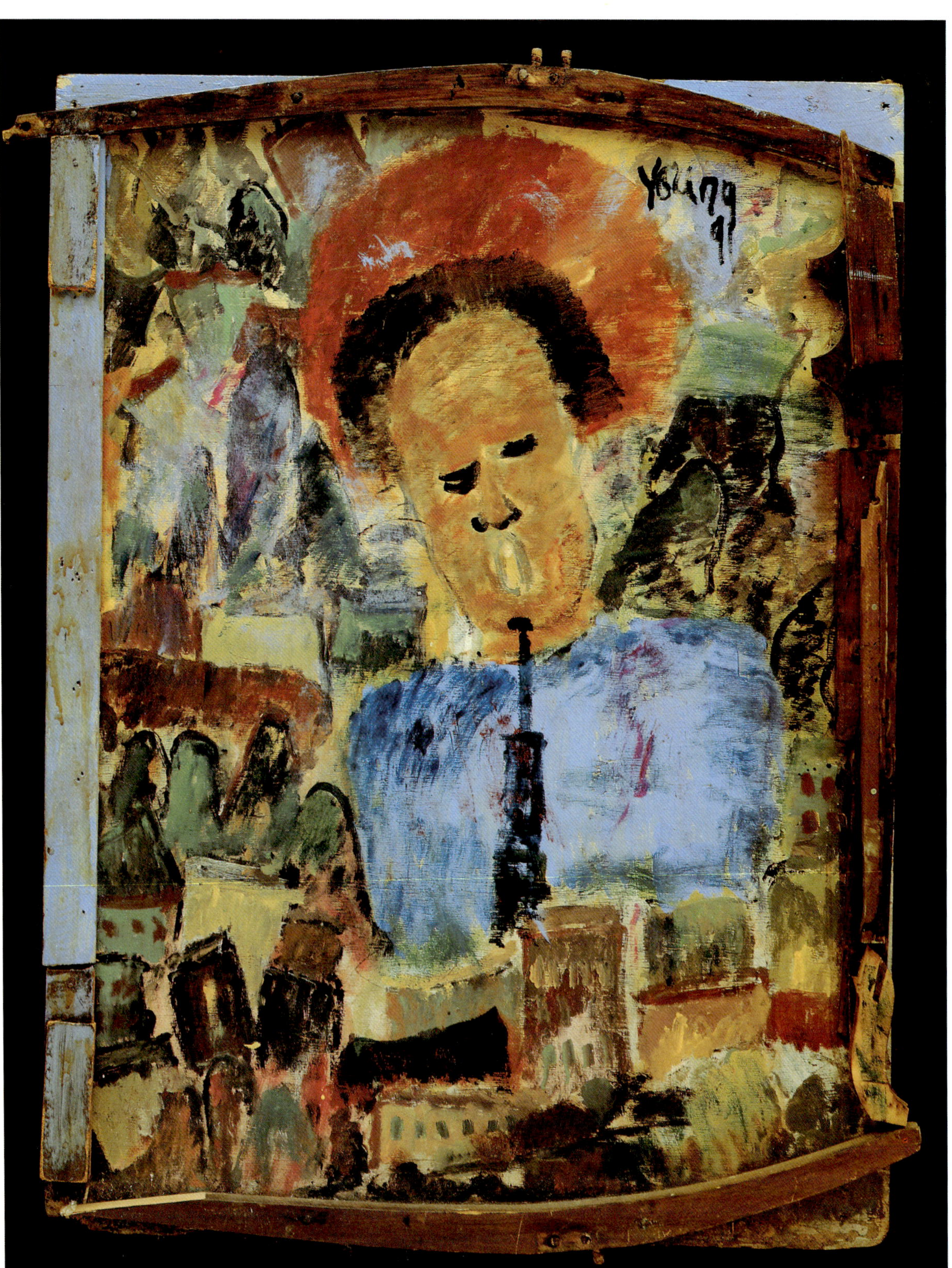

Selected Biography:

1993 Center for the Arts,
Vero Beach, FL;
Art & Culture Center,
Hollywood, FL
1992 "Henry Ray Clark,
Philadelphia Wireman,
Purvis Young",
Janet Fleisher Gallery,
Philadelphia, PA;
"Purvis Young, Sam
Doyle, William
Hawkins",
Edward Thorp Gallery,
New York, NY
1991 "Painting, Books,
Sculptures",
Joy Moos Gallery,
Miami, FL

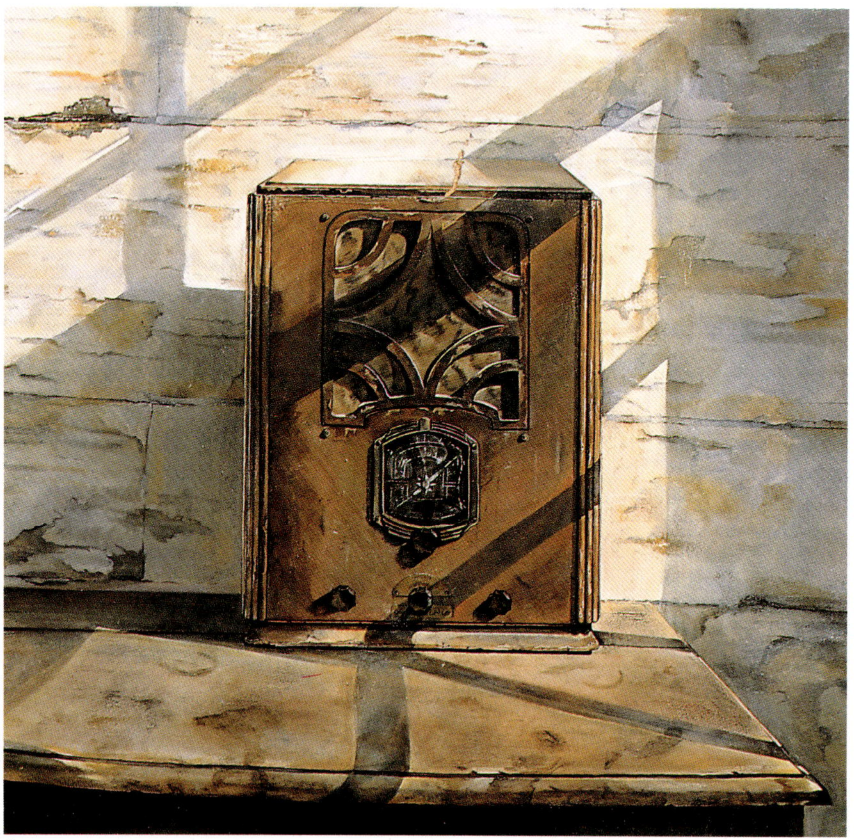

1

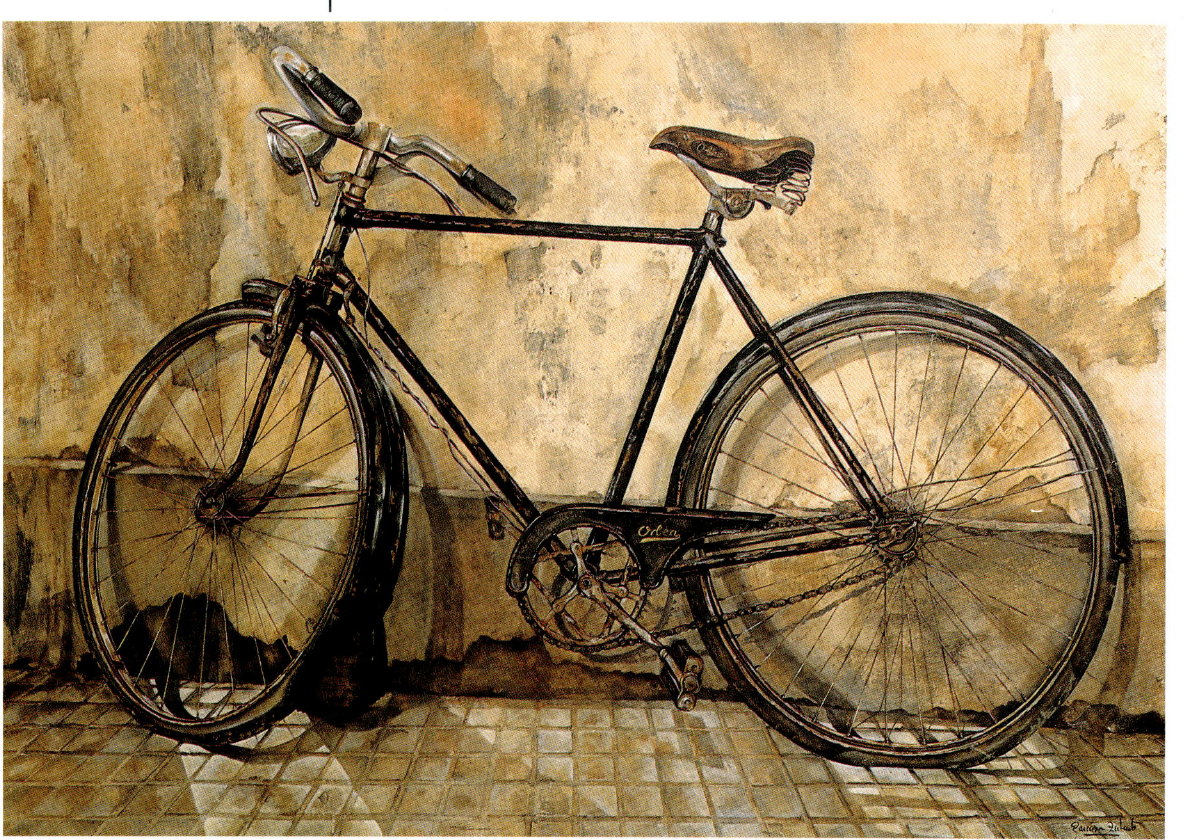

2

MONTSERRAT GALLERY

584 Broadway
New York, NY 10012
212.941.8899
212.274.1717 FAX

Contact:
Marie Montserrat Coll,
Director

Exhibiting:
Contemporary European
and American art

Garcia Zabarte

1. *The Radio*
   1992, Mixed media,
   40" x 36"

2. *The Bicycle*
   1992, Mixed media,
   56" x 40"

Selected Biography:

1994 Montserrat Gallery,
        New York, NY

1993 Bienal National de Arte
        Concello de Cambre,
        La Coruna;
        Fondo de Arte Del
        Museo de Arte
        Contemporaneo,
        Reina Sofia;
        Exhibition Homage
        to Laixero,
        Verin, Orense

1992 Solo Exhibition,
        Estil Gallery, Valencia;
        Solo Exhibition,
        Gallery Trinta

**MARSHA CHILD
CONTEMPORARY**

P.O. Box 364
Solebury, PA 18963
215.297.0414
215.297.0414 FAX

Contact:
Marsha Child

Exhibiting:
Contemporary European,
Eastern European and
American paintings, sculpture
and graphics

Atanas Zgalevski

1. *Memory I*
   1992,
   Mixed media on canvas,
   52" x 44"

2. *Untitled*
   1994,
   Mixed media on canvas,
   10" x 8"

3. *Untitled*
   1994,
   Mixed media on canvas,
   10" x 8"

Selected Biography:

1994 "Mysteries," 101
   Wooster Street
   Gallery, New York,
   NY; " New
   Abstraction," Marsha
   Child Contemporary,
   Solebury, PA;
   "Bulgarian Artists,"
   Prista Gallery,
   Alexandria, VA; "Long
   Island Artists,"
   Hecksher Museum,
   Huntington, NY; "Art
   of the Northeast,"
   Silvermine Galleries,
   New Canaan, CT

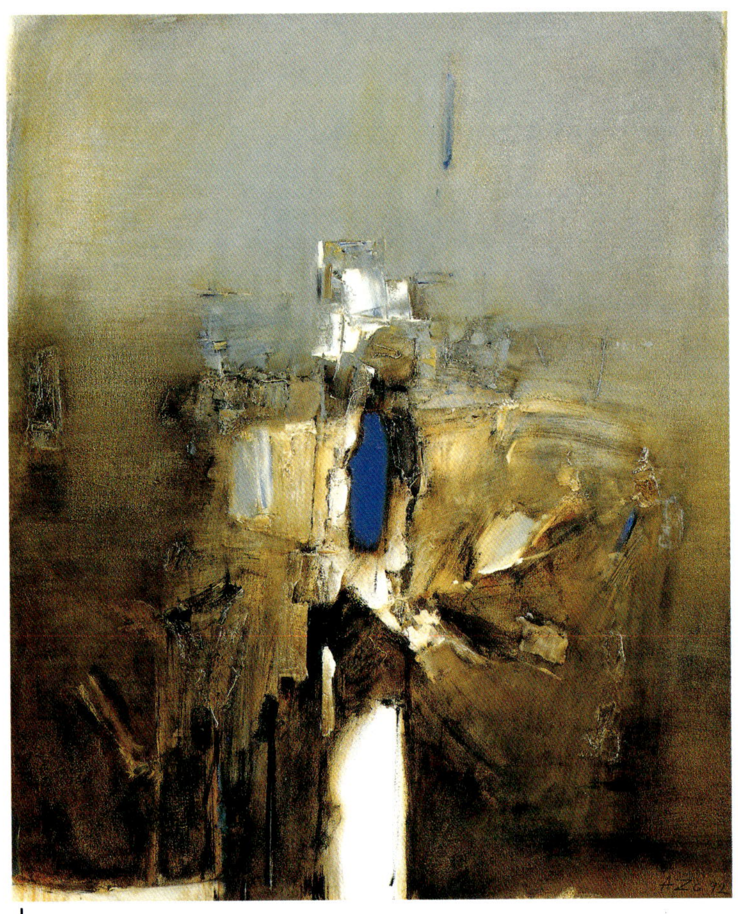

1

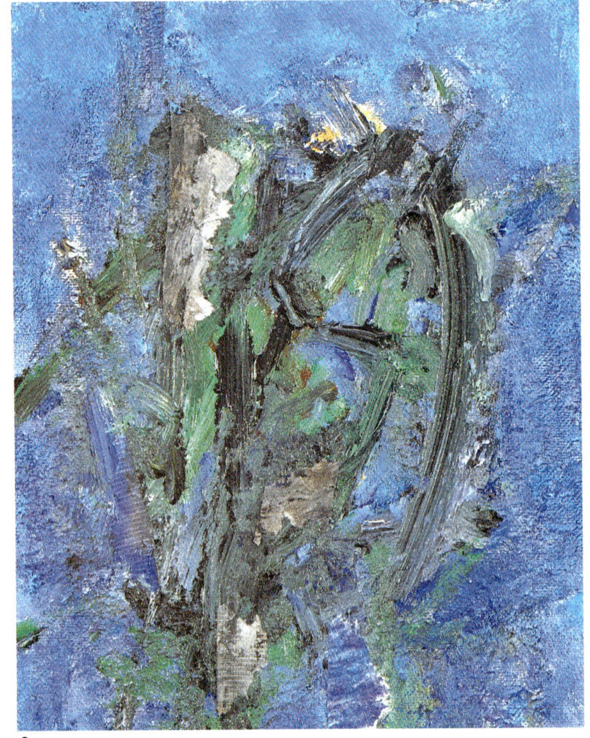

2

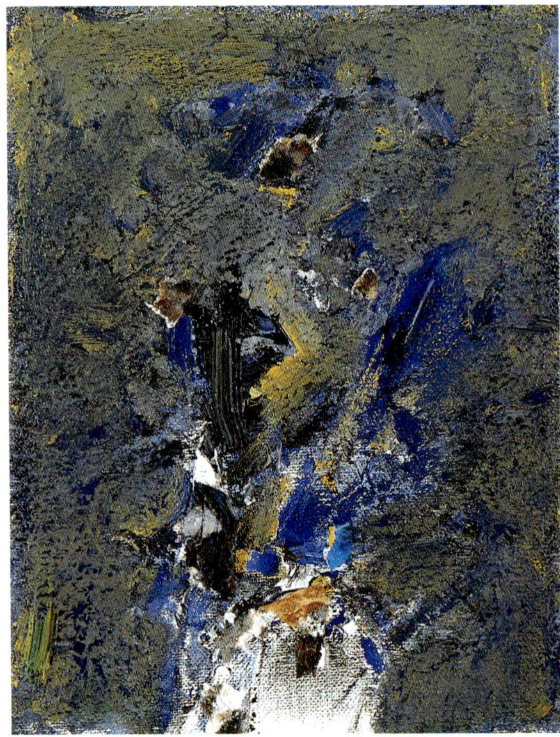

3

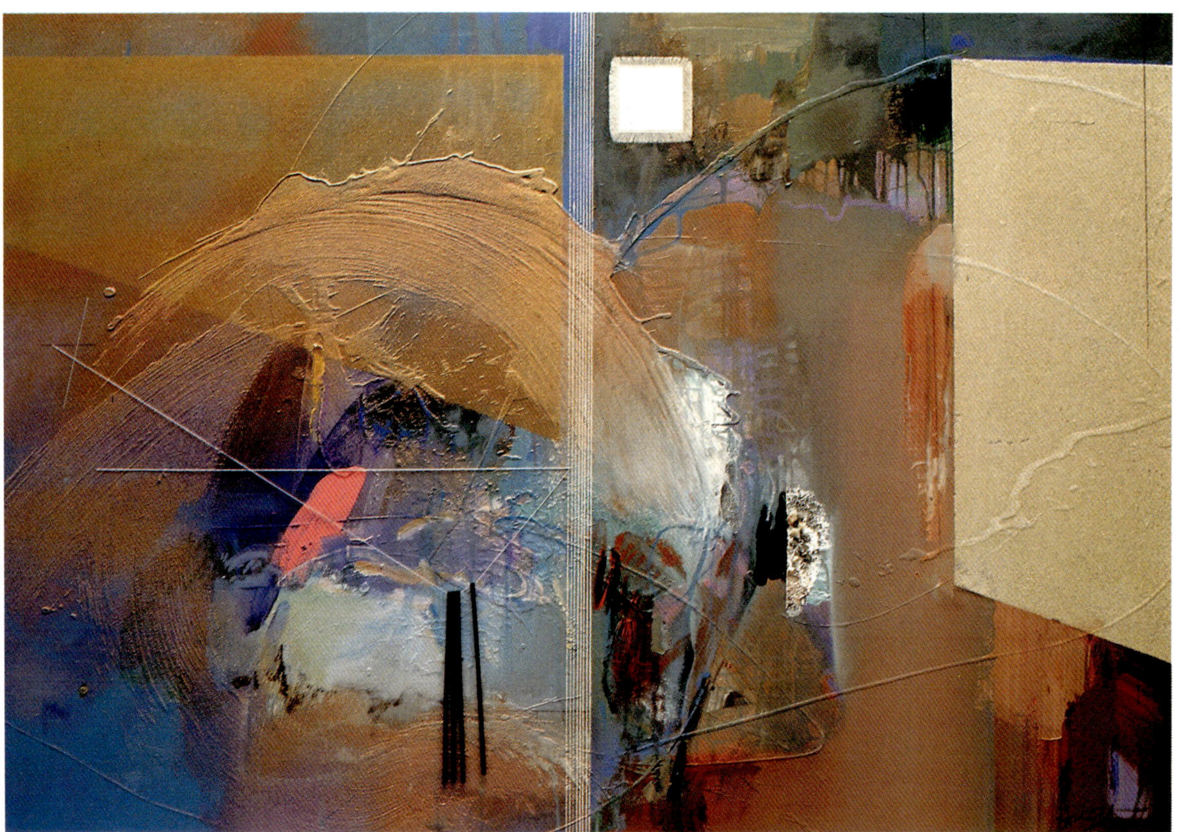

1

CAROLE JONES GALLERY

300 W. Superior Street
Chicago, IL 60610
312.587.8820
312.587.9859 FAX

Contact:
Carole Jones

Exhibiting:
Contemporary International
Fine Art; Painting &
Sculpture

Weiliang Zhao

1. *Golden State no.5*
   1994, Mixed media on
   canvas, 45" x 65"

2. *The Ninth Sun no.2*
   1991, Oil & mixed media
   on canvas, 90" x 90"

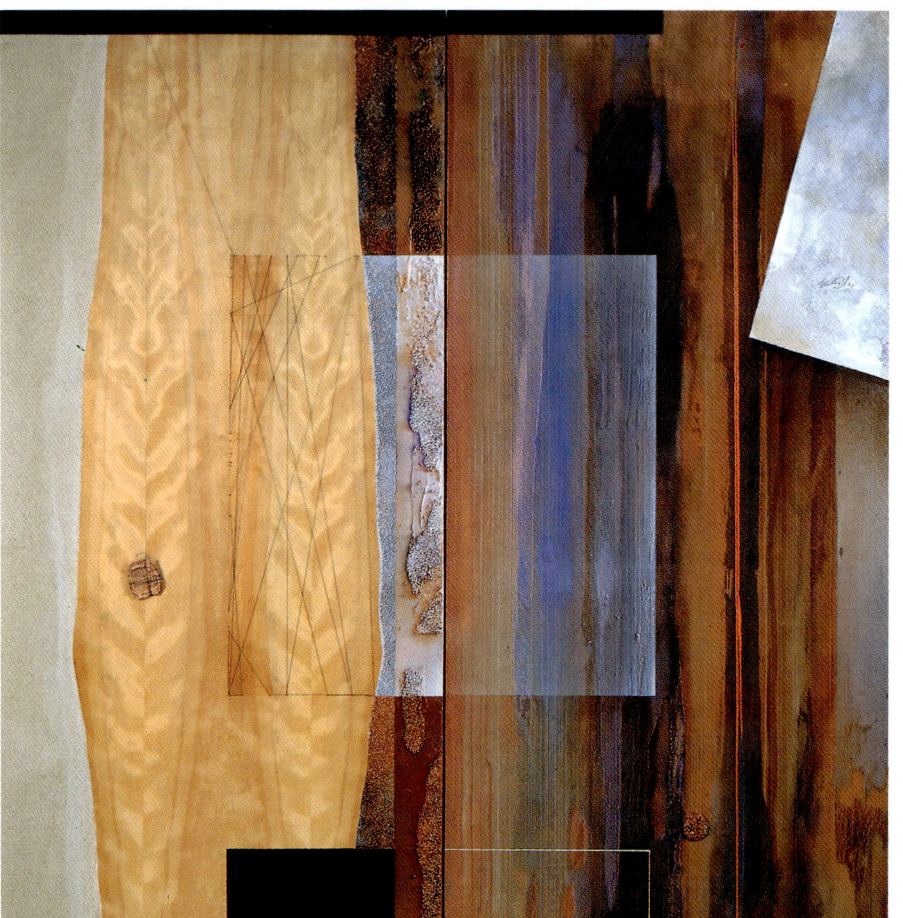

2

Selected Exhibitions:

    Carole Jones Gallery,
    Chicago, IL;
    Pacific Asian Museum,
    Pasadena, CA;
    Hong Kong
    Museum of Art,
    Hong Kong;
    Laforet Museum,
    Japan;
    National Museum of
    Art, Beijing, China

Collections:

    Frederick R. Weisman
    Foundation of Art, CA;
    McDonalds Corp., Oak
    Brook, IL

**ROCFERN
INTERNATIONAL
GALLERIES, INC.**

80 Carlauren Road Unit17
Woodbridge (Toronto),
Ontario L4L 7Z5 Canada
905.850.7647
905.850.8062 FAX

Contact:
Rocco Pannese
Fernando Rocco

David Zucca

Untitled
1993, Mixed media on
paper, 19 ³/₄" x 12 ⁷/₈"

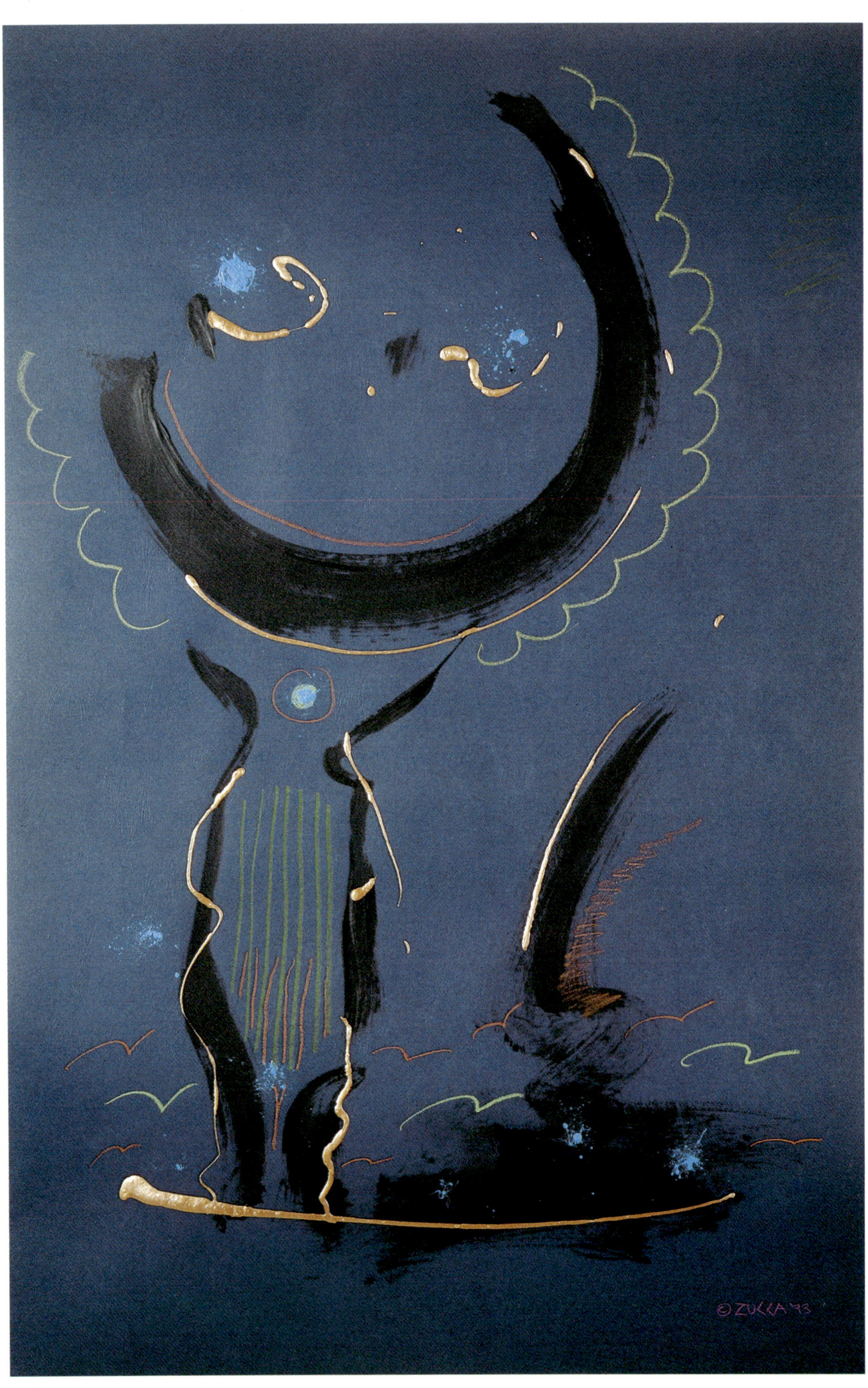

Selected Biography:

1994 Rocfern International
Galleries, Woodbridge,
Ontario, Canada

1993 Art Frankfurt
Frankfurt, Germany

Fine Art Warehouse
Gallery, Vaughan,
Ontario, Canada

Reena Foundation
Toronto, Ontario,
Canada

Fine Art Publishing Inc.
Nobleton, Ontario,
Canada

PRINTS & DRAWINGS

CARIB ART GALLERY

584 Broadway
New York, NY 10012
212.343.2539
212.343.2659 FAX

Contact:
Veronica Ortiz
Sully Saneaux

Exhibiting:
Contemporary art from
Latin America and the
Caribbean

Hochi Asiatico

1. *From Queen Isabella to
   Anaisa Pie*
   1994, Charcoal on paper,
   50" x 100"

2. *The Healer*
   1994, Charcoal on paper,
   38" x 50"

Selected Biography:

1994   XIX National Biennial
of Visual Arts. Gallery
of Modern Art, Santo
Domingo;
Four Dominican
Artists,
John Jay College,
New York, NY;
Beyond the Borders,
Bronx Museum of the
Arts, Bronx, NY

1993   Artistas Dominicanos,
Paterson Museum,
Paterson, NJ

1992   Paper Visions IV, The
Houseationic Museum
of Art, Bridgeport, CT

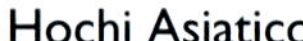

1

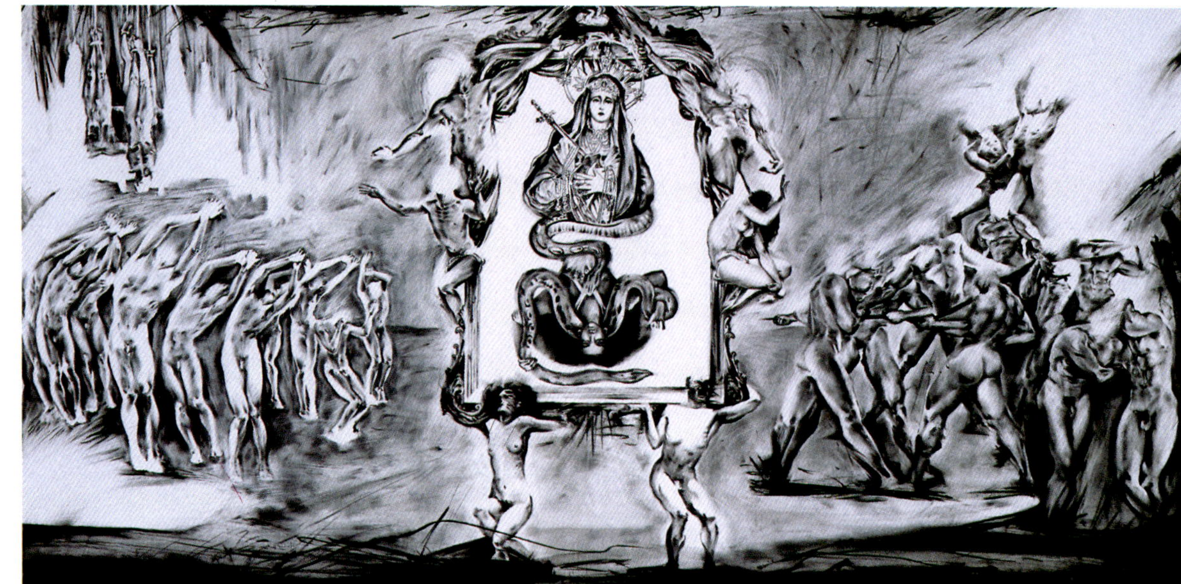

2

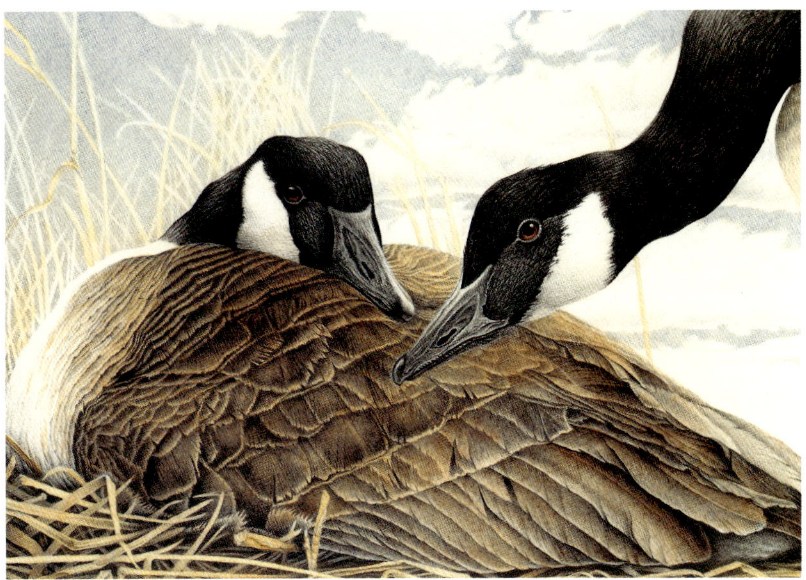

1

LAKE FORD STUDIO

Rt. 5 Box 2340
Cranesville Road
Oakland, MD 21550, U.S.A.
301.387.7010

Contact:
Ken Bauer

Exhibiting:
Drawings, prints; of birds,
landscapes, natural subjects.
Gallery representation
sought.

Ken Bauer

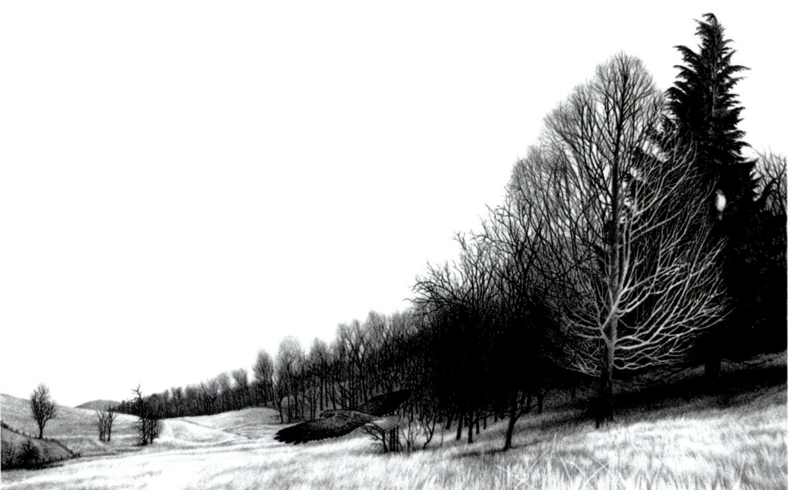

2

1. *Fidelity- Canada Geese*
   1992, Graphite and
   watercolor on rag paper,
   8" x 11"

2. *Simultaneity-*
   Red-Tailed Hawks
   1992, Graphite
   on rag paper,
   $12^{1}/_{2}$" x $18^{1}/_{2}$"

3. *Between the Two- Blue Jays*
   1993, Graphite
   on rag paper,
   11" x $15^{1}/_{2}$"

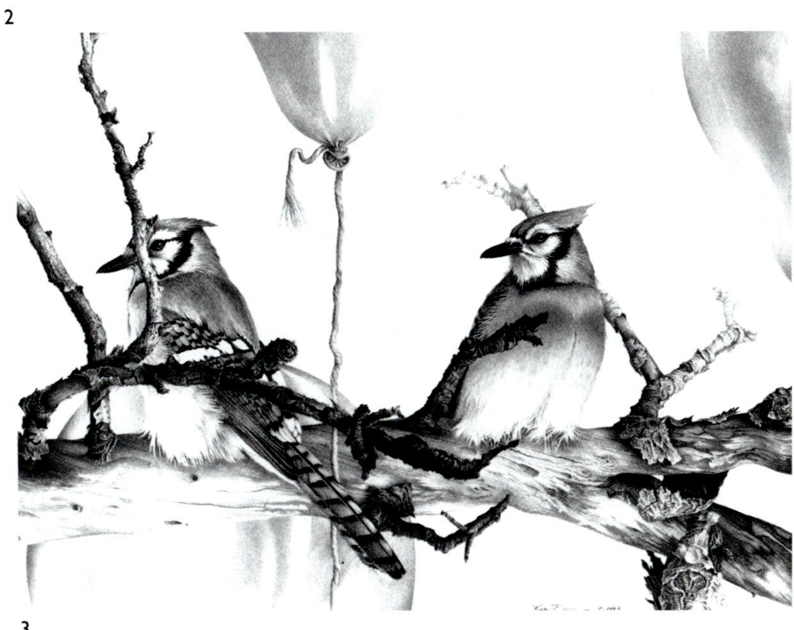

3

Selected Biography:
1993 Associated Artists of
      Pittsburgh "New
      Members Exhibition":
      PCA Gallery,
      Pittsburgh, PA;
1993 Solo Exhibition:
      Contemporary Graphic
      Arts, Morgantown, WV;
1992 Wildlife West Festival:
      San Bernardino
      Museum,
      San Bernardino, CA;
1991 Ward Foundation
      Museum purchased
      drawing, sponsor print:
      Salisbury, MD

FORUM GALLERY

745 Fifth Avenue 5th Floor
New York, NY 10151
212.355.4545
212.355.4547 FAX

Contact:
Robert Fishko, Director

Kent Bellows

JoAnn, May
1986,
Graphite pencil on paper,
22³/₄" × 19³/₄"

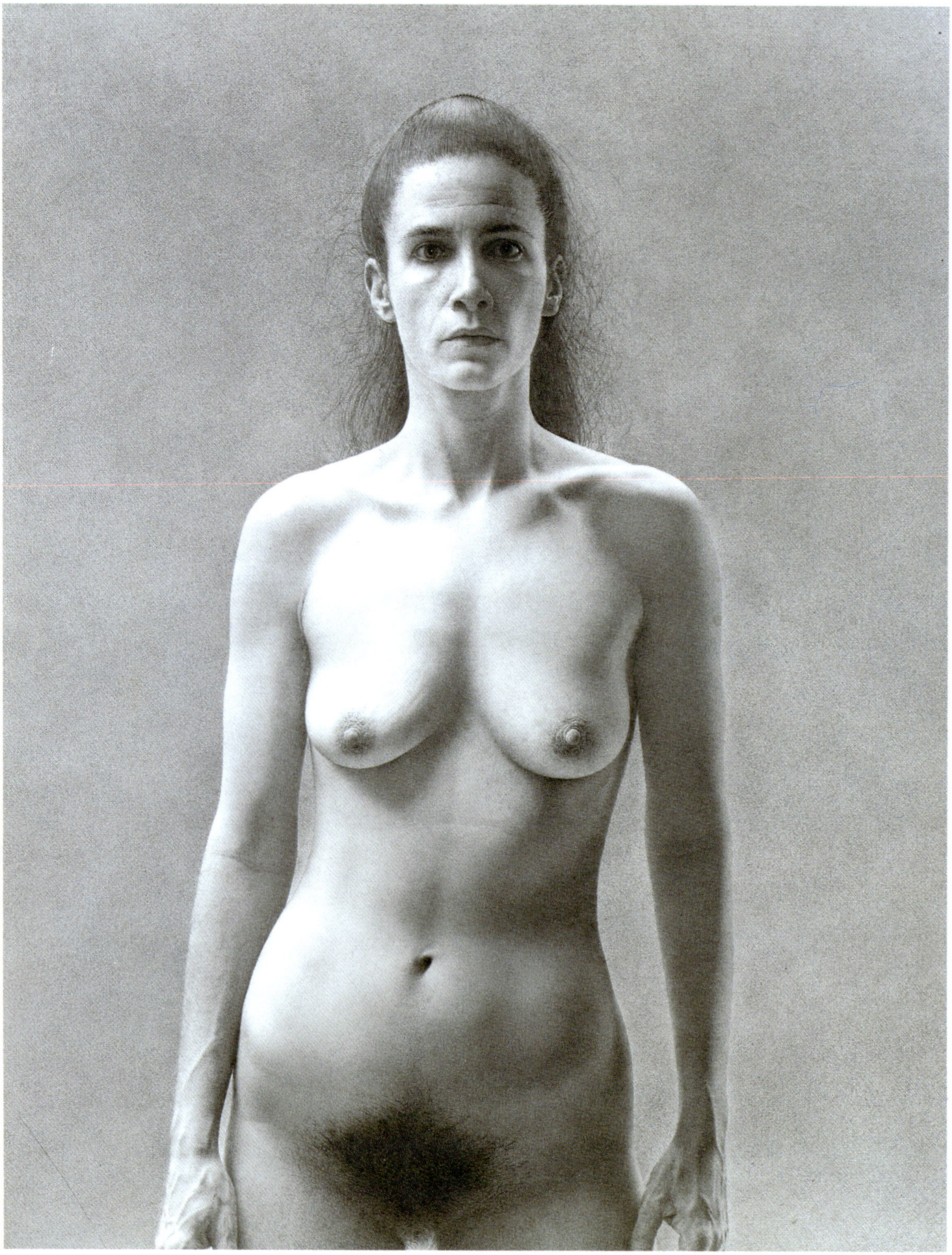

Selected Biography:

Solo exhibitions:
    Forum Gallery, NY;
    University of Missouri;
    Tatistcheff Gallery, NY;
    Midtown Payson, NY;
    Sheldon Memorial
    Art Gallery,
    Middlebury, VT;
    National Academy
    of Design, NY;
    Huntsville Museum, AL;
    Arkansas Art
    Center, AR

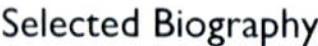

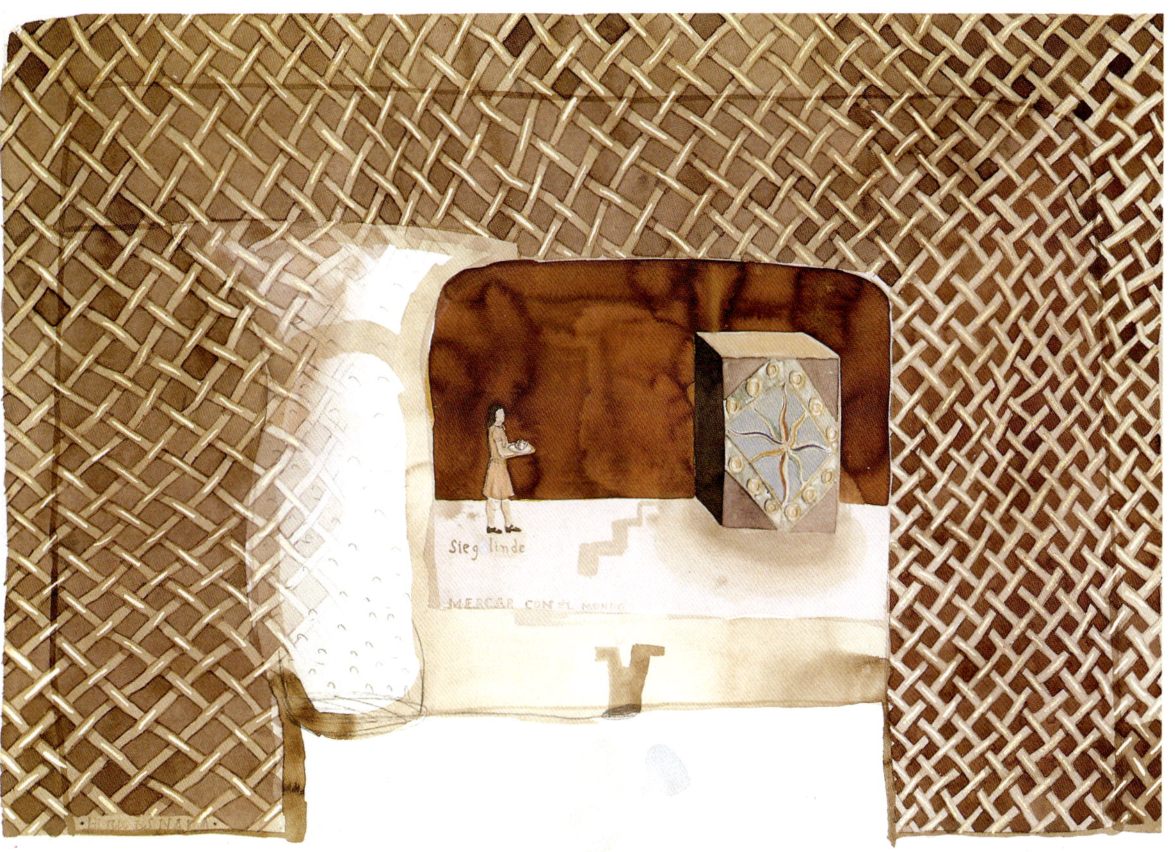

1

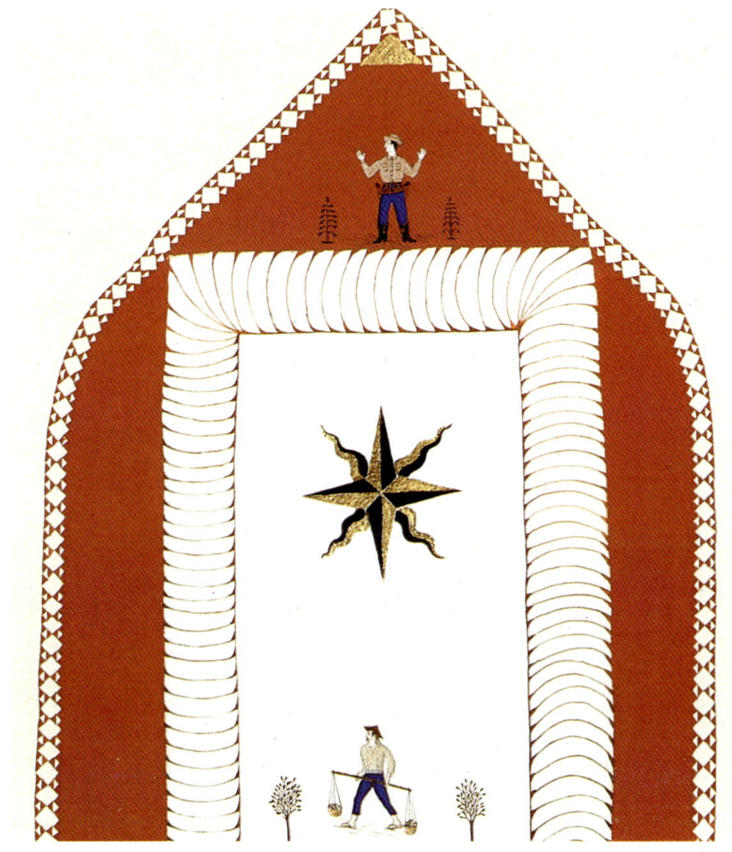

2

Arte do Brasil
souza edelstein

Rua Visconde de Pirajá, 86 slj. 6
22410-000 Rio de Janeiro, Brasil
5521.267.2549
5521.267.1254 FAX

Contact:
Joel L. Edelstein
Miriam Gaudenzi

Exhibiting:
Contemporary painting and
sculpture

Alex Cerveny

1. *Sieglinde*
   1993, Mixed media on
   paper, 41.5" x 30"

2. *Laramie*
   1991, Mixed media on
   paper, 21.75" x 39.5"

Selected Biography:

1993 Chicago International
Art Exposition,
Chicago, IL

Galerie 20x2,
Arnhen, Holland

1992 Contemporary Art
From Brazil-Arte do
Brasil / Souza Edelstein
in Cooperation with
LedisFlam Gallery,
New York, NY

1991 Viva Brasil Viva,
Liljevalehs Konsthall
Stockholm, Sweden

JANET FLEISHER GALLERY

211 S. 17th Street
Philadelphia, PA 19103
215.545.7562
215.545.6140 FAX

Contact:
John Ollman, Director
Nancy Yecies, Asst. Director

Exhibiting:
Contemporary American Art
Self-taught and visionary
artist

Tony Fitzpatrick

1. *Atlantic Nocturne*
    1994, Colored pencil on
    paper, 36" x 49½"

2. *Girl at Ocean City
    with Her Own Lighting*
    1994, Colored pencil on
    paper, 19¾" x 25¼"

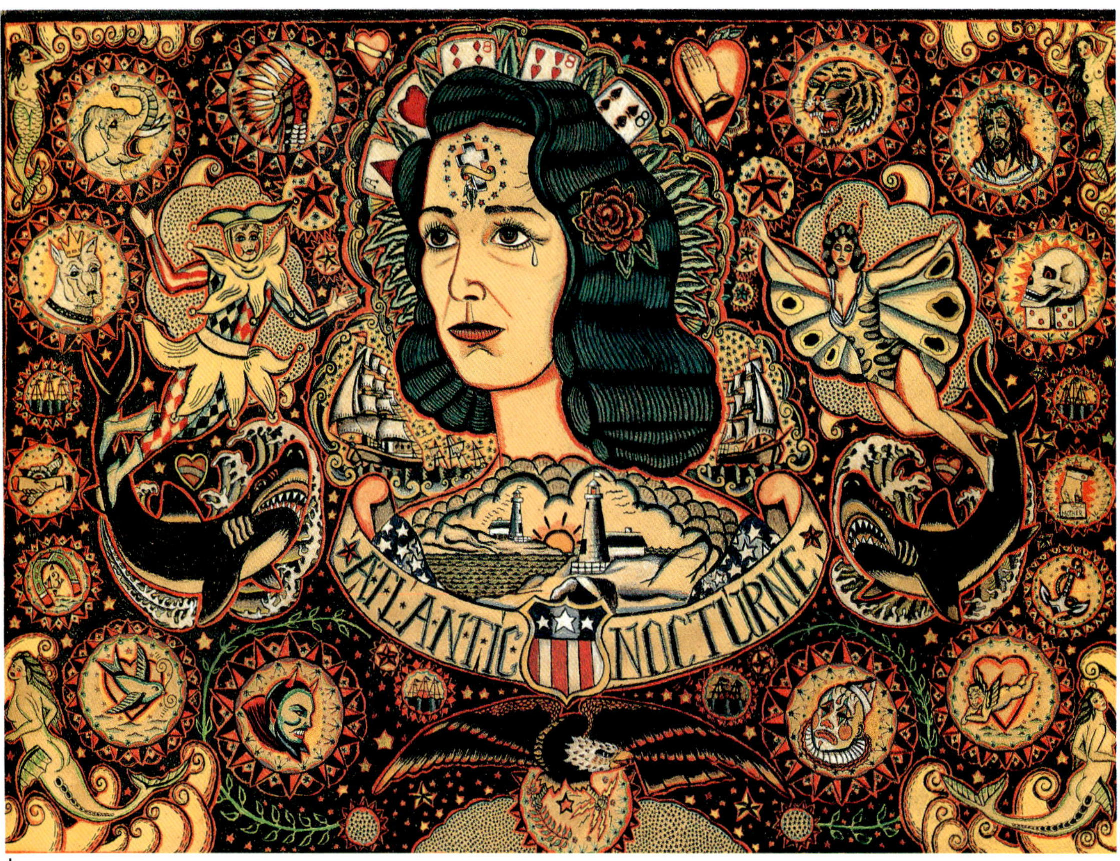

1

Selected Biography:

1994   "Flash" an exhibition of
       tattoo drawings,
       Janet Fleisher Gallery,
       Philadelphia, PA

       "Son of a Sailor",
       Loomis Chaffee School,
       Richmond Art Center,
       Windsor, CT

1993   Janet Fleisher Gallery,
       Philadelphia, PA

       "Eye Tattooed
       America"' Ann Nathan
       Gallery, Chicago, IL

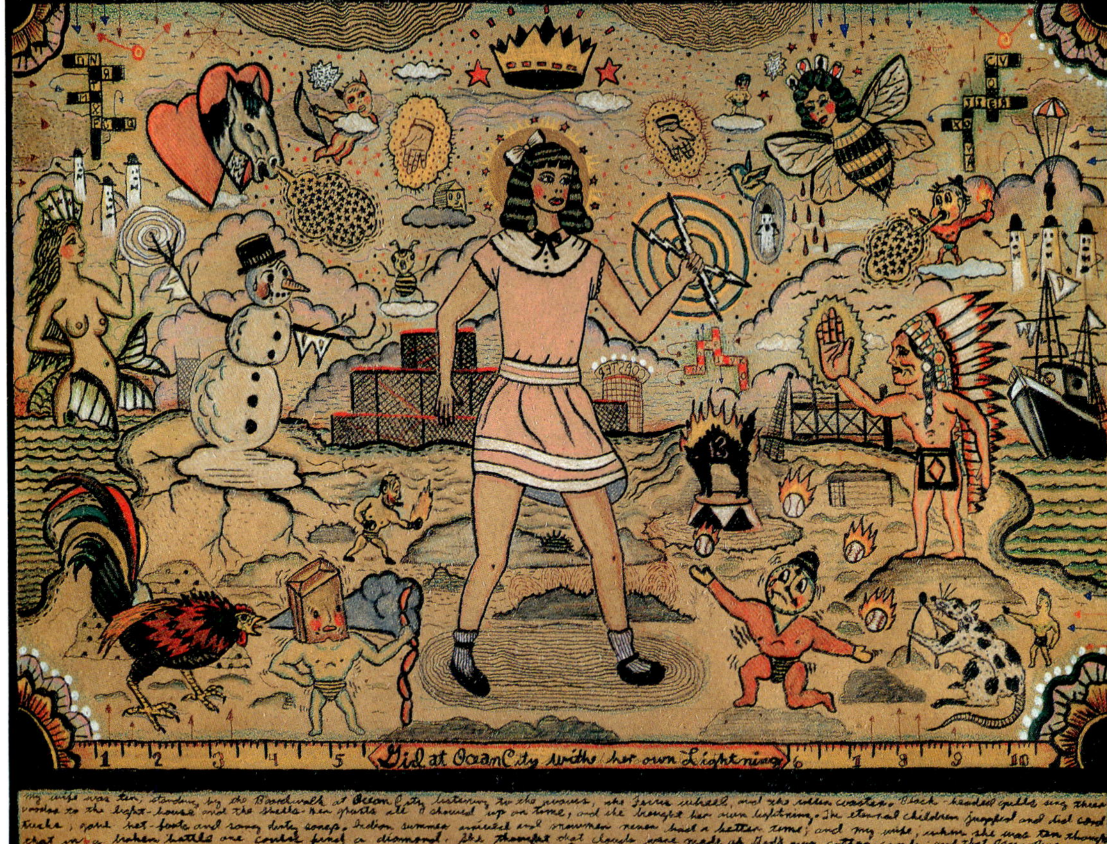

2

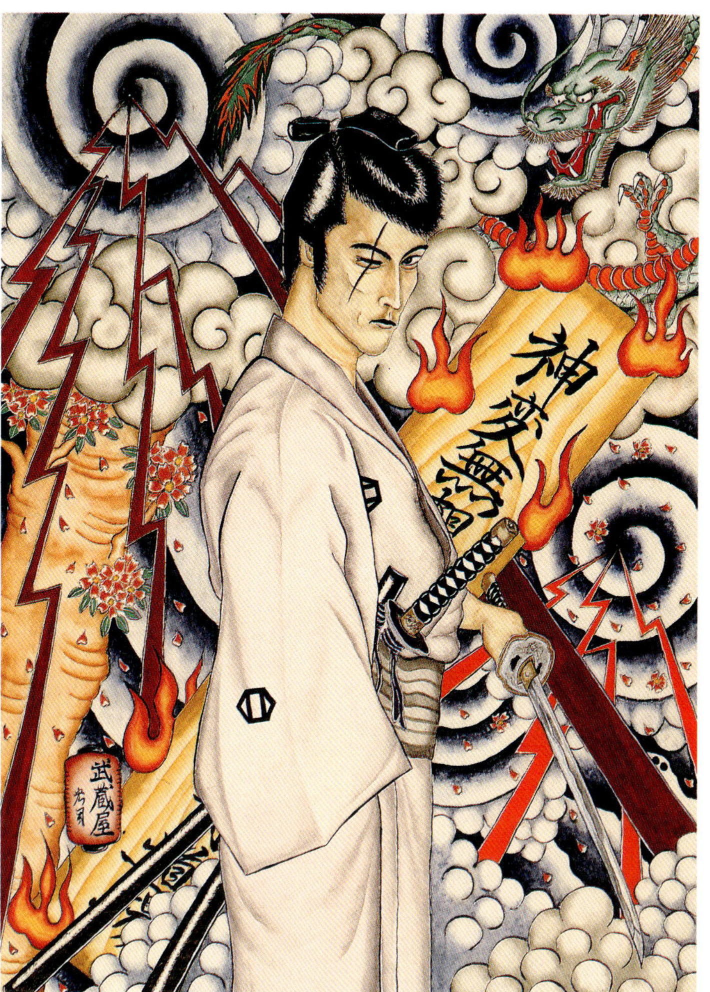

1

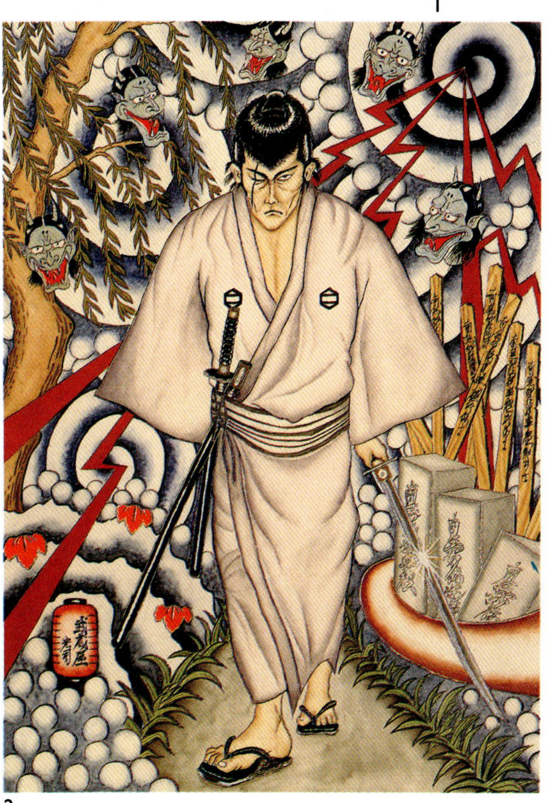

2

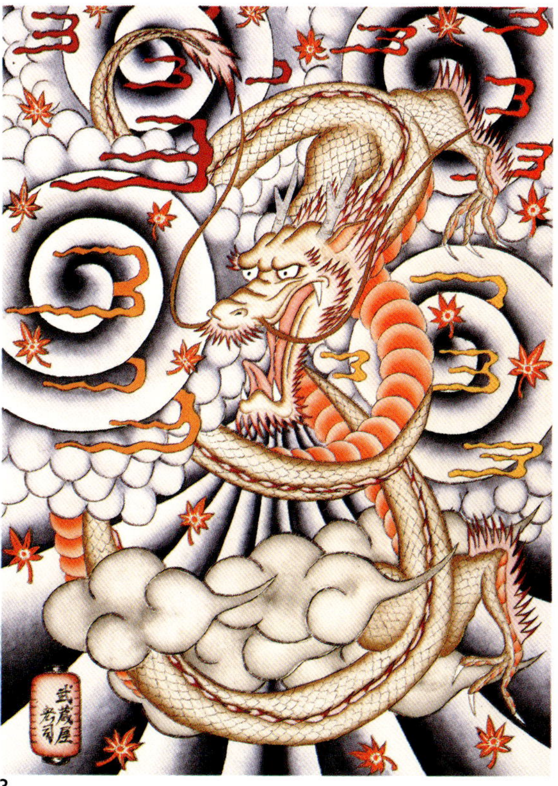

3

MONTSERRAT GALLERY

584 Broadway
New York, NY 10012
212.941.8899
212.274.1717 FAX

Contact:
Marie Montserrat Coll,
Director

Exhibiting:
Contemporary European
and American art

Koji Hayano

1. *One Arm & One Eyed
    Samurai, #2*
    1993, Watercolor,
    13" x 18"

2. *One Arm & One Eyed
    Samurai, #1*
    1993, Watercolor,
    13" x 18"

3. *Golden Dragon*
    1992, Watercolor,
    13" x 18"

Artist Statement:

Today, we are living in such darkness; the world is filled with dishonesty and unfairness. We have now reached the point of no return. There are so many leading people who control our lives using their evil power. We cannot afford to let the evil seeds to grow any more, or they will soon spoil the whole world.

We, powerless and honest people, have been waiting for a hero to come and fight with the evil power to save us.

FRANZ BADER
GALLERY

1500 K Street NW
Washington, DC 20005
202.393.6111

Contact:
Wretha Hanson

Peter Milton

Mary's Turn I:
Visiting Degas, 1994
Etching & Engraving,
ed. of 175
18" x 28"

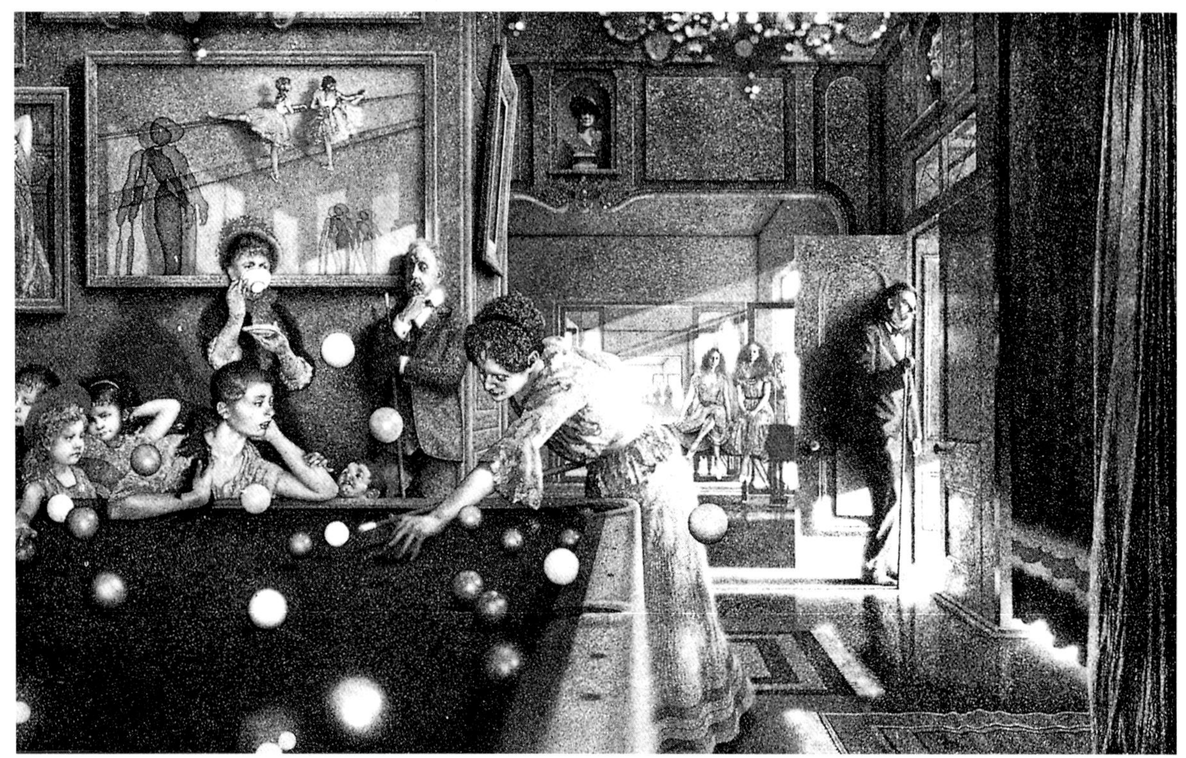

SCULPTURE

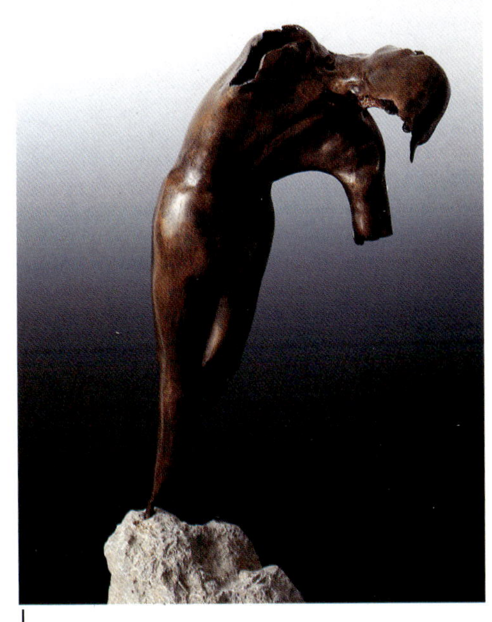

1

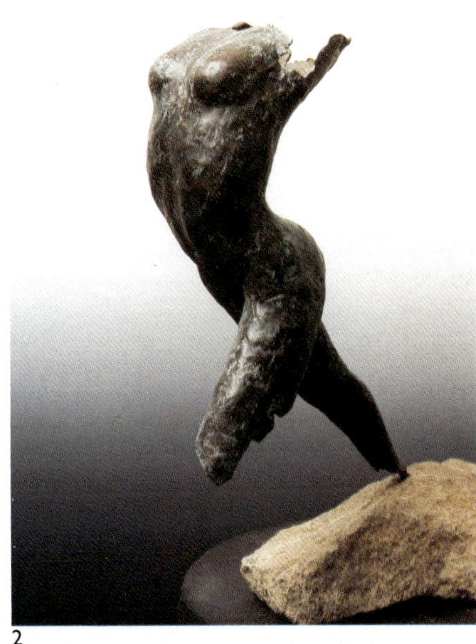

2

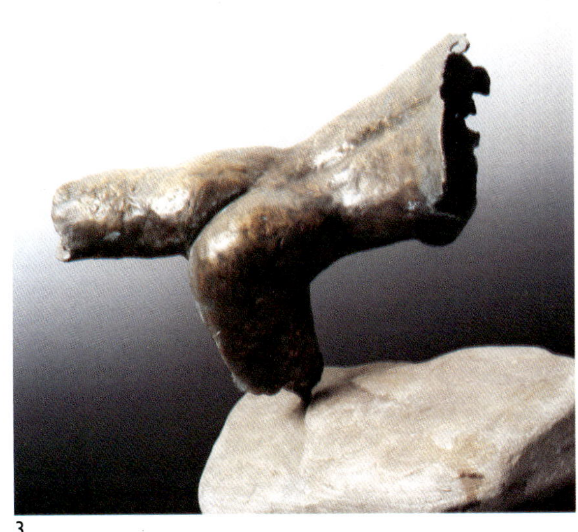

3

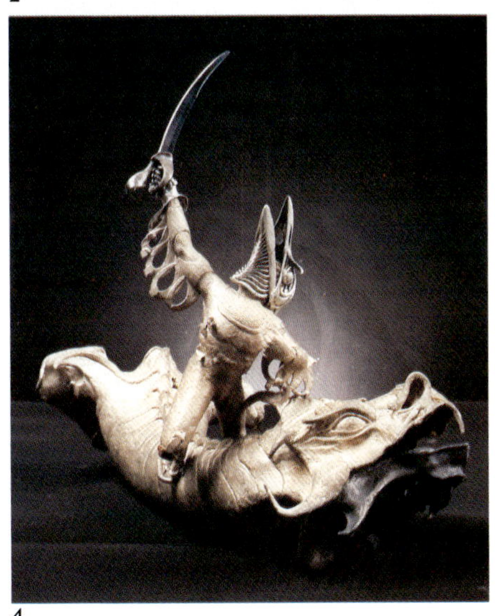

4

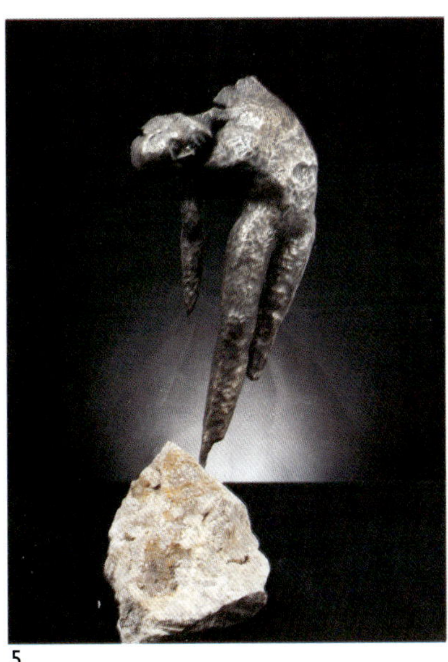

5

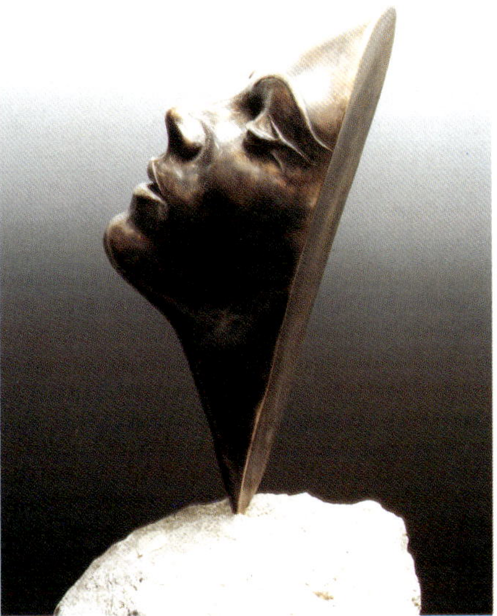

6

ROCFERN
INTERNATIONAL
GALLERIES, INC.

80 Carlauren Road Unit17
Woodbridge (Toronto),
Ontario L4L 7Z5 Canada
905.850.7647
905.850.8062 FAX

Contact:
Rocco Pannese
Fernando Rocco

Arno

1. *Private Sanctuary*
   1993, Bronze, ht. 60cm

2. *Into the Unknown*
   1993, Bronze, ht. 40cm

3. *Orbit*
   1993, Bronze, ht. 30cm

4. *Raven Warrior on Dragons Head,* 1993, Bronze and silver, ht. 30cm

5. *Tattered Rose*
   1993, Bronze, ht. 50cm

6. *Peace*
   1993, Bronze, ht. 40cm

Selected Biography:

1994 Rocfern International
      Galleries, Woodbridge,
      Ontario, Canada

      Lerner Gallery
      Beverly Hills, CA

1993 Art Frankfurt
      Frankfurt, Germany

      Fine Art Treasures
      Toronto, Ontario,
      Canada

1992 Arte
      New York, NY

Arte do Brasil
souza edelstein

Rua Visconde de Pirajá, 86 slj. 6
22410-000 Rio de Janeiro, Brasil
5521.267.2549
5521.267.1254 FAX

Contact:
Joel L. Edelstein
Miriam Gaudenzi

Exhibiting:
Contemporary painting and
sculpture

Marcos Benjamim

Untitled
1993,
Copper leaf on wood,
80" x 40"
Photo by: Ex Machina

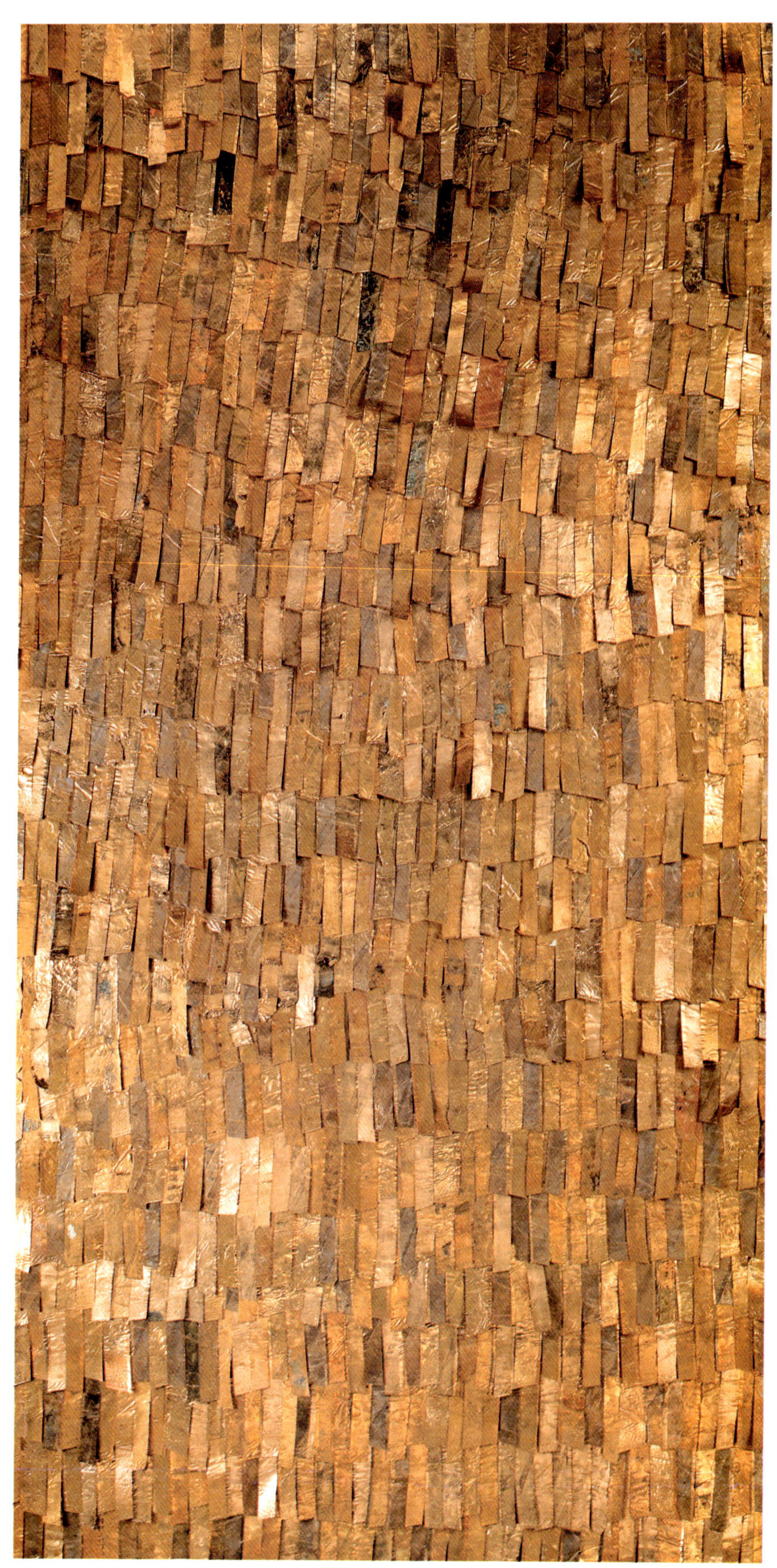

Selected Biography:

1994 Ambrosino Gallery,
     Coral Gables, FL

1993 4 x Minas Exposition,
     Museum of Modern Art
     Rio de Janeiro, Brazil
     & São Paulo, Brazil

1991 21st Biennal of
     São Paulo,
     São Paulo, Brazil

1990 Pulitzer Gallery,
     Amsterdam, Holland

1989 20th Biennal of
     São Paulo,
     São Paulo, Brazil

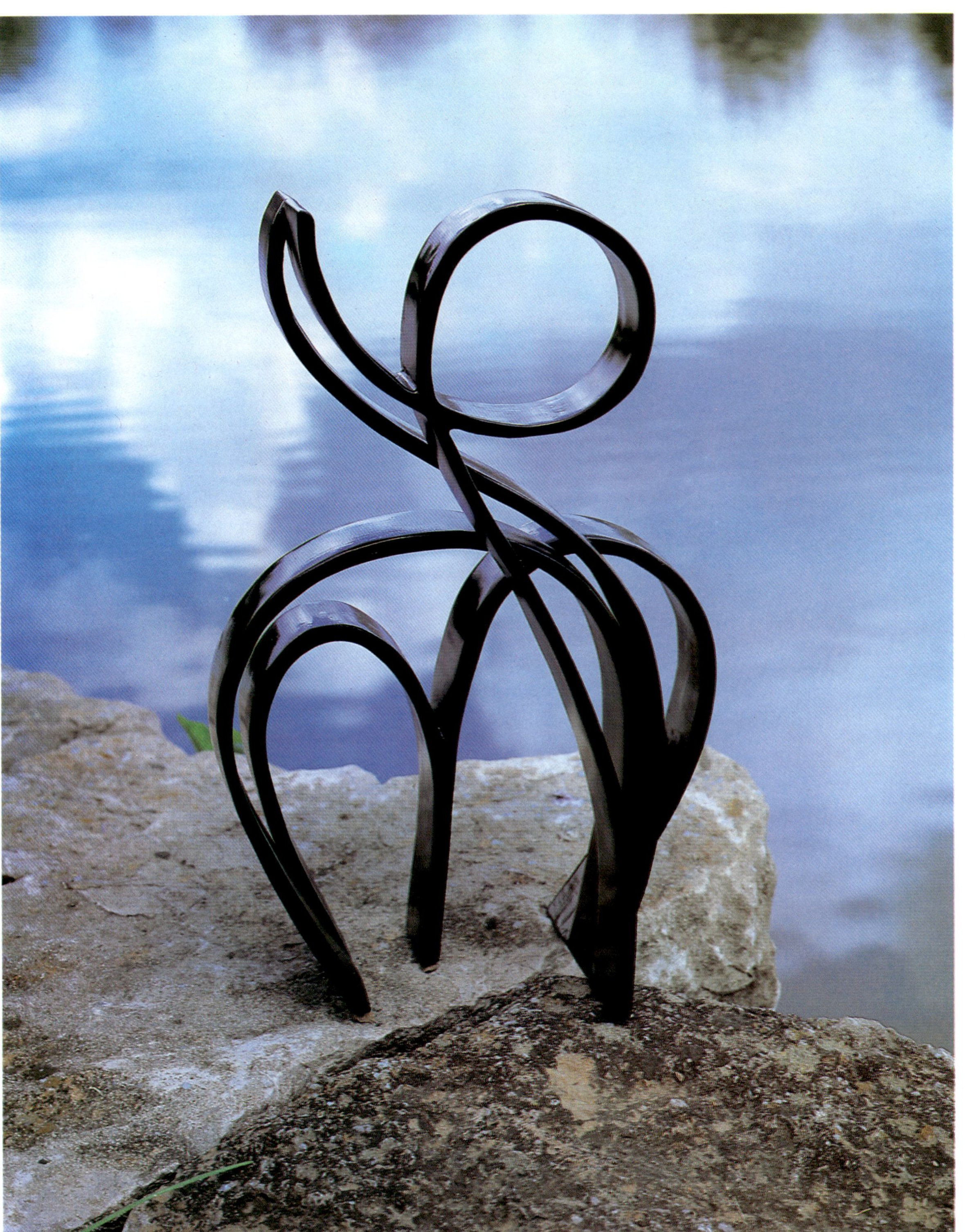

MIA FEROLETO
FINE ART PLANNING

45 West 10th Street #5B
New York, NY 10011
212.529.3744
212.529.4475 FAX

Contact:
Mia Feroleto

Rita Blitt

Happy Day-Mom
1993, wood,
18" x 14" x 7",
to be fabricated in
monumental size
Photo credit: M. Zagalik

Selected Collections:
  National Museum of
  Singapore, Singapore

  John F. Kennedy Library,
  Cambridge, MA

  Aspen Institute,
  Aspen, CO

  Albrecht-Kemper
  Museum, St. Joseph, MO

  Skirball Museum,
  Los Angeles, CA

  Spertus Museum,
  Chicago, IL

THE LOWE GALLERY

75 Bennett St. Space A-Z
Atlanta, GA 30309
404.352.8114
404.352.0564 FAX

Contact:
Bill Lowe

Exhibiting:
Contemporary painting,
sculpture, and objects

James Warner Booth

The Golden Mean Machine
1994,
Mixed media assemblage,
90" x 54" x 12"

Selected Biography:

1994 Solo show,
The Lowe Gallery,
Atlanta, GA

Solo Show,
"My Alchem My",
Velvet Gallery,
Atlanta, GA

1993 Group show,
Hands On Museum,
Johnson City, TN

Group show,
"ACA Video Show",
High Museum of Art,
Atlanta, GA

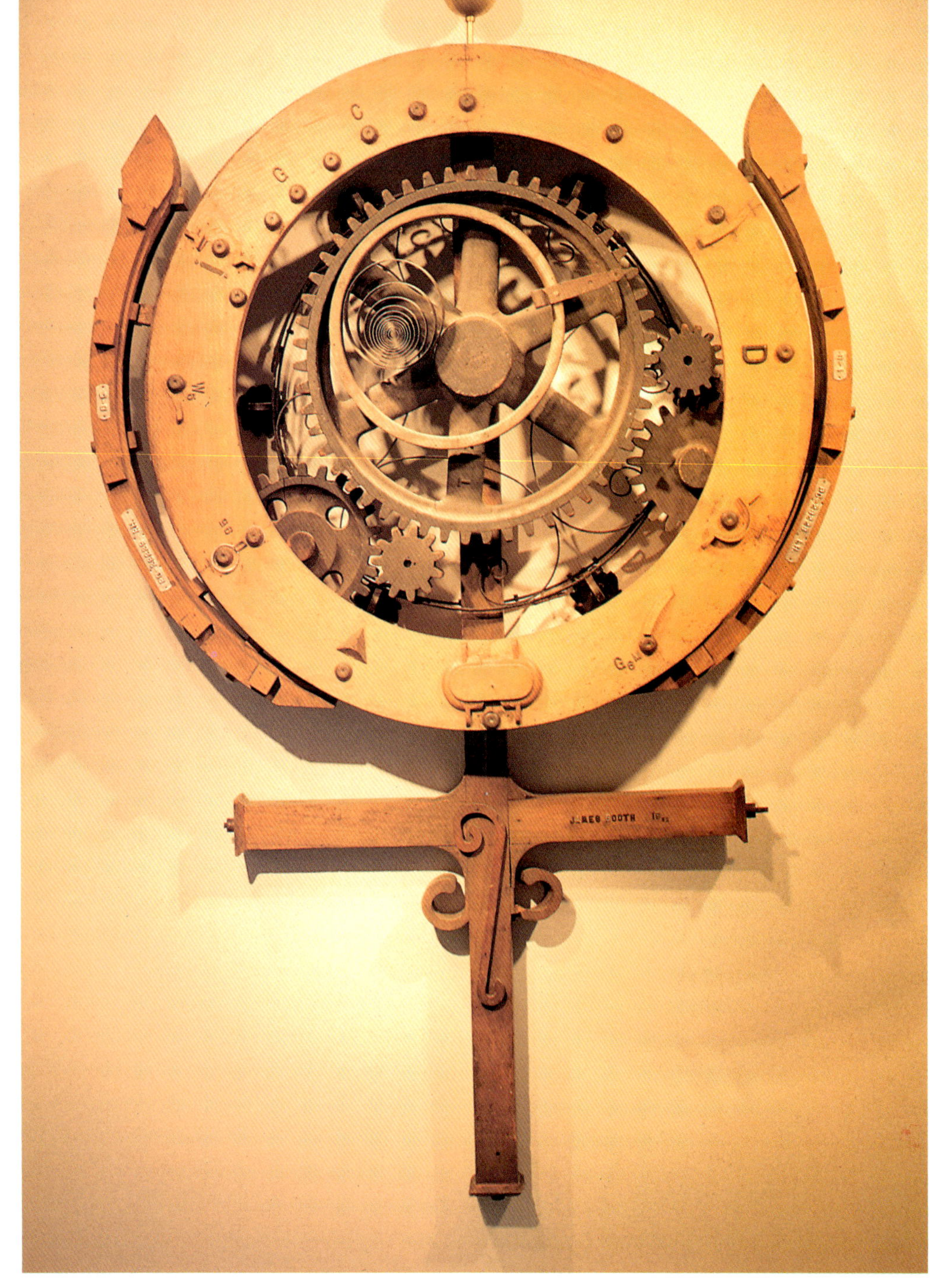

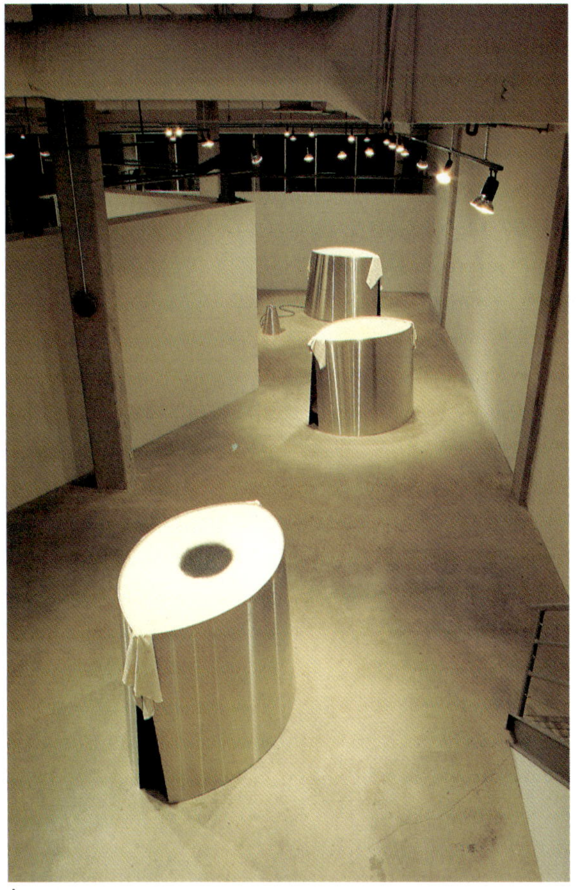

1

DIANE FARRIS GALLERY

1565 West 7th Avenue
Vancouver B.C. V6J 1S1
Canada
604.737.2629
604.737.2675 FAX

Contact:
Diane Farris, Director

Exhibiting:
Contemporary Canadian
and International Art

Claudia Cuesta

1. *Relic of Time*
   1987-88, Stainless steel,
   steel, coal, oil, water,
   propane, sulphur,
   Installation

2. *Symbolic Correspondence*
   1993, Black granite, steel,
   glass, honey, propane,
   plastic tubing,
   Installation detail

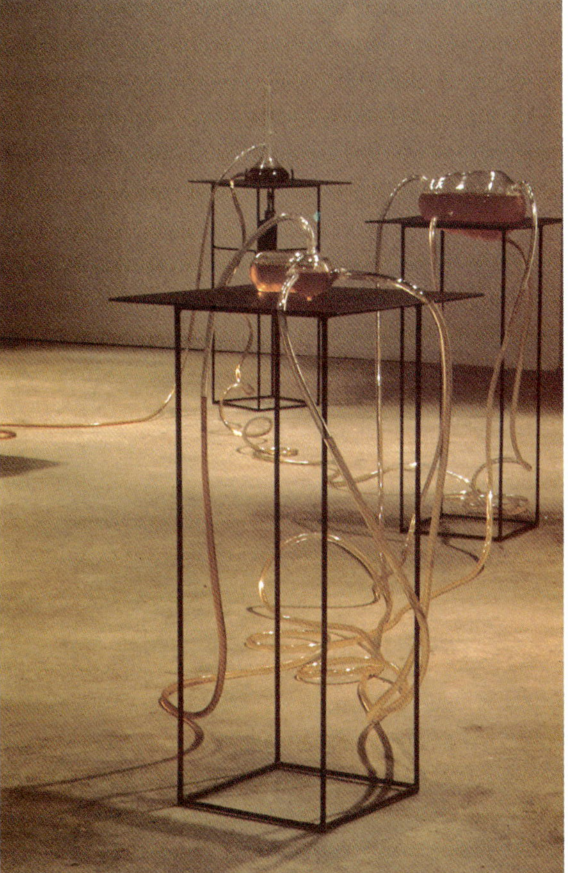

2

Selected Biography:
1993 "Whiteness and
     Wounds", The Power
     Plant, Toronto, ON
     "Out of Place",
     Vancouver Art Gallery,
     Vancouver, BC
     "Sculptures",
     Diane Farris Gallery,
     Vancouver, BC
1991 "Hunting in Time",
     Gimpel Fils Gallery,
     London, England
     "Terra Nova" South
     Bank Gallery,
     London, England
1990 "Low Tech..Artist
     made Machines",
     Center of
     Contemporary Art,
     Seattle, WA

**MARSHA CHILD
CONTEMPORARY**

P.O. Box 364
Solebury, PA 18963
215.297.0414
215.297.0414 FAX

Contact:
Marsha Child

Exhibiting:
Contemporary European,
Eastern European and
American paintings, sculpture
and graphics

Maciek Danilewicz

1. *Face of Depression*
   1993, Bronze,
   24" x 24" x 6"

2. *Lydia*
   1993, Bronze,
   20" x 20" x 12"

3. *Happy Years*
   1993, Bronze,
   35" x 12" x 24"

Selected Biography:

1994 "Mysteries," 101
   Wooster Street
   Gallery, New York,
   NY; "Introspection in
   Bronze," Marsha Child
   Contemporary,
   Solebury, PA; "Face to
   Face," 101 Wooster
   Street Gallery, New
   York, NY; Sodarco
   Gallery, Montreal,
   Canada

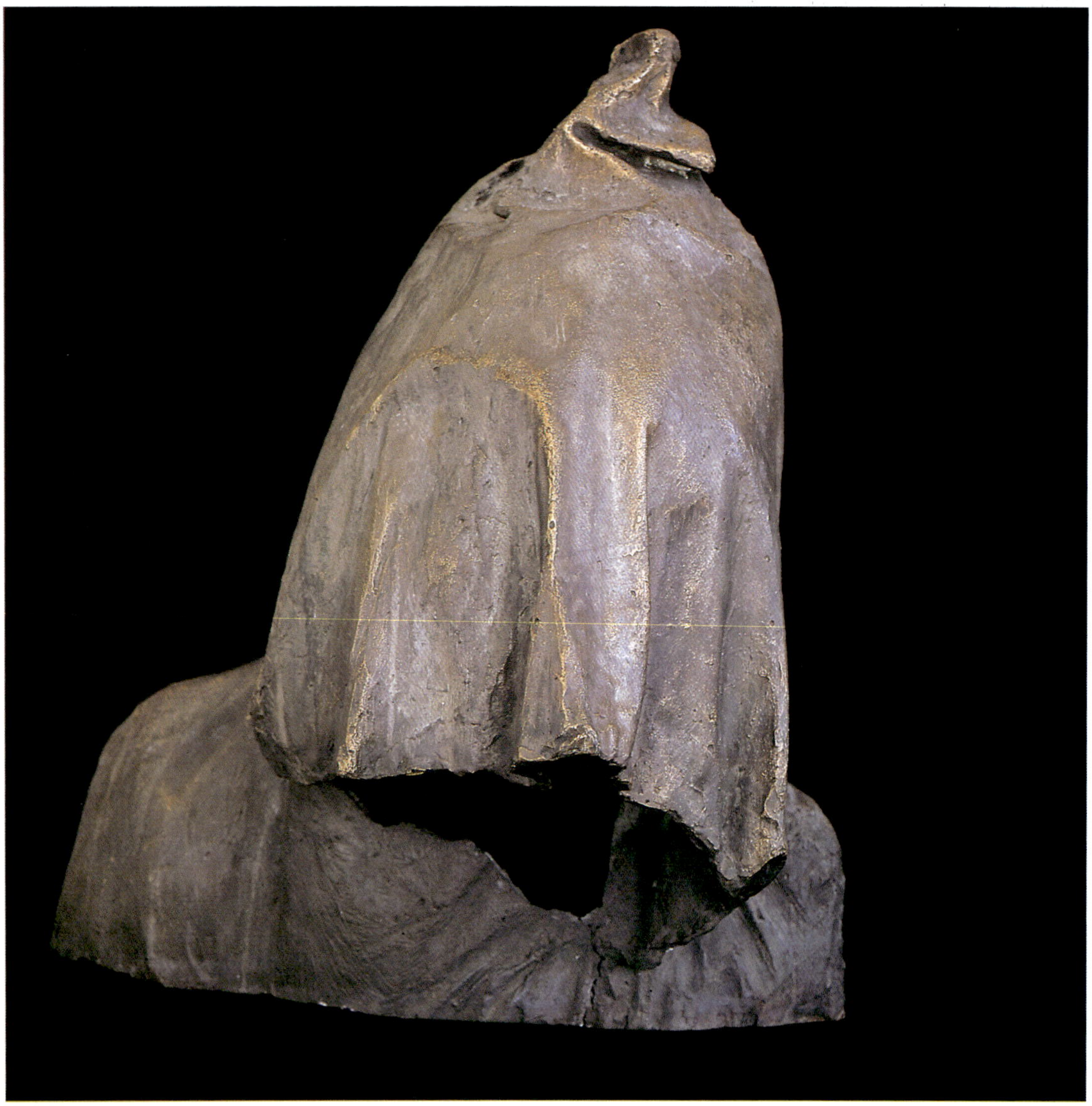

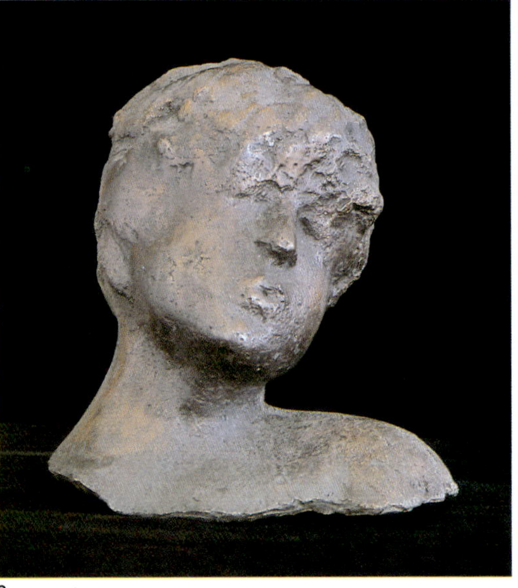

1

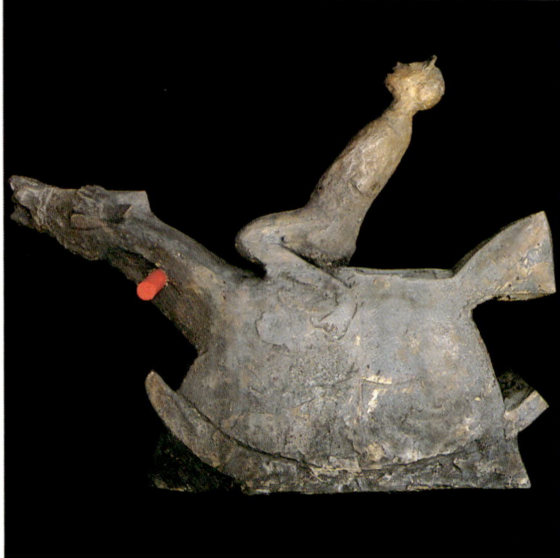

2

3

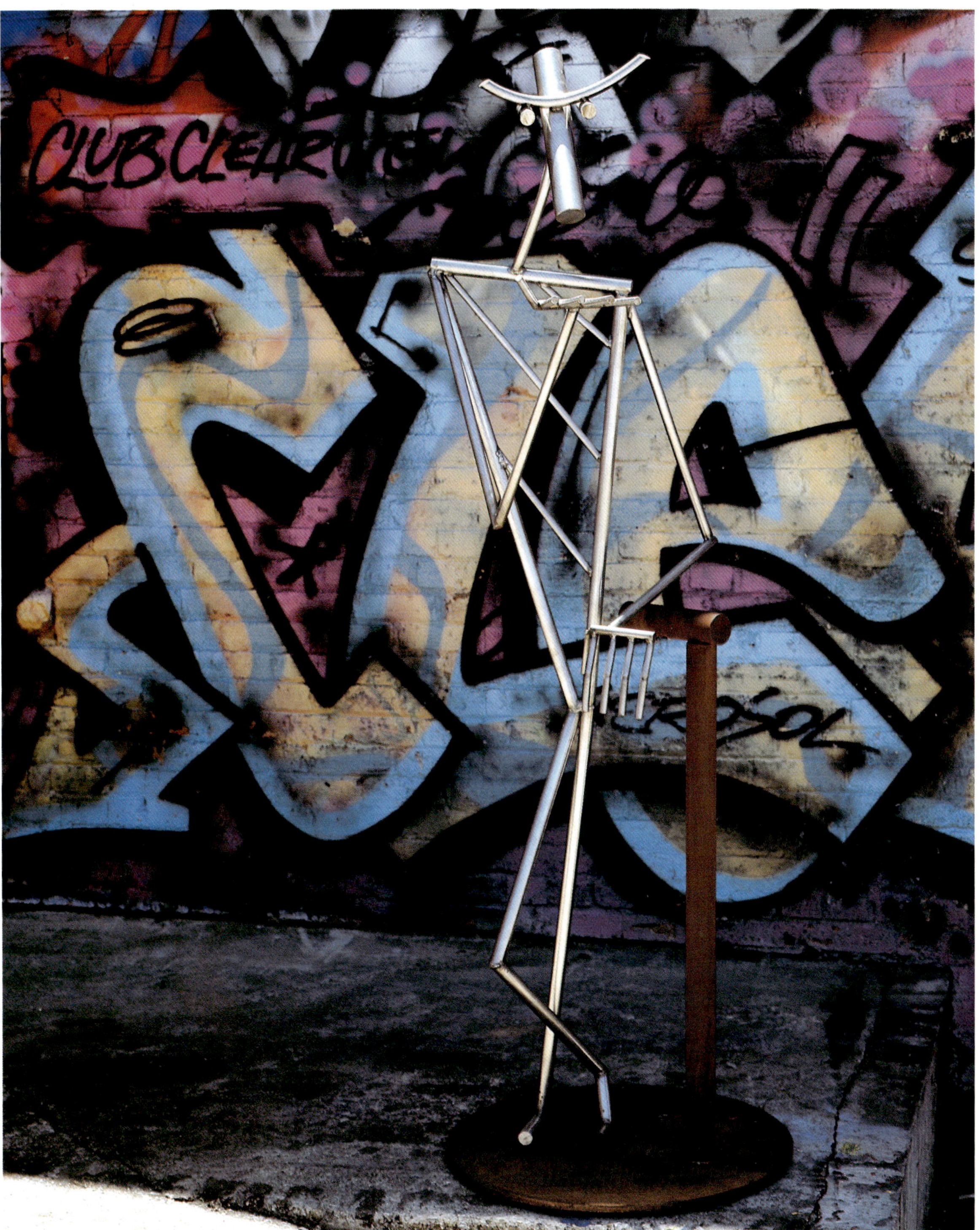

**BARRETT DeBUSK
SCULPTURE**

3813 N. Commerce
Ft. Worth, TX 76106
817.625.8476
817.625.8476 FAX
817.261.8172
817.261.8172 FAX

Contact:
Sue Davis

Exhibiting:
One of a kind & limited
edition DeBusk welded
steel sculpture

Barrett DeBusk

The Beggar
1993,
Stainless & rusted steel,
74" x 28" x 26"

THE LOWE GALLERY

75 Bennett St. Space A-Z
Atlanta, GA 30309
404.352.8114
404.352.0564 FAX

Contact:
Bill Lowe

Exhibiting:
Contemporary painting,
sculpture, and objects

Greg Edmondson

Centaur
1992, Maple wood
with pigment,
79" x 47" x 18"

Selected Biography:

1994 Solo show,
The Lowe Gallery,
Atlanta, GA

1987 Solo show,
Kunstlerwerkstatt,
Munich, Germany

1986 Fulbright Fellowship,
Munich, Germany

1985 Solo show,
Vitrine 002,
Koln, Germany

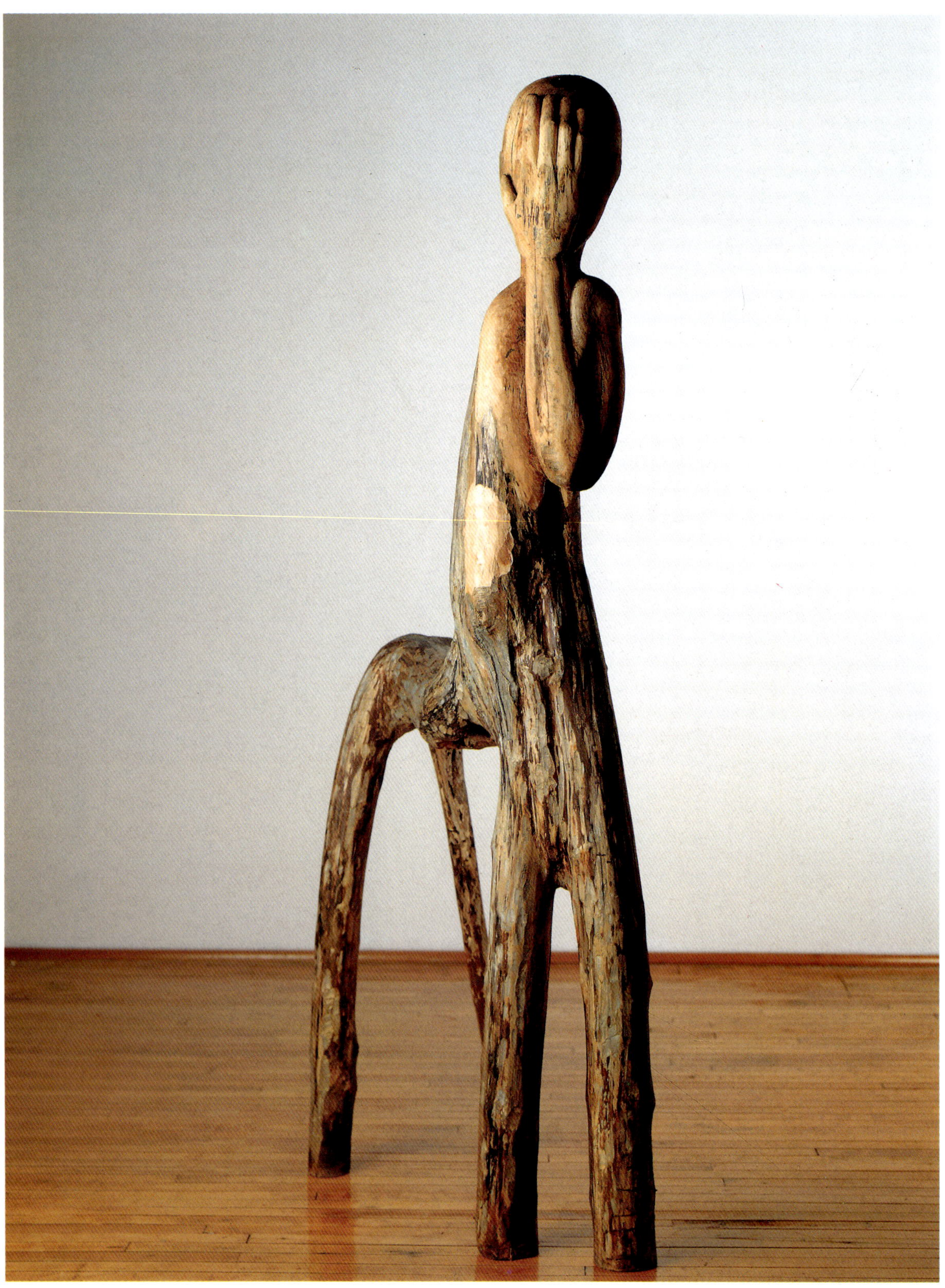

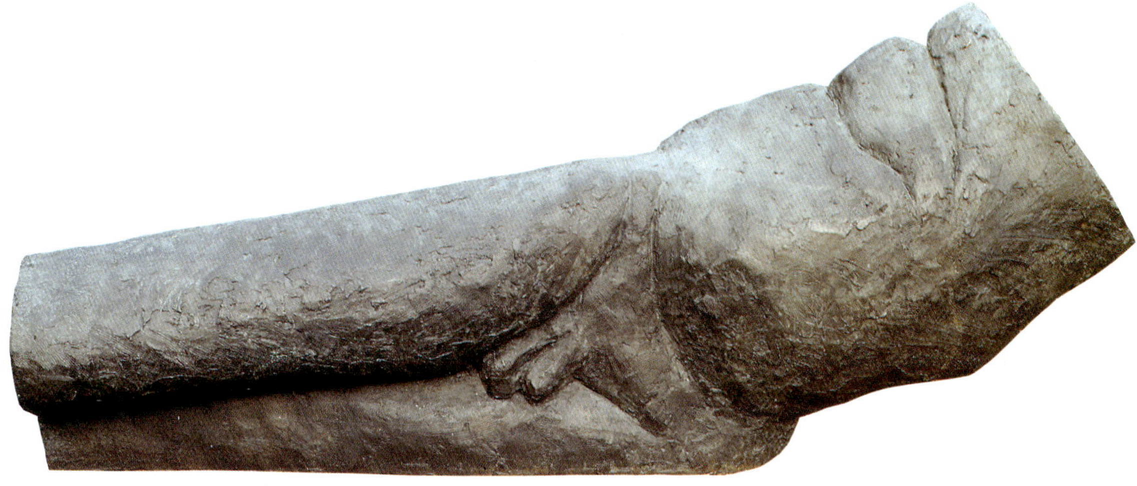

1

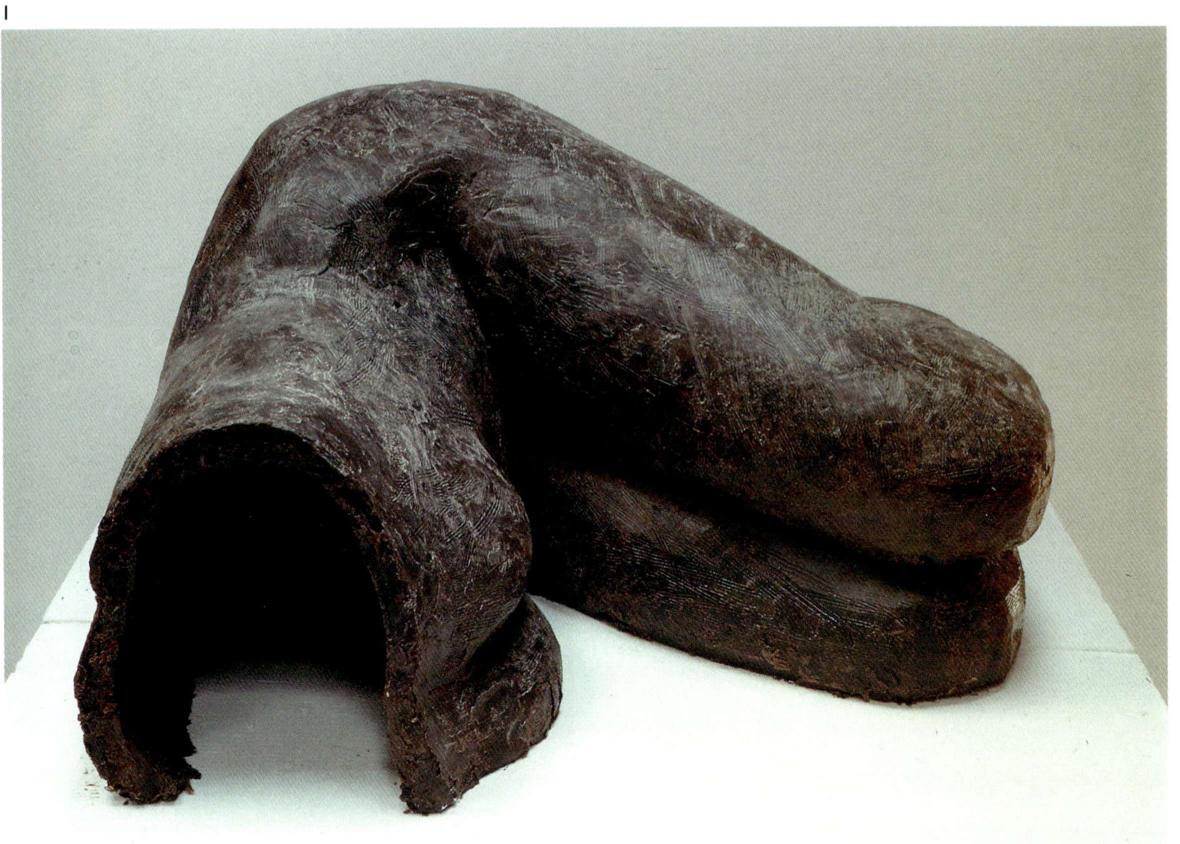

2

CLAUDIA CHAPLINE
GALLERY &
SCULPTURE GARDEN

3445 Shoreline Hwy.
P.O. Box 946
Stinson Beach, CA 94970
415.868.2308
415.868.9436 FAX

Contact:
Margot Merrill

Exhibiting:
Contemporary art

Christoph Fields

1. *Thomas Rising*
   1993, Bronze
   34" x 53" x 17"

2. *Sabrina's Decline*
   1993, Bronze,
   26" x 16" x 28"

Selected Biography:

1994 Claudia Chapline
        Gallery,
        Stinson Beach, CA

        Anya Horvath Gallery,
        Sacramento, CA

1993 I. Wolk Gallery,
        St. Helena, CA

1992 Oliver Art Gallery,
        Oakland, CA

        Gallery Route One,
        Point Reyes Station,
        CA

DONNIE FIRKINS STUDIO

238 Freestone Ct.
Bowling Green, KY 42103
502.842.3337

Donnie Firkins

1. *To the Point*
   1992, Welded Steel-painted, 6'x 8'

2. *Enmeshed*
   1992, Welded Steel-painted, 5'x 6'

3. *Consideration*
   1993, Marble, 4'x 1'

4. *Stain Satin*
   1994, Stainless Steel, 5'x 3'

Selected Biography:

1991 IBC Gallery,
      Washington, DC

      Casa de la Cultura
      Quito, Ecuador,
      South America
      (permanent installation)

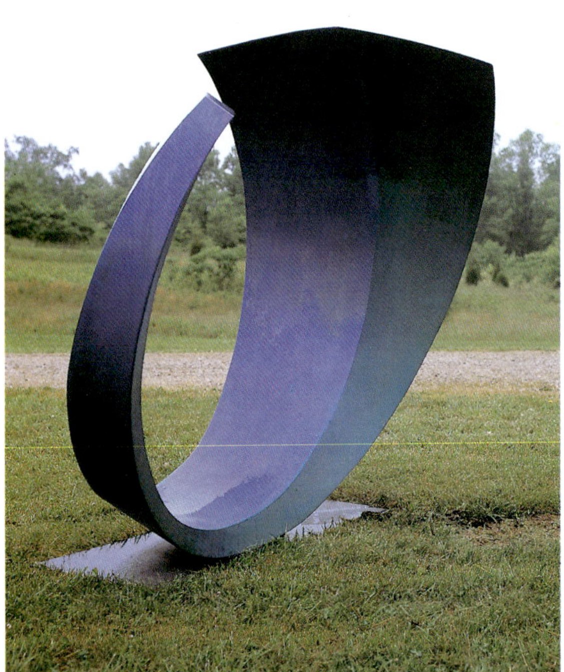

1

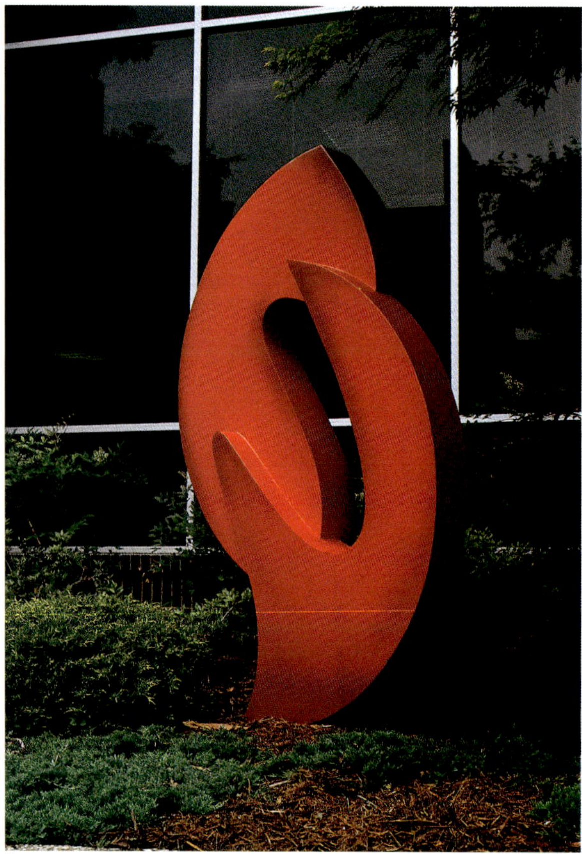

2

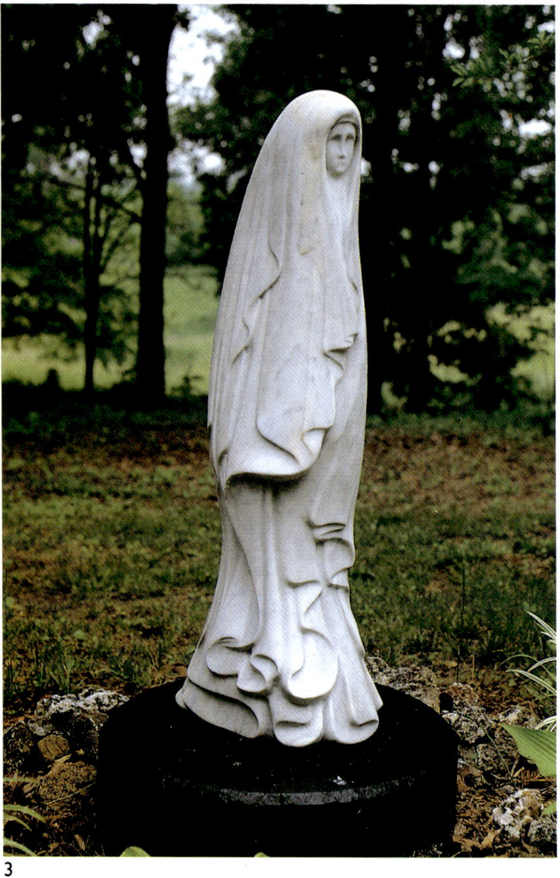

3

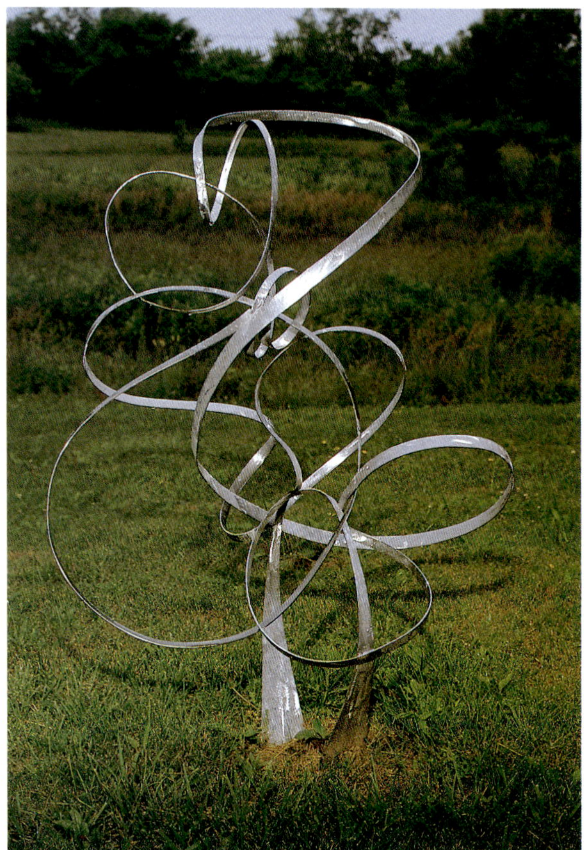

4

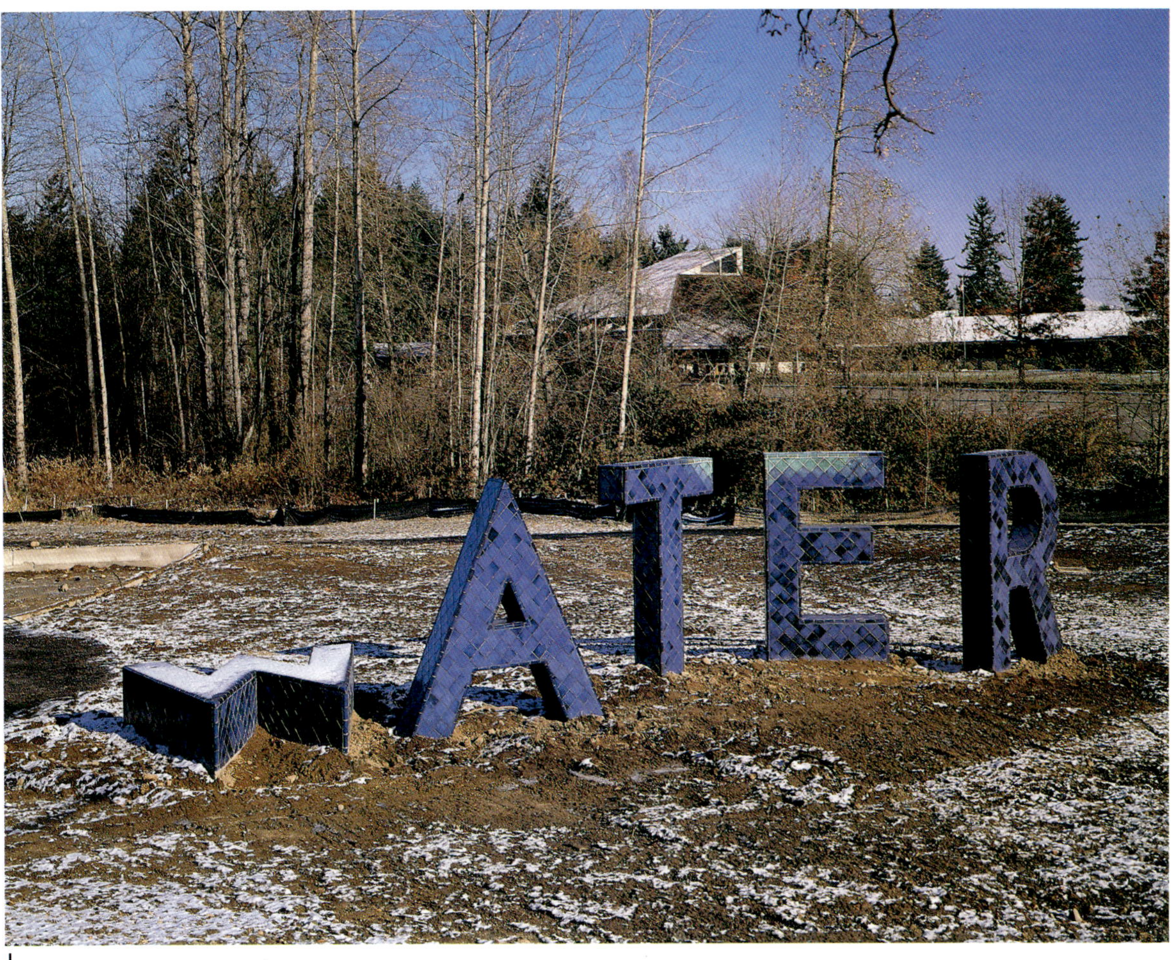

1

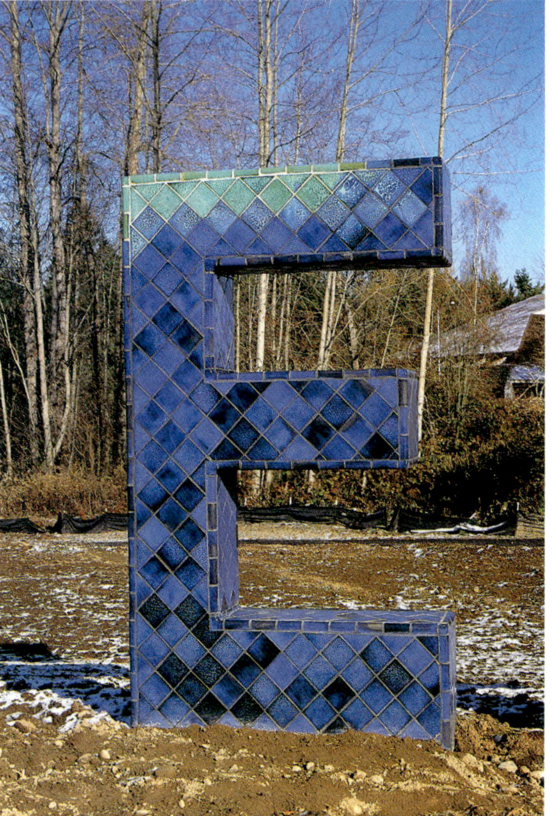

2

RADIX GALLERY

1429 N. First St.
Phoenix, Az 85004
602.256.9252
602.252.8002 FAX

Contact:
Catherine Spencer,
Director

Exhibiting:
Contemporary art from
Europe and America

Barbara Grygutis

1. *Water*
   1993, Handmade ceramic
   tile on cast concrete,
   6' x 30' x 6'

2. *Water, detail*

Public Art Collections:

1994 Garden Of Constants,
      Ohio State University,
      Columbus, OH

1993 Martin Luther King Jr.
      Memorial,
      Columbia, MI

1992 Real Tools, St. Paul
      Technical College,
      St Paul, MN

1991 Cruising San Mateo,
      Albuquerque, NM

LOUIS K. MEISEL GALLERY

141 Prince Street
New York, NY 10012
212.677.1340
212.533.7340 FAX

Contact:
Louis K. Meisel
Diane Sena

Exhibiting:
Photo-Realist painting and
other technically skilled
contemporary disciplines

Oded Halahmy

1. *Babylonian River Banks*
   1989, Bronze Cast,
   96" x 49" x 17.5"

2. *Peace Ride*
   1992, Bronze Cast,
   31" x 21.5" x 6"

3. *What's Peace Got to Do
   With It*
   1993, Bronze Cast,
   27" x 24" x 4.75"

4. *Touching Heaven*
   1990, Bronze Cast,
   87" x 57" x 17"

Selected Collections:

Solomon R.
Guggenheim Museum,
New York, NY;
The Aldrich Museum
of Contemporary Art,
Ridgefield, CT;
Herbert F. Johnson
Museum of Art,
Ithaca, NY;
Indianapolis Museum
of Art, IN;
The Jewish Museum,
New York, NY;
Philbrook Museum
of Art, Tulsa, OK

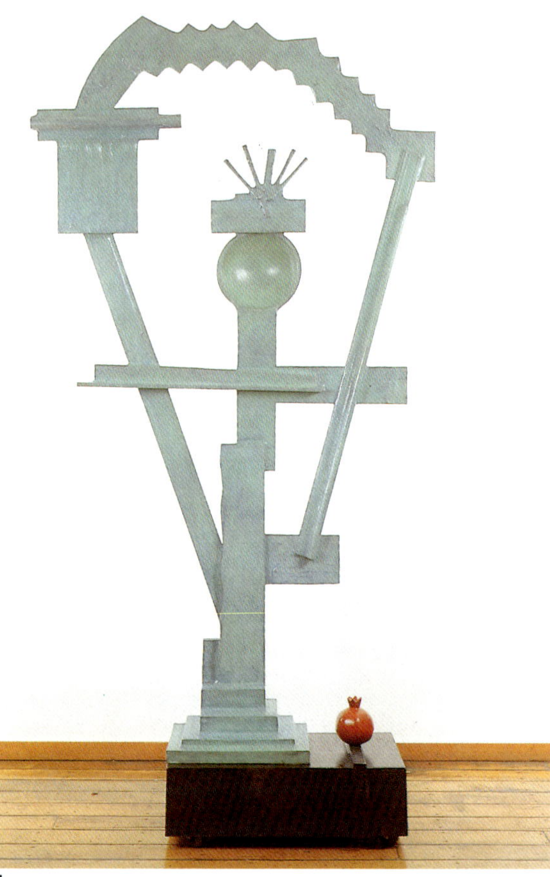

1

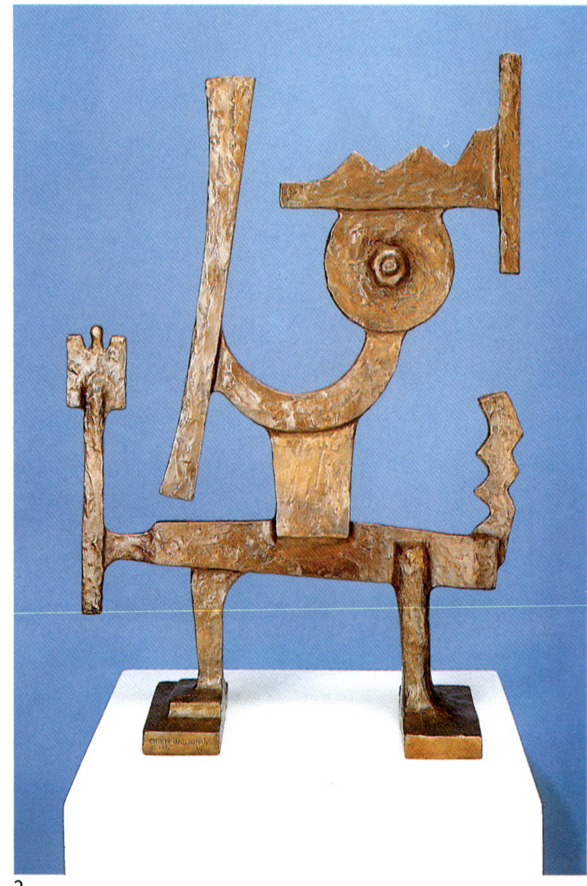

2

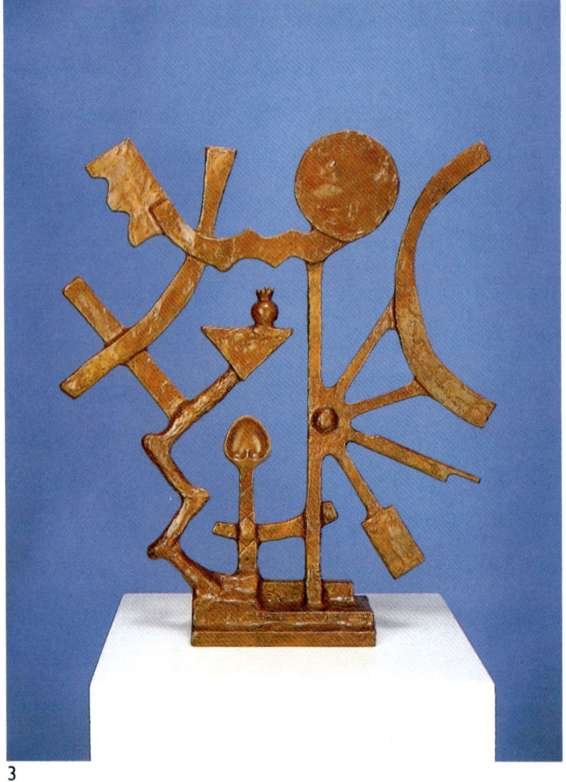

3

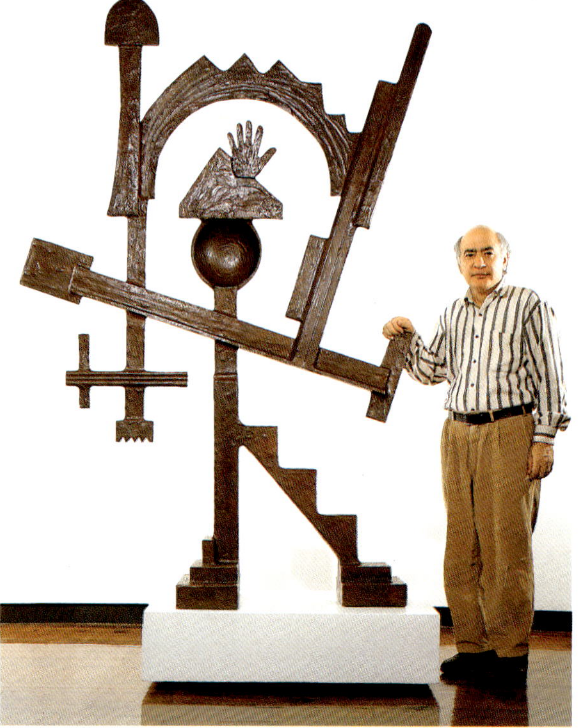

4

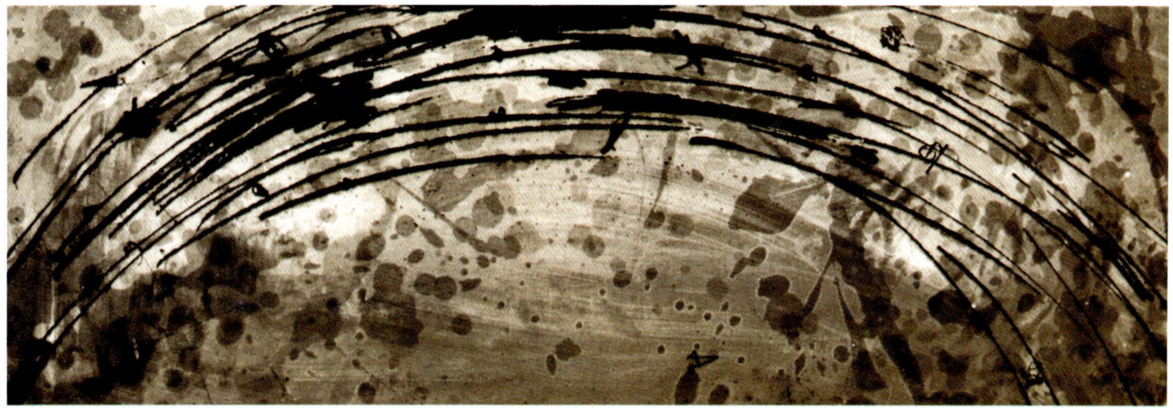

1

CORINNE TIMSIT INTERNATIONAL GALLERIES Inc.

81, rue Lepic
75018 Paris, France
33.1.4255.7682
33.1.4252.4868 FAX

Calle San José 104
Viejo San Juan
00901 Puerto Rico
809.724.1039
809.721.4174 FAX

Contact:
Jaime Otero
Marisa Guevara

Exhibiting:
Latin American and
European art

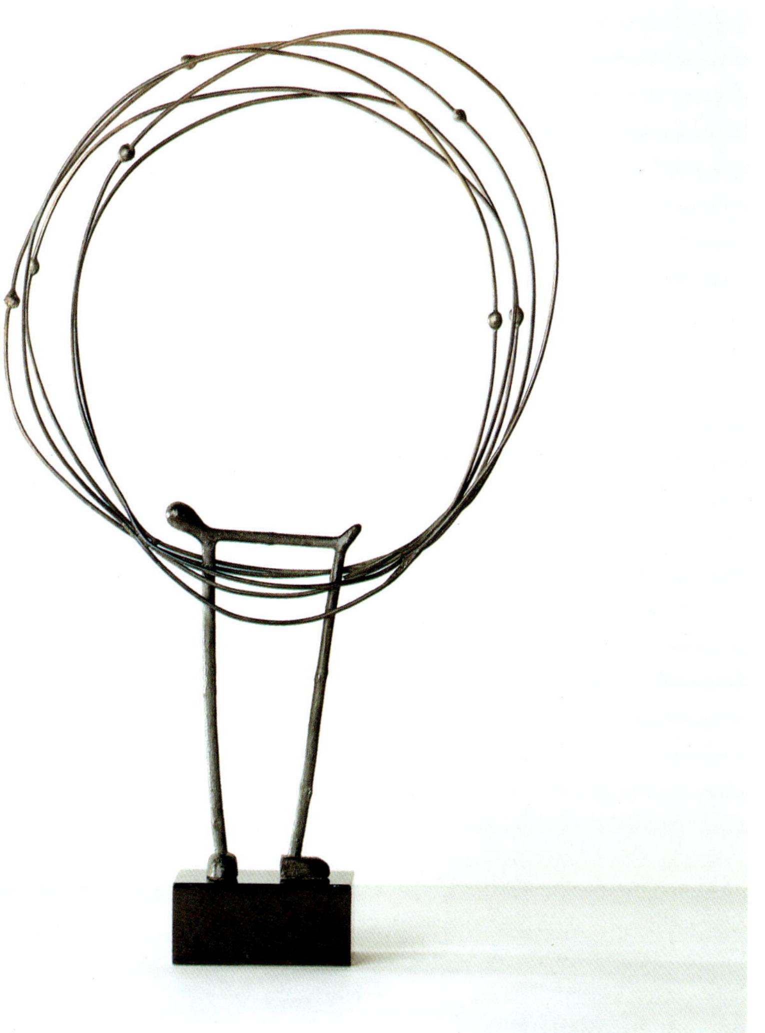

Nora Herman

1. *Explotion Initial*
   1990, Engraving,
   65 × 25 cm.

2. *Univers*
   1991, Bronze,
   46 × 13 × 5 cm.

Selected Biography:

1993　Prize winner of the
FRAC 'Ile de France'

Art Miami '93, Miami,
Gallery Corinne Timsit

1992　Solo exhibitions:
Gallery Corinne Timsit,
Paris, France
Gallery Lucette Herzog,
Paris, France

Europ'Art '92, Genève
Gallery Corinne Timsit:
Art Miami '92, Miami,
Gallery Corinne Timsit

2

THE PACE GALLERY

142 GREENE ST.
NEW YORK, NY 10012
212.431.9224
212.431.9280 FAX

Contact:
Marc Glimcher

Exhibiting:
20th-century paintings,
drawings and sculpture

Donald Judd

Untitled
1990, Orange
anodized aluminum
with clear plexiglass,
6⅛" x 27" x 24" Each Unit
120" x 27" x 24" Overall size

Photo Credit Bill Jacobson

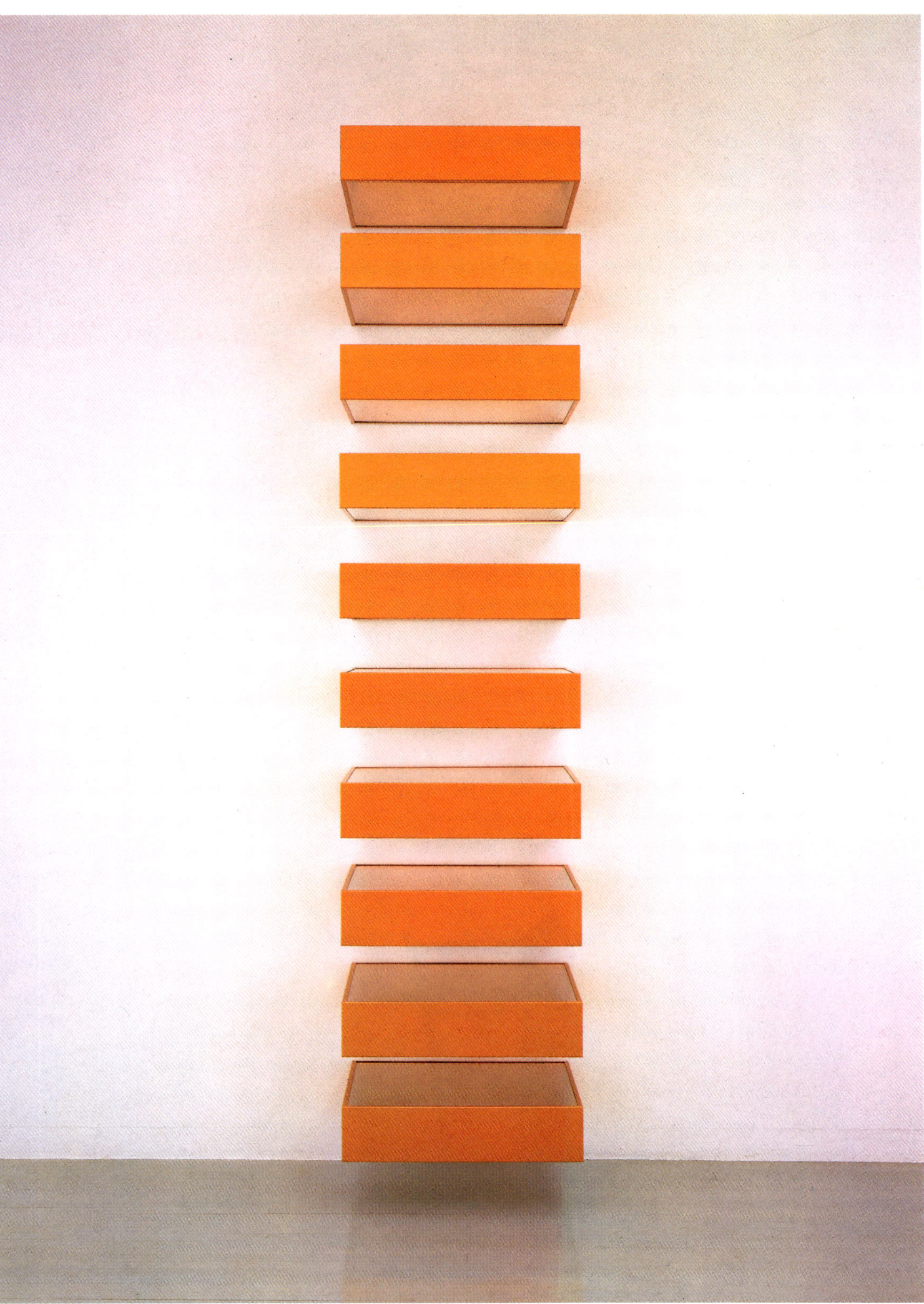

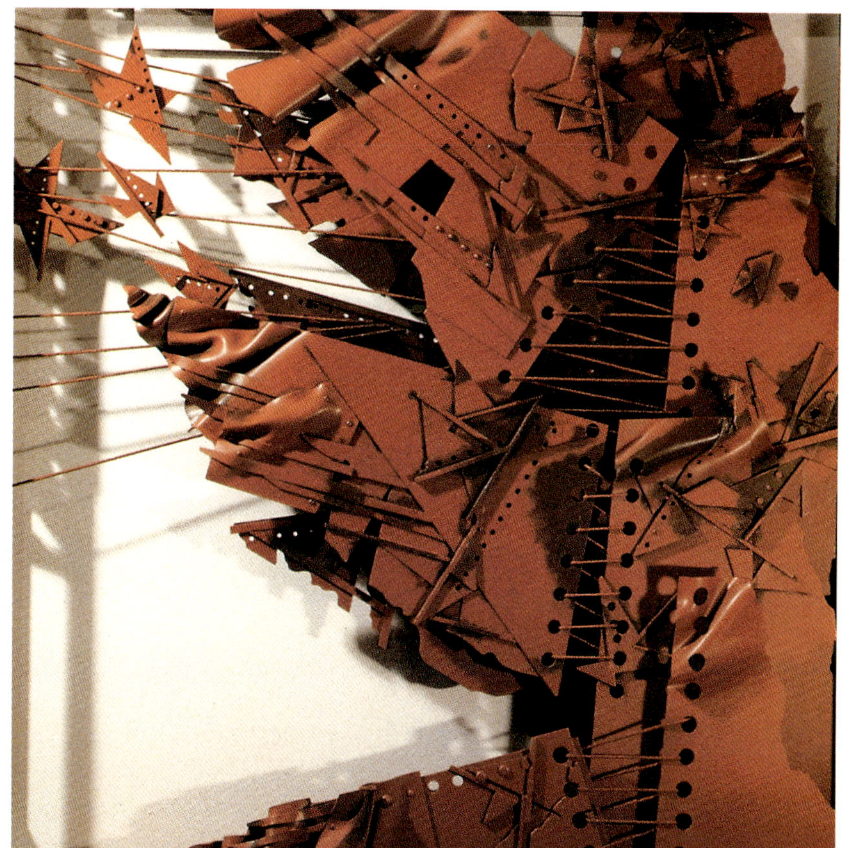

MONTSERRAT GALLERY

584 Broadway
New York, NY 10012
212.941.8899
212.274.1717 FAX

Contact:
Marie Montserrat Coll,
Director

Exhibiting:
Contemporary European
and American art

Alex Klimov

Mutual Feedback
1994, Two piece
wall sculpture, wood,
plastic, acrylic,
42" x 42" x 8" each

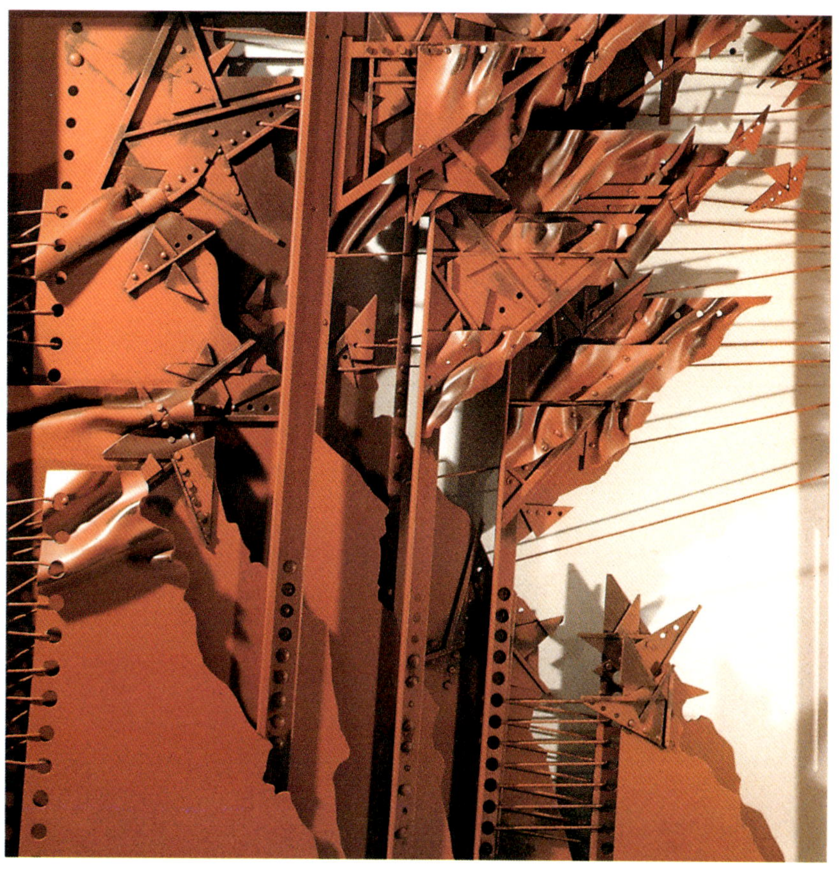

Selected Biography:

1994 Solo Exhibition,
Montserrat Gallery,
New York, NY

Sculptors Drawings,
14 Sculptors Gallery
New York, NY

1993 New York Now,
Montserrat Gallery,
New York, NY

14 Sculptors Gallery
New York, NY

Art Association of
Harrisburg,
Harrisburg, PA

KOCKA EARTHRACKS AND STUDIO

995 Beech Rd. S. E.
Laconia, IN 47135
812.737.2261
812.738.8845 FAX

Contact:
Vickie Hull

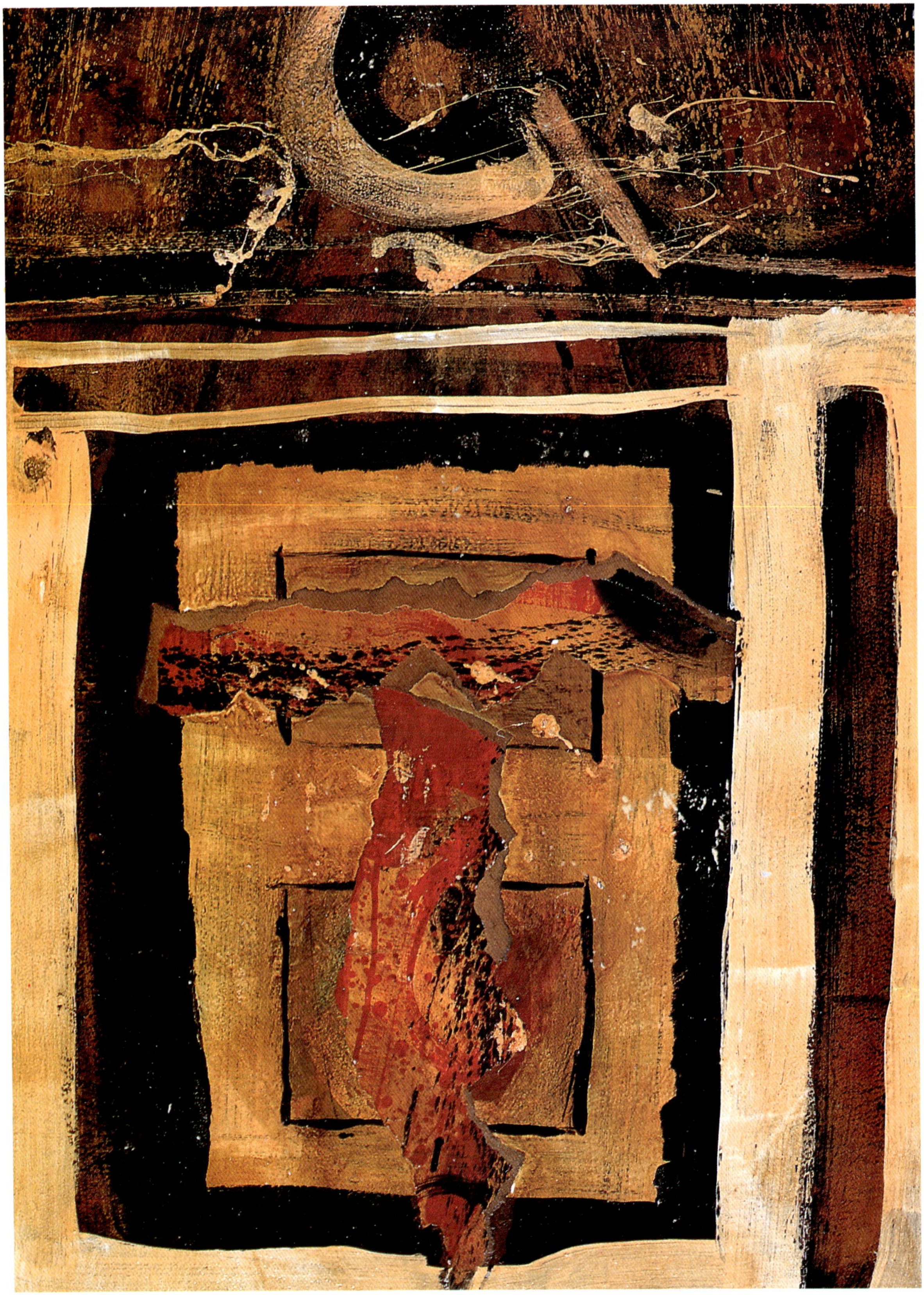

Representing:
Painting and sculpture by
David Kocka

David Mark Kocka

Seraph-Sting
1993, Acrylic/board,
20" x 30"

Selected Biography:

1993 Zehpyr Gallery,
Louisville, KY

1989 Angel of the
Sixth Seal 5 ft.,
New Harmony, IN

1987 Sol-luna Canticle," 6 ft.
diameter Bronze disk

1986 Yoke of Compassion,
Bronze 5 ft.

1985 International Dante
Exhibition

Animalische Seek

These often possess many and varied meanings, so that as in Chinese script, only the context can furnish the correct meaning. This multiple significance of the symbol is allied to the dream's faculty of admitting over-interpretations, of representing, in the same content, various wish-impulses and thought-formations, often of a widely divergent character.

1

The second word, which reminds me of Italian names, and of our discussions on etymology, also expresses my annoyance in respect of the fact that my friend has kept his address a secret from me; but each of the possible first three words may be recognized on analysis as an independent and equally justifiable starting-point in the concatenation of ideas.

The sign reads either:—

> *You are requested to shut the eyes*
>
> or
>
> *You are requested to shut one eye*

an alternative which I am in the habit of representing in the following form:

> *the*
> You are requested to shut   eye(s).
> *one*

2

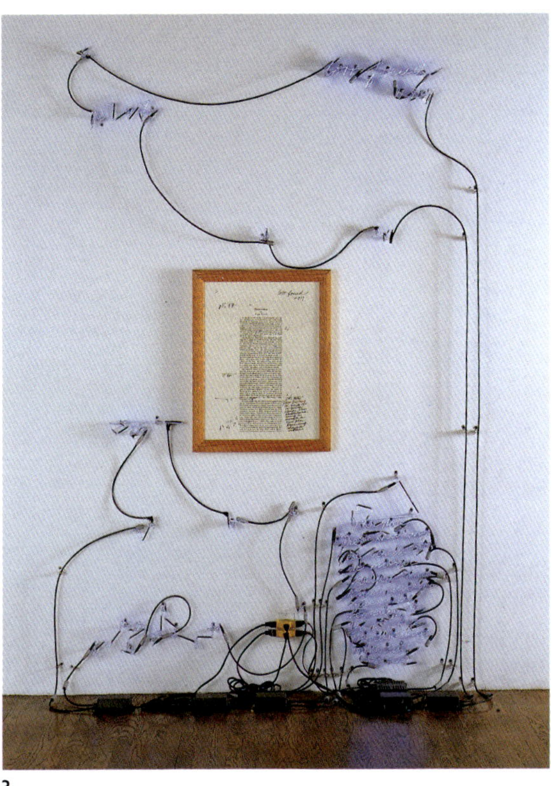

3

LEO CASTELLI

420 W. Broadway
New York, NY 10012
212.431.5160
212.431.5361 FAX

Contact:
Susan Brundage, Director

Joseph Kosuth

1. *The Square Root
of Minus One #11*
1988, Photograph
and silkscreen on
glass, framed,
53³/₄" × 88¹/₂" × 5¹/₂"

2. *Word, Sentence, Paragraph
(V.&N.) #16*
1987, Mounted photo-
graph & neon,
113" × 105"

3. *Fetishism (Corrected) #7*
1988, Offset on paper in
wooden frame, neon and
glass tubing,
(violet neon)
104¹/₂" × 72"
28¹/₂" × 22¹/₂"
(framed offset)

Selected Biography:
1993 Solo exhibitions:
45th Biennale of
Venice, Hungarian
Pavilion, Venice, Italy,
June 13 - October 10;
Joseph Kosuth, Galeria
Juana De Aizpurn,
Sevilla, Spain, April
1992 Solo exhibitions:
"Joseph Kosuth;
Work,"
Hirshorn Museum and
Sculpture Garden,
Smithsonian Institution,
Washington, D.C.,
October 1, 1992-
January 25, 1993

STUART LEVY
FINE ART

588 Broadway, Suite 303
New York. NY 10012
212.941.0009
212.941.7987 FAX

Contact:
Stuart Levy, President

Exhibiting:
Contemporary Russian,
European and American
Artists

Leonid Lamm

Dollar
1990, Wood, 24 kt. gold
leaf and enamel,
107" x 36"x 32"

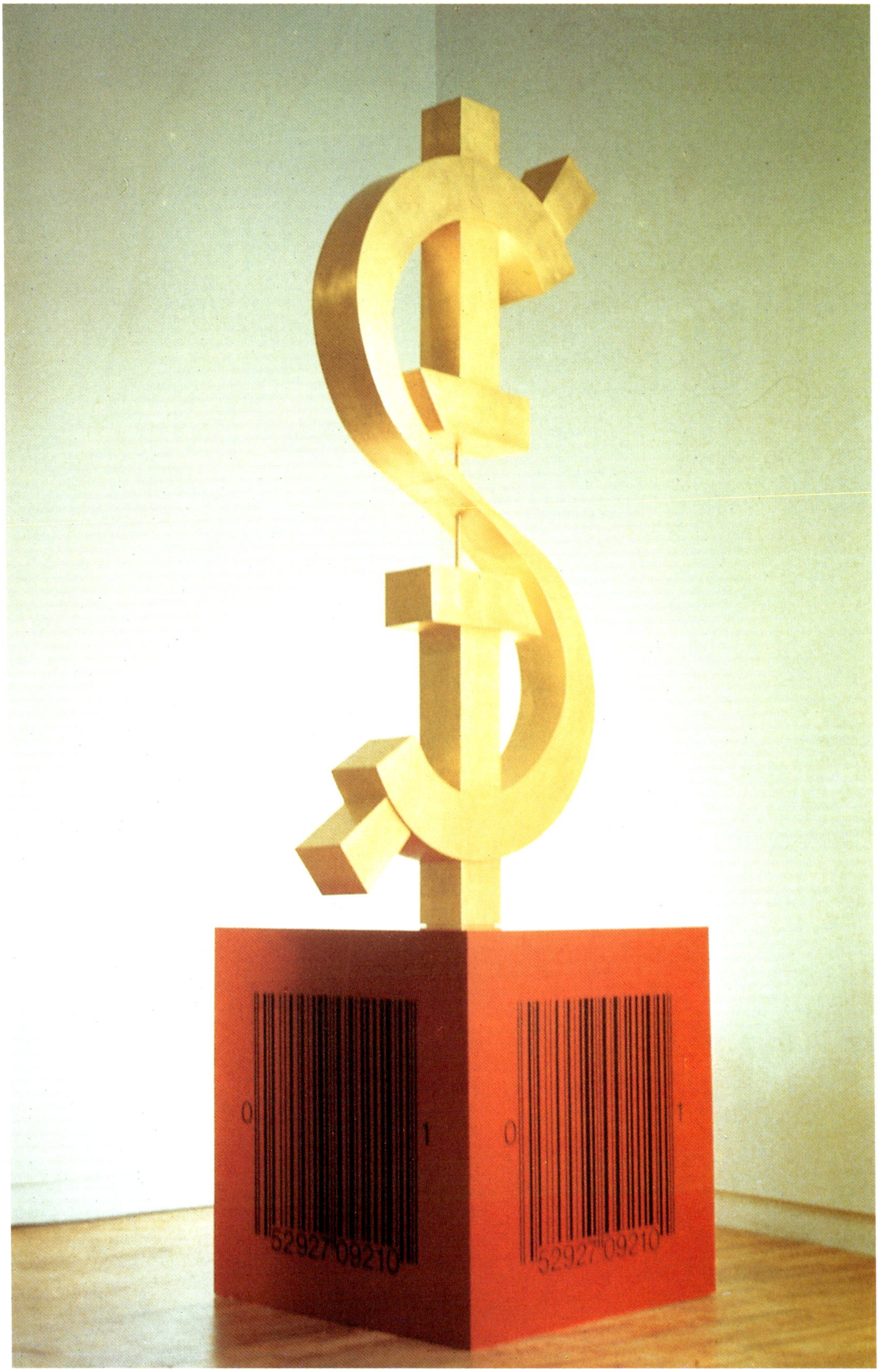

Selected Collections:

The Metropolitan
Museum of Art,
New York

The Jewish Museum,
New York

Stedeluk Museum,
Amsterdam

Russian State Museum,
St. Petersburg

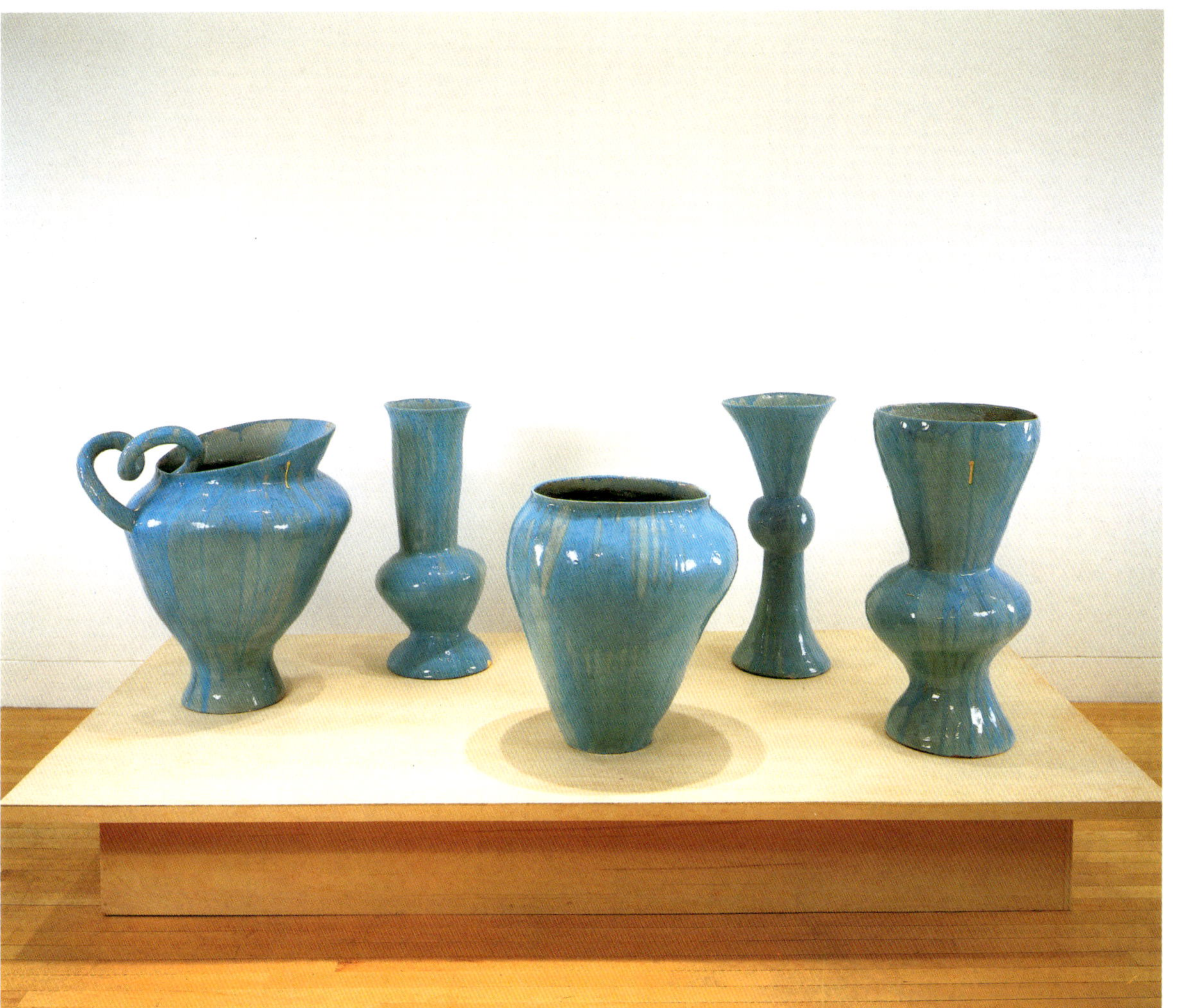

GAGOSIAN GALLERY

980 Madison Ave.
New York, NY 10021
212.744.2313
212.772.7962 FAX

136 Wooster Street
New York, NY 10012
212.228.2828
212.228.2878

Contact:
Melissa Lazarov, Director

Exhibiting:
20th-Century painting
and sculpture;
Abstract Expressionism,
Pop & Minimalism

Andrew Lord

*5 Pieces. Round. Tin and
Copper*
1991-92, Glazed ceramic
with epoxy, gold leaf and
encre de Chine, varying
dimensions.

Selected Biography:

1993 Solo exhibition:
Carnegie Museum,
Pittsburgh, PA

1992 Solo exhibition:
65 Thompson Street,
New York, NY;
Galerie Bruno
Bischofberger, Zurich

1990 Solo exhibition:
Anthony D'Offay
Gallery, London;
Group exhibition:
Gagosian Gallery,
New York, NY

GAGOSIAN GALLERY

980 Madison Ave
New York, NY 10021
212.744.2313
212.772.7962 FAX

136 Wooster Street
New York, NY 10012
212.228.2828
212.228.2878 FAX

Contact:
Melissa Lazarov, Director

Exhibiting:
20th-Century painting
and sculpture;
Abstract Expressionism,
Pop & Minimalism

Walter De Maria

5-7-9 Series:
Variation 9-7-5
1992, Solid stainless
0.steel on granite,
21 ⅝" × 26 ¾"

Selected Biography:
1993 Group show:
Susan Sheehan Gallery,
New York, NY
1992 Solo exhibition:
Kunsthaus Zurich,
Zurich;
Gagosian Gallery,
Wooster Street, New
York, NY
1991 Group Show:
Peggy Guggenheim
Collection, Solomon R.
Guggenheim
Foundation, Venice;
Musee D'Art
Contemporain,
Foundation Edelman,
Pully/Lausanne

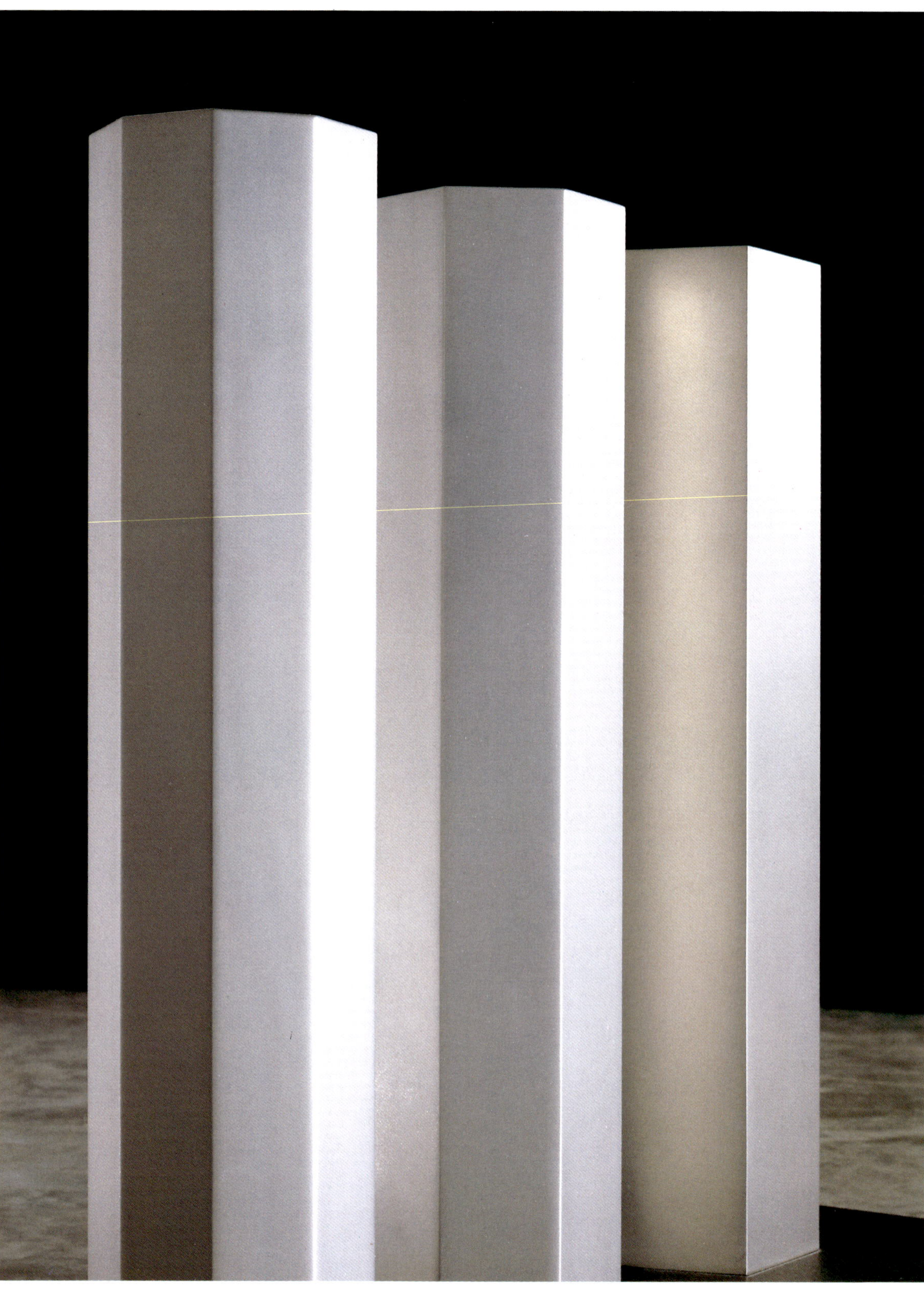

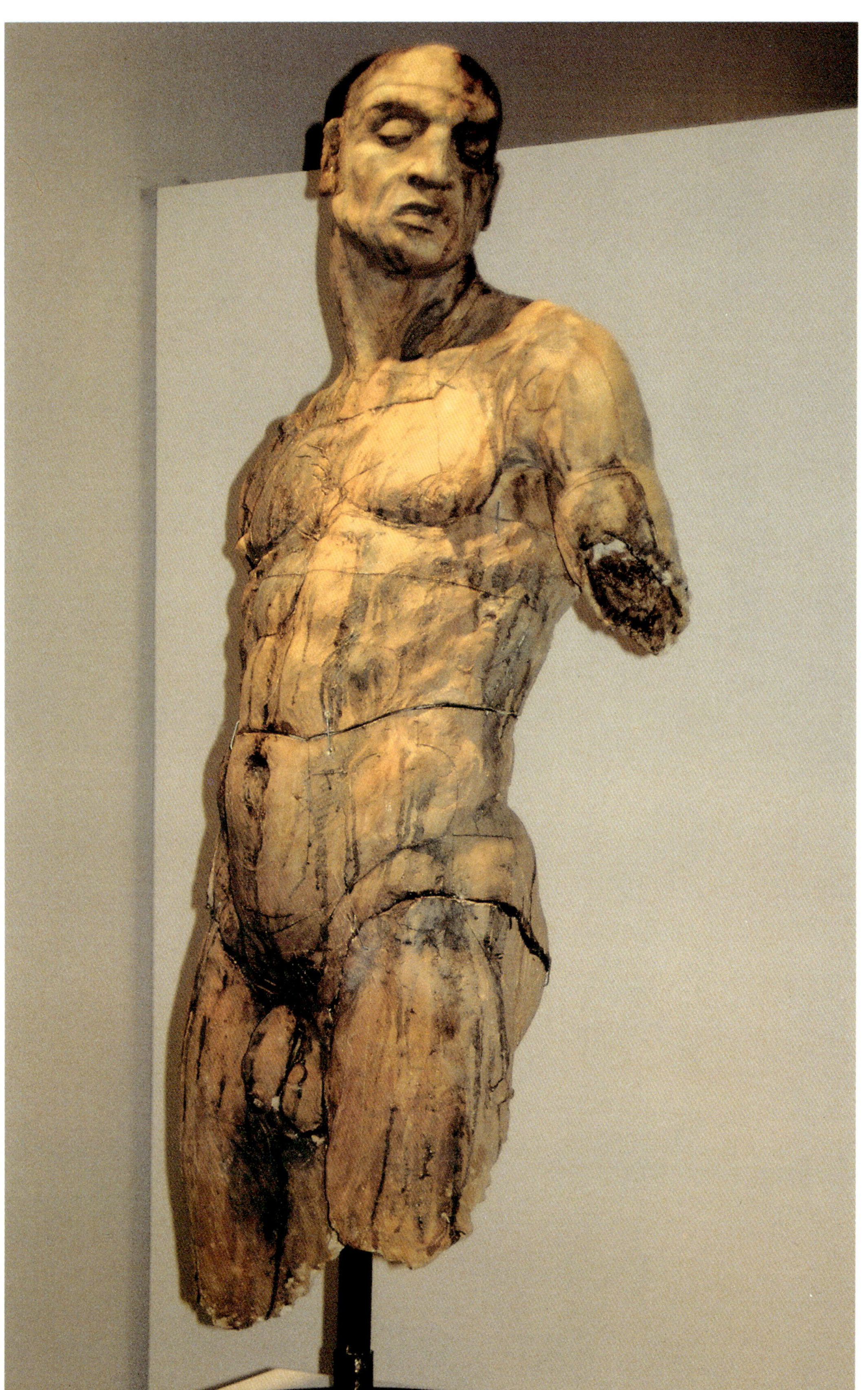

ITURRALDE GALLERY

154 N. La Brea Avenue
Los Angeles CA 90036
213.937.4267
213.937.4269 FAX

Contact:
Teresa Iturralde
Ana Iturralde

Exhibiting:
Contemporary Latin
American Art

Javier Marin

Torso de Hombre Amarillo
1993, Clay from Oaxaca
and Zacatecas with
engobes, 68¾"ht.

Selected Biography:

1994 Solo show, Museo de
Arte Contemporaneo
(MARCO),
Monterrey, Mexico

1993 Solo show,
Iturralde Gallery,
Los Angeles, CA

1992 "Terra Incognita",
Museo de Arte
Moderno, Mexico City

ROSENTHAL
FINE ART, INC.

640 N. La Salle St. suite 582
Chicago, IL 60610
312.642.2966
312.642.5169 FAX

Contact:
Dennis Rosenthal

Exhibiting:
20th century modern and
contemporary international
uniques and multiples

Louis Marinaro

1. *The Presentation*
   1987, Bronze,
   36" x 30" x 12"

1. *Perceptive-hone*
   1990-92, Bronze,
   23" x 22" x 31"

3. *Reflection*
   Bronze,
   33" x 12" x 12"

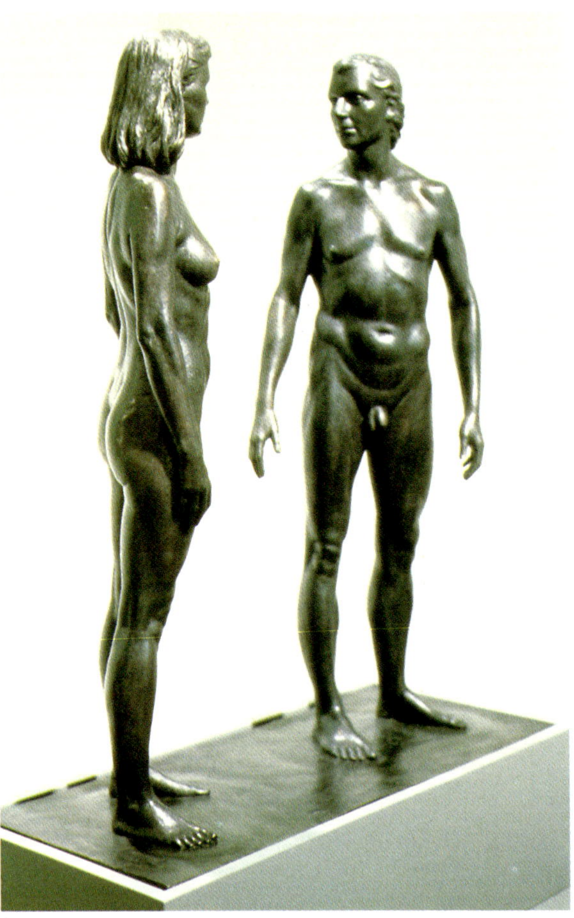

1

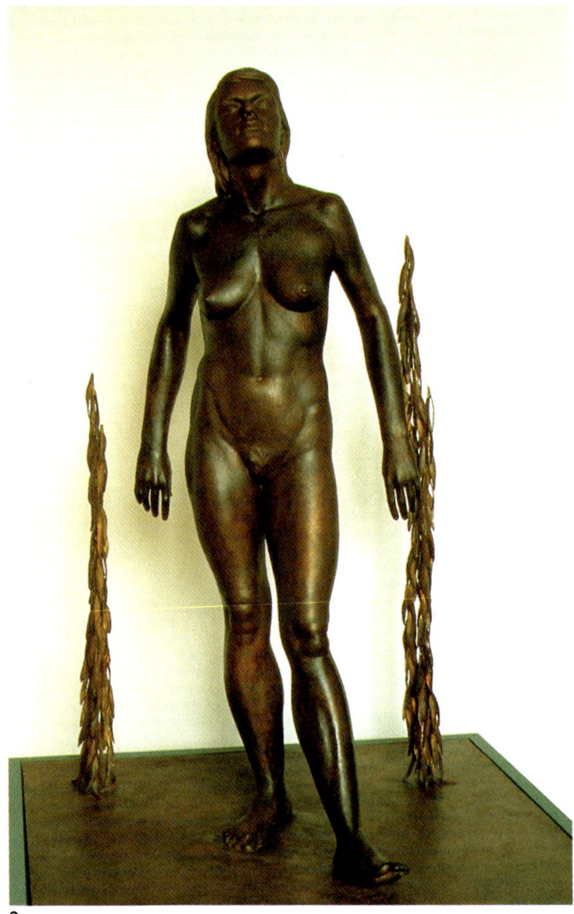

2

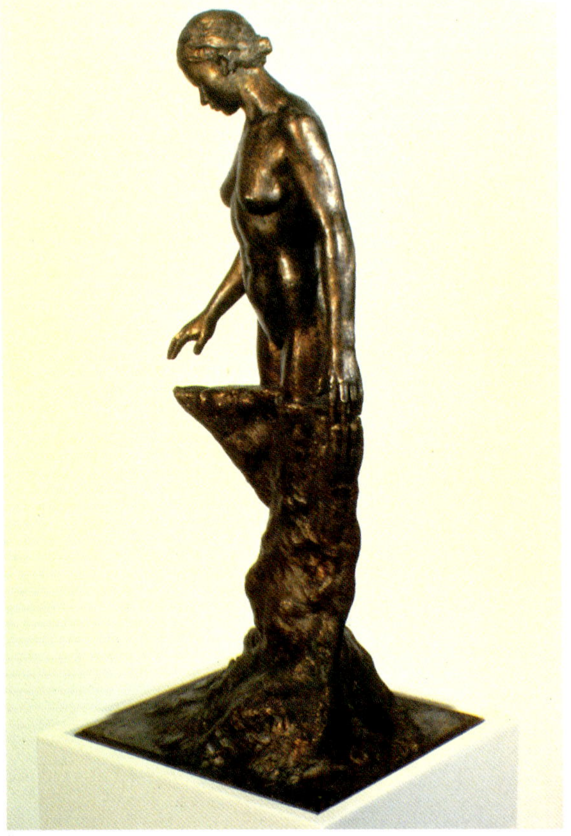

3

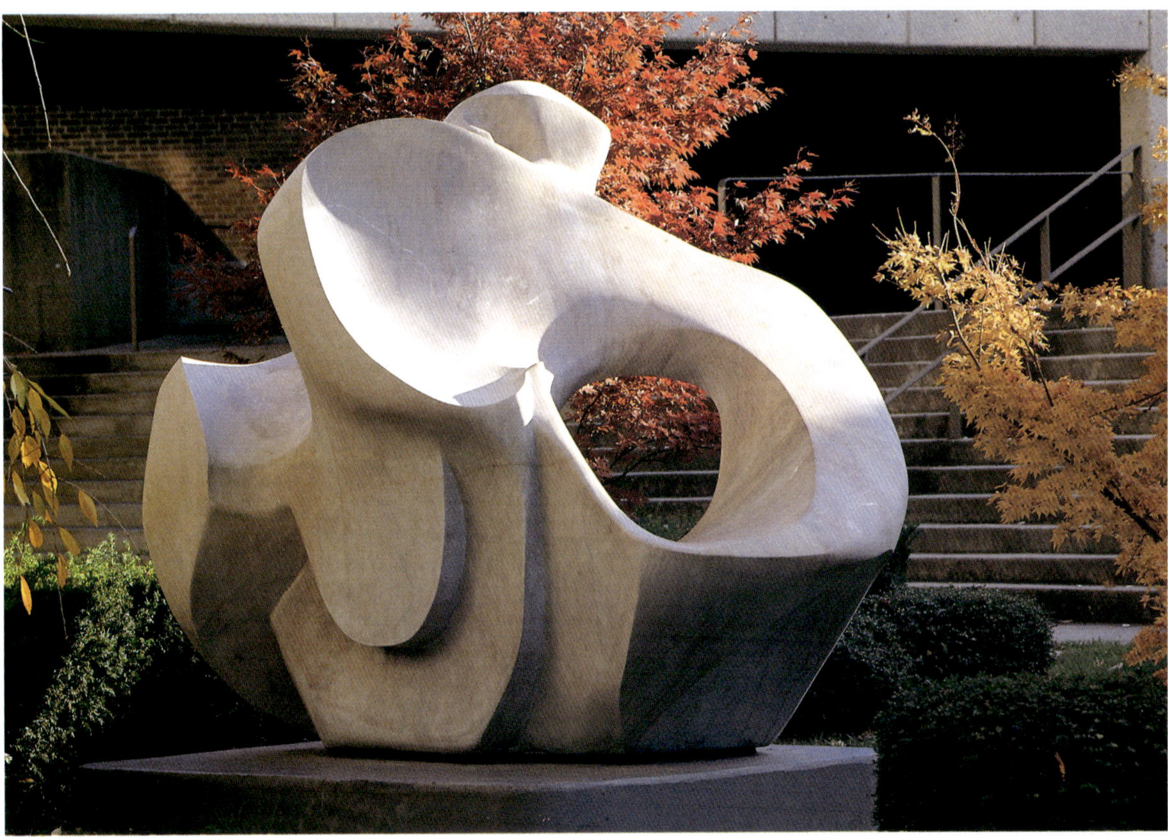

1

ALBERS FINE ART GALLERY

1102 Brookfield Rd.
Memphis, TN 38119
901.683.2256

Contact:
Kathy Albers, Director

Exhibiting:
Contemporary painting
sculpture, clay, glass, and
works on paper

Julie Warren Martin

1. *Genesis/Emergence*
   1987-89,
   Tennessee Marble,
   66" x 96" x 60"
   Located: College of Business,
   University of Tennessee, TN

2. *Flying Wallendas*
   1991, Italian and
   Yugoslavian marble,
   40 ^{1}/2" x 36" x 10"

3. *Passing*
   1992, Italian Marble,
   37" x 15" x 15"

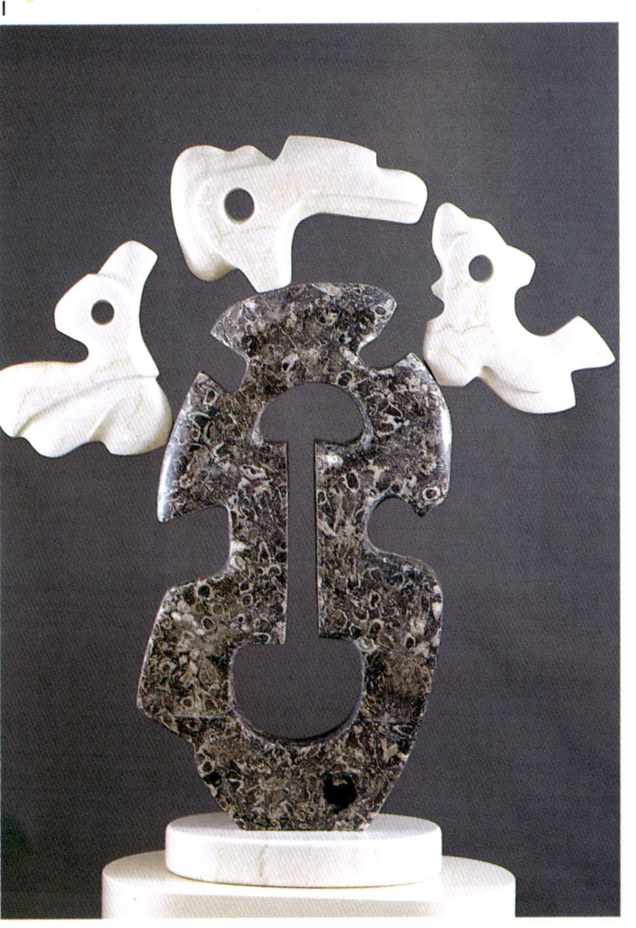

2

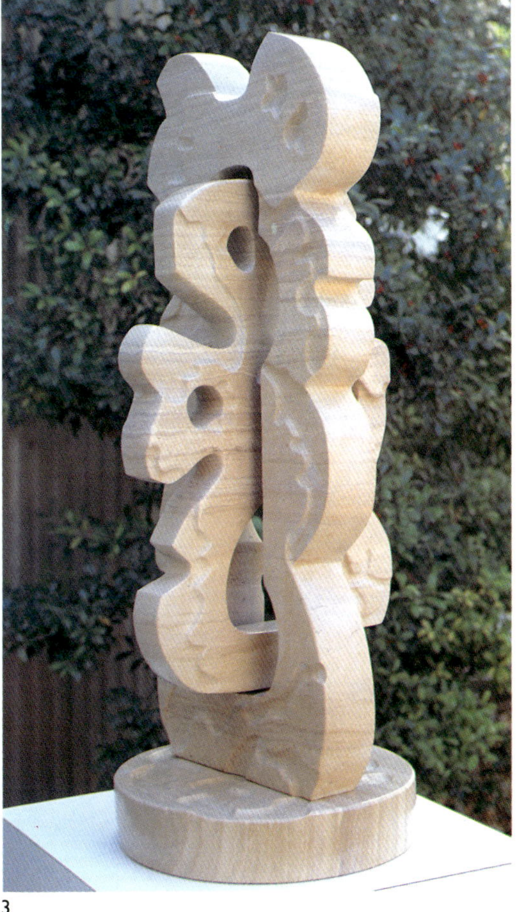

3

Selected Collections:

First Tennessee Bank,
Knoxville/Memphis, TN

Glaxo, Inc., Research
Triangle Park, NC

Hirshhorn Private
Collection

The Hunter Museum,
Chattanooga, TN

Memphis Cancer
Center, Memphis, TN

CHARLES WHITCHURCH GALLERY

5973 Engineer Drive
Huntington Beach, CA 92649
714.373.4459
714.373.4615 FAX

Contact:
Charles Whitchurch

Exhibiting:
Modern and contemporary painting, graphic works and sculpture

Karl Momen

Metropolis
1990, Bronze with patina,
60" x 60" x 60"
also:
19" x 12" x 17⅓", ed. 7

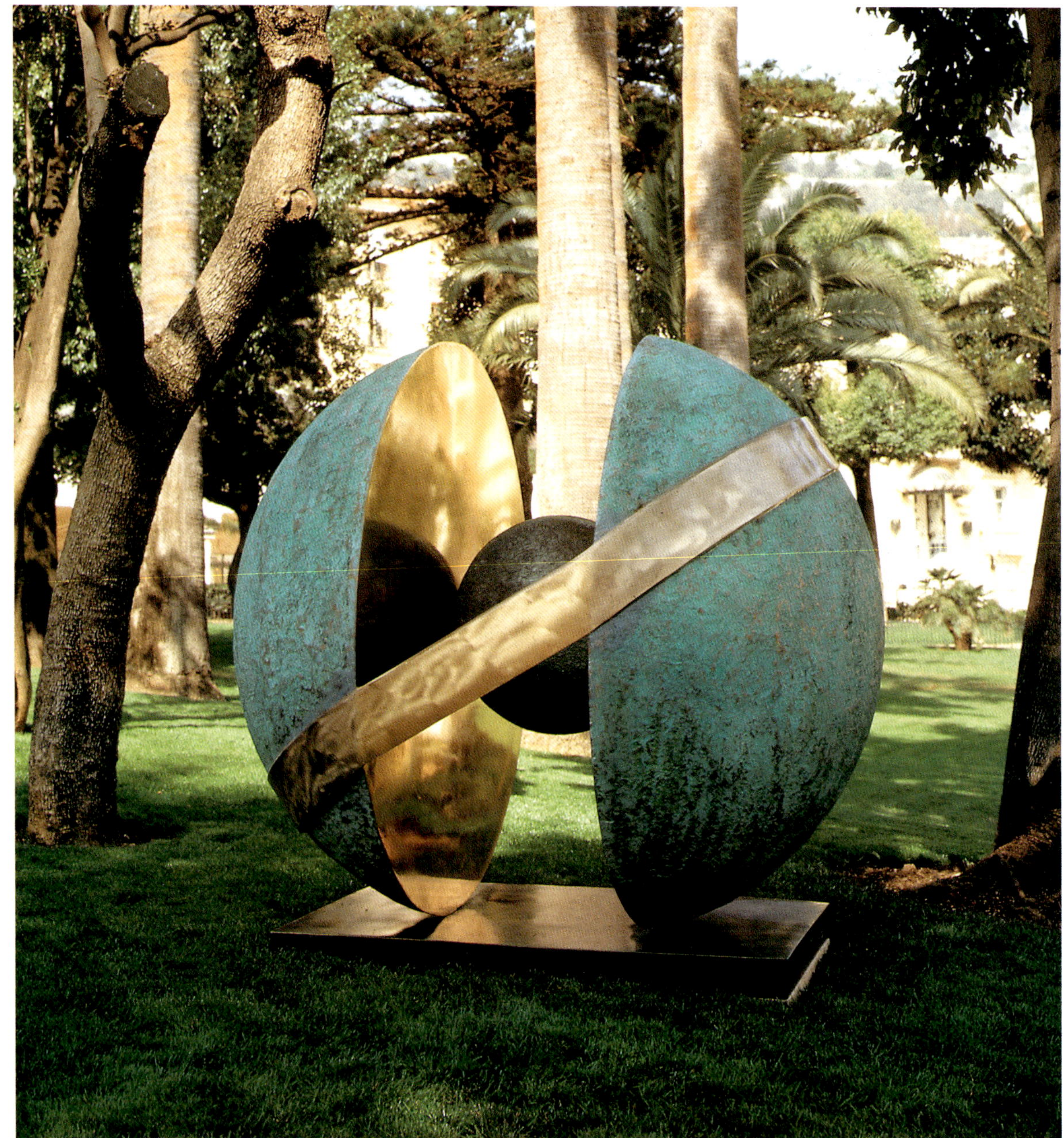

Selected Biography:

1995 Solo exhibition:
Marisa del Re Gallery

1993 Group exhibition:
Biennale de Sculpture,
Monte Carlo

1985 Group exhibition:
Moderne Museet,
Stockholm

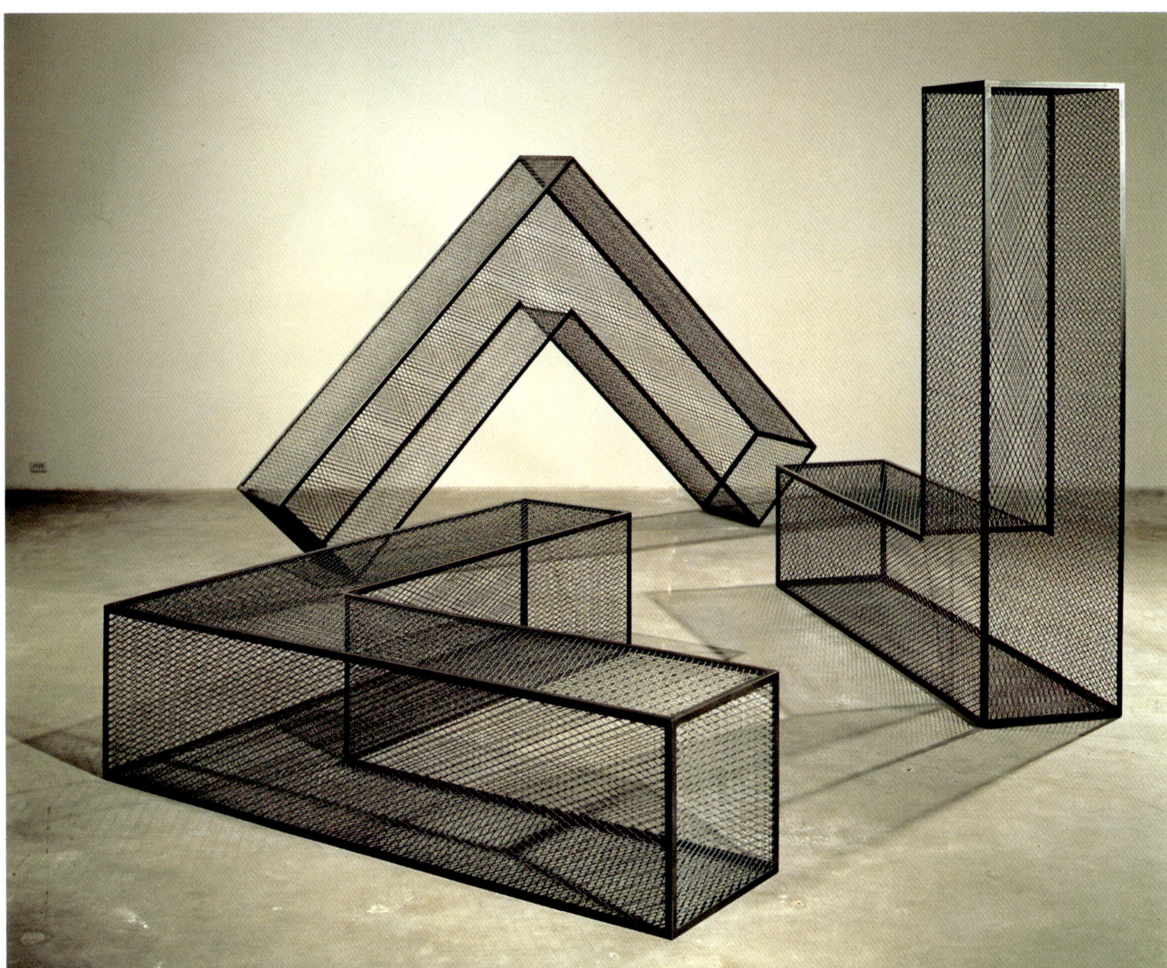

1

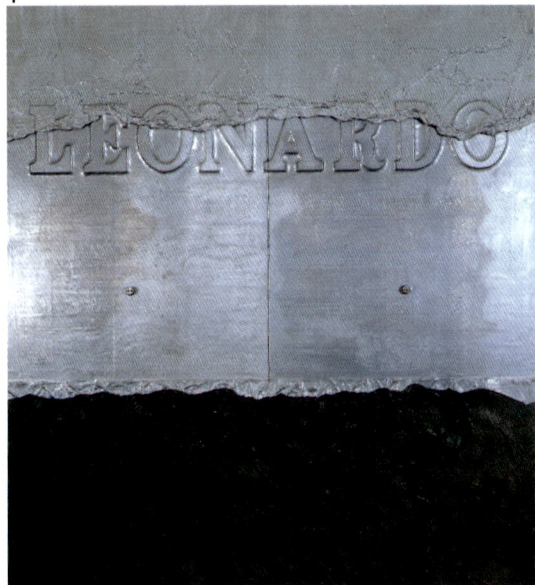

2

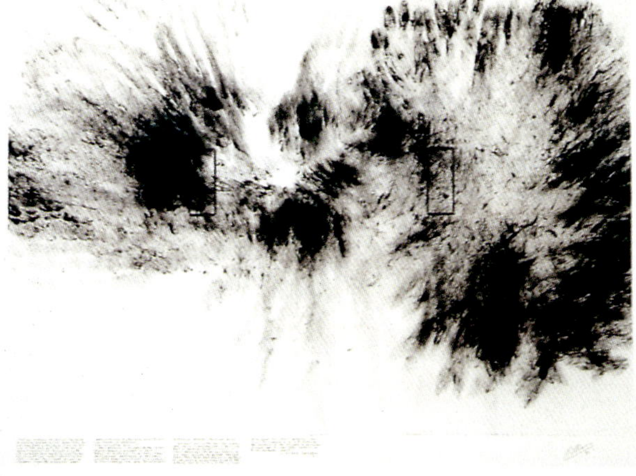

3

LEO CASTELLI

420 W. Broadway
New York, NY 10012
212.431.5160
212.431.5361 FAX

Contact:
Susan Brundage

Robert Morris

1. *The Ells*
   1965-88, Expanded steel,
   3 parts: 96" x 96" x 24"
   each.

2. *Leonardo*
   1990, Lead, steel
   and cast resin,
   91^{1}/8" x 85^{1}/8" x 3"

3. *Blind Time IV, #60*
   1991, Graphite
   on paper,
   38" x 50"

Selected Biography:
1993 Solo exhibitions:
     The Films of Robert
     Morris, Tate Gallery,
     London, March - April;
     "Robert Morris",
     Akira Ikeda Gallery,
     Taura, Japan,
     Aug. 7 - Oct. 30;
     Solo exhibition:
     "Four Corners: I-Beam
     Pieces", 65 Thompson
     Street, New York, NY,
     Sept. 25 - Oct. 23; Solo
     exhibition: "Blind Time
     IV: Drawing with
     Davidson", Leo Castelli
     Gallery, 578 Broadway,
     New York, NY,
     Sept. 25 - Oct. 23

HELLER GALLERY

71 Greene Street
New York, NY 10012
212.966.5948
212.966.5956 FAX

Contact:
Douglas Heller

Exhibiting:
Contemporary glass
sculpture

Jay Musler

1. *Outside World*
    1993, Glass, oil pigment,
    55" x 17" x 7½"

2. *Floating Dream*
    1994, Glass, oil pigment,
    6" x 56" x 10"

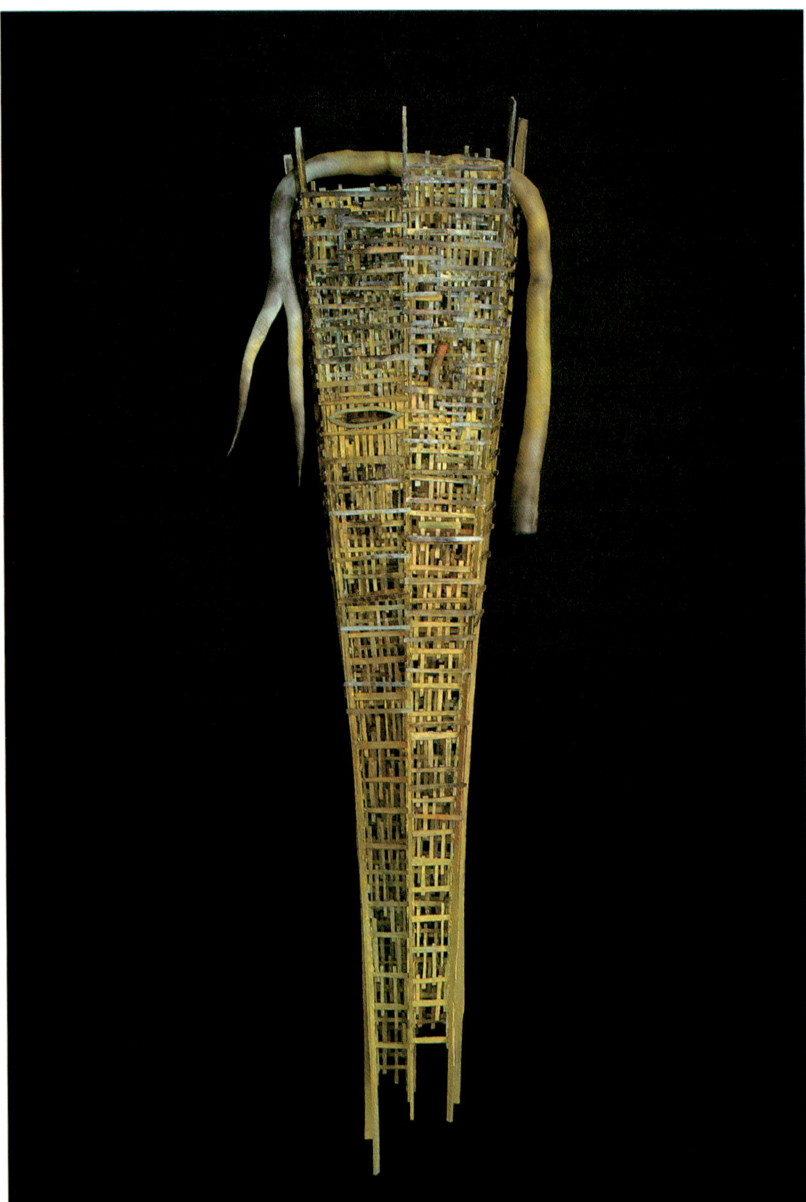

1

Selected Collections:

The Corning
Museum of Glass,
Corning, NY

Hokkaido
Museum of Art,
Sapporo, Japan

Los Angeles County
Museum of Art,
Los Angeles, CA

Museé des
Arts Décoratifs,
Lausanne, Switzerland

Toledo Museum of Art,
Toledo, OH

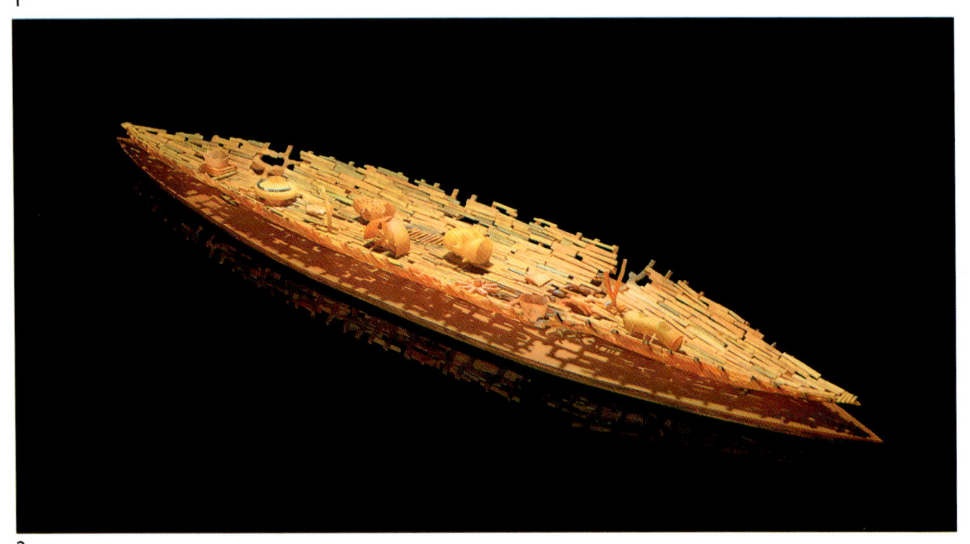

2

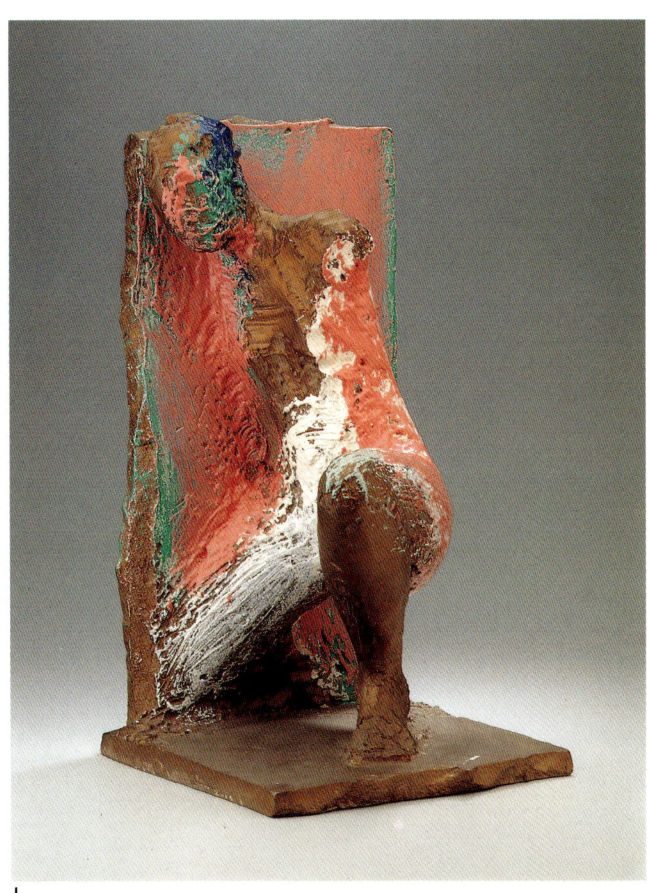

1

ROBISCHON GALLERY

1740 Wazee Street
Denver, CO 80202
303.298.7788
303.298.7799 FAX

Contact:
James Robischon

Exhibiting:
Contemporary fine art

Manuel Neri

1. *Isla Negra II*
   1988/89,
   Enamel on bronze,
   19"h x 10"w x 10"d
   edition of 4

2. *Study for Espanola*
   1993/94,
   Enamel on bronze,
   22"h x 6¾"w x 7"d

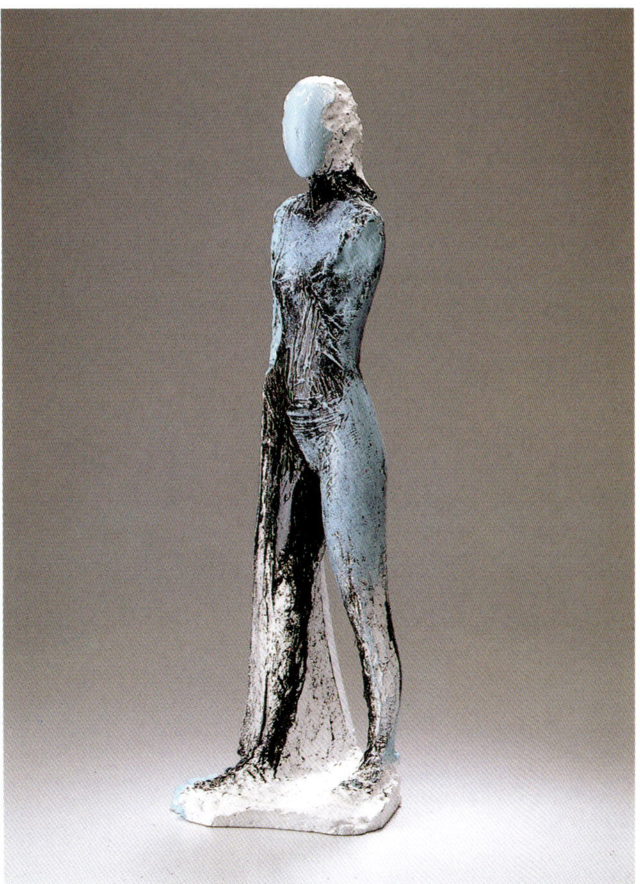

2

Selected Biography:

Solo and group exhibits
in over 100 museum in
the U.S. and abroad
including:

Corcoran Gallery
of Art, DC;
Whitney Museum, NY;
Hirshhorn
Museum, NY;
San Francisco Museum
of Modern Art, CA;
Los Angeles County
Museum of Art, CA;
Denver Art
Museum, CO

ENID OKLA HOMA

233 West Huron
Chicago, IL 60610
312.787.6011
312.787.6617 FAX

Contact:
Celeste Sotola, Director

Exhibiting:
Contemporary painting,
sculpture, and objects

Stephan Nesvacil

*Lazarus
(Death of the Light)*
1992, Mixed

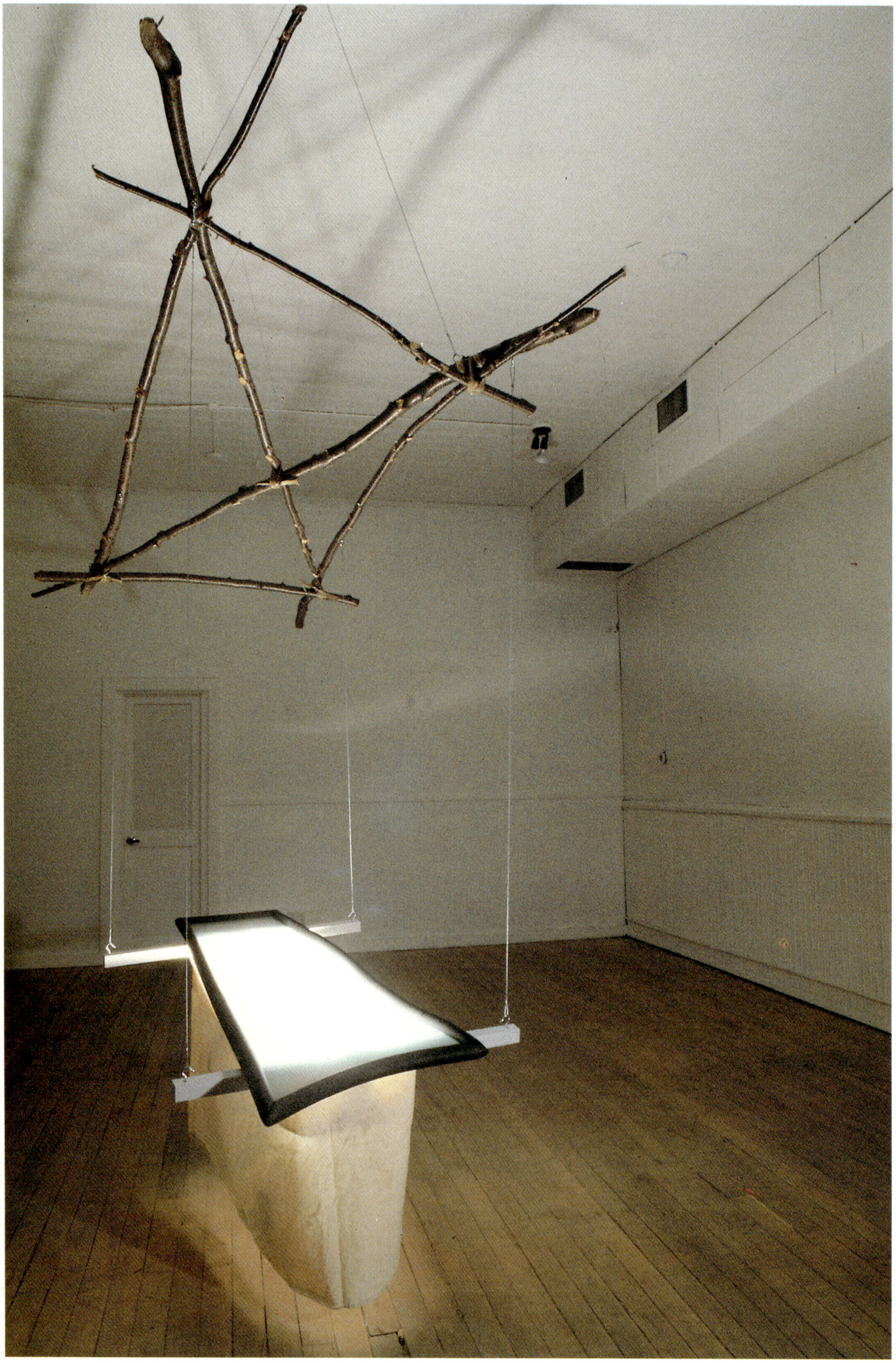

Selected Biography:

1987 to present work
lamont the Loss of
value and qualities
of Life

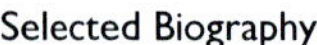

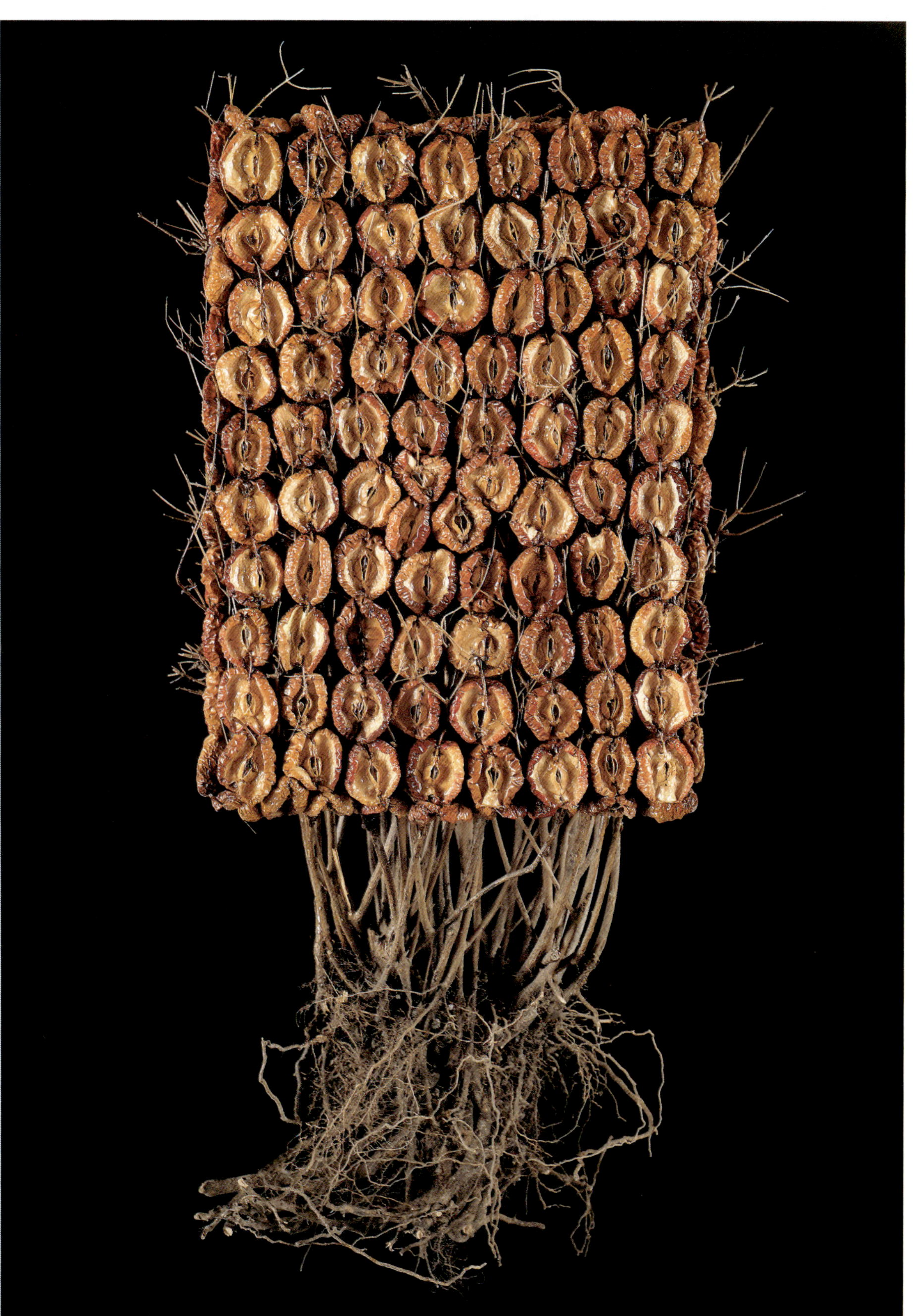

SPACE GALLERY

1945 West North Avenue
Chicago, IL 60622
312.276.5146
312.226.5587 FAX

Contact:
Fitz Gerald

Exhibiting:
Emerging contemporary
paintings, sculpture and
photography

Tom Osborn

Untitled tree box (apple) #9
1993, Mixed media,
46" x 28" x 16"

PAGE PENNA
STUDIO

P.O. Box 4
Harrods Creek, KY 40027
502.228.3149
502.228.0115 FAX

Contact:
Vicki Hull

Exhibiting:
Commissioned fine art
and architectural
installations in glass

Page Penna

1. *Seventy-five*
   Glass, painted and
   mirrored, granite,
   and platinum,
   11" x 7.5" x 7.5"
   Collection: Swenska Tobaks
   Corp., Sweden

2. *The Brown and
   Williamson I. W. Hughes
   Technical Center,
   Dedication Commission*
   Glass, sandblasted,
   etched, and painted
   8' x 10' x 2'; 1,200 lbs.

3-5 *Detail*

Selected Collections:
   Swenska Tobaks
   Corporation, Sweden;
   Vencor, Inc.;
   John Conti Coffee
   Company, Inc.;
   Brown and
   Williamson Tobacco
   Corporation; Alabama
   Power and Light;
   B. W. Fine, V. P.,
   Art in America

Selected Biography:
Page Penna is a third generation
glass artist and painter. Penna has
lived and worked in New York,
Florida, and now resides in
Louisville, KY. The focus of her
work is to combine the skills she
has acquired in her twenty years
in painting, glass, and design, into
creating fine art glass installations

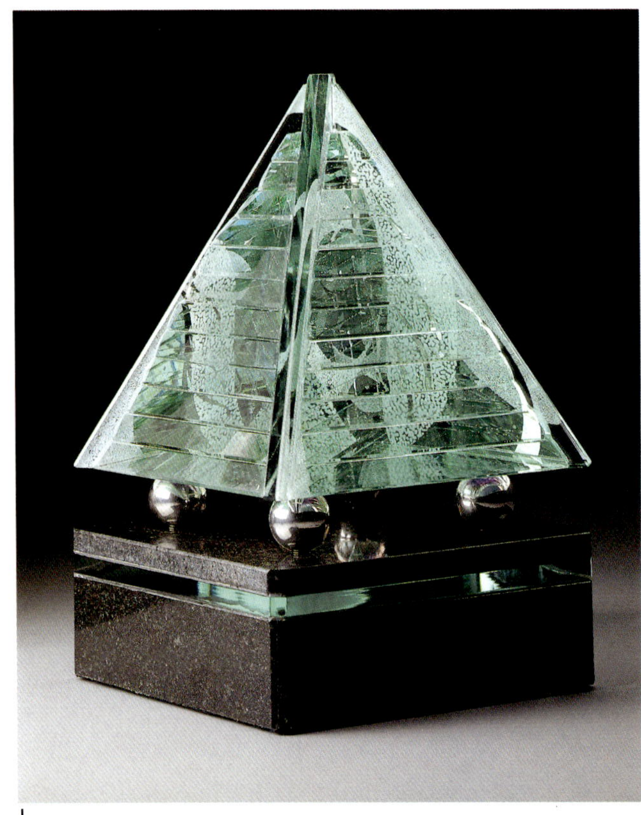

1

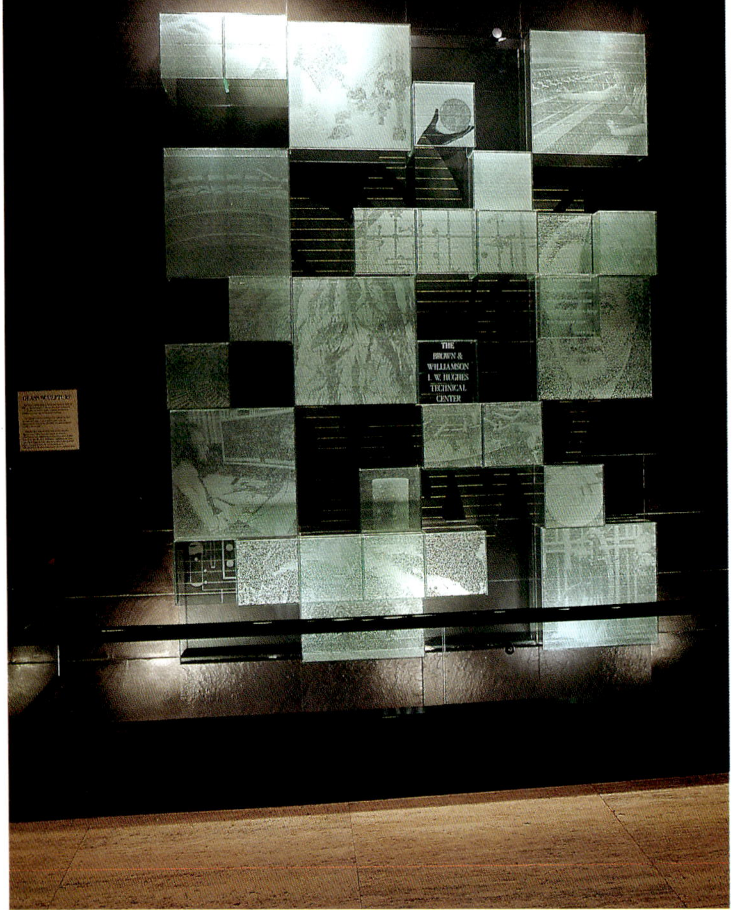

2

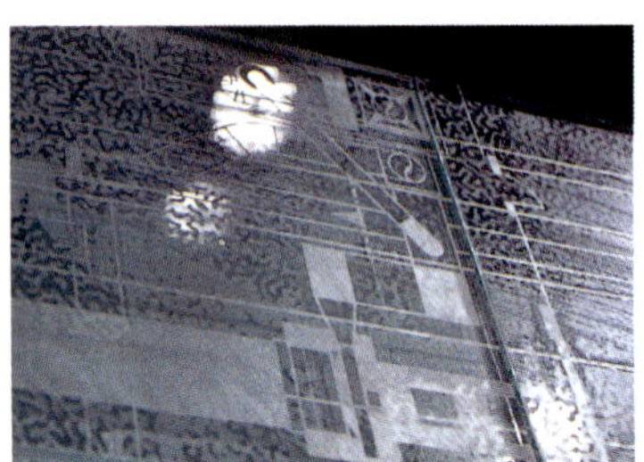

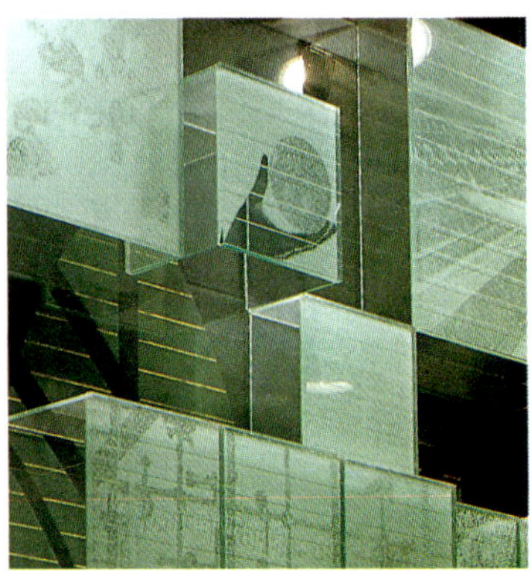

3-5

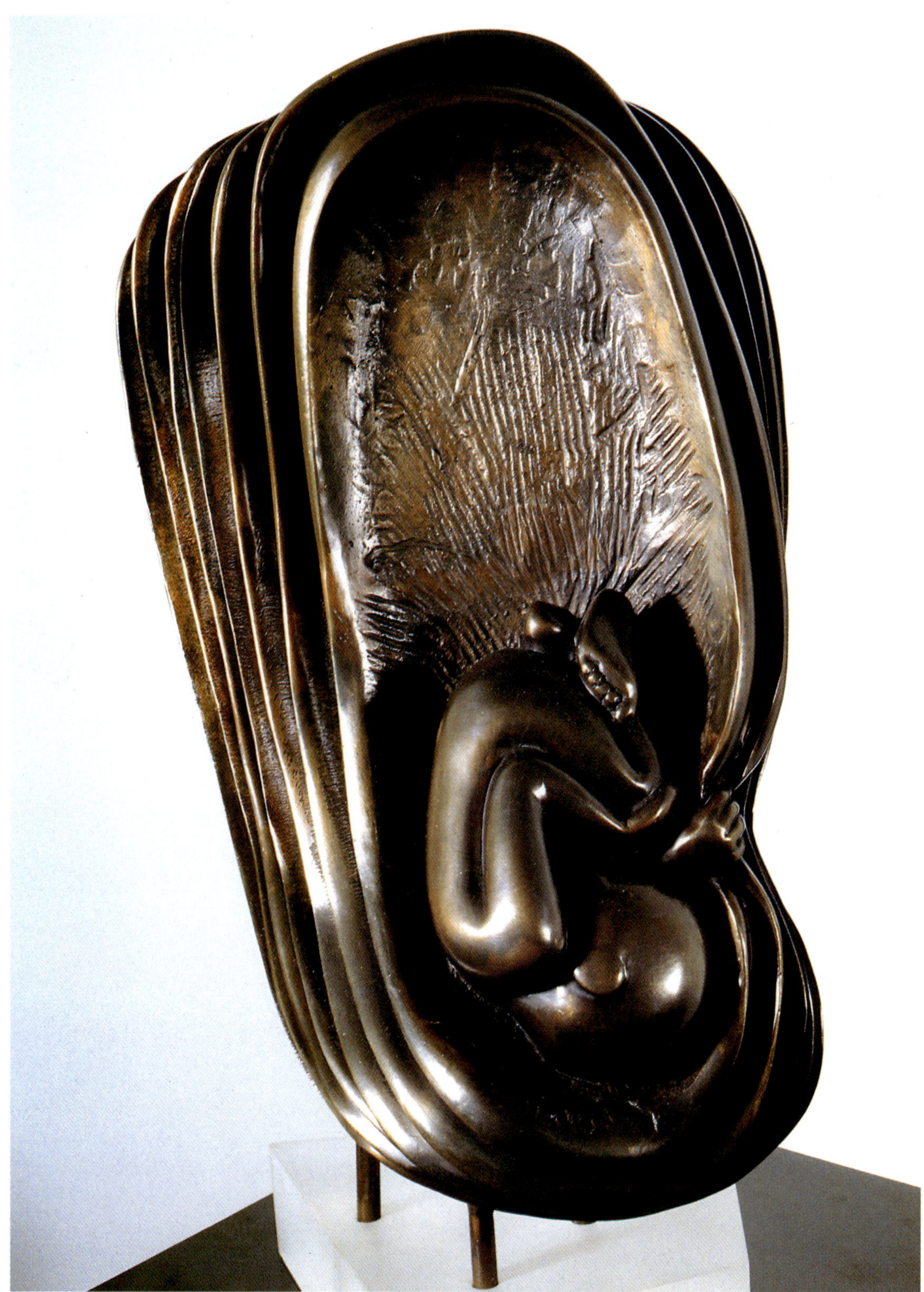

FENIX FINE ARTS

180 N.E. 40th St.
Miami, FL 33137
305.573.2727
305.542.8289
305.576.7707 FAX

Contact:
George Gandelman

Exhibiting:
Latin American Art

Nira Raz

Genesis
Lost wax Bronze

Selected Biography:

1993 Chagall House, The
Israeli Painters and
Sculptors Association
House, Haifa, Israel

Technion, Israel
Institute of Technology,
Haifa, Israel

Haifa Museum,
Haifa, Israel

DIANE FARRIS GALLERY

1565 West 7th Avenue
Vancouver B.C. V6J 1S1
Canada
604.737.2629
604.737.2675 FAX

Contact:
Diane Farris, Director

Exhibiting:
Contemporary Canadian
and International Art

David Robinson

1. *Artifice & Edifice*
   1993, polymer-gypsum,
   egg tempera, steel,
   48" x 22" x 144"

2. *By Any Means*
   1993, polymer-gypsum,
   egg tempera, steel,
   108" x 22" x 75"

3. *Resonant Silence*
   1993 edition of 3,
   polymer-gypsum, egg
   tempera and wood,
   detail of sculpture,
   44" x 19" x 12",

Selected Biography:

1994   Solo show,
       Diane Farris Gallery,
       Vancouver, BC
1994   Solo show,
       Diane Farris Gallery,
       Vancouver, BC;
       London Life Young
       Contemporaries
       (National Touring
       Exhibition), London
       Regional Art Gallery,
       London, ON
1992   "Exalted Humans",
       Solo show,
       Lookout Gallery,
       Regent College,
       University of B.C.,
       Vancouver, BC

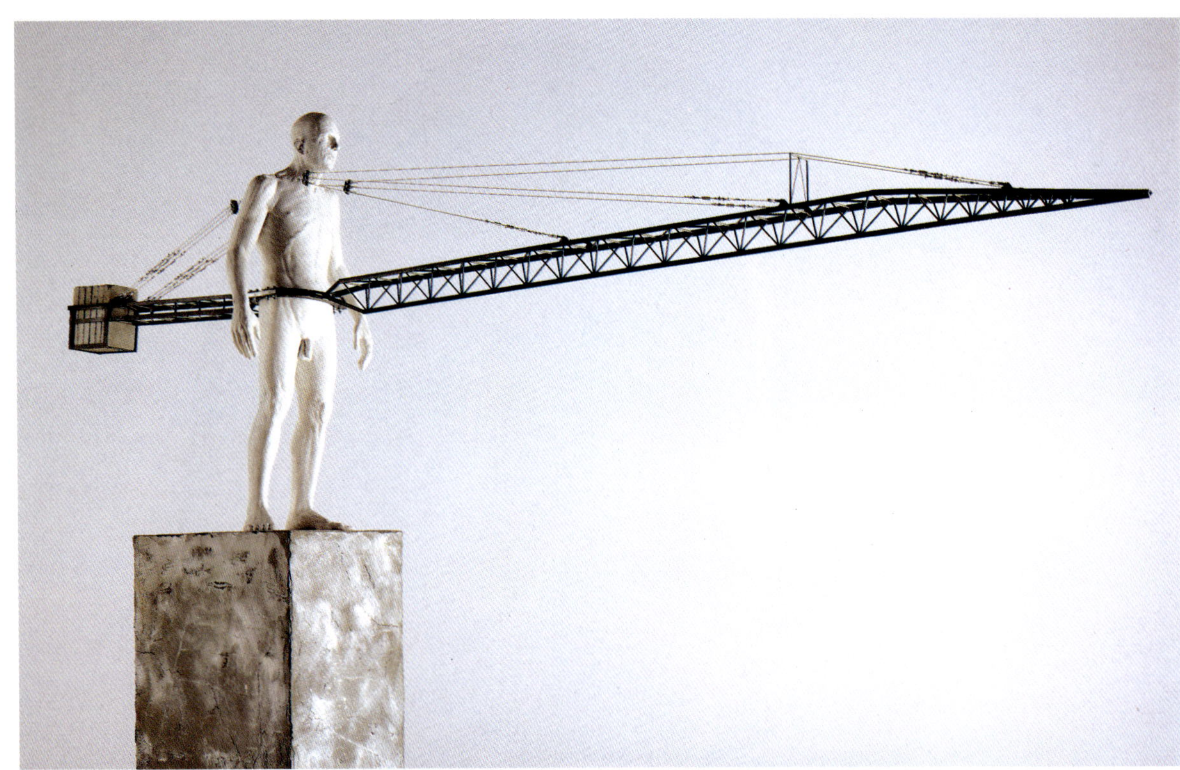

1

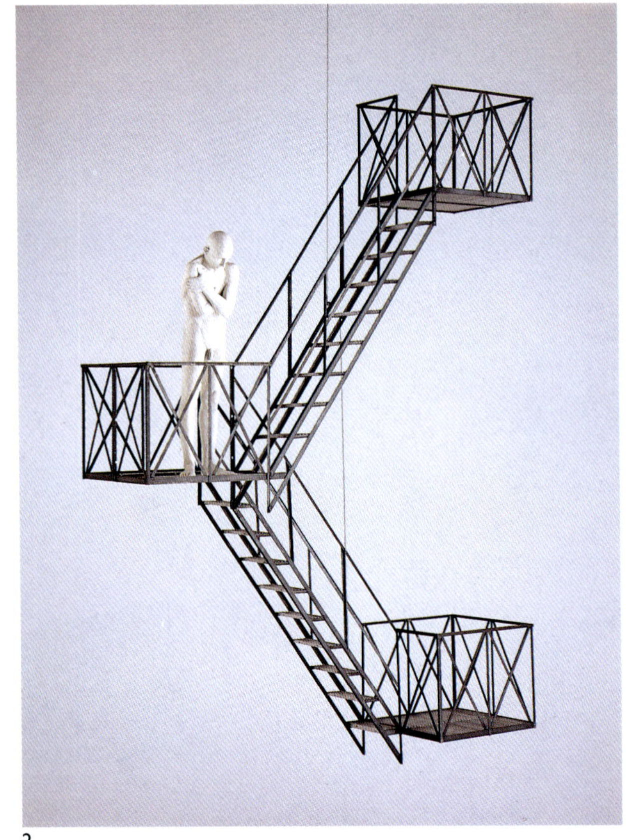

2

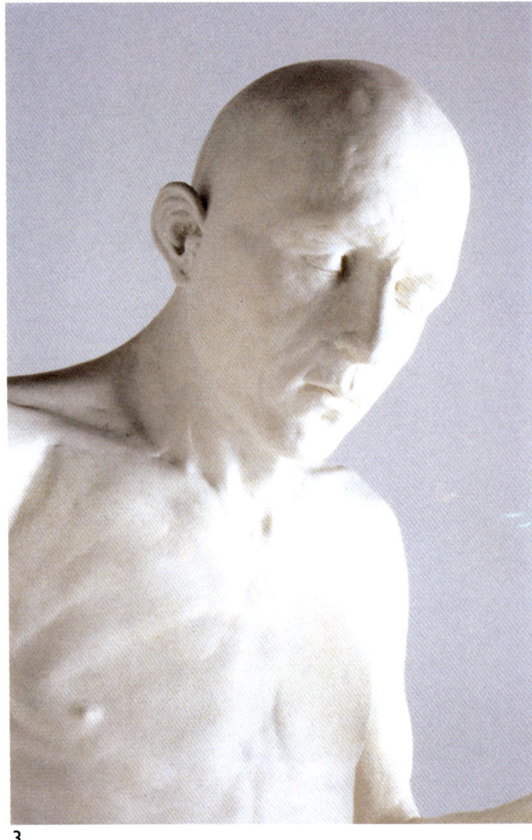

3

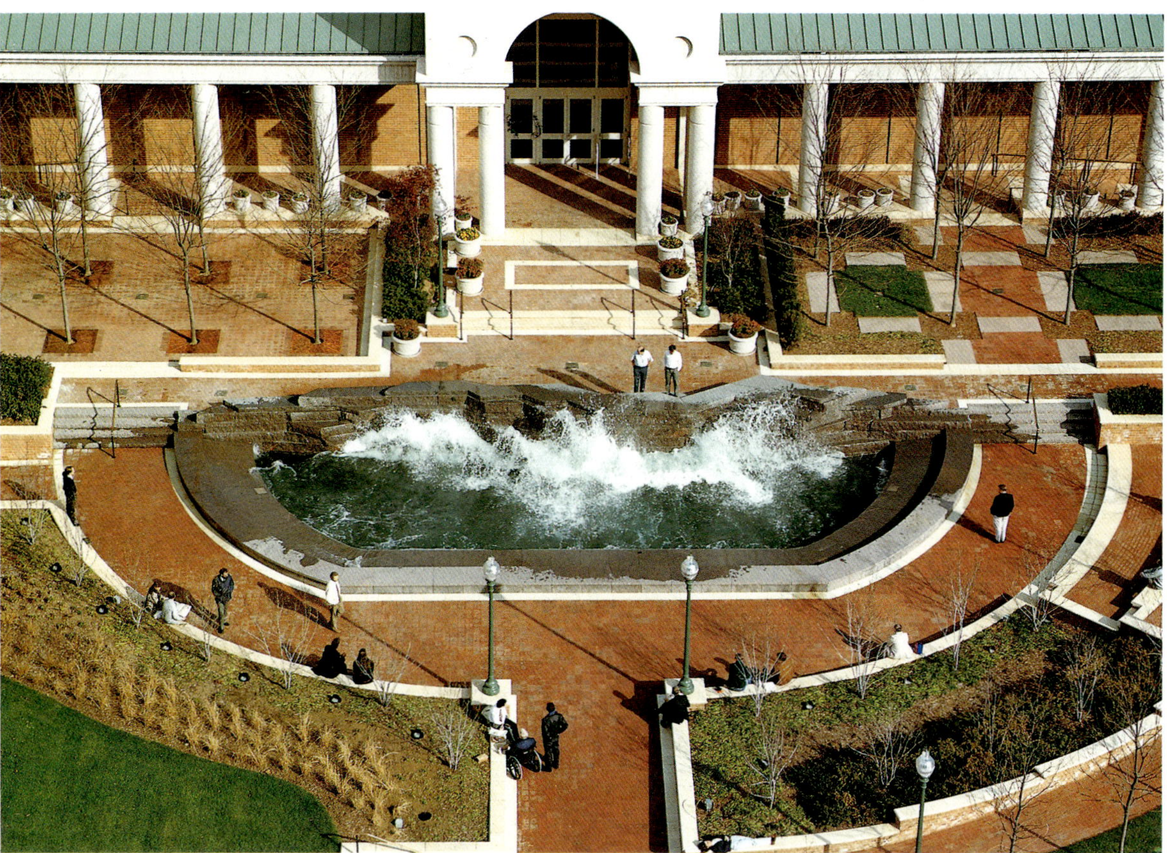

1

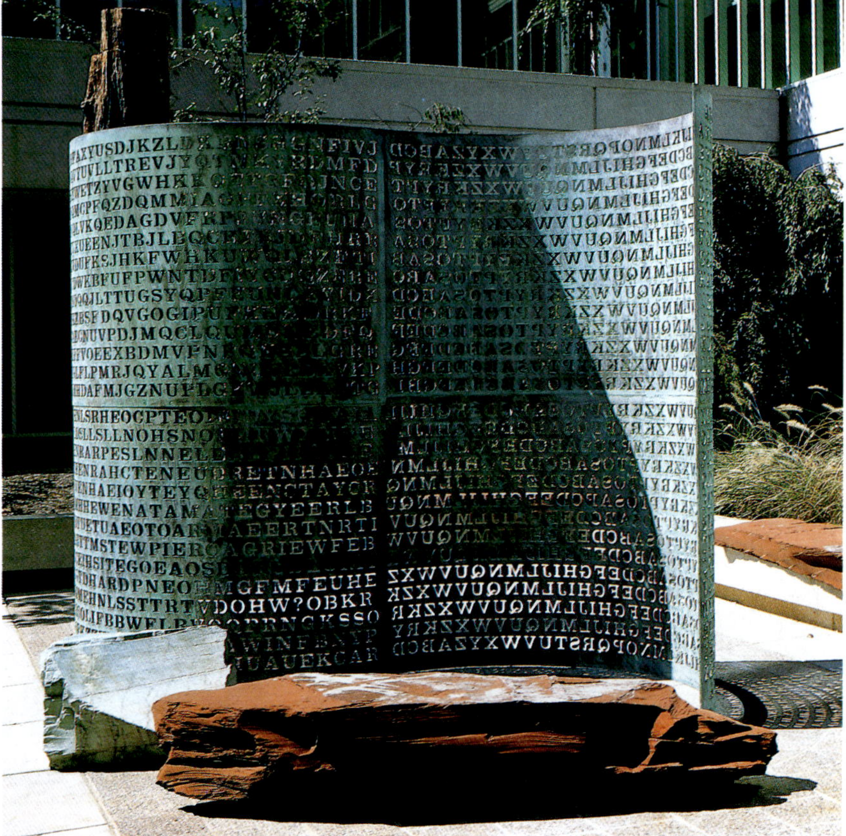

2

NANCY DRYSDALE GALLERY

2103 O Street, NW
Washington, DC 20037
202.466.4550
202.466.4549 FAX

Contact:
Nancy Drysdale

Exhibiting:
Contemporary art
in all media

Jim Sanborn

1   *Coastline*
    1993, Granite, water
    and wave generator,
    Pool: 70 ft. wide x 20 ft.
    Plaza: 300 ft. x 300 ft.
    Site: National Oceanic &
    Atmospheric Administration
    (NOAA), Silver Spring, MD

2   *Kryptos*
    1988-90, Copper screen,
    encoded text, stone and
    petrified tree,
    144 x 360 x 300 inches
    Site: The Central Intelligence
    Agency, McLean, VA

Selected Biography:

1994   "Metaphysical
       Metaphors", High
       Museum, Atlanta, GA

       Nancy Drysdale Gallery
       Washington, DC

1993   Orlando Museum of
       Fine Arts, Orlando, FL

1992   Corcoran Gallery of
       Art, Washington, DC

       "Dialogue with Nature"
       The Phillips Collection,
       Washington, DC

JOAN SHERMAN STUDIO

135 Greene Street
New York, NY 10012
212.387.0866
212.505.8550 FAX

Contact:
Joan Sherman, Director

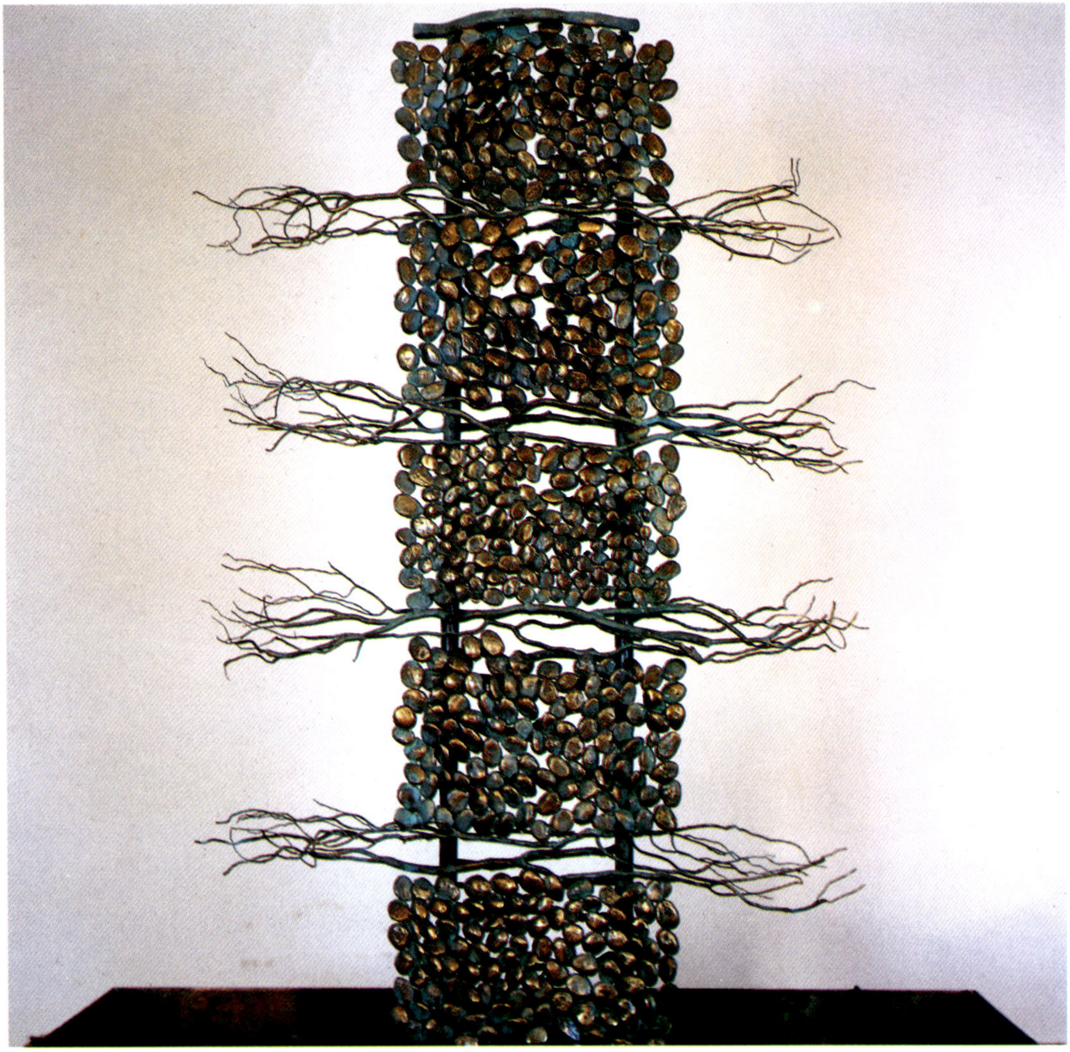

Joan Sherman

1. *Riverbed*
   1993, Bronze, waterfall,
   7' x6' x 2'

2. *Detail of Riverbed*

3. *Garden Path*
   1993, Bronze,
   82" x 16" x 7"

Selected Biography:

1992 Tribeca Gallery,
      New York, NY

1988 Solo exhibition:
      The Evansville Museum
      of Arts and Science,
      Indiana, IN

1985 Concord Gallery,
      New York, NY

1984 Solo exhibition:
      City Center Theater,
      New York, NY

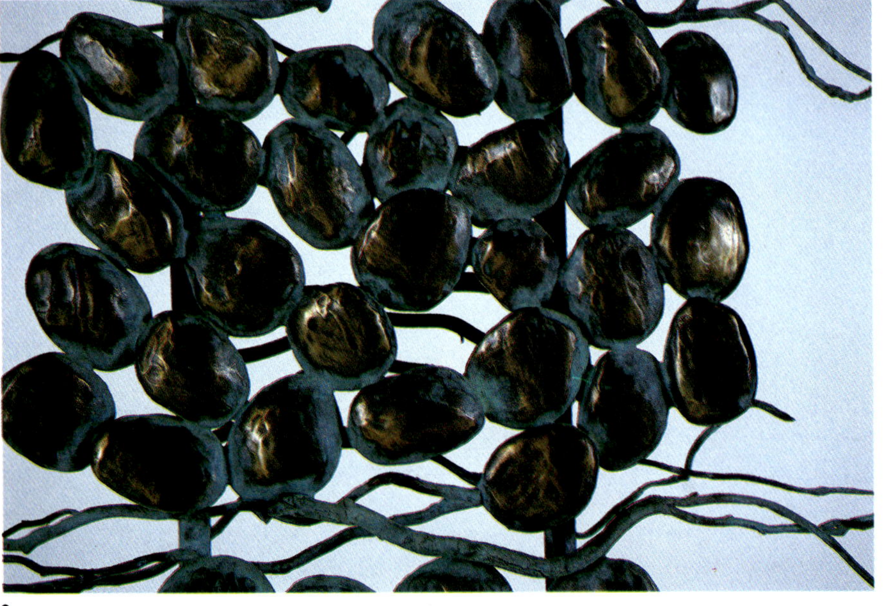

1

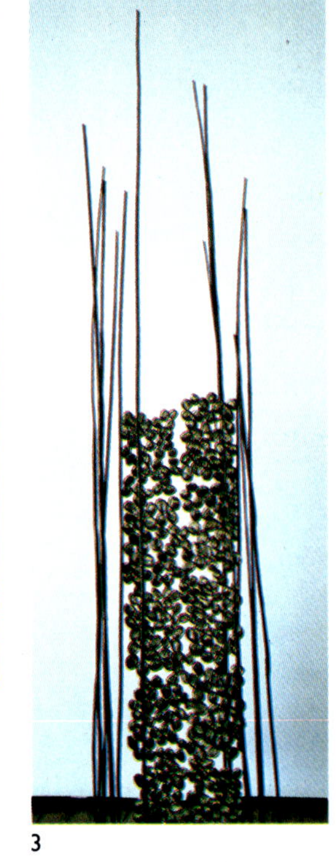

2

3

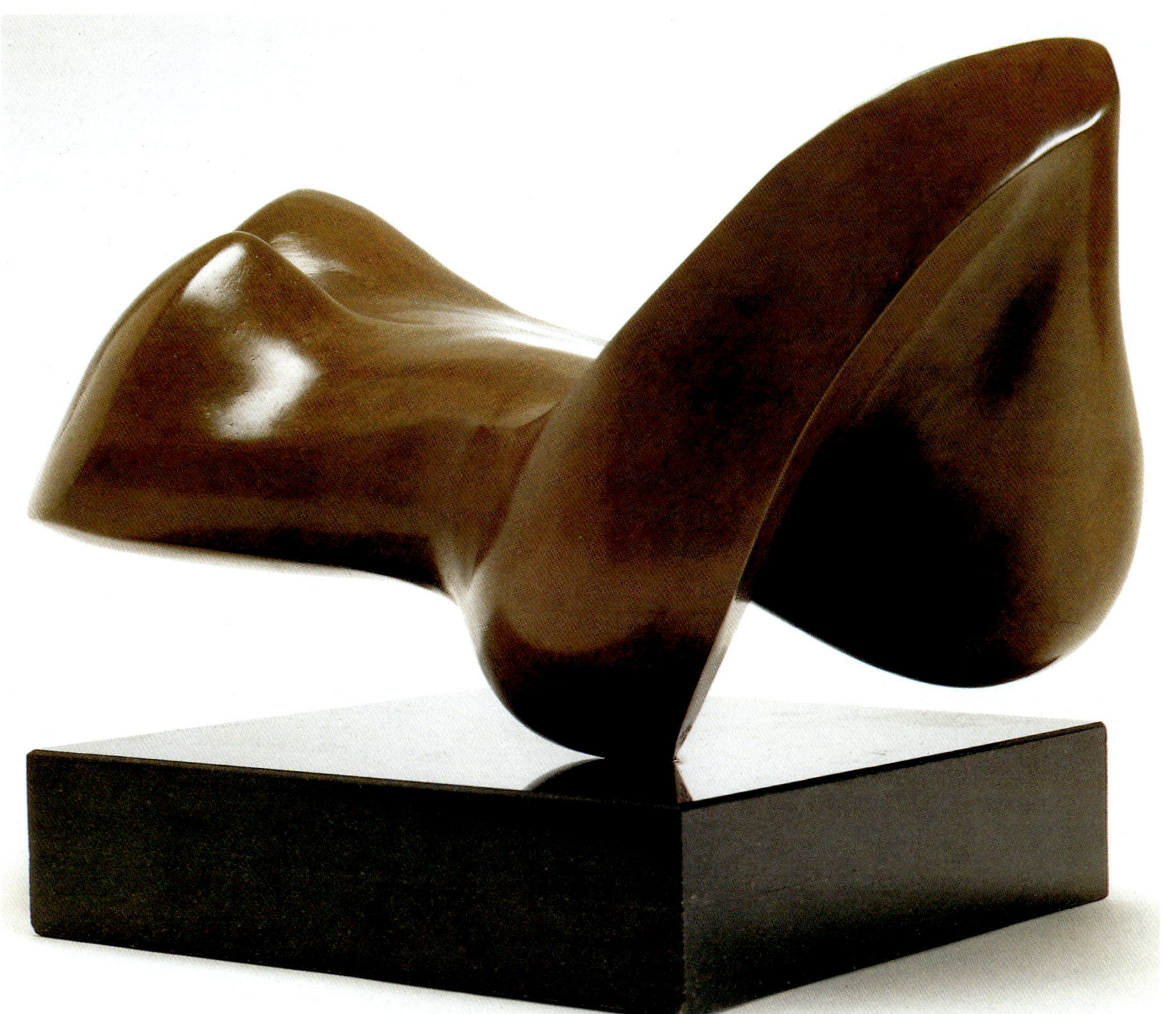

**EDITH LAMBERT
GALLERY**

707 Canyon Rd.
Santa Fe, NM 87501
505.984.2783
800.594.9667
505.983.4494 FAX

Contact:
Edith Lambert, Owner
Anne Ward Burton,
Assoc. Director

Exhibiting:
Contemporary paintings,
drawings and sculpture

Isabelle H. Siegel

Carioca
1980, Bronze,
8" x 17" x 10"

Selected Exhibitions:
1995 Sarah Lawrence
      College, New York, NY
      Memorial exhibition:
1993 Evelyn Siegle Gallery,
      Fort Worth, TX
1992 Edith Lambert Gallery,
      Santa Fe, NM
1991 Kraushaar Gallery,
      New York, NY
Selected Collections:
      Chrysler Corporation,
      Highland Park, MI
      IBM Corporation,
      New York City, NY;
      McGraw Hill, Inc.,
      New York City, NY;
      New Mexico
      Museum of Fine Arts,
      Santa Fe, NM

L.A. ARTCORE CENTER

420 East 3rd Street
Los Angeles, CA 90013
213.617.3274

Contact:
Lydia Takeshita, Director

Exhibiting:
Contemporary painting and
sculpture

Rufus Snoddy

1. *Los Brazos Del Alacran*
   1993, Mixed media,
   94" x 45" x 5"

2. *Icarus*
   1993, Mixed media,
   74" x 60" x 30"

3. *Venus, Circa 2000*
   1992, Acrylic and oil on
   mixed media,
   43" x 79" x 7"

Selected Biography:

1993 Julie Rico Gallery,
      Santa Monica, CA

1992 ENERGY, L.A. Artcore,
      Los Angeles, CA
      and South Bay
      Contemporary Gallery,
      Torrance, CA

1991 L.A. Artcore Gallery,
      Los Angeles, CA

1990 California Afro
      American Museum,
      Los Angeles, CA

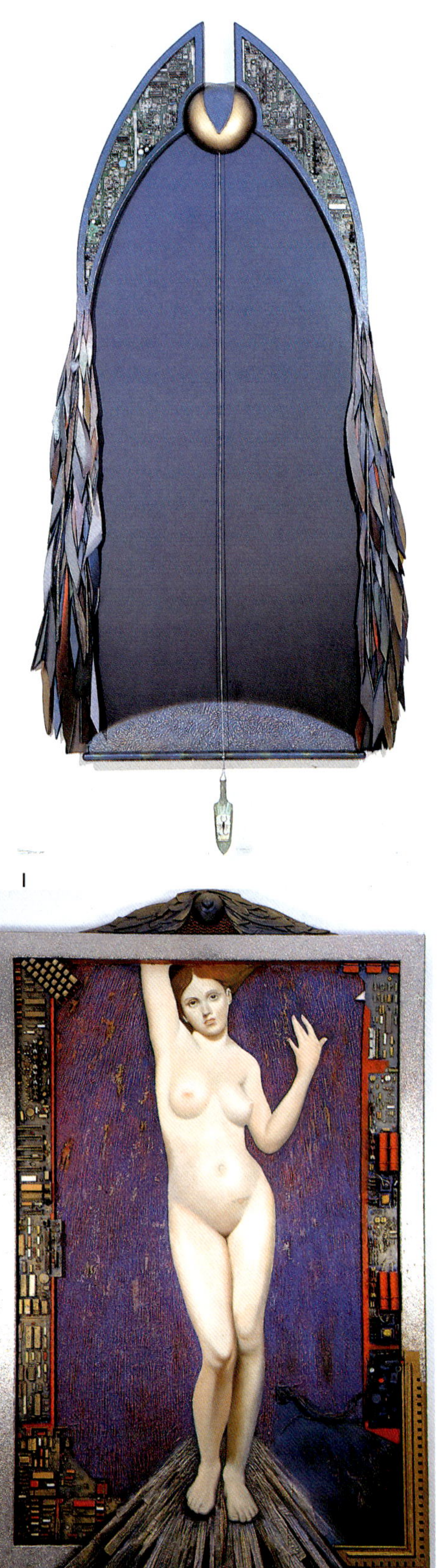

2

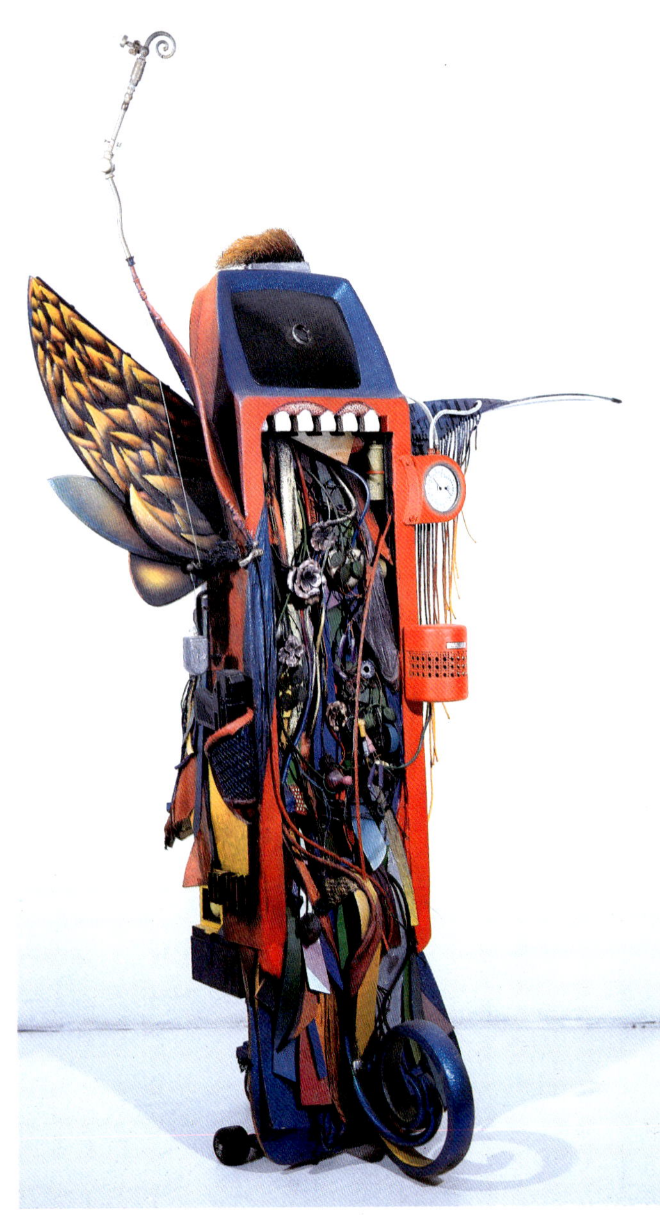

1

3

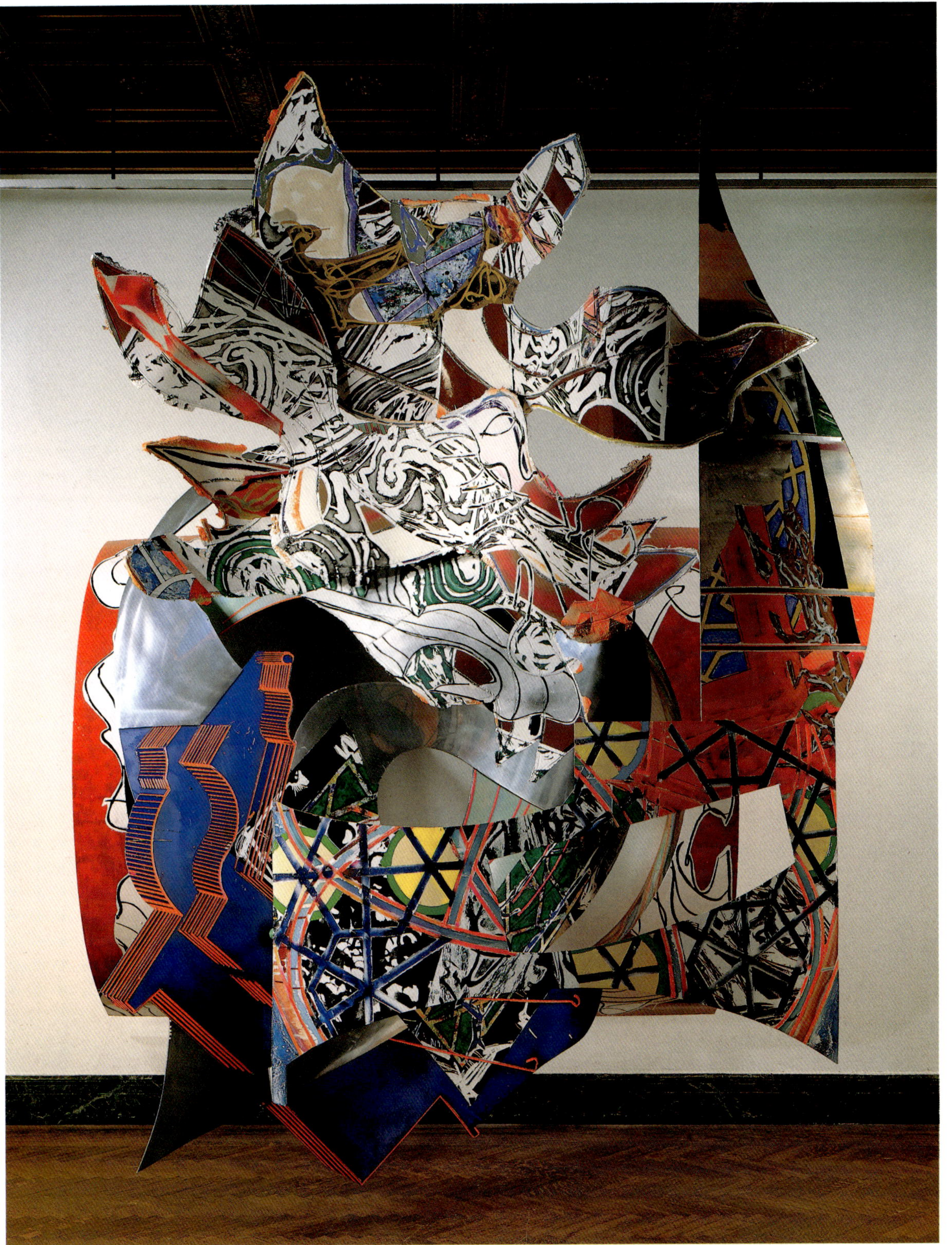

KNOEDLER & COMPANY

19 East 70 Street
New York, NY 10021
212.794.0550
212.772.6932 FAX

Contact:
Larry Rubin
Ann Freedman

Exhibiting:
Contemporary European
and American art

Frank Stella

The Chapel (C-30, 2X)
1990, Mixed media
on aluminum,
139" x 112" x 76"

Selected Biography:

1991 "Frank Stella 1959-
1990," Kawamura
Memorial Museum of
Art, Japan;

Solo exhibitions:
Galerie Daniel
Templon, Paris;
Knoedler Kasmin,
London, England:

Casino Knokke,
Knokke, Belgium;

Galerie Hans Strelow,
Dusseldorf, Germany

LEO CASTELLI

420 W. Broadway
New York, NY 10012
212.431.5160
212.431.5361 FAX

Contact:
Susan Brundage, Director

Robert Therrien

1. *No Title*
   (Black Cloud Relief)
   1991, Steel, paper, enamel & mixed media,
   58" x 106" x 13"

2. *No Title*
   1987, Wood on bronze,
   112 1/4" x 17 3/4"

3. *No Title*
   1985-90, Tempera
   on sketch pad,
   24" x 18" x 1/2"

Selected Biography:
1992 Solo exhibitions:
   "Robert Therrien",
   Angles Gallery,
   Santa Monica, CA,
   Oct. 16 - Nov. 21
1991 Solo exhibition:
   "Robert Therrien",
   Museo Nacional
   Centro de Arte Reina
   Sophia, Madrid, Spain,
   Nov. 27 - Dec. 23;
   traveled to Haags
   Gemeetemuseum,
   The Hague,
   The Netherlands;
   "Robert Therrien",
   65 Thompson Street,
   New York, NY,
   May 21 - June 22

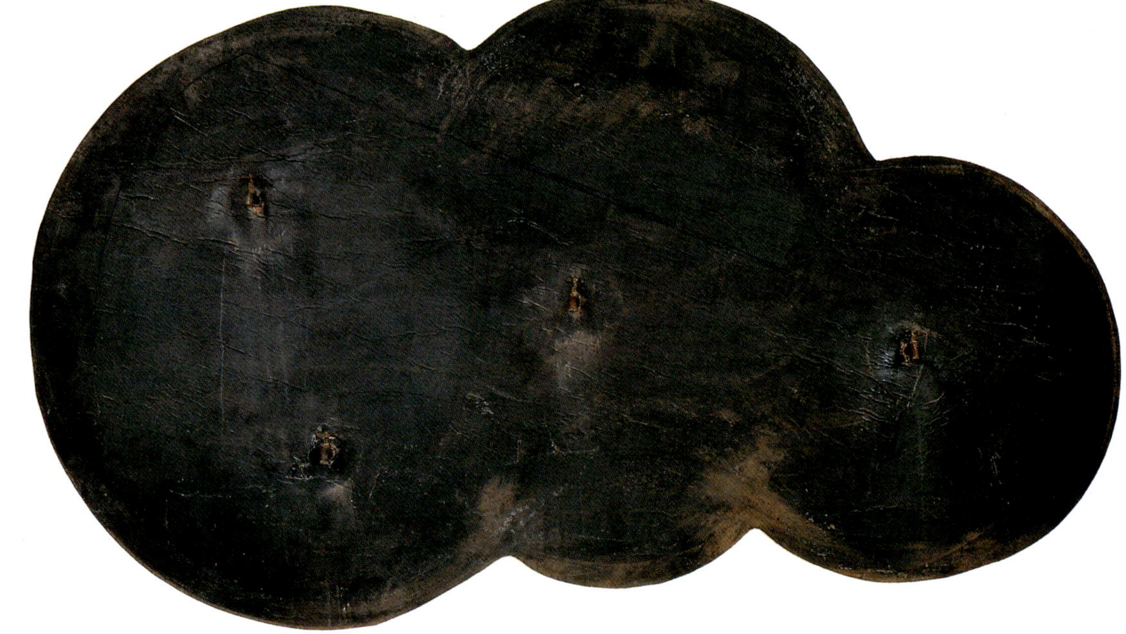

1

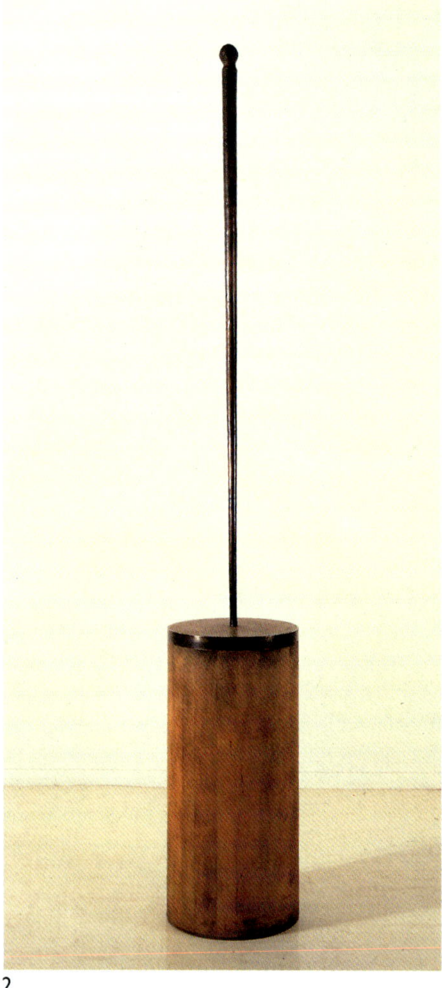

2

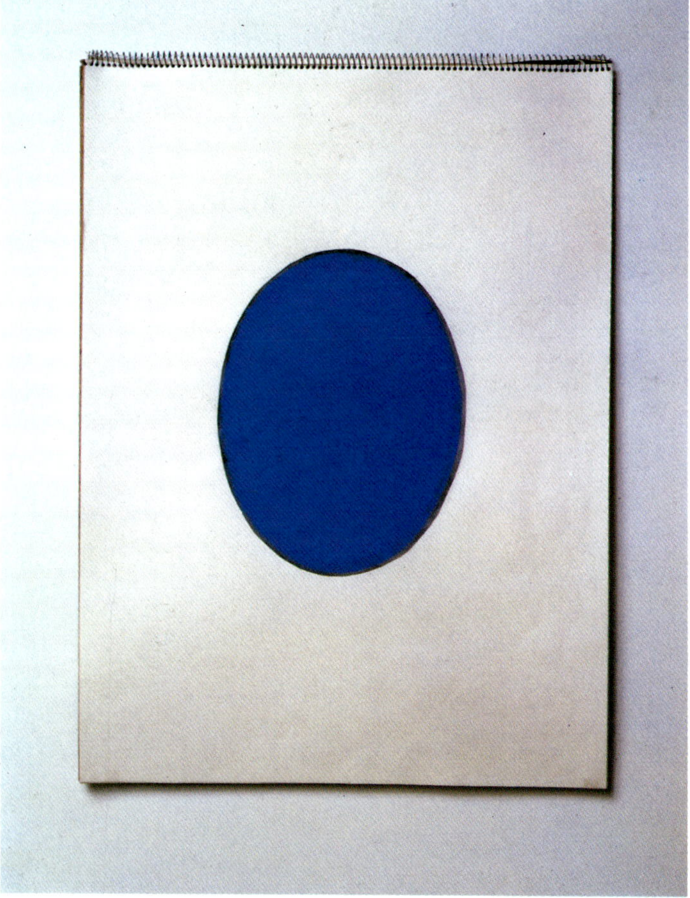

3

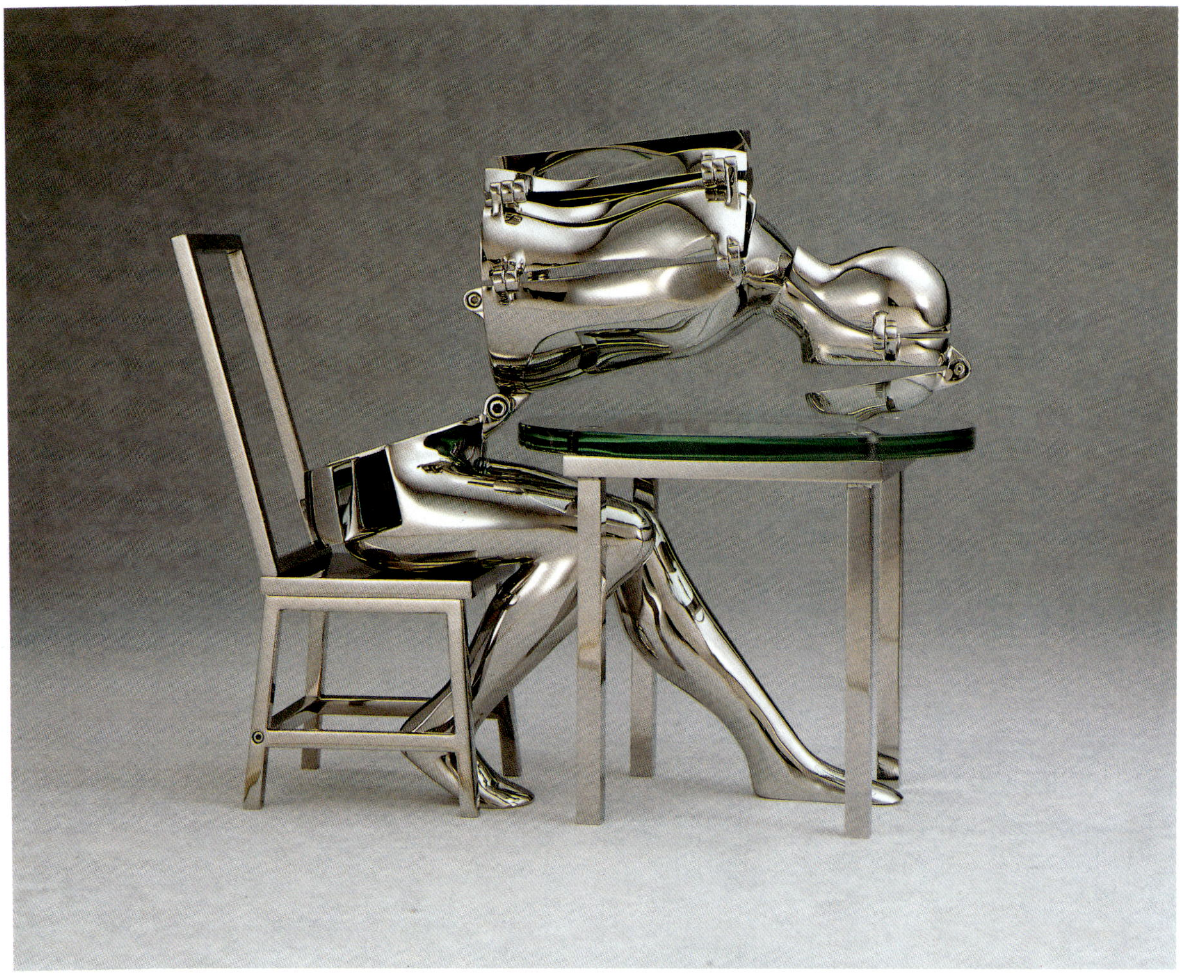

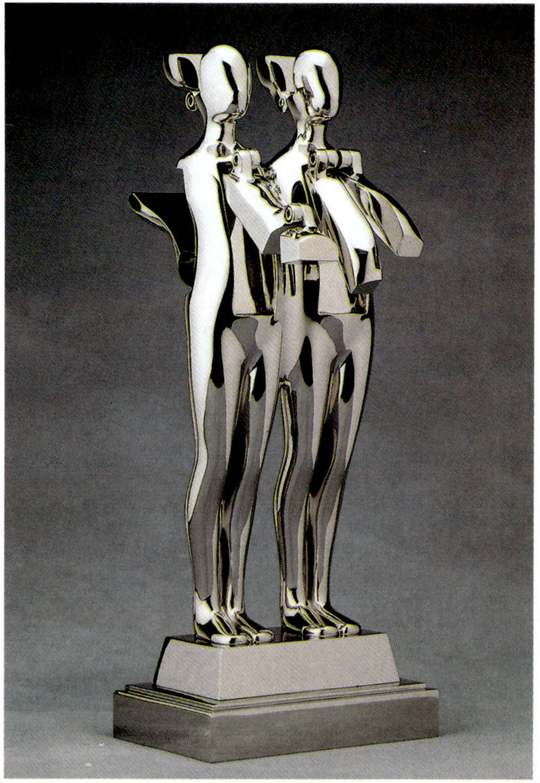

**PHILIP SAMUELS
FINE ART**

8112 Maryland Ave. Ste. 200
St Louis, MO 63105
314.727.2444
314.727.6084 FAX

Contact:
Philip Samuels

Exhibiting:
Contemporary paintings
and sculpture

Ernest Trova

1. *Seated Figure V*
   1990, Stainless steel,
   13 3/4" × 19" × 10"
   Edition: 5

2. *Double Flapman*
   1983, Stainless steel,
   28 1/4" × 10" × 6 1/2"
   Edition: 8 plus 2 artist proof

Friedland Art Inc.
18181 NE 31st Ct.
 N. Miami Beach, Fl
33160
305.935.7544
305.935.3780 FAX
Contact:
Lara Block

Global Art Ltd.
Rue du Chateau 15
2034 Peseux,
Switzerland
41.38.31.10.77
Contact:
Dion Friedland

Selected Collections:
Metropolitan
Museum of Art, NY

Museum of
Modern Art, NY

Whitney Museum
of American Art, NY

Tate Gallery,
London England

FRIEDLAND ART INC.

18181 NE 31st Ct., Ste.1106
N. Miami Beach, Fl 33160
305.935.7544
305.935.3780 FAX

Contact:
Lara Block

Specialty:
Supplies leading art dealers
with available works

Edoardo Villa

1. *Japzi,*
   1992, Steel,
   28" x 26" x 20"
   Edition: 9 plus 1 artist proof

2. *Pesanti,*
   1992, Steel,
   41" x 20" x 24"
   Edition: 9 plus 1 artist proof

3. *Abie,*
   1992, Steel,
   37" x 12" x 16"
   Edition: 9 plus 1 artist proof

Global Art Ltd.
Rue du Chateau 15
2034 Peseux,
Switzerland
41.38.31.10.77
Contact:
Dion Friedland

Philip Samuels Fine Art
8112 Maryland Ave.
St. Louis, MO 63105
314.727.2444
314.727.6084 FAX
Contact:
Philip Samuels

Selected Exhibitions:
1994 Official Opening
      Edoardo Villa Museum,
      Pretoria, South Africa
1983 Valparaiso Biennale
1957 - 69
      Sao Paolo Biennale
1956 - 64
      Venice Biennale

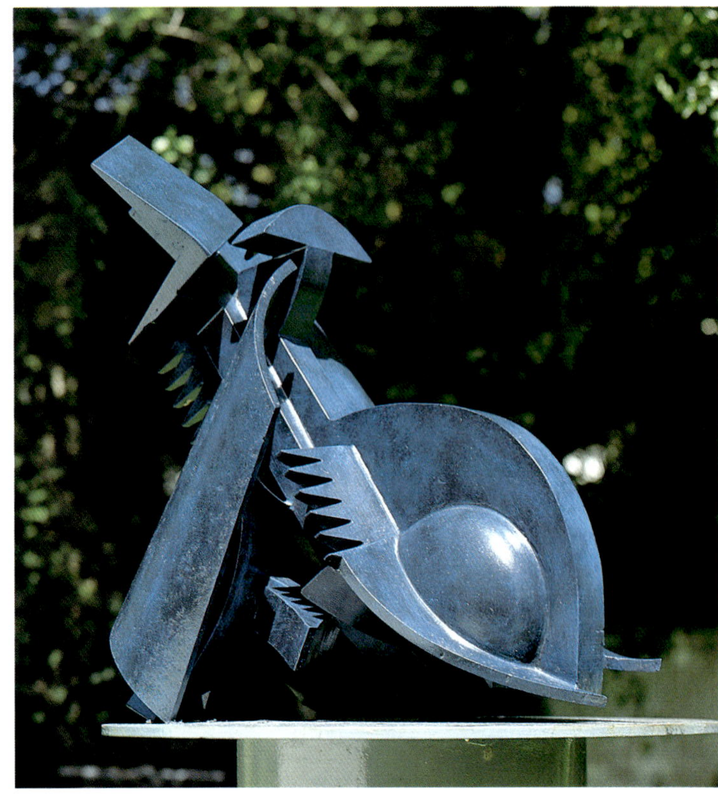

1

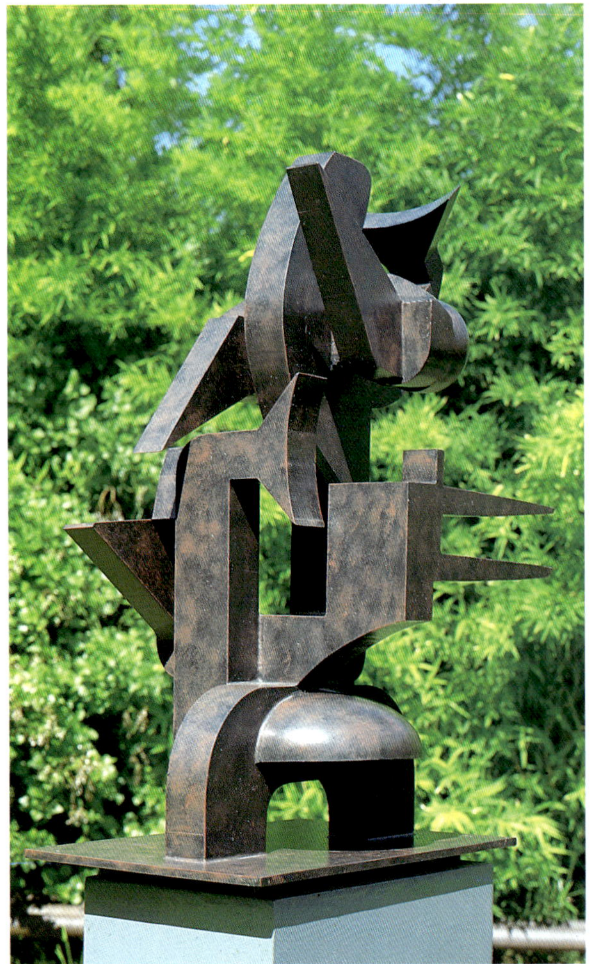

2

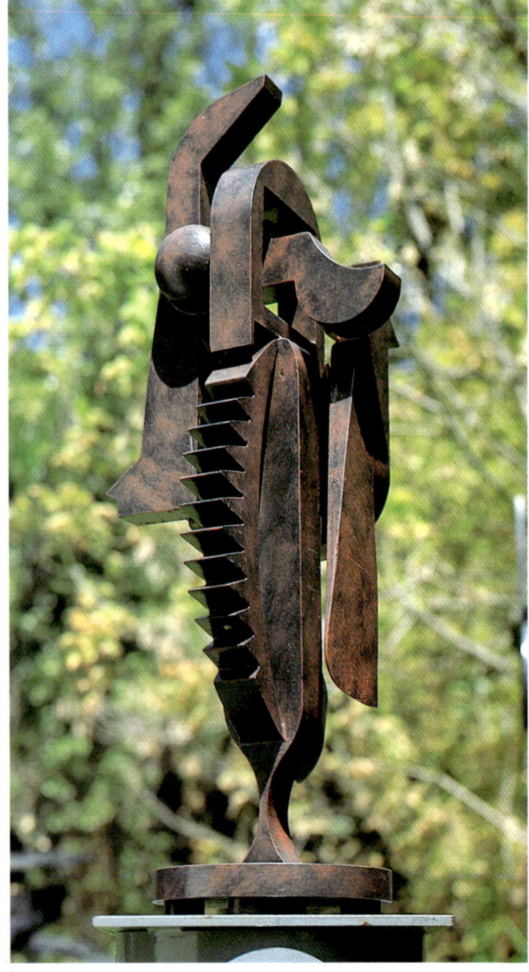

3

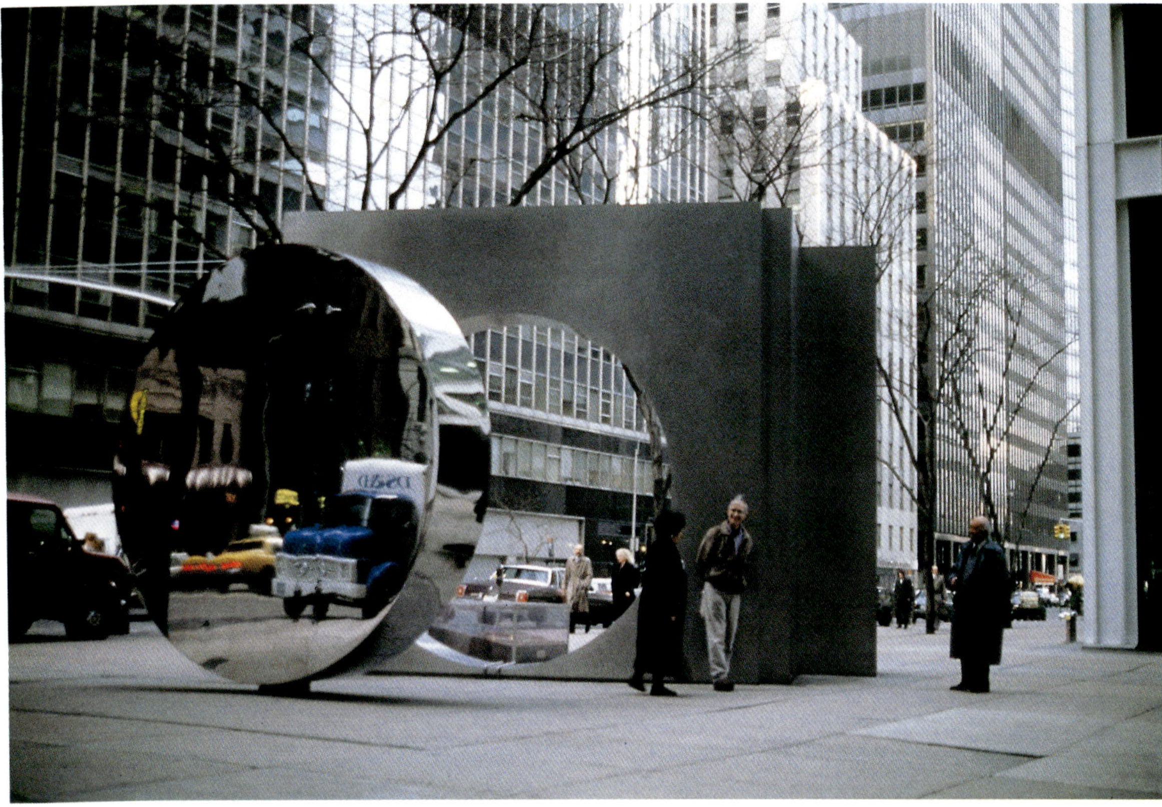

1

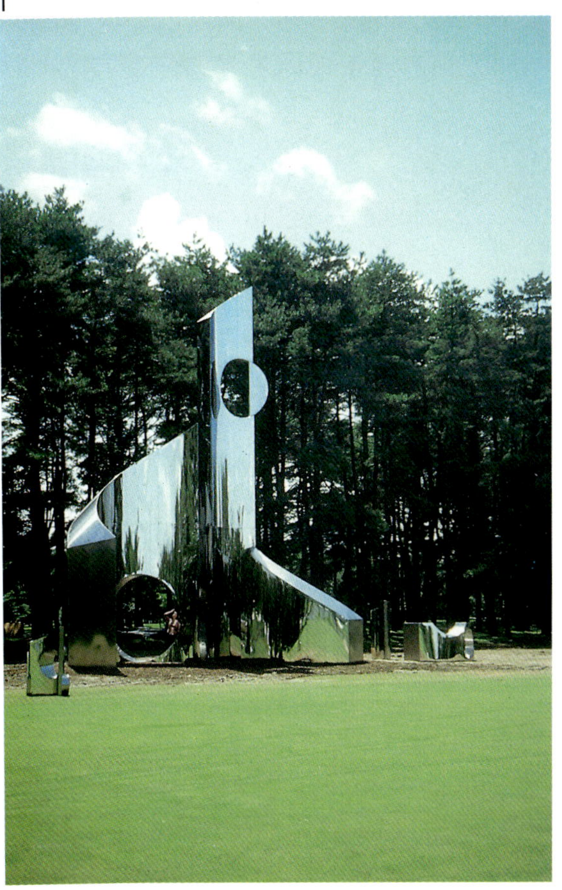

2

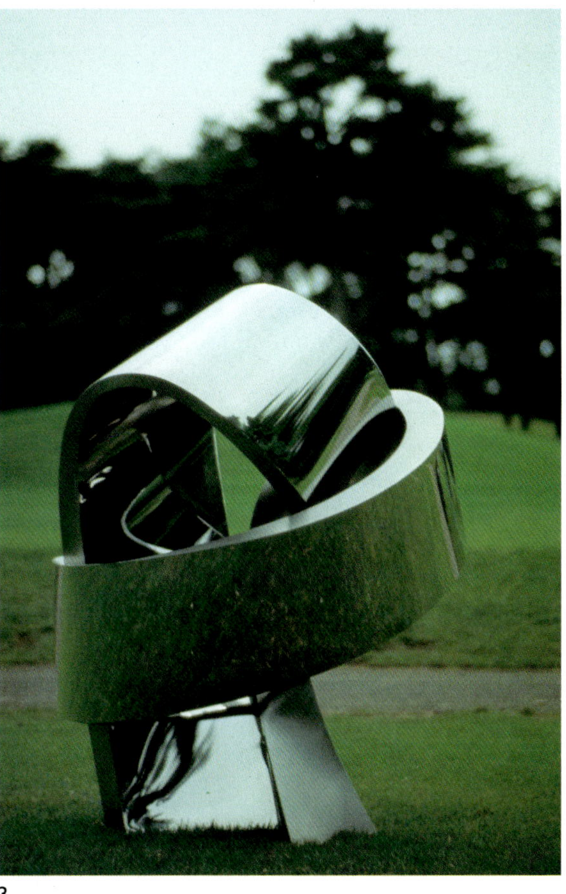

3

MAY GALLERY

31 Chungking S. Rd., Sec. 2
Taipei, Taiwan, R.O.C.
886.2396.1966
886.2396.4850 FAX

Contact:
Ms. Yang Meei Huey,
Director

Exhibiting:
Lifescape sculptures
(stainless steel, bronze),
prints of Prof. Yuyu Yang

Yuyu Yang, Professor

1. *East West Gate (2E Gate)*
   [NY] 1973, Stainless
   steel, 480 x 700 x 550
   cm.

2. *Birth*
   [Tokyo] 1992, Stainless
   steel, 11 m. high

3. *Growth*
   [Tokyo] 1988, Stainless
   steel, 50 x 48 x 50 cm.

Selected Biography:
1992 Spectacular "Birth"
   Stainless steel
   sculptures,
   International Golf
   Course, Tsukuba,
   Tokyo

1990 "Phoenix Scales
   Heavens", Peking;
   "Dragon in Flight",
   Taipei

1973 "East West Gate"
   (QEGATE), stainless
   sculpture, New York

1971 "Peace & Prosperity",
   marble sculpture,
   Singapore

ZAGAMI FINE ART

515 SW 4th Ave.
Ft, Lauderdale, FL 33315
305.463.0014
305.587.7726 FAX

Contact:
Amalia Zagami

Exhibiting:
Contemporary painting
and sculpture

Salvatore Zagami

1. *Car Number Thirteen*
   1988, Steel, wood, plastic,
   30' x 6' x 5'

2. *Three Figures, Three Knots
   (Elvis, Christ, and Mickey
   Mouse)*
   1989, Galvanized Steel,
   plastic, nylon,
   60" x 16" x 6"

Selected Biography:

1994 Solo exhibition,
      Art Miami 94,
      Miami, FL

1992 Ft. Lauderdale
      Museum of Art, FL

1991 Norton Gallery of Art,
      West Palm Beach, FL

      Award for sculpture
      from National
      Endowment for the
      Arts, South Florida
      Cultural Consortium

1988 Art in Public Places
      Commission, Broward
      County, FL

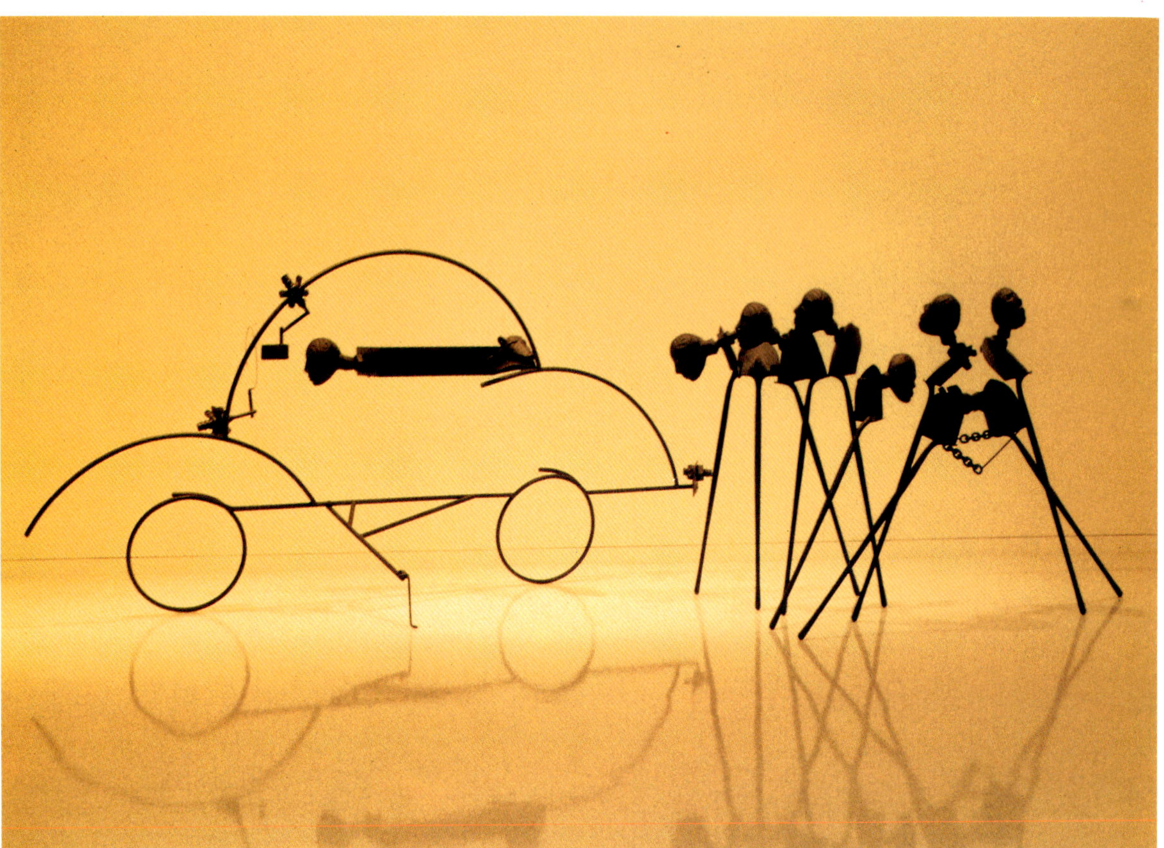

1

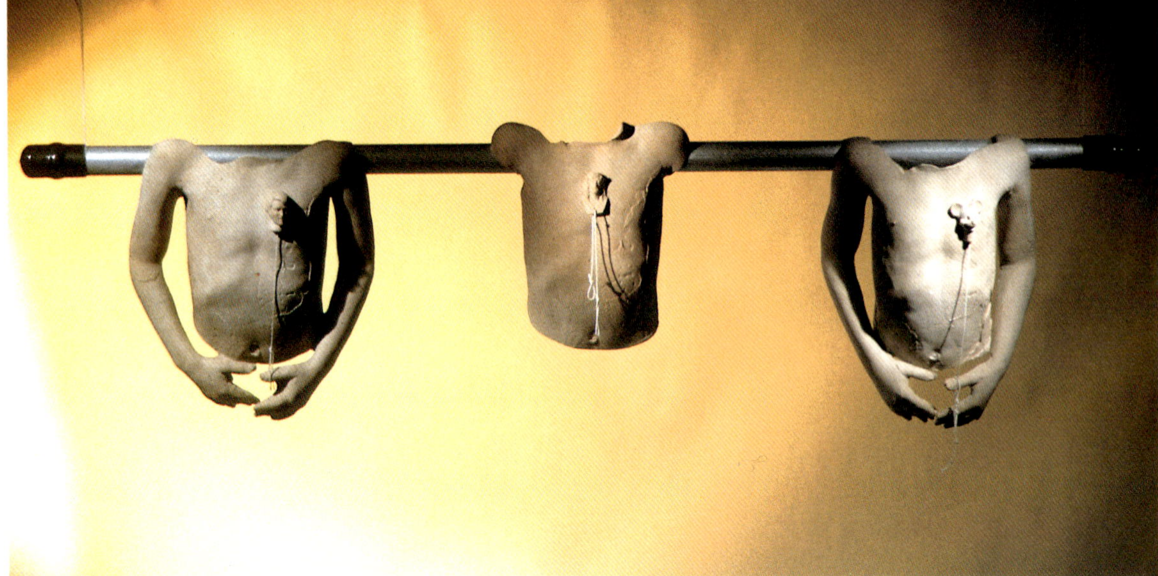

2

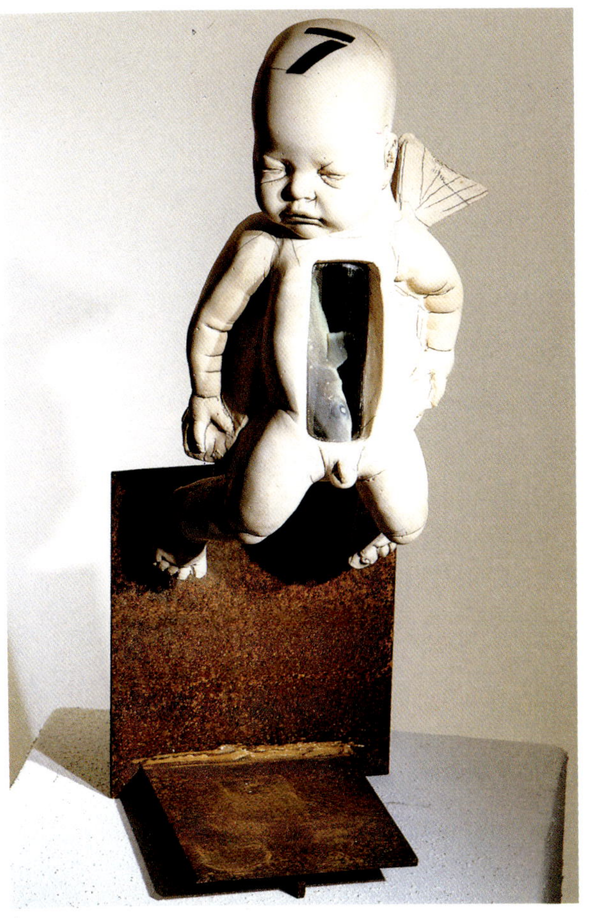

1

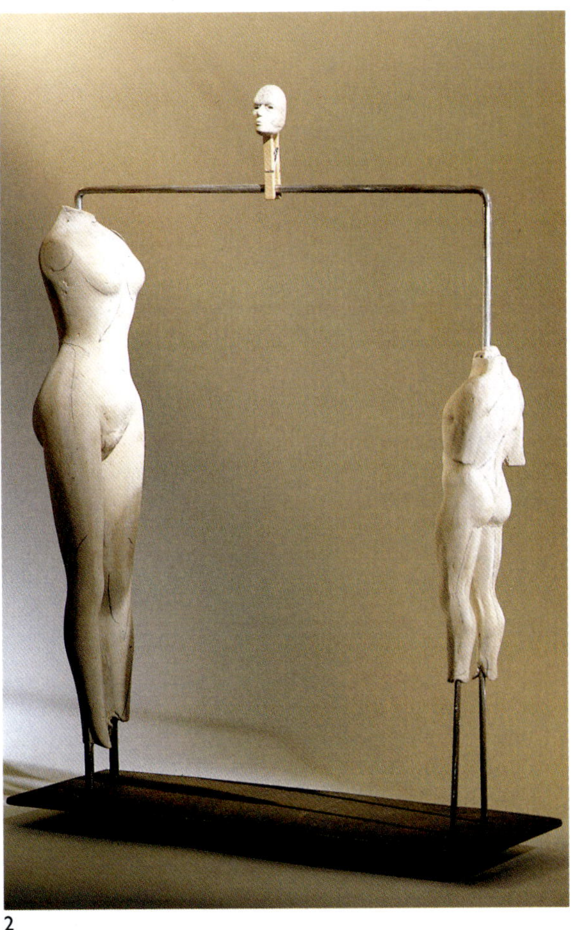

2

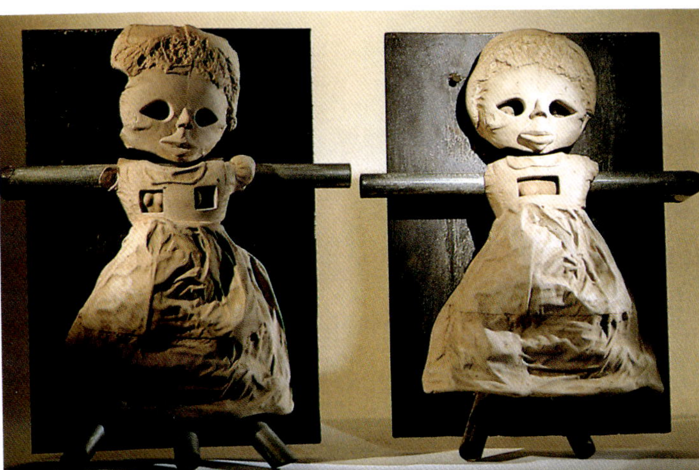

3

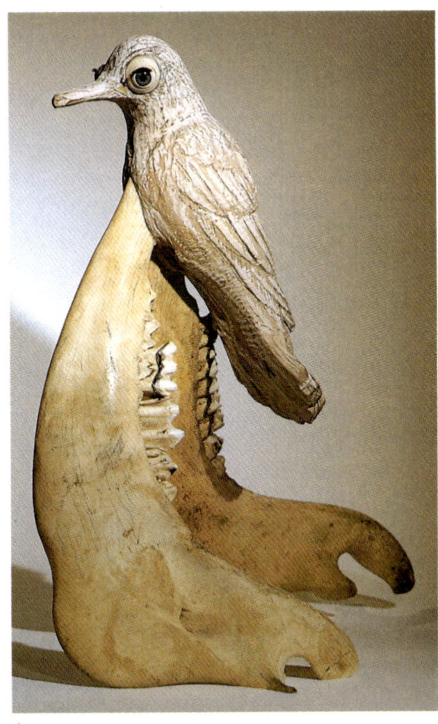

4

ZAGAMI FINE ART

515 SW 4th Ave.
Ft, Lauderdale, FL 33315
305.463.0014
305.587.7726 FAX

Contact:
Amalia Zagami

Exhibiting:
Contemporary painting
and sculpture

Salvatore Zagami

1. *Shark no.7*
   1993, Plastic, Steel and
   shark fetus,
   22" x 8" x 8"

2. *Tic Tac Toe*
   1992, Plastic, Steel and
   wood,
   29" x 21" x 9"

3. *Doll no.1 & Doll no.2*
   1989, Steel & plastic,
   24" x 20" x 10"

4. *Jaw Bone*
   1992, Plastic & bone
   13" x 10" x 7"

Selected Biography:

1994 Solo exhibition,
   Art Miami 94,
   Miami, FL

1992 Ft. Lauderdale
   Museum of Art, FL

1991 Norton Gallery of Art,
   West Palm Beach, FL

   Award for sculpture
   from National
   Endowment for the
   Arts, South Florida
   Cultural Consortium

1988 Art in Public Places
   Commission, Broward
   County, FL

MONTSERRAT
GALLERY

584 Broadway
New York, NY 10012
212.941.8899
212.274.1717 FAX

Contact:
Marie Montserrat Coll,
Director

Exhibiting:
Contemporary European
and American art

Zazé

1. *Abandon*
   1990, Bronze,
   12" x 9" x 4³⁄₄"
   edition of 8

2. *Rencontre*
   1992, Bronze,
   11¹⁄₂" x 9" x 5¹⁄₂"
   edition of 8

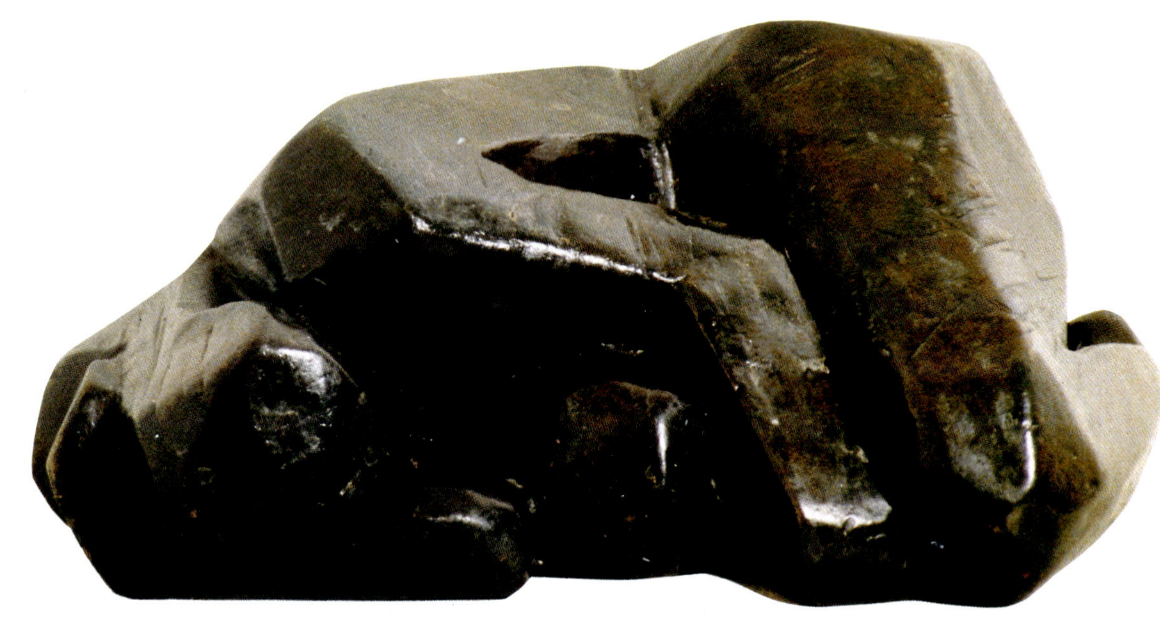

1

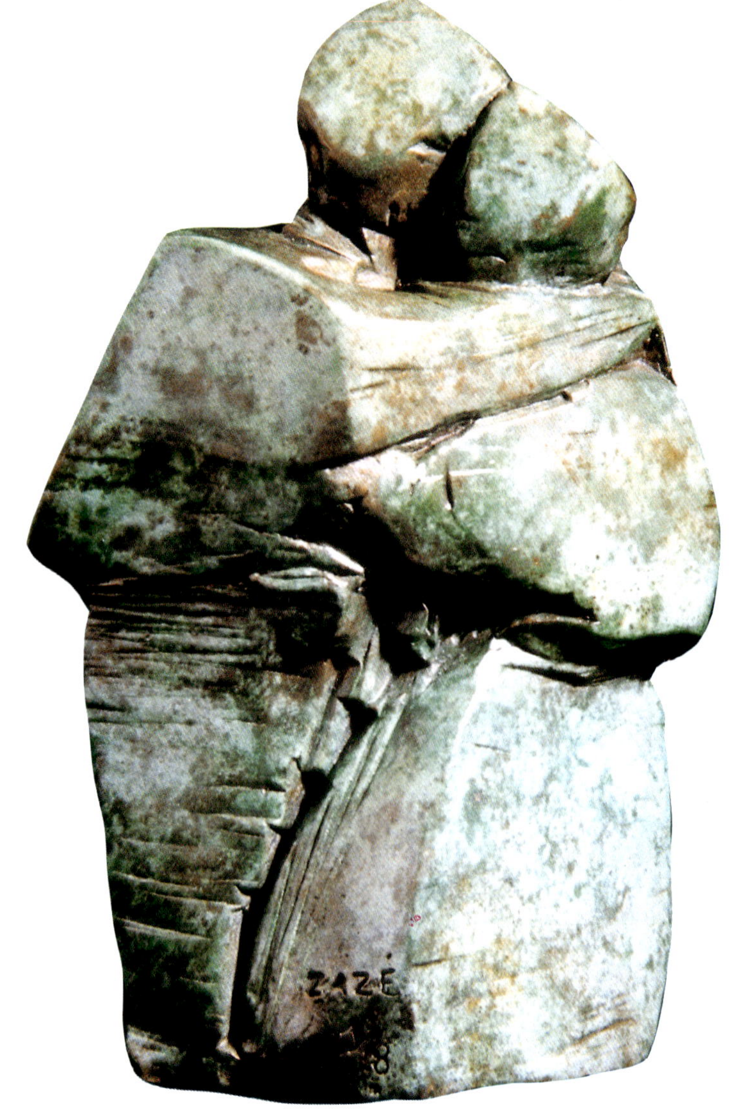

2

Selected Biography:

1994 Solo Exhibition
Montserrat Gallery,
New York, NY

1992 Grand Palais, Paris

Gallery Varga Darlet,
Bordeaux

Gallery de Nesle,
Paris

Rouen

1991 Grand Palais, Paris

PHOTOGRAPHY

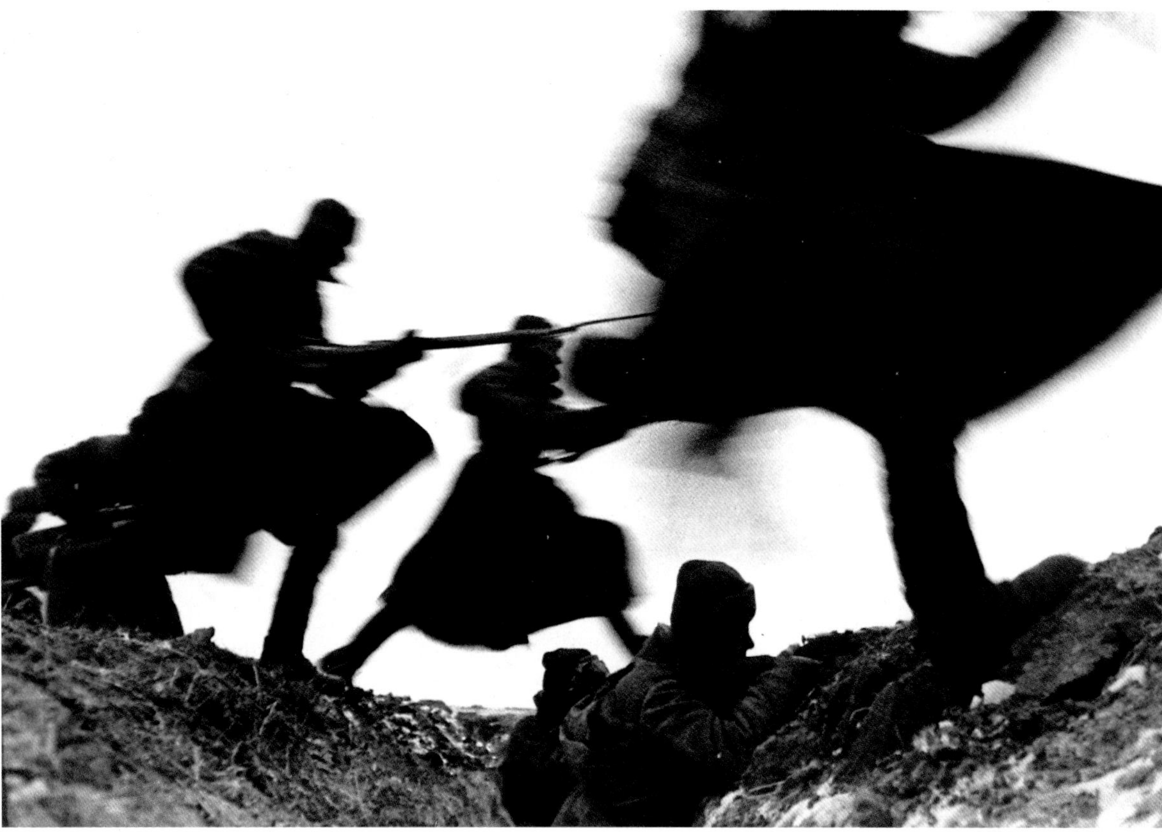

1

G. RAY HAWKINS GALLERY

908 Colorado Avenue
Santa Monica, CA 90401
310.394.5558
310.576.2468 FAX

Contact:
Marla Hamburg Kennedy

Exhibiting:
Fine vintage & contemporary photography

Dmitri Baltermants

1. *Attack*
   1941, Silver print,
   16" x 20"

2. *Behind Enemy Lines*
   1941, Silver print,
   16" x 20"

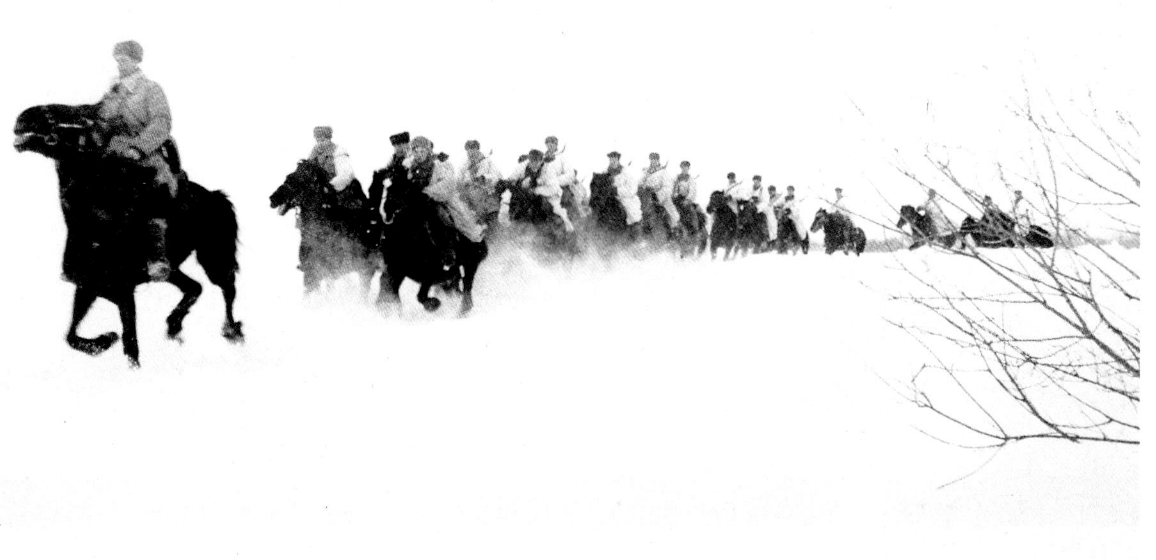

2

Selected Biography:

Dmitri Baltermants (1912-1990)was the premier photojournalist in Russia recording history from 1939-1989 through his powerful images of his nation at war and in peace. He has had numerous exhibitions including a retrospective at the International Center of Photography in New York in 1992

G. RAY HAWKINS GALLERY

908 Colorado Avenue
Santa Monica, CA 90401
310.394.5558
310.576.2468 FAX

Contact:
Marla Hamburg Kennedy

Exhibiting:
Fine vintage & contemporary
photography

Dmitri Baltermants

Tchaikousky
1945, Silver print,
16" x 20"

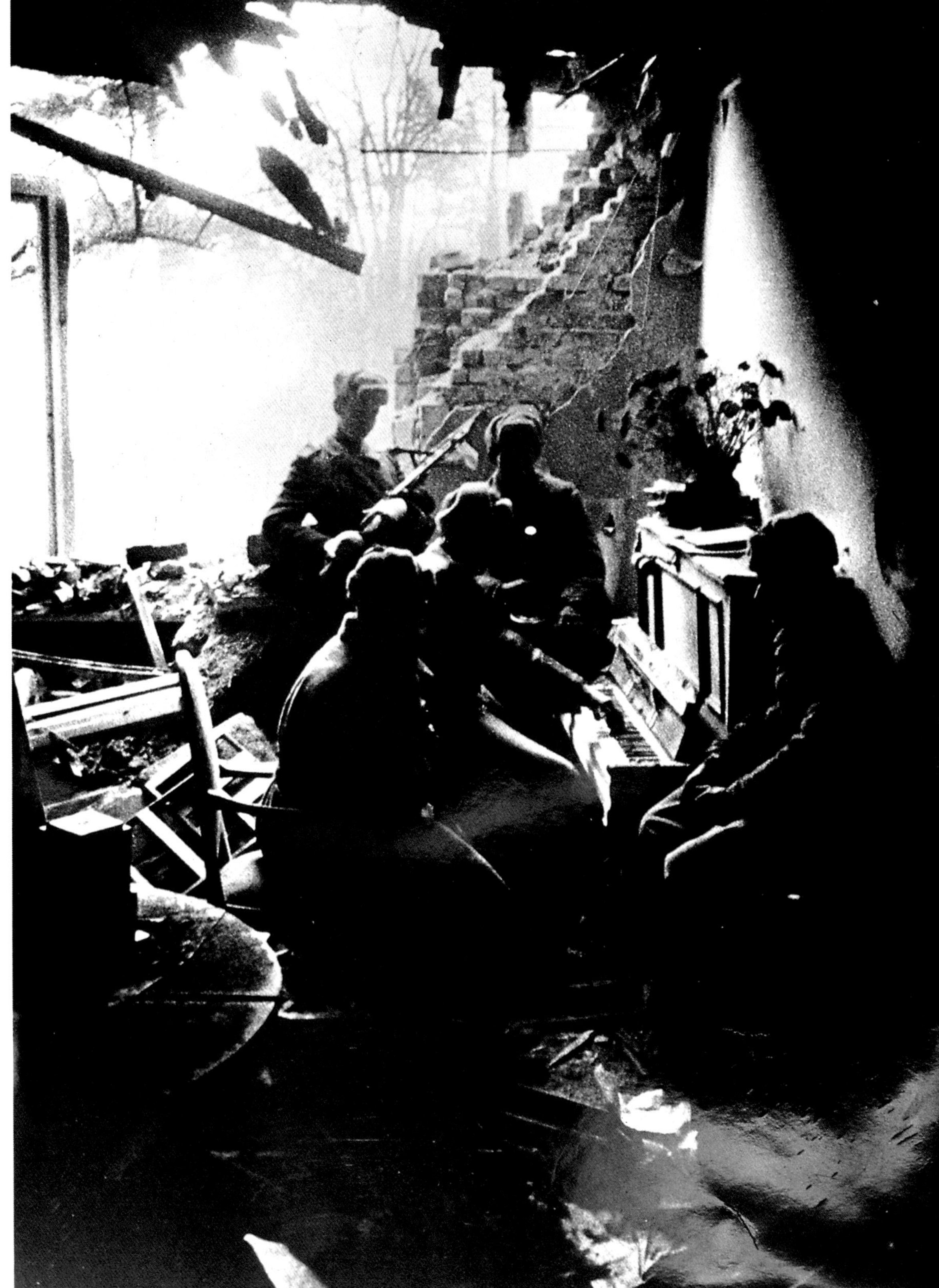

Selected Biography:

Dmitri Baltermants
(1912-1990)was the
premier photojournalist
in Russia recording
history from 1939-1989
through his powerful
images of his nation at
war and in peace. He
has had numerous
exhibitions including a
retrospective at the
International Center of
Photography in New
York in 1992

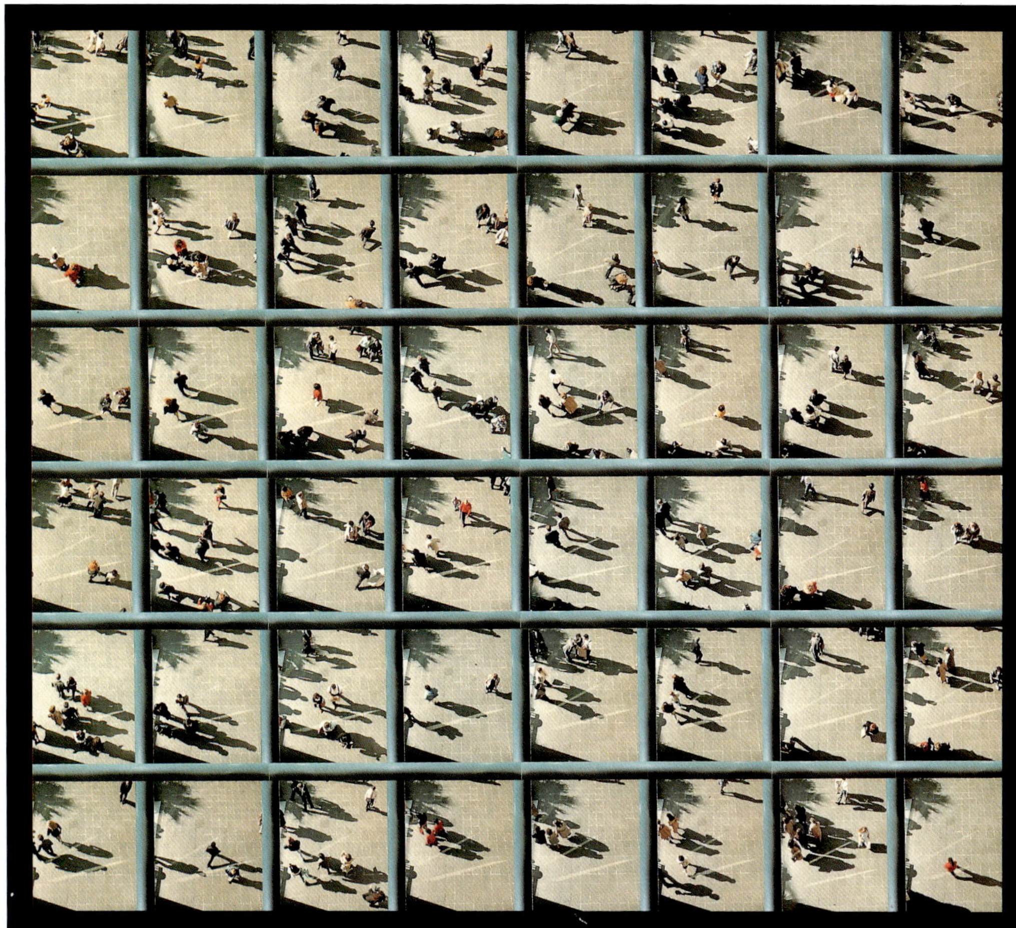

1

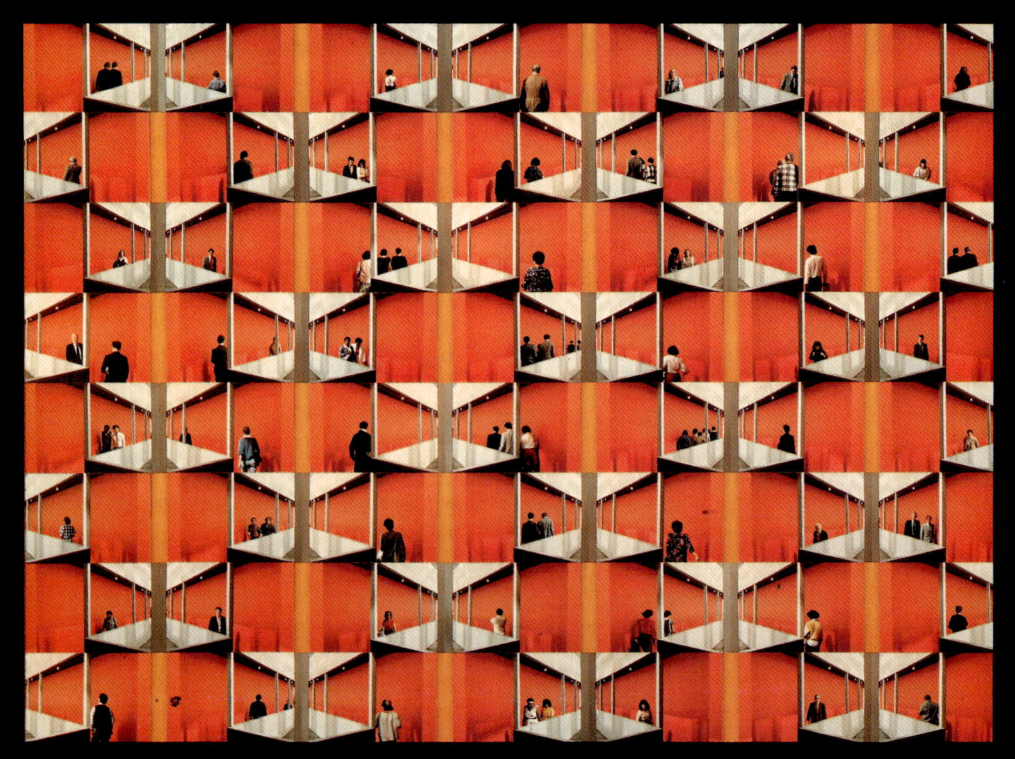

2

J. J. BROOKINGS GALLERY

330 Commercial Street
San Jose, CA 95112
408.287.3311

Contact:
Timothy C. Duran, Director

Exhibiting:
Contemporary paintings,
prints and sculpture;
vintage and contemporary
photography

James Crable

1. *Citicorp Plaza,*
   Los Angeles, CA
   1989, Cibachrome,
   33" x 37"

2. *Commercial Street II,*
   San Francisco, CA
   1988, Cibachrome,
   31" x 42"

Selected Exhibitions:

Otis Art Institute,
Chrysler Museum,
Seattle Art Museum,
High Museum of Art,
Portland Art Museum,
Maryland Institute,
Long Beach Museum
of Art, Virginia Museum
of Fine Art, Monterey
Peninsula Museum of
Art and many others.

J. J. BROOKINGS GALLERY

330 Commercial Street
San Jose, CA 95112
408.287.3311

Contact:
Timothy C. Duran, Director

Exhibiting:
Contemporary paintings,
prints and sculpture;
vintage and contemporary
photography

Lisa Gray

1. *Folds of Flesh*
   1992, Platinum-palladium,
   20" x 16"

2. *Solitary Sin*
   1994, Platinum-palladium,
   20" x 16"

3. *Bird of Prey*
   1993, Platinum-palladium,
   9" x 7"

Selected Biography:

1994 A. Gibson Gallery,
      Seattle, WA;
      Seattle Art Museum,
      Seattle, WA
1993 Platinum Plus Gallery,
      Santa Fa, NM
1992 Anchorage Museum of
      Art, AK; University of
      Arizona, Tucson, AZ;
      J. J. Brookings Gallery,
      San Jose, CA
1991 Fairbanks Arts
      Association, AK; Lamar
      Dodd Art Center, GA
1990 Spiva Art Center, MO;
      Westmoreland Arts,
      PA; Visual Arts Center
      of Alaska, AK

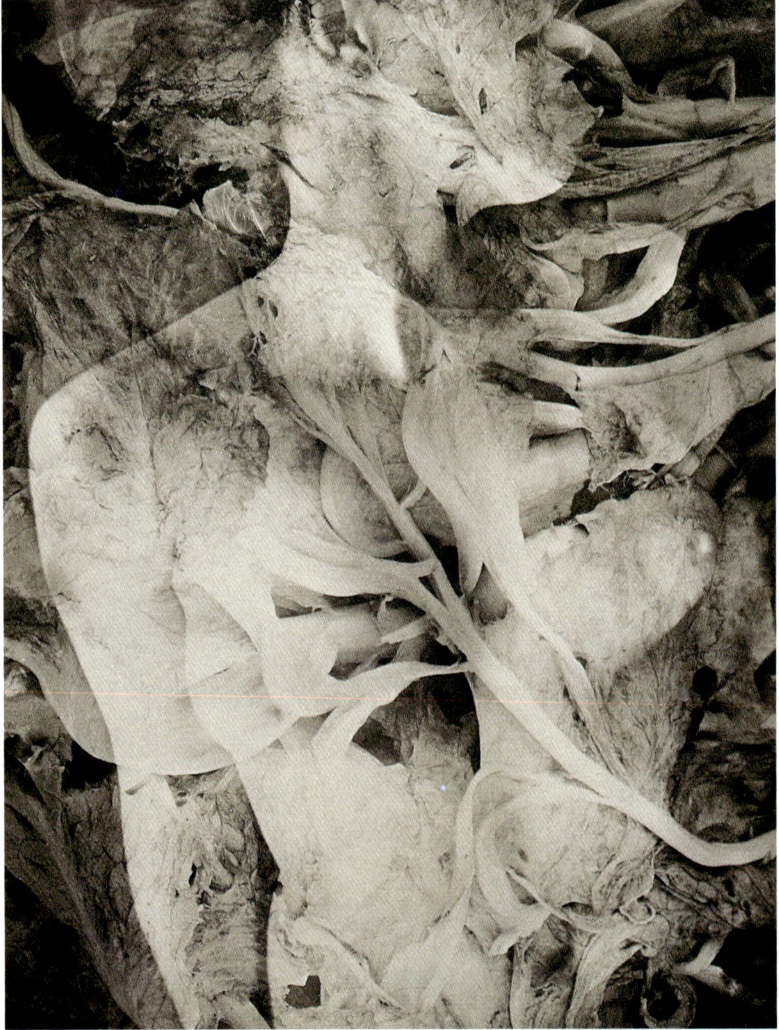

1

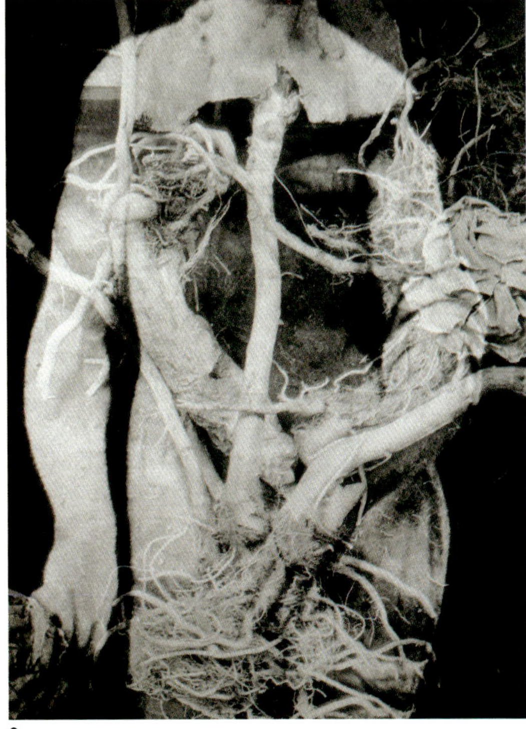

2

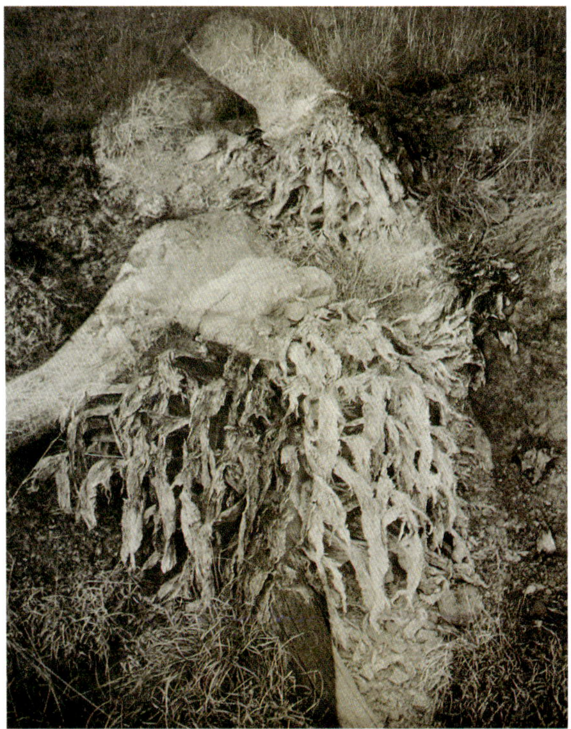

3

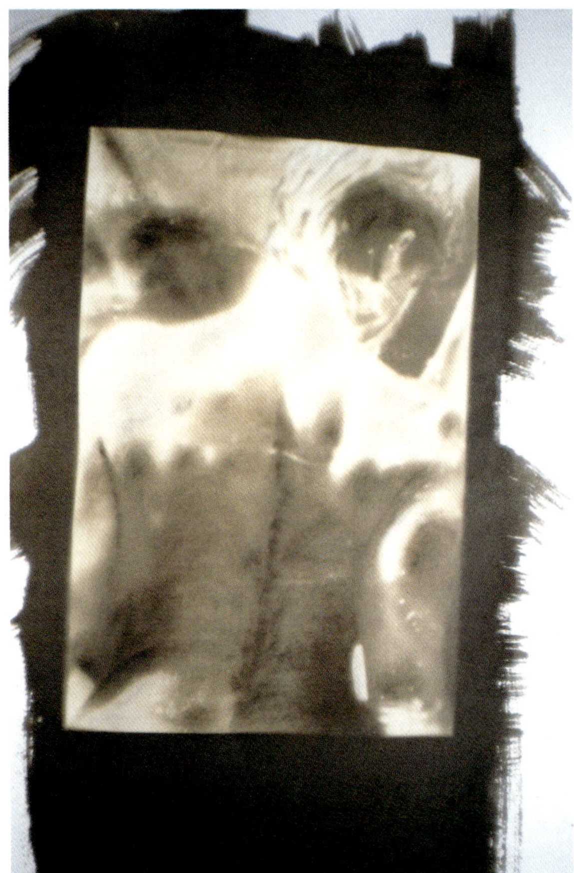

1

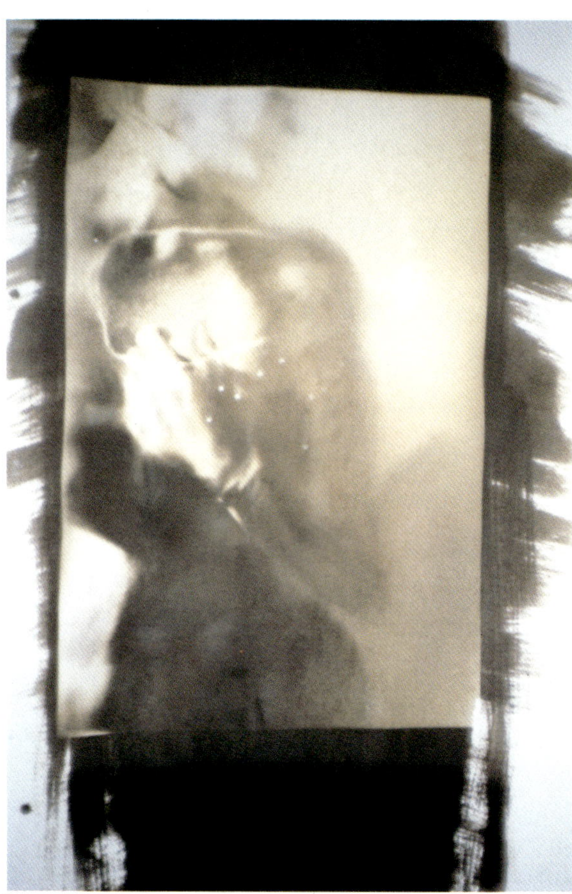

2

ENID OKLA HOMA

233 West Huron
Chicago, IL 60610
312.787.6011
312.787.6617 FAX

Contact:
Celeste Sotola, Director

Exhibiting:
Contemporary painting,
sculpture, and objects

Bryant Johnston

1. *Novembre*
   1993, Van Dke Brown,
   24" x 36"

2. *Tribute to Rosealind*
   1992, Gelatin Prints,
   24" x 36"

HOUK FRIEDMAN

1094 Madison Ave.
New York, NY 10033
212.628.5300
212.861.1030 FAX

Contact:
Susan Arthur

Dorothea Lange

1. *Migratory Cotton Picker,*
   Eloy, Alabama
   1940, Vintage gelatin
   silver print,
   10½" x 13½"

2. *The Road West,*
   New Mexico
   1938, Vintage gelatin
   silver print,
   7¾" x 9½"

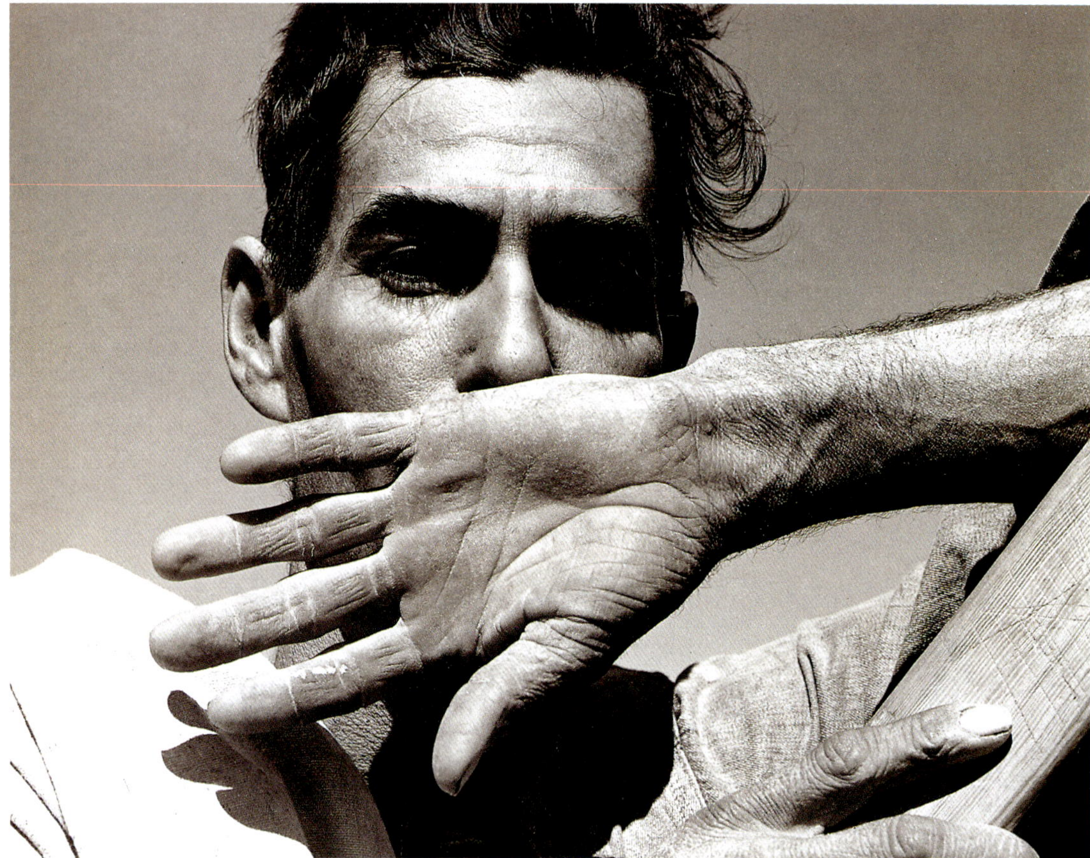

1

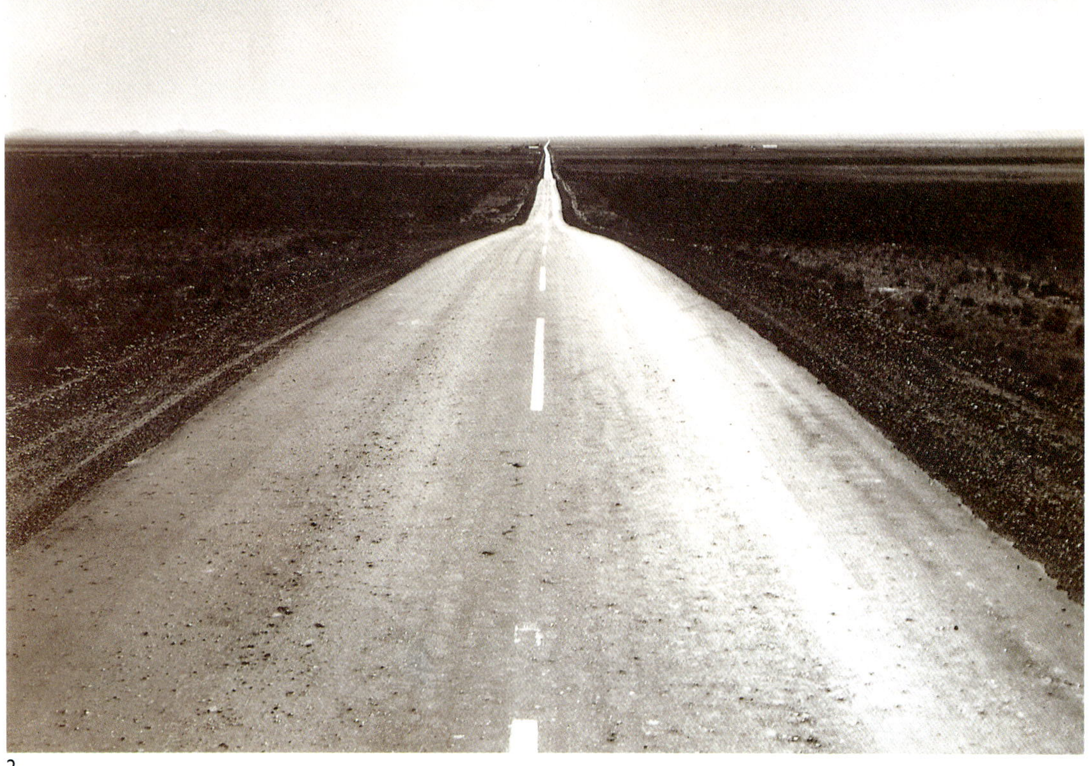

2

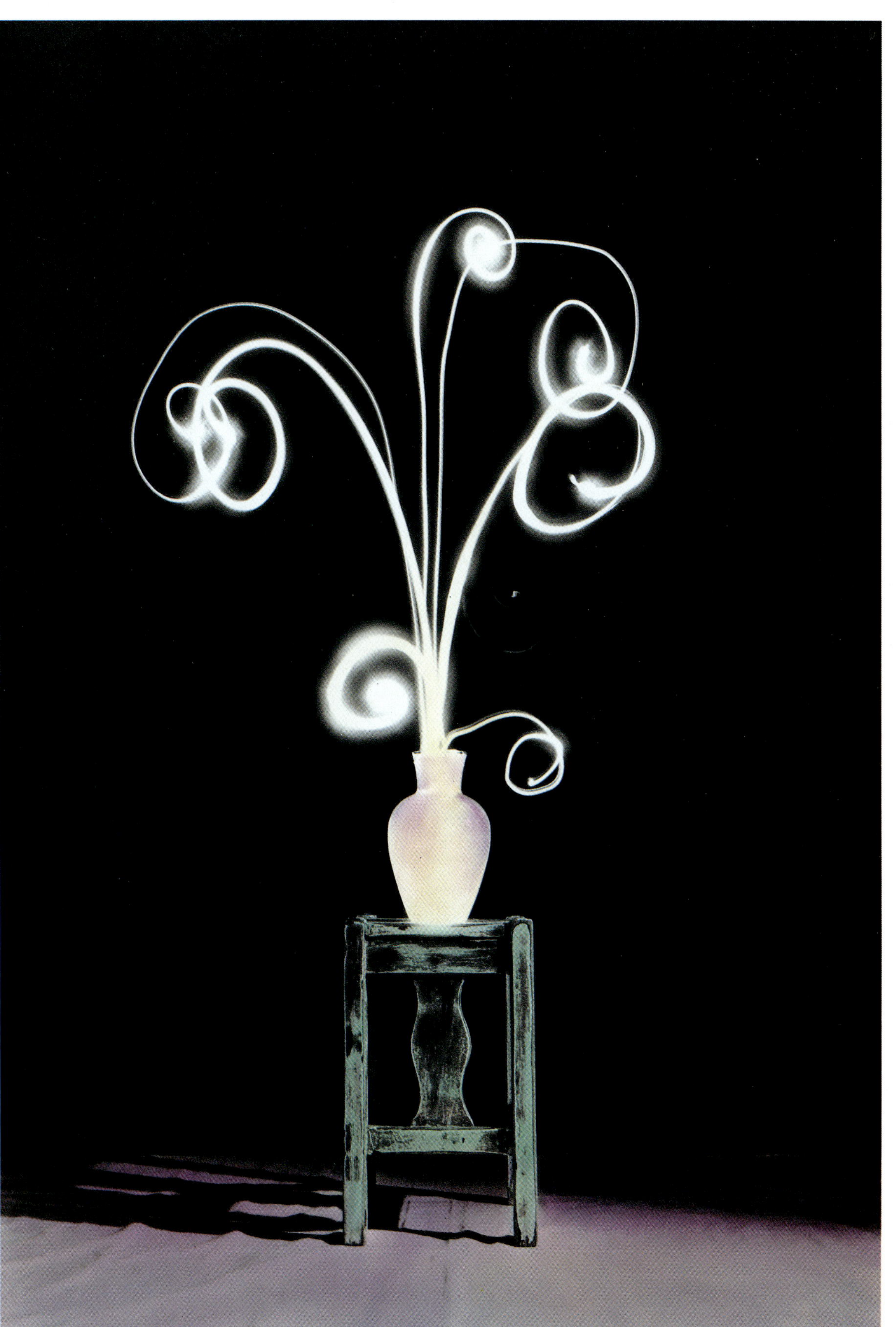

PAUL CAVA GALLERY

22 North 3rd Street
Philadelphia, PA 19106
215.627.1172
215.627.1173 FAX

Contact:
Paul Cava, Director

Exhibiting:
Contemporary art &
photography

David Lebe

1. *Scribble #23*
   1987,
   Painted photograph,
   30" x 20"

Selected Biography:

1994 Paul Cava Gallery,
       Philadelphia, PA

1993 "Flora Photographica,
       masterpieces of Flower
       Photography 1835 to
       the present",
       Traveling exhibition,
       USA & Europe

1991 "Selections from the
       Graham and Susan
       Nash Collection",
       LA County Museum

EAST WEST FINE ART

7 Hallam St. #2C
San Francisco, CA 94103
415.863.3078
408.739.9683 FAX

Exhibiting:
Contemporary Asian and
American Art

Yves Lieou

1. *WPA/SFO*
   1993,
   Color photography,
   16" x 20"

2. *Beam Bam Boom*
   1993,
   Color photography
   16" x 20"

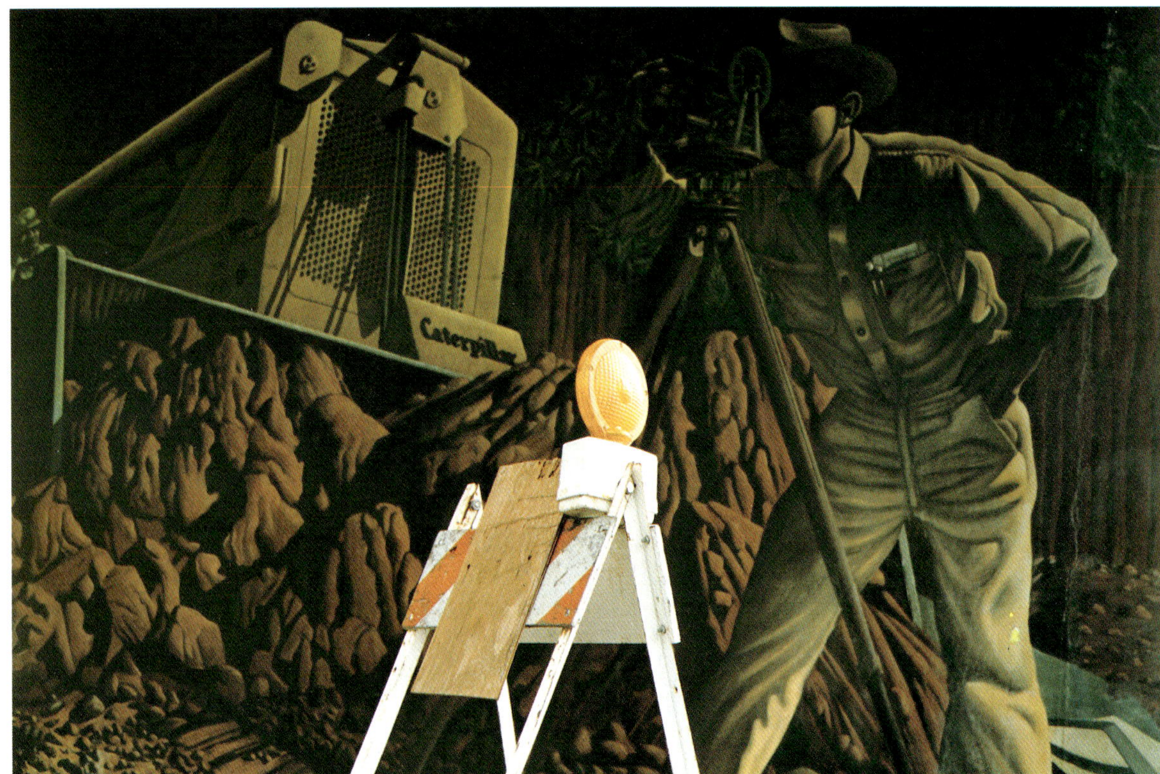

1

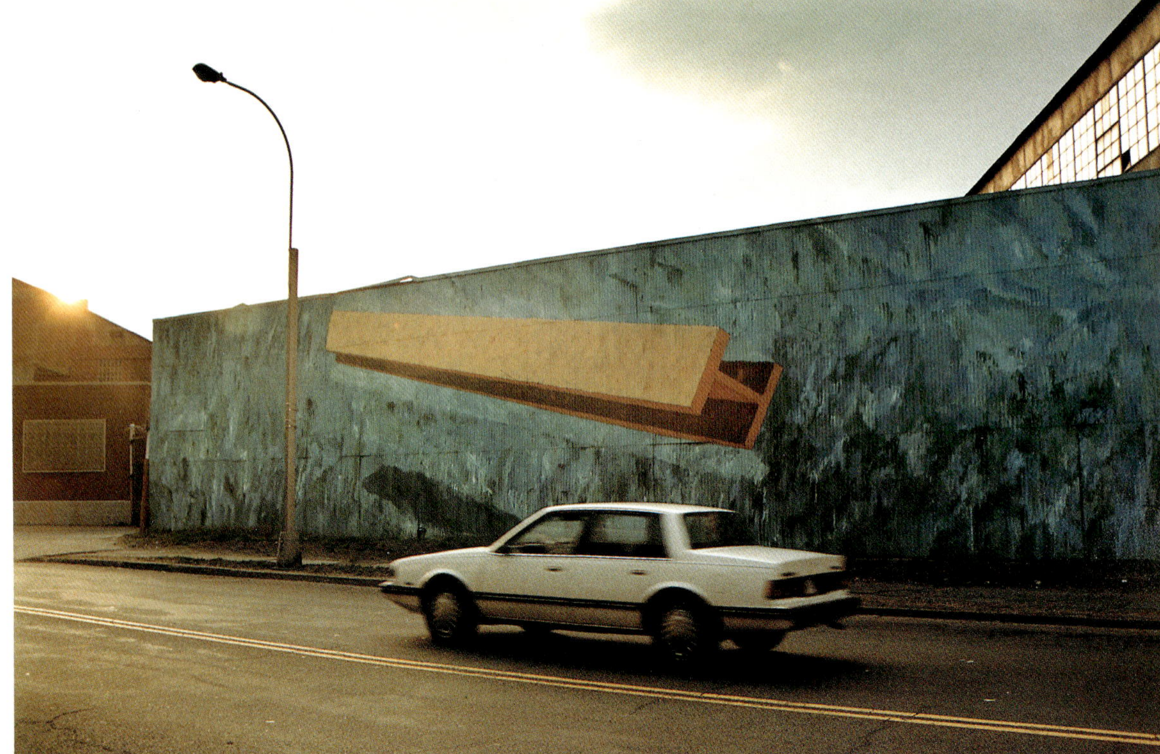

2

Selected Biography:

1993 Museum of Fine Arts,
      Springfield, MA

1990 Musèe Français de la
      Photographie, France
      and Amerika Haus,
      Berlin

1987 The Photographers'
      Gallery, London

1985 "Brief Encounters"
      Hong Kong Art Centre

      The artist was awarded
      the Prix du Ministre de
      la Culture at Bièvres,
      France in 1990

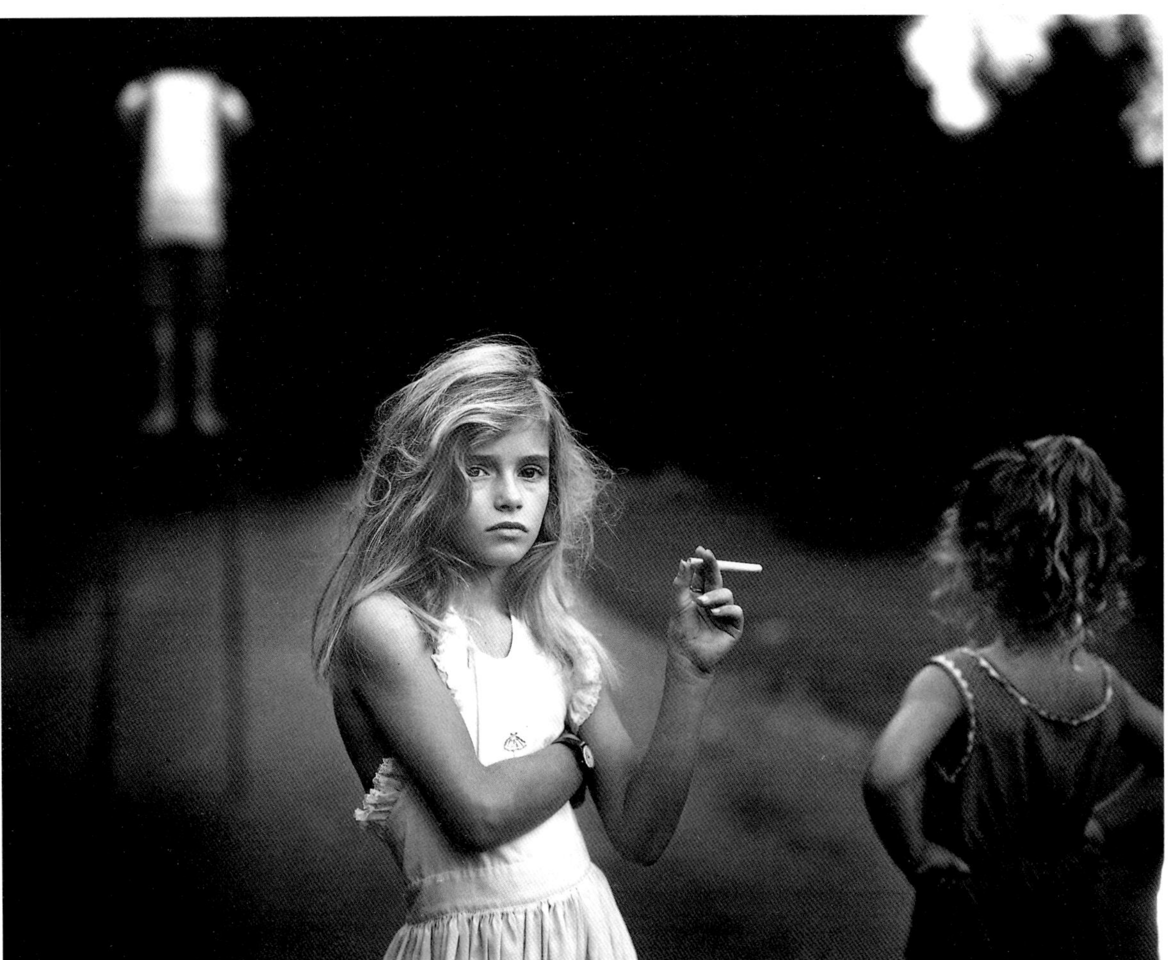

HOUK FRIEDMAN

1094 Madison Ave.
New York, NY 10033
212.628.5300
212.861.1030 FAX

Contact:
Susan Arthur

Sally Mann

Candy Cigarette
1989, Gelatin silver
enlargement print,
20" x 24"

Selected Biography:

1992 "Sally Mann:
Immediate Family,"
Houk Friedman
Gallery, NY

1991 "Biennial Exhibition,"
Whitney Museum of
American Art

"Pleasures and Terrors
of Domestic Comfort,"
The Museum of
Modern Art, NY

The Body in Question,"
Burden Gallery,
Aperture Foundation

POIRIER SCHWEITZER

1545, ave. Docteur-Penfield
Montréal, PQ H3G IC7
514.939.9855
514.939.9855 FAX

Contact:
Robert Poirier;
Decorative Arts

John A. Schweitzer;
Fine Arts

Exhibiting:
20th-century American and
European painting, sculpture,
photography, architectural
and decorative arts; outsider
and tribal art

Robert Mapplethorpe

Ajitto
1981,
Gelatin silver print,
edition 15, 17.75" x 14"
Courtesy the Estate of Robert
Mapplethorpe, New York

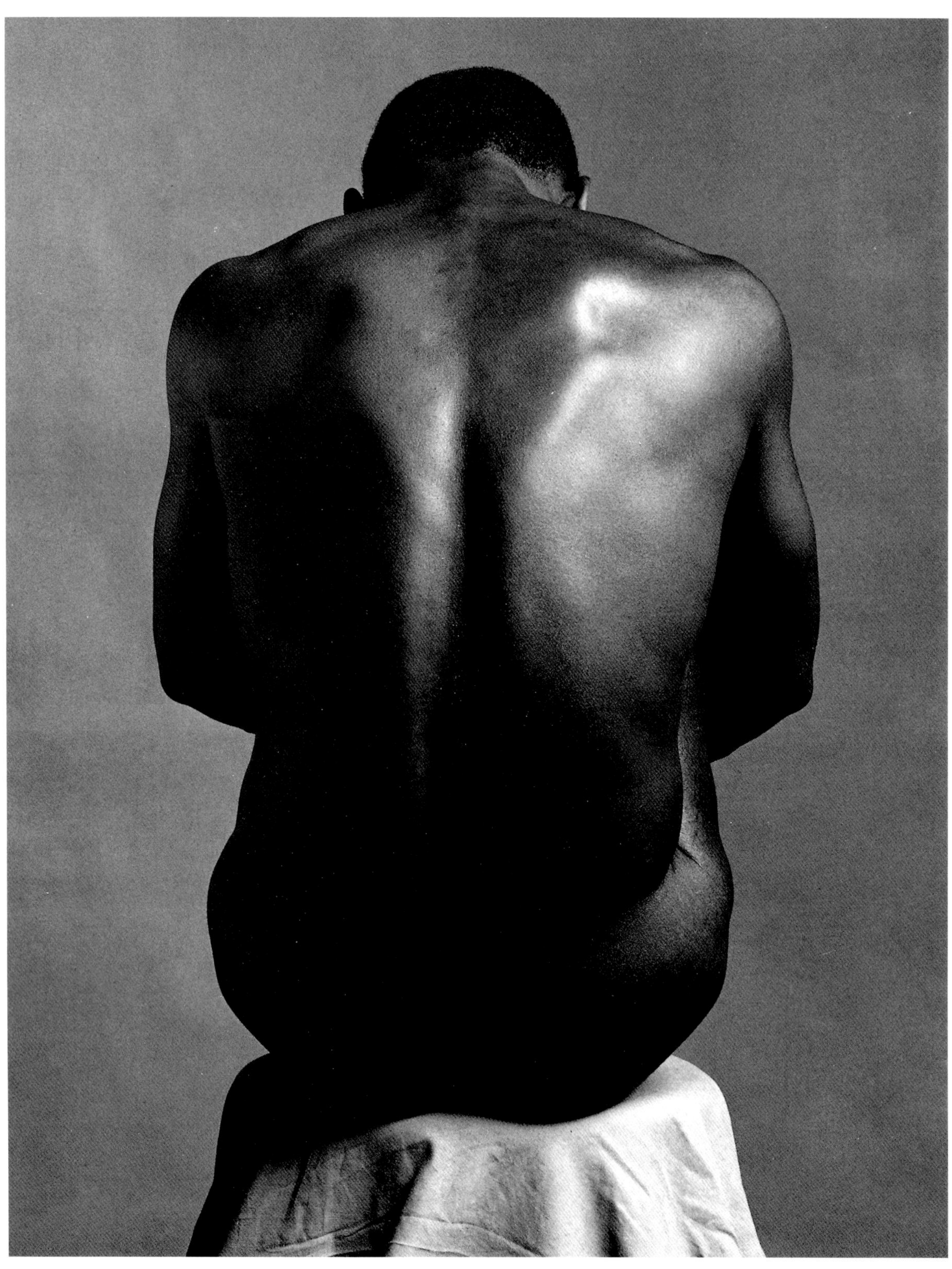

Selected Exhibitions:

1994 "Eros=Thanatos,"
Poirier Schweitzer,
Montréal, PQ

1993 "Self-Portraits,"
Guggenheim Museum,
New York, NY

1990 "In Memoriam:1946-
1989," Galerie John A.
Schweitzer, Montréal,
PQ

1984 "Photographies: 1978-
1984," Galerie John A.
Schweitzer, Montréal,
PQ

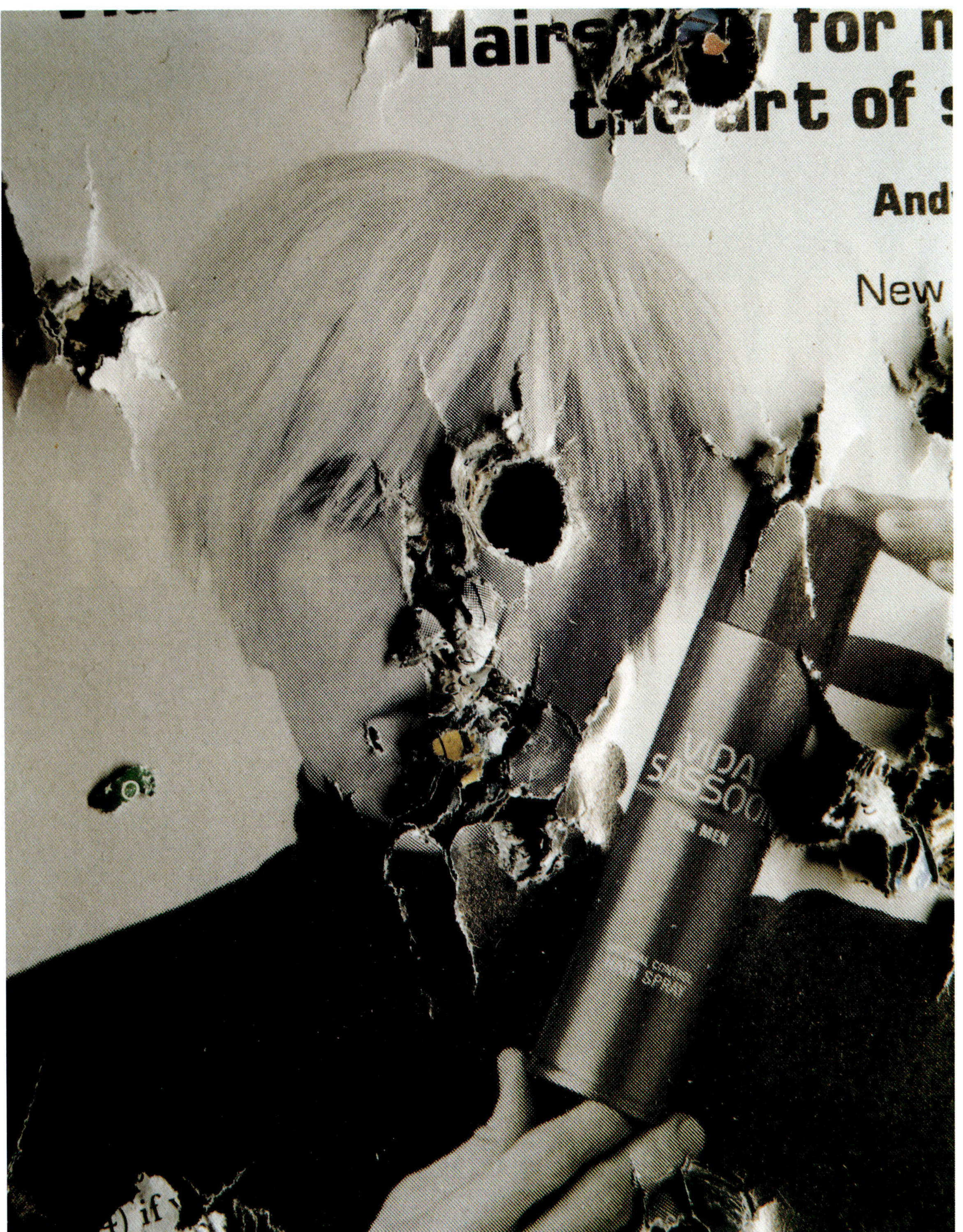

CATHERINE EDELMAN GALLERY

300 W. Superior Street
Chicago, IL 60610
312.266.2350
312.266.1967 FAX

Contact:
Catherine Edelman

Richard Misrach

Playboys #38, 1990
24" x 20", Ektacolor print

Selected Biography:

1993   "Between Home and Heaven," National Museum of American Art, Washington, D.C.

1992   National Endowment for the Arts Grant "The Sporting Life, 1878 - 1991," High Museum of Art, Atlanta, GA

1991   Whitney Biennial, New York, NY

ROCFERN
INTERNATIONAL
GALLERIES, INC.

80 Carlauren Road Unit17
Woodbridge (Toronto),
Ontario L4L 7Z5 Canada
905.850.7647
905.850.8062 FAX

Contact:
Rocco Pannese
Fernando Rocco

Kelly Ross

1. *The Human Condition*
   1993, Photography,
   13¼" x 9"

2. *The Birth of Dawn*
   1994, Photography,
   13 " x 9½"

3. *The Stages of Time*
   1993, Photography,
   9¼" x 12"

Selected Biography:

1994 Rocfern International
Galleries, Woodbridge,
Ontario, Canada

1993 Ryerson Gallery
Ryerson Polytechnical
University, Toronto,
Ontario, Canada

Art Probe International
Inc., Etobicoke, Ontario
Canada

Fine Art Publishing Inc.
Nobleton, Ontario,
Canada

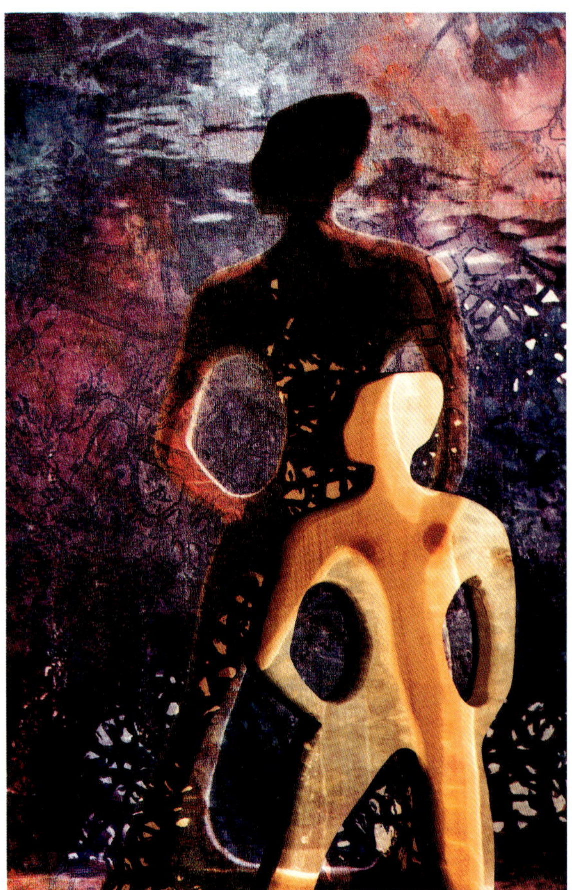

1

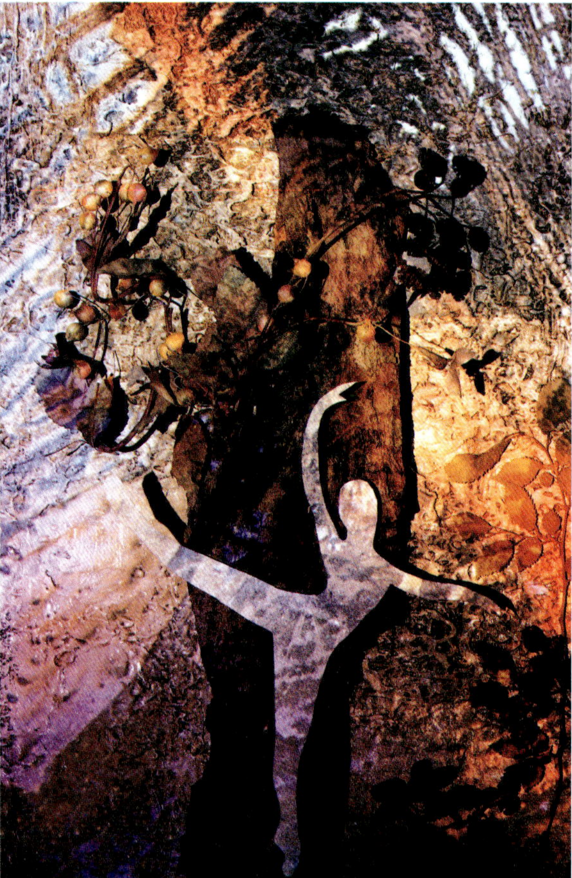

2

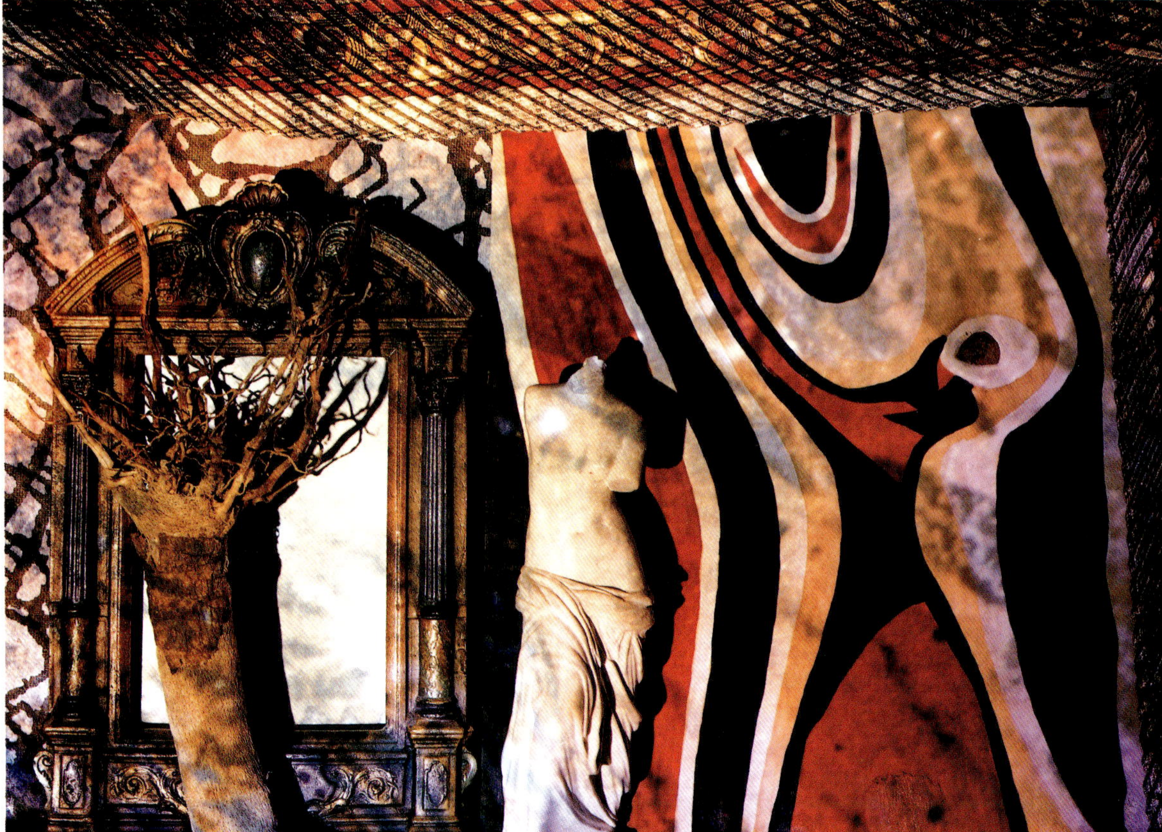

3

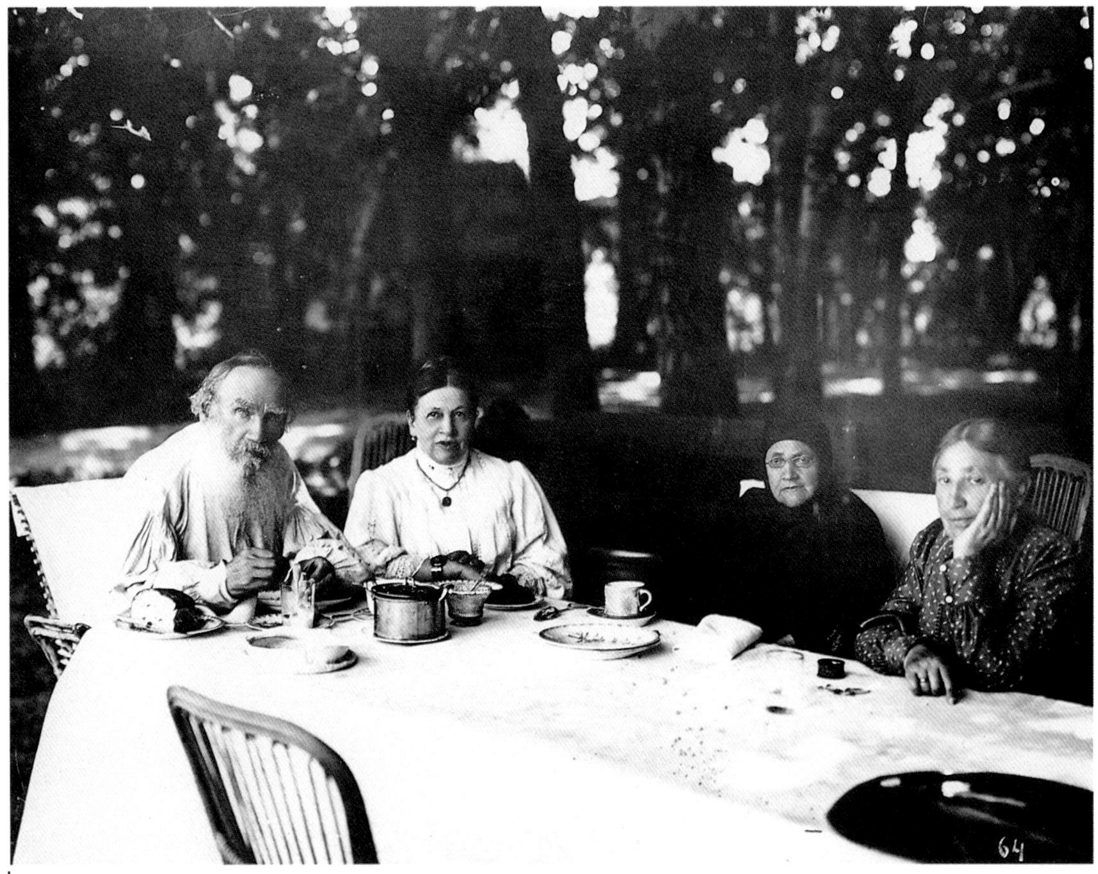

1

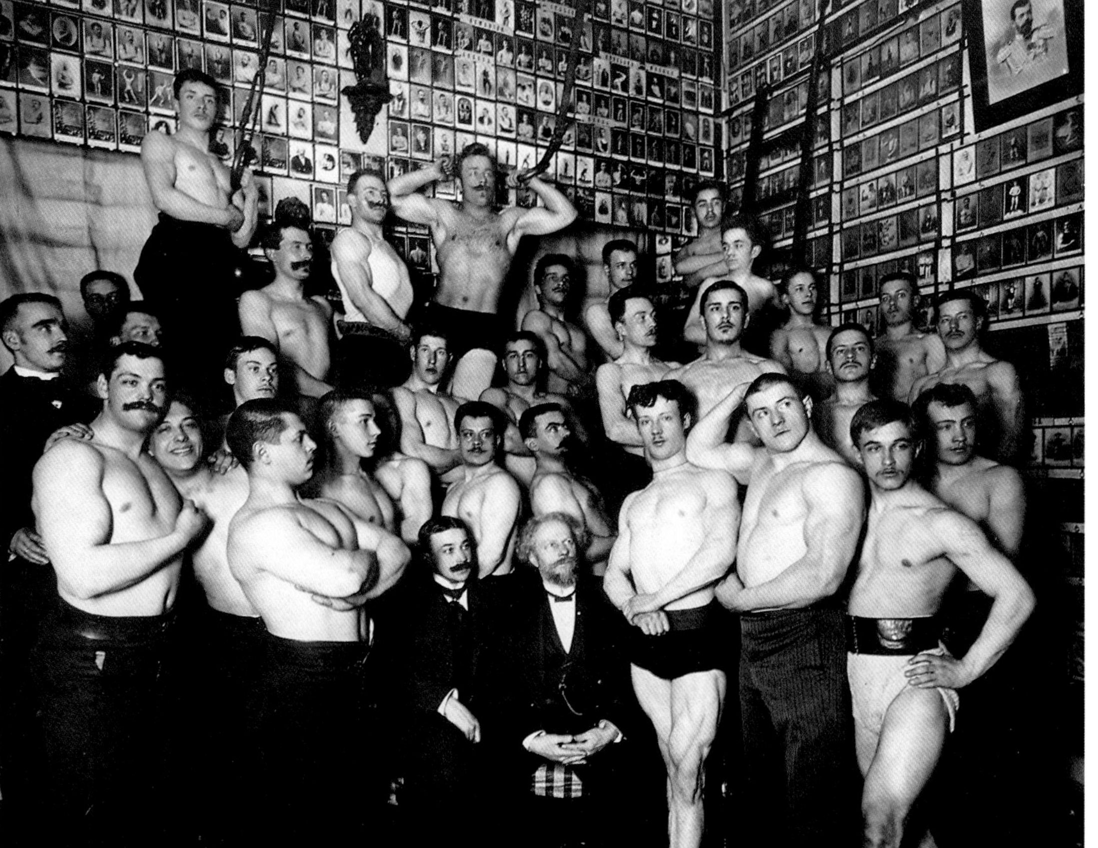

2

**STUART LEVY
FINE ART**

588 Broadway, Suite 303
New York. NY 10012
212.941.0009
212.941.7987 FAX

Contact:
Stuart Levy, President

Exhibiting:
Contemporary Russian,
European and American
artists

**Russian State Archives,
Photographs**

1. *Leo Tolstoy
   with his Sister and Niece,
   Yasnaya Poliana.*
   early 1900s

2. *A Group of Heavy Athletes
   at the St. Petersburg
   Athletic Society,*
   early 1900s

Provenance:

   Printed from the
   original glass negatives
   of the Russian State
   Archives.

J. J. BROOKINGS GALLERY

330 Commercial Street
San Jose, CA 95112
408.287.3311

Contact:
Timothy C. Duran, Director

Exhibiting:
Contemporary paintings,
prints and sculpture;
vintage and contemporary
photography

Ben Schonzeit

1. *Aalto Yellow*
   1992, Cibachrome,
   30" x 30"

2. *Golden Poppies*
   1991, Cibachrome,
   24" x 15"

3. *Venetian Ross*
   1992, Cibachrome,
   40" x 26"

Selected Exhibitions:

Winnipeg Art Museum,
Manitoba, Canada

J. J. Brookings Gallery,
San Jose, CA

Hewlett-Packard,
Palo Alto, CA

Houston Photofest,
Houston, TX

Eve Mannes Gallery,
Atlanta, GA

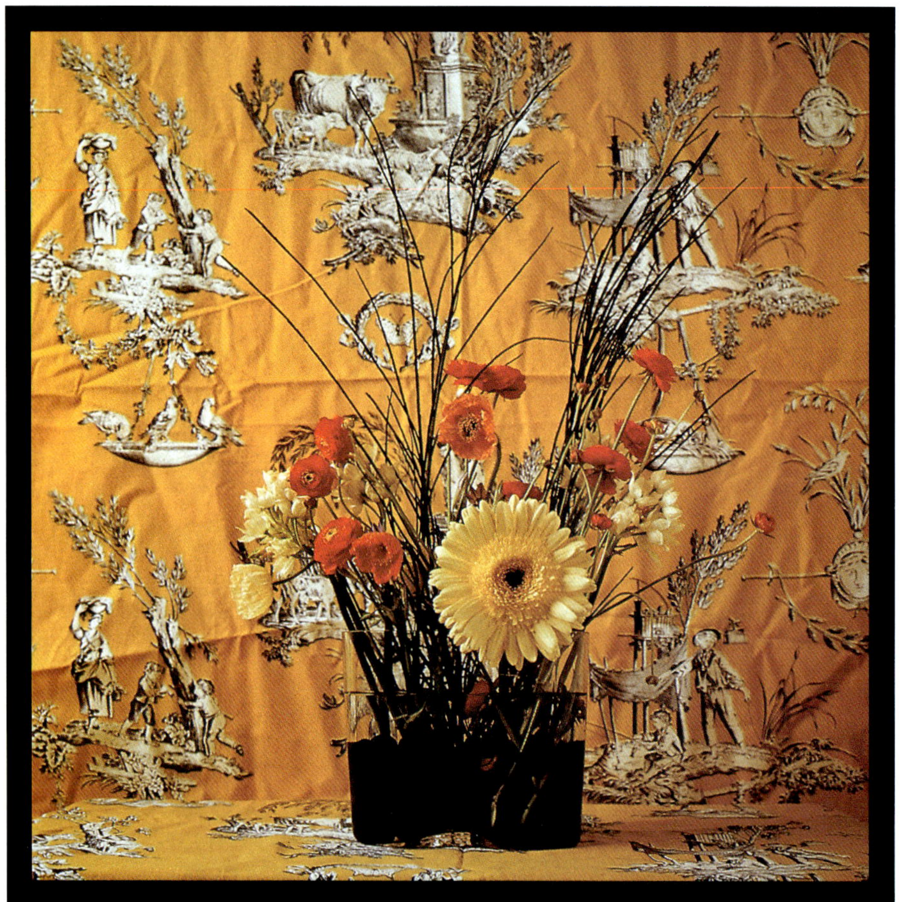

1

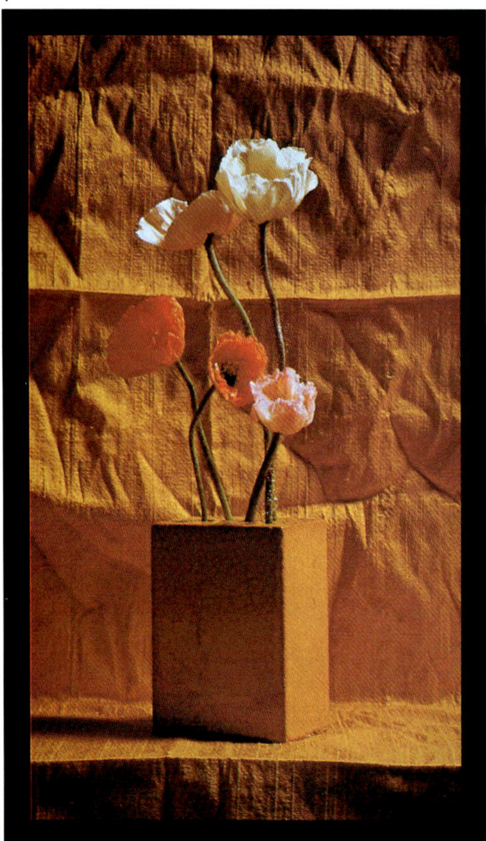

2

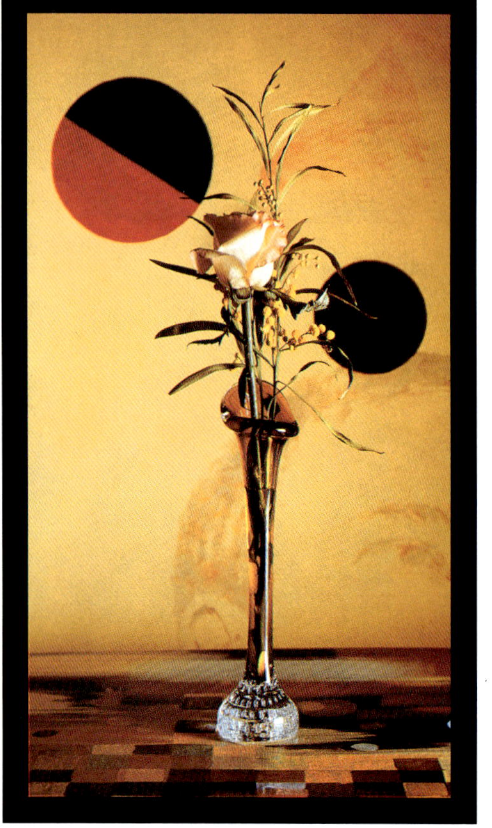

3

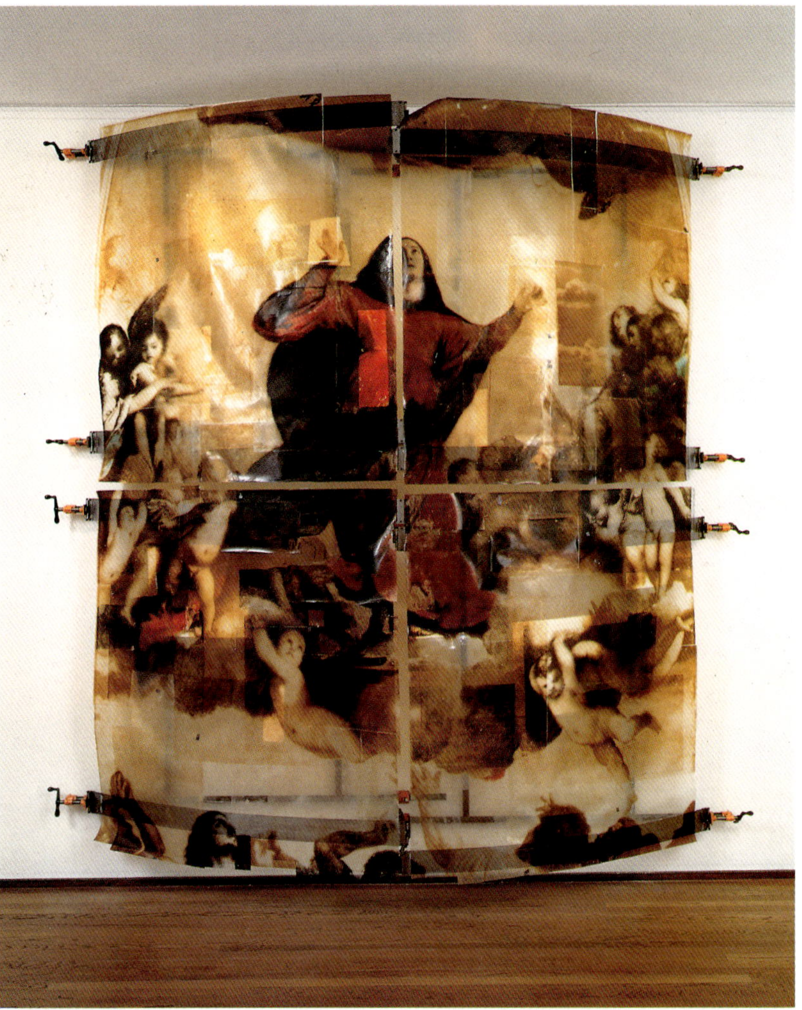

1

LEO CASTELLI

420 W. Broadway
New York, NY 10012
212.431.5160
212.431.5361 FAX

Contact:
Susan Brundage

Mike & Doug Starn

1. *Assumption*
   1992, Toned ortho
   film, silicone, paper,
   pipeclamps, steel, tape,
   114" x 114" x 21"

2. *Rose*
   1982-91, Toned silver
   prints, scotch tape push
   pins and wood measuring,
   15" x 17$^{1}/_{2}$"

3. *Sphere of Influence*
   1990-92, Toned ortho
   film, silicone, tar, steel,
   plexi, pipeclamps,
   12' diameter

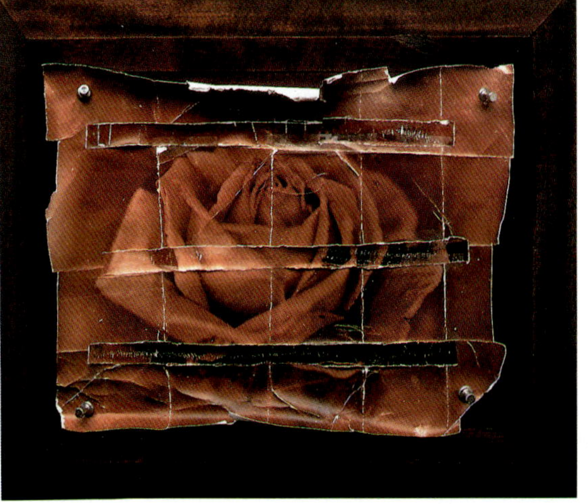

2

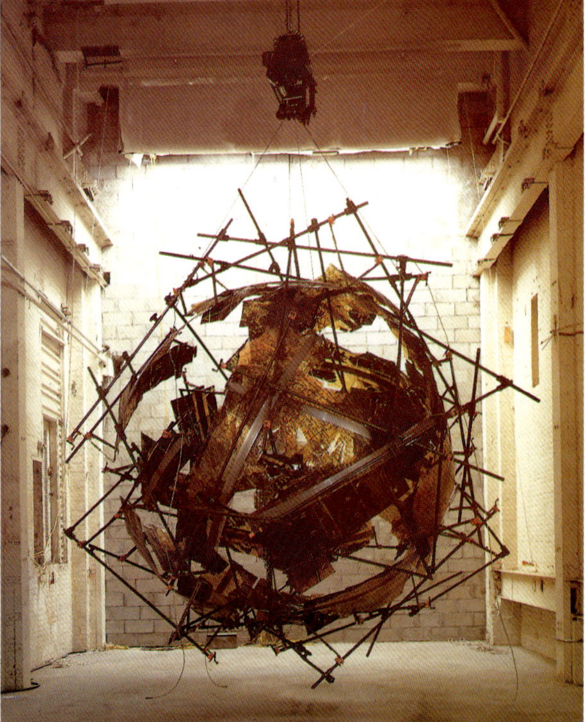

3

Selected Biography:

1993 Solo exhibitions:
      Akira Ikeda Gallery,
      Tokyo, Japan

      Akira Ikeda Gallery,
      Taura, Japan

1992 Solo exhibition:
      Yellow and Blue Louvre
      Floor -A Project,
      Galerie Thaddeus
      Ropac, Paris, France

      Leo Castelli Gallery,
      420 West Broadway
      and 55 Crosby St., New
      York, NY

**STUART LEVY
FINE ART**

588 Broadway, Suite 303
New York. NY 10012
212.941.0009
212.941.7987 FAX

Contact:
Stuart Levy, President

Exhibiting:
Contemporary Russian,
European and American
Artists

Miro Svolik

1. *So I began to
   Wander Around*
   1986, Silver gelatin print,
   from an edition of 15,
   mounted in hand-cut
   mats, titled and signed
   by the artist,
   24.5" x 17.75" overall

2. *And did Not See*
   1986, Silver gelatin print,
   from an edition of 15,
   mounted in hand-cut
   mats, titled and signed
   by the artist,
   24.5" x 17.75" overall

Selected Exhibitions:

1993 "Works Since 1980
from the Collection,"
The Museum of
Modern Art, New York

1992 "Nineteen
Contemporary
Czechoslovak
Photographers,"
FotoFest,
Houston, Texas

1991 "Fotobiennale,"
Enschede, Netherlands

1990 "Winners of Sixth
Annual Infinity
Awards," International
Center for
Photography,
New York

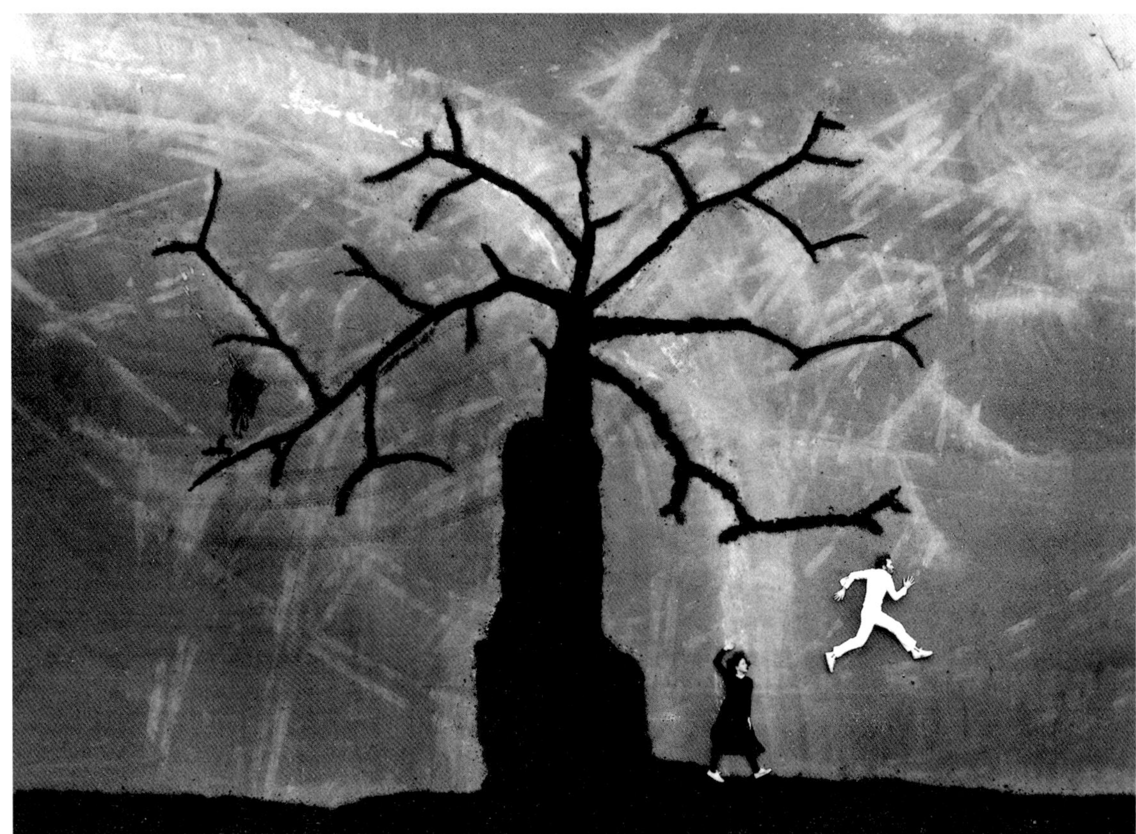

1

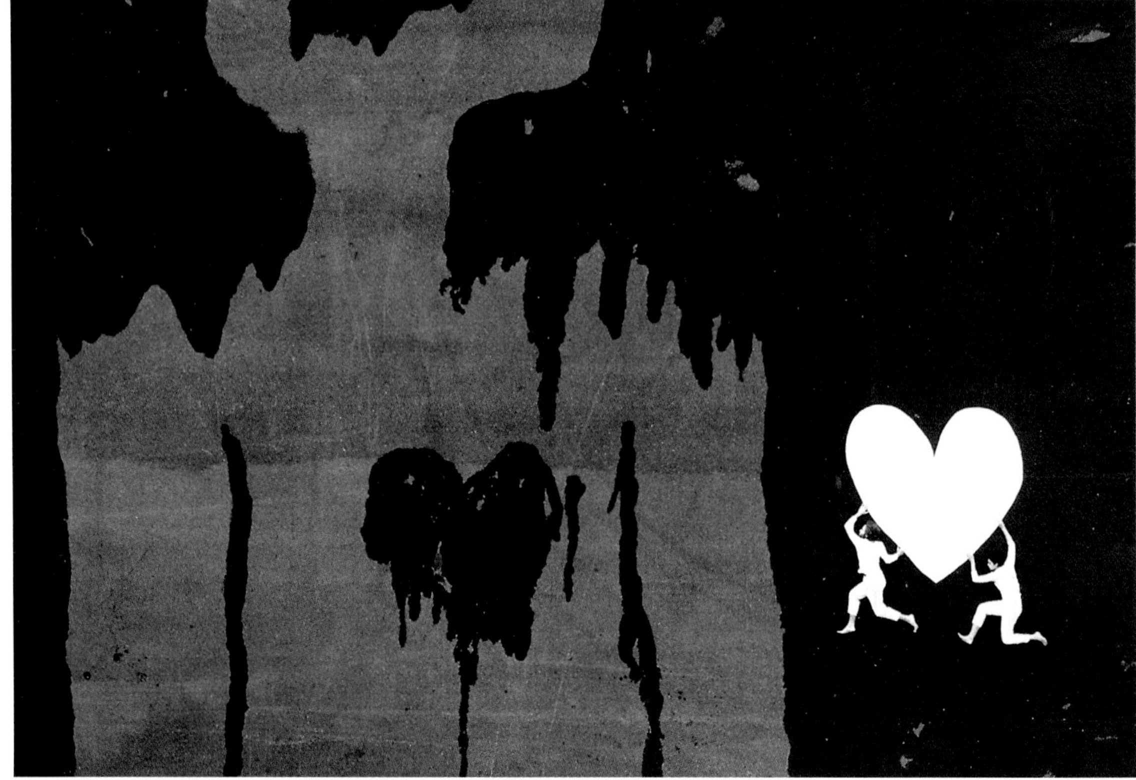

2

GALLERY & ARTIST INDEX

GALLERY LISTINGS

ALBERS FINE ART GALLERY 901.683.2256
1102 Brookfield Rd. Fax: 901.683.2256
Memphis, TN 38119
Hours: Tue-Fri 9:30-5:30; Sat 11-3
Specialty: Contemporary fine art & craft; painting, sculpture, clay, glass & monotypes.

Artists Presented: Iris Harkavy (Page 98), Julie Warren Martin (Page 253)

ALISAN FINE ART 852.526.1091
10 Chater Rd. Fax: 852.845.3975
Central, Hong Kong
Specialty: Chinese Contemporary art

Artists Presented: Chao Chung-Hsiang (Page 66)

AMBROSINO GALLERY 305.445.2211
3155 ponce de Leon Blvd. Fax: 305.444.0101
Coral Gables, FL 33134
Hours: Tue-Sat 10-6:30
Specialty: Latin American and Contemporary art

Artists Presented: Adonay Duque (Page 81)

ANDREAS GALLERIES 703.448.2222
8545 Leesburg Pike Fax: 703.356.3328
Vienna, VA 22182
Hours: Mon-Fri 9-6; By Appt
Specialty: Contemporary European & American art; paintings, drawings, sculpture & limited edition works on paper.

Artists Presented: George Andreas (Page 40)

ANSORENA 1.523.8515
Alcalá 54 Fax: 1.522.0158
Madrid, Spain 28014
Hours: Daily 10:30-2 & 5-8:30
Specialty: Spanish contemporary realism.

Artists Presented: Munoz Vera (Page 207)

ARTE DO BRASIL 5521.267.2549
Rua Visconde de Piraja,86 slj. 6 Fax: 5521.267.1254
22410-000 Rio de Janeiro, Brasil
Specialty: Contemporary painting and sculpture.

Artists Presented: Alex Cerveny (Page 225), Marcos Benjamin (Page 232)

ARTE NUCLEO GALERIA 525.254.3732
Edgar Alan Poe 308, Col. Polanco Fax: 525.254.1942
Mexico City, Mexico 11560
Specialty: Dealer, publisher.

Artists Presented: Agueda Lozano (Page 124), Guillermo Meza (Page 134), Oris Robertson (Page 173)

FRANZ BADER GALLERY 202.393.6111
1500 K St. NW
Washington, DC 20005
Hours: Tue-Sat 11-5
Specialty: Contemporary American sculpture, paintings and works on paper.

Artists Presented: Peter Milton (Page 228)

SARAH BAIN GALLERY 714.257.1440
1112 Brea Mall Fax: 714.257.0192
Brea, CA 92621
Hours: Mon-Fri 10-9; Sat 10-7; Sun 11-6
Specialty: Emerging and established contemporary artists.

Artists Presented: Poly (Page 163)

ROBERT BERMAN GALLERY 310.453.9195
2044 Broadway Fax: 310.453.2383
Santa Monica, CA 90404
Hours: Tue-Sat 10-5; Thu 11-8; Sun 12-4
Specialty: Contemporary, modern & Latin American art in all media.

Artists Presented: Frank Romero (Page 175)

J. J. BROOKINGS GALLERY 408.287.3311
330 Commercial St.
San Jose, CA 95112
Specialty: American contemporary paintings, prints & sculpture; vintage & contemporary photography.

Artists Presented: James Crable (Page 279), Lisa Gray (Page 280), Ben Schonzeit (Page 290)

CARIB ART GALLERY 212.343.2539
584 Broadway
New York, NY 10012
Specialty: Contemporary art from Latin American and the Caribbean.

Artists Presented: Hochi Asiatico (Page 222), Dionisio Blanco (Page 50), Guillo Perez (Page 158), Andres Puig (Page 166)

ROBERT CARGO FOLK ART GALLERY 205.758.8884
2314 Sixth St.
Tuscaloosa, AL 35401
Hours: Sat 10-5; Sun 2-5; By Appt
Specialty: Contemporary folk art, antique quilts, African-American quilts, Haitian voodoo flags.

Artists Presented: Roger Rice (Page 169), Yvonne Wells (Page 211)

ALDO CASTILLO GALLERY 312.525.2536
3513 N. Lincoln Ave., 2nd Fl. Fax: 312.525.2582
Chicago, IL 60657
Specialty: Fine Latin American Art

Artists Presented: Antonio Bou (Page 53)

LEO CASTELLI GALLERY 212.431.5160
420 W. Broadway Fax: 212.431.5361
New York, NY 10012
Hours: Tue-Sat 10-6

Artists Presented: Joseph Kosuth (Page 247), Robert Morris (Page 255), James Rosenquist (Page 180), Mike & Doug Starn (Page 291), Robert Therrien (Page 268)

PAUL CAVA GALLERY 215.627.1172
22 N. Third St. Fax: 215.627.1173
Philadelphia, PA 19106
Hours: Tue-Sat 11-5
Specialty: Contemporary art & photography.

Artists Presented: David Lebe (Page 283)

CENTRO DE ARTE EUROAMERICANO 2.921.204
Calle California, Las Mercedes Fax: 2.915.401
Caracas, Venezuela 1060
Hours: Tue-Fri 9-1 & 4-7; Sat-Sun 11-2
Specialty: Latin American & contemporary art.

Artists Presented: Adonay Duque (Page 81)

CLAUDIA CHAPLINE GALLERY 415.868.2308
3445 Shoreline Hwy., P.O. Box 946 Fax: 415.868.9436
Stinson Beach, CA 94970
Hours: Fri-Mon 12-5; By Appt
Specialty: Contemporary art of Northern California.

Artists Presented: Claudia Chapline (Page 61), Etta Deikman (Page 77), Christoph Fields (Page 239), Sally Roberton (Page 172), Ann Weber (Page 210)

MARSHA CHILD CONTEMPORARY 215.297.0414
P.O. Box 364 Fax: 215.297.0414
Solebury, PA 18963
Hours: Tue-Fri By Appt
Specialty: Contemporary European, Eastern European & American paintings, sculpture & graphics.

Artists Presented: Maciek Danilewicz (Page 236), Georges Mazilu (Page 132), Valerij Skrypka (Page 196), Atanas Zglevski (Page 218)

CONNAUGHT BROWN GALLERY   4471.408.0362
2 Albemarle St.   Fax: 4471.495.3137
London, England WIX 3HF
Hours: Mon-Fri 10-6; Sat 10-12:30
Specialty: Post-Impressionism, modern & contemporary works of art.

Artists Presented: Paul Richards (Page 170)

EUGENIA CUCALON GALLERY   212.472.8741
145 E. 72nd St.   Fax: 212.472.8741
New York, NY 10021
Hours: Tue-Sat 12-6
Specialty: Works by North & South American & European artists.

Artists Presented: Waldo Balart (Page 42), Meret Oppenheim (Page 150)

BARRETT DEBUSK SCULPTURE   817.625.8476
3813 N. Commerce   Fax: 817.261.8172
Ft. Worth, TX 76106
Specialty: One-of-a-kind & limited edition DeBusk welded steel sculptures.

Artists Presented: Barret De Busk (Page 237)

PATRICK DOHENY FINE ART   604.737.7537
2199 Granville St.   Fax: 604.736.8826
Vancouver, Canada V6H 3E9
Hours: Tue-Fri 11-6; Sat 10-5
Specialty: Important 20th-century art.

Artists Presented: Bonifacho (Page 52)

E.M. DONAHUE GALLERY   212.226.1111
560 Broadway, #304   Fax: 212.982.5579
New York, NY 10012
Hours: Tue-Sat 10-6
Specialty: Contemporary paintings.

Artists Presented: Beth Ames Swartz (Page 199)

DONNIE FIRKINS STUDIO   502.842.3337
238 Freestone Ct.
Bowling Green, KY 42103
Hours: By Appt.

Artists Presented: Donnie Firkins (Page 240)

NANCY DRYSDALE GALLERY   202.466.4550
2103 O St. NW   Fax: 202.466.4549
Washington, DC 20037
Hours: Tue-Sat 11-5; By Appt
Specialty: Contemporary art in all media.

Artists Presented: Jim Sanborn (Page 263)

EAST WEST FINE ART   415.863.3078
7 Hallam St., #2C   Fax: 408.739.9683
San Francisco, CA 94103
Specialty: Contemporary Asian & American art.

Artists Presented: Yves Lieou (Page 284), Shan-Shan Sheng (Page 191), Hua-Zheng Wang (Page 209)

CATHERINE EDELMAN GALLERY   312.266.2350
300 W. Superior St.   Fax: 312.266.1967
Chicago, IL 60610
Hours: Tue-Sat 10-5:30
Specialty: Promotion, exhibition and sales of contemporary photography.

Artists Presented: Richard Misrach (Page 287)

ENID OKLA HOMA   312.787.6011
233 W. Huron   Fax: 312.787.6617
Chicago, IL 60610
Hours: Wed-Sat 11-5:30

Artists Presented: Beyant Johnston (Page 281), Mike Linz (Page 123), Stephan Nesvacil (Page 258), Celeste Sotola (Page 197)

DIANE FARRIS GALLERY   604.737.2629
1565 W. Seventh Ave.   Fax: 604.737.2675
Vancouver, Canada V6J 1S1
Hours: Tue-Fri 10-5:30; Sat 10-5
Specialty: Canadian contemporary art.

Artists Presented: David Bierk (Page 47), Claudia Cuesta (Page 235), Judith Currelly (Page 73), Angela Grossmann (Page 93), Kathryn Jacobi (Page 105), John Koerner (Page 112), Sam Lam (Page 114), Attila Richard Lukacs (Page 125), Laurie Papou (Page 154), Taras Polataiki (Page 162), David Robinson (Page 262), Hanneline Rogeberg (Page 174), Chris Woods (Page 215)

FASSBENDER ASSOCIATES   312.421.3600
415 N. Sangamon   Fax: 312.733.6496
Chicago, IL 60622
Hours: By Appt.
Specialty: Contemporary American and European painting and sculpture

Artists Presented: Matt Lamb (Page 115)

FENIX FINE ART   305.573.2727
180 N.E.40th St.   Fax: 305.576.7707
Miami, FL 33137
Hours: Mon-Fri10-5; Sat 11-4
Specialty: Latin American Art

Artists Presented: Mario Madrigal-Arcia (Page 126), David Manzur (page 129), Robertto Milanes-Gala (Page 136), Dario Ortiz-Robledo (Page 151), Albertto Pancorbo (Page 153), Ivan Santos (Page 185), Lina Velazquez (Page 205), Maria V. Velez (Page 206) Nira Raz (Page 261)

MIA FEROLETO FINE ART PLANNING   212.529.3744
45W. 10th St., #5B   Fax: 212.529.4475
New York, NY 10011
Hours: By Appt
Specialty: Contemporary art by major & emerging artists.

Artists Presented: Rita Blitt (Page 233)

JANET FLEISHER GALLERY   215.545.7562
211 S. 17th St.   Fax: 215.545.6140
Philadelphia, PA 19103
Hours: Mon-Fri 10:30-5:30; Sat 11-5:30
Specialty: Contemporary American art, self-taught & visionary art.

Artists Presented: Tony Fitzpatrick (Page 226), Purvis Young (Page 216)

FORUM GALLERY   212.355.4545
745 Fifth Ave., #503   Fax: 212.355.4547
New York, NY 10151
Hours: Tue-Sat 10-5:30; Summer Mon-Fri 10-5:30

Artists Presented: William Beckman (Page 44), Kent Bellows (Page 224)

GAGOSIAN GALLERY   212.744.2313
980 Madison Ave., 6th Fl.   Fax: 212.772.7962
New York, NY 10021
Hours: Tue-Sat 10-6
Specialty: 20th Century painting and sculpture; Abstract Expressionism, Pop & Minimalism.

Artists Presented: Francesco Clemente (Page 67), Peter Halley (Page 97), Andrew Lord (Page 249), Walter de Maria (Page 250), David Salle (Page 184), Philip Taaffe (Page 200)

GALERIA DE ARTE MEXICANO   525.272.5529
Rafael Rebollar #43, Col. San Miguel, Chapultepec   Fax: 525.272.5583
Mexico City, Mexico 11850
Hours: Mon-Fri 10-7; Sat 10-2
Specialty: Contemporary Mexican art.

Artists Presented: Leonora Carrington (Page 59)

GALERIA NORMANDIE 809.725.4252
Ave. Munoz Rivera, Radisson Normandie Hotel Fax: 809.729.3083
San Juan, PR 00902
Specialty: Puerton Rican contemporary arts, scuptures, graphics,
ceramics and crafts.

Artists Presented: Carlos Marcial (Page 131)

GALERIE ARIADNE 1.512.9479
1010 Wien, Beckerstrasse6 Fax: 1.512.4296
Vienna 1010, Austria
Hours: By Appt.
Specialty: Contemporary art.

Artists Presented: Horacio Sapera (Page 186)

GALERIE PIERRE 8864.322.2155
#19 Kuan Chien Rd., 12F Fax: 8864.328.8081
Taichung, Republic of China 404
Hours: Daily 9-6
Specialty: Modern art.

Artists Presented: Michell Hwang (Page 104)

GALERIA VERTICE 3.630.1330
Lopez Cotilla 2285 Fax: 3.630.1330
Guadalajara, Mexico 44120
Hours: Mon-Fri 10-2 & 4-7
Specialty: Contemporary Mexican art.

Artists Presented: Enrique Magana (Page 127)

GALLERY ART & PEACE 407.629.6308
1545 Palmer Ave. Fax: 407.677.8222
Winter Park, FL 32789

Artists Presented: Jim Allen (Page 38)

GALLERY LEU 415.382.9549
49 Pacheco Creek Dr. Fax: 415.883.9714
Novato, CA 94949
Hours: By Appt
Specialty: Contemporary paintings & prints.

Artists Presented: Michael Leu (Page 119)

GALLERY REVEL 212.925.0600
96 Spring St. Fax: 212.431.6270
New York, NY 10012
Hours: Mon-Fri 9-6; Sat 11-6; Sun 12-5
Specialty: Paintings, sculpture and prints by contemporary international
artists.

Artists Presented: Victor Shvaiko (Page 194)

C. GRIMALDIS GALLERY 401.539.1080
523 N. Charles St. Fax: 401.539.2229
Baltimore, MD 21201
Hours: By Appt.
Specialty: Contemporary sculpture and painting

Artists Presented: Mary Shaffer (Page 190)

RICHARD GRAY GALLERY 312.642.8877
620 N. Michigan Ave. Fax: 312.642.8488
Chicago, IL 60611
Hours: Tue-Sat 10-5:30; By Appt

Artists Presented: Luciano Castelli (Page 60)

HARMON-MEEK GALLERY 813.261.2637
386 Broad Ave. S Fax: 813.261.3804
Naples, FL 33940
Hours: Mon-Sat 10-5; Thu 10-9
Specialty: 20th-century American art.

Artists Presented: Colleen Browning (Page 56), Adolf Dehn (Page 76),
Balcomb Greene (Page 91), Bob Kane (Page 107), James Twitty (Page 203)

LISA HARRIS GALLERY 206.443.3315
1922 Pike Place
Seattle, WA 98101
Hours: Mon-Sat 11-5:30
Specialty: Contemporary Northwest and West Coast paintings.

Artists Presented: Gary Nisbet (Page 146)

HART GALLERY 6.0263.8707
23 Main Street Fax: 6.0263.8707
Linby, England NG15 8AE
Hours: By Appt
Specialty: Contemporary British artwork.

Artists Presented: David Blackburn (Page 48)

G. RAY HAWKINS GALLERY 310.394.5558
908 Colorado Ave. Fax: 310.576.2468
Santa Monica, CA 90401
Specialty: Fine vintage & contemporary photography.

Artists Presented: Dmitri Baltermants (Page 277), Dmitri Baltermants
(Page 278)

HELLER GALLERY 212.966.5948
71 Greene St. Fax: 212.966.5956
New York, NY 10012
Specialty: Contemporary glass sculpture.

Artists Presented: Jay Musler (Page 256)

KIYO HIGASHI GALLERY 213.655.2482
8332 Melrose Ave. Fax: 213.655.7016
Los Angeles, CA 90069
Hours: Tue-Sat 11-6
Specialty: Abstract-reductive work (paintings and sculpture).

Artists Presented: Larry Bell (Page 46), Max Cole (Page 70), Madeline
O'Connor (Page 149)

HOUK-FRIEDMAN 212.628.5300
1094 Madison Ave. Fax: 212.861.1030
New York, NY 10033
Hours: Tue-Sat 10-6

Artists Presented: Dorothea Lange (Page 282), Sally Mann (Page 285)

INTERNATIONAL ART RESEARCH 516.352.7399
140 Violet Ave. Fax: 516.352.2156
Floral Park, NY 11001
Hours: By Appt
Specialty: International contemporary, modern & Impressionist art,
including paintings, works on paper, prints & installations.

Artists Presented: Lilo Kinne (Page 108)

ITURRALDE GALLERY 213.937.4267
154 N. La Brea Ave. Fax: 213.937.4269
Los Angeles, CA 90036
Hours: Tue-Sat 10-5; By Appt
Specialty: Contemporary Latin American art.

Artists Presented: Javier Marin (Page 251), Rodrigo Pimentel (Page 160)

JAMISON\THOMAS GALLERY 503.222.0063
1313 N.W. Glisan Fax: 503.224.4517
Portland, OR 97209
Hours: Tue-Sat 10-6
Specialty: Contemporary paintings, sculpture, drawings and prints.

Artists Presented: Rick Bartow (Page 43), Nick Blosser (Page 51)

JASON & RHODES 71.434.1768
4 New Burlington Pl. Fax: 71.287.8841
London, England W1X 1SB
Hours: Mon-Fri 9:30-6; Sat 10:30-4
Specialty: British & international contemporary art.

Artists Presented: Eileen Cooper (Page 71)

CAROLE JONES GALLERY 312.587.8820
300 W. Superior Fax: 587.9859
Chicago, IL 60610
Hours: Tue-Sat 10-5; Thu 10-7; Sun 12-5; By Appt
Specialty: Contemporary international fine art; paintings & sculptures.

Artists Presented: Stan Edwards (Page 83), Eve Hennesa (Page 100), Matt Lamb (Page 115), Joyce Novak (Page 147), Tomas Ochou (Page 148), Charlotte Segal (Page 188), Weiliang Zhao (Page 219)

KATZ 714.497.1098
1914 Upper Rim Rock Fax: 714.497.2569
Laguna Beach, CA 92651
Hours: Daily 9-5
Specialty: Contemporary painting, drawing & sculpture.

Artists Presented: Pamela Wilson (Page 213)

PHYLLIS KIND GALLERY 312.642.6302
313 W. Superior St. Fax: 312.642.8502
Chicago, IL 60610
Hours: Tue-Sat 10-5:30
Specialty: Contemporary American, Soviet, Naive & Outsider art.

Artists Presented: Roger Brown (Page 55), Gladys Nilsson (Page 145), Ed Paschke (Page 156), Karl Wirsum (Page 214)

MICHAEL KIZHNER FINE ART 213.659.5222
746 N. La Cienega Blvd. Fax: 213.659.0838
Los Angeles, CA 90069
Hours: Mon-Fri 10-6
Specialty: California Impressionists (1900-1940) & Russian contemporary art.

Artists Presented: Ilona Severovna Gansovskaya (Page 86)

KNOEDLER & COMPANY 212.794.0550
19 E. 70 St. Fax: 212.772.6932
New York, NY 10021
Hours: Tue-Fri 9:30-5:30; Sat 10-5:30
Specialty: Contemporary European and American art.

Artists Presented: Robert Rauschenberg (Page 168), Frank Stella (Page 267)

KOCKA EARTHRACKS STUDIO 812.737.2261
995 Beech Rd.S.E. Fax: 812.738.8845
Laconia, IN 47135
Hours: By Appt.
Specialty: Representing painting and sculpture by David Kocka

Artists Presented: David Kocka (Page 246)

L. A. ARTCORE 213.617.3274
420 East 3rd St., Ste 110
Los Angeles, CA 90013
Hours: Mon-Fri 8-5; By Appt
Specialty: Contemporary painting and sculpture

Artists Presented: Joseph Piasentin (Page 159), Daniel Storozynsky (Page 198), Ruffus Snoddy (Page 266)

LAKE FORD STUDIO 301.387.7010
Rte. 5, Cranesville Rd., Box 2340
Oakland, MD 21550
Hours: Mon-Fri 8-5; By Appt
Specialty: Drawings & prints of birds, landscapes, natural subjects.

Artists Presented: Ken Bauer (Page 223)

EDITH LAMBERT GALLERY 505.984.2783
707 Canyon Rd. Fax: 505.983.4494
Santa Fe, NM 87501
Hours: Daily 10-5
Specialty: Contemporary paintings, drawings & sculpture.

Artists Presented: Carol Hoy (Page 103), Margaret Nes (Page 143), Isabelle H. Siegel (Page 265)

LANDAU/20TH CENTURY ART 310.474.5155
1625 Thayer Ave. Fax: 310.475.8212
Los Angeles, CA 90024
Hours: By Appt.
Specialty: 20 century sculpture, painting and photography.

Artists Presented: Barry Gordon (Page 89)

UDITA LEBERG STUDIO 718.261.0896
67-38 108th St.
Forest Hills, NY 11375
Hours: By Appt
Specialty: Contemporary art from Europe & America.

Artists Presented: Udita Leberg (Pages 116, 117, 118)

STUART LEVY GALLERY 212.941.0009
588 Broadway, Ste 303 Fax: 212.941.7987
New York, NY 10012
Hours: Tue-Sat 10-5; Sun 10-6; By Appt
Specialty: Contemporary Russian, European and American Artist

Artists Presented: Genia Chef (Page 62), Ueli Michel (Page 135), Osmo Rauhala (Page 167), Leonid Lamm (Page248), Miro Svolik (Page 292), Russian State Archives (Page 289)

THE LOWE GALLERY 404.352.8114
75 Bennett St., Space A-2 Fax: 404.352.0564
Atlanta, GA 30309
Hours: Tue-Fri 10:30-5:30; Sat 12-5
Specialty: Contemporary painting, sculpture & objects.

Artists Presented: James Warner Booth (Page 234), Brad Durham (Page 82), Greg Edmondson (Page 238), John Erickson (Page 85), Kathleen Morris (Page 141), Todd Murphy (Page 142), Andrew Saftel (Page 183), Stephen Schultz (Page 187)

LUCIA GALLERY (SOHO) 212.941.9296
150 Spring St. Fax: 212.941.9296
New York, NY 10012
Hours: Tue-Sat 11-6
Specialty: The neo-iconography of Dr. T.F. Chen.

Artists Presented: Tsing Fang Chen (Page 63)

M-13 GALLERY 212.925.3007
72 Greene St., 2nd Fl. Fax: 212.925.3923
New York, NY 10012
Hours: Tue-Sat 10-6
Specialty: Contemporary art.

Artists Presented: Toon Kuijpers (Page 113), Robin Rose (Page 178)

GALERIA MAREN 525.208.0442
Hamburgo 175-A, Zona Rosa Fax: 525.533.3904
Mexico City, Mexico 06600
Hours: Daily 10-7
Specialty: Modern, contemporary & Mexican art.

Artists Presented: Juan Reyes Haro (Page 99), Adrian Tavera (Page 201)

MARPAD ART GALLERY 305.444.9360
393 Aragon Ave. Fax: 305.888.2877
Coral Gables, FL 33134
Hours: Mon-Sat 10-6
Specialty: Cuban Masters & Latin American Artists

Artists Presented: Héctor Molné (Page 137)

ALFREDO MARTINEZ GALLERY 305.442.0808
2311 Le Jeune Rd. Fax: 305.220.0824
Coral Gables, FL 33134
Hours: Tue-Sat 12-6
Specialty: Contemporary art.

Artists Presented: Marvin Chinchilla (Page 64), Ulrich Gehret (Page 87), Hector Molne (Page 137), Clara Morena (Page 139)

MAY GALLERY
31 Chungking S. Rd., Sec. 2
Taipei, Republic of China
Hours: Tue-Sun 10-6:30
Specialty: Lifescape sculptures (stainless steel, bronze) & prints.

8862.396.1966
Fax: 8862.396.4850

Artists Presented: Yuyu Yang (Page 271)

LOUIS K. MEISEL GALLERY
141 Prince St.
New York, NY 10012
Hours: Tue-Sat 10-6
Specialty: Photo-Realist paintings and other technically skilled contemporary disciplines.

212.677.1340
Fax: 212.533.7340

Artists Presented: Charles Bell (Page 45), Tom Blackwell (Page 49), Paul Giovanopoulos (Page 88), George D. Green (Page 90), Oded Halahmy (Page 242), Ron Kleemann (Page 111), David Parrish (Page 155)

NAN MILLER GALLERY
3450 Winton Place
Rochester, NY 14623
Hours: Tue-Sat 10-5; Sun 12-4; By Appt
Specialty: Graphics and originals by Contemporary artists.

716.292.1430
Fax: 716.292.1253

Artists Presented: Romero Britto (Page 54)

MONTSERRAT GALLERY
584 Broadway
New York, NY 10012
Hours: Tue-Sat 12-6
Specialty: Contemporary European and American art.

212.941.8899
Fax: 212.274.1717

Artists Presented: De La Reina (Page 74), Caroline Degriselle (Page 75), Garcia Erguin (Page 84), Koji Hayans (Page 227), Barbara Kirsch (Page 110), Alex Klimou (Page 245), Victoria McClay (Page 133), Kevin Pinkerton (Page 161), Daniel Prieto (Page 164), Gertrud Promitzer (Page 165), Amalia Ronzini (Page 176), Merceds Roselle (Page 179), John Seratin (Page 189), Francisco Torregorosa (Page 202), Susan White (Page 212), Garcia Zaborte (Page 217), Zaze (Page 274)

LESLIE MUTH GALLERY
225 E. DeVargas
Santa Fe, NM 87501
Hours: Mon-Sat 10-5; Winter Closed Wed
Specialty: Contemporary American folk, self-taught & outsider art.

505.989.4620
Fax: 505.989.4937

Artists Presented: "Uncle Pete" Drgac (Page 79), Ike Morgan (Page 140)

NADER ART GALLERY
Atarazana #9
Santo Domingo, Dominican Republic
Specialty: Fine Latin American Art.

809.544.0878
Fax: 809.565.6204

Artists Presented: Enriquillo Rodriguez Amiama (Page 39), Tony Capellan (Page 57)

O.K. HARRIS WORKS OF ART
383 W. Broadway
New York, NY 10012
Hours: Tue-Sat 10-6
Specialty: Contemporary American & European painting, sculpture, photography, collectibles & memorabilia.

212.431.3600

Artists Presented: John Baeder (Page 41), Leonard Dufresne (Page 80), Josef Levi (Page 120), William Nichols (Page 144)

THE PACE GALLERY
32 E. 57th St.
New York, NY 10022
Hours: Tue-Fri 9:30-5:30; Sat 10-6
Specialty: 20th-century paintings, drawings and sculpture.

212.421.3292
Fax: 212.421.0835

Artists Presented: Chuck Close (Page 68), Donald Judd (Page 244)

PAGE PENNA STUDIO
P.O. Box 4
Harrods Creek, KY 40027
Hours: By Appt.
Specialty: Commissioned fine Art and architectural installation in glass

502.228.3149
Fax: 502.228.0115

Artists Presented: Page Penna (Page 260)

JOSEPH PIASENTIN STUDIO
24356 Baxter Rd.
Malibu, CA 90265
Hours: By Appt.

310.456.4958
310.456.4774

Artists Presented: Joseph Piasentin (Page 159)

POIRIER SCHWEITZER
1545, Ave. Docteur-Penfield
Montreal, Canada H3G 1C7
Hours: By Appt
Specialty: 20th American & European painting, sculpture, photography, architectural & decorative arts; naif & tribal art.

514.939.9855
Fax: 514.939.9855

Artists Presented: Robert Mapplethorpe (Page 286)

PRAXIS INTERNATIONAL ART MEXICO
Arquimedes 175, Col. Polanco
Mexico City, Mexico 11570
Hours: Mon-Fri 10-7:30; Sat 10-3
Specialty: Specializing in Latin American paintings.

525.254.8813
Fax: 525.255.5690

Artists Presented: Santiago Carbonell (Page 58), Roberto Cortazar (Page 72)

PRIOR EDITIONS
1049 Cambie St.
Vancouver, BC V6B 5L7
Hours: Tues-Sat 10-5:30
Specialty: Contemporary Canadian and contemporary prints and paperworks

604.608.0535

Artists Presented: David Ostrem (Page 152)

RADIX GALLERY
1429 N. First Street
Phoenix, AZ 85004
Hours: Tue-Sat 12-5; By Appt
Specialty: Contemporary art.

602.256.9252
Fax: 602.252.8002

Artists Presented: Barbara Grygutis (Page 241)

C.G. REIN GALLERIES
949 Sibley Memorial Hwy.
St. Paul, MN 55118
Hours: Mon-Fri 9-5
Specialty: Contemporary fine art & sculpture; limited edition reduction woodcuts, serigraphs & lithographs.

612.455.7100
Fax: 612.455.1211

Artists Presented: Earl Linderman (Page 122)

JACQUELINE RIPSTEIN
2800 Williams Island Blvd.
William Island, FL 33160
Hours: By Appt
Specialty: Oil paintings lithographs, and a unique, new, invisible technique developed by the artist

305.933.1410
525.202.8296

Artists Presented: Jacqueline Ripstein (Page 171)

ROBISCHON GALLERY
1740 Wazee St.
Denver, CO 80202
Hours: Tue-Fri 10-6; Sat 11-5
Specialty: Contemporary painting, sculpture, photography and works on paper.

303.298.7788
Fax: 303.298.0934

Artists Presented: Manuel Neri (Page 257)

ROCFERN INTERNATIONAL GALLERIES 905.850.7647
80 Carlauren Rd., #17 Fax: 905.850.8062
Toronto, ON, Canada L4L 7Z5
Hours: By Appt

Artists Presented: Pietro Adamo (Page 37), Arno (Page 231), Michael Close (Page 69), Daniel Diaz (Page 78), Ken Kirkby (Page 109), Ernesto Manera (Page 128), Michael Marchese (Page 130), Kelly Ross (Page 288), David Zucca (Page 220)

ROSENTHAL FINE ART, INC 312.642.2966
640 N. La Salle St., Ste 582 Fax: 312.642.5169
Chicago, IL 60610
Hours: Tues-Fri 10-6; Sat 11-5
Specialty: 20th century modern and contemporary international uniques and multiples.

Artists Presented: Hubert Shuptrine (Page 193), Louis Marinaro (Page 252)

PHILIP SAMUELS FINE ART 314.727.2444
8112 Maryland Ave., Ste. 200 Fax: 314.727.6084
St. Louis, MO 63105
Hours: Mon-Fri 9-5
Specialty: Contemporary paintings & sculpture.

Artists Presented: Nico Roos (Page 177), Michael Rubin (Page 181), Ernest Trova (Page 269), Edoardo Villa (Page 270)

ANITA SHAPOLSKY GALLERY 212.334.9755
99 Spring St. Fax: 212.334.6817
New York, NY 10012
Hours: Wed-Sat 11-6; By Appt
Specialty: Abstract painting & sculpture, first & second generation abstract expressionism.

Artists Presented: Buffie Johnson (Page 106)

JOAN SHERMAN 212.387.0866
135 Greene St. Fax: 212.505.8550
New York, NY 10012
Hours: By Appt
Specialty: Abstract painting & sculpture.

Artists Presented: Joan Sherman (Page 192), Joan Sherman (Page 264)

RUFUS SNODDY STUIDO 310.552.0696
4848 W. Jefferson Blvd
Los Angeles, CA 90016
Hours: By Appt

Artists Presented: Rufus Snoddy (Page 266)

SOO BIN ART GALLERY 65.738.0488
81 Oxley Rd. Fax: 65.733.1294
Singapore, 09023
Hours: By Appt
Specialty: Fine contemporary ink & oil paintings.

Artists Presented: Wu Guanzhong (Page 95)

SPACE GALLERY 312.276.5146
1945 W. North Ave. Fax: 312.226.5587
Chicago, IL 60622
Hours: Daily 9-6
Specialty: Emerging contemporary painting, sculpture and photography.

Artists Presented: Adam Siegal (Page 195), Tom Osborn (Page 259)

SPECIAL THINGS GALLERY
1407 Greenleaf Fax: 708.869.8909
Evanston, IL 60202
Hours: Tue-fri 11-6; Thu 11-8; Sat 10-6; Sun 2-5
Specialty: Art of emerging artists, ethnic art, fine reproductions & framing.

Artists Presented: Zhao-Yu Wan (Page 208)

STIEBEL MODERN 212.759.5536
32 E. 57th St., 6th Fl. Fax: 212.935.5736
New York, NY 10022
Hours: Tue-Sat 10-5
Specialty: Contemporary representational paintings & drawings.

Artists Presented: David Ligare (Page 121)

STROKOVICH FINE ART 305.576.6587
40 NE 40th St. Fax: 305.534.0868
Miami, FL 33137
Hours: Mon-Fri 11-6; Sat 12-5; By Appt
Specialty: Modernistic, national & international art, including paintings, drawings, sculpture, installations & themes.

Artists Presented: Eszter Gyory (Page 96)

DANIEL STROZYNSKI STUDIO 310.455.3874
1525 Bainum Drive
Topanga Canyon, CA 90190
Hours: By Appt

Artists Presented: Daniel Strozynski (Page 198)

TAMENAGA GALLERY 212.734.6789
982 Madison Ave. Fax: 212.734.9413
New York, NY 10021
Hours: Tue-Sat 10-6
Specialty: Contemporary realist & figurative paintings.

Artists Presented: Tom Christopher (Page 65), Frank Holmes (Page 101)

CORINNE TIMSIT INTL GALLERIES 1.42557682
81, rue Lepic. Fax: 1.42524868
Paris, 75018
Hours: Daily10-1; 2-7
Specialty: Latin American Art.

Artists Presented: Fernando Varela (Page 204), Nora Herman (Page 243)

CHARLES WHITCHURCH GALLERY 714.373.4459
5973 Engineer Drive Fax: 714.373.4615
Huntington Beach, CA 92649
Hours: Mon-Fri 12-5; By Appt
Specialty: Modern & contemporary paintings, graphic works & sculpture.

Artists Presented: James Groff (Page 92), Karl Momen (Page 138), Karl Momen (Page 254), Michael Rubin (Page 182)

ZAGAMI FINE ART 305.463.0014
515 SW Fourth Ave. Fax: 305.587.7726
Ft. Lauderdale, FL 33315
Hours: Daily 10-5
Specialty: Contemporary painting & sculpture.

Artists Presented: Salvatore Zagami (Page 272), Salvatore Zagami (Page 273)

ZAPLIN-LAMPERT GALLERY 505.982.6100
651 Canyon Rd. Fax: 505.988.2142
Santa Fe, NM 87501
Hours: Mon-Sat 9-5
Specialty: Fine 19th & 20th-century American art.

Artists Presented: Lindsay Holt II (Page 102)

ZEE STONE GALLERY 852.845.4476
Forum, 111 Exchange Sq., #11 Fax: 852.877.2859
Central, Hong Kong
Hours: Mon-Sat 10-6:30
Specialty: Contemporary Chinese paintings, antique Chinese & Tibetan carpets.

Artists Presented: Wu Guanzhong (Page 94)

ARTIST INDEX

EXPOSITIONS

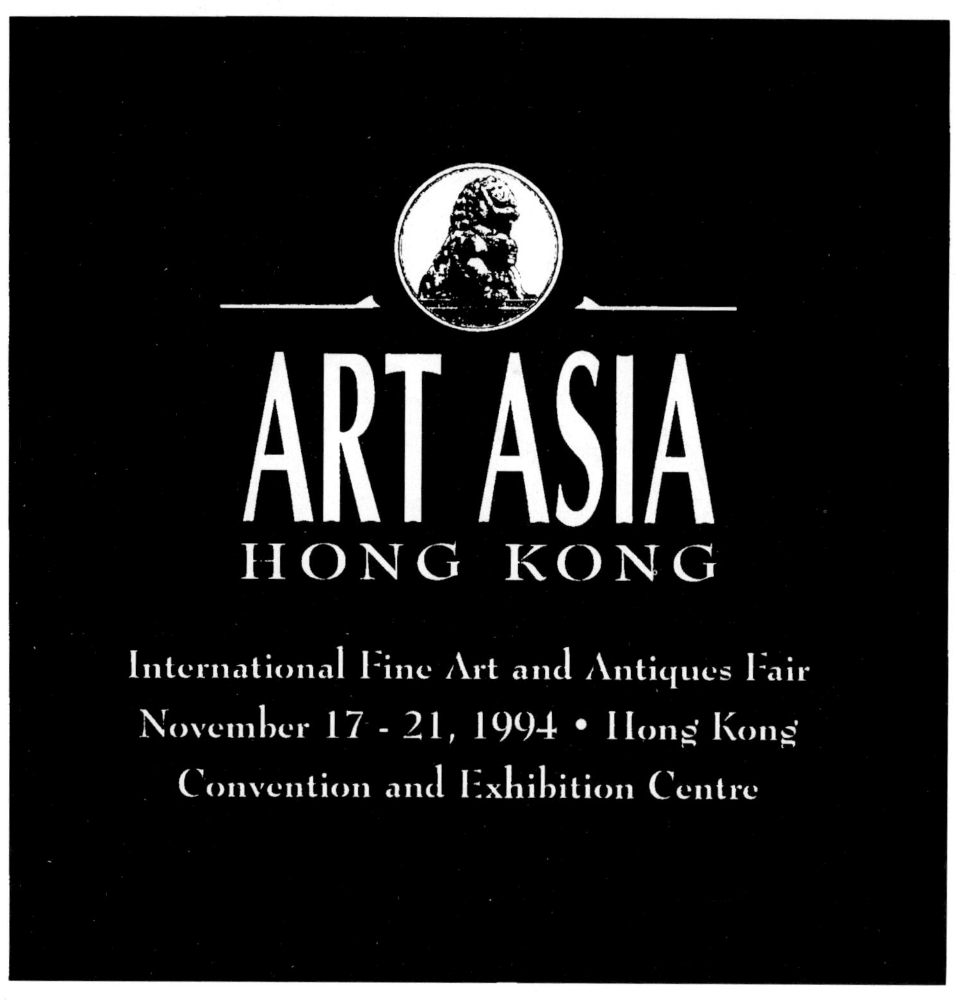

ART ASIA'94 INTERNATIONAL ANTIQUE & FINE ARTS

Location:
Hong Kong Convention & Exhibition Center

Date:
November 18 to 21, 1994

Hours:

Friday, November 18, 94	noon to 9 p.m.
Saturday, November 19, 94	noon to 9 p.m.
Sunday, November 20, 94	11a.m. to 7 p.m.
Monday, November 21, 94	noon to 6 p.m.

Show Schedule subject to minor modifications

Charity Gala Preview:
Thursday, November 17, 94   6 p.m. to 10 p.m.

Preview Benefitting:
Society for Promotion of Hospice Care
Business Attire
Gala Ticket intormation:
852.868.1211
852.530.3290 FAX

Organizer:
International Fine Art Expositions
3725 SE Ocean Boulevard, Suite 201
Stuart, FL 34996
407.220.2690
407.220.3180 FAX

Press Contact:
International Fine Art Expositions
3725SE Ocean Boulevard, Suite 201
Stuart, FL 34996
407.220.2690
407.220.3180 FAX

Travel Arrangements:
Art Tours
815 NW 57th Avenue, Suite 301
Miami, FL 33216
800.226.6972
305.857.0619
305.854.3872 FAX

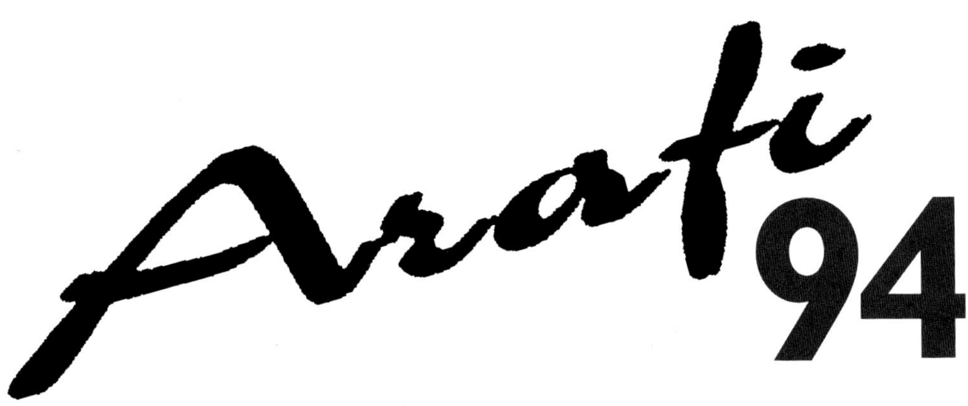

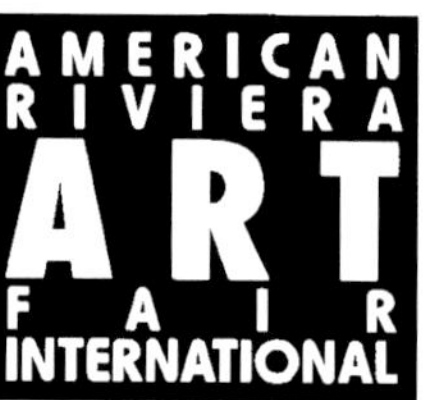

AMERICAN RIVIERA ART FAIR INTERNATIONAL

Location:
Sheraton Bal Harbour Resort
9701 Collins Avenue, Bal Harbour, Florida

Date:
November 24 to 27, 1994

Hours:
Thursday, November 24, 1994   11 a.m. to 8 p.m.
Friday, November 25, 1994   11 a.m. to 9 p.m.
Saturday,November 26, 1994   11 a.m. to 10 p.m.
Sunday, November 27, 1994   12 p.m. to 7 p.m.

Vernissage:
Wednesday, November 23,1994

Organizer:
American Riviera Art Fair international
420 Lincoln Road, suites 393-394
Miami Beach, FL 33139
305.672.2333
305.672.2887 FAX

Cultural Program:
Guided Tours, Lectures, Chamber Concert,
Beach Jazz Festival

Fair Infomation:
American Riviera Art Fair international
420 Lincoln Road, suites 393-394
Miami Beach, FL 33139
305.672.2333
305.672.2887 FAX

Travel / Hotel Arrangements:
Bestway Travel & Conventions
USA
800.226.6972
305.672.3035
305.672.2580 FAX
ITALY
0971.471.400
0971.471.403 FAX
ARGENTINA
541.314.3732
514.314.7211 FAX
AUSTRALIA
7.236.1944
7.236.1202 FAX

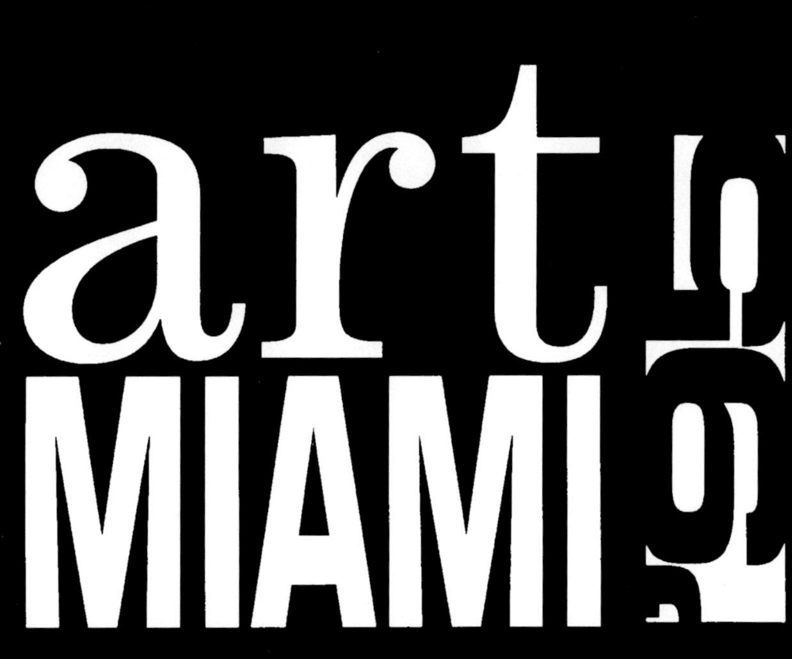

ART MIAMI '95

Location:
Miami Beach Convention Center
1901 Convention Center Dr.
Miami beach, FL 33139

Date:
January 6 to10, 1995

Hours:
Friday, January 6, 1995   12 a.m. to 10 p.m.
Saturday, January 7, 1995   12 a.m. to 9 p.m.
Sunday, January 8, 1995   12 a.m. to 7 p.m.
Monday, January 9, 1995   10 a.m. to 9 p.m.
Tuesday, January 10, 1995   10 am. to 2 p.m.
Show Schedule subject to minor modifications

Vernissage:
Wednesday, January 5, 1995   6 a.m. to 8 p.m.

Organizer:
International Fine Art Expositions
3725SE Ocean Boulevard,Suite 201
Stuart, FL 34996
407.220.2690
407.220.3180 FAX

Press Contact:
International Fine Art Expositions
3725SE Ocean Boulevard,Suite 201
Stuart, FL 34996
407.220.2690
407.220.3180 FAX

Travel Arrangements:
Art Tours
815NW 57th Avenue, Suite 301
Miami, FL 33216
800.226.6972
305.857.0619
305.854.3872 FAX

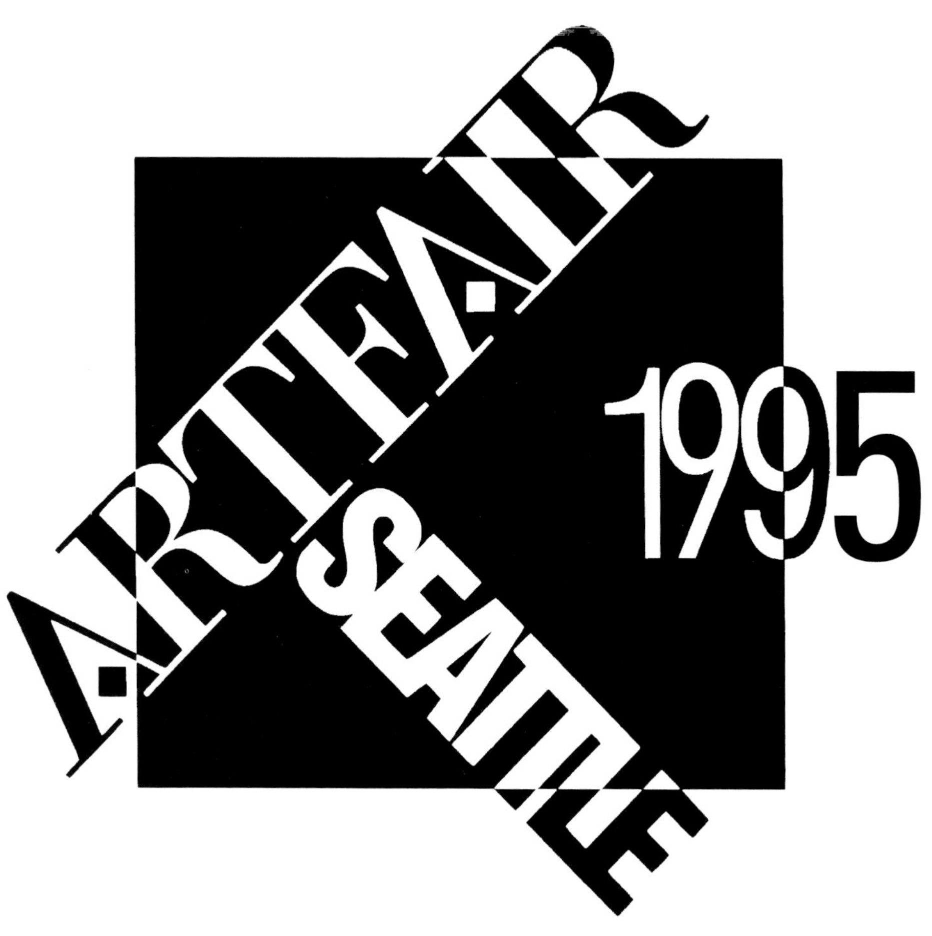

ART FAIR/SEATTLE 1995

Location:
The Westin Hotel, Seattle, Washington

Date:
February 3 to 6, 1995

Hours:
Daily 12 p.m. to 8 p.m.

Vernissage:
Thursday, February 2, 1995   6 p.m. to 10 p.m.

Anticipated Number of Gallery Exhibitor:
50

Anticipated Number of Visitors:
8,000

Organizer:
ArtFair/seattle
270 S. Hanford St. Ste 208
Seattle, WA 98134
206.624.7363
206.583.0345 FAX

Press Contact:
ArtFair/seattle
270 S. Hanford St. Ste 208
Seattle, WA 98134
206.624.7363
206.583.0345 FAX

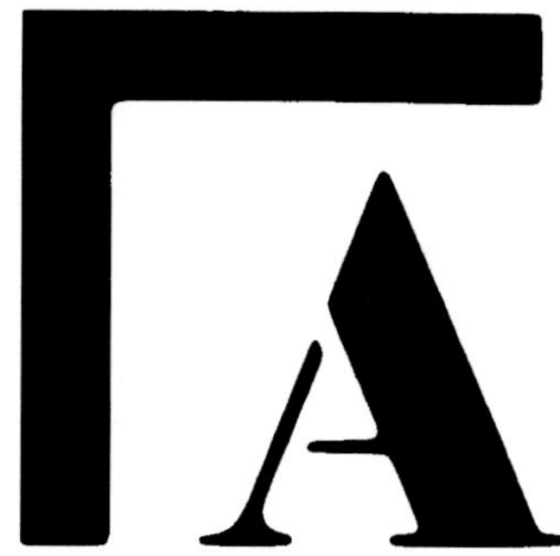
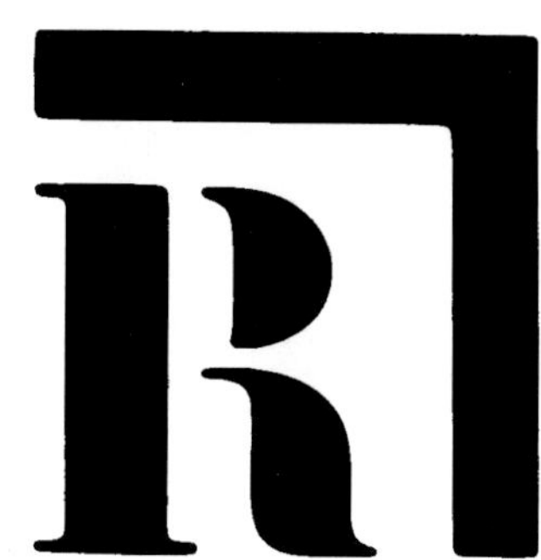
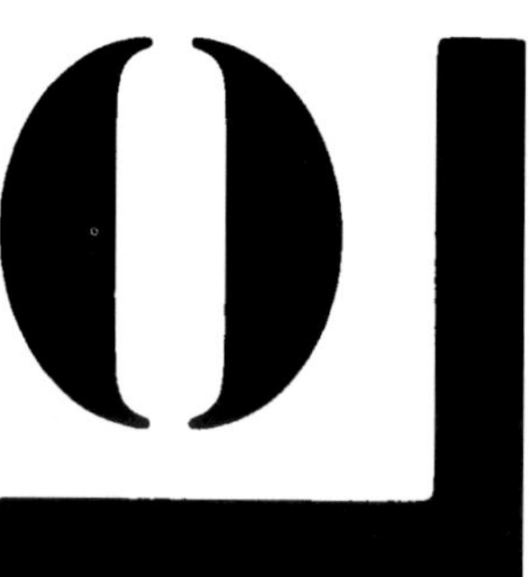

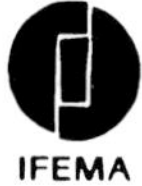

IFEMA

ARCO '95 INTERNATIONAL CONTEMPORARY ART FAIR

Location:
Juan Carlos I Exhibition Centre (Madrid)

Edition:
Fourteenth

Date:
February 9-14,1995

Hours:
Daily Noon to 9 p.m. uninterrupted

Professional Visit:
Wednesday, February 8, 1995   1 p.m.

Vernissage:
Wednesday, February 8, 1995   8 p.m.

Activities:
"U.S.A. at Arco"
Current American Art Galleries, selected by a
curator (to be determined)
FOTOARCO
PHOTOGRAPHIC GLIMPSES

Organizer:
Feria Internacional
Parque Ferial Juan Carlosl
28067 Madrid
Apdo. de correos (P.O. Box)
67.067- 28080 Madrid
34.1.722.50.00
34.1.722.57.98 FAX

Arco Management
Director: Mrs Rosina Gómez-Baeza
Deputy Director: Mr. Carlos Urroz

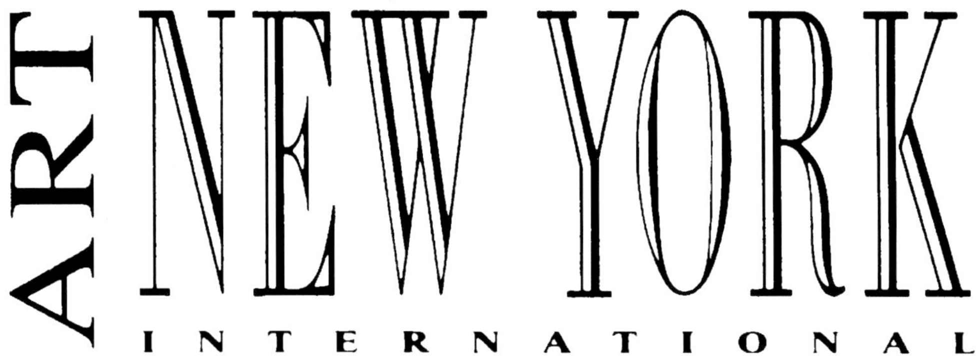

ART NEW YORK INTERNATIONAL '95

Location:
New York, New Jersey
Passengership Terminal
Piers 90 & 92

Date:
April 29 - May 2, 1995

Hours:
Saturday, April 29, 1995   11a.m. to 8 p.m.
Sunday, April 30, 1995   11a.m. to 6 p.m.
Monday, May 1, 1995   11a.m. to 8 p.m.
Tuesday, May 2, 1995   11a.m. to 6 p.m.
Show Schedule subject to minor modifications

Vernissage:
Friday, April 28, 1995   6 p.m. to 10 p.m.

Organizer:
International Fine Art Expositions
3725SE Ocean Boulevard, Suite 201
Stuart, FL 34996
407.220.2690
407.220.3180 FAX

Press Contact:
International Fine Art Expositions
3725SE Ocean Boulevard, Suite 201
Stuart, FL 34996
407.220.2690
407.220.3180 FAX

Travel Arrangements:
Art Tours
815NW 57th Avenue, Suite 301
Miami, FL 33216
800.226.6972
305.857.0619
305.854.3872 FAX

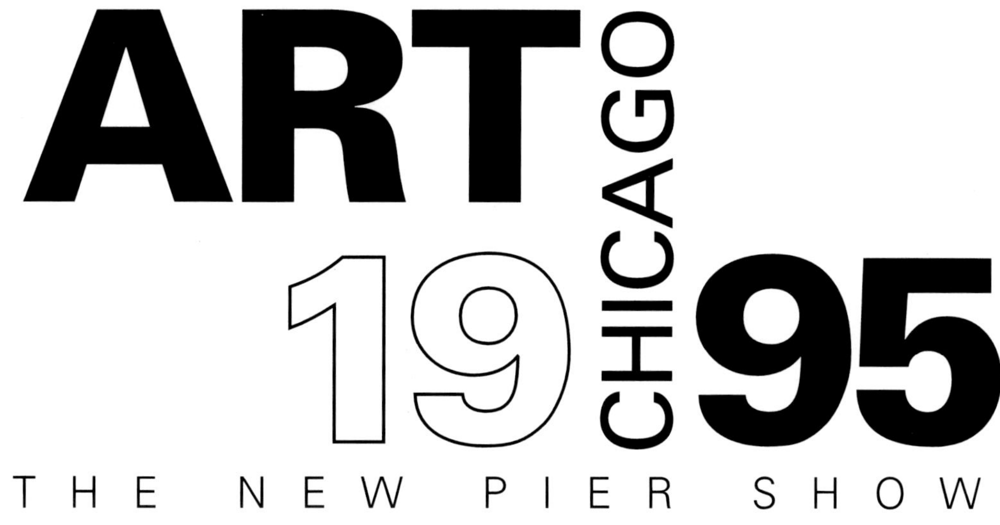

ART 1995 CHICAGO: AT NAVY PIER

Location:
Chicago Navy Pier - Festival Hall,
600 E. Grand Aveenue
Chicago, IL 60611

Date:
May 11 - 16,1995

Anticipated Number of Gallery Exhibitor:
Over 130

Anticipated Number of Visitors:
30,000 to 40,000

Organizer:
Thomas Blackman Associates
215 West Houron
Chicago, IL 60610
312.587.3300
312.587.3304 FAX

Press Contact:
Thomas Blackman Associates
215 West Houron
Chicago, IL 60610
312.587.3300
312.587.3304 FAX

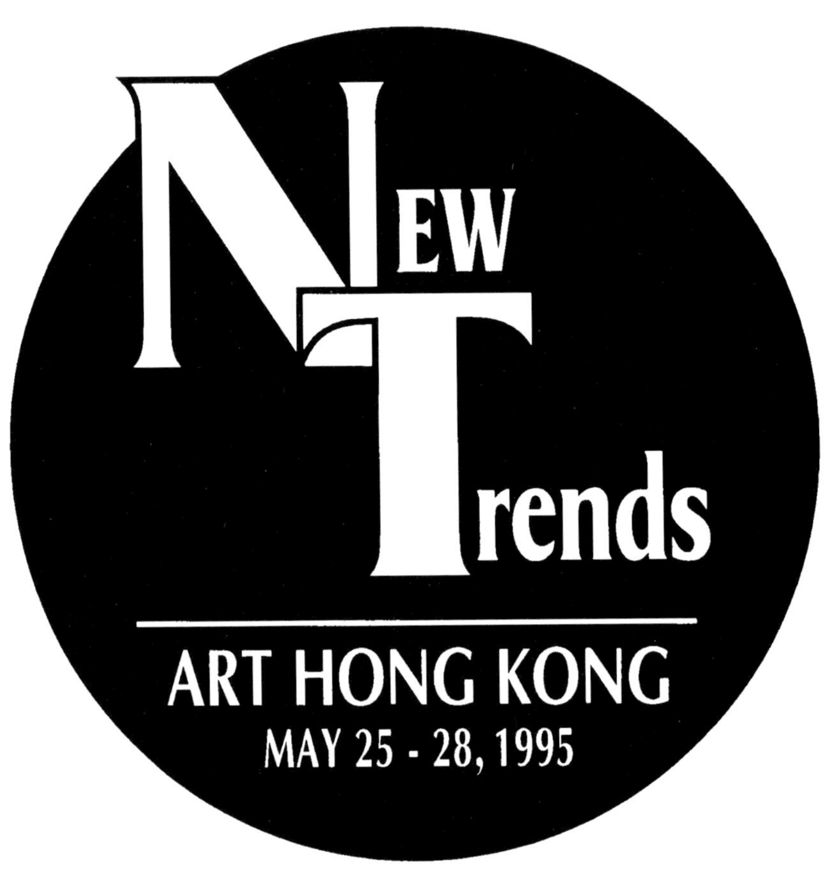

NEW TRENDS - ART HONG KONG '95

Location:
Hong Kong Convention and Exposition Centre

Date:
May 25 - 28 1995

Hours:
Thursday, May 25, 1995   noon. to 10 p.m.
Friday, May 26, 1995   noon. to 10 p.m.
Saturday, May 27, 1995   noon. to 10 p.m.
Sunday, May 28, 1995   noon. to 10 p.m.
Show Schedule subject to minor modifications

Vernissage:
Wednesday, May 24, 1995   8 p.m. to 11 p.m.

Organizer:
International Fine Art Expositions
3725SE Ocean Boulevard, Suite 201
Stuart, FL 34996
407.220.2690
407.220.3180 FAX

Press Contact:
International Fine Art Expositions
3725SE Ocean Boulevard, Suite 201
Stuart, FL 34996
407.220.2690
407.220.3180 FAX

Travel Arrangements:
Art Tours
815NW 57th Avenue, Suite 301
Miami, FL 33216
800.226.6972
305.857.0619
305.854.3872 FAX

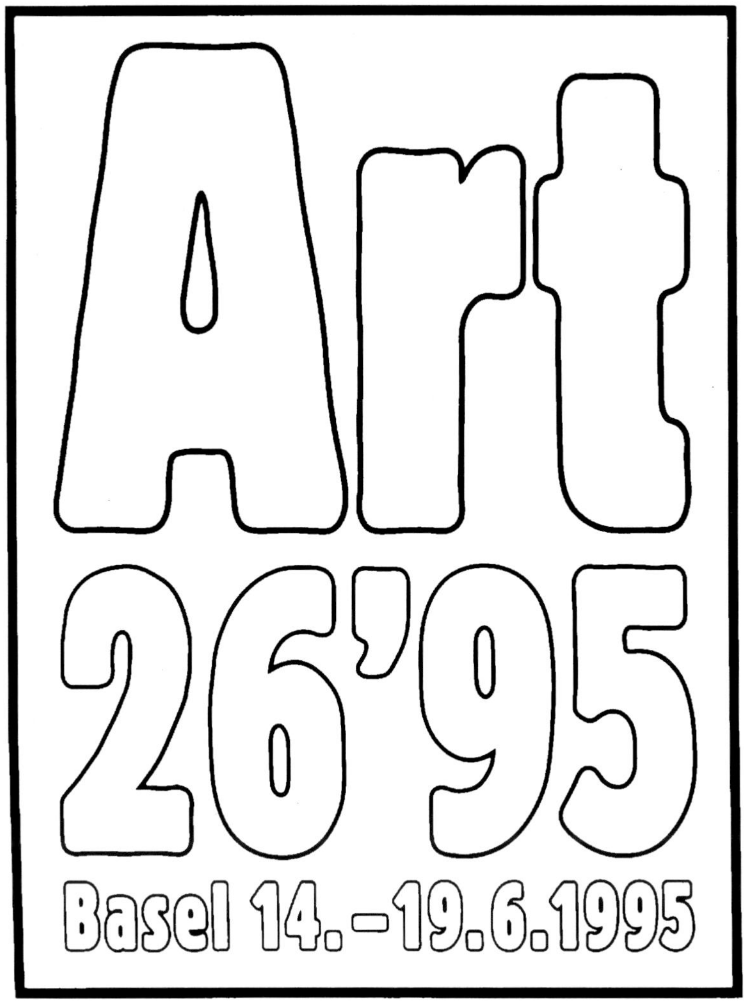

ART 26'95

Location:
Basel Fairgrounds, Basel, Switzerland

Date:
June 14 to 19, 1995

Anticipated Number of Gallery Exhibitor:
300

Anticipated Number of Visitors:
50,000 to 60,000

Organizer:
Basel Fair
The International Art Fair
Art 26'95
Schweizer Mustermesse in Basel, CH - 4021
Basel, Switzerland
061.686.20.20
061.686.21.88 FAX

CHICAGO
INTERNATIONAL FINE ART FAIR
Navy Pier
September 7 - 11, 1995

ART CHICAGO '95

Location:
Chicago Navy Pier-Festival Hall
600 E. Grand Avenue
Chicago, IL 60611

Date:
September 7 to 11, 1995

Hours:
Friday, September 8, 1995 — noon to 9 p.m.
Saturday, September 9, 1995 — noon. to 9 p.m.
Sunday, September 10, 1995 — noon. to 9 p.m.
Monday, September 11, 1995 — noon. to 9 p.m.
Show Schedule subject to minor modifications

Vernissage:
Thursday, September 7, 1995 — 6 p.m. to 10 p.m.

Organizer:
International Fine Art Expositions
3725 SE Ocean Boulevard, Suite 201
Stuart, FL 34996
407.220.2690
407.220.3180 FAX

Press Contact:
International Fine Art Expositions
3725SE Ocean Boulevard, Suite 201
Stuart, FL 34996
407.220.2690
407.220.3180 FAX

Travel Arrangements:
Art Tours
815NW 57th Avenue, Suite 301
Miami, FL 33216
800.226.6972
305.857.0619
305.854.3872 FAX

GEORG BASELITZ

ALEXANDER CALDER

JOHN CHAMBERLAIN

CHUCK CLOSE

GEORGE CONDO

JOSEPH CORNELL

JIM DINE

JEAN DUBUFFET

BARRYFLANAGAN

DAN FLAVIN

ROBERT IRWIN

ALFRED JENSEN

DONALD JUDD

ROBERT MANGOLD

AGNES MARTIN

LOUISE NEVELSON

ISAMU NOGUCHI

CLAES OLDENBURG

PABLO PICASSO

AD REINHARDT

MARK ROTHKO

ROBERT RYMAN

LUCAS SAMARAS

JULIAN SCHNABEL

RICHARD SERRA

JOEL SHAPIRO

SAUL STEINBERG

ANTONI TÁPIES

32 EAST 57TH STREET NEW YORK CITY 10022

142 GREENE STREET BNEW YORK CITY 10012

THE PACE GALLERY

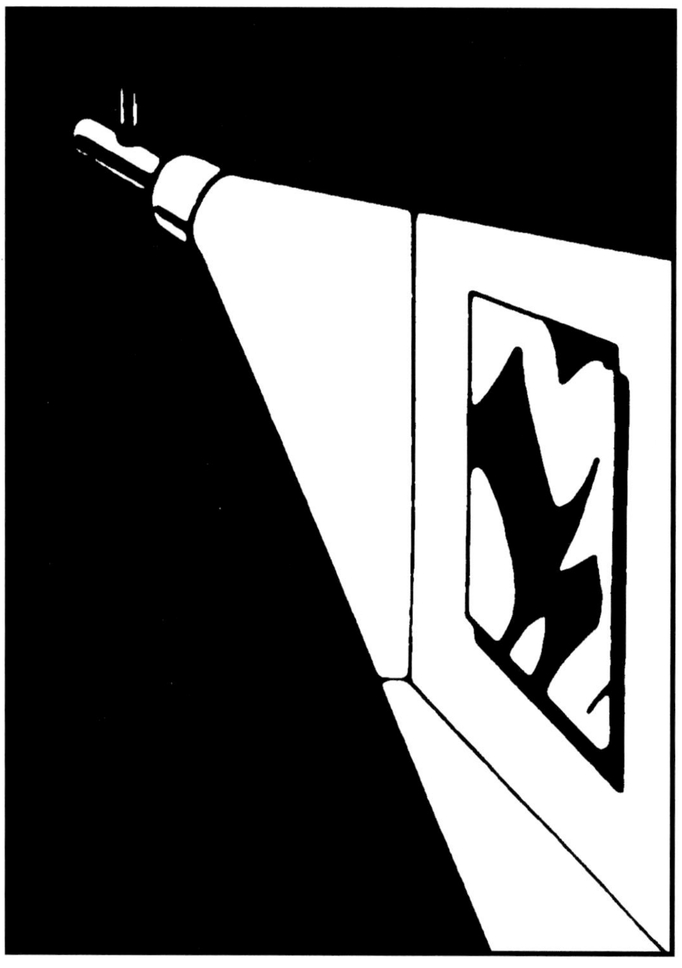

The Golden Gallery

Richard Diebenkorn • Jim Dine • Helen Frankenthaler

David Hockney • Jasper Johns • Alex Katz • Roy Lichtenstein

Robert Motherwell • Claes Oldenburg • Larry Rivers

Jim Rosenquist • Sean Scully • Frank Stella • Wayne Thiebaud

CONTEMPORARY MASTER PRINTS

207 Newbury Street
Boston, Massachusetts 02116
Tel: 617-247-8889
Fax: 617-247-0990

NOTES